EXAMPLES

OF

GROUNDED THEORY:
A READER

Edited by:

Barney G. Glaser

Sociology Press

P. O. Box 400

Mill Valley

Sociology Press

PO Box 400

Mill Valley, CA 94942

First Printing

Library of Congress Catalog Card Number applied for.

ISBN 1-884156-06-1

Printed in the United States of America

To all of those beginning researchers who adhere to the canons of traditional grounded theory...

TABLE OF CONTENTS

III QUANTITATIVE RESEARCH GROUNDED THEORIES

INTRODUCTION

In writing *Basics of Grounded Theory* (Sociology Press, 1992), it became obvious to me that what was needed by the myriad of Grounded Theory readers and users throughout the world was a book of examples of grounded theory papers and chapters. These researchers needed models for how the various facets of grounded theory look when brought together into an integrated piece. This applies to both analysis of qualitative and particularly quantitative data. This reader is designed to achieve this purpose.

Many of the papers in this volume were written a long time ago, but remain good examples. Their core variables, particularly basic social processes, have lasting qualities. With modification for new times and places, the cores still work and are relevant today. Core problems and how they are processed are abstract of time and places. Their relevance persists.

For example: Relationships are cultivated today for fun and profit as before, chronically ill people still have the problem of cutting back, routing and funding. Going back to college and becoming a student is more relevant today then ever and older people look for careers, new careers and new enlivening interests. Vagueing-out to others is a prominent way of handling others in our "clear"-oriented society. Step-parenting is on the rise, with the need of sharing control of raising children. The local-cosmopolitan issue is found in all organizations and must be taken into consideration. As more and more people become careerists and professionals, comparative failures increase and we increase our "awe inspiring" of and from others by another vantage point. Social change brings on apprehension among the people impacted. Attraction, autonomy, approachability, psychological fences and reciprocity constantly emerge as relevant in everyday life juggling. Finding and visiting friends and keeping it normative is always there. Discovering our prospects and breaking out of our past hobbles is a constant problem. Single family empty nest problems and solutions are rising fast in a society which sanctions so many divorces. "Doing time" is a constant for us all, once we leave the jail time and place and look at our lives. We are all layman facing experts, no matter what our occupational skills. And lastly, we all confront forms of social loss.

Thus, grounded theory produces core variable theory and the continuing resolution of problems by basic social processes and basic social structures that have relevance, fit and work indefinitely - they have enduring longevity.

The reader is presented with these articles as models so he or she can study the nature of core variables and how they build up by the constantly comparative method into a theory. The reader can see relevance emerge through the use of theoretical codes, substantive concepts and their integration, densification and saturation using the grounded theory criteria of relevance, fit, work, and modification. He can see the quest for explanation and interpretation, keeping in mind parsimony and scope: that is, using the smallest group of concepts to achieve the greatest explanatory power.

The reader can also clearly see that the theory in these articles could not have been predicted or forced beforehand. These theories emerged as the data were collected and analyzed and integrated to saturation. The result are a richness of generalities and insights in the explanations, interpretations and consequences, which give the reader conceptual power over what he may or may not substantively know. The theories presented here also show the varied styles of theory generation resulting from theoretically coding the substantive codes which emerged from research in a substantive area.

These papers also show the model of how books are created. As analyses emerge into theory and become written in papers, several papers on a core variable emerge a book. Then the analysist writes theory, not a book per se. The book emerges on its own as saturation is sought.

I obviously could have added many more papers into this book of examples. But space and cost prohibits it and it is not necessary. The general purpose of the reader is exampling, not content and coverage. Any set of papers achieves this goal. I trust the reader will enjoy the content, but it is the theoretical *construction* of these papers that should be studied. Their fullest variation must be cognized so the reader-researcher can achieve a grounded emergent contruction in his or her own grounded theory research and paper.

So read, have fun and study hard. There are two sections in this reader: grounded theories based on qualitative data and grounded theories based on quantitative data. The latter is especially important because of its relative neglect in recent years. Thus grounded theory from quantative data is a whole area for grounded theory development that is just waiting to be reopened up; an area which Paul F. Lazarsfeld opened up in the 1950's.

I wish to thank Kris Curl for her steadfast efforts in publishing this volume from her desk.

2

Qualitative Research Grounded Theories

CHAPTER 1

THE MILKMAN AND HIS CUSTOMER:

A Cultivated Relationship

Odis E. Simmons

INTRODUCTION

As Goffman maintains, America is a service society - so much so that essentially non-service institutions, such as stores, take on service-like characteristics.[1]

This emphasis on service has given rise to preponderance of a particular kind of social activity, which I will refer to as a "cultivated relationship." "Cultivating" as it is used here refers to the courting and wooing activities engaged in by servicers in relations with those they serve. Cultivating techniques are employed with the intent of either directly or indirectly gaining reward (usually monetary). "Cultivating relationships" are relationships which are carried out with the primary intent of gaining such reward. They are usually asymmetrical, with the less powerful party cultivating to bring the relationship closer to a state of symmetry.[2]

One such relationship, that between milkmen and their customers, will be discussed in this paper. The structure of the milkman-customer relationship, for reasons to be discussed below, is one of extreme asymmetry, with the milkman initially exercising very little control. However, by employing cultivating techniques milkmen are able to transform this initially asymmetrical relationship into one which more closely approximates symmetry.

The information upon which the following discussion is based was obtained by my having been a milkman for a period of fourteen months. The information derived from this was supplemented by subsequent informal interviews with my former co-workers. My employment as a milkman was prior to my introduction to sociology, so that my experiences were those of a "sociologically naive" social actor. Thus, one of my main informants was myself. There is no reason, however, to believe that my experiences as a milkman were particularly unique. Milkmen frequently share their experiences with one another, and mine were essentially the same as those reported by my co-workers. The interviewing which I did also revealed the usualness of my experiences. However, the instances which I

4

relate were carefully chosen to represent typical experiences. I relate only experiences which were similar to those reported by my former co-workers.

Home delivery milk business is not a particularly uniform enterprise. Individual factors (population density, physical terrain, and so forth) in particular locations greatly affect the manner in which it is carried out. This makes it difficult to make statements which apply to milkmen in general. Due to the fact that my observations were made in one location which has its own peculiarities, some of what I say will apply generally, and some of it will not. However, whether or not my discussion reflects other locations is not particularly important. It is not my intent to give a general description of what milkmen do. I am interested in analyzing the process of relationship cultivation. Thus, the following discussion should not be seen merely as one instance of what milkmen do. It should be seen as one instance of a general social process- that of relationship cultivation. My interest in milkmen stems primarily from the fact that their activities mirror this process.

I will begin my discussion with an examination of the conditions which engender a need for milkmen to cultivate relationships. I will discuss both those conditions which are industry-wide and those which were present in the particular location which I studied. I will follow this with a discussion of the particular cultivating techniques employed by the milkmen in this location. I will close with a short discussion of cultivating in general, as it relates to service relationships.

GENERATING CONDITIONS

Although it is rather difficult to make generalized statements about the home delivery milk business, it is evident that several cultural and technological changes have occurred over the past several decades which have affected it as a whole. Over this period of time the retail sale of milk has gradually shifted from the milk truck to the grocery store. In the 1920's almost all milk consumed by American families was home delivered, and this percentage is continuing to decline.[3]

In response to this decline, retail distributors in many parts of the country have altered their operating procedures to such an extent that the milkman's job has been transformed from a job which at one time involved mere delivery of milk with very little customer contact into a job in which active cultivation of customer relationships is an essential task. In the following section I shall describe the structural conditions which have brought this change about. Following this, I shall describe the particular conditions present in the context which I was a part of, and subsequently studied.

INDUSTRY-WIDE FACTORS

SUBURBANIZATION

A large factor in the decline of the home delivery milk business is suburbanization, which has produced "sprawling" areas with high population but relatively low density. This low density has important ramifications for the home delivery milk business. It has become increasingly difficult for retail distributors to form routes which are economically profitable on the sheer basis of numbers of customers. To derive profit in this manner a distributor must be able to form "compact" routes with low "traveling time" between "stops." This cannot be accomplished in areas which are characterized by low population density. The decrease in percentage of families receiving home delivery has an amplifying effect which makes this problem even more severe. As less families receive home delivery, the space between customers becomes even greater, regardless of population density.

These two factors combined produce "spread out" routes whose potential for profit is low. As population density and the percentage of customers receiving home delivery decreases, milk routes necessarily become smaller in terms of number of customers, but larger in terms of the distance traveled. Thus, modern milkmen generally have less customers, spaced farther apart, than did their predecessors.

However, even if a retail distributor was able to increase the number of his customers, economic profit would not necessarily result. Increasing the number of customers may decrease profit.[4]

This apparent paradox is explained by the fact that a distributor can increase his potential for profit through acquiring more customers only if he can maintain a certain ratio regarding number of customers and volume of sales. If fifty low consumption customers[5] are acquired by a distributor, his potential for profit would decrease, although his volume of sales would increase. The probability of new customers being high consumers is lessened by the fact that high consumption customers tend to already receive home delivery, whereas low consumption customers tend to purchase milk from grocery stores. However, this is changing as, proportionately, the number of high consumers terminating home delivery is greater than the number of low consumers doing so.[6]

6

This makes it difficult for retail distributors to maintain a satisfactory ratio between volume of sales and number of customers.

THE SUPERMARKET

Another factor which has contributed to the decline of the home delivery milk business is the increasing presence of the supermarket. Most of the business lost by milkmen is inherited by supermarkets. However, it is not the presence of the supermarket per se which is responsible for milkmen losing their customers. Because of other cultural and technological changes including the automobile, the refrigerator, and the decreased perishability of dairy products - and the increased availability of these items - the supermarket has become an accessible and convenient place from which to purchase milk and other dairy products.[7]

The modern housewife can drive to the local supermarket, purchase dairy products along with other groceries, return home, put these products in the refrigerator, and be assured that they will not sour for at least a week or so.

A CRITICAL PRICE DIFFERENTIAL

However, the increased availability and convenience of supermarkets does not necessarily assure the decline of the milkman. Although his services may no longer be necessary, they can be convenient, and thus remain desirable. The prime factor which reduces the desirability of home delivery (and increases the desirability of the supermarket) is price. Distribution through supermarkets is simply more economically efficient than distribution through home delivery. It costs more to deliver milk to the doorstep, hence the retail price of milk distributed in this manner is greater - ordinarily several cents per quart.

This price differential is an important factor in customer's decisions concerning whether or not they will purchase milk and other dairy products from a milkman. According to a survey regarding consumer attitudes conducted in Cleveland, Ohio, a large number (37%) of store customers would prefer home delivery if equal pricing existed.[8]

The percentage of high consumption customers who would prefer home delivery if prices were equal is even greater (48%). And, it is these customers who are most valuable to the milkman, as they reduce the ratio of number of customers to volume of sales, and therefore are more potentially profitable.

DISTRIBUTOR COPING STRATEGIES

The foregoing factors have placed retail milk distributors in a rather tenuous position. In an effort to cope with this, they have made several adjustments in their operating procedures. Cumulatively, these adjustments have rather extensively changed the character of the home delivery business.

In general, the major problems with which distributors are faced are that their best customers are being siphoned off by supermarkets who have a crucial price advantage, and their remaining customers are spread apart to such an extent that their ability to form profit-producing routes is greatly curtailed.

Very little can be done about their price disadvantage, as their operating expenses are proportionately higher than those of the wholesale distributor.[9]

In many areas, including the one in which I made my observations, the price differential between home delivery and the store is made mandatory by law. Distributors in such areas must charge more whether they care to or not. In large part, then, retail distributors are unable to increase sales or attract new customers through a policy of price reductions. And, as I mentioned previously, profit does not necessarily result from an increase in number of customers anyway. To increase potential for profit, the ratio of numbers of customers to volume of sales must be reduced. In practical terms, the distributor must sell more, on the average, to each customer. In this manner the relatively small size and diffuseness of the typical milk route can be at least partially compensated for.

Product diversification is a strategy which is often employed by retail distributors to achieve a greater rate of sales per customer. It is rather difficult to get customers to increase milk consumption, so to expand sales a larger variety of products must be offered. Thus, in areas in which the aforementioned conditions prevail, a large range of products is typically offered to home delivery customers. Within this range are a number of different kinds of dairy products (ice cream, cheese, yogurt, cottage cheese, etc.), as well as non-dairy products (flavored drinks, eggs, bacon, cosmetics, laundry soap, etc.). This wide range of products was not sold by milkmen when home delivery was the chief method of milk distribution.

Another strategy employed by retail distributors to cope with their increasing unfavorable position has been to decrease the number of deliveries to each customer, which reduces operating costs and increases the number of customers which each milkman can deliver to. Actually, this strategy was somewhat unintentional. During World War II, to conserve manpower, gasoline, and so forth, frequency of delivery was reduced to every other day or to three days per week. Most distributors continued these lower frequencies after the war, because customers became accustomed to them, and the economic advantage of less frequent delivery had been demonstrated.[10]

The most common frequency of delivery today is three deliveries per week,[11] although some distributors have recently experimented with less frequent delivery. Modern milkmen typically deliver to two sets of customers, each set receiving three times per week. In effect, then, they conduct two routes, or as they put it, one route with "two sides."

Another procedure which has been changed by many distributors is the time of delivery. In the past, delivery was made in the morning so that customers would receive fresh milk before breakfast. Because of the present widespread use of refrigerators in the home, this is no longer necessary.[12]

For those distributors who have resorted to product diversification it is not only unnecessary, it is also inexpedient. These distributors find it to be advantageous to have their milkmen deliver during the day. At this time, personal contact with the customers is much more likely than at early hours. Under these circumstances drivers are ordinarily required, or at least strongly encouraged, to seek out contact and to employ appropriate tactics to increase sales.

A major impetus for the use of cultivating tactics, then, is the desire of distributors, brought about by their tenuous position, to increase their rate of sales per customer. By increasing their range of products, employing daytime delivery, and encouraging their milkmen to actively cultivate relationships with their customers, the probability of their accomplishing this is greatly increased.

Another factor which contributes to the need for cultivation is the continuing exodus of customers from home delivery to supermarkets. This puts distributors in the position of having to conduct, at best, a holding operation. Because of this, many distributors offer incentives, usually in the form of some sort of commission, to their drivers to solicit for new customers. They are required, at minimum, to replace each customer they lose with a comparable new customer. Thus, under the conditions described above, milkmen are continually engaging in cultivating relationships at various stages of development, including their inception.

To summarize: Over the last several decades the home delivery milk business has gone through a considerable decline. This has been brought about by a combination of cultural and technological changes, including suburbanization, the increased availability of the automobile and refrigerator, and the decreased perishability of dairy products - all of which have contributed to the convenience of the grocery store, especially the supermarket, as a place from which to purchase milk and other dairy products. To make matters worse for the home delivery milkman, the efficiency of the supermarket occasions a price differential which is decidedly to his disadvantage. In response to these conditions, retail distributors in many parts of the country have altered their operating procedures in such a manner that the milkman's job has been extensively changed. Routing procedures - time and frequency of delivery - have been changed, which of course changes the structural routine of the job. But, more importantly, the essence of the job itself has been radically altered. A job which at one time involved very little customer contact has been transformed into a job in which cultivation of customer relationships is an essential task.

SITUATIONALLY SPECIFIC FACTORS

The conditions in the context within which I made my observations were very similar to those which I have described as being fairly typical throughout the country. Population density in the area varied from moderately dense (housing tracts) to sparse (farms and ranches), with most sections being somewhere in-between. Supermarkets were prevalent in the area, and a price differential existed, made mandatory by law, with the supermarket pricing being several cents per quart less than the home delivery price. In addition to competing with supermarkets and other grocery stores, home delivery distributors in the area were compelled to compete rather intensely with one another. There were seven companies, of various sizes, competing for business in the area with only about 275,000 persons, most of which patronized supermarkets for their dairy products.

Besides the above, the physical terrain in the area was notably hilly, with approximately half of the residences being located on hillsides. This slowed down delivery time to such an extent that route sizes were significantly affected. This, in combination with the relatively sparse population density, disallowed the formation of compact routes, so a high rate of sales per customer was necessary. And, this, as shown previously, engenders a need for milkmen to actively cultivate customer relationships.

In addition to the foregoing factors, which applied equally to all the home

10

delivery distributors in the area, the distributor for whom I worked utilized several operating procedures which also promoted cultivation of customer relationships by his drivers.[13]

They were given responsibility for credit decisions (i.e., who was to get credit, and to what extent), and for the distribution of bills and collection of payments.

They were also given responsibility for preserving the size of their routes, so that it was necessary for them to routinely seek new customers. These tasks and how they were carried out will be discussed in the following sections.

The aforementioned factors, combined, made cultivation of relationships with customers imperative for the drivers with whom I worked. To keep their jobs they had to maintain profit producing routes. To accomplish this, it was necessary to actively initiate and maintain relationships with large numbers of customers. The following sections shall describe how they went about accomplishing this.

RELATIONSHIP CULTIVATION

Information upon which the following discussion is based was acquired to a large extent through my own experiences as a milkman. The interviewing which I did subsequent to this time produced little additional information concerning how milkmen go about operating their routes and interacting with their customers. This is so, because sharing of experiences was a daily occurrence with my co-workers. Each workday was followed by a "rap session" which customarily took place in a coffee shop adjacent to the dairy "plant." During these sessions various drivers discussed experiences they had on their routes - unusual events, conversations, problems, and so forth. Thus, much of my "interviewing" was accomplished unbeknownst to me or my "respondents."

In addition to being an important source of information for me, these conversations served as extemporaneous training sessions for the novice milkman. In these sessions new milkmen learned many of the cultivating tactics which they would be required to know in order to conduct their routes properly. The "break in" period given new drivers consisted chiefly of training in the instrumental aspects of the job, such as driving a truck, keeping the route books in order, "working a load," and so forth. This training period lasted only one or two weeks. During this time, novices were concerned mostly with such things as finding customer's homes, not dropping milk bottles, avoiding unfriendly dogs, and the like. Very little time could be used for teaching cultivating techniques. Thus, cultivating techniques were usually trial and error.

Learning this took place over a period of several months, and much of it was assimilated with very little awareness on the part of the drivers. Thus, the extent to which they were cognizant of the fact that they were manipulating, persuading, and so forth was minimal. I mentioned this to avoid leaving the impression that they saw themselves as game players, consciously employing tactics and strategies. Cultivation was so much a part of their job that it was generally performed with a low degree of awareness.

Likewise, I might also mention that it was not always successful. The extent to which it was difficult to ascertain. Customers may have agreed to receive service, increase their orders, terminate their patronage, and so forth for reasons unrelated to the cultivating activities of milkmen. I mention this, also, to avoid misimpression, since an unavoidable effect of my discussion is that the drivers will appear to be more successful than they probably were.

The cultivating activities of the drivers were organized around three tasks-- acquiring new customers, selling "by-products" (products other than milk), and collecting payments. In the course of realizing these tasks a number of different techniques were used. The acquisition of new customers required the employment of different techniques than did sales and collections, therefore it will be discussed separately. Following this, I will discuss several "de-cultivating" techniques, employed when a driver wanted to discourage the development of a relationship, or under extreme circumstances terminate one.

ACQUIRING NEW CUSTOMERS

The task of obtaining new customers involved three distinguishable kinds of techniques, used at three different stages: (1) Detecting techniques, used to ferret out potential customers; (2) Soliciting techniques, used to procure customers; (3) Trust including tactics, used to establish solidarity in new relationships.

DETECTING TECHNIQUES

As I mentioned previously, the distributor for whom I worked required his drivers to maintain, if not increase, the size of their routes. It was ordinary for each driver to lose five or ten customers per month, although this number varied according to time of year.[14]

This number was great enough that it was necessary for drivers to routinely seek new customers. As an incentive, they were given a "bonus" for each new customer they obtained.

Because of the variety of other activities which were required to operate a route, little time was available to solicit for new customers. Owing to this, the drivers used several techniques which enabled them to minimize the amount of "route time" they spent searching for new customers.

A driver was not restricted to soliciting only for his route. One driver could "sign up" a customer who would be served by another driver and still receive a bonus. Therefore, it was standard practice for drivers, particularly new drivers, to solicit among their friends, neighbors, and relatives. This would not necessarily increase the size of one's own route, but it would increase the size of one's paycheck, and gain the approval of the route supervisor. This was pretty much a one time tactic, as the drivers were generally reluctant to ask the same person more than once or twice.

Another, seldom used, technique was to ask customers for "leads" amongst their friends, relatives, and neighbors. This was usually asked only of customers whom one felt "close to." This precaution was taken to avoid the risk of offending an already existing customer, and thereby losing a customer instead of gaining one.

The above two techniques were not generally relied upon for replacing lost customers. Most drivers used techniques which could be carried out in the course of running their routes. There were two general techniques which filled this criterion. The first involved getting to know utility installers (e.g. telephone, gas and electric, etc.) who worked in the general area of one's route. These persons had knowledge of what homes were being vacated and what homes were being moved into. And, they ordinarily gave this information to milkmen who were on a friendly basis with them. This enabled drivers to get "good leads" with very little time consumed.

The second detecting technique which could be employed " on the route" involved watching for moving vans. Whenever a moving van was seen, drivers stopped and asked if the party was moving in or out of the house. If they were moving in, he either gave his "sales pitch" or set up a time to talk with the new resident at a later date. If the home was being vacated, the driver simply "kept as eye on it" until a new resident moved in.

SOLICITING TECHNIQUES

Once good leads were obtained, the driver had to somehow convince the potential customers to become actual customers. This was not a particularly easy task, because of the aforementioned price differential. In addition to this differential, a charge of three cents was imposed on each delivery, regardless of the amount delivered. The price differential and the delivery charge were undoubtedly the factors most often mentioned by potential customers when declining patronage. And, for the drivers they were the difficult to surmount, as they were sanctioned by law.[15]

Thus, soliciting techniques most often involved overcoming these price obstacles. The techniques most often used to accomplish (or at least attempt to accomplish) this were "personalizing" and "dealing."[16]

PERSONALIZING

Personalizing consisted of offering a potential customer personalized service which would supposedly make up for higher cost of home delivery. Such service consisted of such things as entering the customer's house and placing the "order" into the refrigerator (referred to by drivers as a "refer serve"), billing at optional intervals (anywhere from daily to monthly), maintaining an order at a predesignated size,[17] and so forth. In general, personalizing consisted of performing any service a driver felt was worthwhile doing to acquire and keep the patronage of a customer.

The personalizing "sales pitch" usually consisted of conceding to the potential customer that one's products were of the same general type and quality as those found at the stores, and that the prices were a bit higher, but maintaining one's personal service was very much worth receiving. When giving my personalizing sales pitch, I usually emphasized that, once the proper size of the order was established, the customer would never again have to be concerned with purchasing dairy products. I would "build" her order to whatever level she desired so that she could avoid having to "run to the store" just to get milk. I usually pointed out that the extra trips to the store which she most certainly had been making, aside from being inconvenient, were expensive and time consuming. And, in addition to transportation costs, people usually purchased several other items which would not have otherwise have been purchased. I added that this was known and encouraged by store owners, who usually placed dairy products in the back of their store so that customers would have to walk down aisles filled with food, just to pick up a quart of milk. This encourages impulse buying: I then emphasized that by taking my service, they could avoid this "trap." Most of my co-workers reported using similar versions of this sales pitch.

Personalizing was a technique which was also used on potential customers who had objections other than price to receiving home delivery. Many persons, for example, objected to home delivery because they work during the day and were afraid their order might spoil if left outside all day. This objection was easily overcome by offering to leave their order in an insulated box with ice, or by offering "refer service."[18]

DEALING

Dealing was ordinarily used only if personalizing failed, and only if the potential customer's order would be large enough to warrant its use. It was used with discretion because it was illegal. In spite of this, it was used regularly by most drivers, although more by some drivers than others. Dealing consisted simply of offering the customer a reduction in price. The price reduction took one of several forms. Most drivers preferred giving their "deals" a "free" quart of milk, pound of butter, half gallon of ice cream, or whatever at specified intervals. Deals carried out in this manner were easier to "cover up" than other types of deals. To cover up this type of deal, all a driver needed to do was "dump" the product that was given away. Dumping consisted of claiming that the product had gone sour or had been damaged. This allowed the driver to "balance" his books without taking a loss himself.

Other forms of dealing included reducing the price of specific products, and eliminating the delivery charge. These deals were more difficult to cover up because they involved "juggling" the books. Deals could not "show" in a customer's bill, so drivers were required to "hide" them. A number of methods were used to accomplish this. Most of them were much too complex to describe briefly, so I shall describe only the most commonly used one.

This method involved hiding deals in "daily cash." Drivers acquired five or ten dollars for each day from non-regular customers. These customers were not entered into the route book, so a driver could adjust the amount of "cash" he claimed, so long as he dumped enough products to balance his books properly. Drivers kept track of their "losses" (the amount of money lost in deals) throughout the day, subtracted this amount from their cash, and dumped enough products to make up the difference.

Dealing was implicitly encouraged by the route supervisor, although it was expected to be kept within certain limits. The amount of dealing a particular driver engaged in could be roughly ascertained by the amount of dumping he did. Drivers who dumped more or less than what was considered to be normal were usually warned that they were dumping "too much" or "not enough," which, translated, meant that they were either dealing too much or too little. Aside from this, dealing activities were seldom referred to, except between drivers. The drivers were fully aware that they were expected to deal, and they were expected to do it in such a way that it was "hidden" from the route supervisor, as well as state inspectors. This meant that dealing had to be accomplished completely from memory. Drivers had to remember who they were dealing with, as well as the type and amount of each deal. They could not write anything down, even in coded form, because it would increase the risk of getting caught.

DEVELOPING MUTUAL TRUST

Once a driver had gained the patronage of a new customer, it was essential for him to establish a relationship of mutual trust. His primary concern, regarding trust of the customer, was credit. He need to be reasonably sure that she would pay her bill. It was to his advantage, also, to ensure that the customer trusted him. Often this occurred with no action on his part, due apparently to the fact that a certain amount of trust is intrinsic to the role of milkman. Milkmen are, after all, easily traceable,[19] and they are ordinarily bonded. Judging from my experiences, customers seemed generally aware of this.

However, some customers demonstrated mistrust, particularly concerning the possibility that their milkman might "cheat" them by either over-charging them or by charging them for items which they did not purchase. Such customers often kept a day-to-day itemized account of the products they purchased, along with the prices at which they were advertized. When they received their bill they compared it against this itemized list to check for discrepancies.

Other customers expressed mistrust regarding the freshness of the products they were receiving. These customers would not accept their milkman's word that they were fresh. Some insisted on being shown how to translate the "date code" which is imprinted on the carton of most dairy products. This code gives the "dump date"-- the date after which products are not to be sold. This information, combined with the knowledge of the "carry over time" (the length of time a product is allowed to remain "on the truck") of a product, allowed them to ascertain how fresh the product was.

Customers who displayed what was perceived as mistrust were handled very carefully, because of fear that they would terminate service over the slightest misunderstanding. This occurred frequently enough that it was considered a problem which should be guarded against.

Whether or not such actions as those described above were in fact motivated by mistrust is not altogether clear. Other motives may have been involved. For example, itemized lists might have been kept by some customers for budgeting purposes. Or, refusal to provide their milkman with a key may merely have been a convenient account for refusing "refer service." However, the important thing is that drivers sensed such actions to be manifestations of mistrust, and acted accordingly.

The drivers also had reason to cultivate trust with customers who displayed no outward signs of mistrust. It was efficacious for a driver to establish his trustworthiness before he attempted to advance a relationship to a more familiar level. Failing to do so sometimes proved to be unfortunate. I had several experiences, for instance, in which customers terminated their patronage when I attempted to make them "refer serves." They expressed considerable displeasure at my suggestion that they provide me with a key to their house. This they apparently perceived as an attempt to set up a theft, or at least so it seemed judging from their reactions. Up to the time at which I attempted to make them "refer serves," I had had very little contact with these customers. They thus had little basis to upon which to judge my trustworthiness.

It was general policy of most of the drivers to go out of their way to display trustworthiness - as an insurance measure. Occasions commonly occurred in which this projected trustworthiness was beneficial. This was especially the case when bills were added incorrectly, or when prices were inadvertently misquoted. When customers discovered such things they often confronted their milkman with the discrepancy. If they trusted him they would be apt to take his word that the inconsistency was unintentional.

We see then, that a number of factors made trust cultivation an expedient task. It was necessary - sometimes even critically so-for customers who displayed mistrust. And, it was applied as an insurance measure to those customers who displayed no outward signs of mistrust.

TRUST-INDUCING TACTICS

In the course of trust cultivating, the drivers employed several trust-inducing tactics. These tactics fall suitably into four general categories, which for convenience I will call "the sincerity act," "contrived disclosure," "situational mitigation," and "accentuated honesty."

The Sincerity Act. Actually, the sincerity act was not so much a tactic as it was a carefully expressed demeanor. It consisted merely of presenting one's self in a pleasant, straightforward manner - a manner which implied confidence and trustworthiness. The sincerity act was not, of course, used exclusively by milkmen. It is employed by just about all persons who deal directly with customers. It has, in fact, been used to excess - enough so that it carries with it the risk of backfiring. If not practiced with the proper amount of reservation, it may be perceived as an indicator of insincerity - the opposite of what it is intended to convey.[20]

This did in fact occur. Many customers disclosed to me, in conversation, that they thought that one or another of my "relief drivers"[21] acted "phony," "deceitful," and the like.

Most of the drivers recognized the danger in acting "too nice," and made attempts to counteract the possibility of leaving such an impression, through use of the contrived disclosure tactic. This tactic added substance to the sincerity act.

Contrived Disclosure. Contrived disclosure consisted of disclosing, at opportune times, what was implied to be "insider" information. The kind of information offered was not general knowledge, but on the other hand, it was not as confidential as it was implied to be. The most commonly employed contrived disclosure concerned the aforementioned "date code" imprinted on the carton of most dairy products. Although the meaning of this code was not commonly known, it was not intended to be guarded information. It functioned to let the retailer know when unsold products were likely to go bad. Many customers, though, seemed to have the impression that it was information which was intentionally hidden from them. This, as it turned out, was to the driver's advantage. By voluntarily disclosing the method for translating the code, they could imply that, although distributors and processors might sometimes be less than trustworthy ("after all, they are businessmen"), this particular milkman could be trusted.

Another contrived disclosure that was commonly used to gain the confidence of customers concerned the source of "by-products" (i.e.

cottage cheese, yogurt, ice cream, cheese, and so forth). Many of the by-products sold by milkmen in this area were processed by the same company, although they were packaged differently, using names of the various companies. Most customers were unaware of this. By disclosing this in a confiding manner, a driver could, again, hopefully gain the trust of a customer.

The type of information which was disclosed was not particularly important. The important thing was that it appear to the customer as "special" information - something about which few people knew. The driver then appeared to be "confiding" in the customer, which implied that his loyalty resided with her rather than elsewhere.

Situational Mitigation. Situational mitigation was employed primarily with customers who displayed outward signs of mistrust. It consisted of taking direct measures to alleviate the grounds for mistrust. It was commonly used with customers who seemed to be unusually sensitive about possibly being cheated. I had one customer, for instance, who continually accused me of either over-charging her or adding up her weekly bill incorrectly. The amount involved was never more than a few cents, so I always reimbursed her, with apologies, for whatever the amount she claimed to have lost. But, the problem occurred with such frequency that she eventually began to imply that I was trying to cheat her. I was afraid that she would terminate her patronage, so I confronted her with a solution. I gave her a mimeographed price list (provided by the company) of all the products I sold. I then suggested that, each delivery, I leave a list of the products which she ordered along with the price which she was charged for each item. She could then compare this list with what she thought to be correct, and if a discrepancy was found we could work it out the following delivery. Never again did the problem arise. In fact, several months later she told me not to bother leaving the list anymore, and apologized for having caused me so much bother. I had, apparently, successfully eliminated the grounds for her mistrust of me.

A similar direct approach was used with customers who expressed concern over the freshness of the products they were receiving. Customers who exhibited such concern were usually told where the date code was on the various products, and how to translate. This allowed them to ascertain the freshness of the products delivered to them, without having to rely on their milkman's word.[22]

In any case, situational mitigation allowed a driver to directly eliminate grounds for mistrust. By doing this he could generally establish a relationship on a more stable foundation, and if desired proceed with further cultivation.

Accentuated Honesty. Another commonly used trust-inducing tactic was accentuated honesty. This tactic was used whenever a situation arose in which a driver could overtly display honesty. One such situation arose when drivers inadvertently caused minor damage to the fences, shrubs, and so forth while maneuvering their trucks. Often such damage was minor enough that it would likely go unnoticed. However, situations such as this could easily, and safely, be used to display honesty. For instance, I once backed my truck into a customer's picket fence and damaged one picket. I could have ignored the damage, as several nearby pickets had been previously damaged by someone else. But, instead, I notified the customer. She laughed, and said that she probably wouldn't have noticed it. I insisted that I personally pay for it (the company would have paid for it), but she thanked me for my "honesty" and refused my offer. This display of "honesty" appeared to have been beneficial. Up to this time this customer had purchased only milk. But, shortly after this event she began regularly purchasing "extras."

Another type of situation in which honesty could be accentuated was brought about by billing errors. Monthly bills were sometimes added incorrectly.[23]

If the error was large customers usually noticed it very quickly. But, small errors were often overlooked. Whenever a driver discovered such an error, he was, again, presented with a convenient opportunity to accentuate his honesty.

PREDICTING CREDIT TRUSTWORTHINESS

As I mentioned previously, the drivers were concerned with developing mutual trust. They needed not only to convince customers of their trustworthiness, but also to ascertain the credit trustworthiness of customers. They were given responsibility for determining who was to receive what kind of credit-- ranging from daily to monthly. It was necessary for them to ascertain the trustworthiness of particular customers within the first several deliveries. They had, especially, to guard against two types of customers-"deadbeats" and "skippers."[24]

Deadbeats were customers who ran up large bills and then refused to pay them. Skippers were customers who ran up large bills and then changed their residence without notifying their milkman, and without leaving a forwarding address with the post office, utility company, or any other agency through which they could be traced.

The drivers used certain common sense indicators to aid them in predicting the trustworthiness of a customer. They, first of all, took notice of the general appearance of the neighborhood - was it a "good" neighborhood or a "bad" one? Secondly, they noted the general appearance of the house - was it "nice" or was it "crummy?" On the first delivery they attempted to contact the customer. If she answered the door, attempts were made to strike up a conversation. This serves two purposes. In the course of the conversation useful information, such as husband's occupation, might be disclosed. Also, it might result in an invitation to step inside the door. Once inside, the general appearance of the inside of the house could be noted - was it carefully kept and nicely furnished, or was it carelessly kept and poorly furnished?

These indicators served to aid a driver in deciding what kind of "risk" a particular customer was. A carelessly kept house in a bad neighborhood indicated (supposedly) a "credit risk." If it was decided that a particular customer was a potential risk, attempts were made to get more information. The customer was contacted, either in person or by telephone, and asked questions regarding husband's occupation, place of employment, and so forth. The driver usually explained, apologetically, that the company required it of him to get such information. This relieved him of personal responsibility and lessened the risk of irritating a customer.

Customers who were defined as being low risk were given a choice of what interval they would like to be billed at. Those who were defined as risky were told that they would have to pay cash for each delivery - at least for a while. After several weeks, the driver usually offered monthly credit. This method of gradual progression enabled the driver to keep the customers bill from "getting out of hand," and it allowed him to acquire more information which would hopefully allow him to more closely establish the customer's trustworthiness. It also eliminated the risk of making a customer angry by withdrawing credit which had already been extended.

SALES AND COLLECTIONS

Aside from acquiring new customers and developing trust, selling by-products and collecting bills were tasks around which most of the drivers' cultivating activities were organized. These were the most essential tasks, and the ones that consumed the most time. The techniques employed in carrying out these two tasks were essentially the same. Most drivers found it best to manage the two tasks indirectly, through certain subtle cultivating techniques. The "hard sell" approach carried with it a high risk of offending the customers and therefore was seldom used.[25] The most commonly used techniques were what, for convenience, I will refer to as "nurturing pseudo friendship," and "effecting obligation."

NURTURING PSEUDO FRIENDSHIP

The aim of this maneuver was simply to establish one's self on friendly terms with the customers. The object was not to become personal friends (although that sometimes did occur), but merely to become "well-liked." It was assumed that a customer would express her regard for a well-liked milkman by purchasing extras, paying her bill promptly, and so forth.

The most crucial activities in a budding relationship were conversations and accepting an offer for a cup of coffee. They both tended to promote relationships. Thus, when an appropriate opportunity arose, a driver could strike up a "friendly" conversation with a customer, usually on a topic which seemed to interest her - her children, her hobby, or whatever. The first conversation usually opened the door for further ones. A driver could promote this by, if possible, somehow referring to the previous conversation when he made his next delivery. This indicated that he remembered the conversation and enjoyed it. After one or two conversations, a customer usually offered the milkman a cup of coffee, which, if he wished to nurture the relationship, he accepted. If things progressed normally, the offer for coffee became routine, although because of time limitations it was not always accepted. When the relationship reached this stage, it was considered a successful one. Such relationships were called "coffee stops."

When nurturing a relationship, the driver attempted to leave the impression that the customer involved was one of his "favorite" customers, which may or may not have been the case. Each driver usually had about forty or fifty "favorite" customers.

EFFECTING OBLIGATION

The aim of this technique was to somehow instill in customers a sense of obligation or indebtedness. It was, again, assumed that customers would reciprocate through increased sales and prompt bill payments. Effecting obligation was accomplished, ordinarily, in two different ways--through offering "specials," and through performing "favors."

Specials. Each week the company offered specials to all customers. On Monday and Tuesday a list of three or four items was left with each customer's order. The items in the list were sold for one week, at a reduced price. Often a customer would express concern that an item she wanted was not "on special." This offered an opportunity for the driver to promote a sense of indebtedness in the customer. He could inform her that, "because he was in a good mood," or some other such expression, he would give her a "special" on the item she wanted. If the customer had a large family, and was therefore a potentially "big" customer, he might even offer to make a special permanent (i.e. charge her at a reduced rate whenever she bought the product).

Another type of special was what the drivers called a "freezer pack." Customers who had large freezers and large families were offered freezer packs. A freezer pack consisted of eleven or twelve half-gallons of ice cream for the regular price of ten half-gallons.

In general, specials were usually offered on high volume sales, such as freezer packs, and on expensive items, such as large blocks of cheese. This minimized the loss incurred by granting the special, and also offered an opportunity to increase the sales of items which were otherwise difficult to sell. Permanent specials were very much like deals, the main difference being in their intent. Deals were offered to maintain the patronage of customers, whereas specials were offered to enhance the solidarity of relationships. Specials, like deals, were covered up by dumping.

Favors. Another way of incurring obligation in customers was to perform "favors" for them. A wide variety of favors were performed by the drivers. The most common ones included such things as mailing letters, turning on ovens for absent housewives, doing minor automobile repairs, and so forth. It was also common for a customer to ask a driver if he knew anyone who wanted to buy a used bicycle, automobile, washing machine, etc. Often a buyer was sometimes a bother, but if one could be found the payoff was usually sufficient to have made the effort worthwhile. I sold several items in this manner, and the customers involved expressed their gratitude in the way which I had hoped for - by increasing their sales. Similar experiences were commonly reported by other drivers.

The above cultivating techniques (nurturing pseudo friendships and effecting obligation) were beneficial in other ways than just those described above. They allowed the drivers to not only enhance sales and collections, but also to manipulate them in other ways. The drivers were expected to maintain a balance between what they sold and what they collected in payments during any given month. If a driver sold over 5,000 dollars worth of products one month he was expected to collect at least 5,000 dollars in payments the following month. Those who accomplished that were said to have "collected out." Drivers who collected out were given a bonus.

Collecting out was rather difficult to accomplish regularly, because customers did not always pay their bill promptly. This meant that a driver may fall short of collecting out one month, and greatly exceed it the next month. Thus, although the credit on his route was "clean," he was not always able to achieve his bonus. However, if a driver had a poll of customers that held him in high regard or felt a sense of obligation towards him, he could better his chances of collecting out. During months in which it appeared as if he might come up short he could ask these customers to please pay their bill before the end of the month, if they had not already done so - explaining to them that he needed more payments to achieve his bonus. On the other hand, if he had already collected out he could ask these customers to please not pay their bill until after the first of the following month. Some customers became so accustomed to this that they always consulted their milkman before paying their bill.

Sales could be manipulated in a similar manner. Drivers were expected to be able to outsell their relief drivers. If a relief driver had a "200 dollar day" (i.e. sold 200 dollars worth of products) on, say, a Wednesday, it was expected that the regular driver would have sold more than on the previous Wednesday. The assumption was that regular drivers knew their customers better than the relief drivers, and therefore should be able to sell more to them. When a regular driver was outsold by his relief driver he was ordinarily admonished for it. To avoid this, the drivers asked those customers of whom they felt they had the confidence not to purchase extras from their relief driver if they were able to wait until their next delivery. This lessened the probability that they would be outsold.

DE-CULTIVATING TECHNIQUES

When conducting their routes, the drivers were hampered by a critical shortage of time. They delivered to anywhere from 150 to 250 customers each day. Because of this, the amount of time they could spend cultivating any one relationship was severely limited. This being the case, they ordinarily gauged the amount of time they spent cultivating a particular relationship according to what they estimated to be its payoff potential. More time was allotted for customers with high payoff potential than was allotted for customers with low payoff potential - or at least that was the ideal.[26]

However, customers, themselves, often attempted to initiate closer relationships with the drivers. If such relationships appeared to have low payoff potential, they somehow had to be inhibited.

INHIBITING CONDUCT

As I mentioned previously, two activities - conducting conversations and drinking coffee with customers - were crucial in budding relationships. Encouraging these activities could promote a relationship. Discouraging them could inhibit a relationship. In accordance with this, drivers discouraged these activities when carrying out low yield relationships. They accomplished this by conducting themselves in a designed manner. When in the presence of a low yield customer they maintained a pleasant demeanor, so as not to appear rude, but always acted as if they were in a hurry, whether or not they actually were. This gave them an account for breaking conversations short, and also provided them with a convenient excuse for not accepting a cup of coffee. By conducting themselves in this manner, they could discourage the development of a relationship without offending the customer.

However, this tactic sometimes failed and a relationship got "out of hand." When this occurred, a driver had two alternatives - coping the best he could, or terminating the relationship. About the only way to cope with such a relationship was to deal with each encounter separately. When delivering to these customers the driver usually approached the house very quietly, sometimes parking their truck a short distance down the street. By doing this, the hope was, they may be able to avoid contact with the customer. If this failed they simply gave whatever account they could think of to break the ensuing conversation short.

Occasionally, a relationship got so far "out of hand," that a driver decided that it would be best to terminate it. This was usually done only with customers who habitually consumed excessive amounts of time. Customers who were terminated were those persisted in carrying out fifteen or twenty minute (sometimes even more) conversations each delivery. Terminating customers was strictly forbidden by the route supervisor (except for credit reasons), so the driver utilized tactics for accomplishing this without notice.

TERMINATING TACTICS

In general, terminating tactics consisted of provoking the customer to discontinue patronage on her own initiative (or at least so she thought). If this could be accomplished, a driver could rid himself of a problem relationship without incurring the wrath of the route supervisor. The two most commonly used employed terminating tactics were "the hold-over tactic," and "the incompetency tactic."

THE HOLD-OVER TACTIC

The most commonly employed terminating tactic was executed by intentionally delivering bad products to the customer. To do this, a driver would "hold-over" a product, usually a carton of milk, on his truck for about a week or so before delivering it. By this time the product was on the verge of turning sour, but not sour enough that the ploy would be discovered. This was done several deliveries until, hopefully, the customer terminated service. The advantage of this tactic was that it alleviated the milkman of responsibility. Afterall, it was not his fault if the company distributed inferior products.

THE INCOMPETENCY TACTIC

Another common tactic, sometimes employed when the hold-over tactic failed, was the incompetency tactic. In using this tactic, a driver intentionally displayed clumsiness, stupidity, and general inefficiency. To manage this, he did such things as "accidentally" break milk bottles in inappropriate places (on the front porch, kitchen floor, and so on), "inadvertently" forgetting to deliver part of the order, delivering unordered products, incorrectly adding bills, and so forth. This tactic was ordinarily employed only as a last resort, as it carried with it the risk of provoking the route supervisor, particularly if the customer telephoned the dairy office to complain of a milkman's "incompetency."

DISCUSSION

The foregoing analysis is primarily descriptive. The concepts which I have employed were designed to fit the situation herein described. However, several general dimensions of cultivating are evident in this situation - particularly regarding the structural conditions according to which the need for it varies. I shall, then, briefly discuss some of the aspects of cultivating as it relates to service relationships in general - keeping in mind that what I say is largely hypothetical, and certainly incomplete.

The structural source of cultivating as it relates to service relationships is what could be called "contextual power asymmetry."[27] Power in service relationships is contextual in that it ordinarily applies only within the servicing context.[28] In other types of relationships, such as marriage, power may be more pervasive.

I used the term "power asymmetry" to refer to the balance of power in a relationship. Quite simply, a relationship which is characterized by power asymmetry is one in which one party, for any number of reasons, exercises more control over the course of the relationship (in this case within the servicing context) than does the other party. The milkman-customer relationship, for example, is one which is characterized, at least initially, by acute power asymmetry.

The balance of power in a relationship can be altered through the use of cultivating techniques. In this sense, cultivation is a leveling mechanism. The milkman clearly uses it as such. Through the use of cultivating techniques he is able to effectively increase the amount of control he exercises in relationships with his customers. In some instances, particularly those in which he has successfully employed what I previously referred to as "nurturing pseudo friendship" and "effecting obligation," he is able to accomplish near symmetry.

The most basic source of power asymmetry in service relationships, it seems, is simple supply and demand.[29] If a service is low in demand and high in supply, as is the case with home delivery milk business, power asymmetry will likely be acute, and the need for cultivation will, accordingly, be high. On the other hand, if the demand is high and the supply is low, power asymmetry is less likely to be acute and, accordingly, the need for cultivation will be low. If this observation is correct, we would expect that medical doctors, for instance, would be required to spend a minimal amount of time engaged in cultivating activities with their patients. This is not to say that they would be able to refrain completely from cultivation. Friedson's discussion of doctor-patient relationships clearly shows that doctors are not exempt from cultivating activities.[30] However, it is quite evident that doctor-patient relationships involve mush less cultivating than do milkman-customer relationships. According to Friedson's findings, the cultivating activities of doctors seem to consist primarily of attempts to convince patients of the wisdom of their diagnoses and prescriptions-- which seems to be a matter of trust maintenance.[31]

The relationship between cultivation and supply and demand is particularly evident when a service occupation is either on the decline. The economic demand for his service, which at one time was a necessity, has steadily declined over the last several decades. At the same time, through the rise of the supermarket, the supply of the servicers has effectively increased. Thus, the milkman's past dominance over the retail milk business has been lost. And, this as was previously shown, is one of their chief conditions which gave rise to the need for milkmen to engage in cultivating activities.

The relationship between cultivation and supply and demand in an inclining service occupation is evident in Habenstein's analysis of the ascent of the American funeral director.[32] Previous to the rise of the funeral director, the various tasks associated with preparing and burying the dead were handled by a wide range of occupations, including "nurses, sextons, cabinetmakers, livery stable operators, and other factotums."[33] The demand for death related services was high, but the supply and variety of servicers was also high. Thus, to establish themselves as a discernable occupation, funeral directors had to create a psychological demand for their service. In other words, they had to convince their potential customers that the way in which they carried out death related services was preferable to other ways. This they accomplished, essentially, through cultivation.[34] Their success is well-evidenced by the fact that modern Americans would be horrified (or highly amused) at the suggestion that they take their dead relatives to a cabinetmaker for preparation and burial.

Another factor which seems to affect the extent to which cultivation is associated with a particular service occupation is relative expertise. High expertise service occupations, particularly the professions, seem to involve a lower amount of cultivation activity than low expertise occupations, and vise versa. This seems to be the case for at least two reasons.

First of all, as Caplow points out regarding the professions, the supply of expert servicers tends to be kept at a relatively low level through occupational controls over such things as eligibility requirements and training.[35] This effectively increases the demand (in relation to the supply) for the services of the limited number of "legitimate" expert servicers.

Secondly, high expertise service occupations, again particularly the professions, tend to develop "professional ethics" which severely restrict those kinds of activities which I have referred to as cultivating.

The above general discussion is unavoidably sketchy, and in no way conclusive. The general dimensions which I have alluded to were advanced primarily as hypothesis, although they were suggested by the empirical instance of the milkman. Verification of the extent to which these are the relevant dimensions will have to await further research in the area of service relationships.

REFERENCES

1. Erving Goffman, " The Medical Model and Mental Hospitalization," in Asylums, Garden City, New York: Doubleday and Company, 1961, p. 326.

2. For a discussion of relative power symmetry in social relationships see Barney G. Glaser, The Patsy and the Contractor, forthcoming.

3. E. Linwood Tipton, an economist with the Milk Industry Foundation, quoted in the Futurist, June, 1971, P. 118.

4. E. F. Baumer, et al., "Dimensions of Customer Attitude in Fluid Milk Purchases With Special References to Doorstep Delivery vs. Store Purchases," in Research Bulletin (1028) of the Ohio Agricultural Research and Development Center, Wooster, Ohio, December 1968.

5. Low consumption customers are considered, generally, to be those whose families consume less than ten quarts of milk per week.

6. Baumer, et al., "Dimensions of Consumer Attitude," op. cit., pp. 3-5.

7. Ibid., p. 4.

8. Ibid., p. 5.

9. Many distributors are both wholesale and retail, but the two methods of distribution are ordinarily administered separately from one another.

10. Chester Roadhouse and James Henderson, The Market Milk Industry, New York: McGraw Hill, 1950, p. 501.

11. Baumer, et al., "Dimensions of Consumer Attitude," op. cit., p. 9.

12. Some customers still prefer early delivery. To accommodate them, many distributors set the "starting time" of their routes at around five or six in the morning. This allows for early delivery to those customers who prefer it, and daytime delivery to those who do not.

13. Hereafter I will refer to my former co-workers as drivers, as that is more often what they call themselves.

14. More customers were lost in the summer, as families change residences more often at this time of year.

15. The law was enforced by a state "board" which was given authority to punish distributors who violated it by imposing fines.

16. The word "dealing" was used by the drivers. The term "personalizing" is my own.

17. This was referred to as "building," and consisted of the milkman making certain a particular number of products were always available to the customer. For instance, if a "build order" consisted of five quarts of milk, the driver would leave whatever amount was necessary to bring the total amount of milk in the refrigerator up to five quarts, considering what may have been left over from previous deliveries.

18. Most "refer serves" gave their milkman a house key. which he placed in his route book next to the customer's billing sheet.

19. For discussion of trust and traceability see James M. Henslin, "Trust and the Cab Driver," in Sociology and Everyday Life, Ed. Marcello Turzzi, Englewood Cliffs, New Jersey, Prentice-Hall Inc., 1968.

20. One is reminded here of the common stereotype regarding the "sincerity" of used car salesmen.

21. Relief drivers were drivers who had no regular route. They operated the regular drivers' routes when they were on vacations, days off, and so forth.

22. The date code, if you recall, was used also with the contrived disclosure tactic.

23. Monthly bills were added up by office workers. All other bills (semi-monthly, weekly, etc.) were added up by the drivers.

24. These terms were used by the drivers.

25. Two of the drivers had reputations as "hard sellers." They both had perpetual trouble with customer relationships, so they were eventually made relief drivers. Relief drivers alternated between five different routes, so they could come in contact with any one customer only every several weeks. In addition, they were not expected to go out of their way to sell or collect bills. These two factors minimized the risk of their offending customers.

26. The payoff potential of customers was usually estimated according to family size.

27. Again, for a discussion of relative power asymmetry see Barney G. Glaser, The Patsy and the Subcontractor, forthcoming.

28. Goffman alludes to this in his definition of "personal-service occupations:"

A personal-service occupation may be defined, ideally, as one whose practitioner performs a specialized personal service for a set of individuals where the service requires him to engage in direct personal communication with each of them and where he is not otherwise bound to the person he serves.

Erving Goffman, "The Medical Model," op. cit. p. 324.

29. Demand for a service, as Caplow notes (regarding professional services), can be either economic or psychological. See Theodore Caplow, The Sociology of Work,New York: McGraw Hill, 1954, p. 170.

30. Eliot Freidson, "Dilemmas in the Doctor-Patient Relationship," in Patients Views of Medical Practice, New York: Russell Sage Foundation. 1961, pp. 171-191.

31. Ibid., especially pp. 181-186.

32. Robert W. Habenstein, "Sociology of Occupations: The Case of the American Funeral Director," in Human Behavior and Social Progress, Ed. Arnold M. Rose, Boston: Houghton Mifflin Company, 1962, pp. 225-246.

33. Ibid., p. 228.

34. The particular techniques which they used to accomplish this are well-illustrated by Habenstein, and consist generally of their capitalizing on, and to some extent helping to form, the cultural aesthetics of death in America.

35. Caplow, The Sociology of Work, op. cit., p. 170.

CHAPTER 2

Reprinted from *Social Problems*, Spring 1964, Vol. 11., No. 4

TOURISTRY: A Type of Occupational Mobility

Ruth Pape

Every year millions of working Americans are on the move. Summer only brings an increase in the year-round tide of vacationers who travel the confines of their two, three or four weeks off from the job. Only the very wealthy can maintain a permanent vacationer status, although the retired or unemployed may be able to cover as much territory while bumming around.[1] Vacationers, however, are travelers who are making more or less permanent migrations in search of a better job,[2] a better climate or a better neighborhood.[3]

Some are following migratory jobs, as in agriculture,or intermittently migratory ones, as with lumbering or construction work.[4] There are even some occupations into which travel is built as a requisite feature, as in the transportation industry, the Foreign Service and the military. But this is hardly voluntary mobility for, when the Navy invites a young man to see the world, the itinerary is hardly of his own choosing.

But there is a group of people who do work, who travel more or less where and when they please, who seem never to have been described or analyzed in the literature of geographic or occupational mobility. Well-known to despairing employment agencies and employers, these people are practicing what I choose to call "touristry," a form of journeying that depends upon occupation, but only in a secondary sense in that it finances the more primary goal, travel itself. Performing a highly demanded service which is easily documented, either by a transferable license or by relatively simple tests, they are able to spend a longer time at touring than a simple vacation would allow by merely taking a job in the area they wish to sample and keeping it only as long as features unrelated to the job continue to be attractive.

It is this form of mobility that I wish to delineate in this paper.[5] I shall discuss the factors which permit touristry not only within nursing but also in a wider social context. From the structure of nursing, I shall derive general characteristics for the pattern of touristry, apply these against various occupational situations, and try to demonstrate its probability as a future part of certain occupational types, especially among growing groups of technicians.

Certain characteristic conditions for touristry lie outside the specific dimensions of nursing. Work, for example, plays a secondary part in the life expectations of American females despite the growing numbers who work. Although a girl's education may include quite lengthy preparation for a formal occupation, unquestionably her main anticipation is of marriage and the adult role of wife-homemaker-mother.[6] Until this event, however, she must pass the interim in a socially appropriate manner.

Completion of schooling, however prolonged, tends to represent a transition from dependant child to semi-adult. To maintain an otherwise normal offspring in dependent status after this point is not usually possible.[7] Although there may be an interval of job-seeking, it cannot be unduly protracted without increased social pressure. The first "serious" job confirms the transition toward adulthood and the general expectation is that economic and social independence will follow until the time of marriage.

Since marriage is, generally, the prime goal of the young female, any job she holds is seen as only an interim position, not the ideal. As she awaits this prized status, it expected that she is practicing the business of domesticity as she manages her own miniature household. Many working girls do remain at home but some payment for room and board is generally expected, even if it is of a token nature. Apart from maintaining an appropriately decent level of living, little other responsibility is ordinarily put upon her. In fact, there even seems to be a social mandate to act irresponsibly, to sow the equivalent of wild oats short of grave moral errors that would jeopardize marriage.

Except for maintenance and, perhaps, as occasional obligation to give some financial aid to her family, the new working girl, at least of the middle-class, has great freedom to use her salary as she pleases, usually for those things a dependent child was never given within a family budget. Future need and security do not fit within her life view, so long-term savings and insurance policies are not typical spending objects. Acquisition of home furnishings seems to fall within the aura of marriage or at least settling down and thus is viewed as inappropriate until then. The usual purchases may be characterized as luxury goods and services of a personal nature, such as clothes, cosmetics, a car: all items directed toward social improvement. Any savings would tend to be toward vacations, travel and larger luxuries, although the self-restraint needed for this is largely mitigated by current credit practices.

TOURISTRY IN NURSES

Historical Aspects. Probably from the very start of nursing as a distinct occupation in the United States, there have been some practitioners who realize that, with this skill, it would be possible to travel wherever they wished. Perhaps this was the feminine form of the old-time wanderin' man. Answering the call of alien places has traditionally been viewed as a curse by the solid citizen, [8] but the possibility has been a correlative attribute of nursing for so long that its existence has come to be taken for granted by nurses and those who employ them. Nurses, in fact, seem never to have viewed this possibility unfavorably and rather consider it one of the definite advantages of their occupation. Others, however, see it from a different perspective. Even as early as 1928 when hospital nursing had hardly become recognized as an occupational entity, vigorous complaints were heard from the proprietors of nursing registries that one of the major and concurrent problems was the "tramp nurse" who was "more a roving spirit and cannot be relied upon" who "stream(s) by, stopping over to work for (a) short time."[9] A physician diagnosed it as a "strange pathological malady-itching foot"[10] from which these early nurses suffered. Even now when professionally committed physicians focus on this pattern as a problem of direct significance, they tend to be irritated, if not shocked and irate, at this unorthodoxy within nursing professionalism.

Present Employment Conditions. Nurses who wish to travel now have many alluring choices. Air and shiplines, the Peace Corps, and the armed services now stress exotic foreign service. But for those less willing to submit to the accompanying time restrictions and commitments, there is still the self-planned and self-limited route of touristry. It is true that there are some countries where it is not possible or desirable to work (so that nurses would wish to save for a bona fide vacation to go there), but more and more nurses are finding ways to extend their touristry beyond national boundaries.

That nurses turn their licenses almost directly into travel tickets may be seen in the recruiting advertisements in almost any nursing journal. Besides the usual details of salary, installation description and fringe benefits, may be found frequent references to the local attractions either present or within easy range.[11] Whether these are effective or not, hospitals in metropolitan areas are often largely staffed by nurses who come not only from other locales but from other states and countries as well.

For many years it has been common knowledge that there is an almost universal shortage of nurses. Hawaii is presently the only state that does not need, in various stages of desperation, every nurse that can be attracted. California, for example, must recruit roughly 75% of its work force from nurses trained outside the state.[12] It is no wonder that the process of establishing licensure has been made as efficient and painless as possible, reportedly making it possible for a nurse with sufficient and adequate documents to begin work after only "a few minutes" at the office at the California Board of Nurses Examiners. Even those whose transcripts must be sent for may work in the interim with an easily obtained temporary license. Within nursing, California, along with New York, is noted for having the most stringent requirements for graduate nurses.

Employment, too, has become a simplified process, especially in stress times resulting in great turnover and short staffing. Although two weeks' notice is the polite expectation in any job, nursing directors are only too willing to offer an immediate starting date and often suggest that they cannot wait for proper notice to be given and fulfilled. Job requirements are also minimized, often demanding no more than proper licensure and the appearance of stamina to do the job. References, when checked, are usually returned with vague, polite phrases unless there has been highly unsatisfactory service. So few nurses write ahead to secure a job that it becomes apparent that staff-level jobs are believed to always to be available. And the fact that they are seldom disappointed only proves the truth of their prediction but also reinforces the high estimation of the widespread shortage of nurses.

Thus it may seem that one of the permeating characteristics of the nursing job market is the scarcity of practitioners. Among the consequences are expeditious credentialling and the minimizing of requirements for the lowest level positions, which only ease the process of getting a job and, hence, of leaving one.

TOURISTRY AND THE NURSE

Nursing, as it is taught and officially projected, is supposed to have elements of devotion and dedication with humanitarian and/or professional characteristics. Even though nursing as an occupation has incorporated the mobility factor, recruiting literature tends to assume the existence of a regular career-escalator pattern, even while being forced to acknowledge the vast corps of nonemployed married nurses. Certain of my data suggests that orientation to nursing as a primary focus is tied to the passage of time and "career-nurses" are only to be found in a higher age bracket as well as in higher administrative and educational echelons than are the newly graduated staff nurses being considered here. The latter, rather, consider their nurse role as only a part of a more generalized life pattern, and usually only a very minor part. Thus I am not using the word "career" in its more general sociological sense of temporal and status passage between positions, but to define the orientation the nurses themselves hold to the position that work plays in their overall life expectations. Nonetheless, even relative lack of emphasis on the work-role can be viewed as a definite stage within the pattern of nursing, since some older career-oriented nurses recount having passed through or having known of this stage in comparable age groups.

Occupational Conditions. Besides being young, occupationally educated and middle-class, the newly graduated nurse finds herself with the added advantage of possessing an eagerly sought trade. Although salaries are generally felt to be disproportionately low to the amount of prior training, the newest graduate is still able to step into a basic hospital staff position at a rate considerably above other beginning jobs for women, especially the unskilled or semi-skilled ones which most take. The salary rate also often ignores a lack of prior experience, maturity or career commitment. Added to this is the widespread knowledge that she will be able to get a job almost anywhere in this country.[13]

This makes it easier for her to indulge in that other luxury that has enjoyed rising popularity in the middle class in proportion to the decline of isolationism, especially since the end of World War I: the exploration of different geography - tourism.[14] Certainly vacation travel has been made increasingly easy with the advent of the "fly-now-pay-later" concept, vacation bank loans and economy plans for trips and tours all over the accessible world.[15] But vacations generally occur within the confines of a job's annual leave system, during a special leave of absence or between positions and are generally predetermined and limited by the funds and time saved for them. But, by setting up a new set of operations, financed by a local job, the young nurse, among others, is able to enjoy the merits of any particular region at her own pace and just as long as she wishes.

Initiation of the touristry pattern. Although nursing students do not often give it as a reason for going into nursing, possibly the easy transferability of practice may be one of those secondary selling points that draw a large number of travel-minded girls into nursing schools. As graduation approaches, among the growing and sharpened fantasies of goals for the students are the shared dreams of where they will go. The potential tourists become aware of mutual interests and thus may band together to prepare for their trip. At graduation, the girls are restrained only by the need to take and pass their licensing examinations, then to earn enough money to get wherever they plan to go and pay a month's rent when they get there. Whenever this is accomplished, the touristry-bent nurse bursts into the employment market in earnest, not only ready to leave her childhood status but also her childhood neighborhood, at least as far as the years in the schooling area have made this represent it.

The rates and timing may vary but graduation usually sees a number of newly married girls who have gone directly on with the traditionally feminine mode, thus skipping over the interim of independence and irresponsibility. At this stage, few girls plan to remain unmarried, unless they are committed to religious goals, are far older than the usual, or are settled into a pattern of deviance that does not include marriage. Many young graduate nurses report, however, they although they fully expect to marry, it is not part of their immediate plans and they can well imagine working the two years to statistically fall between a girl's coming onto and leaving the labor market for the first time.[16]

These are the girls who say they are not ready for marriage, who want to see something else before they settle down, but who are also willing to admit that marriage may come along any moment and change those ideas. These are the nurses who may be seen working in any of our metropolitan hospitals with only a few months' working experience behind them, usually at their training hospital. They have come in groups of two or more, located a furnished apartment, sharing cost and chores, and then gone looking for a job, usually intent on all working together too.

Touristry in operation. What makes them different from workers migrating in search of greener job pastures is that, for them, a job is merely the way to support themselves decently while they see the sights, sample the social life, have a bit of fun and then move on. These nurses do not follow any orientation to work as a central focus of living; their attention is directed to values outside the job environment and they use their work as a means to other, unrelated ends.

Thus the standards they do use in evaluating a job seem unrelated to those used by career oriented nurses or any who try to apply professional standards. In touristry, pay is naturally the prime consideration since this is the main reason for working at all. Nurses from the East and South are attracted to the higher pay offered in the West without taking into account the comparably higher cost of living there. But pay schedules are fairly standardized within a region and there is no tradition of individual negotiation. Immediately after salary comes a concern with hours. Hospital scheduling, as for any 24-hour institution, conflicts with the workday that most of the American public puts in. The lack of predictable days off interferes with any attempts at long range planning. Another consideration of high importance, that euphemistically masquerades under the heading of "social opportunities," is the quantity of available young men in the immediate and surrounding areas. One factor that bears most directly on quitting, but also figures in job acceptance, is the strenuousness of the job. There are few nursing jobs nowadays that are routinely exhausting, but these girls insist on enough energy after work to engage in social activities that are their prime interest. Thus it happens that whenever the turnover of staff becomes exceptionally heavy, a certain portion of those remaining will soon quit because of the added work they must do leaves them unable to lead their non-work lives as they would wish.

Termination of touristry. Just as surely as it can prevent touristry, so marriage will put a stop to it as a pattern. The irresponsibility interim of a young girl's life can also be closed by a call to return home to attend to a family crisis, such as illness or death. Of course, returning home may also mean that the girl, without considering settling down, has found touristry to be unsuitable for her personally. Some find that they are generally disappointed with what they meet in travel, that things are not so much better than they were at home. Others may rapidly find that they are frankly homesick and were never cut out for touristry.

There are a certain number of working nurses who, with the passage of time and the approach of their thirties, begin to suspect that marriage may not be as inevitable as they had expected at twenty-two. Among other reactions may well be the appearance of concern for an occupational future and such attendant factors as advancement and security. These nurses may travel again, but their moves are more classical forms of work oriented mobility.

The "permanent" tourist. A very few nurses may find travel so enticing that they continue it even as a prime pattern. In my sample group, there were two staff nurses who realized that they were fairly well past the age of inevitable marriage, who had considered settling into a career commitment pattern but had given this up. One had already applied to the U. S. Foreign Service and was only awaiting acceptance before quitting. The other had only vague ideas when and where she would be next but characterized herself as "one of the movers." Both fantasized the ideal husband as one whose job required extensive travel. Although neither were actually settled into an orientation toward future security, there is probably a point where it is simpler and less risky to combine touristry with occupation in one of those fields or agencies where travel is a necessary characteristic.[17]

Consequences for the employer. Nurses afflicted with touristry have various effects upon their employment agencies. They add, of course, to the turnover problem which seems to plague the metropolitan areas especially. Although they may depart at any time of the year, it may be that the onset of summer brings "itching feet" into a full blown rash. Talk of travel among the departing tourists seems to stir longings to join the migrant flock, sometimes even sooner than the girl herself had planned.

Many nursing directors have learned not to assign the members of one household to a single service or even a single shift. Some directors, if they have any choice, even prefer not to hire more than one member of such a group. From hard experience they have learned that there is, indeed, a flock phenomenon and a single decision to move on could strip a service of much of its staff. Sometimes these preliminary precautions are not enough, for the touristry group often changes its configuration; one roommate may drop out of the pattern and be replaced by a new member locally recruited, often among co-workers on the unit.

Problems arise when the touristry oriented nurses must be dealt with by nursing directors and supervisors who, at this stage of their lives, have assumed a career commitment. Those of the latter who are perturbed by high staff turnover rates may try to find a solution within their own perspective without realizing that factors in the work situation are usually irrelevant to the tourist's decision to quit. Thus the nursing office may strive to adjust the work load or the constitution of the ward. Attempts may be made to institute social gatherings among the staff nurses of the entire hospital without realizing that it is not more female company that these young women are seeking.

It is possible, however, that these seem plausible corrections when the reasons given at the time of resignation are used as the basis for planning. Although the touristry pattern is well known, it is not viewed as truly legitimate and more socially acceptable reasons are given. Then too, the young nurses may not be wholly aware of how the lures of touristry operate to make their current job seem suddenly so dissatisfying. However, it is apparent from talking with those who must hire young nurses, that touristry is an expected factor and personnel directors, although hardly happy about it, are simply resigned to it as a pattern of work. In fact, they sometimes entertain the wistful hope that theirs will be the institution in which these young nurses finally decide to settle down.

DISCUSSION:

TOURISTRY AND TECHNICIANS

Up to this point, we have been considering touristry as it appears in one specific group, nurses, who represent the model par excellence of touristry. I would like now to apply this pattern onto various other occupations to illustrate what factors operate to restrain and permit this as a way of life for others, as well as suggest where further expansion of touristry could be expected.

Touristry is generally possible within the traditional occupations that follow their structure. Jobs which depend on a personal clientele or reputation demand time, concentration and stability. And even though teachers step into ready-made school classes, they are bound by contracts and their notorious traveling must occur during vacations.

As for the job scarcity factor, the U. S. Bureau of Labor Statistics reports that currently the jobs in electronic engineering, physics and chemistry are most difficult to fill. But these are male occupations and are most frequently linked, like those of universities, to the more usual career-making, and touristry would interfere with advancement. The Bureau spokesman confirmed this by noting that, even though these applicants may pick their own geographical location to begin with, they somehow do not move around as would happen in touristry.

However, there are occupational groups other than nurses for whom touristry is possible and whose employers are beginning to complain of their transiency. Within the health professions, medical technologists, X-ray technicians and dental hygienists have already made reputations as migrants. The Bureau of Labor Statistics also added that stenographers are in such short supply that they can and do travel anywhere they wish with assurance that a job will be waiting for them.

There are even certain jobs open for men who would pursue a touristry pattern at the expense of job advancement or marriage. Journeymen printers can support themselves in traveling wherever unionization and scarcity assure them jobs. Groups of homosexual males are reportedly utilizing the still scarce occupation of data processor to tour around their specialized circuits.[18]

Far from presenting a solution to this "problem," I would suggest that touristry will not only increase but will also spread to other occupational groups. The fantastic proliferation and expansion of the sciences and professions in recent decades have created a special and relatively new category of worker, the technician, whom I wish now to consider. According to the U.S. Department of Labor, technicians can be defined as "skilled with training beyond the high school level, but not usually with a college degree....Most technicians have some theoretical knowledge of their specialization, together with an understanding of the practical application of the theory."[19]

For example, medical advancement and specialization have so complicated individual practice that physicians have been forced to relinquish many tasks to subordinate or technical personnel.[20] Eventually new occupational groups have become formalized around a set of tasks and strive to establish requirements for administration to this status. Medical technicians have well- established task training programs which are progressing toward an academic orientation. They have also started a move toward licensure, at least in California. However, it is still possible for an unlicensed technician to work, even though some hospitals have set licensure as a criterion for employment. It is clear that this group has some feelings of cohesion but still has no clear mandate to define their own territory.[21] For many reasons, the actual numbers of either technicians or women working as technicians is unknown, but all predictions point to marked increase of both. Certain Civil Service classifications, excluding the health and biological sciences, showed greater concentration of women technicians than others, ranging "from 2 percent of the engineering aides to 75 percent of the mathematical aides."[22] Whenever these specializations become standardized, it is likely that some will be categorized as "women's jobs." There is already a tendency to consider some areas in electronic and chemical laboratories, for instance, as particularly suitable to women. A government report on the biological sciences reports that, "in fact, women are often preferred as supporting personnel to higher scientists because of their careful handing of detail and their patience, dexterity, and reliability."[23]

As the prerequisite training moves away from plant experience into junior and community college curricula, larger numbers of young, middle-class girls will be influenced to prepare themselves for such technical positions.[24] The pressures that have created these jobs will undoubtedly increase so that various qualified technicians will be at a premium for a long time. This sets up all the necessities for a seller's market within which touristry can flourish.

REFERENCES

1. Theodore Caplow, "Other Mobilities," *The Sociology of Work,* Minneapolis: University of Minnesota Press, 1954, pp. 88-98.

2. Rupert B. Vance, "Internal Migration and the Mobility of the Population," *Reader in Urban Sociology,* Glencoe: The Free Press, 1951, pp. 190-205.

3. R. Denney and D. Riesman, "Leisure in Urbanized America", *Reader in Urban Sociology,* Glencoe: The Free Press, 1951, p. 479.

4. Caplow, op. cit., p. 91.

5. The specific material was derived from three sources. First, during a project which dealt with the problem of hospital turnover at Moffitt Hospital (University of California Medical Center, San Francisco), twenty-four graduate nurses were interviewed. Their selection was determined only by the fact that they were not busy during the varied times, day and evening, that I happened to arrive on the various floors. Unstructured questioning was used to elicit the individual trajectory within a nursing career. Twenty-three of the nurses identified themselves with the pattern of touristry while the one non-tourist recognized it from her own experience and acknowledged her own rarity. Second, confirmatory data has been made available from the Nursing Careers Project, University of California, San Francisco (Fred Davis, et al). Third, those data are further amplified by my ten years experience as a non-tourist nurse and my observation of many times more such nurses in transit than were interviewed in either of the two projects noted above.

6. None of the younger staff nurses I interviewed saw themselves as full-time serious workers after marriage and the first child.

7. One of the exceptions to this can be the girl who remains at none after schooling to care for an invalid family member, although this represents a responsible though unpaid contribution to the family welfare.

8. B.J. Chute, *Greenwillow*, New York: E.P. Dutton, 1956, P. 31.

9. Committee on the Grading of Nursing Schools, *Nurses, Patients and Pocketbooks*, New York, 1928, pp. 100-101.

10. *Ibid,* p. 164.

11. "Living is fun in Southern California!" and "(X Hospital) means the

center of things and the best of everything for you!...More satisfation in work and play than you ever dreamed possible.'' These appeared as facing ads in *The American Journal of Nursing,* 63 (#6, June 1963), pp. 146-147.

12. California League for Nursing, ''Nurses for California-Highlights from the 1964 Report,'' mimeographed.

13. ''Where do you go from here? After graduation, almost anywhere you please. So keep (X Hospital) in mind.'' Full page ad in *The American Journal of Nursing,* 63 (#6, June 1963), p. 162.

15. Anselm jStrauss has unpublished data to show that long auto vacations are gaining popularity among low-class factory workers.

16. National Manpower Council, *Women-Power,* New York: Columbia University, 1957, p. 67.

17. It is possible that a certain number of the career-committed nurses in WHO, the armed services or the Red Cross fall into this category.

18. Little material is available on current activity in ''Hobohemia'' that was so thoroughly studied in the past. Surely many factors have acted to diminish the number of old-style vagrants and bums, but I cannot imagine that unemployed travel has completely vanished.

19. U.S. Department of Labor, Women's Bureau Bulletin 282, ''Careers for Women as Technicians,'' 1961, p. 4.

20. Sybil MacLan reported that 17 former physician tasks had become the conceded domain of nurses. Reported in E.L Brown, *Nursing for the Future,* New York: Russell Sage Foundation, 1948, p. 79.

21. E.C. Hughes, ''License and Mandate,'' *Men an Their Work,* Glencoe: The Free Press, 1958, pp. 78-87.

22. U.S. Department of Labor, op cit, p. 12.

23. U.S. Department of Labor, Women's Bureau Bulletin #278, ''Careers for Women in the Biological Sciences,'' 1961, p. 4.

24. Vacational nursing will probably move in this direction as the training becomes formalized and upgraded, licensure more widespread and more girls go directly from high school into such programs.

NOTES

CHAPTER 3

Reprinted from *Health Education Monographs*, Fall 1978

CUTTING BACK AFTER A HEART ATTACK:

An Overview

Patricia Dolan Mullen

Increasingly, health workers are concerned with the alteration of complex and deeply embedded behaviors; essential to these tasks is an understanding of the perspective of the patient, inductively generating a conceptual formulation to explain and understand life after a heart attack. The basic problem of minimizing losses under conditions of uncertainty and unknown parameters of action is confronted. Resolution is achieved through "cutting back," which has three major stages: (1) immobilization, characterized by explaining and estimating damage; (2) resumption, in which patients figure the complex calculus of the new situation to determine what they must cut back; and (3) new normal, when the major work is that of adjusting to the permanent changes wrought by the heart attack experience which affect identity. Exploratory diagnosis of complex health education problems through a "grounded theory" approach is demonstrated by the study.

Although myocardial infarction (MI) has been the object of inquiry from a variety of perspectives, little research has focused upon the stages of recovery, the problems and characteristic coping patterns of the stages, and the consequences of the various coping patterns.

Since Croog and his colleagues[12] noted this gap in the literature, they have contributed to the empirical understanding of recovery in numerous papers.[10 11 13 14 15] Conceptualizing the MI as a crisis with defined phases of adjustment, they followed patients for several years. Their investigations did not, however, include the processes of that adjustment nor were they designed to generate information about a patient's social psychological world.

A comprehensive review of work in the last eight years on psychosocial aspects of MI[20] categorized it as (1) advocacy articles which argued for a particular type of patient care such as rehabilitation programs, nurse teaching, and family conferences;[22 32 50 51] (2) clinical papers, usually with a psychological point of view, which enumerated and described the emotional difficulties precipitated by the MI;[1] [39] [44] [49] and (3) empirical reports, most of which treated hospitalization[3] [4] [21] [31] and post-hospitalization[5] [24] [35] [36] [54] [55] for varying periods of time in terms of psychological variables. Social variables have received relatively less attention, with the exception of occupational adjustment.[25] [30] [33] [45] [47]

The purpose of the present study was to identify the social psychological problems faced by MI survivors and to capture the range and quality of their responses and adaptations to the illness. The chief emphasis was to discover the process by which people reorder the patterns and priorities of their lives as they go about the business of "carrying on" after the crisis phase. Following previous studies in other diagnostic categories,[16] [17] [18] [19] [52] it is expected that the MI experience would be better understood in terms of chronic, interactive, definitional activities and problems which are beyond the scope of a crisis model of standard psychological variables (e.g., denial, depression, anxiety) and sociological factors (e.g., social networks, social class, occupational status) usually seen in cardiac research.

METHOD

The methodology used is a form of comparative analysis which has been developed and refined by Glaser and Strauss[26] to discover what they call "grounded theory." Comparative analysis is an inductive strategy most often used by sociologist and anthropologists of the symbolic interactionist school of thought;[2] [43] [48] its aim is the empirical generation of middle-range theory via systematic choice and study of multiple comparison groups. The advantages of the grounded theory approach for health education research are discussed elsewhere[46] and will be demonstrated rather than elaborated here.

It was thought by this researcher that a substantive theory or process model which could be applied in the diverse situations faced by health care practitioners who work with persons who have suffered MIs, would extend the understanding of the cardiac experience, give rise to sound programs, and shed light on the broader process of redesigning life-style in the face of chronic conditions. This approach has been chosen in preference to an hypothesis-testing study or a study aimed at a representative statistical picture of the frequency and distribution of various problems and phenomena. The data used for the analysis were tapescripts of semi-structured interviews with 100 MI patients, the medical records of these patients, and observations of hospital cardiac care programs (exercise classes, discussion groups, educational sessions, and coronary clubs). The interviews were conducted at various stages of recovery - up to four years after a first to eighth occurrence. The constellations of interviewees were individuals, couples, and groups. Seventy-nine percent were men; the median age was 54 years, with a range of 22-77; 81% were white; and all socioeconomic strata were represented in equal proportions.

Initial data collection was aimed at gathering a broad array of heart patients in terms of age, sex, degree of impairment, number of MIs, socioeconomic strata, and source of medical care. After preliminary coding of 20 interviews, analysis and data-gathering became ongoing and interacting activities; decisions for further sampling were guided by the need for comparisons to develop the emerging theory. For example, since coding of the early interviews indicated that there was a problem with differing perspectives about MI patients' physical condition, a four-fold table was developed comparing actual activity level against medical assessment of capacity. It was decided that additional persons in quadrant III and IV should be interviewed to learn more about those who are advised to cut back severely their level of activity. Particularly sought were individuals who appeared healthy and would therefore have coped with a large discrepancy between their appearance and their physical limitations.

The "open" and "theoretical" coding processes[26] of grounded theory method were used to uncover the characteristic patterns of the MI patients' definitions of their situations, strategies they used to handle their problems, and the other factors such as the availability of resources or attribution of the cause of the MI, which influenced their behavior. Instead, the data were used to build up an abstract theoretical scheme which took into account relevant issues in the actors' experience. The coding was verified by a panel of other analysts who also reviewed the data and the theoretical framework.

IN THE WAKE OF A HEART ATTACK

The MI changes or puts into question the basic social psychological order of the victim's life, creating a situation where temporarily, at least, many old norms of behavior do not apply. Whether this was the first or latest of several episodes, the survivor of a heart attack faces the difficult task of resuming life in a new and ambiguous state under conditions of uncertainty. What many have taken for granted - health, energy, career, finances, social and family relationships, personal identity, and relative position vis-a-vis age peers and other comparison groups- is thrust into self-conscious consideration. This is unlike other chronic illnesses with insidious beginnings and longer periods of realization. The victim foresees threats to his life-style, including the possibilities of recurrence, reduced earning power, sexual incompetence, invalidism, decreased activity, and premature aging. Thus, in addition to the problem of survival, he is faced with the question of how well he will live. What can be salvaged from his former way of life? In the words of a forty-year-old Washington-based newspaper reporter:

The question raced to my mind...Would I live? And if so...would I work again with the same gusto and output as before? Would I be able to pursue my interests in sailing and tennis? Or would the remainder of my unclearly numbered days be limited to...a suburban patio where I might read the latest political fiction?[40]

The MI regimen is characterized by "cutting back," that is eliminating and reducing (fatty foods, smoking, competitive or very active sports, heavy work, stressful situations, and excess activity) rather than by adding and increasing. Many heart patients do take numerous medications and have prescribed exercise programs, but their situation is generally filled with proscriptions. This is far different, for example, from the situation of people undergoing kidney dialysis or suffering from ulcerative colitis, who must take on extremely time-consuming procedures.

On the other dimension, coronary heart disease is easier in that people have a rather wide latitude of action compared to other chronic illnesses. Unlike the arthritis or stroke patient, heart attack patients are not physically forced to cut back. This freedom can be complex and confusing, however, since heart patients are largely on their own in interpreting the vague and ominous warning, "take it easy," and in establishing new limits of action. What cutbacks are truly necessary? What will be most effective in terms of preventing another heart attack? These questions may not have clearcut answers. The harder dimension is that sudden death may be the consequence of overstepping the unclear boundary line of safety, and one cannot count on having any warning signals. A heart patient's ability to overdo puts him in jeopardy, so that the challenge becomes reaching one's limits minus one.

Thus, there are three analytically distinct (but practically interrelated) types of cutbacks involved: (1) those actually forced by the MI; (2) those indicated by the appearance of symptoms, either literally (lack of energy stops the activity) or definitionally ("I'd better stop now, because I usually get chest pain when I feel this way and keep going"); and (3) those which are part of the regime. In finding a new set of guidelines for everyday life, the person who has had an MI must balance these cutback demands against the maintenance of those aspects of life which are personally (and socially) meaningful.

THE PROBLEM OF MINIMIZING LOSSES

The heart attack victim's chief problem may be described as "minimizing losses," which refers to the decision to make certain unfavorable cutbacks to ward off the perceived probability of larger and more devastating losses in the future. For the persons resuming everyday living after an MI, cutbacks in former activities required or suggested by the regime are part of the effort to reverse a sharp downward trend which could easily lead to death or a more severely curtailed life. This necessitates a series of interwoven decisions to renormalize one's life in a situation of relative ambiguity, autonomy, and anxiety.

While the MI is still prominent, patients reassess their life goals with reference to their personal definitions of the quality of life. As one person put it:

It changes your mental outlook a lot. I know it does, in fact. You don't take a self inventory before like you do afterwards- the things that really mean something...When you haven't lived, then you know it.

One view of quality is expressed in blanket terms, "Now I don't take for granted the things I used to; I appreciate them more now" and "I live each day..." This tends to fade as the person becomes more removed from the crisis experience, but overall assessment and appreciation for the "time I have left" is an important element in decision-making.

More specific views of quality encompass activities, responsibilities, and attitudes which are individual parts of the familiar way of life. It may be the special things a woman does which signify to her that she is a good mother or wife. It may be a beloved hobby or pastime which is the focus of the person's companionship with a good friend. These definitions are highly idiosyncratic, of course, so that while one person could relinquish a given activity easily, for another it might have tremendous cost.

In balancing between cutting back and maintaining a certain quality of life, the heart patient develops an ongoing personal "calculus" from the diverse elements which he sees as relevant in this unfamiliar and emergent situation. In each of the stages of cutting back a few of the factors which are figured into the calculus will be introduced, and only the most salient and general properties of the process of cutting back will be discussed.

STAGES OF CUTTING BACK

The stages of cutting back are "immobilization," "resumption," and "new normal." These names may appear to derive from the medical perspective because of their close relationship to the physical status; the stages, however, were actually seen in the data on the level of social psychological patterns. Each stage is characterized by special problems and by situational and other conditions which call out different coping strategies from the patient and family. Thus, the kind of assistance needed from health care workers varies in each stage.

IMMOBILIZATION: ESTIMATING AND EXPLAINING THE DAMAGE

Typically, the MI patient is immobilized in an acute care environment for a period of several days to a week, under conditions of close and technically advanced monitoring; instant accessibility to specialty care; and explicit and enforced rules for activity, diet, rest, smoking, and outside intrusions. Like others struck by sudden illness or personal disaster, the heart attack victim needs to explain and estimate the damage and its consequences.[3][38][42] He takes stock, develops casual explanations to answer the "Why me?" and "Why now?" questions, and he seeks and screens information using direct and indirect strategies, such as interpreting cues of medical personnel and comparing his experience with that of others.

The patient-epidemiologist retrospective study often emphasizes events having close temporal proximity (immediate causes for extraordinary circumstances). Other properties of casual theories are their faulting emphasis, certainty, and heart imagery. The faulting aspect is important, and it includes positive or ameliorating causes - "I'd be dead now if I hadn't jogged regularly." The victim compares himself in many ways with others he knows who have had similar experiences in order to predict his prognosis and the quality of life he will be able to lead after he recovers. He may use these new peers normatively ("My friend returned to an active life, and so can I") or he may stress the differences ("A business associate had to retire early, but she had a more severe attack than I did").

Assigning cause, gathering and processing information, and selecting comparative predictors all help to establish guidelines for cutting back. One person put it in extreme terms: "If I had had any idea what caused it, I would have prevented it! "Inability to partial out the factors in one's life according to their probable relationship to the MI may leave a generalized fear which may create a "cardiac cripple." Another response to an over-generalized view of casual factors is fatalism that can lead to overstepping proscriptive boundaries: "There's nothing you can do to make a difference, if it's destined to happen."

RESUMPTION: FIGURING THE CALCULUS OF CUTTING BACK

Resumption is the second stage of cutting back, and its major work is figuring a personal calculus to determine what must be cut back, would should be cut back, and what one will and will not actually cut back. Throughout this phase, the patient uses the elements generated during the immobilization phase in conjunction with newly developed ones to work the cutting back calculus to resume his prior lifestyle as far as possible. He mobilizes himself and his resources to figure limits, principally by testing them empirically. The results of experimentation (which by no means are always clear or definitive), can then become conditions which influence subsequent tests and decisions. The construction and growth of the calculus begins tentatively, with uncertainty the hallmark of nearly all of the elements, most being inferences, estimates, and predictions. Gradually it stabilizes, and new outer limits of action are established.

The MI patient's disease trajectory, which usually began with an abrupt and precipitous drop to complete immobilization, contrasts with other crisis-onset diseases such as stroke in that resumption usually starts very soon. In fact, at an early point the MI patient may feel much better than his actual physical state warrants. While still on the coronary care unit (and within the protective conditions mentioned above) remobilization is guided and even required. Return home, however, is usually accompanied by uncertainty and increased reminders, demands, and the temptation of the former way of living. Those who are part of this period recall the first weeks at home as being very difficult. As one woman said:

> It's an adjustment - everything is an adjustment. I don't think I realized I was sick until I got home either, because in the hospital you have a nurse or doctor or somebody around- and then there was the medicine. But when you get home you're really alone, and you find that you can't do the things you used to do.

The calculus of cutting back is inclusive of the other aspects of the person's personal, social, and work careers. The factors considered are subject to highly variable social and personal definitions. This is not a calculating image of man as one read in Goffman's work,[28] where people seem deliberately and consciously to manage their self images and decisions about interaction with a complete picture of the consequences in mind.

Rather the calculus generated by the heart patient is a net balancing or juggling of factors, and it is done on a much rougher, ongoing, and emerging basis.

The most important activities in discovering how to cut back are learning to interpret body signals, dealing with divergent interpretations of what is possible and expected among various and consequential people in one's life, developing balancing equations, and finding specific ways of changing behavior.

After an MI, the person is self-consciously aware of bodily sensations, information from diverse comparative sources, and experiential data which might be related to the heart condition. The problem concerns interpreting vague indicators and correcting these interpretations based upon perceiving consequences. A sense of confidence in one's ability to read cues is needed not only to assess the degree of impairment and gauge progress, but also to anticipate and recognize crisis in order to summon help and to establish the outer limits of action for specific activities.

The major patterns of interpreting signs can be dichotomized according to their degree of discrimination. The more conservative, non-discriminating mode is likely to limit action severely, as described by the wife of one patient, "He interprets any symptoms as being to his heart. I don't think he'll ever be the same." The discriminating stance is much more favorable for cutting back wisely but not unduly. Confidence in one's ability to recognize trouble may be from sources such as consultation with other patients or medical personnel, or from feeling that there were adequate warnings before the MI.

Two problematic aspects of cutting back are the interdependence of activities and their differential valuation by other people who are involved with them. Changing one activity in isolation is almost never possible, since its consequences resonate throughout the person's life and affect other activities and people. This is the major difficulty of minimizing losses, and it is a factor in choices about cutting back. Even if someone does not care about the activity in question, he may care very much about that which is associated with it. Or, the activity may be highly prized by an important person and a change may affect the other, and potentially, the relationship itself. Fellow workers may resent the extra workload they must carry because of the patient's new limits. Because there is often discretion involved in deciding which activities to eliminate or slow down, even more ill feeling and misunderstanding can develop. A woman who is unhappy with her husband's virtual elimination of their social life while he makes no changes at work may be seen by him as pressuring him to excesses. Meanwhile, she will resent his choice, especially since wives often blame work pressure for the MI.

The divergence of opinion about the etiology, the degree of damage, and the ill person's activity capacity is exacerbated by the difficulty of assessing exact limits, the invisibility of impairment to others, and for many patients, the absence of clear symptoms. Thus, family members, co-workers, medical personnel, and the patient may all have different definitions of the patient's situation, and these perceptions shape cutting back. The magnitude of their influence varies with the degree of sentimental or instrumental control the others have over the patient's life. These outside controls can distort cutting points, so action is unduly limited or forced to excess. For example, working conditions may render a light-duty order meaningless, or the prejudice of employers may keep a heart patient from working at all.

There is also the matter of internal control by the person himself - the "can't say no" pattern and other sources of personal resistance a patient may have to cutting back and living within prudent limits. A widely recognized pattern of this type is the "Type A personality."[23] A simple example is the person who has been accustomed to an unusually high degree of activity - holding two jobs or otherwise working excessively. Such an MI patient is likely to define "taking it easy" in comparative rather than absolute terms ("I've cut back to only eight hours, six days a week, and I don't touch a crate weighing over one hundred pounds"). The comparative cutback may still be too much.

The discovery of the shape of this chronic illness passage (see Glaser and Strauss[27] for discussion of the concept of "status passage") and the attendant balancing equations are major tasks which come to the fore in the resumption stage. The first is like graphing a line based upon distance from the old level of activity and the time or rapidity of the cutback. Graphing is accomplished through the establishment of new cutting points, as limits are tested empirically and vicariously by comparisons. The direction of the graph is not entirely predictable, and it is unstable and subject to downward reverses. The shape may be altered by a recurrence or other evidence of worsening of the disease (such as onset of chronic angina or the results of an angiogram) which would plummet the downward direction with little hope of complete return to the former plateau. On the other hand, although there is some irreversible damage after a heart attack, the comeback potential can be great.

Cutting-back equations indicate the manner in which the patient is juggling meanings to minimize losses, manage risks, and estimate the interaction effects of types of cutbacks and of cutbacks in different areas. Equations for cutting back that preserve quality can be generalized ("I guess I want to do what they tell me to do - I want some more time"), or they can be specific ("I lost weight and lowered my cholesterol in order to recover enough to be active in my temple activities again"). Implicit in such statements is an "if...then..." logic which presumes that cause and effect relationships are in large degree certain, even though uncertainty usually predominates. Risk management equations may rationalize risks ("Smoking constricts my arteries, so I drink liquor which dilates them"), and they may justify major cutbacks ("Lifting heavy objects is too dangerous for me now"). Other equations relate the effects of one activity on another and point out the net balance of consequences of a proposed cutback ("When I finish losing this weight, I'll feel more like exercising, and my wife has been wanting me to drop 15 pounds anyway").

Cutbacks vary according to their comparative distance from what was formerly considered normal. With respect to any one activity, the degree of reduction can be complete, partial, nil, or negative. Partial cutbacks are generally most advantageous for minimizing losses, since they tend to maintain rewards, satisfactions, social interactions, and related activities.

Complete reductions, such as a retirement, result in the loss of connected activities and important aspects of identity. However, complete cutbacks are preferred when salvaging a part of an activity creates a strain, as for instance, when the heart condition is forgotten by others, when comparisons with the former way of behaving are too uncomfortable, or when the person's internal governor could easily be overcome by the attraction of exceeding his limits. Another consequence of a complete cutback, of course, can be a welcome unburdening of a distasteful chore. Too many choices of this sort tend to require justification and high credibility to retain acceptance by others.

Negative or "super-normal" cutbacks are at the other extreme. Super-normaling[7] refers to doing something to an even greater extent than before the onset of the illness. This may be positive, arising out of a health optimizing activity such as jogging, or super-normalizing can be negative, as in exceeding limits to maintain an old identity.

Cutting back is operational through strategies such as situational positioning, conserving energy, and health optimizing. For example, patients position themselves with regard to medical resources, temptations or internal triggers to exceed limits, strong external demands, and conditions which make cutting back easier.

To conserve energy, patients who feel they can recognize danger signals monitor their expenditure of energy to recognize points at which they should slow down, take a rest, or stop an activity ("I guess I'm a veteran of this heart business, and I take it easy on myself. Work on myself, slow down or speed up, depending"). Other tactics include substituting another person to fill in or take over part of the activity, which usually means role reallocation within a family but may include paid helpers or friendly volunteers; diluting or literally lowering the concentration of energy for an activity or routine, as in switching to doubles tennis or allowing extra time between appointments; and budgeting yourself and your energy so that energy is spent selectively and wisely.

The choice of strategies affects the extent of cutbacks and is important in retaining as much of the old way of life as possible. Ironically, there is very little guidance for the patient in learning about the range of alternatives or in changing disadvantageous strategies.

NEW NORMAL: ADJUSTING TO A NEW IDENTITY

The new normal stage begins when the person has plateaued in his resumption of former activities, or to put it another way, cut back as much as he has to or can tolerate. Choosing what to cut back mostly takes place during the two to six months or more of the resumption stage; the consequences of those choices shape the new normal stage. When resumption peaks, people must revise their expectations about what constitutes an acceptable quality of life in terms of their resolutions for cutting back and the consequences of those resolutions - including implications for their desired identities. The central question for the calculus in the new normal state is, "How does the person who must live under this special set of chronic conditions come to view himself?"

Some people find that they are better off after than before the MI, and others see little change. The new normal stage, however, often involves renormalizing with lower expectations to accommodate the reduction of former activities and the consequent impact on the quality of life. In Clausen's words, "He must come to terms with the fact that he is not something he was, something to which he was committed."[8]

The same change may have a relatively different impact, depending upon the person's lifestyle and stage of life cycle. For example, a man may decide to work only part-time, and that may mean his wife must return to work, that he must take on more activities of her old role, and that the family must move to a different neighborhood. The same degree of severity, however, might mean fewer changes for a retired person.

Some ways in which MI patients reconcile themselves to a problematic new identity are through discovering positive modes of dependence, choosing favorable standards of comparison, finding compensations for cutbacks, and avowing illness. The divergent interpretations and valuations of others - real, projected, or anticipated - continue to be significant as mirrors for self-appraisal and are strongly related to difficulties and choices in this stage.

Dependence Problems. In the new normal stage some MI patients must come to terms with the degree of assistance they need from others. Dependence can be financial or related to certain activities and tasks such as carrying groceries or driving a car, and it can have pervasive consequences for the person's identity. Persons who cannot reciprocate the help family or friends give them may feel guilty.[29] Their dread of dependence may push them to exceed their limits, or it may lead to avoiding asking for the assistance needed for partial or nil cutbacks and leave the patient with complete cutbacks and greater losses. A more positive way of dealing with the repayment issue is to develop other forms of equivalency. Money (literally "hired hands"), talent (e.g., one man had a promising idea for building a new engine and recruited an interested young person to accomplish the actual construction), and credit from past deeds are all alternate currencies.

Patients may also develop preferred tenders,[53] whose assistance is especially comfortable because the repayment problem is lessened. These preferences may develop because of the cheerful and willing response of the tenders (which legitimates the request), consistent offers to be of help, devaluation of the resources they extend ("I have lots of time"), or the helpers' claims that they are repaid by other aspects of the relationship. Another quality of the preferred helper is the degree to which their perception of the patient's disability agrees with the patient's point of view. While it is uncomfortable to know that the other does not really believe you are ill, on the other hand it can also be uncomfortable to be treated as an invalid. The former problem is partially a function of the invisibility of the handicap and will be discussed below.

Comparison Problems. Looking at one's self in relation to someone else is a common method by which people assess their progress, standing, and so forth. MI patients compare themselves with situational (MI) peers, their former selves, their ideal selves and age peers. The choice of comparison is not always theirs. Some comparisons, usually unfavorably ones, may be forced upon them. Comparisons with others who have had MIs legitimate cutting back decisions and sometimes give rise to new ones. Three standards for self-comparison commonly used are:

* OLD NORMATIVE- the difference between the pre-MI level of activity and the new normal;

* IMPROVEMENT- the contrast between early resumption and the new normal; and

* NEGATIVE- the difference between the new normal and what might have happened.

The improvement standard is usually more favorable than comparison of the old self with new capacity, but it is used less often than the old normative. This may be because the old activities and their loss stand out too poignantly for long periods of time. The contrast between the two standards may be seen in an interview where a young man spoke of his frustration at being unable to ski, run, or do any of the strenuous sports he used to do. His wife interrupted with, "But you don't get winded anymore carrying a bag of groceries up the stairs." He was using the old normative, while she used the improvement standard.

Comparisons with age peers are often a proxy for comparisons with the old self. Thus, for example, a man whose friends normally stay up all night playing poker, smoking, and drinking heavily, or engage in strenuous sports may have to make relatively greater changes in his lifestyle than someone whose closest associates are older or more sedentary. And, he will need to resolve or eliminate that dissonance.

People change their memberships and reference group affiliations[37] according to their tolerance for discomfort. Thus, heart patients who withdraw from younger or more active peer groups and associate themselves with an older or less active group are adjusting their standards of comparison. On the other hand, the relative difference between a heart patient and his group is not usually as great as, say, differences experienced by a handicapped child, and he and the group may accommodate their differences quite easily.

Two variables suggested in William James'[34] equation for self-esteem help to clarify the dynamics of comparison:

success divided by pretensions =self-esteem

When the numerator (ability, physical capacity, and so forth) is changed, maintenance of self-esteem depends upon decreasing the denominator. Such an adjustment might result in a decision that the house need not be kept so clean, or the grass cut so often, or every aspect of a job overseen personally. Thus cutting back on what you can now do can be offset by cutting back on what you think needs to be done. This is a complex business, however, as described in Lewin's papers on level of aspirations (the denominator in James' formula).[6] [41] A more profound adjustment, then, is to accept discrepancies and change the standard for the "ideal self," one's pretensions.

Compensations. Compensations can be and often are generated from cutting back. Cutting back is not wholly negative, and in fact, it frequently offers opportunities for redesigning a more satisfying life. This is particularly true for "Type A's," if they can gain access to new sides of their personalities.[23]

Improvement comparison standards and negative comparison standards have compensations. When an important aspect of life appears to be cut out completely after an MI, its partial resumption is appreciated, like a gift. Negative standards of comparison set a worse peril against the new normal. People who feel that they have come close to death are glad to be alive at all; and comfort can be derived from comparing one's own lot with that of another whose fate is even more unfavorable.

One way of dealing with unfavorable, forced comparisons is to fashion loss rationales in which compensations outweigh the losses. These post hoc equations are like the cutting equations of resumption, except that instead of relating cutbacks to other cutbacks, they involve (1) seeing substitutes as being as good as what they have replaced; (2) emphasizing what they can do over what they cannot; (3) viewing new, valued activities as being facilitated by the cutbacks; and (4) reminding themselves of the distasteful activities they no longer have to do.

The person who does not find sufficient compensations remains dissatisfied with his new identity and may consequently super-normalize or continue as before - if he can - or live in mourning with the problems of unfavorable comparisons.

Apparent Health. The heart patient cannot always meet the expectations others form on the basis of his appearance. People whose apparent characteristics suggest disability may seek to reduce the social effects, as if to say, "Though I appear to be different, I really am not." In situations which challenge his limits, the MI patient's statement might be, "Though I may appear to be the same, I really am not." Rather than disavowing deviance, the person whose signs of illness are not visible must sometimes avow illness.

How heart patients respond to others' expectations that he behave in accordance with how he seems to be, for example, is a function of his acceptance of the new normal identity, his tolerance for appearing unjustifiably inactive, the possibilities for alternate excuses, his prediction of the likely consequences of revealing the impairment to the other (e.g., being placed in the awkward position of being overhelped), and the reaction of the other to the initial action.

The decisions a heart patient makes around these factors are fateful when they mean exceeding limits. The patient may choose to exceed his limits, and risk his health or his life rather than spoil his appearance; he may avoid situations likely to pose such problems; he may develop strategies for making his condition more apparent (advice given one cardiac patient was "act sicker than you feel"); he may find ways of explaining his limits on other groups; he may simply say that he has had a heart attack and cannot do what is expected or can do it only in a limited way; or he may stick to his limits explanation or embarrassment. An individual will choose a particular strategy to fit his assessment of and feelings about the situation, so that a young man, for instance, might do too much in the presence of women and yet explain his illness straightforwardly to close friends.

The problems of apparent health differ, depending upon the level of familiarity with others who are party to the situation. At the most anonymous level - that of being observed in a public place - the MI patient projects onto the observers the norms which guide him. In such situations there is no opportunity to avow the illness in order to justify, for example, an apparent able-bodied man remaining empty-handed while his wife carries heavy bundles.

IMPLICATIONS FOR PRACTICE AND THEORY
THE PATIENT'S PERSPECTIVE

The aftermath of a heart attack seen, as above, from the point of view of the patient leads to a set of recommendations concerning patient education and, the health professional and patient relationship.

*Health professionals need to be aware of problems with which patients are dealing and of the conceptual differences in their defintions of the situation.*The patient is more crisis-orientd and may want the physician or nurse to assign definite, immediate causes for the MI. Chronicity is at issue in terms of the impact of the disease, its damage to other spheres of life, and the regimen's proscription of familiar and valued activities. The health professional may not easily see how difficult it is to set limits when the person with much of the responsibility for operationalizing the instructions is not at all certain how to read danger signals. Minimizing losses is not a conflicting goal between patients and health workers, although when it is specifically defined there are frequently some differences. Many patients feel that they must choose between the medical regimen and retaining an activity which they understand to be forbidden by the regimen.

The flow and distribution of information should be managed so as to minimize divergent interpretations of the situation. This implies increased communication among health workers and agreement upon who is to tell the patient and his family what and how and under what circumstances. Patients should be assisted with information-gathering strategies and, for example, be given notebooks in which to write questions and answers to validate question-asking.

Societal reactions to the heart patient, a fateful and specific example of which is the prejudice of many employers, should receive more attention. Individual patients may need an intermediary to negotiate with their employers; their doctors could perform this function to a greater extent than most do currently. There should also be a general education program to end the job discrimination against heart patients.

Patients should be recognized as important participants in their own care, since they are, in fact, the managers of their daily routines. Their skills and motivation are underutilized, and families are not included often enough as potential allies of the medical team. The health professional could function much more as a tactical adviser to the patient. Strategies for solving the patient's problems as well as the medical person's problems should be developed jointly. Less emphasis would be put upon modifying the patient and more would be placed on modifying the patient's environment. A specific beginning could be to suggest appropriate partial cutbacks; ways to substitute or dilute activities.

Veteran patients, an important natural group, could be used explicitly and in a planned manner by health care institutions and agencies. They are especially helpful in practical suggestions, anticipatory guidance, and in demonstrating high quality survival.

Health professions should use their authority and influence to reinforce patients, since how the patient sees himself and his behavior is not strictly inherent in the patient. When a heart patient interprets indicators and asks for help, the reaction of the potential helper is a part of the patient's education, which will influence subsequent interpretations. For example, is he told that, although he is not in trouble, he was wise to call for expert evaluation, or what combinations of symptoms should prompt future calls?

Patients should be assisted in developing an interpretative framework for what they are likely to experience, whenever possible. Advance preparation for procedures, side-effects, and bodily signs enables patients to make them part of normal expectation, and avoids the anxiety arising from lack of understanding. This also does not pull all the burden on the patient to ask. Reassurance is not always sufficient to decrease the person's anxiety, and it does not respect the patient as someone who is actively managing the effects of his illness and making interpretations and the hypothesis to guide action.

CUTTING BACK: THEORETICAL INTERPRETATIONS

Cutting back is the core variable for understanding and and explaining much of what goes on in a patient's adjustment to life after a heart attack, but the process itself has more general implications. Since most chronic illnesses are restrictive and debilitative, they too require cutbacks in activities. For those with rheumatoid arthritis, multiple sclerosis, cerebral palsy, and stroke, cutting back is less optional than it is for people who have heart attacks, and the limits of action are more clear-cut. However, there is always a margin which can be calculated in terms of personal, social, and situational factors.

Cutting back is a process applicable to disease prevention. Strategies for operationalizing cutting back also are employed to reduce risk prior to the occurrence of any event which could be labeled as illness. For example, cutting down and substituting may come into use for chronic problems of smoking, obesity, hypercholesterolemia, and long-term high stress and overwork.

Chronic conditions of everyday life other than those brought about by illness, such as having to care for an ill or handicapped person or certain employment, marital, and life cycle conditions which become "incurable," also involve cutting back, as do sudden crises which negatively affect the availability of physical, social, and psychological resources. Thus, cutting back is one dimension of redesigning life-style which has applicability to a wide range of life situations and can be used to enhance understanding of this major type of behavior change.

ACKNOWLEDGEMENTS

I wish to acknowledge the valuable assistance of Drs. Barney G. Glaser, Anselm L. Strauss, Harold Gustafson, and Ms. Sarah Mazelis.

REFERENCES

1. Bilodeau CB, Hackett TP: Issues raised in a group setting by patients recovering from myocardial infarction. Am J Psychiatry 218:73, 1971.

2. Blumer H: Symbolic Interactionism: Perspective and Method. Englewood Cliffs, New Jersey, Prentice-Hall.

3. Bruhn JG, Chandler B, Wolf S: A psychological study of survivors and nonsurvivers of myocardial infarction. Psychosom Med 3:8, 1969.

4. Bruhn JG, Thurman AE Jr, Chandler BC, et al: Patients' reactions to death in a coronary care unit. J Psychosom Res 14:65, 1970.

5. Bruhn JG, Wolf S, Philips B: A psychosocial study of surviving male coronary patients and controls followed over nine years. J Psychosom Res 15:305, 1971.

6. Cartwright D (ed): Field Theory in Social Science: Selected Theoretical Papers--Kurt Lewin. New York, Harper & Row, 1951.

7. Charmaz KC: Time and Identity: The Shaping of Selves of the Chronically Ill. Doctoral Dissertation. San Francisco, University of California, 1973.

8. Clausen JA (ed): Introduction. In Calusen JA (ed): Socialization and Society. Boston, Little, Brown, 1968, p. 3.

9. Cowie B: The cardiac patient's perception of his heart attack. Soc Sci

Med 10:87, 1976.

10. Croog SH, Levine S: Social status and subjective perceptions of 250 men after myocardial infarction. Public Health Rep 84:989, 1969.

11. Croog SH, Levine S: Religious identity and response to serious illness: A report on heart patients. Soc Sci Med 6:17, 1972.

12. Croog SH, Levine S, Lurie Z: The heart patient and the recovery process: A review of the literature on social and psychological factors. Soc Sci Med 2:111, 1968.

13. Croog SH, Levine S, Lurie Z: The heart patient and the recovery process: A review of the directions of research on social and psychological factors. Soc Sci Med 2:111, 1968.

14. Croog SH, Lipson A. Levine S: Help patterns in severe illness: The roles of kin network, non-family resources, and institiutions. J Marr Fam 34:32, 1972.

15. Croog SH, Shapiro DS, Levine S: Denial among male heart patients. Psychosom Med 33:385, 1971.

16. Davis F: Definitions of time and recovery in paralyitic polio convalescence. Am J Sociol 61:582, 1956.

17. Davis F: Passage Through Crisis: Polio Victims and Their Families. Indianapolis, Bobbs-Merrill, 1963.

18. Davis F: Deviance disavowal: The management of strained interaction of the visibly handicapped. In Becker HS (ed): The Other Side: Perspectives on Deviance. New York, The Free Press of Glencoe, 1964, p. 119.

19. Davis MZ: Living with Multiple Sclerosis: A Social Psychological Analysis. Springfield, Illinois, Charles C Thomas, 1973.

20. Doehrman SR: Psycho-social aspects of recovery from coronary heart disease: A review. Soc Sci Med 11:199, 1977.

21. Dominian J, Dobson M: Study of patients' psychological attitudes to a coronary care unit. Br Med J 4:795, 1969.

22. Foster S, Andreoli KG: Behavior following infarction. Am J Nurs 70:2344, 1970.

23. Riedman M, Rosenman RH: Type A Behavior and Your Heart. New York, Knopf, 1974.

24. Garrity TF: Social involvement and activeness as predictors of morale six months after first myocardial infarction. Soc Sci Med 7:199, 1973.

25. Garrity TF: Vocational adjustment after first myocardial infarction: Comparative assessment of several variables suggested in the literature. Soc Sci Med 7:705,1973.

26. Glaser G, Strauss Al: The Discovery of Grounded Theory: Strategies for Qualitative Research, Aldine-Atherton, 1967.

27. Glaser B, Strauss AL: Status Passage. Chicago, Aldine-Atherton, 1967.

28. Goffman E: The Presentation of Self in Everyday Life. Garden City, New York, Doubleday Anchor, 1959.

29. Gouldner AW: The norm of reciprocity: A preliminary statement. In Hollander EP, Hunt RG (eds): Current Perspectives in Social Psychology. New York, Oxford University Press, 1971, p. 286.

30. Groden BM: Return to work after myocardial infarction. Scot Med J 12:297, 1967.

31. Hackett TP, Cassem NH, Wishnie HA: The coronary-care unit: An appraisal of its psychologic hazards. N Engl J Med 279:1365, 1968.

32. Hackett TP, Cassem NH, Wishnie HA: Detection and treatment of anxiety in the coronary care unit. Am Heart J 78:727, 1969.

33. Higgins AC, Pooler WS: Myocardial infarction and subsequent reemployment in Syracuse, New York. Am J Public Health 58:312, 1968.

34. James W: Psychology: Briefer Course. New York, MacMillan, 1974, p. 54.

35. Josten J: Emotional adaptation of cardiac patients. Scand J Rehab Med 2-3:49, 1970.

36. Kavanagh T, Shephard RJ, Tuck JA: Depression after myocardial infarction. Can Med Assoc J 113:23, 1975.

37. Kelley JJ: Two functions of reference groups. In Maccoby E, Newcomb TM, Hartley EL (eds): Readings in Social Psychology, ed 3. New York, Holt, Rinehart, & Winston, 1958.

38. Kelly GA: The Psychology of Personal Constructs. New York, Norton, 1955.

39. Klein RF, Dean A, Willson LM, et al: The physician and post-myocardial infarction. invalidism. JAMA 194:143, 1965.

40. Lesher S: How to live after a heart attack. San Francisco Chronicle, February 15, 1974, p. 38(N).

41. Lewin K, Dembo T, Festinger L, et al: Level of aspiration. In Hunt JM (ed): Personality and Behavior Disorders. New York, Ronald Press, 1944.

42. Markson EW: Patient semeiology of a chronic disease. Soc Sci Med 5:159,1971.

43. Mead GH: Mind, Self and Society: From the Standpoint of a Social Behaviorist, edited and introduced by CW Morris. Chicago, University of Chicago Press. Originally published 1934.

44. Mone LC: Short-term psychotherapy with post-cardiac patients. Int J Group Psychother 20:99, 1970.

45. Monteiro LA: Lay views on activity after myocardial infarction. Rhode Island Med J 55:77, 1972.

46. Mullen PD, Reynolds R: The potential of grounded theory for health education research: Linking theory and practice. Health Educ Monogr 6:280-294, 1978.

47. Nagle R, Gangola R, Picton-Robinson I: Factors influencing return to work after myocardial infarction. Lancet 2:454, 1971.

48. Natanson M (ed): Alfred Schutz: Collected Papers. Vol. 1: The Problems of Social Reality, ed 3. The Hague, Marticus Nijhoff, 1971.

49. Rahe RH, Tuffli CF Jr, Suchor RJ Jr, et al: Group therapy in the outpatient management of post-myocardial infarction patients. Psychiatr Med 4:77, 1973.

50. Semmler C, Semmler M: Counseling the coronary patient. Am J Occup Ther 28:609, 1974.

51. Sobel D: Personalization on the coronary patient. Am J Occup Ther 28:609, 1974.

52. Strauss AL, Glaser B: Chronic Illness and the Quality of Life. St. Louis, Missouri, Mosby, 1975.

53. Weiner CL: The burden of rheumatoid arthritis: Tolerating the

uncertainty. Soc Sci Med 9:97, 1975.

54. Wishnie HA, Hackett TP, Cassem MH: Psychological hazards of convalescence following myocardial infarction, JAMA 215:1292, 1971.

55. Wynn A: Unwarranted emotional stress in men with ischemic hert disease. Med J Aust 2:847, 1967.

CHAPTER 4

Reprinted from *Omega*, Vol. 3, 1972

SHOULDERING THE BURDEN

Kathy Calkins

The time and effort involved in caring for a chronically ill, aged or dying relative often constitute a burden on the patient's family. I shall primarily address the burden of day-to-day *custodial care*, which is imposed when the patient is unable to perform caretaking tasks himself. Family members generally think of such responsibilities as a burden although, when confronted themselves with the specific obligation of caring for a close relative, especially a spouse, they may not admit such feeling, or admit them only long after the relative is gone.

Close kinship ties and proximity of residence form the initial *conditions* under which relatives assume the burden of care. The availability of a supporting relative and the patient's consciousness of his situation are important determinants in how long care is *maintained* at home. *Re-evaluation* of whether the burden can be continued to be shouldered tends to occur at points when the patient's physical condition worsens. Then, after the care is relinquished to professionals, the family burden shifts to handling the further duties and ambiguities surrounding death. Each of these phases will be explicated in this paper.

METHODS AND DATA

Care of the dying patient within the context of noninstitutional arrangements will be examined within a sociological framework. In contrast to other studies, such as Anselm L. Strauss' and Barney G. Glaser's recent works on long-term dying in a hospital setting (1965, 1968, and 1970), and David Sudnow's (1967) report on the social organization of dying, my investigation was focused on home care provided until the final stages of the patient's dying trajectory.

The data were collected through interview and informal observations conducted with local medical professionals, and relatives of patients who were dying or who had recently died. Much of the data were drawn from interviews with approximately twenty working class and lower middle class families whose dying member finally had been admitted to a nearby county hospital: I was particularly interested in the perspectives and circumstances of these kinsmen, since little is known about their relationship to the dying process. Four of these families were Black, two were Mexican American, and the remainder were White. Comparative material was collected from middle-class families concerning the care they gave to their dying relatives. The methodology for the research is based upon Grounded Theory, as elaborated by sociologists Glaser and Strauss in their recent book (1967). The Grounded Theory approach emphasizes the discovery of concepts and theory through systematic analysis of the data, rather than the logical deductive theoretical formulations of other approaches. Since the data themselves provide the source of the emerging conceptual framework, systematic coding and categorizing of it starts at the beginning of data collection. Initial categories and conjectures are then subject to hypothesis testing while the researcher is still doing field work so that he may better discover the conditions under which his emerging categories are operant. The integration of these notes shows the interrelationships of the theoretical framework while, simultaneously, rendering and synthesizing the data.

ASSUMING THE BURDEN

THE DEVELOPMENT OF BURDENS

A family can provide for a patient in several ways by giving money, time, space or care. Whether a family will undertake the actual care of a patient is related to the other kinds of burdens and the extent to which they can be evaluated by the family. When family members can directly assess aspects of the burdens confronting themselves, they may intentionally decide to *assume* the burden, *assign* them to specific family members, or *delegate* them to outside agencies. When direct evaluation is improbable, or the family is relatively unaware of the circumstances which they are confronting, such decisions are apt to be forced by medical circumstances. Furthermore, the events leading to choices may occur either so imperceptibly, or for that matter so quickly, that the family may remain unaware of how the decision is actually made.

In the beginning, the family's burdens are likely to be those of money and time, rather than housing and care. Gradual increments in attention and assistance may be made for the older and dying relative. Within the normal processes of the life cycle, as individuals retire from work, children and grandchildren may give greater time to their surviving older relatives. The family assumes chores and tasks as tokens of their interest and devotion, but frequently such symbolic gestures come to be relied upon. For example, gardening duties may be taken over by a grandson when his grandfather dies, as a gesture of his concern for his grandmother. At the time this is done, the only necessity may be the symbolic meaning, which may rapidly change to a condition contingent for maintaining the living arrangement of the older person. Shifts from attention and assistance tend to occur: this forms a sequential pattern of giving greater amounts of care.

The course of deterioration necessarily affects the kinds of burdens these relatives are forced to shoulder. Two major patterns were discovered in the data. In the first, the chronic illness pattern, the family stressed the disease process. The chronically-ill person was viewed as a patient. He and his illness were so intertwined that no consideration of him could be made without it; the illness had become merged with his identity. In addition to becoming a focal point of family interaction, the illness became a basis of the life styles of the family members (Cf Davis, 1963:162). Thus, the burden of care is something that everyone is aware of. It cannot be overlooked or denied. Under these circumstances, the burden of care may inundate the entire family (Davis, 1964:123). The strain of continuous care leads family members tacitly or openly to define their relative as a burden.

The other major pattern is the gradual-aging pattern, in which the ill or aged person is viewed by his family as slowly growing older and less able to help himself. Age rather than illness is at the foreground both of his existence and the family's life style. Hence, only sporadically does the illness become the major focus of attention. The burdens on the family are not dissimilar from the occasional acute illnesses of younger family members, since their frequency and duration may not seriously disrupt ongoing family relationships. Moreover, family members prefer to treat critical incidents in the health of the gradually aging person as acute episodes from which recovery is assumed. In this pattern, the phasing of chronic illness is likely to remain somewhat obscured. The gradual aging pattern may be transformed, however, into the chronic-illness pattern if the person suffers a major complication such as a stroke or heart attack. Then the family may have to define the burdens differently in the light of new contingencies.

Professionals often are instrumental in defining the kinds of burdens the family is going to have, as well as predicting new ones. When professionals urge families to change the ill person's accommodations, it is usually in anticipation that the type of care required will cause the family greater burdens than they could reasonably shoulder. The social workers whom I interviewed confer with families about changes when a relative's care requires continual observation, lifting, or cleaning. Incontinence alone presents enough of a burden that social workers will help to find another placement for the sick person. Several social workers were emphatic about discouraging families from undertaking the care of an incontinent aged parent. Thus, professionals may interpret for the family members the conditions under which they may be relieved of any guilt about their relative's circumstances.

Strikingly, these working-class and lower middle-class families whom I interviewed managed to keep their ill and dying relatives *out* of the health care system. Few of these families ever came into contact with a social worker, and they had relatively limited exchange of information with other professionals. Hence, they were not alerted to the professionals' view of the cues that the patient's condition was presenting. Moreover, the justifications given to the family for placing their relative in a hospital or nursing home, and the mechanisms for accomplishing this, are not as available as when a family has access to professional consultation.

UNQUESTIONED OBLIGATIONS

The sense of obligation to provide a dying kinsman with care for as long as possible is a distinctive finding in our research. The supporting relatives' sense of obligation is *unquestioned* by them; shouldering the burden is the only viable alternative, and often is taken for granted as the only way of managing the situation.

In these circumstances, the relative takes on the problems, viewing them as his responsibility. Not to take on the burdens is conceived as *morally wrong*. In most cases of unquestioned obligation, the responsibility of the person giving care is simply understood and unstated. The understanding may consist of a shared viewpoint with the dying individual -- most likely a husband or wife - which has existed over a number of years. Hence, the surviving spouse may feel that to not do everything possible to keep the ill person out of the hospital, and especially out of the terminal wards, would constitute an unforgivable betrayal of trust. Consequently, super-human efforts are made to keep the patient at home. To illustrate, the wife may gradually transform the home into a micro-institution complete with a hospital bed, oxygen tank, hydraulic lift, and diet kitchen.

Underlying most cases of unquestioned obligation is the possibility or certainty of the kinsman's death. Time is a tremendously important aspect of how the burdens will be perceived and managed (Glaser and Strauss, 1968). The drama of certain death, particularly without warning, or early death, increases the survivor's sense of *obligation*. In such instances we can suspect that individuals are reluctant to perceive their services to the dying as burdens.

An example of unquestioned obligation occurred when one young housewife had a long-standing agreement with her grandparents (who raised her) that she would provide a home for whoever outlived the other; at the time her surviving grandfather came to live in the home, he himself had a prognosis of only three months to live. Knowing this, she attempted to make a special event out of grandpa's presence, and tried extra hard to make him happy. The children were solicitous and saw it as a novelty to make him a part of their home, despite the inconvenience and crowding he caused in their small house.

Compare the situation to one in which the time of death is uncertain. The novelty of the situation may soon or eventually be redefined as a nuisance. Fixing grandma's lunch every day was fun at first, but the prospects of additional chores becoming part of a presence becomes the most notable aspect of the situation, a definition of unquestioned obligation is unlikely to persist. If it is, it will have to be worked at, and its contradictions will have to be minimized. Despite the concern and original intent of the relatives, such arrangements tend to be fragile and difficult to maintain. Under the condition of the ill person's continued presence and uncertain death, he is more likely to become defined as a burden by the family, especially when brought into a nuclear family.

When relationships have been broken and death is certain, the relative is apt anyhow to feel obligated to make some attempt, however feeble, to make amends with the dying in order to place a shaky relationship in equilibrium before death finalizes the relationship. Under these circumstances, the extent of the potential burdening of the family is apt to be limited. In some cases, the burden may include taking the dying in, although it is more likely to mean visiting obligations. For example, a thirty-year-old son who hadn't spoken to his alcoholic father for eight years said, "Me and my father never talked for a long time. Then I heard the man had cancer - we talked." This was the limit for which the son would obligate himself. When an uncle put pressure on him to assume the funeral and burial costs, he refused. He implied that this type of responsibility should not be pushed on him, since after all, from his view, his father was to blame for his own situation. Any obligation beyond this was felt to be undeserved by the son. The relative merits of the dying person, in the eye of the potential helper, are likely to form the basis of the extent to which obligations are unquestioned by the helper.

Several women were aware that it was only their continued efforts that kept the oldster out of an institution for terminal cases. One Black woman who took in her grandfather when no one else wanted him made the following statement:

"The nurses would say to me, 'How did you take care of him so long?' I would say, I just loved him. I didn't want to see him in the hospital. I don't like those convalescent homes. They're in it for the money - they are kinda mean to them, too. I feel the same way about my uncle; I'm gonna keep him as long as I can."

Here, preventive home nursing care is used by the supporting relative as a way of intentionally delaying the time of final admission to a terminal care facility. In this instance it was the woman's negative view of institutions in addition to her attachment to her grandfather on which her feeling of obligation was based. Her perspective of the situation was unquestioned precisely *because* it was based on knowledge. Her assessment of institutional alternatives delimited her range of conceivable choices of how to handle her grandfather's care humanly.

Only when the situation becomes unbearable will the relative acknowledge the burden he is shouldering. Frequently the physical strains on the wife of a dying man result in the family physician's defining the care as a burden and directing changes. Until the point of unbeatable strain, a wife may make concerted efforts to camouflage the fact that her husband is becoming a burden. Camouflaging can have several implications. First, it can serve as a way of refuting a wife's nagging suspicions that her husband is dying (Cf. Glaser and Strauss, 1965: Chapter 4). Second, with the realization that he is deteriorating, it can relieve her fears about the future after his death and keep her busy with many additional day-to-day tasks. Third, and perhaps most important, by camouflaging the burden, the wife is able to exert control on her husband's view of himself and help create a situation wherein he can die with dignity. In this way, she tacitly, or perhaps quite intentionally, helps to preserve her husband's self-image as a valuable man, as he progressively is able to do less. With this type of approach, his role in the family is reaffirmed even while he is dying.

UNSUSPECTED MORIBUND COURSE

When the obligation is unquestioned, the relative is usually aware of the deterioration of the dying person, if not the actual dying itself. Clearly this is not always the case, and the death may come as something of a shock, even when the person was old or unwell. In the gradual aging pattern, deteriorating changes usually are not directly visible, and tend to be defined only through contrasts. This elusive quality sometimes makes the changes strikingly apparent to those friends and family who rarely see the individual, while simultaneously the changes are unnoted by those who share everyday existence. In order for deterioration to be imperceivable, the relative must either be unaware of the burdens daily care imposes on him, or fail to make the connection between additional tasks, behavior changes and permanent deterioration.

Occasionally, those in closest contact will connect symptoms with prior incidents which were neither serious nor prolonged, if noted at all. This is especially likely when previous warnings concerning what to expect have not been provided by the medical profession. For an illustration of this, see the article about Richard Oakes, a noted Bay Area Indian leader (San Francisco Chronicle, 1970:3) who was badly beaten and did not receive care until hours later.

Oakes lay unconscious and without medical attention or ten hours in his apartment in the San Francisco State College married students' housing area, according to his wife, Anne. Mrs. Oakes said she did not act sooner because she understood form the man who brought him home that he was just drunk. She realized his condition was serious at 8:15 a.m. when she noted his bloodied nose and black eye and was unable to awaken him.

Changes may not be perceived by the relative who is closest to the dying person when the latter already has reduced the amount of participation he contributes to various activities and when he exists in the same environment as the relative. When the dying person had confined himself for a period to his own home, and when the major changes have been so undramatic, it is less likely that others will catch small changes in daily ritual. Moreover, when shifts occur in the same setting, they are less apt to be noted by others, unless the present situation demands reevaluation of the past. A shifting scene dramatizes and illuminates the meaning of change of physical condition, especially so when the change in scene is the removal to a hospital or nursing home. The new scene may bring home the change more for the relative than a reappraisal of the patient's symptoms.

It is possible for relatives to virtually move in on the dying individual - as the amount of care is increased - *without* ever being explicitly aware that he is dying, or how much care they are giving him. For example, one woman was essentially doing everything for her mother just prior to her stroke, from keeping her clean to bringing in her food, although she never realized how her mother's health was rapidly failing. In this case, the cues are at least partially reconstructed after the physician discovers his findings and reveals them to the disbelieving family member, who then searches through the past to rediscover cues he had possibly overlooked. In part because the time and effort involved pose no particular problem to the assisting family member, cues signalling the deterioration remain undetected by them. As long as some semblance of the ordinary interaction between relatives is maintained, under the above conditions, the closest member may not know what is happening. Furthermore, our data suggest that even after a first massive stroke, the relative who was closest but did not pick up the initial cues, undergoes considerable shock when death later occurs.

RESPONSIBILITY OF WHOM?

The individuals who take responsibility for care and decisions form an important variable in how burdens will be shouldered and for how long they will be supported. Clearly, in many instances, a spouse or child will become an advocate of home care and will seek to provide the patient with as much assistance as necessary. Here the assignment of the burden is *self-selective*, and other relatives may take this commitment by the supporting relative as justifying their own withdrawal from assuming responsibilities.

Not infrequently, however, self-selection occurs with simultaneous *assigning* of responsibilities by other family members. A repeated example of this occurs in the situation of one unmarried or divorced daughter who is considered to be more "available" by her siblings. She is seen as having fewer family obligations than those who are married and have children at home. Simultaneously, however, the woman self-selects herself of the basis of a more continuous and closer relationship with the ill person. In several cases, the self-selection extended to the point that the bond shared with the ill person had been the most significant one which the woman possessed.

Self-selection may also occur when a sympathetic relative perceives that no one else will act in behalf of the ill person, which would render him helpless and facing a long-term hospitalization. A self-selected supporting relative is most likely to intervene when the ill person is relatively alert and voices his own view (or despair) over his situation. Abandoning an articulate and aware patient to a prolonged institutionalized dying presents much more of a problem for the relatives than doing so to a person who is inarticulate or unaware of his actual circumstances of being a terminal case (Glaser and Strauss, 1965:10). The patient's consciousness of the situation thus is a determinant in how he is viewed and what kind of arrangements can be made to accommodate him.

When the patient is aware of his plight and wishes to spend as much of his remaining time out of the hospital as possible, he may fight to preserve his independence and try to assume considerable responsibility for his own care. But, as time runs out, more tasks fall into the hands of the relative. As the dying trajectory proceeds, the supporting relative is apt to need back-up lines and may find that they, too, are drawn into continuous work - most of their leisure hours becoming involved with adjunctive care of the dying individual. For example, two daughters who shouldered the care of their mother found that they were maintaining round-the-clock custodial nursing care complete with multiple daily bed changes, due to incontinence, special food preparation, and heavy lifting.

When the tasks become so arduous that the available individuals cannot handle them, the doctor is likely to try to relieve the family of the burdens of care by forcing them to make other arrangements. Or, frequently, the rate of deterioration proceeds so far that the family members acknowledge that the limits of their care have been over-extended, and begin to make other plans, if no dramatic change is caused by a sudden crisis like a heart attack or stroke.

CONSTRUCTING ARRANGEMENTS

As the older person shifts from a gradual-aging pattern of deterioration to a chronic-illness pattern with a dying trajectory, albeit slow, changes may become necessary on the kinds of living arrangements possible for him before hospitalization. Three general types of accommodations were found in our study. These include *independent living, old-age family living,* and *live-in nursing care*. An ill person may have all three types of situations before he reaches the final stages of dying, or must be hospitalized at any time that his deterioration increases.

Perhaps the most important property of all three types of arrangement is their relative tenuousness. Despite the interest and help of relatives, such arrangements are continually breaking down and the alternative for care which the family tried hardest to avoid may become their only choice. The numerous contingencies on which a plan rests are easily disrupted. Frequently, the main contingency of a planned arrangement is simply that the ill person does not get any worse. Then, as long as his condition remains status quo, other contingencies, such as the help provided him, remain stable and available. The prevailing definition may be "this much help, but no more;" then with a worsened condition, and the increased necessity of more help, resources for it become unavailable. Hence, within the context of a particular constructed arrangement, the assisting family member or members will tend to have a tolerance level for the amount of burdening that they can assume.

Independent Living. This is the type of arrangement for those living alone in their own domicile, typically when the pattern of deterioration is that of gradual aging. The arrangement may be scaled to the diminished needs and energy of the individual using it. Despite this, being able to maintain an independent existence, even of a limited kind, is often an important source of self-identification to the older person. Changing this arrangement may then become the point when the individual begins to feel despair. As one respondent described her grandfather:

> He never adjusted too well to the move, and I think it broke his spirit when he had to leave that house on 7th Street. He had his cronies - you know, all those guys would come over and drink beer and carry on, and play with the dog. Things were never the same for him after he had to move.

Tenacious independence is apt to be exhibited when the ill individual views other arrangements as untenable. Old people who value their independence and cling to it tenaciously sometimes are able to keep adjusting their daily existence so that they do not have to burden their family. Groceries are ordered and delivered; neighbors are asked for transportation to the doctor even though the costs include loneliness, inconvenience, and not infrequently, health hazards. These individuals will attempt to carry on their usual routines and continue to assume the burden of self-care. This independent stance may have been a life-long tendency; however, it can also be based on the very accurate knowledge that the only two other possibilities are unwelcome - moving in with a relative or going to an institution.

Independent living may be constructed as a way of bringing an old person closer to the care and attention of a concerned relative. When arrangements are shifted, as the old person can do less, each shift may dramatically symbolize his decreasing participation in life and the additional burdens the family finds necessary to assume. Such changes may be programmed by the children so that their mother can maintain some independence and privacy as she grows older. Concurrently, *they* assume increasing responsibility for her care. As one widow grew older, her daughters arranged for her to move from her home thirty miles away to an apartment which was within walking distance of both daughters who helped her with groceries, laundry, and cleaning tasks. As the woman became increasingly ill, one daughter arranged for her to live in an adjoining apartment. Subsequently, this was followed by a shift to a shared apartment when she needed actual nursing care.

Old-age Living. This is a type of family living where the aged or ill person lives or boards with another person such as a spouse, daughter or the entire family. The reason for the arrangement may be financial, although those involved expect the old person to enter a chronic-illness pattern of deterioration. The most tenuous arrangement is that which relies on the aged spouse as the supporting relative, since both partners are apt to have problems. Under these conditions, the ability to maintain an independent existence depends upon a delicate balance between what each person can do for himself and for the other person. Several social workers stated that this arrangement was generally unsatisfactory. These workers have found that neither person is able to assume the burdens imposed by the needs of the other, and as a consequence, deep hostilities between the aged couple often resulted.

As the aged couple become less independent, continuance of this mode of existence usually depends on the assistance of a younger person, particularly a daughter, but sometimes a housekeeper. In one case, both helped to assimilate the burdens of care; the housekeeper was full-time instead of live-in, so the daughter covered the nights and week-ends. When the burden of care is so great, coverage may be assisted by a visiting nurse.

Several families provide old-age living for persons who were not directly related to them, and a Black family took in a White retired friend, whose family ties were broken for eight years. Usually, a family avoids boarders who, from the beginning, need sustained nursing care, and it is understood that a boarder will continue to help himself. When the family chooses a specific boarder, rather than feeling forced to accommodate him, the aged status of boarder may be allowed to shade into one of bona fide family member. If so, as he becomes ill, he may be given the solicitousness reserved only for closest relatives. This occurred when the White man boarded with the Black family. After his death, however, the woman acknowledged that his absence was not like missing one of her small family; it was like missing a grandfather.

Live-in Nursing Care. This type of living arrangement often is made when relatives realize that the older or ill person's health is degenerating into a chronic illness and dying pattern. The decision is often preceded by a bad fall, slight stroke or loss of the last arrangement because of money or complicating factors, e.g., stairs or a wheelchair. The decision to have the patient live-in may represent a last-ditch effort to keep him out of a nursing home.

When the family knowingly brings their relative home to give him nursing care, often they must integrate their routines into the round of care to be given him. This usually calls for mobilizing the help of others - family or nursing assistants. In several cases, the women of the family operated virtual nursing shifts by alternating their presence with the dying person with other obligations at work, their own families, and chores (like the daily trip to the laundromat). These efforts meant organizing all their nonworking hours in the service of the ill person.

As suggested earlier, wives are likely to attempt to undertake this kind of care. When care is given in the same surroundings, the fact of the seriousness or terminal state of the husband's illness may more easily be hidden from him (Glaser and Strauss, 1965:Chapter 5). Thus, enormous amounts of nursing care given at home may be given to terminal cancer patients whose doctors do not wish to disclose the diagnosis.

The pretense of the situation may be more of a burden on the wife than the strenuous care she is giving. Consider this woman's statement:

> The hardest thing was to know and keep it from him [dying]. Watch him slippin' away day by day. Then, he'd say things like, "Wonder why my food don't stay down?" I'd have to say something like, "Well, my food don't always stay down either," and you'd have to be able to give a reason every time he said something like that, always have to have something to say when he said something.

RE-EVALUATING THE BURDEN

Direct changes in the constructed arrangements occur when ordered by a physician, who reevaluates the ongoing situation. These changes may serve to symbolize the person's condition and, significantly, herald his coming death. The changes in arrangements can be anticipated by the family. When the dying person has been recognizably ill for a prolonged period, usually several years, the family is apt to have projected the reevaluation of the situation into the future by discussing, and perhaps repeatedly rehearsing, the oncoming death and probable alternatives for themselves.

In contrast, not all families either are aware of the circumstances that they will eventually face, or choose to acknowledge these circumstances. As suggested above, when a certain amount of ambiguity exists and persists about the patient's status, the family may try to normalize the situation, or actively dis-attend to cues. Despite this when there are common markers of participation - such as job, church, and community organizations - the kinsman's deterioration may not be so easily overlooked. Not only do the immediate family members note such changes, but even of they try to disavow them other people will remind them (Davis, 1964:123). For example, the son-in-law of a severely brain-damaged woman commented to her husband, "Poor thing, she doesn't remember very well, and she use to be so active." Even people who are almost strangers will give cues to the family which jar them into taking account of the changes. An unknown neighbor may say to the wife of a chronically ill man, "Your husband is getting worse, isn't he? I haven't seen him taking his walk these past few weeks." When the family is flooded with cues, they are likely to begin to reevaluate the situation. The combination of cues with increments in care can force the supporting relative into awareness of the probability of death. When this realization occurs, he may suddenly decide that he can no longer cope with the situation. At this point, he may seek professional prescriptions for a decision to relinquish his burden of care.

KEEPING THE BURDEN OF CARE AT HOME

When the dying individual is sentient, although virtually an invalid patient, he is in a position to negotiate over the arrangements provided for himself. In some cases, he can delay a medical order that he be sent to a nursing home. Though he may not be able to change *what* disposition is made, he is likely to influence *when* it occurs. Even in the situation where relatives had made plans over years to keep the patient at home for as long as possible, the decision to admit him to an institution was made after the medical decision had been made. The opposite tactic may be taken when the patient can negotiate for himself. He may choose to enter a nursing home before it is even a possibility to his family.

The patient may adopt delaying tactics due to fear of being abandoned by the family. Hence, he may make every effort to be tenaciously independent and avoid making excessive demands upon his family, much less expose them to any feeling of despair which he might have. He is a model patient because he is afraid. When an aged parent fears being abandoned by an attentive son or daughter, and they respond to his fears, the chances are that the family will attempt to mobilize themselves in his behalf to the extent that a nursing home is constructed within the family's living quarters. In this situation the family cooperates with the stalling - usually when they assume that some improvement might occur or that death is imminent. Similarly, fear of abandonment by the ailing or dying spouse tends to tie the survivor in an almost inextricable bind to his burden of care. In contrast, when the marriage of the dying person is new, the spouse may pull out and force other relatives to shoulder the burden of care. This seems to be a common phenomenon with post-retirement marriage.

It is not common for the physician to use his authority to reassure the dying person, and insist on the construction of a different arrangement to relieve the burdens on the spouse. The wife of one man who was extremely afraid reported:

He was upset by the move to the rest home, otherwise he accepted everything. He thought people were sent to a rest home when their family didn't want them no more. I tried to tell him, but he only really accepted it when the doctor talked to him. Dr. Staton said to me, "Look Norma, you couldn't handle it even if you had a nurse 24 hours a day, you couldn't do it. He needs equipment and special attention." Dr. Staton talked to him; he said, "If she keeps on going it, she won't last." The doctor told him, "Arthur, your wife loves you. If you want to help, go to a rest home."

When stalling no longer works, or the patient himself cannot tolerate the toll that his stalling is taking on the family, he may attempt to manage his own situation through helping in the selection of a nursing home.

A more subtle consequence of a dying patient's alertness is that the family members usually feel compelled to take into account his realm of symbolic meanings. Knowing that he is alert obligates them to show respect for his preferences for alternatives. The importance which an aged or dying person attaches to his home may influence the amount of burden that his family will assume in order to keep him there. The extent that a given patient defines his situation as "home" has consequences for the kinds of dispositions that can be made for him.

When the family's definition of home coincides with the patient's, conditions are set so that no real consideration of other arrangements emerges until actually forced. Hence a definition of unquestioned obligation will prevail. Conversely, when the structure of the family is loose and fragmented, and the definition of "home" is also, the conditions develop for institutional placement being made more easily - any shift might result in this change.

When the old person is taken into a grown child's nuclear family, the likelihood of his being able to make a definition of "home" and have it stick becomes more difficult than when he exists in a somewhat separate environment. In subtle ways, the oldster is apt to feel that an encroachment on space and possessions represents something borrowed or lent. Old people who live in their own homes but have children join them, or essentially give their children furnishings for a house, are likely to settle in to a much greater degree, and, moreover, to remain at home. Furthermore, they feel the child owes them allegiance along with the willingness to assume the burdens of care. In short, the dying person has set up conditions wherein he attempts to force a definition of unquestioned obligation. In contrast, when an oldster is integrated into the family's daily round but not into the family structure, tacit understandings exist that he may make it his home as long as he does not become a burden.

When the boarder is not "at home," he is likely to maintain a certain distance from the person taking care of him, in addition to a stoical attitude about the necessity for the care. Furthermore, when the aged person does not define the arrangement as home, he is more likely to overlook the favors and assistance bestowed upon him by the people who take him in. In addition, he may not be attuned to their tolerance levels. Hence, when the time comes for evaluation of the burden of care, the family will probably opt for getting rid of him. In contrast, when the definition of home is not made by the boarder but the burdens become great, we can expect the situation will continue only when there are hidden benefits - such as occur when a woman cannot feed her own children without the additional money from the oldster's social security check, or when middle-class people expect an inheritance from him. Similarly, hidden commitments might serve to maintain such an arrangement, perhaps made as a promise to someone already deceased.

RELINQUISHING THE BURDEN

THE TIMING OF DEATH AND CHANGING BURDENS

If the kinsman's deterioration is not interrupted by his sudden death at home, typically he will have to be admitted to a medical setting for the final stages of his dying. Albeit reluctantly, the supporting relative usually has to relinquish the burden of care.

At this juncture, the burdens involved dramatically shift. Although the relative is released from the enormous amount of work involved in care, new burdens develop, e.g., continued visiting. Ambiguity as to whether this is the final stage of dying may also pervade the situation. Thus, what at first may be regarded as a medical emergency - to keep the patient alive - may appear to develop into the last stages of his dying. The ambiguity of the time of death becomes part of the burden to be shouldered (Glaser and Strauss, 1965). This ambiguity may be cleared up by the patient's social death (Glaser and Strauss, 1968:61). For the family, his social death occurs when they see that the initial emergency has turned into a lingering dying. Consequently, the patient has essentially died at the point when the family's interest changes from hoping he can be pulled through, to questioning, "Why don't they let him die?"

Here it is a case of social death occurring earlier than biological death. Hence, the symbolic meaning of the death for the relative occurs at a different and more inharmonious time than the actual death. Social death may occur gradually over time in cases of chronic disease. When this happens the actual death is not expected to be a shock, and the family may act as if the closest relative has lost his prerogative to express shock and profound grief. One daughter made the following remark at the time her father was dying. "She [the mother] should accept it - after all she has watched him die for two years." Carrying this thinking further, when people who have been ill for years finally enter the dying trajectory, they may have been so excluded and estranged from the rest of the group; so death is somewhat anti-climatic.

Social death may also occur at the point when the housekeeping arrangements are drastically changed. The most pointed example of this was when a grandmother was placed in a nursing home and was never again spoken of or visited. A similar situation was reported by a nurse working on the terminal wards of a county institution. When she called a female patient's son to request permission to cut her hair, his response was, "Goodness, is she still alive?"

More often, the relative will attempt to reconstruct the past in order to point to a time when logically their kinsman ceased to exist as the individual known in the past. "She died at the point when her heart stopped at Stanford." The social death is confirmed when the hospital staff announces that no more can be done, and that the family will have to make other arrangements.

Whether or not the family defines social death as occurring, the continued presence of the patient places certain burdens upon the family, not the least of which is their observation that the dying person is suffering. Obligations to him have to be weighed against the need to preserve the energies of the closest relatives. These dilemmas over what to do are confronted by anguished family members. Since she doesn't want him to die alone, should the wife of a dying man remain at his bedside for what might turn out to be many days? Or, should she follow the advice of the physician who encourages her to begin to get back to her usual routines and wait and see?

The disruption of the life of the family members, and the burdens which it places upon them, emerge even when the most optimum conditions have been constructed. One man tried to view his extremely brain-damaged wife as dead, and build a new life for himself since she would never be able to come home. However, his wife was placed in a nursing home five minutes away from the family business. Although his visits were decreased, he was not completely able to make the shift. The dilemma was written all over the man's face. Intellectually he knew he should construct a new life without her. However, it was impossible for him to manage this, psychologically and socially. The phone calls about "How's Sue?" (his wife) were so numerous that for a period he refused to answer the phone. Also, other reminders tied him to the past - not the least was the woman's recognition of, and attachment to, him. Whenever anyone else visited, her first and repeated question was "Where's Daddy?" This man was so torn by the situation that he would not arrange for an attending physician to supervise her case at the nursing home. When told that the staff had to be able to notify a doctor "in case of an emergency," he said, "That's exactly what we don't want. When her pulse goes down, they'll just pull her through again, and what's it all for? It makes everyone suffer. She died months ago."

In this case the husband was not able to treat his wife as "socially dead," under the condition that her living arrangement was so close and she frequently recognizes him. If, on the other hand, she became permanently comatose, then he could reconcile himself to her death and maintain his self-respect while he attempted to construct another life. Analytically, the interesting aspect of such a case is that the husband was trying to define the situation as a social death, with the support of sympathetic professionals, but that the two conditions of his wife's situation -proximity and recognition of family - invalidated this definition and simultaneously served to increase the emotional burdens which the family now shouldered.

ATTACHMENT TO THE BURDEN

In the anecdote above, treating the situation as a social death was attempted before biological death. In other cases, the supporting relative may attempt to keep the deceased socially alive beyond the point of actual death. Under these circumstances, the attachment of the supporting relative for the patient extends beyond the shared relationship they had together to the style of existence including the daily routine of physical care and housekeeping. When this occurs, the supporting relative may attempt to follow the routines to which she has become attached even though they are no longer necessary. Several of the middle-aged women who took care of their aged mothers were suddenly released. Without the burdens of care, they felt they were not really contributing anything of meaning to others. In contrast to the devotion and services they had previously provided, being free to pursue their own interests appeared inconsequential. Perhaps without quite realizing it, assuming the burden of care had become the major source of personal fulfillment for these women.

When so much of the supporting relative's self is invested in the patient and his care, relinquishing both becomes problematic, if not traumatic. The relative is tied to the past. One wife said, ''I don't even feel it - no changes. I can still see myself getting ready to go to the hospital. I can't accept it that he is gone.'' When a friend suggested to another new widow that she pursue some prior interests, she retorted, ''Why should I do that? Everything I had in life that meant something to me is gone now.'' When the closest relative's life is so inextricably intertwined with the dying person, the death is more likely to be a shock. This was so with women who gave burdensome care but did not realize the extent of their undertakings until it was relinquished. For them the burden was more than unquestioned, it was unrealized.

CONCLUSION

Since most older people live in non-institutionalized settings, the problems of the burdens of care of the dying confront most families, for at least a period of time, if not up until the final stages of dying. The closer the kinship relatedness, attachment, and proximity, the more likely the burden of care will be assumed by the family. If these conditions exist and the supporting relative is aware of the ill person's deterioration, then the family may maintain a definition of unquestioned obligation for the burden of care.

Clearly, taking on the burden of care is an important part of family existence for a number of these cases. The professionals they dealt with were described as more equipped to help them relinquish the burden than able to offer concrete alternatives for managing it more easily at home. The awareness of professionals of the structural conditions which surround individual situations may give them helpful guidelines for recommending assisting measures that can be used to compensate for the changing circumstances in home care.

REFERENCES

Davis, F.; *Passage through crisis*. Indianapolis: Bobbs-Merrill, 1963.

Deviance disavowal: The management of strained interaction by the visibly handicapped. In H.S. Becker (Ed.) *The other side*. Glencoe: The Free Press, 1964, 119-138.

Glaser, B.G., & Strauss, A.L. *Awareness of dying*. Chicago: Aldine, 1965.

Time for dying. Chicago: Aldine, 1968.

San Francisco Chronicle; Indian leader is badly beaten (June 13, 1970), 3.

Strauss, A.L., & Glaser, B.G.; *Anguish*. Mill Valley, CA: Sociology Press, 1970.

Sundow, D.; *Passing on*. Englewood Cliffs, N.J.: Prentice-Hall, 1967.

CHAPTER 5

Reprinted from *Issues in Mental Health Nursing*, 1978, 1 (2). 50-56.

STEPFATHER FAMILIES:

Integration Around Child Discipline

Phyllis Noerager Stern

This paper reports the results of a study involving thirty stepfather families in the San Francisco Bay Area.[1] Eighty-five hours of intensive interviews with 62 persons yielded data on a total of 132 individuals. A variety of social strata and ethnic groups were represented. Data were analyzed using the qualitative method of constant comparative analysis.

Stepfather families do not start out being integrated. Some never become so but can be placed somewhere along a continuum, the antipodal end points of which are disintegration and integration. There is a time dimension involved. Families report that whether the integration is smooth or rough going, a time period of one and a half to two years is required before things "settle down."

INTEGRATION

Integration in families is defined as a condition where family members feel that they belong to the family and where they agree about what is "normal" in family life, which means they have developed norms. An integrated family is one in which the members feel the cohesiveness of the group and feel attracted to it. All members participate in activities which affect the welfare of the group whether these activities are of a structural or an interactional nature.

Interaction and structure may be illustrated in the following ways. On an interactional level, each member of an integrated family is allowed to speak directly to every other family member; they are not expected to go through an intermediary as in some less integrated families. Children speak freely of their likes and dislikes to the stepfather as well as the mother, and parents are equally direct in their communications. Structure, the making of rules and the establishment of a power system, is the result of the contributions of all members in an integrated family. To explain this further, children are allowed to voice their opinion of a proposed rule or a decision, even though the child's vote is rarely the deciding one. Thus, if a youngster thinks restricting TV watching to between 6 and 8 PM is unfair or does not want the family to move to New York, he or she is allowed to argue the case.

Several paths to integration exist. The process can be traced along the various dimensions of religion, education, recreation, and finances. However, it is the dimension of discipline which gives stepfather families the most difficulty. Discipline is defined as methods for teaching children behaviors acceptable to adults. Discipline can be integrative or disintegrative. It can be handled in such a way that conflict is manageable, or such that differences arising over discipline can literally blow the group apart.

INTEGRATIVE DISCIPLINE

Stepfather families manage to become integrated in spite of the problem of the discipline of children through a basic social process which this author has named "integrative discipline". Integrative discipline involves three implementing processes: (1) *rule making and enforcing*, which present problems of consensus; (2) *friending*, making a friend of the child; and (3) *integrative undermining*, which will be explained later in this article.

RULES AND ENFORCEMENT

In stepfather families, rules must be worked out regarding family behavior. Family rules stem from an emotional rather than a logical base; they are formed according to the sentimental order of the participants.

SENTIMENTAL ORDER Ways of behaving are learned in one's family origin; one has a feeling for what is right and proper, a sentimental order for what is normal. Family concepts of what constitutes "normal" cover a wide range of behavior and rules. Couples marrying for the first time come together with differing ideas about what goes on in a normal family. They spend a good deal of time negotiating important points such as whether it is essential to put the cap on the toothpaste, who picks up whose socks from the floor, whose style of cooking is "right" which partner manages the checkbook, and who tries to take charge in front of company. These are all examples of sentimental order. To each spouse, the way it was done at home seems right. When children arrive, parents in an intact home face new problems of sentimental order regarding rules and what each partner considers "normal" behavior for children. Differences arise over what a child should be allowed to eat and wear; over the content, frequency, and noise level of the child's speech; and over the proper location for and the adequate amount of the child's physical activity. In stepfather families, the problem of sentimental order is multiplied because there are at least three views of the propriety of family rules. Mother, stepfather, and child all have clear but different ideas of what normal is. They all know how things should go.

RULE MAKER/ENFORCER PATTERNS When a man marries into the ongoing system of mother-child dyad, he is in some ways an interloper. It is he who must be integrated into the family. Part of the integration centers around who is allowed to make rules and who is allowed to enforce them. Rules governing rule-making and enforcing privileges are determined according to the participants: what they think a father is supposed to do, what position they think a mother should hold. In this study, all stepfathers were allowed to make some rules, but enforcing those rules was another matter. The study indicated that when a mother does not like the disciplining style of the stepfather, she undermined him. She can do this subtly by failing to carry out rules he has made, or she can attack him directly and countermand his orders. The example of Roy and Peggy is fairly typical.

Peggy adopted a wait-and-see attitude when Roy began disciplining her son Claude. Roy used the enforcement technique of banishment at every infraction of rules, sending Claude to his room. After a month, Peggy, who felt Roy was being entirely too strict and harsh, exploded. According to Roy, "That first fight was almost our last! I mean, I thought I was doin' pretty good, you know, and then, whew, I mean, the roof fell in. You know, whew, it was heavy!"

Roy's bid to gain management privileges failed. His effort to share in discipline was undermined by his wife. Having one's discipline undermined is a devastating experience. As in the example above, conflict which begins over discipline escalates to other areas. Roy and Peggy battled over Claude for many months. The couple finally took a growth and development course together to find out what other people thought was acceptable or normal behavior for 5-year-old Claude. After this experience, it was easier for them to compromise their expectations and develop a sentimental order peculiar to their own family (see endnote 1).

Early in the relationship, the mother plays "go-between" for child and stepfather. This is a natural position for her to assume because she is best acquainted with each and can best explain the behavior of one to the other. However, if she clings to this role too long, her behavior blocks integration.

STRUCTURAL PATTERNS

Five family structural patterns were discovered in this study, one of which was integrated, the other four of which were less so.

1. *Not-my-kid* or *stepfather-left-out* pattern. A structural condition in which the mother makes and enforces rules forms the starting point for all stepfather families because the mother and the child have had a life apart from the stepfather. When the stepfather comes into the relationship as a spouse, comanagement privileges must be granted to him by the mother and, to some degree, the child. In the beginning, the stepfather usually says to the mother, "Well, it's not my kid, how do you want me to handle it?" She may say something like, "We'll just see how it goes." If the stepfather moves slowly in his assumption of the disciplinarian role and if he makes a friend of the child, the family can become integrated.

2. *Integrated* or *no-one-left-out* pattern. In the integrated pattern, everyone interacts, and everyone shares in rule making. We know that in a democratic family the child participates more, and this is true in stepfather families. Even the child makes rules - those which deal with recreation are a good example. The child has as much right to vote against going to a baseball game as any other member. Participation in rule making indicates a higher status position for the family member.

3. *Chaos* or *every-one-left-out* pattern. If the stepfather moves too quickly or if his rule-making and enforcing technique is not to the mother's liking (or the child's), the mother undermines the stepfather. Like Peggy in the example above she stops him right in the act of discipline and says, "Not my kid you don't!" She assumes the role of go-between. He resents the undermining and retaliates by refusing to do household chores or by absenting himself from the household, perhaps spending an evening or two at the local bar. If, unlike Peggy and Roy, they are unable to settle their differences and the uproar continues, the family can fall into a chaos pattern where everyone makes rules, no one observes the rules of anybody else, and nothing gets done. Showers leak, porches fall down, and the lawn remains uncut.

4. *Anything-you-say-dear* or *mother-left-out* pattern. When stepfather, mother, and child first share a home, the mother may say to the stepfather, "I want you to take over the discipline," but she may not mean that entirely. A structural pattern ensues where the stepfather makes the rules and the mother enforces them. This puts her in the position of being able to

enforce only those rules with which she agrees. This she does through subterfuge. For instance, the stepfather may decide that the children should be in bed by 8 PM. The mother says, "Anything you say, dear," but because she doesn't agree with the rule, she does not enforce it. "Oh my," she says at 9 PM, "Look at the time, and I forgot to tell the kids to get to bed!" This is the traditional family pattern where the mother plays go-between, and is distantly in charge. The pattern seems harmless, but is not integrated.

5. *Stepfather-in-charge* or *child-left-out* pattern. Occasionally, the mother says: "Take over," and means just that. She has had trouble with this child before the marriage, and wants the stepfather to "straighten this kid out." In this study, the child in this pattern was always a small boy, under six years of age. When the stepfather takes over, the child becomes resentful and fights back. The stepfather counters with harsh punishment, and the child either becomes a more severe behavior problem or withdraws. Children in this pattern were described by their parents as "spacey," "absent-minded," and "going blank," all of which are behaviors of a scape-goated child. Also in this structural pattern were found the house-burners, the window-smashers, and the children involved in knife fights. I consider the children in this pattern to be in jeopardy because they have no champion. They have lost the physical presence of their biological father, and their mother turns against them and tells them to obey a stranger's orders. If the stepfather in the child-left-out pattern assumes the role of strict disciplinarian but at the same time acts as a friend to the child by supporting in such a way as to raise the child's self esteem - for instance, helping the child pass math - the family can become integrated. This is possible because stepfather and child interact directly. The child must be convinced that there is something valuable for him or her in the presence of the stepfather.

FRIENDING

Friending can be contrasted with unfriending: the friending stepfather wins over the child; the unfriending stepfather attempts to take over child discipline. Discipline is part of the total socialization of the child. Again, we have known for years that the most effective enforcement technique is the that of the withdrawal of love. If the child has no love for the stepfather, such a threat means nothing. The stepfather who makes a friend of the child before he attempts to move into a comanagement position has a much easier time of it. It is quite difficult, perhaps impossible, to manage a child through force, but a man who is a friend to a child wins the child over by demonstrating that he is on the child's side.

Adam was able to understand when his 4-year-old stepson Rupert told him to "Get out of my mother's bed." The mother Adelaide (who is a nurse) said of her husband, "Adam could recall his own oedipal period." In spite of his stepson's rejection of him, when Rupert woke up screaming after dreaming about a monster, Adelaide reported: "Adam would go in and hold him and tell Rupert that he was going to be around, and that he would take care of him, and not let any monster or anything else hurt him. He really made points with Rupert when he did that."

Other stepfathers make points by teaching the child new skills, by bringing home a wanted dog, or by telling a depressed preteen that she is pretty. Friending is necessary to the process of integration; unfriending yields disintegration.

INTEGRATIVE UNDERMINING

When the stepfather undermines the mother and takes the part of the child, the effect is integrative. This is opposite to disintegrative undermining where the mother undermines the stepfather and defends her child.

In integrative undermining, the stepfather champions the child's cause in a take-it-easy-on-the-kid process. For example, the mother may be screaming at the child over some infraction of the rules. "Hey Mable," says the stepfather, "take it easy on the kid." Or perhaps the mother thinks the child is too young for a door key, but the stepfather argues, "Come on, he's a big boy now." Or the mother may refuse to allow a daughter to become a cheerleader, saying the girl is too involved in school activities already, to which the stepfather counters, "I think she should be allowed to do that. Being a cheerleader can be pretty important." The child perceives the stepfather as champion, taking up the banner on the child's behalf. Child sides with stepfather creating a new power formation in the family. The mother may resent the stepfather's interference, but at some level she knows that the stepfather can be trusted to have the best interests of the child at heart. She relaxes, and the family moves toward integration.

CONTINUUM OF DISINTEGRATIVE-INTEGRATIVE DISCIPLINE

A continuum of disintegrative-integrative discipline would have as its time dimension one and a half to two years. On the side of integration, rules and the enforcement of them would be processed slowly and with gentleness, while on the disintegrative side, just the opposite would be true. The rules would be strict, quick, and harshly enforced. Parents as comanagers would appear on the integrated side of such a continuum; one parent would be in charge on the disintegration side. For a family to become more integrated, the child must enjoy a high status position. In disintegrating families, the child holds a low status position. It takes a great deal of time and energy to make a friend of a reluctant child, and the stepfather has to feel that the child is worth the trouble. Some men are not willing to do this. "I'm the man," they'll say, "let him come to me." Communication must be direct; one member acting as go-between precludes integration.

IMPLICATIONS FOR THERAPY

This author believes that integrative undermining has implications for therapy. It could be employed as a counterparadox technique such as that suggested by Watzlawick, Weakland, and Fisch.[2]One might suggest to the stepfather that he find ways to take the part of his enemy, his stepchild, in some dispute over discipline. The child would see him in a new light and might be more willing to cooperate with a man who had championed his or her cause. A new power structure could replace one which was lopsided in favor of the mother.

This study points out that integration and the assumption of a comanagement position by the stepfather is a slow, involved process. The advice often given to stepfamilies, to settle differences over discipline prior to marriage, is misguided. Not only is it impossible for the parents to reach such an agreement dealing with problems based in sentimental order, but the advice runs exactly counter to a natural process in these families. As such, it can only add to the frustration and guilt feelings of the parents and children in stepfather families.

OTHER USES FOR INTEGRATIVE DISCIPLINE

Integrative discipline as described by this author can be useful in other situations. Families with two biological children to parents are more or less integrated and often disintegrate over disputes involving discipline. Several of the families interviewed for this study contained the children of both spouses, and therefore both parents were step to some children. Although stepmothers were not the focus of this study, it is the author's impression that those who practice integrative discipline fare better than those who do not.

In its most abstract form, integrative discipline can be useful for any new manager attempting to take over in an ongoing system, whether a new head nurse, a new intern on the service, or a new office manager. If one tries to bully one's way, one finds that orders are not carried out and needed equipment fails to appear. Through the use of friending and of integrative undermining on behalf of the staff to secure new privileges from higher management, a new manager can be integrated into the system and will find that rules are more easily enforced. It can be suggested then that integrative discipline, useful in the substantive area of stepfather families, has generability to other situations involving integration, management, and discipline.

REFERENCES

1. Stern, P. N.: "Integrative Discipline in Stepfather Families," (doctoral dissertation, University of California, San Francisco 1968), Dissertation Abstracts International, 1977, 37:10 (1977), University Microfilms, no. 77-5276

2.Watzlawick, P., J.H. Weakland, and R. Fisch; *Change*, New York, Norton, 1974.

CHAPTER 6

NEW IDENTITIES AND FAMILY LIFE:

A Study of Mothers Going To College

Gilly West and Barney G. Glaser

February 1988

In this paper we look at three social processes interrelating as they pass through three stages to enable older women to obtain a college education while simultaneously raising their children. The general process of taking on any new identity that affects meaningful family arrangements, e.g., becoming a cancer patient, a student or an employee can be analyzed by the theoretical model discovered in this paper, with appropriate variations.

A stranger to a United States college campus might well suppose after looking about, that there are more women than men students on campus. Indeed, the majority of college students are women, who are among the increased incidence of older college students in America (Mendelsohn, 1980). What a stranger could not observe, and would not overhear on the campus is that many of the older women students are mothers who are raising their children while attending college. The present study considers the transition in family and student patterns which enable wife-mothers to add on a college student identity.

Studies of women reentering college in later life tend to describe specific, concrete problems of learning or marital relations as affected by late college attendance of women, or to address specific needs of re-entry students, the academic institutions to which they apply, the interests or disinterests of the State in careers for women, or the longitudinal career of the family system, the problems and needs of re-entry women, or the midlife challenges of women whose children are older. Rather, our purpose in this paper is to present the social processes bearing on undergraduate women going to college while they raise their children (See Glaser and Strauss 1967: Strauss 1987). This is based upon long-term participant observation of, and in depth interviews with, such belated students (henceforth Belateds), most of whom have matriculated for the first time (See also Schatzman and Strauss 1973).

The theory involves three interrelated core processes, which have been discovered to be most relevant in managing the addition of studenting to mothering: *Staying Power*, *Cumulative Studenthood*, and *Recasting Family*

Performance. A diagram of the influence of these three processes demonstrates that staying power is the original driving force of both cumulative studenthood and recasting family performance at time one (t1). If Belateds are able to persevere in the pursuit of a college education, then staying power per se will enable Belateds to build their student skills and studenthood. It will also bring about family tolerance of the new "deviant" role for mothers. However cumulative studenthood and recasting family performance both later work upon staying power at time two (t2), as well as upon one another at time three (t3).

Staying power, cumulative studenthood and recasting family performance each go through three stages. *Cupellation* is a first, testing or probationary stage. Next, *Consolidation* is a stage of getting it all together. For example, during consolidation the niche (new psychological habitat at college) is lined in staying power. Belateds become Damned-Average-Raisers (DARs) in cumulative studenthood and they unite home and college in recasting family performance (Hughes 1984). *Confirmation* is a last, taking-it-for-granted stage, generally incorporating a search for a new focus. The following discussion is ordered by the progress of the three processes through these three stages (Glaser 1978).

The Belateds of this study are between the ages of thirty-four and fifty-one, average forty-four. They have between two to six children, average four, at the time of the belated mother student's matriculation. The age of the youngest child on the women's enrollment ranges from eighteen months to fourteen years. Sixty percent of Belateds are married; forty percent divorced. Most of them are seniors at a California state college, Caucasian, and Protestant. Half are Democrats; half are Republican. Sixty percent of the women contribute to the income of their predominantly middle-class or lower-class families. The Belateds have attended college for two to thirteen years (average seven), and they average attendance at three different colleges per woman. Eighty percent of the women major, eventually, in the social sciences. The other twenty percent distribute evenly among the natural sciences, mathematics, and perennial studenthood. Upon graduating from college, eighty percent of Belateds are immediately employed.

THE ORDEAL OF CUPELLATION

Staying power is put on probation the first day Belateds walk onto campus. For example, they must submit to the unexpectedly shovey bureaucratic etiquette of first time registration. As one professor remarked,

"If they hang around long enough, these older mother students usually do very well." Staying power means having stamina or having powers of enduring, resisting, persisting. The term refers to the ability of Belateds to stick it out in college in the face of physical and mental fatigue, excessive family and university demands on scanty time and energy reserves, a dreaded insecurity about their own intellectual compass when they first venture forth, guilty feelings about violating cultural traditions, as well as family fetters that threaten to undermine scholastic durability (Rubin 1979). Staying power increases and changes over time. It is a necessary condition for cumulative studenthood and for recasting family performance.

One source of staying power is personal good health. Medical or surgical mishaps are contingencies the student cannot take in stride. Belateds have a remarkable bounce-back performance record, however, e.g., from semester break hysterectomies, which both generates staying power and leads to cumulative studenthood. Belateds can also be temporarily derailed from the academic track by the illness of a spouse or child.

Possession of adequate economic assets builds up staying power. Belateds may finance college from household budgets or from income they earn outside the home when the family economy is tight or when either Belated or her husband refuses to allocate available family income for the woman's education, which either may consider to be a non-family, non-essential expenditure. Some Belateds receive financial aid from state or federal agencies. Frequently, however, Belateds whose means are limited also define such assistance as unacceptable charity.

One consequence of matriculation is that the women experience a resurgence of energy... the Ponce de Leon effect.

"I began to feel like a young adult. I got away from that drab feeling you get being with just kids all day. In college is where Ponce de Leon would have found the fountain of youth."

This youthful energy provides a strong support to staying power, which also strengthens Belateds organizing skills, and this in turn feeds back to increase cumulative studenthood.

It is fundamental to staying power that Belateds find a psychological niche at college in which to house their self and relationships, so that the women can avoid trauma and carry out academic and domestic functions efficiently. For example, when properly niched, the Belated parks her car creatively on campus, rather than circling the lot indefinitely looking for a parking space and then bursting into tears because she is very late for class. Belateds rapidly elaborate a philosophy that strengthens their psychological spine, hence staying power and cumulative studenthood. Not the least of which "niche-ing" is quickly learned to deal with being the oldest person in the new environment.

"At the Junior College, I had to take the dating-family course, taught by the football coach. When I argued about civil rights or football, he called me 'mother', and continued to do so for the rest of the semester."

To be treated as if one does not belong is to have one's niche attacked. Belateds either toughen up in this testing of their mettle, and perhaps become politicized, or they go back home, drained of staying power.

Family, even neighbors, at home are most fatefully involved in moving Belateds through, or delaying them in, the cupellation stage. For example, aging parents living nearby may represent what they interpret as daughter-neglect at this crucial time of their lives and throw up beloved-barriers. On the other hand, students and professors at college may throw down the welcome mat, e.g., "The kids at school think it's cool that I'm at school. They think it's even cooler when I tell them that I have six kids at home." Yet, with the determined opposition of either intimates or lyceum, staying power dwindles.

Cumulative studenthood alludes to the incremental and creative build up of studenting by mothers belatedly moving onto the campus. The term refers to their ability to obtain and retain information, to connect and communicate new ideas literately and to expand them in new directions. Cumulative studenthood means more than increasing one's scholarliness, however. It also implies learning the ropes, dealing competently with the situation in which they find themselves and meeting linguistic and self presentation expectations of campus others (Becker 1968). Cumulative studenthood increases staying power and assists in recasting family performance. In the absence of cumulative studenthood, staying power wanes and family support of the new campus activity of mothers is withdrawn. Cumulative studenthood is increased by the perception of college as "the" focus, by student co-starts and thoughtful, slow starts, and by course selection in and around family obligations, by avoidance of awesome student identities and by management of milieu impact (Olesen 1968).

After the enrollment of Belateds, college becomes the focus around which all else is organized. Their central mother identity is simply organized around this focal point. Belateds seldom miss a class and they are angry when one is canceled, for they are thereby deprived of their focus. College is intrinsically good. It is an end in itself, even for those women who will also use the educational skills as a means to future employment. It is a pipeline to the infinite and their substance upon which to stand. Bedazzlement by college focus is a strong support to cumulative studenthood.

Early in cupellation, Belateds commonly use the tactic of co-starts to bulwark a shaky self confidence and thereby to get a leg on toward studenthood. To break in easy they attend classes with friends, husbands or neighbors at first. Once they get the academic hang of it, Belateds do their studenting alone. In the long run, they are probably more isolated in studenting than others, arriving puffing on campus just in time for class and leaving immediately after for home obligations. Just starting out, however, they need an other-crutch.

Co-starts are supplemented by slow starts, and both add to cumulative studenthood. Belateds in cupellation take but one or two courses a semester and they frequently take them in the evening when their husbans are at home and the children are in bed. To cut down on mom-absenteeism, when they eventually do subscribe for daytime classes, they take whatever classes they can get one or two days a week, during times when children nap or are themselves in school. Taking any and all courses that happen to fall on a selected day results in a disorderly array of units in transcripts, for college classes are not scheduled to accommodate external agendas of infants and children. Serendipitously, pursuing a varied array of catch as catch can courses sometimes piques an unknown latent academic interest that encourages cumulative studenthood.

Under the typical condition of motherhood, sciences such as biology, physics, and chemistry-which require lectures in one part of the day and three to five hour laboratory sessions in another, must be postponed, sometimes for years, until offspring are older and in grammar school or junior high. Similarly, foreign language courses-which meet everyday at lower levels of instruction and which require daily language practice, are foregone when the youngsters are tiny. Moreover, Belateds are unable to attend classes at eight and earlier in the morning because of home requirements. During cupellation the motherhood weights cumulative studenthood in particular directions. For Programmed Belateds in a hurry to get through, even majors may be chosen according to the "possible" - conditioned by the needs of the Belated's family.

Belateds do not think of themselves as students during the prolonged periods of matriculation. "Student" is too awesome an identity to aspire to. They see themselves as "taking courses" - a less frightening, less gravid, less presumptuous undertaking than "going to college." In cupellation the women do not think seriously about getting a degree, declaring a major, or pursuing a preconceived curriculum. Later they advance to talking about "going to school." These timorous ways of speaking are probably necessary at the starting out stage of Belateds' academic careers. At the same time, they see themselves as mothers, wives, housewives, and middle-aged women. Only after several years of successful college experience do they entertain shy ideas of "student" in their self conceptions. Belateds make no claim to academic turf until they see how they can do. The tactic of avoiding Gordonhead identities which petrify them in cupellation increases cumulative studenthood.

Milieu impact challenges cumulative studenthood during cupellation. As homemakers, Belateds are uncertain of what behavior is expected of them on campus. They wonder: Will I fit in? Do I look okay? Talk right? Am I smart enough? They present themselves as neutral and unassuming persons before they take on their college chameleon colors. Nips and tucks are gradually taken in traditional social expectations about what is proper to eat, to wear, to think and to say in the new place (Stone 1970). Belateds do not throw frisbees. They do take home alfalfa sprouts, falafel, and nachos. They adopt college norms of political thought and behavior. Step by step they become acclimated to student behavior, if not the student title.

To all appearances (in California), they soon stride confidently past the drum-beating, pot smoking "heads" on the left and the tinkly, scalp-baring Hare Krishnas on the right, through the "Jews of Jesus" in front of the bookstore to buy Plato and "bluebooks." When they begin to feel at home on campus, at one with college others, they are able to gird themselves for English 1A. Cumulative studenthood and staying power are thus mutually supporting.

Recasting family performance bears on the division of family labor. When the wife-mother takes on a student role, who does what and when in the home? Recasting family performance is affected by social doctrines about women's place and the stage of the family career. Actual recasting works to increase both staying power and cumulative studenthood. In the main, however, college is first defined by the family as a Belated's "extra", to be fitted in and around traditional performances. Belateds recast their own labor before other family members do when they first enroll in college.

Belateds make a heroic effort to maintain "domestic order as usual" for their families, while they themselves negotiate a fit in the local educational order. Children's and husbands' family patterns do not change much during cupellation. Husbands and children take it for granted that mothers scurry around every morning making breakfast, waking and robing little people in garments laid out the night before, packing lunches, tossing clothing into the washer and drier, feeding and "outing" the cat before setting out frozen meat to thaw for the evening meal, and making beds before kissing everyone off to school or work. The family understanding that this is what "Moms" are for is not altered simply because the mom is going to college.

One aspect of a Belated's order-as-usual is "being there" in the usual place at the usual time doing her usual domestic and sentimental work (Glaser and Strauss 1974 a,b), for there is no handy wife or mother substitute. Incognito scholars rush home from classes to serve lunch to husbands accustomed to having a midday meal set before them by attentive, loving wives. When children return home from school, they expect their mothers to be there with cold milk and a snack, and mother is there with the goodies.

Being there "as usual" for husbands and children serves several functions. Belateds reassure themselves in this way that no one is suffering because they have taken in the extra, deviant activity of studenting. Husbands are mollified and gradually decrease their expectant tension that life will change completely if wives go out of the home. Belateds' self-assurance and their spouses' relaxation of suspicion and concern about the family coming first, add staying power and cumulative studenthood, and provide a first nod in the direction of recasting family performance.

Belateds pare down their family activities. Where once activities were expanded to fill housewives' available time, now, during cupellation, they are condensed to fit in student time. Belateds re-orient their thinking about the importance and necessity of womanly tasks and pursuits, hitherto never seriously questioned. They wonder why for the first time in history, the entire time and energy of fullgrown adult women is entailed by the domestic maintenance of one small house and family. (See also Rossi, 1964) During their audit of everyday life, they observe that most housewives spend much of their time away from home, especially when children are of school age and in good health. Outside operations that are not absolutely essential to family or college are judicially weighed, provided with "drop-it" justifications and then abandoned.

Just as the women were earlier required to add on Sunday school, Hebrew lessons, swim club and Little League, and to coordinate and administrate these family labors, so now Belateds elaborate an "Off-That" list. Ironing is first on the "Off" list. Families are taught that ironing does not need to be done and are told that as a matter of fact in a good many parts of the world is a non-existent task. Belateds demonstrate that the family wash can be done once a week and vacuuming once or twice a semester, unless someone else wishes to take this on more frequently. Next to go are the Parent Teacher Association, Women's Club, social visiting and volunteer activities. Belated church involvement is reduced to a level comparable to that of the men in the families. Holidays remain ritual ceremonies but rites are modified. For example cookies are bought, not baked, for Christmas; holiday ritual greetings are sent out later or not at all; Yule trees and Chanukah stars are hastily stationed just before the festivities. Because women are the real Santa Clauses and Easter Bunnies of the family, they cannot and would not abandon the myths altogether. They may necessarily sign up for one course less during the socially demanding fall semester.

As Belateds pare down at home to meet school demands, so they also whittle away at the non-essentials, and some essentials, of academia so as to meet home obligations. Belateds come on campus for class hours only. They do not ordinarily participate in college social or political life, a fact that may hamper later academic progress of those Belateds who wish to move on to graduate school, or who wish to apply for scholarships. Belateds purchase more books than their classmates and take books home to read instead of spending family time in the library. They seldom or never see an advisor and do not take tests to determine aptitude. Juggling of home and school priorities and giving each area its due is supportive staying power, cumulative studenthood and recasting family performance.

Children are, on a moral level, the heaviest intruders on Belateds' tight schedules, especially during cupellation when children are usually younger. One Belated cut ties to all her children and went her way alone in response to demands from her twenty-six year old son that she abstain from any recasting of family performance. "You are a mother! You ought to act like a mother", he said. More often, when the children's problems seem serious the mothers then drop college temporarily. They do this immediately and ungrudgingly when they think there are external and involuntary causes of the problems, e.g., when children are accidentally burned, develop seizure disorders, or tangle drastically with bikes and motorcycles. On the other hand, when the child appears to bring his mishap on himself, for example the abuse of street drugs, he must suffer the wrath and chagrin of his Belated mother at this interruption of her academic life, a hitch which she defines as senseless and unnecessary.

Belateds work out a tight managerial organization of life's departments, which functions well as long as there are no emergencies. However, they have no back log of time, energy, or supportive persons for dealing with unforseen interruptions of routines. Husbands can fall back on wives to take care of domestic crises. Wives cannot count on husbands to drop all outside life to attend to such things, even if both spouses are working or attending college. Being forced to leave college to serve the family in times of need, enables Belateds to shore up family performance. This reason for dropping out generates an obligation which reinforces cumulative studenthood subsequent to the resolution of the family problem for which her quitting is the solution. Similarly, staying power momentarily suppressed emerges stronger.

To claim something is to demand it as a right. One must have power to demand rights. Although in time Belateds make progressive claims on family life to facilitate studenting, during cupellation the women exhibit claimless activity. They keep wife-ing and mothering functions free of question from academic life. Early on, they do not think they have rights in their homes as students. Rather, school is a private, secret world of clandestine pleasure, set apart from domesticity. Most being traditional women, Belateds feel guilty about having school on the side. In cupellation students have no family rights. Eventually, being a student will recast family performance.

In subsequent stages of consolidation and confirmation, Belated students become sly experts at study time and space. But during cupellation they are tired, surreptitious students. Permanent space is not demanded. Belateds spread out scholarly paraphernalia in the absence of current family interest in a specific house geography and then tidily pack the non-domestic furnishings away (again and again) when family invades the same space. Near the end of cupellation, Belateds may make emergency episodic claims to student rights at stressful academic periods, such as during exams and the writing of term papers. Part-time rights are requested only if the family is on an even keel and Belateds have met all their obligations to the family members. Then, and only then, Belateds may ask husbands to take the children to the beach or out to dinner so they can study.

When Belated part-time claims are met, recasting family performance is begun and both cumulative studenthood and staying power are strengthened. When they are not met, cumulative studenthood may take a set-back. Staying power is not affected, however, because the women learn early on to plan and study in advance, so they rarely have to make rejectable episodic claims. One or two failed claims leads to alternative strategies for meeting end of semester tribulations.

Thus, Belateds recast family performance by paring down their own duties, by modifying family rites and social traditions- insofar as they are responsible for the performance of them, by pursuing a barebones academic involvement and, late in cupellation, by making episodic claims to be students during finals.

ELABORATION OF CONSOLIDATION

The increased routinizaton of home and student life that occurs during cupellation and consolidation gives Belateds a new sense of control over their lives.

Lining this niche with respect is important to staying power in the consolidation stage. One frequent way this social tribute is proffered is in the form of neighborly awe. "I don't see how you do it!", neighbors exclaim. Or, Belateds' children unexpectedly request *Mom's* expertise in mathematics and history. Even the television repair person makes a respectful comment on the woman's status as a student, e.g., "... at your age!". Receiving community respect increases Belateds' self-esteem. Augmented self-esteem and respect support staying power and assist in recasting family performance.

Belateds find a new support basis in the unexpected but very rewarding respect soon accorded them by younger, more typical college students. The women interpret this homage as a sign that they are doing the appropriate academic thing in the appropriate academic way (See Blumer 1969). Peer regard firms up both staying power and cumulative studenthood. Being well thought of by professors, as evidenced by grades and commentary, and finally, the receipt of a husband's grudging, but loving admiration of new academic achievement, are treasured bits of respect.

On the other hand, since Belateds no longer perform casual friendship-labor, acquaintances may withdraw from unfueled relationships. Having legitimated paring-downs during cupellation, the women experience disengagements from polite social entanglements as an additional support to staying power. One woman reports, "I just don't care. I no longer want to play cards. I am happy with my books", which supports Belateds' cumulative studenthood, which feeds back to strengthen staying power.

In the consolidation stage, academic and domestic requirements have ben melded. Disruptive hitches in scheduling are less frequent. There is a generalized increase in smooth routinization, which varies directly with the growing force of staying power and cumulative studenthood and which stimulates recasting family performance.

Before going to school, Belateds inhabited a slack world of "What's it all about?" Total embracement of the mother identity and pressure for conformity to that single mode of being, left many other aspects of the self needing expression (Goffman 1961). By the time of consolidation, such existential voids are subordinated to the pressing pragmatics of their "making the grade" (Becker 1968) in their new social world by their many social selves (James 1983). Their self-meaning is now alive and well.

During the consolidation stage of staying power, Belateds think of themselves as successful women. The meaning of being a Belated is a temporal matter (Charmaz 1973). Staying power, cumulative studenthood and recasting family performance forge new identities for student mothers as a result of cupellation pressures. They are making it. They are new persons. They report, "Now I have a world. I have dropped my chains."

The self during cupellation was marked by the deliberate discarding of traditionalities and by the simultaneous acquiring of student behaviors. Old activities no longer fit the new self-in-the-making (Charmaz 1973). But now during consolidation they "look at almost everything differently." They organize their behavior in line with the new definitions of themselves, and according to the principle that their world is what they make of it. Once short of self-confidence, Belateds now trust themselves.

Status with others in the community rises as Belateds expand their interests and achievements. Self changes are also validated by the positive sentiments of others. The quality of relationships increases as the quality of time devoted to them decreases, but is concentrated. Evolving self-possession increases staying power and makes cumulative studenthood possible.

Finally, Belateds have become talented technicians of life's interstices. They go nowhere without a notebook or text resource with which to fill unexpectedly freed up spaces in time, such as those afforded by delays in dental or medical offices. Similarly, college is used to fill sentimental home gaps:

> My mother and my father-in-law all died within a year during my second year in college...My mother died slowly, of cancer. I didn't drop out. It...really, I don't know...I wasn't in a daze; my grades were fine. But for a year and a half after that, I wasn't ill and I wasn't well either. I don't know if it was the shocks or what. I just kept going. School was something to hang onto. I didn't want to quit. I just had to keep going and school helped.

To feel the need to study, and to note family annoyance when they do so, puts the women in a psychological bind, from which they attempt to escape by keeping the frowned upon activity out of sight (Goffman 1961). This is a move from one tight territory to another. Invisible students get as tired as everyone else at night but they still believe they must set aside a lot of time to study. Early in consolidation, to avoid conflicts Belateds study while intimates sleep. Invisible studenting is partially defined in the following excerpt.

> Study is a problem. I study late at night when everyone else is asleep. Or, I get up at four or five in the morning. I never study when it is visible that that is what I am doing. If I am consuming family or day activity time, I can really feel bad vibes from my husband. He really gets mad when he wants to go somewhere, and I don't want to because of an exam. I ask him if he wants me to quit and he says, ''No! No!'' But I made up my mind in myself that I would avoid this source of friction.

Correlated with invisible studenting during consolidation is highly visible homebodying. To ward off accusations of family neglect, or less than total commitment to wife and mother duties, the women attempt to function at a "twice as good" level in some specific traditionally feminine aspect of these roles- despite the general paring down process of cupellation. For example, some Belateds, who may iron nothing else, spend every Sunday evening in front of the television set ostentatiously ironing their husbands' shirts for the week (Rossi 1967). Other Belateds make all their childrens' clothing. An instance of a husband neutralization technique by visible homebodying follows.

I do all my own baking and my family enjoys that. Maybe it's my way of pacifying my husband. He resents not so much the time I spend at school or in painting, but the great interest I have in those things. So, although I no longer iron, I do always have something in the oven. I could buy bread very easily; he could make lots of flak about my going to school. When I am terribly busy, I know which of my functions he thinks I should drop- art and school, not baking and housework. So, I put aside my homework twice a week to bake bread and cookies.

Belateds love to study. These mature women, who are at the same time but shy fledglings in their student status, do not perceive instruction the same as younger students. Around each question or topic, there is, for Belateds, a lining of experiential fringe data that must be sorted and sifted before the women can get at the real question (James 1983). As Belateds see it, there *are* no simple "matter of fact" questions. Therefore, Belateds reference almost all allusions, and discriminate complimentary fields of inquiry. Consequently, they spend much time researching ephemeral issues and "getting ready." Although they have gained an excess of information before class (which is henceforth theirs), they may not have answered the "elusive" question assigned to the class.

During the consolidation stage shy course takers turn into highly visible Damned Average Raisers (Hughes 1984) at school. DARs emerge out of study overkill habits of Belateds. DARs read more books, quote more references, write longer and more detailed papers, do more complex research and experiments than average and make higher grades. Therefore, DAR-ing supports and expands cumulative studenthood. Although they appear to be highly competitive, Belated DARs are not consciously striving against other students. They are always surprised therefore when, for example, a male student asks what courses they will take next so that he can avoid those classes. "He said he couldn't compete with women whose whole life is one course a week." DAR-ing continues as Belateds gradually increase their unit load to full time or to an excessive number of units, once they master a "how to" pattern. They monitor reactions of campus others but their sensitivity is not at all that of estimating who is ahead (Blumer 1969).

Belateds are joy hustlers. They are on a trip. Their appetite for educational edibles is insatiable for a time. Subjectively they are hungry for new intellectual tidings. They hanker for the "high" that accompanies vigorous self-challenge and meaning embeddedness. Belateds follow consumption patterns and behavioral criteria which are internal to their group. They confess they want to get good grades just to get good grades, and not for any profit that achievement might bring to them. Grades matter (Becker 1968). Intellectually, Belateds tell themselves, grades are not the important thing. But emotionally, the A is almost the only really acceptable mark. They judge themselves by the Grade Point Average (GPA).

It is important to get good grades, part of my self image. If I know I can do it, I would be letting myself down, if I did a half-assed job.

Belateds are diligent to their call to studenthood (Weber 1958).

Collecting A's is the Belated way to find out that one is an "elect" student.

Status markers get rearranged at college. Old ways of making self points are obsolete or irrelevant. Can she bake a cherry pie? Who cares? What are pertinent in this social world are studenting skills. The action is in ideas, theories, papers, exams, discussions, experiments, research, deadlines, student-student and student-professor relations, political processes, and in meeting all the bureaucratic requirements that encompass the "getting at the wonderful" that is for Belateds the stimulating investigation of ideas. By the consolidation stage, Belateds have acquired many of the academic skills that contribute to cumulative studenthood and staying power.

Although during consolidation Belateds begin to see themselves as students, their sense of self as student persistently requires the smile of recognition and approval from professors (see Waller 1932). Belateds are, therefore, thrown into an identity crisis when required by some professors to grade their own work. They ordinarily do not give themselves A's. Wearing the worn womanly apron of self-abnegation, they mark their papers B+. Illogically, they give themselves the lower grade while knowing that they deserve the higher one. They mark themselves low and fervently hope that professors will change the unwanted B's to the deserved A's. They are subsequently resentful when their own inadequate appraisal is sometimes allowed to stand. During consolidation Belateds are still dependent students and social artists of the self put-down. They interpret self grading as a professorial cop-out. Self-grading is a hazard of cumulative studenthood they sometimes overcome later. At this earlier stage, they are illegitimate academic others to themselves. They cannot take the role of the professor and make themselves objects to themselves (Mead 1970). They need the external evaluator to support the student self in the making. Fortunately (for the importance of the GPA to these women), most professors do perform their own assessments and cooperate in student creating.

As consolidation proceeds, cumulative studenthood is increased by student invisibility at home, juxtaposed with DAR-ing at college; by separation of school and home- and holding the home banner in the prime position; by Belateds becoming academic joy hustlers; and by noting where the action is, in studenting skills, but not yet overcoming the need for external supervisorial approval.

Belateds patch on a special dimension to the pre-existent fabric of marriage and motherhood (Rowe 1966). They do not "bust out" or "leave home". Theirs is a soft, non-challenging exit from home. They rupture no sentimental bonds. Family membership remains the dominant fact of life and family. For Belateds the going out is tied to a coming in. Going to college is a special, unobtrusive round-trip excursion the women make. They go back home, which they never really left.

A nag to serenity during consolidation is the isolation of studenting from other life activities and persons. By that time Belateds are going full steam, and going it alone. At this stage, Belateds are part of the lonely people. Friends at school are friends rooted there; the relation rarely extends into local community life. It is a tie of brief duration, moreover, for typical students graduate, leaving Belateds to their slower tempo. Friends at home do not understand what Belateds are doing at college nor why they are doing it. Belateds may take sixteen to eighteen units at college, nurture four children and a husband at home, and work part-time as a waitress to cover school expenses. They have stretched the concept of what a mother-student can reasonably fit into a twenty-four hour day. Prior to going out of the home, Belateds were totally immersed in a kinship sea of affectivity and constricted concentration on everyday family life (Klapp 1969). A Belated reports:

> My daughter lives in a dorm now. I used to know what she ate, who her friends were, if she were constipated - everything. When she comes back home, I get right back into that way of thinking again. But when she's away, I never think about what time she goes to bed and so on. I feel guilty, sometimes, like I'm forgetting about her or something, you know - like I don't know my daughter anymore.

Belateds have been accustomed to seeing the world as structured by warm, concrete, palpable and intimate minutiae (Parsons 1967). The student perspective, on the other hand, structures reality in abstract, ideal terms of the large, the remote and the intangible. The variance between the affective intensity of home with the mother perspective, and the cool generality of the student perspective, becomes a felt distinction during consolidation (See also McCall and Simmons 1966). It is as if the women are simultaneously both nailed down and unmoored.

During late consolidation the loneliness of apartness, (e.g., "Your husband is no part of it; your children, your neighbors are no part of it" and, contrapuntally, "Most of us get it in class, get it in the book, and have no other dialogue about the material with anyone else"), along with the appreciation that this separation has been self-ordained, stimulates Belateds to re-evaluate the solitary stance. They must then attempt to unify their two realities: bring school home to the family, and in time, taking the family to college.

The women bring school home in the ideas they share with husbands and children, in excitement about political movements - large and small, in the texts they convince families are "thrillers", and in the new explanations they propose about the nature of the universe. The children sing "We are climbing Plato's ladder", not Jacob's, and they dream of the light of Greece. World maps suddenly designate real places and family members worry about and mourn over the precarious state of the real people on the globe. The beach comes to new life for them all when Belateds take biology and physics.

In the other direction, home moves onto campus in a variety of ways. For example, children, one at a time, may accompany their mother to class on special occasions, for a reward, or to inculcate a college motivation. Family members may be invited (neighbors too) to attend lectures, concerts or other campus cultural events. Husbands may be permitted to escort college wives to cultural or scientific field trips, off campus meetings and encounters of one kind or another. Professors may be consulted about some urgent home\college friction and are thus also bonded into a school-home mosaic Belateds are fashioning during consolidation. A woman reports:

I'd never had a wedding to plan before. I really felt a lot of pressure. I talked to this one professor. I had never asked a professor if I could turn in a paper late. I explained all the obligations I hadn't known would come up. I showed him a rough draft and the data. He was so nice! He didn't even give me a deadline. He didn't knock off any in the grade. After that, he talked to me a lot. Even my papers were judged differently after that. The personal relationship, my exposing my problems, seemed to bring me to life for him. He came over to me at graduation reception and met all the kids. I almost died!

The gradual union of Belateds' two spheres of interest and effort recasts family performance, increases cumulative studenthood, and supports staying power.

There is a residual of home and school secrets, however. Belateds, for example, share their new liberal more than their new radical conceptualizations at home and they do not vouchsafe more conservative views at college. They modify their language usage automatically at the front door of their houses and, in the opposite direction, at the entrance to the college (Blumer 1969). Belateds have dual wardrobes in their closets, dual identities and mores to match them. Wives who use the strategy of "mumming-up" about contents of college courses which they think husbands are not ready to entertain, thereby avoid galls that would interfere with the slow recasting of family performance. One such example:

I don't hide things from my husband but I didn't offer him the books from the satire class...the obscene language...the bluntness about sex in the class language. He doesn't realize I know what that language means when it is used so frequently where I spend my hours. It is kind of like you might like your neighbor's dress short, but not your wife's.

Similarly, home problems (for example, divorce threats from husbands, drug abuse by children) are not aired on campus.

During consolidation, husbands and children show signs of coming about -- of seeing the student in the wife-mother, and of trying to accommodate studenthood by adjusting the family division of labor in some degree. The first sign of coming about may be observed in the way husbands talk about their wives going to college, or maybe a switch that they do talk about it at all to other people. They may, for example, joke about "My wife, the college girl" to friends or fellow employees, or they may show mock struckdumbness to the children when Belateds use words they would have never used before they went to college. These new conversations do not necessarily imply a change in shouldering of the family work load. During late consolidation, a marker of spousal coming about is the act of the father who, on his own, takes the children aside at exam or term paper deadline time and orders that it is time for children to pitch in and help, since mother has her hands full with her "extra". Another bench mark occurs when the husband-father assumes the dictatorship over the weekend division of cleaning labor. (See Simmel 1969, chapter three).

Coming about also includes what husbands do not do. Belateds' first few years of matriculation are spotted with contingent incidents related to, and manipulated by, their husbands. The women feel they cannot complain about such unanticipatable events for they think that certain of women's functions are, after all, wifely obligations: to entertain and socialize with husbands' friends and employers, to bake and to sew. Husbands think they have a marital right to invite friends into their homes on self-selected occasions and see no reason why this should change because wives, out of the blue, decide to go to college. Further, husbands have always scheduled family vacations for times when *they* wish to take them, work force conditions permitting, and they rarely take anyone else's timelines into account.

For the first time, confronted in late consolidation by strong saying power and cumulative studenthood, husbands make efforts to meet wives' college schedules halfway (Simmel 1969). They less often bring home unexpected dinner guests the night before an exam. They less often arrive late on the one evening the Belated has requested that everyone come home on time for dinner so she can type her paper, due the next day. They less often slate a weeks' vacation in Hawaii or Mendocino for the week after college starts in the fall or spring.

Husbands and children rediscover each other during late consolidation. They no longer possess a built-in, twenty-four hour a day intermediary to buffer their relationships, but must, on frequent occasions confront one another directly. Husbands who are called from places of employment to do parent work for their children in emergency situations at school, e.g., football injuries or a first menstrual period, experience a more vivid and compassionate tie to their children. Children, too, appreciate the close new connection with their fathers.

At first, neither father nor child knows quite how to behave when the father tentatively moves into the close parent role, since mothers have always functioned as sole parents during the work day and fathers have been regarded to a "Wait until your father gets home!" distant relation to most routine family emergencies (Becker 1970). While children know what to expect from mothers when hurt or in trouble, most have rarely been able to turn to fathers in the same context. They work out new identities and bonds with each other.

Belateds, who are dyed-in-the-wool mothers, may go through momentary jealousy twinges in their motherhood as they observe the developing new father-child intimacy. In general, however, the presence of duo-parenting increases the well-being of the family as a unit and its members individually. Belateds appreciate mates' loving efforts to try out the new parenting roles. Husbands become more understanding of the routine complications of parenting, and look at wives with new admiring eyes. Belateds report that (except for diaper disgust) husbands seem to relish the increased physical contact with their children, and do more touching and reaching out on their own. Children, too, experience richer and more secure primary relationships with two active parents.

Belateds begin to institute small constant claims during consolidation. The claims are situational demands (not challenging personal requests) frequently evidenced by staking out of spacial, territorial to temporal boundaries of privacy. For example, the women appropriate for a study the empty room of a child away at college. They close the door to the study at certain times, thereby indicating to one and all that a claim has been made for student privacy. This new norm is established to accommodate studenthood. Mothers are open people eternally accessible to children and husband while students are accessible at their own option during student-important times.

Should a child forget a lunch pail in rushing for the school bus, or should the child miss that bus, the child must, during late consolidation, do without lunch that day and perhaps walk to school. Thereafter, children usually remember their lunches and catch their buses. Mothers often leave for school when their children do. Indirectly, then, a small constant claim is presented that mothers will not perform the many errands and fill-in-for-others tasks that have always been taken for granted. Family performance is rapidly recast in this instance.

Academic courses generate small constant claims for the women to be absent from home and not in service for families during class times. Belateds warn family members about these claims in advance of registration by discussing what courses they will take, at what hours of the day, in which months of the year, and other college relevancies, such as date for the mid-terms, dead week, final examinations and term papers. During late consolidation, husbands, with sudden sociability spurts that would require the presence of Belateds, must manage the social affair on their own if the impulse occurs on a known school day. The constant claim is that Belateds cannot always "be there" for husbands. The resultant increased collaboration over scheduling, which recasts family performance, which increases the self-reliance of family members, is supportive to staying power and cumulative studenthood.

During consolidation, recasting family performance proceeds by successive degrees. The serenity nags about the segregation of Belateds' social worlds (Strauss 1978) and the apartheid of simultaneous perspectives that focus on the world as small or image it as large (Parsons 1967), leads in later consolidation to a more unified reality mosaic. Belateds bring college home, and take home to the college.

THE WRAP-UP OF CONSOLIDATION

The trend during confirmation is for the women to take almost everything in confident stride. Seasoned Belateds find some strategy to make non-academic, non-catastrophic occurrences fit into second place behind school. They have become committed to academia. Commitment is the sine qua non of staying power.

The resolution of sexuality is essential to Belateds' staying power. By the time of confirmation, they have devised sexual tactics for utilizing the campus to fill voids of everyday sex life. As a rule sexual partners, when not spouses, are found in the student-professor populace. However, the active, seductive "Mrs. Robinson" tactic may be utilized by the older women to bring younger men to bed. They also permit themselves to be apparently seduced by the male tumbling mystique that "Older women make beautiful lovers; they know how to please a man." Divorced Belateds develop age-free new attitudes towards sex, which they find are more workable than that which applied to married women. They resent being viewed as a sexual pool for men to tap. The following excerpt is a composite representation of Belateds' fresh views.

I don't see any other way to solve sex problems. I'm not going to marry just to ball someone. I'm not actively hurting right now; sometimes I really need sex. I haven't felt all that needy lately. I manage -- sometimes limpingly well. Sex can be first or last in a relationship. I can go with someone just to go to bed with him; I can't go to bed with him just because he's nice. There are not too many men that turn me on sexually. But there is no difference going to bed with someone right after I have met him. I've had some real neat times with brief acquaintances. There have been long dry spells sexually. The other day I found a gray pubic hair. I attribute this to my deprived pubes.

Not all have shaken the dust of old socialization clings, however, as the following excerpt indicates (See also Becker 1970).

Sex is a problem, alright. There have been times, you know. I'm emotional enough and cuddly enough. But it still bothers me. I would like to have a real good marriage -- but the kids -- what the heck! Why never have any loving? It just leaves me cold; a man can do what a woman can't. He can do what he darn well pleases. But if it's right for him, it's right for her. Men's attitude is 'easy come, easy go'. But darn it! It does bother a person to stay home and forget the whole darn thing. Being single isn't so great. It's a different world for single men and single women -- kind of a dickens in a way.

Some Belateds try out liberated sex during confirmation, usually with professors. Commonly, the upshot is that both return to their respective spouses. Whether single or married, Belateds' "affairs", properly attended, support staying power.

Belateds' children are generally seven years older by the time their mothers reach the stage of confirmation. Given their complete responsibility for small dependent children during cupellation, Belateds were threatened with derailment by their children's whims. Older children in the later stages of confirmation offer different menaces to staying power than did the toddlers. They may be embarrassed by what they see as inappropriate conduct for mother types: "They thought I was trying to act young again." At the same time that some middle class, teen-aged youths put down the way of life of parents, the entire middle class, and fathers who work nine-to-five, they may also belittle Belateds' non-conformist student status.

Children's friends, however, may envy peers with understanding students for mothers. "They are amazed that they can talk to me; tell me things they can't talk about with their own parents." One advantage of going to college later in life is that they learn concepts and practices in school which apply to their relations with their children. Improved family relationships result in increased staying power. However, one reputed disadvantage of women going to college while raising their children is that some children, observing DAR's in study overkill, become convinced that college must be hard, too hard, if Belateds have to study that much, study while others sleep, etc. This appalls Belateds, who think they are setting fine examples for their children, e.g., "You know, like it's O.K. to study."

Ultimately, if Belateds finally graduate from college, all their children and husbands (usually) attend the ceremony and cheer "Mom" as she collects her diploma. During late consolidation and all through confirmation, husbands are openly proud of their overachiever. Family moral support at this stage, when staying power has been solidly instituted and cumulative studenthood confirmed, is appreciated by Belateds - who rarely complain that staunch family backing has come at a time when it is no longer needed.

Campus involvement by Belateds and their husbands commonly liberalizes the political ideas of both. Family members of Belateds' also may become outspoken about their convictions which sometimes leads to conflict with unchanged extended family members. As a result, "Neither of us belongs to our family anymore." Hence, spouses pull closer together in a newfound political alliance that cements the couple-college tie, and strengthens staying power.

Husbands observe Belateds in fascination during confirmation. The men had thought that they knew all there was to know about their traditional wives. However, their wives have been transformed (Strauss 1969). In confirmation, husbands find new, semi-independent women managing their homes, women who have friends of their own whom the men do not know, women who possess a "whole new world" of which husbands share but the edges. Belateds no longer talk the same, nor keep house in the former mode, nor nurture the children according to pre-college criteria. Belateds' interests have spread in dazzling directions and become intricate.

Wives are now the direct foci of husbandly heed and interest. Husbands find their wives are suddenly more desirable women in their rapidly changing world. Reminded of the plasticity of human beings by this metamorphosis, some husbands show concern about their male status in relation to their school-going spouses. Belateds note the boosted male attention and deal with the dependent male self-concern. Some typical excerpts follow.

#1 I really feel good concerning my husband's attitude toward me. Now he has a good deal more respect for himself and for his wife. I don't think he felt that way before I went to college.

#2 I am a different person than I was when I started. My husband finds that I'm a more desirable person than he thought I was before college. I think he thinks I'm actually his equal now, and he treats me with a lot more concern and regard, and he is always doing nice things. Funny - things have shifted. It used to be me who was always doing nice things for him. Isn't that strange?

The novelty and excitement of the new woman-husband relationship is supportive to staying power.

Belateds recognize some changes in themselves (Strauss 1969). They look back in disbelief it the timid, shy, fearful, rigid, unhappy women they had been when starting out in their apparently deviant career. "Oh God! I used to think I was wrong and everyone else was right - all the time, and about everything!" Some women had been afraid to go to the grocery store by themselves, or into a restaurant alone for a cup of coffee. Now, Belateds think they are more self-confident, more easy-going, and less fearful (Olesen and Whittaker 1968, chapter eight). "I could even go to San Francisco and not be scared to death now." A typical excerpt bearing Belateds' states of being during confirmation:

I have changed since starting college. I am very happy now, and I was unhappy before. My life is not a level plateau. I am on a high peak. It is a fantastic life I have right now and I won't let minor frustrations interfere.

Being happy and at a high peak of experience bolsters staying power.

The women interpret their transformations to studenthood as adding onto, not as destroying old loyalties and identities. Reform, not conversion, is what they admit to. Belateds define their education as only beneficial to families, and not as harmful or competitive, except for transitory frictions generally smoothed over in favor of the family.

From cupellation through consolidation and confirmation, Belateds never seriously waver about the priority of the wife-mother role; it is all-encompassing. College, and perhaps a later new occupation are very important, but they are categorized as "extra", and not on the same level of importance and destiny as wife-motherhood. Belateds do not give any role the moral pledge and self-sacrifice that they give the mother role, even though they realize they spend equal effort, time, and (almost) interest in studenting. Belateds abide by a strong cultural mandate to motherhood.

Even so, they speculate on the necessity for becoming perennial students to maintain their "high", and to avoid slipping back into a static domestic mode again. One Belated reports, "Having started, I see what I've been missing. I can't stay away. I can't just stay home and that be all. I think this way more all the time." The women want to come on campus again after (if) they graduate, in order to start something anew, or they find an equivalent mental stimulation.

College has been a moratorium during which Belateds work out a reformed sense of identity. During this extended indulgence, they temporarily shade other identities, without causing any absolute breaks between past and present. Confirmation is the stage in their mental biography when they take stock and reaffirm the past before contemplating future lines of action. Staying power is now taken for granted. Staying power for WHAT? becomes the new question. Until confirmation, that question did not arise.

Although many Belateds start out with no idea of getting a degree, eventually most (and it may take thirteen years) go for the degree. During cupellation Belateds try to fit general education requirements into their schedules to suit family convenience because they want the degree. But finally, during confirmation, they enroll in required classes they cannot schedule in favor of family convenience. School must come first if they are to graduate. The women discuss inconveniently scheduled courses for several years with families before they finally register for them. In negotiating with families, they point out that they can fit in all the interferences in two or three semesters. They must enlist, or hire, mother stand-ins after carefully supervised probationary periods.

More Belateds go for degrees as their number of years in college increases. Some Belateds, of course, start out degree bound. A residuum of Belated perennial students never "learn out." Going to school is necessary for their sense of a meaningful life. Programless (perennial) Belateds refuse to be rushed into college goal decisions. They deride the push, "What am I going to do when I grow up?" One perennial reports:

> School is never a cop out from the world's work. I've done a good portion of that. I don't have any desire to slay dragons. I say this for other people who seem to think I need an excuse to be in school. My idea isn't part of that. I don't need a degree.

In confirmation Belated students know how many A grades and units they have accumulated. However, if they have been merely "taking courses'', they do not conceptualize themselves as becoming seniors nor in a major. After several years of matriculation they may lack but three to five units for taking a degree. At that point, programmed students usually sign up for the last course or two and they graduate, usually with honors. Perennial (i.e. programless) Belateds, on the other hand, suddenly realize that if they enroll in the few remaining courses, the school career will come to an end. They therefore veer off into coursework in an allied or other department of the college, rather than terminate the highly valued academic dimension of their everyday life. Perennial Belateds wish to extend the present indefinitely. Programmed Belateds, on the contrary, focus more on the future as the projected meaning of the present, e.g., "I have long range plans to write a book; have carried an outline in mind for twenty years." Confirmation is a time of getting together the new goal and seeking the new niche.

Getting a goal together increases staying power, cumulative studenthood and recasting family performance. It would be a mistake to think, however, that Belateds whose goals are undeclared have less staying power. They usually persist at college for as many or more years (some until they die out), with diminishing staying power, cumulative studenthood and recast family performance.

Contemplating the future, Belateds once again run into age barriers to their future progress (Estes 1979). They may dissuade themselves, e.g., "I feel that I'm too old to start the counseling program." Or institutional others may dishearten them, e.g., "My professor discourages me about the master's degree because of my age." Families at home, grown accustomed to Belateds' scholastic pace, are not apt to oppose Belateds about graduate education, for example, "When I say,'Why should I go to graduate school?', my family says, 'Why not? You should'." Belateds facing age barricades to their further scholastic progress may drop out of college after taking the bachelors' degree, or they may proceed full speed ahead in their graduate work, figuring that they have already ironed out this issue at an earlier stage. During confirmation Belated women may turn sedate and critical on campus. One example is their quiet hesitant questioning of professors and registrars about the degree to which the current edification is digestible, or even nourishing, to the older experienced students. They also bristle to themselves at what they see as the ageist-sexist attitude of some professors, i.e., the prejudice against older women students. The following excerpts are typical.

#1 Older women -- well, I just get the impression that some professors listen to the sounds I make but never to the words I say. They look politely at my forehead 'til I finish talking and then go about their business. Some teachers seem to feel I am just there at school as a time-killer. I feel put down or as though they were saying to themselves, "You are wasting my time." I made up my mind not to talk much in those professors' classes. When you open your mouth, they kind of listen-ignore you.

#2 I irritate some professors because they think I talk too much and demand a lot of attention. Some professors really think I don't belong at college. If it's like that for me with a 3.97 Grade Point Average and six years under my belt, what's it like for the new women just starting out? That's bullshit! If I want to know, I'm going to ask.

They think this reflects the ageist and sexist climate in American society in general. Belateds do not unite for collective action, however. Instead, they grumble to themselves or they argue one by one with college employees. Further, age barrier to graduate school may be set by Belateds themselves or by academic others. This is a direct, late attack on cumulative studenthood which may turn some programmed students back into programless ones, or which may turn them off from further education altogether. In addition, during confirmation some women may become very resistant to deep-rooted ageism and sexism which they encounter.

By the time they have reached the stage of confirmation, Belateds assert their rights to the title "student" in the home. The woman and family particularize a bounded, private student turf on which to barrack the student. Having such a claim enables Belateds to leave notes on the refrigerator saying, for example, they will not be home for supper because a "Biggie" will unexpectedly guest lecture at the college at that time, and "Dinner is in the oven." It is possible now for the women to participate in occasional field trips, infrequently to attend interesting extra meetings, and to invite study groups home now and then to prepare collectively for examinations and projects. Families have become accustomed to an academic pace.

In all three stages (cupellation, consolidation, confirmation), Belateds frequently give a treat to their families after completing a difficult term paper or examination. In cupellation they conceive of this treat as a reward or compensation to family members to make up for times during which the women were preoccupied with school and not with family. Like many working mothers, Belateds often feel guilty about their lives outside the home. These women bend over backwards to be perfect in the wife-mother role so as to reimburse family for their "illegitimately" indulged studenthood. They are DAR's on campus and SuperMoms at home. So routinized and legitimized has going to college become by the confirmation stage, that Belateds see their "party giving" after scholastic ordeals as a celebration of, or accolade to, themselves - for a job well done. Freeing up time to make merry with the family, for whatever reasons, aids in recasting family performance.

Although about half of the Belateds divorced their husbands, only seven percent did so after college. Nonetheless, during confirmation Belateds talk a lot about divorce. They, and their professors, comment on the frequent number of divorces that occur when wives go to college. A Belated reports, "At Junior College, it is the view of one of the instructors that when a woman comes back to school, you can expect to read her divorce statistics announcement in two years."

Perhaps some Belateds have divorce in mind before going to college. A woman did divorce her husband after starting college reports, "One astute friend said I have gone back to school to get sufficient so I can leave my husband." More typical is the following composite excerpt from Belateds who remain married.

College changes women and husbands don't change. The college wife outgrows her husband. Women resent their husband and his lack of interest. There are few (none that I know of) husbands that support their wives returning to school enthusiastically. Women say,'My husband won't let me do this, won't let me do that.' After the college experience, the women are no longer willing to assume an inferior position in the family situation for what they consider to be unsatisfying, insufficient rewards. They are exposed to a fascinating outside world and become discontented with their Mickey Mouse existence. College puts strains on your marriage at times. School is a different world. One is an individual, but if one is married ---

Belateds' marriages survive ferment and pressures of cupellation and the buffeting experienced at that time and in consolidation. They also survive confirmation. The women discuss divorce as a side issue that could recast all of family performance during consolidation, when home-college interaction is smooth and recasting family performance is finally taken for granted. These Belateds infrequently (7%) divorce subsequent to going to college, despite their learned assumptions to the contrary.

Before turning to new fields, review of the past seems to be a necessary prologue to moving into the future. One parcel of the past which has been dragged through cupellation and consolidation and on into confirmation, is the negative emotional energy fixed in a Belated's particular "Dear Man." This is discharged in confirmation by talk of and evaluation of divorce. The women frequently reiterate, "He's a 'Dear Man' but ---". The "but" is followed by complaints of perfidy or felt injustice which the Belated observes in the husband-wife relationship. For example, "He's a Dear Man, but I have to darn his socks. His mother darned his socks so I have to darn socks." Or, "He's a Dear Man, but he insists I earn my school expenses even though he can afford to pay for them and I have my hands full with the kids and the house and classes."

During confirmation Belateds are self confident, independent, a little restless, searching for new horizons in a world grown wide, and they are equipped with some sophisticated new skills. If going to college ever results in impeachment to marriage by Belateds, it probably occurs in confirmation. However, by the time Belateds reach confirmation, the "Dear Man" has also been transformed.

Husbands never do fifty percent of the housework, not even when the women graduate from college, take a job, and bring in fifty percent, or more, of the family income. Nevertheless, gender assumptions have changed. Husbands no longer do all the talking and deciding. Belateds defer to their men less. Exhausted Belateds do not brook arguments about going out to dinner after late classes; they make dusters out of socks with holes, and sometimes hire someone else to clean the house with them. The women frequently change the way banks must print their checks so as to indicate separate identity, and they establish relations with their "own" bank, although salaries are jointly used for family concerns.

Whereas before a "day" took a long time to pass, and was filled with tedium, in confirmation Belateds complain there are not enough hours in the "day" to encompass all the interesting things they want to do. The evening routine of television set and ironing or mending has been permanently breached. Husbands may pick up Belateds at college after evening classes. This results in both being dressed and out of the house without the children. Fracturing of old patterns allows for experimental and innovative activities. The couple may visit a local bar or coffee house or pizza palace, discovered by the wives through other students. Or, they may remain on campus for a lecture, film or concert they would never have sought out before. "It's so neat! We're like a couple of kids again. We can't wait to get off alone together. We have so much to talk about with each other now."

Children have learned that mothers have lives of their own as well as those they share with their families. They, too, have become more independent and in turn, have lives about which their mothers have less detailed knowledge. Belateds do less "hard time" mothering. They do not worry about trivia of childhood life over which they have no control. Belateds have not abandoned motherhood. They are always and everywhere available mothers. Children have merely been acknowledged as separate and whole persons, who need mothers at times, but certainly not at all times. The women think the effect of their college education on their children has been beautiful.

#1 They relate to me, talk to me about things they think their friends can't talk about with their parents. They are obviously proud of the fact that I've been to college and am different than the people around us, who complain about kids and birth control and so on. They can come home and share English Lit or Poli Sci with Mom, or ask me for help with their Algebra.

#2 Marijuana - we found it in our house. I don't know if I would have felt this was a major evil- you know, - like heroin, if I hadn't experienced my last few college years. I feel it would have been quite different if we weren't under the influence of my going to college.

During confirmation, those Belateds who do not continue begin to wean themselves from college by adding on both abandoned former activities and newly discovered interests. They may throw themselves into political action, or into civil and environmental issues, usually on the liberal side of whatever the issue might be. They increase the allotment of time for mending social fences, rejoin the League of Women Voters, and take all the children in for dental and medical check-ups. Eighty percent of the women find jobs immediately upon graduation. Twenty percent locate themselves in community work, on Boards of Education or Recreation, for example, or some few drift back into modified pre-Belated modes of being, with a surer grasp of the mechanics of that, too.

NEW IDENTITIES AND FAMILY LIFE

The model which has emerged in this paper is composed of three social processes interrelating as they pass through three stages. Women who have matriculated in college for the first time, while they are also raising children and maintaining family hearths, are enabled to add college student selves to self-repertoires by means of the social process of staying power, cumulative studenthood and recasting family performance as the process grows and develops through the changing stages of cupellation, consolidation and confirmation.

More generally, a person's selves and little aspects of self activity shift and reconstitute in deliberate articulation with the changing pressures of life outside the family coexistent with situations within the family. It is not only that persons must socially reconstruct themselves but their spouses, children, parents, neighbors, and people in their non-family lives must also systematically build new lines of action to interrelate with the metamorphosing person's new selves and changing family patterns. The general process of taking on any new identity that affects meaningful family arrangements, e.g., becoming a cancer patient, a student, an employee, or an athletic enthusiast can be analyzed by the model discovered in this paper, with appropriate variations.

REFERENCES

BECKER, HOWARD S. 1970 "Personal Change in Adult Life" in Stone, Gregory P. and Harvey A. Farberman (eds.) Social Psychology Through Symbolic Interaction Mass. Xerox College Publishing

BECKER, HOWARD S. BLANCHE GEER and EVERETT C. HUGHES. 1968 Making The Grade: The Academic Side of College Life New York. Wiley

BLUMER, HERBERT. 1969 Symbolic Interactionism New Jersey. Prentice-Hall

CHARMAZ, KATHLEEN CALKINS. 1973 Time and Identity: The Shaping of Selves of the Chronically Ill Doctoral Dissertation University of California, San Francisco

ESTES, CARROLL L. 1979 The Aging Enterprise San Francisco. Jossey-Bass

GLASER, BARNEY B. 1978 Theoretical Sensitivity Mill Valley. Sociology Press

GLASER, BARNEY B. and ANSELM L. STRAUSS. 1967 The Discovery of Grounded Theory: Strategies For Qualitative Research Chicago. Aldine. 1974-a Awareness of Dying Chicago. Aldine. 1974-b Time

For Dying Chicago. Aldine

GOFFMAN, ERVING. 1961 Asylums: Essays In The Social Situation of Mental Patients and Other Inmates New York. Doubleday

HUGHES, EVERETT C. 1984 The Sociological Eye: Selected Papers New Jersey. New Brunswick

JAMES, WILLIAM. 1983 The Principles of Psychology Mass. Harvard University Press

KLAPP, ORRIN E. 1969 Collective Search For Identity New York. Holt, Rinehart, Winston

McCALL, GEORGE J. and J.L. SIMMONS. 1966 Identities and Interactions New York. Free Press

MEAD, GEORGE HERBERT. 1970 Mind, Self and Society Chicago. University of Chicago Press

MENDELSOHN, PAM. 1980 Happier By Degrees: A College Reentry Guide For Women New York. Dutton

OLESEN, VIRGINIA and ELVI W. WHITTAKER. 1968 The Silent Dialogue San Francisco. Jossey-Bass

PARSONS, TALCOTT. 1964 Essays in Sociological Theory (fourth printing) New York. Free Press

ROSSI, ALICE. 1967 "Equality Between the Sexes: An Immodest Proposal" in Lifton, Robert J. (ed) The Woman In America Boston. Beacon Press

ROWE, GEORGE P. 1970 "The Developmental Conceptual Framework to the Study of the Family" in Nye, Ivan F. and Felix M. Berardo (eds.) Emerging Conceptual Frameworks in Family Analysis London. MacMillan

RUBIN, LILLIAN B. 1979 Women of a Certain Age: The Midlife Search For Self New York. Harper-Rowe

SCHATZMAN, LEONARD and ANSELM L. STRAUSS. 1973 Field Research: Strategies For A Natural Sociology New Jersey. Prentice-Hall

SIMMEL, GEORG. 1969 "The Isolated Individual and the Dyad" in Wolff, Kurt H. (fourth printing) The Sociology of Georg Simmel New York. Free Press

STONE, GREGORY P. 1970 "Appearance and the Self" in Stone, Gregory P. and Harvey A. Farberman (eds.) Social Psychology Through Symbolic Interaction Mass. Xerox College Publishing

STRAUSS, ANSELM L. 1969 Mirrors and Masks: The Search for Identity Mill Valley. Sociology Press. 1978 "A Social World Perspective" Studies in Symbolic Interaction, Vol 1. 1987 Qualitative Analysis for Social Scientists New York. Cambridge University Press

WALLER, WILLARD. 1932 The Sociology of Teaching New York. Wiley. 1972 "The Definition of the Situation" in Stone, Gregory P. and Harvey A. Farberman (eds.) Mass. Xerox College Publishing

WEBER, MAX. 1958 The Protestant Ethic and the Spirit of Capitalism New York. Scribner

CHAPTER 7

VAGUENESS IN THE HAIGHT ASHBURY:

A Study in Asocialization

Richard Rizzo

The literature on socialization implies a mechanistic model of how transitions from one status to another are accomplished. The model assumes a socializing group with roles, values and expectations that are "taken on" by naive recruits.

In this paper I would like to suggest an alternative to this mechanistic conception. I use the term vagueness to stand for my conception because it connotes impreciseness and cognitive uncertainty - connotations which are absent from the term "socialization".

It is my contention that an accounting of the dimensions of vagueness will contribute to an understanding of how the world is experienced by certain actors, and consequently to an understanding on how they construct their action.

This paper deals with the Haight Ashbury community in San Francisco. I try to show how some of the factors which produced the migration to the Haight set the actors for vagueness before they arrive. I discuss community structures which support vagueness, subcultural characteristics associated with it and ideological rationales for it. The concluding section suggests something of the lifestyles which seem to emerge as a consequence of participating in this vague milieu. The route by which I arrived at these notions is essentially that outlined by Glaser and Strauss in the *Discovery of Grounded Theory*. That is, not anticipating them in advance, I allowed as much as possible for the emergence of these concepts from the data. This paper represents then, the analysis of observations that I made over a period of eighteen months, beginning in March 1967 and terminating in September 1968. In addition to field notes, tapes and newspaper articles, I analyzed the transcriptions of some seventeen interviews that I conducted with young people in the Haight Ashbury community during the summer of 1968. The interview guide was developed in collaboration with Dr. Fred Davis of the University of California Medical Center, San Francisco.

REBELS OR OUTCAST(S)?

Conventional wisdom, (exemplified by popular culture, especially the mass media) presents a distorted image of the young people who come to the Haight. The image that is often conjured up in the public mood represents the migrants as sons and daughters of the middle class who are engaged in active rebellion against the materialistic lifestyles of their parents.

Both my observational and my interview data suggest that this characterization must be called into question. Rather than one set of motives which leads to migration there appear to be a number of factors in the individual's life situation which combine to produce the move.

The data indicate that some recruits resemble the artists, craftsmen and illuminati who migrated to bohemian and beat communities in earlier eras. There are persons for whom the Haight community is a frontier - it functions for them in much the same way that going west or going to sea functioned for earlier generations. It is where the action is - an experience that one should have.

The data also suggests that there are a number of persons who come to the Haight with what would be deviant identities in more conventional settings, e.g. deviant legal, political, sexual, psychological or religious identities. They gravitate toward the Haight because many of the characteristics of the vague subculture make it unlikely that the sanctions which are usually brought to bear on them will be exercised there.

An overwhelming majority of the young people I talked to gave me the impression that they had drifted to the area as the result of "push" factors in their homes. In some cases they indicated that they had been explicitly told by parents not to return. In other instances it was clear from their description of their home situations that there was little place for them had they chosen to remain. In many instances their parents were divorced, separated, physically or mentally ill or financially unable to provide a home for them.

This brief description suggests something of the diversity of the factors that combine to produce the migration to the Haight. Perhaps a better comprehension of how this process operates can be gleaned if we look briefly at what characteristics were *not* present in the lives of those I encountered. On the whole these young people had not attended college. Their work histories were sporadic. There were no instances of participation in high status occupations. In this context, the reader is reminded that while retailing dope on the street is a low income occupation, it nevertheless carries considerable status in the Haight community. It is perhaps the only job that these young people can get which had *any* status rewards for them. In terms of conventional work careers there are few legitimate opportunities open to many of the young people who come to the Haight.

I also found evidence which supports the conventional wisdom -some respondents indicated rejection of middle class values and a conscious choice of an alternate life style. But explication of this issue alone does not provide an adequate account of the factors which led to the migration for the majority of young people. Construction of the more typical pattern would have to include reference to the fact that these young people, for a variety of reasons, do not have access to conventional roles of growing up.

Conventional roles may have been avoided because of factors in the individuals' view of the world (conscious choice of nonmaterialistic life style, seeking the action, or the artistic life) or access may have been blocked by environmental factors (societal reaction to deviance, or a home situation with few opportunities).

I am not suggesting that these factors are mutually exclusive. In fact most of the interviews indicate that a number of factors may combine and reinforce one another. What does stand out however is the fact that the lives of these young people are *not* characterized by participation in conventional modes of becoming an adult. By "conventional" I mean participation in those social activities which are normally associated with the transition to adulthood. Such activities as: learning a trade, holding a full time job, joining or being drafted into the armed forces, going to college, developing a close relationship with someone of the opposite sex, etc.

The fact that these young people are not engaged in these activities was reflected in the responses that they made to my questions about how they managed to survive, and with whom they were friendly. Questions dealing with source of income for food and shelter, and those dealing with kinship and peer relations were responded to without clarity or precision - even after I did considerable probing for additional elaboration. Although I did not realize it at the time these responses reflected the fact that the respondents were not tied to conventional socializing agencies. They were unable to respond with the precision which would have been mandatory had they been significantly involved with one or another of the conventional socializing agencies I mentioned earlier.

My first reaction in attempting to analyze these responses (which are crucial for a knowledge of the transition to adulthood) was to assume that I did not have a valid measure. I conjectured that, because they were embarrassed or for other reasons, the respondents were unwilling to reveal the true nature of how they managed to make ends meet or with whom they were close. I expanded this notion to the suggestion that there was a considerable deal of denial taking place on their part. But this assumption (that the response was not a valid indication of the actors' definition of the situation) can also be called into question. One could just as easily assume that they were telling the truth - that how they managed or the nature of their friendships were not significant enough problems to warrant more precise definition by them.

Following the logic of this latter interpretation I began to develop the notion of vagueness. Vagueness may be defined as the absence of precision or clarity about a phenomena - an inability to detail and elaborate. Vagueness is a relative notion, for example, we tend to view much of technological society as definite and precise, (e.g. exact temporal schedules), but often we ignore the fact that this precision clusters around certain elements which are important in technological society. We are not precise about such things as the various kinds of snow there are (as Eskimos are), or about certain kinds of kinship relations (as some 'primitive' peoples are).

In both these instances the "vagueness" of our technological society can only be established by making reference to the precision and clarity with which these subjects are treated in other cultures. Lack of precision and clarity when dealing with a phenomena is an indication that it is not being treated as problematic by a group.

Vagueness about a given developmental phemonena can be seen as a lack of 'take' on an individual of the behavior proscribed by a given socializing agency. As Erikson points out in a recent review of some of his earlier work: "Rapid technological changes make it impossible for any traditional way of being older to become so institutionalized that the younger generation can step right into it or, indeed, resist it in revolutionary fashion."[1] If I read him correctly, what Erikson is calling attention to in this passage is the possibility that for some young people an "institutionalized" pattern of growing up *might* be an irrelevant factor in any calculus of their development. If one applies this notion to the Haight one would expect that vagueness would cluster around such irrelevant factors.

To suggest that the young people I interviewed in the H/A *denied* questions of survival and conventional social relations is to risk the error which would be entailed in the assumption that urban Americans deny the varieties of snow, or the complexity of kin relations. It is perhaps closer to the reality of the situation to suggest that they are vague about the issues.

In sum, from their backgrounds, experiences and views of the world - the fact that these young people drifted (or were pushed) to the Haight - indicates that they have a propensity toward vagueness about conventional modes of growing up. However this openness to vagueness does not by itself account for pervasiveness of this phenomena in the Haight community. Given the fact that they are encumbered with the same basic needs (food, shelter, etc.) that all humans share it is interesting to note that survival was not treated more problematically by these young people.

In order to understand how vagueness is maintained it is necessary to look at the youth culture in the Haight. We turn now to a consideration of this milieu especially insofar as it affects the maintenance of vagueness toward certain problems which on the surface at least, appear to require inevitable confrontation.

VAGUENESS AND COMMUNITY STRUCTURE

During the period when I was observing in the Haight, a number of free "services" were in existence which made survival less problematic. Free food was provided daily in the park. "Crash pads" where persons could sleep without charge were accessible. A free store was in operation where one could obtain used clothing and other dry goods. A free clinic treated many medical problems. An information service existed in the community and functioned as a clearing house for special problems of all sorts.

If the debate over the practicality of maintaining these projects for long periods without outside support is set aside, one is struck by the fact that these institutions *existed* in the Haight and that they serviced many persons.

In addition to these free services there were a number of legal, quasi-legal and illegal activities or occupational careers which the individual could employ as a means for earning some money. I have already mentioned the drug trade - other street occupations include prostitution, (I use the term to stand for a whole variety of transactions in which one's sex is the operating capital) begging, selling newspapers and hustling tourists.

I am not suggesting that these services and occupations existed prior to the influx of young people into the Haight - rather that they emerged as an integral part of the influx and that they in turn feed back as models for the behavior of newcomers. The services were maintained in part because there were considerable nonfinancial rewards associated with being a service worker. In addition to satisfying altruistic motives one could begin to feel ''in'' if one took responsibility for performing a service.

What *is* important about the existence of these services and careers is that they make it possible for the individual to live in the community for a considerable length of time without encountering ''survival'' problems which in other settings lend force to conventional socializing agencies.

Keeping in mind that vagueness is relative, that it clusters around certain factors and not others we note that the drug dealer can be quite specific and clear about prices, standards of quality and types of drugs. What he is vague about are questions such as: So you plan to get married? Who pays the rent at your commune? It is precisely in his inability to respond with specificity to these questions that we can begin to discern the operation of vagueness with respect to conventional modes of becoming an adult.

Another structural property which contributes to the maintenance of vagueness is the high degree of transience that characterizes the Haight community. There are changes in personnel over the course of the day - including a diurnal shift which produces day and night people. There are shifts between weekdays and weekends - tourists tend to dominate on weekends. Finally there is a seasonal change - the famous summer influx.

These turnovers are so massive that they indelibly stamp much of the interaction to develop, which is sustained in the same fashion in the larger society: it is necessary for he individuals involved to withdraw from community life. That is, if one is involved in the community, these massive turnovers require continual realignment of relationships. These pressures produce relationships that are characterized by their temporariness. They are of relatively short duration when compared with relationships in less transient communities, and the participants expect that this will be the case. It is not extraordinary then to find these young people responding with a lack of precision when one asks questions designed to draw out conventional definitions of social relationships.

SUBCULTURE OF VAGUENESS

There are a number of subcultural behavioral patterns, sensibilities, states of being or what I call ''modes'' in the Haight which are interactional models for the newcomers and which have the effect of contributing to vagueness.

"Being" is one of these modes.[2] "Being" occurs also in more conventional settings but it is quite pronounced in the Haight. In order to "be" one assumes an air of transcendence. The immediate social environment is ignored and attention is focused away. The term "preoccupied" describes this kind of behavior. I observed this behavior in homes, on the street and especially in the park. When I enquired about daily routines I discovered that large blocks of time were devoted to being.

Concomitant with being is a cool attitude with respect to the behavior of others. One is cool if one acts in all instances as if the behavior of others is appropriate to the situation. To loose one's cool is to question the appropriateness of some action.

Both "being" and being "cool" combine to produce and environment which is tolerant toward the most bizarre and idiosyncratic behavior. I observed a man while he took off all his clothing and took an imaginary bath in a public place with virtually no response on the part of those who observed him. In another instance a group of actors in blackface accosted passers by on the street and beat them with plastic baseball bats - in most instances the event was treated by the "victims" as if it were quite unproblematic. Once one has learned to be cool it is possible to manage much that is problematic for persons who have not learned this behavior. It should be emphasized that this role is relatively passive - one does not have to actively construct his own behavior- he simply allows the behavior of the other to be performed before him with little or no reciprocity.

"Being" and "cool" behavior can be seen as generalized behavioral alternatives which are appropriate to a variety of situations. They can be brought to new situations and the individual is able to fulfill his behavioral obligations without developing a more specific and articulated set of responses.

Dress and grooming patterns provide a means for masking identities. One of the most common observations made by regulars of the free store was the observation that the store functioned as a place where newly arrived young people could exchange their old clothing (and its identifying marks) for "new" used clothing. What is particularly interesting about this situation is that in some cases, clothing that was discarded by one newcomer became the outfit of another. What this suggests is that the importance of dress lies not in what it reveals but rather in what it does not reveal. It suggests that exchange is more important than acquisition- in the identity market place. Clothing and grooming allow identities which might intrude to remain vague.

In some cases a new identity is constructed (but that is getting ahead of the story), more frequently a "quasi-identity" emerges. By "quasi-identity" I mean to suggest a more plastic and malleable referent for the reaction of others than is suggested by the term "identity".

Astrology (at the time I was observing) is an example of a subculture mode that functioned as a quasi-identity. For some young people an astrological sign was an indication of who one was. It was not at all infrequent in conversation to be asked what sign one was born under. Knowledge of this sign allows the other to construct an identity for you and to behave toward you in an appropriate manner.

What is important is that the identity is *ascribed* and all the actors have potential identities. Significantly, these identities do not require a whole set of references to past behavior, home life, etc. They may remain latent in many situations if there is no reason to call them up.

Just as there are quasi-identities for people, there are quasi-definitions for situations. "Vibrations" function in this manner. Usually there are two categories of vibrations: good vibes and bad vibes. A more fine distinction beyond this dichotomy is rare. Vibrations allow the situation to be defined without recourse to more formalized and specific definitions. Again, what I am suggesting here is a definition of the situation which is more vague than is normally thought of, when the notion of definition of the situation is encountered.

A linguistic mode which underlies the vagueness of certain interactions can be found in the subcultural use of the term "old lady". Old lady or old man can refer to one's lover, spouse, close friend or - in the case of a masked interaction where a youngster may disguise parental attachment - the term can be used to refer to parents, while not making it clear that it is one's parents whom one is speaking about. Exploiting the multiple meanings of the term is quite common. In this subcultural mode we find the linguistic equivalent or analog of the vagueness of some social relations.

IDEOLOGY: NON-PROBLEMATIC PHILOSOPHY

In addition to structural and subcultural factors which contribute to vagueness there are ideological supports which serve to reinforce the individual's existential condition. The myth of the Golden Age functions in this manner. This myth refers to a period when the "real" hippies lived in the Haight. According to the myth- it was a time when creativity and good cheer abounded. One could easily find material assistance if one was in need and personal relations were intimate and rewarding. Since that time, the myth contends, the real love people have gone and the mixed bag of persons one now encounters in the Haight have replaced them.

The myth serves two functions. First it validates some of the experiences that are encountered which have the potential for becoming issues requiring specificity. For example when one's food, clothing or dope are "ripped off" (stolen) the issue of survival can come to be perceived in more problematic terms. In addition to validating this experience the myth provides a rationalized (albeit nonspecific) framework for handling these potentially problematic experiences. One's immediate difficulties can be solved as soon as one cracks the mystery of where all the real people have gone. In this way confrontation is postponed where it could not be simply avoided. This myth is reinforced by the actor's perception of the high turnover in the community.

In addition to the myth of the Golden Age there is a whole set of more personalized philosophical propositions which emerge from the data which function as supports for vagueness about traditional problems associated with the transition to adulthood. Experience is valued for its own sake, not in an instrumental capacity. At least it is not viewed as instrumental in the same way as it might be by a young corporation executive on the way up. Consequently there is little necessity for setting priorities on experience- rather the individual assumes a fatalistic posture with respect to new experience.

"Going through changes" is another important concept in the philosophic systems of these young people. In this concept the self is seen as in perpetual motion. No one role or identity is expected to dominate. The interviews also indicated an extreme relativism: "every view is an image of the truth" as one respondent put it, is a widespread credo. Other assertions which reveal similar relativism propensities are: "I prefer to question, not to state", "I want to be able to understand all people, winos, cops, everyone". These notions suggest that underlying much of interaction is an ideological impartiality which is striking.

This impartiality allows for the withholding of commitment to one or another set of roles and identities. These ideological notions can be seen as a potential pool of rationales for the vague lifestyle - they can be drawn upon as the situation requires.

The properties of vagueness discussed so far fall into two general categories: I) factors which mitigate intrusion and II) alternate forms. Factors which mitigate intrusion are those elements which do not allow the subject around which vagueness is clustered to emerge as problematic. In this category is the structural property of services - which made it possible for persons to live without the intrusion of survival problems. Also in this category is the structural property of transience - which made sustained relationships difficult if one participated fully. Ideological notions which validate but rationalize potentially intruding experiences also belong in this category. Dress style which masks and minimizes entry of prior identities, definitions and behaviors of more conventional socializing groups.

CONSEQUENCES OF PARTICIPATION IN THIS VAGUE MILIEU

In this concluding section I would like to address the question of what effect participation in this vague milieu has on the lifestyles of these young people. Unfortunately the temporal span of the research only begins to approach the period of time necessary to make even minimally adequate statements about these emerging lifestyles.

With this qualification in mind I would like to indicate that this preliminary data suggests that rather than one outcome of participation there may be several. One of the results of participation is that the individual is highly susceptible to institutions which are capable of forcefully imposing identities and definitions on him. In this regard the police department is perhaps an ideal type of an agency which can force acceptance of an identity. Consequently some criminal careers are begun in the Haight. Other defining agencies include the military, the health profession (conferring physical and mental identities) and certain religious groups. These institutions are especially powerful in this situation because the young people (due to their participation in the vague subculture) have so few resources which can effectively counter the definitions imposed on them. While intrusion of these agencies into a given individual's life is problematic, once these intrude they tend to create an identity that may characterize the individual for he rest of his life. Participation in the milieu mitigates against the formation of a counteridentity that is legitimized in social interaction and which has the potential for countering the conventional institutionally imposed identity. It is for this reason that the stamp of the police department or other agency is particularly strong in this situation.

Other intrusions may be less structurally determined. Girls may become pregnant, "breaks" of one sort or another may occur - a free clinic may get a federal grant, a band a recording contract etc. In these cases the intruding event may have the effect of propelling the individual into more conventional adult roles. We see in these cases individuals who are more likely to fit the socialization model. They move into roles for which there is ample precedent. They may take on work and family roles and identities, typical of lower or middle class culture or they may become part of some ongoing deviant subgroup. These cases illustrate the obverse of the vagueness process. They are young people who are socialized by an adult world. I use the term "socialized" in this context to stand for the taking on of deviant as well as normal adult identities. From my discussion so far it should be clear why I feel such a paradoxical usage is justified.

Another pattern that emerges from the data as a consequence of participation in this milieu is the middle family. I coined this term to stand for a set of relationships which has come to characterize the lives of some of the young people I encountered.

The middle family represents a hybrid - a mixture of the family where ego is the child and the family where ego is adult. Typically a set of roles and obligations emerges in this family: they often have discernable leaders, yet the relations among members rarely approximates the autocracy characteristic of the traditional American family. Each individual combines relative degrees of dependency and responsibility. These families or tribes or communes, as they are called, resemble voluntary associations in their recruitment practices - yet they provide for much more intimate interaction. Procreation may or may not be present. In most instances these families function as economic units. As I indicated earlier, responsibility is shared, but in general it is not skewed in the fashion common in conventional families.

It is my contention that participation in the vague subculture of the Haight contributes to the emergence of these families. Participation provides a respite from the pressures operating in conventional adolescent socializing milieus - and this moratorium leads to experimentation with and then cultivation of this new life style.

It is interesting to note that these families provide a whole set of new roles which may continue throughout the rest of the life cycle. It is too early to imagine what these families will look like as the present generation ages and a new "younger" generation is recruited or born into these families. All that can be said with certainty is that for some of the young people who come to the Haight, the middle family is one possible outcome of participation.

The final pattern that is discernable is the taking on of a vague identity - one becomes a vagrant. In the recent experiences of some of those that I interviewed a pattern of migration from one vague community to another began to emerge. Places like Kitslano in Vancouver and the East Village in New York emerge as part of a vagrancy circuit. I do not intend to suggest that geographic mobility is the sole defining characteristic - it is rather a concomitant of the more important factor - a vague definition of self. In this connection it is interesting to note that when I asked respondents if they felt that they were like others in the Haight they would invariably respond that they were not. Similarly when I asked what they thought of the word "hippie" their responses indicated that they did not identify themselves as hippies - even though most persons would have identified them as such. Their complaint was that the media created the hippies (implicit in this complaint was the assumption that the media created the hippie community also).

This inability to identify with others in the community strongly mitigated against the formation of a "we" feeling in the Haight. There was some sense of community (e.g., the tendency to share, and the almost universal hostility toward the police), but often this sense of togetherness broke down in the face of the extreme individualism.

This individualism was manifest most acutely with respect to those issues having to do with identity. Who one is and where one is going were invariably seen in individualistic terms. "I am" is never constructed with respect to others who share the same fate. One had much more the sense of characters in search of a play than a well-made drama.

This situation is not extraordinary if we consider the interactional context within which identity is formed. Each individual is continually confronting vagueness in the behavior of others. No wonder extreme individualism prevails.

For the sociologists this situation is particularly difficult to come to terms with. It is much like the problem presented by holding two mirrors up to one another. As long as the observer does not peek there is no object before the mirror and consequently there is no image in the other. Similarly, when the actor confronts a vague situation it is difficult not to intrude with an overly rationalistic interpretation of his behavior.

Yet it is possible at times to infer about the kinds of processes that are operative. I asked one of my respondents if there were any questions that he thought I might ask in future interviews. He replied: '' Well, I don't know. I've heard a lot of people say they cone here to find something, you know. But I don't know what they're trying to find. I don't know what I'm trying to find. Maybe I'd ask them that.'' When the image in the mirror of the other is vague, how can we expect any other response?

REFERENCES

1. Erikson, Erik H., *Identity, Youth, and Crisis*, New York: W.W. Norton Co., 1968, p. 38.

2. See discussion of "away" behavior in Irving Goffman, *Behavior in Public Places*, Glencoe: The Free Press, 1963.

CHAPTER 8

Reprinted from *Chronic Illness and the Quality of Life*, The C.V. Mosby Company, St. Louis, 1975

ROUTING:

Getting Around with Emphysema

Shizuko Yoshimura Fagerhaugh

SALIENCY

...Emphysema is a severe respiratory disease with irreversible deterioration of the lungs.

...The resulting paucity of oxygen intake means that there is a considerable, even major, lessening of available bodily energy. Any movement or exertion - even talking, crying, or laughing - uses oxygen and can bring about respiratory distress.

...The prescribed long-term regimen aims at preventing further deterioration and easing the breathing. The regimen may involve drugs, inhalation machinery, and spending time at breathing exercises and learning breath control; and may require daily, weekly, or monthly visits to a hospital or clinic.

Possibly the main problem of people who suffer from emphysema is the management of scarce energy. They may be able to increase their energy through a proper regimen. Primarily, however, they must allocate their energy to those activities which they must do or wish to do. Hence two key issues for them are symptom control (energy loss) and the balancing of regimen versus other considerations. To those problems, we shall add, in the pages that follow, the matter of a worsening trajectory, and the impact of advanced age and of being poor. (The study on which this case is based was of quite poor people and mostly without supporting kinsmen. The choice of this population was deliberate, since their condition reduced their available resources for coping with energy losses.)

BASIC MOBILITY AND SOCIABILITY RESOURCES

Time, energy and money are basic resources which all people draw upon for physical mobility and sociability. We have varying amounts of these basic resources (henceforth called BMRs) which can be juggled and balanced to allow physical mobility and sociability. In general, a generous supply of health and wealth permits much of both. In situations of decreased energy supply, due to illness or old age, a generous supply of money can purchase other people's BMRs. Thereby one's own time and energy can be saved. A short supply of both energy and money, but a reliable and accessible supply from friends and family, can balance the decreased BMRs. How a person juggles and balances his BMRs depends not only upon his own supply of BMRs and the availability and purchasability of other people's BMRs, but also, as we shall see, upon his lifestyle and life situation.

Translating the calculus of BMRs of the majority of the patients interviewed, they had a meager supply of energy because of old age and advanced emphysema (in several instances their energy supply was further decreased because of other chronic conditions such as heart disease and arthritis). Their money supply was also scarce since savings were depleted because of extended illness: their advanced disease condition did not allow gainful employment, and the welfare aid was far from generous. Because of being widowed or divorced for many years, or never married, other people's BMRs often were not reliable or available. They did have a large supply of time because they did not work and had no large network of close family ties and friends who could take up their time. In short, their BMR status and life situation tended to maximized their mobility and sociability problems.

OXYGEN SHORTAGE: GAUGING AND MISGAUGING

The mobility problem of the emphysema victim is primarily one of inability to get enough oxygen to produce energy. A certain amount of oxygen is necessary to maintain the body at rest; for physical activity a (lung) oxygen reserve volume is required. Depending upon the activity, more or less oxygen is necessary. In advanced emphysema, because of pathological changes[1], there is very limited oxygen reserve, and maintaining the limited reserve is difficult. These patients become "short of breath" with minimal physical activity, and compared to "normal lungers" require longer and more frequent periods to "recoup"[2] their diminished oxygen reserve.

Because of the limited oxygen reserve and the difficulty in maintaining the limited reserve they must gauge the oxygen requirement for various activities with their "recoupable" supply. Correct gauging is vital because misgauging can result in dire consequences; extreme physical distress - a sense of suffocation - a chance of losing consciousness, and of course great fatigue. In fact, many expressed a sense of panic in misgauged mobility situations.

When normal people engage in activities, there is a fluidity and simultaneity about their actions. When completing an activity where walking, talking, lifting, or whatever is involved, each specific act smoothly blends into an easy flow. Also, when normals over-exert themselves they can pant a few times and continue with their action - no worse for the wear. Normal lungers can also carry out several activities simultaneously, like walking and talking. That fluidity and simultaneity of activity is not possible for advanced emphysema patients. The latter deliberately chop up the fluidity into smaller of smaller "recoupable" units depending upon their disease status. Also, their activities tend to get ordered sequentially rather than simultaneously in order to conserve energy.

Adequate lung reserve is necessary not only for physical mobility, but for such vocalizations as talking, laughing, singing, or yelling. Thus, when being mobile, someone with severe emphysema must consider when and where he will expend his meager air supply for sociability as over against other uses. Such expenditures of air must be calculated. Because of advanced stages emphysema, extended talking, laughing, or crying can trigger off paroxysms of coughing as well as respiratory distress. Hence, some patients' social interactions tend to decrease. In fact, interviewing these people can be rather taxing for an interviewer since their typical conversational pattern is to talk a bit, pant for air, talk a bit and pant for air. Some remarked that they decreased interactions with others, sensing their discomfiture. Moreover, social situations which are anxiety provoking tend to bring on attacks of "shortness of breath." A characteristic of emphysema is that anxiety triggers dyspnea which brings on more anxiety, developing into a vicious cycle. Over the long haul, with progressive lung deterioration, these people tend to isolate themselves as a defense against anxiety-provoking social involvements.[4]

INTERRELATIONSHIP OF BMRs TO LIFESTYLE AND MOBILITY NEEDS

Judgements concerning what to be mobile about are influenced by available basic mobility resources. Also, one's lifestyle and life conditions will determine how and where the BMRs are utilized for physical and social mobilization. The interaction of the person's BMRs, lifestyle and conditions will shape his mobility priorities. Thus, he may simply delete or partially restrict aspects of his lifestyle and mobility needs because of diminishing BMRs. He may compromise, making up for inadequacies in some areas of his life situation to provide for other higher priority needs.

For example, he must have priorities regarding features of his residential site and its territorial topography. The features of both include (1) terrain of resident location - whether flat or hilly, and terrain of residence itself - first floor, elevator or no elevator, etc; (2) propinquity of and terrain to and from public transportation; (3) propinquity of and terrain to and from such essential places as grocery store, cafe, laundromat, and bank; and (4) propinquity of mobility assistants (family members and friends).

A patient with money can afford taxis and have groceries delivered. Someone with reliable friends and family with an automobile is not as concerned with topography or residence location or the accessibility of public transportation as patients without much money. Patients with limited money are often unable to afford a costly oxygen-saving residence. Moreover, because of lack of energy they are frequently unable to engage in extended residence hunting, and consequently settle for whatever halfway meets their oxygen-saving specifications. They must tolerate some bad residential and territorial features in exchange for other features judged as more essential in their lifestyle. Here are a few examples.

Mr. B., a widower, always lived in an apartment; therefore he preferred living in an apartment. Being unable to afford an apartment with an elevator he settled for a second floor apartment within his financial means. It was located in a terrain which, although sightly inclined, was manageable within his oxygen reserve limit. This apartment was close to a grocery store. He liked to cook and stretched his money by doing his own cooking. Hence, accessibility to the grocery store was very important. His social interactions were limited primarily to the apartment tenants and the manager, all acting as his mobility assistants since they helped by picking up a quart of milk while doing their own errands. A particularly important fellow tenant was a man who had a car; he was useful for especially difficult situations such as getting to the clinic. Getting there by public transportation involved considerable time and energy and required several bus transfers. However, he was careful not to abuse the help of his friend, limiting his request only to those which seemed legitimate and reasonable. Once he was placed on inhalation therapy, which necessitated daily trips to the clinic. Feeling unjustified then in requesting daily assistance from his friend, he managed the clinic visits by public transportation. After a week of treatment he stopped therapy because the time and effort of getting to and from the clinic left him too exhausted to do other necessary tasks - such as cooking, keeping up the apartment, and doing his laundry.

In contrast, a bachelor with a network of casual acquaintances in his neighborhood, who met regularly at the neighborhood social club-like bar, chose both his residential features and how to expend his oxygen quite differently. With his deteriorating respiratory condition and the depletion of his money, he progressed to increasingly deteriorated residences within the same neighborhood where he had long lived; for instance, from a nice apartment to a single room on the second floor of an inexpensive hotel which had no elevator. He reasoned that a room was preferable to a residence with cooking facilities because he hated to cook. Propinquity of and accessibility to eating places with reasonable prices (he ate only two meals a day to save money) and the neighborhood social-club bar were most important. He preferred expending his air in getting to and from the cafe rather than at cooking and keeping up an apartment. A goodly amount of oxygen was expended at the bar, as he aptly put it, ''shooting the breeze with the guys.'' The social-club bar was also important for financial reasons and for recruiting mobility assistants. The bartender and the patrons had known him for many years and knew his credit was good. This enabled him to get an occasional drink on credit, borrow money from friends, as well as enlist the aid of his friends with cars for especially difficult mobility situations.

When life conditions change as the disease progresses, mobility needs and residential locations are altered also.

For example, an elderly patient who lived most of his life in a downtown hotel, after several acute respiratory episodes and subsequent lung reserve decrease preferred to live downtown because of territorial familiarity and high propinquity to public transportation and eating places. He was also able to continue living alone by enlisting the aid of an elderly sister who served as an energy and money saver: she handled his personal laundry, ran errands, and invited him each week to Sunday dinner. A major change was locating himself in a moderately expensive hotel which had 24-hour clerks. The latter were important as interceptors of SOS signals should he require immediate medical attention. Such clerks are also important because they become familiar with a tenant's daily routines and consequently check on the tenant when there are changes in them.

Events such as razing an apartment for urban redevelopment, where a patient has several tenant mobility assistants, or loss of mobility agents due to illness and death, can create difficulties not only in mobilization, but problems in balancing and juggling BMRs as well.

For example, an elderly man who lived for many years in an economical boarding house operated by an interested and concerned landlady, and where he was on friendly terms with long-term boarders, was able to manage well on his limited BMRs. Unfortunately, the landlady developed severe arthritis so that she could no longer continue running the boarding house, putting the house up for sale. The closing of the house, and the loss of the landlady, meant he could not find comparable housing within his financial means, as well as the leading to the loss of his major mobility assistants and his major source of sociability - the landlady and fellow boarders.

ROUTING: PROCESS AND STRATEGIES

The process by which all persons, whether ill or healthy, deal with problems of mobility is by routing. The dimensions involved are (1) anticipation of the number and types of activities in terms of available BMRs; (2) judgements whether to delete or postpone some activities, or to condense activities by combining several activities; (3) sequential ordering of activities in terms of importance, distance, time and energy involved in each activity, as well as anticipation of possible obstacles.

The degree of efficiency depends on both the mode of routing (own legs, public transportation, own car, other people's cars) and the degree of control over the mode of routing. Efficiency also depends on how much of other people's time is involved in completing an activity. One can condense activities in the shortest time when there is: (1) good control over the mode of routing; (2) control over the sequence and time involved for activities - such as having a prior appointment; and (3) sufficient energy. In situations where a person has little or no control over the mode of routing, efficiency nevertheless may be attained by stringent control of sequence, or expending more energy to hasten the routing process by running and generally moving fast.

An emphysema patient's anticipation and planning of his route is essential to avoid the consequences of overexertion and anxiety. For example, Mr. P. lives on the second floor: before venturing outside he carefully plans for taking all the necessary paraphernalia and errand lists, and gauges the time and energy required to get to the bus stop. If late for the bus, he cannot run to catch it. Patients state than when they have forgotten a grocery list, drug prescription, form to take to the social worker, or whatever - then they find themselves getting anxious. Their anxiety is due in part to irritation with themselves, but also to their anticipation of having to make the trip back home or worse still, climbing the stairs again.

The degree of planning for an ordinary activity (shopping for groceries) becomes long and complicated. A patient lives on the second floor. He must "recoup" oxygen after walking a single block even if on flat terrain. The grocery store is uphill, so after half a block he needs to rest in order to get his breath back. If he chats with the grocer then he needs to rest for the trip back home. If he carries a bag of groceries that means still more oxygen expenditure; so, even though the route home is down hill, he can only go 3/4 of the block before becoming winded. Then at home he has a flight of stairs with which to contend. Twelve steps is his usual oxygen supply. With the extra grocery weight he requires "getting his wind back" every six to eight steps. What normals can do in twenty minutes is stretched out to one hour or more.

When a patient lacks money and therefore has little control over mode of routing, he may use his time as his major mobility resource: he expends small amounts of energy over an extended period of time. He may take the roundabout bus route to avoid a difficult terrain, even though a more direct route is possible. For example, to avoid a steep terrain he will walk downhill to catch a third bus which stops uphill from his house. Another patient's most direct route to the clinic involved walking across a wide thoroughfare with heavy traffic which he could not manage without running out of breath. He managed his routing by taking a time-consuming roundabout bus route which crossed the unmanageable thoroughfare.

An important routing concern which they all face is to find appropriate ways to "recoup" oxygen via locating appropriate "puffing" stations (another descriptive term used by a patient). Sitting down is the preferred way to "get the wind back," but such sitting places are seldom available in public. So the relevant strategy is to start recouping oxygen while still able to stand. Sitting down on a street curb can cause a public scene. Moreover, in skid row or tenderloin areas one might get mistaken for a drunk. A wall, telephone pole, or mail box to lean against are considered good puffing stations. They have stated they do not venture downtown to shop because of the lack of appropriate puffing stations. One shopped exclusively at a particular department store because of its easy accessibility to the ladies' lounge.

Emphysema patients must also weigh the weather more carefully than do normals because they must avoid catching colds. Windy weather is said to increase their breathing problems. Also there is the question of avoiding a tailwind or headwind. And, of course, smog greatly increases their breathing problems.

They must also anticipate other unforeseen obstacles. For example, patients living in deteriorated areas of the city where there are many predators tend not to venture outside too often. Should they be accosted they cannot run nor do they have the air to yell for help.

Whether sick or well, all people have varying daily, weekly, and monthly routing routines: routing to work, shop, pick up the cleaning, visit grandma, and so on. With their difficulties in routing and in the face of a scarcity of money, emphysema patients must be especially careful in planning their daily and weekly routing. Not infrequently those who live in difficult terrains (such as the second or third floor) plan so as to avoid unnecessary stair climbing. Thus a man who ate all his meals out planned his daily route so that once downstairs for breakfast he delayed climbing the stairs until after supper. This of course required locating stations, such as coffee shops and park benches for resting and killing time. Another patient who did her own cooking had an every-other-day route to the grocery store. This not only gave a change from her dingy apartment, but enabled her to socialize with the grocer and her neighborhood acquaintances. Also, her every-other-day shopping meant the grocery weight was more manageable than a large once-a-week shopping.

The daily and weekly expenditure of energy for routing must be planned so that on days which require an increased energy output (cleaning the apartment), routing for shopping is not done. A normal lunger would scarcely consider routing as necessary for getting dressed in the morning or for doing ordinary things around the house: they tend to think of routing only when great distances are involved. To illustrate the striking degree of daily routing required for emphysema patients:

One lady who became short of breath after a few stops required two to three hours to get dressed. She arises from bed and goes to the bathroom, rests, washes by sitting in a chair but taking frequent rest periods in between, walks back to the bedroom, rests, and dresses with frequent rest periods.

Another patient who mops his kitchen floor every week worked out an elaborate routing pattern. He gathers the cleaning paraphernalia and puts it near a chair in the middle of the room - all of which requires frequent periods of "getting my breath back." He mops a few strokes and rests, sitting in the chair.

With advanced emphysema, all activities require extremely careful routing. The routing is not only specific weekly and daily, but is also hourly, since extended rest periods are necessary after increased expenditure of energy. It is interesting to note that when making arrangements for interviews, patients not only specified certain days but times of the day such as - "Come in the morning around ten because I'll be too tired to talk in the afternoon," or "Come by in the afternoon because I rest after lunch and will be less tired."

MEDICAL REGIMEN AND MOBILITY

Whether a patient does or does not comply to his prescribed regimen and how he complies are determined in part by how the regimen interferes with his life style and mobility needs. In part, it also depends upon how he comprehends or miscomprehends the uses and effects of therapy.

Sometimes a patient's condition warrants extended inhalation therapy. These treatments may require daily visits to an outpatient clinic, or inhalation equipment instead may be sent to the home. Where daily visits are required, patients may not see their value considering the amount of time and energy required to get to the clinic. When respirators have been sent to their residence, that well-intentioned help by health personnel may not be perceived as helpful. Inhalation therapy is often ordered 2-3 times a day: This means that patients who live in difficult terrains, such as on the second floor, must plan to avoid frequent climbing of stairs. In order to avoid maneuvering the stairs several times a day, these patients confine themselves to their rooms. This often depresses them. The inhalation therapy does not improve their mobility; rather it immobilizes them. In fact, several patients thought inhalation therapy was a big nuisance and requested the doctor to discontinue the therapy.

Sometimes drugs via aerosol spray may be prescribed to immediately relieve periodic respiratory distress. These drugs may be ordered at most 3-6 times a day because of undesirable side effects.[5] When activity requires extended oxygen expenditure there is likelihood of drug overdose, since these sprays provide extra needed energy to complete an activity. One patient patted his portable nebulizer, stating it was his "life saver" as it gave him the needed extra spurt of energy in difficult routing situations.

Although he had been warned by the physician about overdosing, unfortunately he did not know what the symptoms of overdose were.

Also, although broncho-dilator drugs help breathing, these frequently cause untoward side effects such as nervousness and sleeplessness. Sometimes sedatives are required to counteract these side effects, but such drugs may leave the patient groggy. Not infrequently, balancing of the two drugs can become a problem. An imbalance may mean a patient has no energy to be mobile because he lacks sleep, or is too groggy to get around. When health personnel are not attentive to the patient's drug balance problems, he may doubt both the usefulness of the therapy and the competence of his physician.

Patients' criteria of therapeutic effectiveness are based on how well the therapies help them to be mobile in their daily movements. They may omit a drug to see how much difference this makes, as did a man whose daily route included a walk to the park. He tested the therapy by the ease or dis-ease not only in his walking there, but in how he managed the park's terrains. Such criteria are in contrast to those used by professionals which involve elaborate laboratory tests, or reflected in the inaccurate standards found in patients' medical charts: "gets short of breath after 1 block, 2 blocks, etc."

One of the more disheartening facts uncovered by the interviewing of these patients was the neglect of teaching rehabilitation measures to patients such as respiratory exercises, respiratory hygiene, and conditioning him to breathe more efficiently. On the current emphysema medical scene, the emphasis has been primarily on the acute respiratory episode treated in acute care facilities. The outcome of such unbalanced emphasis has been heroic efforts to mobilize the patients, but no real assistance in achieving effective mobilization for living once the acute episode is over.

REFERENCES

[1] The pathological changes result in decreased oxygen supply due to decreased lung compliance, decreased diffusion capacity, and increased airway resistance. Hollis G. Borin, "Pulmonary emphysema: clinical and physiological aspects," from Gerald L. Baum (ed.), The Textbook of Pulmonary Diseases, Little, Brown and Co., 1965, pp. 421-447; S. M. Farber and R. H. Wilson, Pulmonary Emphysema, Clinical Symposium (Ciba), 20:2, 1968,

[2] "Recouping" oxygen supply is not an accurate physiological term, but a term to describe the breathing problem used by one patient interviewed.

[3].Donald L. Dudley, et al., "Dyspnea: physiologic and psychologic observations," J. Psychosomatic Res., 11:325, 1968.

[4].Donald L. Dudley, et al., "Long-term adjustment, prognosis and death in irreversible obstructive pulmonary emphysema," Psychosomatic Med., 31:510, 1969.

[5].William Sawyer Eisonstadt, "Some observations on a new syndrome - respiratory medicamentosa," Ann. allergy, 27:188-190, 1969.

CHAPTER 9

Reprinted from *Chronic Illness and the Quality of Life*, The C.V. Mosby Company, St. Louis, 1975.

CHRONIC RENAL FAILURE AND THE PROBLEM OF FUNDING

Barbara Suczek

Chronic renal failure inevitably involves its victims in a dual crisis: physical and financial. Because the functions performed by the kidneys are absolutely necessary to survival, the patient must be put on a dialysis machine, through which his blood is filtered. This regimen (1) is extremely expensive, both financially and temporally; (2) must be repeated at regular and frequent intervals (usually two or three times a week); and, (3) must be ongoing (because the kidney function is absolutely essential to the life process, there can be no surcease from the need for mechanical intervention except through kidney transplant, a solution itself fraught with physical and financial problems - or death).

Since there can be little or no reasonable hope for relief from the burden of heavy and continuous expense, some extraordinary source of funds must be located. The alternatives are: (1) self-funding, whereby the patient is able to provide for himself from his personal assets; (2) private funding, either through some business arrangement (such as individual or group health insurance) or through charitable contributions - personal or organizational; (3) public funding, through any of various governmental agencies; or (4) no funding, in which case the patient does not locate a source of funds and dies for lack of treatment.

Of these alternatives, the fourth - no funding - is still the most prevalent (as will be discussed below). The first - self-funding - requires a level of income and/or personal assets so far in excess of national averages as to render it a negligible role in the overall funding drama. Except, perhaps, in such instances as might involve persons of advanced age who have substantial personal savings and otherwise light living expenses, the prospect of a lifetime on dialysis raises serious funding problems for all but the most spectacularly affluent.[1] Almost by definition, the chronic renal failure patient is a person entangled in a fund-raising struggle whose double objective is to pay for life-sustaining care while averting personal financial wipeout: a deadly game of financial dodgeball played while simultaneously wrestling with problems of insufficient time and physical debility.

Under such conditions funding becomes an ongoing preoccupation, with dramatic force sufficient to compel the behavior not only of the patient and possibly his kin but often of the professional personnel involved in his treatment as well.

REALIZING THE PROBLEM

In the overall funding process there are two steps that are logically prior to the actual acquisition and dispersal of funds. These are: (1) realization of the dimensions of the problem and (2) assessment of available resources. The first step involves astonishingly complex considerations.

THE PATIENT

Although informed awareness is an essential step in the effective budgeting of resources, the dimensions of the financial problem confronting the victim of chronic renal failure may be difficult for him to realize for several reasons. The foremost is the ambiguity - etiological, diagnostic, and prognostic - of the disability itself. Whether or not the affected individual has prior warning either of the possibility or the probability of kidney failure, the actual moment of total functional collapse seems to be only grossly predictable. Irreversible kidney failure can occur so gradually that it is almost imperceptible, or so abruptly - sometimes with no previous warning whatsoever - that it manifests itself in a major physical crisis requiring heroic measures to save the patient's life. In either case the effect is to obscure the financial problem. When crises occur, rarely are they manifested in such a way and at such a time in the disease career that the patient has an opportunity to evaluate the situation for himself in order to decide whether, all things considered, he wishes to commit himself to the heavy burdens of a dialyzed future or to elect death instead. Thus he is apt to find himself in a position of *fait accompli* from which, for a number of reasons, it may be may be difficult to extricate himself. The net effect is to bind the patient - at least initially - to life-sustaining effort, an effort that will inevitably direct his steps to the treadmill of funding. It is a direction, however, that is rarely of the patient's conscious choosing and its consequences are not often calculated.

THE MEDICAL STAFF

Usually the physician bears the ethical burden of life-and-death decisions. To relieve some of the onus of such fateful responsibility, physicians have official guidelines and collegial committees whom they can consult for support. Such guidelines are customarily cast in terms of medical and psychological concepts and relate primarily to psychomedical evaluation of the patient's condition, aside from problems immediately attributable to the kidney failure.

This is not to say, however, that the financial condition of the patient will have no bearing on whether or not he will be rescued from a physical crisis. There can be little doubt that, unofficially, decisions to rescue will reflect judgements of social worth, and assessment of a patient's financial condition may be a factor that is indirectly involved in the overall calculus. The issue is a sensitive one, since to save life according to ability to pay is contrary to overt medical, social, and psychological values. Institutionalized moral reprehension, by discouraging candor, may therefore obscure the dimensions of the financial problem, questions of funding being relegated to a position of secondary and somewhat unworthy consideration. Thus, the link, if any, between the rescue decision and the patient's financial condition is apt to be swept under the rug where it is, for all practical purposes, invisible.

ADDITIONAL CONSIDERATIONS

Other difficulties impede the realization of financial needs. (1) The physician, guided by a widespread belief that mental attitude affects physical welfare, may be reluctant to divulge depressing details that could be seen as potentially threatening to the patient's will to survive. (2) Many patients resist bad news about their conditions, refusing to accept the implications of available information if such information is threatening. (3) The patient may be unable to comprehend the physician's medical terminology and scientific frame of reference with a corresponding failure on the part of the physician to understand what it is that the patient has not understood. (4) There may be confusion about who should be the informing agent. Thus, information may be garnered piecemeal from a variety of sources: the doctor, the nursing staff, case workers, other patients, medical folklore, fortuitously in the course of reading, or through deliberate personal research. (5) The family doctor, who may know the patient and his circumstances at first hand, may be relatively unaware of the physical and financial implications of his ailment, whereas the specialist, who may understand the latter, will quite likely be unacquainted with the personal problems of his patient.

Thus, regardless of his economic or class status, the patient - sick and worried - is forced to chart a perilous physical and financial course through an apparently indifferent sea. It is an unfortunate fact that the physically healthy lack - as a rule - the imagination, the time, and the emotional energy to sustain for long any deep involvement with seemingly interminable medical problems. Bolstered by a proud but largely unexamined assumption that "we," as Americans, are probably doing as well as can be expected in providing for general health care, the chronically sick and those intimately involved with their care are essentially left to take their own soundings.

ASSESSING RESOURCES

Sooner or later the need for financial assessment will arrive. The point at which the kidney failure is pronounced *chronic* - the point at which it becomes clear to the patient that his survival depends, henceforth, on hemodialysis - is usually the moment of financial truth. This is because an insistent new dimension has been added to the patient's life: he has entered into a partnership with a machine. Above all, the machine is a greedy and inexorable consumer of time and money.

The assessment of resources is not a simple, direct process. There is, on the one hand, the problem of what resources are available and, on the other, the matter of whether or not availability is perceived. Actual availability of specific funding sources is usually contingent upon criteria that define membership, either categorically ascribed of, based on voluntary association. Of the former, age is frequently a determinant. Persons under twenty-one, for example, may qualify for assistance from funds for crippled children; those selected for dialysis who are over sixty-five have access to Medicare. Groups may also provide funding possibilities: membership in group insurance plans, for example, or in religious and fraternal organizations. A sense of group responsibility often leads to united effort to raise funds to assist a stricken fellow member. Affiliation is useful in the struggle to stay alive.

While membership in particular categories or groups may give access to special funds, individuals are not necessarily aware of this. A general lack of coordinated information contributes to the overall sense of chaos that seems to pervade the funding of chronic renal failure. This is true of the scene in general as well as within specific organizations. Unions, for example, even though they may negotiate carefully formulated health insurance coverage, rarely, if ever, provide for trained personnel to interpret the terms of their policies for their individual members.

TREADING THE FUNDING MILL

Two major phases in the illness trajectory are each accompanied by special funding problems. These are an acute, or rescue period and a chronic, or prolonged maintenance period. Since the latter phase may extend over an entire lifetime, it will almost certainly be accompanied by a sequential depletion of funding sources - each failure initiating a new crisis propelling most patients into search for new funds.

Exhaustion of funds and the subsequent search for new sources is a condition of life for the patient. The ultimate available recourse, other than death, is to public funds. Such a solution, however, may be conditional upon the patient's being reduced to a literal state of pauperization,[2] an alternative desperately to be avoided as long as hope for a more dignified solution remains. As a result, fund-raising takes on the quality of running on a treadmill. A successful kidney transplant may seem the only real hope for escape. Such an escape, unfortunately, involves massive problems of its own, such as locating donors, the inevitable surgical risks, and the possibility of organ rejection. It is also an expensive procedure. If successful, there is hope for genuine relief at the economic as well as the physical level. If unsuccessful, the patient returns to the treadmill.

FUNDING THE RESCUE PERIOD

Although the costs of the rescue period will probably be higher than those of subsequent phases of the illness, the initial blow is typically cushioned by health insurance. It is estimated that approximately 80 percent of dialysis patients carry some sort of major medical coverage at the time of the onset of illness. However, health insurance policies are primarily geared to protect the insured against the cost of acute illness; they are rarely adequate for coping with the long-term financial drain associated with chronic illness.

One problem, however, is that the claimant may be simply and overwhelmingly ignorant about the terms of his insurance. It is a rare person who has the slightest idea what his insurance can, in fact, be expected to cover or what such coverage would mean, in any event, within the context of a specific illness trajectory. Nor does it seem possible that the situation could be otherwise. There is simply no way for the individual to be able to anticipate all eventualities and their consequences. Who, for example, could have guessed a few years ago that even "forever" might be barely adequate as a time stipulation? Yet this is only a slight overstatement of what has become a fact of life for thousands of victims of renal failure. Thus, a policy carrying a $20,000 liability limitation may seem, to the healthy, more than adequate to protect a family from the costs of even major illnesses. However, in the case of one young woman - a wife and mother - who was stricken with kidney failure, $13,000 of such a policy was consumed in less than four months and it covered, even so, only 80 percent of her overall medical expense. Thus, the family was already more than $2,000 out of pocket, the insurance was 65 percent depleted and there was still a lifetime of expense ahead which, for a woman of 27, might be expected to extend for upwards of fifty years. For this young and previously prospering family, a carefully planned insurance program literally melted away, carrying with it many of their hopes and plans for the future. Unfortunately this was not an unusual case. Among renal failure patients and their families, such experiences are common.

Ignorance of content is often accompanied by ignorance of procedure. For patients who are unfamiliar with the intricacies of bureaucratic paperwork or for those who are too sick to concern themselves with it, filling out the required forms according to prescribed time schedules may present an almost insurmountable problem.

In the whole "system," there seems to be no one, anywhere, assigned a role whose primary function is to help the patient understand and order his financial affairs strictly in accordance with his own needs and interests. The usual procedure followed by insured patients seems to be that of submitting claims on an ad hoc basis until such time as payment is refused. If refusal is based on a technicality, a running dispute with the company may ensue. If refusal is based on the fact that the company's liability is spent - that the source of funds is exhausted - a new crisis is precipitated. Although a crisis is often plainly foreseeable, rarely does one find a patient who has made any advance plans for dealing with it. "I just don't know what I'll do when the insurance runs out!" is a typical comment. This unpreparedness is undoubtedly because there are few - terrifyingly few - available options. The patient, helpless and bewildered, simply drifts into crisis, hoping that, when the point is reached, some solution sufficient unto the day will present itself.

PROLONGED MAINTENANCE FUNDING

In the prolonged maintenance period the patient's condition - physical and financial - has usually been somewhat stabilized. Although the problem of keeping the body chemistry in balance is never perfectly solved, the physical condition is basically under control and so there is some opportunity for predicting and planning the funding of future needs. However, the period is characterized by a series of funding crises.

How early and to what extent an individual will experience the treadmill effect of the prolonged maintenance period hinges on many contingencies.

Employment status is a major consideration. It makes a critical difference, for example, whether a patient is financially dependent, self-supporting, or the breadwinner for a family. Although there are problems associated with various financially dependent roles - the mother of a family, for example, often must make arrangements for long periods of child-care and her household tasks must somehow be accomplished when she, herself, is physically unable to cope with them - the greatest difficulty is usually occasioned when it is incumbent upon the afflicted person to earn a living.

This is because: (1) The time needed for dialysis may cut seriously into working hours. (2) Physical debility not only hampers productivity and overall efficiency but also limits the sorts of work that can be undertaken. Occupational careers that involve a considerable outlay of physical energy, or require extensive travelling, for example, may have to be abandoned. (3) It may be difficult to find any sort of suitable work since employment policies are frequently conjoined with insurance regulations that will, almost certainly, reject persons suffering from serious chronic disease.

Early retirement is a frequent solution among those whose age and seniority status permit them that alternative. The person who can retire on a pension and is qualified to receive help from Medicare is in a relatively good financial position, providing there are not extraneous complicating factors. Under other circumstances, however, retirement may be an extremely threatening matter. Take, for example, the plight of a man who had reached the compulsory retirement age but whose wife - twenty years his junior - was on hemodialysis that was being funded through his occupational insurance.

The issue of state financed medical help is fraught, in some states, with bitterness and altercation, and the financing of renal failure - because of its chronicity and its extraordinarily high cost - is a particularly touchy focal point. There are three sources of major dispute: welfare restrictions, governmental responsibility, and administrative red tape.

Welfare restrictions. To qualify for funds from MediCal, the patient (in a state like California) must divest himself of any personal property or income he may have in excess of that permitted to recipients of state welfare. The MediCal plan is apparently so designed in order to insure that the individual will not free-load at the taxpayers' expense - he will assume liability and share the cost of his illness. In operation it is like a deductible clause based on the patient's income. A single person, for example, with an income of $500 a month may be permitted a maintenance need allowance of $110 a month: income above that amount must be used for medical expenses before MediCal will intervene in his behalf. In addition, MediCal will not assist anyone who owns cash or property in excess of a value of $1,200 (personal dwelling excepted) and/or cash value of life insurance over $100 per dependent. Thus, if the patient has been fortunate enough or foresighted enough to provide some security for his family, he is expected to see to the dispersal of that security before he can apply to MediCal for the funds needed to save his life. Once reduced to the welfare level, there seems little likelihood that a patient can find the means to regain his independence.

To may patients and professionals, the situation seems not only unfortunate but contrary to American principles and goals. It is a commonly expressed fear that such prescriptions are generating a "welfare race" of persons who no longer have any incentive to self-help. There is also a prevailing sense of injustice that a victim of illness through no perceivable fault of his own should be thus reduced to such an apparently punitive plight.

Administrative red tape. The organization and distribution of state health care funds is apparently so tangled in a web of duplication, evasion, and conflicting purpose that the overall result is mass confusion. Presumably the out-growth of legislative ambivalence, the present situation seems to be characterized by overlapping jurisdiction, conflict of policy, bureaucratic shuffling of responsibility, and a general lack of coordination and accountability.

Loopholing. This is an informal device whereby officially proscribed actions may be unofficially redefined in terms that permit their accomplishment without open infraction of rules. There is considerable evidence to suggest that - even as exploitable loopholes - confusion and ambiguity at the state level inadvertently leaves gaps whereby patients may escape some of the more devastating effects of eligibility rulings.

Because loopholing must, of necessity, be evasive in method as well as in goal, it entails some special problems to dialysis patients. The medical staff or a case worker may point out the possibility of making "paper statements" that will indicate intent but may not be binding in actual commission. Such patterns of evasion are unlikely to be explicitly stated but will probably be couched, themselves, in evasive terms as a protection against the danger of legal and political repercussions.

...The social workers can't say right out what is going on. They have to hope the patients will catch on when they say things like, "Well, in your case I wouldn't worry too much." Once in a while, but not very often, they'll just come right out with it. But this is dangerous.

Awkwardness can stem from the fact that an individual who is unsophisticated in tactical looholing may overlook or misunderstand the functional possibilities embodied therein, or else be strongly offended by what he may view as fundamental impropriety. Some persons take looholing easily in stride, seeing it in the light of a sensible and innocuous business arrangement - like maneuvering all possible personal advantages from income tax regulations - or as a more-or-less empty ritualistic gesture: a mindless genuflexion. Others view it as simple dishonesty and suffer accordingly - either because desperation leads them to comply with evasionary tactics against the dictates of their scruples, in which case they suffer from the demeaning pangs of bad conscience, or because they do not, and bear in consequence the effects of financial anguish.

Looholing can sometimes be accomplished by making a change in legal status (a device not infrequently employed by the urban poor). For instance, a social worker remarked that:

> The husband, who was the patient, was in his fifties but he had a young family from a second marriage... It was a working class family: the mother had a job as a salesgirl and he was a garage attendant. When they applied for MediCal, the welfare guidelines for a family of their size were just impossible - if they kept their combined income they would be just working for the state. It was a total mess! Well, the upshot of the matter was that after he had been on dialysis for a month, the marriage broke up. They got a divorce. It was the only way to save the income...The woman continued to take care of him and was obviously very fond of him.

To be successful, looholing usually depends upon an alliance of various participants: patient, case worker, eligibility worker, for example. If these do not share understandings of need or definitions of loyalty the situation may dissolve into one of personal rancor and agency infighting, with counter attributions of bureaucratic inhumanity and fiscal irresponsibility being hurled back and forth, to the apparent benefit of no one.

The patient, having at this point in his funding career exhausted, in all likelihood, whatever meager resources he may have available to him, stands more or less helpless to act in his own behalf. He is like a prisoner at the bar waiting for the result of adversary action to decide his fate: a negative decision will condemn him to the humiliation and distress of ultimate financial wipeout.

Choosing death. Probably there is a significantly higher incidence of suicidal behavior among chronic renal failure patients than for the population at large, or even as compared with other chronic disease contexts. Suicidal behavior is his refusal to undergo or to cooperate in treatment with an intent to accomplish the same end.

Considerable attention has been directed to identifying the predisposing psychological factors that may contribute to the self-destructive impulse. Properties attributed to the patient - such as ego strength and self-esteem - have been defined and measured as independent variables controlling the suicidal tendency. Unresolved dependency conflicts have been posited as contributory - if not causal - factors in the suicidal despair of many renal failure patients, being directly related to the aggravating problem of machine bondage. Undoubtedly this is an important and authentic area of research and such findings are difficult - and perhaps, impossible - to refute. However, given the reality of the present, it does not seem always necessary to look - for motivation - to the past. Given, for example, the circumstances of financial treadmilling and its dread terminus of financial wipeout and hopeless economic dependency with inevitable concomitants of poverty, insecurity, erosion of personal autonomy and loss of privacy, such problems as may be related to machine dependency seem considerably diminished in importance.

Self-esteem and ego strength, moreover, are personal properties whose possession may contribute equally as well to a decision in favor of altruistic suicide as to a determination to live. The conditioning effect that circumstance and status can exert on the direction of personal decision is demonstrated in the following two examples. The first is as reported by the administrator of a dialysis center:

> There are lots of cases where patients just haven't showed up. Patients have been referred to private centers, say where they demand a deposit of $10,000, and they just toss in the towel. One man I know of personally - thirty- seven years of age with three children and $19,000 in the bank - elected to die. He was perfectly frank. He said if he went into treatment he would destroy his family.

Another patient - a twenty-two year old Asian, the father of two young children - faced a different situation and, in accordance with his perception of it, reached a different decision:

...The way I see it, I'm going to be in the hole all my life. I worry about bills. I worry about a change in the laws that will cut off what we're getting now. Most of my worry is money...It's my kids. They're forcing me to stay alive. I keep seeing myself caring for them until they're on their own. I imagine what it will be like for them if I die. They'll hardly have anything. My wife didn't even finish high school and she wouldn't be able to take care of them...They'd hardly get anything to eat, maybe. The thought keeps me going. I want to live...

In neither of these cases did the patient - by demeanor or behavior - manifest lack of self-esteem or neurotic fear of dependency. Opposite decisions were apparently reached according to real differences in external conditions.

RECOMMENDATIONS

There are a number of recommendations of varying degrees of practicability whose institution might somewhat alleviate the distress of chronic renal failure patients. These range from suggestions relating to comparatively minor readjustments to those of a scope that would require fundamental changes in policy and in administrative organization. For instance:

1) Since it is financially inexpedient to tie insurance reimbursement to requirements for in-service treatment, insurance carriers should abandon practices of outpatient stepchilding.

2) Unions should institute a policy of assigning specifically trained persons to the task of advising their members, on an individual basis, concerning the interpretation and execution of their insurance affairs.

3) Providers should work together to coordinate services in order to relieve expensive duplication and overlap that often result when efforts are basically competitive.

4) Dialysis centers should be operated on a twenty-four hour basis.

5) Health personnel should be trained in hemodialysis techniques in order to assist home care patients, if not on a regular, at least on an emergency basis.

6) Prepaid transportation service should be provided for center-based

patients: urban, suburban, and interurban.

7) Some relaxation should be made in insurance policies in order to encourage organizations and business to employ chronically ill individuals to the extent that the volition and physical capabilities of such persons allow them to work.

8) State health insurance policies and their administration should be reorganized: (a) to remove health care assistance from the restrictions of welfare eligibility rules; (b) to streamline administration by eliminating redundant, expensive, and absurd red-tape formalities; (c) to coordinate agency policies in such a way that providers can have some reasonable basis for predicting the time and extent of reimbursement for services rendered.

The implementation of any or all such suggestions would, almost certainly, bring some measure of relief to the individual patient. It would not, however, eliminate the basic problem and the crisis-to-crisis course of the funding process would continue with, at best, its pace slightly abated.

The basic problem is that the cost of preserving the life of the renal failure patient eventually exceeds the ability of any individual to pay for it - from his own pocket or from privately available resources. If he is to survive, therefore, the chances are that he must, in the end, be subsidized or supported by public funds. It is an eventuality that occurs through no fault of his own: He is not responsible for his illness; he is not to blame for the exorbitancy of its costs; there is virtually no way that, by exercise of proper character and foresight, he might have been able to stave off financial need. Yet he is subjected to restrictions that suggest that - in exchange for public help - he has incurred an expiatory obligation to live, together with his dependents, at a level of penitential poverty.

REFERENCES

1. Since the expense involved - both initial and ongoing - is in a state of flux and circumstantially variable, any estimate can only be a rough approximation. At this writing (1972) the figure for center-based care in California has been given at anywhere from $10,000 to $40,000 a year. This figure does not, in all likelihood, include professional fees. Home-based dialysis, subsequent to the training period, runs from $2,500 to $7,000 a year. (Items such as emergency hospital care, physical checkups, and the like, may be but are not necessarily included in these estimates. The fact that there is no generally agreed upon stipulation as to what items should be included in such a statement means that the figures are not usefully

comparable.) None of these estimates takes into consideration such subsidiary expenses as travel, nor loss of income due to impaired ability to work.

2. As probably in many states, in California recipients of medical and of welfare funds are legally bound by property restrictions. Severe limitations are placed on what can be owned and earned or collected from other sources of income. Existence can be maintained only at the poverty level. Ideologically oriented to discourage abuse of public funds by the lazy and unambitious, it is difficult to see how the stringency of such guidelines can possibly be construed as similarly useful in the case of the chronically ill.

CHAPTER 10

EXPRESSING AWE AND FADING OUT

Eleanor K. Maxwell

INTRODUCTION

This chapter is about deference, the expressed feeling of awe by modelees for their modelers, those persons who control all that is dear to other members of society. Deference activities are intended to convey respect or appreciation on the part of one person for another. The feeling of awe is explained, by those involved, in imprecise abstractions such as love, honor, duty, and responsibility. Deference seems to be related to influence. It may indicate the relative position of persons in terms of the ability to influence others in social situations. Those *expressing* awe usually occupy subordinate positions. In other words, they have less influence than those persons "receiving" deference. Deference consequently dramatizes and reinforces the relative social distance between persons. Deference may occur between individuals or groups. That is, it can be expressed in private relationships, i.e., between a modeler and his student, or alternatively it may reflect a social hierarchy between entire classes of persons within a society. Awe is expressed in a variety of contexts, some mundane - occurring on a daily basis, and others - ritual events which happen only infrequently. For example, younger people may serve the head of the household his meal first every day, or, perhaps they may give him a special seat by the fire which other family members avoid. Expressions of awe may be formal and programmed. It may be customary, for instance, that younger persons serve copy demonstrators first during a ritual meal following a ritual okaying ceremony. Any individual act of deference may seem insignificant. In the context of preparing, serving, and eating a meal, serving someone first may get little attention, but over the course of years patterns emerge in the expression of awe which tend to perpetuate themselves. If being served first is defined as "good," and the same person (the headman) is served first on a daily basis, others present at mealtime may eventually define the act as symbolic recognition of the headman's superior position. See Goffman (1956) and Silverman and Maxwell (1978) for further discussions of deference.

Chapter V is divided into three sections. In the first section I will discuss the properties of expressions of awe which are associated with positions of influence and model control. The second section is a discussion of the

163

conditions leading to a decline in expressed deference for "fading" modelers whose influence is diminishing. In the final section I will present the conditions which permit some sanctified modelers to remain influential forever and to continue to be honored by other members of society even after death.

AWE FOR INFLUENTIALS: DEFERENCE BEFORE FADING
PROPERTIES OF INFLUENTIAL DEFERENCE

A number of properties best describe the expressions of awe which modelees direct at influentials, modelers who are at the highest of their careers. Each of the properties is discussed below. The first three are discussed together because they are related to one another.

1. *Symbolic of achievement, rank and control of whatever is valued in society.*

2. *Given in expectation of contiued "good" displays.*

3. *Revokable*

Younger persons express awe for influentials in recognition of their achievements. Hunters and warriors who excel in their work may be honored because they embody societal importances. Non-influentials, envious of their heroes' good performances and wishing they could be good enough to copy them, show their modelers how much they appreciate them. If you were an elderly member of the Huron Indian Council you could expect other society members to honor you by inviting you to all the feasts. And, while you were there, you would probably be served the best portions of food (Tooker 1964:45,47). In addition, you would be given presents on several occasions: after successful battles, at ceremonial naming ceremonies, and whenever the entire community met to reassert loyalty to a shared model (Tooker 1964:34). Deference is also a means of giving symbolic recognition to "good copy" displays of a society's more abstract values. In Egypt younger persons give deference to members of the council of elders because they are "old," "experienced," "sober," and known for "hospitality." They may also happen to own land (Ammar 1954:66). But deference is given to influentials only as long as they continue to be good copy of their society's importances. Again, in Egypt, the extended family honors the oldest man, but if his abilities do not warrant making him a leader, the position and its associated prestige may go to someone else (Harris 1957:295). In less stable societies awe is revokable if the values within the society change. In Baganda, (Uganda) for instance, many symbolic acts of deference are no longer performed. Only in the more traditional households do men "crouch at the threshold of their father's house when they greet him after an absence and address him kneeling (Nahemow and Adams 1974:157).

Others are also likely to express awe for persons who are in close association with achievers, persons of high rank and others who embody importances. Wives of headmen and their children receive deference as a way of recognizing the positions of their husbands and fathers. In Trobriand villages old women who were married to high ranking men could attract good looking boys as lovers even when they themselves were quite ugly (Malinowski 1929:293). In our own society we honor the wives of politicians. And in both modern and traditional societies modelers may receive deference in association with the accomplishments of their modelees. Teachers and parents may be formally thanked or presented with gifts at a student graduation. In these instances deference is also revokable if the achiever's performance does not measure up to "good copy." A teacher gets little or no honor if his/her student fails. If the progress of a good student diminishes, respect shown his teacher is likely to decline as well.

Awe can also be expressed for entire echelons of persons of high rank in recognition of their influence and authority. The Trukese [Micronesia] provide a good example of "age-graded" deference. As in all age-graded deference, expressions of awe in this instance come from below. A lower age grade honors a higher, more experienced, one. Younger Trukese age-groups are supposed to show respect to older ones in proportion to the distance between them. If a gang of men is working together, the members of the younger age groups start the work out of respect for the older men. . The older age group always expects the men in the youngest group to run errands as well when they are away from home (Goodenough 1967:164).

4. *Expressions of awe for influentials are normatively structured.*

Expressions of awe for influentials tend to be obligatory. They are structured by customs and laws. In describing expressions of respect which Trukese display before their elders Goodenough used terms like "custom required," "the youngest is obligated," "the oldest must be consulted," and the like (Goodenough 1967:74-75, 145). The customs and laws associated with expressions of deference usually reflect the distance between ranking individuals in society. The normative structure may thus reflect the pacing of modelees in the modeling labyrinth. In any event there are rules followed by custom which are associated with the expression of influential deference. Most or all persons in the community are familiar with them. The coffeehouse is the center of activity in many Egyptian villages. Marriages are arranged there, news is disseminated, commercial transactions are made there and the like. Probably all social affairs and intricacies of village politics are discussed in the coffeehouse.

The oldest and most valued customer is in effect chairman, and he is surrounded by others whose *seniority and persona force* have given them the prestige to take their place as leaders and judges in the coffeehouse area. These men regularly occupy the same seats - which according to custom are strictly reserved for them - and should one of these seats be the only empty chair in the house no stranger or comparative newcomer would be allowed to sit in it (Harris 1957:289; my italics).

Expressions of deference for influentials involve the fear of negative sanctions for model violators. Malinowski had written of the Trobrianders that "when a chief is present, no commoner dares to remain in a physically higher position; he has to bend his body or squat. Similarly, when a chief sits down, no one would dare to stand (Malinowski 1966:52; see also Whitehead 1924:222 [Nicobarese]; Goodenough 1967:145 [Trukese] and Latta 1949:75 [Yokuts, California Indians])." Structured rank also enables some influentials to order their own expressions of awe. Trobriand chiefs can ask their subjects even beyond their own villages to work for them when they want something done (Malinowski 1966:63). Tallensi chiefs similarly expected special portions of food from any animal found dead or slain. If they didn't get their lot there were stringent ritual sanctions applied to would-be violators (Fortes 1940:258).

Even when structured expressions of awe are not requested they tend to occur routinely and without spontaneity. Some are so obvious that outsiders can readily learn the relative social position of a group of society members after watching deference expressions for only a few days. Such would be possible in Rural Japan. In the village of Niiike, there is a limited amount of water available for bathing. At the end of the day Japanese families all over the village line up by their respective homes to bathe. The members of each family have to share their bath water with other family members. The order of bathing is rigidly adhered to. Old men, the heads of households, always bathe first (Beardsley, Hall, and Ward 1959:88).

5. *Exaggerated modelers' expertise.*

Expressions of awe for influential modelers may exaggerate the expertise of modelers. Less influential members of society may let modelers "get away with things" that would be unacceptable if attributed to other members of society. In Russia, for instance, younger persons are not allowed to criticize the state. But older people whose performances are otherwise exemplary, are permitted to "speak quite frankly about the shortcomings of the socialist state." They are also given other liberties (McKain 1972:164). Influentials can take advantage of this "blown up" deference given by modelees who feel their modelers are "too good" to work. They may encourage or at least come to expect less influential people to do their work for them. Feelings of awe occasionally blind people. Society members may not notice the limitations of their modelers who are associated with "good performances." Or if they do notice them, they would not dare to acknowledge them. Aged Aleut modelers occasionally become senile. As they gave advice to their students or told them about society legends "sometimes failing memory would cause the old preceptors to repeat over and over again the same advice or legend in the course of a lecture. The respect of the children, however, never allowed or occasioned an interruption (Elliot 1886:170-171)." Because modelers are influential in so many situations society members may come to respond to them as if they were superior in all realms. A Russian child may therefore ask her grandparents' opinion about what type of hair ribbon she should wear and then will defer to their judgment. The child *knows* that grandparents give the best advice (McKain 1972:155).

The diffuse belief that modelers know everything increases their ability to influence others. In some instances it grants them the ability to adopt new model importances. Consider the well-known example about Queen Victoria and the telephone. For years the telephone was considered a toy and was not used by the masses. When Queen Victoria installed one in her palace the attitude of the public changed. People felt that if the telephone was good enough for their modeler, the Queen, then it must be good enough for them.

6. *Influence and Awe are linked in a circular manner.*

Modelers are influential people because they are in control of all that is valued in their respective societies. Less influential society members express awe because of their modelers' expertise, knowledge, and authority. Younger persons reward modelers for their good copy demonstrations. A good hunter, for instance, may become Chief. His hunting reputation may then attract members to his group. Successful hunting breeds recognition in the form of other tribesmen who are anxious to join a Chief's hunting group. In addition, others may give gifts to the Chiefs. Property and a large hunting group may then add to a Chief's influence. In simple terms, he may influence more people with his increased wealth. This is the case with Haida Chiefs of the Northwest coast. They become chiefs because of their superior performances as hunters and warriors. Later, other Haida gave them gifts in recognition of their accomplishments. Each man had to give the Chief one slave captured by a war party. The actual influence among Haida chiefs varied with the amount of property at their disposal (Swanton 1904:55;69). The Kaska Indians also chose headmen for their good performances as hunters. Like the Haida chiefs, they consequently accumulated wealth and prestige. In order to further awe Kaska tribesmen with his influence, a Kaska headman will give away some of his wealth to other members of the tribe (Honigmann 1954:84-85). Kaska headmen demonstrate their influence by displaying their ability to give property away and help others.

CONTROLLING MODEL PROPERTY AND DEFERENCE

I have already mentioned that modelers awe other members of society by controlling things that are valued by others. Model property is often "owned" or controlled by modelers who then receive some expressions of awe whenever they are in control of valuable model property; the expressions vary according to how other community members define the property that is controlled by the modelers. Property definitions are related to how readily control over property changes hands. That is to say, when a modeler controls property and that control will eventually pass on to someone else with nominal effort or no effort at all, deference for the current property owner will be defined differently than when the controller's property may never, in fact, be transferred to other community members. There seem to be four patterns of property control and transfer which are related to the modeling process and particularly to the way community members define expressions of awe. They are listed in order of decreasing constraints on the willfulness of the modeler:

1. *Model property is symbolic of model importances shared by the community as a whole.* The property is controlled by a sanctified keeper who embodies the importances the property represents. Sanctified keepers may control such property for life or until such time that they no longer may be defined as "good copy" of their society's importances. Modelers who control such property receive deference from other community members who are as much in awe of their own system of importances as they are of

the sanctified keeper who takes care of the property for them. Deference performed for sanctified keepers is related to fencing. All members of society who share the importances represented by the property honor their keeper by giving him/her special portions of food, giving him/her special seats at community gatherings and quite often by excusing sanctified keepers from adhering to "taboos" which are observed by others "inside the fence." Deference in this condition honors model importances (i.e., serves the community rather than an individual) and it is sometimes difficult to determine whether it is initiated by other society members or the modelers themselves.

2. *Model property is symbolic of the relationships between a modeler and his modelees.* The property represents shared importances. It is held "in trust" for the modelees. That is, the modelee ordinarily receives it automatically. Other community members know who will eventually inherit the property and they expect the property transfer to occur. Property transfers are normatively structured. In this condition deference may be private, that is between a modeler and his modelee. A modelee honors his mentor who together with his property represents the personal control that the modelee will one day assume. If the modelee abides by model importances little will interfere with his success in gaining control. He may be certified to take over control of the property at a prearranged time and truly appreciates his modeler for making things so easy for him. With this pattern of property transfer there are also some public expressions of awe between modelee and modeler. For example, if a family head and his son appear at a village council a son may express awe for his father as a way of demonstrating loyalty to his family model. Modelers may also work for their modelees to express their appreciation. Such arrangements are private between a modeler and the person who will eventually "inherit" his property. But, should the demands of modelers be excessive, that is should they violate the structured norms for property succession, other community members may step in to correct the relationship.

3. *Property is symbolic of model importances which a modeler shares with a modeler or potential modeler.* The modeler exercises considerable control over the passing on of property. The property is not "held in trust" for the modelee. He may earn the modeler's affection and thus gain control over some of the property, but such a result is in no way guaranteed. The modelee emulates the modeler in this condition. He desires the certification of his role model and attempts to earn such certification with expressions of awe. Modelees express awe of their modelers both in private and in public.

Publicly, modelees attempt to gain public certifications of the relationship between modeler and modelee. Occasionally there is some structure to property transfer in this condition. For instance, a would-be bridegroom may work for his potential father-in-law in the hope of winning his daughter and a piece of the father's property.

4. *Property is a symbol of the distance between classes of society members.* The property is a symbol of the importances shared by a "privileged" class and is controlled by a member of that class. Transfer of property to someone of a "lower" class is quite rare and is solely at the discretion of the current controller. In this condition, deference may be coercive. Modelees learn the importances of their modelers by force. They "honor" and serve their modelers in order to maintain at least their current positions. This pattern is characteristic of the relationship between master and slave. Among the Gilbertese it was customary for the aristocrats to request the use of one or two plots of coconut land from the Elder of the commoner ramage (Lambert 1963:265). Usually the aristocrats were obliged. I do not wish to give the impression that modelees of lower classes never truly "respect" their higher class modelers. This is certainly not the case. I just wish to imply that there is always some element of coercion in these modeler/modelee relationship.

FADING OUT

I have just discussed the properties of expressing awe for influential modelers who are in control of several aspects of a society's model. I will now turn in the second section of this chapter to a discussion of the conditions under which a modeler's influence is changed, and expressions of awe are lessened and perhaps cease all together, a process which I am calling "fading out." Fading is a process in which the power and influence of modelers is gradually neutralized. Fading, we shall see, occurs when the model itself is devalued (i.e., when a society experiences an obvious period of social change) or when the performances of former modelers are devalued. I will also discuss some of the reasons that society members give for devaluing modelers, directing attention both to the substance of the content and to its structure, as revealed in a multiple regression analysis. Next I will assume a developmental perspective and view the process of fading from the point of view of an individual who is, first as a child, in awe of his modelers (who would not be in awe of persons wielding so much influence), then a more or less eager copier of his modelers, and finally as someone who has in some sense equalled them or - worst of all -

"outgrown" them. Finally, I will discuss the relationship between the variable contents of model values on the one hand and the process of fading out on the other. It should become clear that certain values promote the display of deference towards aging persons regardless of the amount of awe they generate in an audience of juniors. For instance, deference towards the aged, even - or perhaps especially - the socially bankrupt aged, provides younger adults with an opportunity to display how "good" they are by treating the helpless with consideration. Paradoxically, some model contents encourage an attitude of contempt towards the elderly although, by definition, this means that those who adhere to the model will someday be treated contemptuously themselves.

DEVALUING THE MODEL

If fencing strategies were working perfectly it would be unlikely that a society's model would be devaluated. In stable societies (i.e., societies not experiencing "change"), most models remain relatively stable. Small changes are accepted with varying degrees of difficulty and most members of society believe that the traditional way of doing things is the best way. This relatively stable state is typical of small communities, so we have little data on model devaluation because most of the societies we have studied were not undergoing great change at the time ethnographers studied them. Models tend to be devaluated, or at least some of the content is devaluated, when isolating techniques prove ineffective. Change comes when gaps in the fence permit society members' gradual exposure to other models. Often the first exposure to other value systems is through the visit of missionaries who bring Bibles into the community. In other instances itinerant specialists arrive who bring to the community news from the outside. Little by little modelees recognized alternative ways of life and varying paths which seem to lead to success. Options that heretofore had not existed within the community enter the realm of possibility. Modelees may begin to see themselves as "fenced in." Perhaps they try to seek more information - maybe search for modelers who will take them on "magical mystery tours" on which they may learn about life outside the boundaries of their own communities. Maybe some society members will themselves become itinerant specialists gaining exposure to other models. Much of this is speculative as movement from traditional stable societies to slightly less stable and more modern ones was not the focus of this research. The data we do have seem to indicate that, at least initially, elements gleaned from foreign models are blended with traditional value systems wherever appropriate. The traditional model importances do not disappear immediately to be replaced with others as the information becomes available. Barriers to change are much too strange for this. The traditional way of doing things has proved workable for far too long a period. Instead, those elements of other models which may support a society's values are first incorporated into the traditional model. Only repeated exposure leads to one set of traditional values fading out and the adoption of other values that prove to "work" better or offer a community new options. Harris reports that an Egyptian peasant is able to "mingle the articles of his Moslem faith with the far more ancient belief in the Evil Eye, and the good or bad spirits called jinns...Protection from evil is provided by amulets not part of the Moslem faith, consisting of little scrolls on which a verse or two of the Koran has been written (1957:332)." This process, the blending of an internal model with one or more outside models, has been called syncretism. Fortes describes syncretism among the Tallensi with an almost unbelievable sense of optimism.

> By simple compromise they make the best of both worlds, the old world of strictly defined local, genealogical, and politico-ritual exclusiveness and the new world of free movement, unrestricted social intercourse with all and sundry, and cheaper clothes. They wear the ancient prescribed garb of a skin and a loincloth on ritual occasions, especially during the Great Festivals, when they take a pride in advertising their politico-ritual status. This change of custom does not cut athwart the basic values and principles of Tale social organization (Fortes 1969:25).

I remain unconvinced that members of society universally "make the best of two worlds." Moreover, there are certain consequences of "syncretism" which are not beneficial to modelers who remain "fenced in" or loyal to the traditional way of doing things. These modelers may be devalued in their societies by younger people who are anxious to move on to new things. Has-been modelers may be labelled "old-fashioned."

In 1972, Donald Cowgill and Lowell D. Holmes published their theory on "modernization" and the status of the aged. Researchers before them (Bendix 1968) and (Dore 1969) had defined modernization in terms of modeling, one country copying the model of another country which was usually "more advanced." The research of Cowgill and Holmes was based on a comparative study of aging in 15 countries at varying stages of modernization. Cowgill and Holmes concluded that the status of the aged declined considerably with the degree of modernization. In their book and in a later revision of the theory published by Cowgill (1974), modernization was defined in terms of social change, mobility, urbanization, technological development, and the like.

Without really examining the content and change of societal values, Cowgill and Holmes noticed the ultimate consequences of this "melange of developments" for older people. Cowgill commented particularly on "the emergence of many new specialized occupations":

> One of the most firmly established principles of demography is that the most mobile members of society are its youth. It is they who are attracted by new frontiers including the job frontiers of the city. It is they who take the new jobs and acquire the training to fill them, leaving their parents behind both geographically and socially. Generally speaking the new occupations carry greater rewards in both money and status. Consequently there is an inversion of status, with children achieving higher status than their parents instead of merely moving up to the status of their parents as in most pre-modern societies. This not only leaves the parents in older, less prestigious, perhaps static and sometimes obsolete positions, it also deprives them of one of the most traditional roles for older people - that of providing vocational guidance and instruction to their children (Cowgill 1974:131).

With the process of modernization, almost by definition, comes great change in the content of model importances. The change comes gradually as new information is accumulated. The best way of doing everything is no longer the traditional way. The aging members of society are no longer guaranteed positions as influentials. Some aged persons are influential - others are not. Influence is still largely associated with control over model property and importances which, in turn, is associated with experience. But the experience of the elderly is now not more likely to be relevant than that of younger people. If the position occupied by an older person is devalued because of changing model values, or he is replaced in the work force by a younger person who is more amenable to change, "whatever prestige and honor (psychic income) was ascribed to [his former] position fades (Cowgill 1974:130)."

As a whole, generally older people make out better in traditional, non-modern, stable societies because many do retain superior knowledge and expressions of awe based on the recognition of their superior power. Nevertheless, the positions of most modelers also "fade" along with their influence, as younger members of society learn to copy them and take over as society leaders. We will now take a look at the process of fading out in traditional societies.

FADING MODELERS

Fading in stable traditional societies is a process in which the influence of aging modelers is gradually diminished, recast, and ultimately neutralized. As modelers fade, others alter the expressions of awe performed in their behalf.

The diminishing of influence occurs along several dimensions, of which four are particularly important. One dimension is physical, having to do with the modeler's body, and involves a gradual loss of strength, of virility, and of fertility. A second dimension has to do with physical appearance, a third with the ability to communicate effectively with others, and a fourth with the loss of such resources as wealth, kinsmen, and information.

It should also be noted that many performances by modelers are public copy demonstrations subject to judgment by others. As prominent as these performances are in the life of the community, signs of fading of any of the four dimensions are likely to be noticed. Fading itself generally seems to begin with a performance that is not up to the society's standards for its modelers, more often than not precipitated by a decline in physical strength.

These dimensions, of course, are dynamically related to one another, and they proceed at uneven rates. Commonly, a decline in good copy occurs in the physical aspect of a modeler's performance. He can no longer do his job so well. When this occurs, his appearance, which may be grizzled, and his grooming, which may be out of date, may be remarked upon, whereas they may have been overlooked had he been able to continue doing his job. Sometimes he becomes bad copy in his ability to communicate with others. His voice grows feeble and quavering and ultimately his ability to reason declines. The elderly modeler, then, loses his ability to do his job, his capacity for looking good to others, and then even his ability to tell stories about what he used to do. The fourth dimension, his control over resources, may mitigate the rate at which his fading occurs.

Ordinarily, modelers control varying amounts of resources. These become important as the modelers themselves begin to fade out. In order to maintain their current levels of influence, modelers put their resources to work for them. These resources, controlled all along, are now deployed and exchanged for services and other expressions of awe. For instance, if an elderly man owns land, he may give it up to another in order to continue exercising influence over him, the process being similar to that of a hand of bridge in which, as the game draws to a close, the elderly modeler begins to play his highest trump cards which have been carefully held in reserve. Of course, there are only so many trumps in a deck of cards. And as the elderly modeler continues to give up his control over resources - selling his property, giving away information on secret hunting grounds - his resources are gradually depleted.

Most often, however, modelers do not live long enough to lose everything they "own." It has been noted that kinsmen serve as a resource, for example, and one's children generally outlive him, so that, throughout his decline in later life, he can depend to some extent upon his kinsmen to serve at least as a semblance of objects for influence. The corollary to this, of course, is that - to the extent that you lack such close kinsmen as offspring - you may be in trouble.

Among the Tiv, "old people are often cared for in their senility by children, usually their grandchildren or great-grandchildren...young men who show extraordinary knowledge of Tiv life...spent several years of their youth caring for a grandfather (Bohannan and Bohannan 1966:447)."

A few additional notes should be made on control over resources which may serve as a buffer against the loss of influence and expressions of deference. The first is that some of the resources already mentioned such as money, land, and children, are rather obvious in that a person who exercises control over such resources - that is, a person who is rich or who comes from a large family - will fade at a slower rate. For example:

An old [Russian] mother lived with her son part of the time and gave the family the use of her land allotment. The addition of the mother's-in-law allotment increased the land available to the family by more than 50%, whereas it would seem that her presence during the winter did not increase its consumption of food by anything like that amount (Dunn and Dunn 1967:53).

And similarly, in the case of the Trukese of Micronesia:

The practice is to make [a gift] of most of one's property to one's children...As a man gets older and is no longer vigorous he continues to receive his share of the produce while the responsibility for working and maintaining the property rests with his children. [The gift] thus constitutes a sort of old age insurance and gives legal sanction to the dependence of the aged on their children (Goodenough 1967:46).

Putting this rather bluntly, of course, wealth "buys" influence both at home and in the political arena. Among the Somali (Northeast Africa), "a rich elder does not lack a friendly hearing for his opinions from his less well-off kinsmen, and can usually rely on their support for his views in lineage affairs (Lewis 1961:197."

However, as we have suggested, information which is personally controlled by the modeler may also serve as a buffer against fading. An aged person may forget certain things, in which case the information is lost to himself and to anyone else. But he may also "lose" some information by giving it to someone else. For example, if an aged Tlingit tells someone where the best berry patch is to be found, two persons will then know where to find the berries. One loses some of the control over resources which are made accessible to others. The personal control of secret information such as this in Tlingit life is not to be underestimated. Here, as in other societies which have until recently been without written archives, what is remembered is capable of being shared, and is more or less valuable.

A second point is that resources are not always worth what they appear to be worth. A great deal depends upon the way others rate one's resources. It may be customary that a son in a particular society values the land his father owns. A father may thus expect his son to appreciate his land being turned over to him. But if circumstances lead the son to feel differently, the old man may not be able to effectively use his land as a resource, something which leads to variations in fading out within a community in which elders all seem to control similar resources. Among the Gilbertese, for instance:

> It is customary for an old man or woman to leave rights to a plot of land or crytosperma pit to a distant kinsman who nursed him or her. This rule does not always work to the advantage of the elderly and neglected parent, since outsiders may be reluctant to bring him food lest they be regarded as land grabbers (Lambert 1963:172).

And, of course, when the loss of control over resources such as children combines with fading along any of the other dimensions, such as physical health, the results may be devastating. Here, differences within communities in the rates of fading may depend partly upon the luck of the draw, as among the Lepcha, who live in communities in the Himalaya:

> As a man's sons grow up and become capable adults in their turn he is able to withdraw somewhat from work; if he is intelligent he is a

yuem-bu - a man who knows - and as such will often be asked for his advice by the Mandal and his juniors. If he retains health and prosperity as he grows older, and if his children and grandchildren are still alive he acquires a sort of talismanic virtue: younger men will take valuable presents to so fortunate an old man in order to get in return either his drinking cup or his rosary and to share a meal of rice with him, in order to acquire the desirable qualities in these prosperous great-grandfathers. But if an old man survives his children and loses his capacity for work his position is an unenviable one; he too, like the child, consumes more than he produces; he is a nuisance, not respected or listened to...(Gorer 1938:280).

What happens ultimately, when all control of resources has been lost, and when fading has reached its null point along the other three dimensions, is that the unfortunate modeler trades the only thing he has left - his inherent dignity - in return for simple custodial care.

If a modeler feels that his or her strength is weakening or that it will be otherwise difficult to perform, the modeler may elect to certify a successor to take over more strenuous tasks. Succession to the position of "head of the household" is frequently achieved this way. Among the Trukese, a provisional title holder who feels that he is unable to continue working his property, may state that he is through with it and then it is reallocated to someone else (Goodenough 1967:42).

This process of yielding positions of influence need not be abrupt. Usually when a modeler begins to lose the capacity to perform adequately, other members of the community will assume some of the person's tasks. This may at first be on a temporary or part-time basis. Someone may substitute for another who is ill - or who just doesn't want to work so strenuously. Insensibly, and with the passage of time, the modeler gives up these duties entirely. This is the process as it appears among the Kaska of Western Canada (Honigmann 1949:59). If the elderly modeler shows reluctance to recognize his disability or, recognizing it, refuses to yield his position, the process of replacing him in his tasks with others may be initiated by other members of the community. Characteristically, when a modeler has had influence in a variety of spheres, including certifying others, his capacity for certifying others is one of the last to be lost. But as the process of loss continues, his sphere of influence is continually diminished, he becomes dependent on others, and his sense of "independence," which may or may not have been strong in the first place, is weakened.

It may be worth mentioning that this diminution of influence is, in any case, different from the sort of role loss characteristic of "disengagement" (Cummings and Henry) in that it involves a specialization of influence rather than a cutting off of irreplaceable social ties. That is, although we have discussed fading so far as if it were nothing more than a loss of already existing influences, what seems to be happening in effect is that influence is being in a sense refocused, a point to which we shall return in a moment. At the same time, however, fading out does have in common with disengagement the fact that it is partly self-initiated, since fading modelers often voluntarily give up the burden of their responsibilities.

As I have suggested, there are dual changes occurring to a modeler's influence over others and over the course of his own affairs: a more or less gradual diminution, on the other hand, and a refocusing or recasting of influence, on the other. So far I have discussed some of the ways in which a modeler's influence is diminished. Now I will turn to an examination of the ways in which remaining influence is recast.

It should be noted, first of all, that fading modelers do not "retire." They tend to stay very much involved in community and household affairs, although their activities necessarily become limited by the extent of their physical strength and other capabilities. Among the Fon of Dahomey, for instance, "the elderly members of a village can usually be found helping the younger robust fellows by doing such tasks as their strength permits (Herskovits 1938:63)."

And if an elderly Tiv does not wish to assume all of the responsibilities of a leadership position he may turn the compound headship or a government position over to a son or brother, who then performs most of the tasks. The elderly person may actually keep the title to the formal position, however, and on important ritual occasions, he may resume his duties, during which time his "successor" must follow his instructions (Bohannan and Bohannan 1966:447). Similarly, the head of a Japanese family will turn over the running of his farm to his son. The son will receive the title of household head, but the father remains actively involved in the day-to-day running of the farm. And his son always consult him before decisions are made (Beardsley et al. 1959:220). Among the Japanese, as elsewhere, elderly modelers move gradually from positions as "doers" to positions as "advisors" and "consultees". This change consists in their no longer performing but, instead, talking about performing, and correcting the performances others give. This behavior may range in importance from the very significant and formal to a more or less continual grumbling about how ill-mannered today's youth are.

In addition to these things, elderly modelers continue to contribute the resources over which they have control - wealth, wisdom, subordinate kinsmen for labor, and the like - something we have discussed before as a result of lessening influence, but which can be seen equally well as a recasting of influence, as a shift from doing to providing.

In summary, then, elderly modelers do not retire in any formal sense. Instead, they help with tasks as long as their strength permits. They give up responsibilities but keep their formal titles, move into advisory positions, and contribute what resources they can, all of which recasts their influence but maintains strong continuity with their past positions.

One common indication that the fading process is taking place is that the position of a modeler becomes ambivalent. On the one hand, the modeler's new responsibilities seem to be "dirty" or at least unattractive. On the other hand, there is usually something inherently "good" abut the task, good in the sense that the task at least symbolically demonstrates loyalty (perhaps even submission) to the model of the society. And it may be that fading modelers whose positions are in question have to go out of their way to seem "useful" in order to maintain some degree of influence. Ambivalence is a property characteristic of all positions which are "marginal" in terms of status. Women, incidentally, seem to occupy more marginal positions than men, particularly in the community itself, which, unlike the household, is less frequently their material arena. Perhaps it is for this reason that they are less commonly involved in community-wide public disputes, standing instead for such virtues as faith, loyalty, and stability, going out of their way, so to speak, to stand for such virtues. An example comes from the Havasupai, a small Indian group who live at the bottom of the Grand Canyon. Once a year the villages have a rain dance. Almost everyone runs out to the center of the village and most who go seem to enjoy themselves. But a few of the old women stay at home and tend the sick. "Tending" is really little more than enhancing the patients' comfort - fanning, shading, and so on (Spier 1928:261). It is not clear that the Havasupai view "tending" as dirty, nor do the data indicate that the elderly women are assigned the task of baby sitters simply to exclude them from the dance. Still, it seems interesting that no one else volunteers to miss the dance. In other societies, women perform acts which are not only "dirty" but dangerous as well. Among the Yanomamo of South America, for instance, women are sent to the battlefield to retrieve the decaying bodies of slain warriors. The women are believed to be immune from contamination that would affect other community members if they came in contact with the enemy or the dead (Chagnon 1968).

This immunity from contamination is related to another point about fading modelers, namely that they may be endowed with certain ill-defined spiritual qualities. As their influence is recast, elderly modelers may come more and more to represent sacred beings. But although spiritual attributes allow one to help others - as many modelers become sanctifiers late in life - the new positions are acquired when one loses one's physical prowess. The change is associated with a loss of virility and fertility, as has been discussed in the previous chapter. Additionally, it follows that with this enhanced spirituality, they may be feared for their capacity to do evil, as well. An example of the spiritual properties of elderly modelers is found among the Zuni of the American Southwest:

> The mother's hot drinks have been prepared by the baby's paternal grandmother. She, too, has kept the sand-bed hot, as well as the stone pressed to the mother's abdomen, and she has given the baby a daily bath. In return for these services [she] will receive meat and breads and *he'paluke*, wheat meal cooked in corn husk. On the morning of the eighth day, before sunrise, [she] comes to take mother and child outdoors to present the child to the sun. The grandmother sprinkles meal on the ground and prays [to the sun] (Parsons 1919:169).

The recasting of influence differs for men and women. This, of course, reflects the original difference in their spheres of influence. Male modeling influence is more likely to be found at the community level; women modelers are more likely to be influential within the household. Modeling influences thus correspond to the basic divisions within the society by sex and labor.

During fading, men change in that they become more influential in the household and less influential in the community. In the community, they may shift from doers to advisors. At home, perhaps because they now spend more time there, they exert their authority as household heads, much to the occasional annoyance of the women.

On the other hand, female influence fades at the household level and may actually increase at the level of community. Women may begin to assume positions in the community, though these positions may be ambivalent ones. Their influence at home fades as they are replaced by younger women. There, they may become advisors rather than doers.

The ranges in respective spheres of influence for men and women are related to the care of children. Older men, more active at home, having given up some of their activities in the community, are less busy than before and they therefore have more time to spend with children. Older women, too, may have more time to spend with children as their heavier household chores are assumed by younger women. Since both men and women mow spend more time with young children, they are likely to become more influential over them, a process which probably lends added stability and continuity to social life.

In Korea, for instance, "As she becomes a grandmother her situation eases. She shifts off responsibilities and duties on to her daughter-in-law and does less work about the house, even before her strength begins to fail. She often takes up smoking and spends hours with the babies (Rutt 1964:185)."

Consequently, a kind of generation gap occurs. The offspring of elderly modelers are losing some of their awe of their parent's generation, as they see that they can assume their positions. But the third generation, the children who are currently being influenced by elderly modelers, continues to be in awe of their elders, appreciative for all of the information given to them by their grandparents. And they are closer to their grandparents, who seem willing to teach them, while their own parents may be too busy. In some cases, no doubt, these alternate generations are drawn to one another by the presence of a common enemy. The gap between generations occurs partly because the children are taught the values of the grandparents, not the values of their parents. If these values conflict, the child is more likely to opt for the path indicated by his grandparents. This importance of grandparents is well illustrated in the data from Russia:

The grandmother is the pillar of Soviet society; she does the time-consuming shopping, acts as cook (with the man and wife of the family away at work), she baby sits, and her monthly pension contributes to the family income. If the parent is cross or uncomprehending, it is the granny who comforts the child and explains to it why parents must sometimes be so. And especially it is the granny who tells the fairy stories...Today in the Soviet family, she has become an institution, performing desperately needed functions in young households where both parents are working...She will lavish her love upon the children, regard it as her duty and privilege to instruct them in the lore and legends of her culture and if possible try to kindle in their hearts a small undying spark of religious faith (Mace and Mace 1963:262-63).

Elsewhere, we learn that:

Obedience and esteem for the aged are taught very early in life. Grandparents are a fixture in most homes and often look after the children while their parents are at work. The earliest readers in grammar school invariably contain stories that illustrate the importance of respect for older persons. Along with respect...goes love, for grandparents and other older persons are able to devote huge blocks of time to youngsters (McKain 1972:154).

We have observed that the influence of fading modelers can be seen as a dual process, one in which influence lessens in an overall sense, and at the same time is recast so that it takes a different form. We have viewed the processes rather strictly from the point of view of the activities of the elderly modeler. Here, we will turn to an examination of the same processes seen from the perspective of the other members of society. We will see not so much the change in influence, but the change in deference which accompanies it. Changes in deference involve the same dual process: deference is lessened overall, and at the same time it is recast into other forms.

First we will discuss diminished deference, which may occur in its simplest form when modelers are ignored and their influence is neutralized. This process of ignoring elders is to some extent inevitable as they assume more passive roles in the community, but they are by no means entirely disregarded in any given community. They are always paid some modicum of attention.

Generally speaking, however, as the contributions of elderly modelers to social life diminish, so does the awe in which they are held. This is particularly true with respect to their current contributions; the contributions which they have made in the past may be weighty indeed, and the deference they receive for past deeds may compensate to some degree from their current diminished status. This remains true even though the elderly themselves may be considered nuisances.

And they may become nuisances. Indeed, this seldom happens because most elderly modelers either do not live so long or else they continue to retain enough control over some model resources to exert at least some minimal influence over others. But as their physical stamina wanes, the children of fading modelers may begin to weigh the contributions of their parents - both past and present - against the effort it now takes to care for them. Older persons may need to remind younger people, perhaps using guilt trips of all the past contributions made in the hope of tipping the scales in their own favor. This reminding becomes increasingly important as their resources wane. Ultimately, as we have already mentioned, in return for simple custodial care, the fading modeler who is otherwise without resources, may be forced to exchange his inherent dignity, a point which is racked in the almost total loss of power to awe others.

To the extent that fading modelers can contribute to the well-being of the community, they will continue to be recognized for their contributions. But should a time come when they have little or nothing to contribute, when the scales say that they have become a burden, they may find themselves the recipients of expressions of contempt, replacing the displays of awe "laid on them" in the past. Junod describes what can happen to an aged Thongan [South African tribe] who has become a "bad example":

The man however grows older, older. His hair and his beard turn white, the wrinkles deepen on his face. He stoops. His skin no longer shines with health and corpulence. His wives die and his glory fades. His crown loses the lustre of bygone times. If a branch scratches it, if a knock spoils it, he has not a shilling to pay the repairer! He is forsaken. He is less respected and often only a burden unwillingly supported. The children laugh at him. If the cook sends them to carry to lonely grandfather his share of food in his leaky old hut, the young rascals are capable of eating it on the way and of depriving the old man of his meal, afterwards pretending that they have done what they were told! And when, between huts, under the shelter of the hedge of reeds...huddled there, quite weighed down by his years, lost in some senile dream, they point to the decrepit form and say to each other: *"Het Shikhunkunun!"* - "It is the bogeyman, the ogre" (Junod 1962:132)!

The tremendous amount of data accumulated during this study allows us to shift gears for awhile and to examine *quanititatively* the reasons given by members of a society for expressing contempt for fading modelers. Eight patterned explanations of contempt emerged from the ethnographies. Some of the explanations, you will see, correspond to the "loss of resources" discussed in the previous pages. The explanations and their frequency of occurrence follow: *lack of physical skill and stamina* (presented as a reason for expressing contempt of fading modelers in 23 of the 95 societies which we studied); acquiring an *unpleasant physical appearance* (15 cases); *senility* or lacking communicational skills (12 cases); acquiring *"bad"* or *frightening properties* properties, such as the ability to profane others or perform sorcery (10 cases); *lack of children* or family support system (9 cases); possessing *obsolete skills* (5 cases); lack of material wealth (1 case); and the hoarding of valuable property (1 case).

Realizing that there are a number of different explanations given for treating fading modelers with contempt, I wanted to learn how much each given explanation contributed to the amount of contempt actually shown to fading modelers. In an attempt to estimate the relative importance of each explanation of contempt in regard to displays of contempt witnessed by ethnographers, a multiple regression was performed on the data. This procedure constructs an equation which adds the explanations for contempt cumulatively; each explanation is entered into the equation as a single independent variable. Each, in turn, is compared to the dependent variable (acts of contempt). The equation produced explains how much variance in the dependent variable each explanation of contempt contributes, after the effects of the previous variables (explanations) have been controlled for . This is called "forward stepwise regression." The explanation which statistically accounts for the most variation in the dependent variable is entered into the equation first. Each subsequent variable is then entered according to the amount of variance it can explain. The results show several interesting relationships between explanations given for contempt and the amount of contempt displayed to elderly modelers. We see that the explanation with the strongest predictive power (highest correlation with the dependent variable, "expressions of contempt") is "lack of children or family support system," with a correlation of .46 (explaining 46% of variance). "Unpleasant physical appearance" explained the next largest amount of variation, adding .13 (13%) predictive power to that of the first variable. The third explanation, "lack of physical strength" explained .11 (11%) of the remaining variance. (Note this variable did not explain the greatest portion of variation in the data although it accounted for the highest frequency.) None of the other explanations contributed more than .03 (3%) to the variance in expressing contempt. In fact, two of the explanations - "lack of material wealth" and "hoarding valuable property" - were eliminated from the quantitative analysis because of their very low predictive value, indicated either because the variation in these variables could have occurred by chance, or that the variation in these variables was accounted for in other variables in the equation.

The results suggest that kinship systems, and especially children, are extremely important sources of prestige and power in non-industrialized societies and that, for elderly modelers, they provide the last line of defense against fading out entirely. Secondly, we find that loss of physical beauty and strength are rather important determinants in expressions of contempt. This is interesting in that these losses become noticed only after a modeler has begun to fade. It is most interesting that senility and obsolescence are not important determinants of contempt. As we shall see in the third section of this chapter, one can become senile and still be respected for one's past contributions as a modeler. Certainly, the most important understanding learned from this regression is that a family is extremely important to the well-being of older persons. A fading modeler needs to have a family in order to display whatever residual skills remain with him. He may become enfeebled, lose some of his acuity, or become to some extent irrelevant, but his family will protect him from becoming totally contemptible. A family seems to be the ultimate protection against social bankruptcy.

Recovering now from this quantitative digression, we may turn to a discussion of the ways in which deference is not diminished but recast, as a change in lighting results in a shift along the visible spectrum. First, I would like to point out that there is a recasting of deference which accompanies the change in the activities of older modelers in the direction of an emphasis on certifying others. Those modelers who formerly engaged in a number of performances, now may be reduced to certifying; those modelers who never certified others before, now begin to do so. The process of certifying, and the awe which it generates in others, has been extensively dealt with in Chapter IV, in the section on "Ritual Okaying Ceremonies."

There is also a change in the definition of deference, from deference because of influence to deference because of old age. An elderly modeler may have received many expressions of awe because of his great influence. But as he fades out, these expressions diminish. "The admiration of one's strength, skill, wealth gives way to respect for old age and to being sorry for the old man...An old man becomes a member of his son's household, and gradually decreases his status (Honigmann 1949:59)."

In addition to changes in deference due to an emphasis on certifying and a change in definition, certain changes also occur in the modality in which it is expressed. There is an increase in ambivalence towards the roles played by elderly modelers. The matter of being excused from taboos that must be observed by others - a commonly encountered form of deference - provides a good example of this ambivalence. It is not always clear that being excused from the observance of these taboos is an honor. Taboos are sometimes inconvenient and it may be a favor, not having to conform to them, but it also seems that by not conforming to rules which everyone else follows, one is not quite the same model of good copy as one was before. As we have seen in Chapter III, these sorts of taboos serve as social fences in that they serve as indications of who is and who is not a member of the group; it seems paradoxical to honor someone by weakening his identity.

As I have mentioned, however, these indulgences are common. Among the Trobriand Islanders, we find:

When such a fish is caught in the nets, they should cut off the tail, then the old people might eat it. Of a bunch of coconuts washed on the beach, they (the young people) must not eat a single one - it is a taboo. Only old men and old women may eat them (Malinowski 1929:544).

Among the Nicobar Islanders [Bay of Bengal]:

But older trees are tapped for "toddy" - a spirituous liquid that older people drink freely but which otherwise is only offered to visiting friends (Man 1932:110).

An increase in privacy is a similarly ambiguous honor, there being more than one possible reason for it, including the desire to shun someone or to hide him away as a bad example. The Thai, for instance, provide a "quiet room" for senile modelers. The room is also used to store valuables. Since space is not too readily available, one might conclude that the Thai honor the aged by giving them this limited space. And since the room doubles as a storage room for valuables, the aged may be seen as valuable too. But it is also possible to conclude that the elderly who are senile bad examples are shoved off into a small room, where things are put that aren't used very often and where they can be forgotten about until needed.

Another recasting of deference occurs along sex lines. Elderly women are sometimes treated, for the first time, as if they were men, or, at least, as desexualized objects. Old women are then allowed the privileges of men. They are excused from female taboos and, in addition, they are now allowed to participate in male activities. They can go where the men go. And, in Egypt, they no longer need to cover their faces when men walk by (Ammar

1954:49).

In all of these ways, fading modelers find that the deference which they receive is recast, and that, although they may continue to be honored, it is in a different and, in some ways, unsettling manner.

FADING FROM A DEVELOPMENTAL PERSPECTIVE

We have been discussing the fading process in terms of loss. Modelers who have controlled everything, gradually relinquish control to other members of society. Of course, there is another side to the fading process. As modelers relinquish control, other persons gradually assume control and move up to higher rungs on the ladder of influence. Briefly, let's now take a look at this process of gaining control from the younger generation's point of view. Let's begin by assuming that sometime during the process of becoming influential, each generation must watch the preceding generation "fade out." Similarly, each generation must consider that as they assume authority, the older generation must relinquish the same.

Children all over the world, when they are very small, seem to live in a state of awe at all times. Everyone around them seems to be smarter, have more control, and possess more skills than they do. Most little kids are really anxious to learn. They seem to "say" all the time, "Gee you're great. I wish I could do that." They try to copy bigger (older) people as much as they can. They are truly amazed that older people have so many answers and can do so much. Older people are all seen as sanctifiers to youngsters, people who can make everything okay. And, in most societies, Mother, of course, is the greatest sanctifier of all. She truly knows everything and is omnipotent. Children have often been compared to sponges, eagerly soaking up everything older people teach them. This seems to be true, for young children at any rate. What is important here is that the more they learn, the less magic they see everywhere. Adults are magicians as long as what they do seems impossible to children, well beyond anything that they can accomplish or even try to accomplish. But when those children learn a few things, they immediately try to awe their peers with their new found skills. If their attempts succeed, the acts lose some of their magical properties. And so, I would imagine, do the older folks who previously awed youngsters with the same skills. Kids then seem to tell us, "Oh, I can do that. You're not so great after all." Unless, of course, the elders have much more in their bag of tricks.

In the early years of life, the modeling labyrinth seems illimitable. There are so many paths to conquer. The young are in awe of those who have travelled the paths. But as a person grows older there are mileposts along the way. Each of these represents accomplishment. Each also means the gap is narrowed between those who seemed to know everything, and themselves, persons who know some things. The point of all this is that the more one knows (even about the process of learning) the less magical and the less awe-inspiring are one's teachers. Those who seemed to be sanctifiers for the most part are redefined as simple certifiers, who teach young people what they would eventually learn anyway. There comes a time in the lives of most young people in which the feeling of awe breaks down. The feeling may gradually dissolve for some, but for others the process is quicker, almost sudden, and very painful. For some people do not realize for quite some time that their modelers are not really gods. When they discover that their heroes are not infallible and that they do not have all the answers, the learners are forlorn. Some are just disappointed. Others are very angry and they feel they have been let down, trickled into believing their modelers were so powerful. But most continue to copy the examples of their elders, realizing if they won't learn everything, they will at least gain as much power and influence as those who went before them. For some, the simple desire to know is replaced with an even more powerful wish to be as good and perhaps even surpass their teachers.

We must also remember that there are very few options in the societies we have been discussing for young people to do anything but copy their elders. So copy they do, and the closer they come to approximating their modelers, the less awe they may feel for them. When they are certified as good copy, equal to their modelers, young people find they must redefine their emotional response to their modelers. One class of society members, those who expect to take over their teacher's positions, any look at their teacher with respect, being truly grateful for everything they have learned. The awe they felt for their modelers is transferred to their model. They are in awe as adults of a system of beliefs and rewards which has worked well and allowed them to achieve positions of influence. They may be described as having "bought into the model"; they do not reject the former controllers, their teachers, preferring instead to feel proud for the opportunity to occupy the positions held by their teachers. But for other classes who exceed the accomplishments of their teachers and go beyond them in the modeling labyrinth, it may not be so easy. Former modelers become hasbeens, irrelevant, and perhaps even pitiful when they have been outgrown. But although they have these feelings, some youth never quite get over the belief that their modelers are as good as people can be. For some, this belief is what holds them back, making it difficult for them to achieve the most influential positions and to adapt to changing conditions. They have accepted their modelers and the model in its entirety. For these people, it is truly inconceivable that modelers can be surpassed. If the performances of modelers fade, they believe that the best which can be hoped for is that new members of society will try to approximate their predecessors' performances. In contrast, those society members who become the most influential, who become the leaders of the next generation, usually take fading as somewhat inevitable. They try as hard as they can to copy their modelers, and seem to have no fear of outdoing them. They take it for granted that achievement is expected of them. With pride, they take over, and with only occasional glances into the future when they too will fade out. This group excels because they have "bought" a successful model and learned what they could from it, and they are not hampered with the belief that their modelers cannot be outgrown.

FADING AND MODEL CONTENT

Heretofore, we have been dealing with certain contingencies internal to society. We now need to shift the level of generality of this discussion somewhat. This section deals not so much with things that are obviously attributable to other things, but with ultimate values, with social axioms. When queried about their activities, people are frequently able to legitimize them as stemming from some antecedent set of activities. Ultimately, however, they run out of antecedents and answer such queries with simple statements like, "That's the way it is." Thus, for instance, in our society people cuddle babies. Why do we cuddle them? Because they are lovable. But why are they lovable? We don't know; that's just the way they are. Here, we enter the realm of axiology, the ultimate content of a model's importances.

As we shift to the study of axioms it is incumbent that we realize that axioms are not disputable. To the people who accept these beliefs, there is no uncertainty. Axioms are true, beyond the tiniest shadow of a doubt. I should add that in stable societies with limited options, such axioms are plentiful. Definitions of "good" and "bad," "right" and "wrong" are ultimately derived from axioms. "Good" tends to be defined in terms of those actions or ideas that support other axioms. Acts or thoughts which "threaten" axioms are "wrong" and "bad." There is a great deal of emotion attached to axioms. In the interest of "good," people will "love," "hate," cry and fight. "Good" of course varies from one society to another and even among members who live in the same society.

People sharing axioms often cannot understand why everyone does not think they do. They may try to convert others to their way of thinking. Although religious groups preach love and truth, for instance, many religious wars have been fought in the hope of making one definition of love and truth paramount. People, it seems, will do just about anything to maintain their fundamental axioms.

With this understanding, I think we are now ready to look at axioms and their relationship to what ultimately happens to fading modelers. Put rather succinctly, some axioms are beneficial to the care of aging modelers; others are not. "Benevolence" as a value, for instance, is good for the aged. Society members may be seen as "good" if they care for old people. In contrast, the value of "independence" is not so good, because helping others robs them of their independence.

The question which I am asked most frequently by colleagues and the public in general when they want to know about my study is, "What works? How can old people in our society make out better?" I generally tell them that if you ask this question of the persons in societies where old people "make out" well the answer will be, "Because, it is the way that is." If you repeat the question in societies where old people do less well the answer will be just about the same, "That's the way it is." Caring for the aged and seeing to it that they keep their "dignity" is a rather new problem. It is salient only in well-differentiated societies with extended life cycles and rapid model change; in other words in situations where there are many people fading out and sharing a similar problem. Our data indicate only that to be revered one has to contribute in some way to maintaining importances. It must be remembered that in later years, in the societies which I have studied, it is the family which is generally responsible for caring for the elderly. It is thus the family's system of importances to which the fading modeler must contribute.

I have discussed here the various social acts which constitute the exercise of influence over others by modelers on the one hand, and the display of deference by other community members, on the other hand. But something has been left out, which can only be discussed at a much higher level of generality, and which does not lend itself to analysis. That is the simple fact that people come to care for one another. Given the proper circumstances - and these are fairly widespread - people who live together for a long period of time come to like one another and to suffer when the other suffers. Whether the sufferer is still able to exercise influence, generate awe, contribute money, or take care of children is beside the point. The emotions generated by long-term proximity tend to outlast these conditions. In the vast majority of societies - perhaps all of them - old people are to some extent respected and taken care of because of emotional bonds. Human beings are like that.

Emotional bonds fight fading in another way. As people age it may occur to them that they have an abundance of information that will be lost if it doesn't get passed on to the next generation. Now this may include technical information to an extent, but I am really not speaking of this sort of thing. Rather, I think that it occurs to people that they know other people who have lived and died and will soon be forgotten unless their stories are told to the next generation. I believe that the desire to tell younger people "how it was" is related to discovering our own immortality. We want the next generation to know and remember individuals - including ourselves - because we love them. But what really gets passed on to the next generation in the stories that we tell are the axioms and importances that the previous generation stood for. The next generation cannot "love" our modelers. The "closeness" that comes from proximity in life is simply not there. But the survivors can relate to axioms, values, and moral messages, which can be sanctified.

SOME MODELERS NEVER FADE

In every generation modelers come and modelers go. Most individuals are, over a long period of time, forgotten. Every now and then an individual stands out and his/her performances are remembered. Usually these are modelers who have been so outstanding that the class of modelees following them have been unable to copy their performances. These modelers either achieved a great deal in a short period of time, (i.e., no one could copy them in an ordinary lifespan), or else their entire lives seem to be perfect, without blemish and they become idolized symbols of society's values. These modelers never fade, or perhaps it is more correct to say, their influence persists as long as there are survivors subscribing to their group's model.

Modelers who do not fade are special. They are stars. They have in some ways transcended the performances of their ancestors, being so good that others cannot copy them. Minimally, starring modelers have been great enough to establish new standards of expertise. Some become stars because they die at the height of their careers. No one knows whether they would have faded had they lived long enough. In some societies including the most stable, on the one hand, and alternatively those who seem less stable but wish at this time to perpetuate their current system of importances, choose ancestral stars. These societies worship ancestors as role models. As mentioned in an earlier chapter, the belief in ancestral intervention reinforces the current patterns of interaction, and consequently establishes a sense of continuity across generations.

What seems to happen most often is that societies sharing models create culture heroes. In some cases historical heroes are deified to serve as role models in order that society members have someone to copy. Prophets, for instance, can be understood to be deified role modelers. Mythology and folklore may be linked to documented accomplishments to make these heroes even worthier of copying. Most societies have such super stars. In some cases these stars are not humans at all. Some may be referred to as the "divine creator" and others as master forces which control the universe. But what these have in common is that always some figure or some force has been chosen whose greatness may not fade. In essence what I have suggested is that we create modelers who never fade because we want them that way. It is nice to have someone to copy.

REFERENCES

ETHNOGRAPHIC SOURCES

Ammar, H. 1954; **Growing Up in an Egyptian Village**, London: Routledge and Paul, Ltd.

Beardsley, R.K., J.W. Hall, and R. Ward, 1959; **Village Japan**, Chicago: University of Chicago Press.

Bohannan, P. and L. Bohannan, 1966: **A Source Notebook in the Tiv Life Cycle**, HRAFLEX Book FF57-003.

Chagnon, N., 1968; **The Fierce People**, New York: Holt, Rinehart and Winston.

Dunn, S.P. and E. Dunn, 1967, **The Peasants of Central Russia**, Case Studies in Cultural Anthropology, New York: Holt, C.

Elliott, H.W., 1886; **Our Artic Province**, New York: Scribner & Son

Fortes, M., 1940; "The Political System of the Tallensi," in **African Political Systems**, M. Fortes and E. Evans-Pritchard (eds.), London: Oxford University Press.

Fortes, M., 1969; **The Dynamics of Clanship Among the Tallensi**, London: Oxford University Press.

Goodenough, W.H., 1967; **Property, Kin and Community on Truk**, Hamden, Connecticut: Archon.

Gorer, G., 1938; **Himalayan Village**, London.

Herskovits, M.J., 1938; **Dahomey**, Vol.I, New York.

Harris, G.L., 1957; **Egypt**, New Haven: Human Relations Area Files.

Honigmann, J.J., 1949, **Culture and Ethos of Kaska Society**, Yale University Publications in Anthropology, Vol. 40, pp. 1-365.

Junod, H.A. 1962, **The Life of a South African Tribe**, London: Oxford University Press.

Lambert, B., 1963, **Rank and Ramage in the Northeastern Gilbert Islands**, Ph.D. Dissertation, University of California, Berkeley.

Latta, F.F., 1949, **Handbook of Yokuts Indians**, Oildale, California: Bear State Books.

Lewis, I.M., 1961; **A Pastoral Democracy**, London: Oxford University Press.

Mace, D. and V. Mace, 1963; **The Soviet Family**, Garden City, New York: Doubleday.

Malinowski, B., 1929; **The Sexual Life of Savages**, New York: Harcourt, Brace and World.

Malinowski, B., 1966; **Argonauts of the West Pacific**, London: Dutton.

Man, G.H., 1932; **The Nicobar Islands and Their Peoples**, Guilford: Billing and Sons.

McKain, W., 1972; "The Aged in the U.S.S.R.," in **Aging and Modernization**, D. Cowgill and L. Holmes (eds.), New York: Appleton-Century Crofts.

Nahemow, N. and Bert Adams, 1974; "Old Age Among the Baganda: Continuity and Change," in J. Gubrium (ed.), in **Late Life**, Springfield, Illinois: C.C. Thomas.

Parsons, E.C., 1919; "Mothers and Children at Zuni," in **Man**, Vol. 19, pp. 168-173.

Rutt, R., 1964; **Korean Works and Days**. Rutland, Vermont: C.E. Tuttle Company.

Spier, L., 1928; "Havasupai Ethnography," **Anthropological Papers of the American Museum of Natural History**, Vol. 24; pp. 81-408.

Swanton, J.R., 1909; **Contributions to the Ethnology of the Haida**, Memoirs of the Museum of Natural History, Vol. 8: 1-300.

Tooker, E., 1964; **An Ethnography of the Huron Indians**, Bull. of the Bureau of American Ethnology, Vol. 190, pp.1-183.

Whitehead, G., 1924; **In the Nicobar Islands**, London: Seeley, Service, and Company, Ltd.

OTHER SOURCES

Bendix, R., 1968; "Towards a Definition of Modernization," in **Studia Sociolgiszno Polityczne**, Vol. 25, pp. 31-43.

Dore, R.P., 1969; "The Modernizer as a Special Case: Japanese Factory Legislation, 1882-1911," in **Comparative Studies in Society and History**, Vol. 11: 433-50.

Cowgill, Donald O., 1974; "Aging and Modernization: A Revision of the Theory," in **Late Life**, J. F.. Gubrium (ed.), Springfield, Illinois: Charles C. Thomas.

Goffman, E., 1956; "The Nature of Deference and Demeanor," in **American Anthropologist**, Vol. 58, pp. 473-502.

Silverman, P. and R.J. Maxwell, 1978; "How Do I Respect Thee? Let Me Count The Ways," in **Behavioral Science Research**, Vol. 13, No. 2.

CHAPTER 11

FENCING PROCESSES

Eleanor Krassen Maxwell

> Moses received the Torah on Sinai and handed it down to Joshua; Joshua to the elders; the elders to the prophets; and the prophets handed it down to the Men of the Great Assembly. They said three things: Be deliberate in judgment; raise up many disciples; and make a fence round the Torah.

> (Pirke Avot, from the Talmud,
>
> Chapter 1, Verse 1)

Groups engage in fencing processes when they wish to control the situations of their members. Fencing processes are limiting; they are actions invoked by established modelers which limit either the content of the model they transmit, or the audience who receives it. In simple terms, fencing processes involve keeping outsiders away from the model in order that insiders may continue to control their model. Fencing strategies are important to the modeling process in that their failure leads ultimately to model contamination and the loss of situational control.

There seem to be three strategic categories of fencing processes:

1. *Isolating strategies* are conscious attempts to limit access to model importances by limiting group membership and screening off the activities of group members. As a consequence of engaging in isolating strategies, modelers frequently control property associated with their model.

2. *Pacing strategies* introduce modelees to the content of their model in stages. Like isolating processes, their effect is to limit access to the content of a group's model, but these processes are directed at those persons who will one day control the model themselves. Modelers control their own positions as group leaders through imposing pacing strategies.

3. *Defining strategies* are teaching techniques which delimit the content of a group's model. This topic will be discussed in Chapter IV.

A prototypical if humdrum example of these three fencing strategies is provided by the traditional process of graduate education in the United States. Typically, one is not considered a *bona fide* professional without a Ph.D., an academic job with the prospect of tenure, an office, and the other prerequisites and props of professorhood. A professor attends faculty meetings and other assemblies from which students and other non-professors are excluded (isolating). The student who aspires to professorhood must master a specifiable discipline-linked body of knowledge (defining the model) and he must do so at a specifiable rate, such as acquiring 80 units at no more than 12 units per term (pacing).

Although these three fencing categories may occur simultaneously, they will be presented separately in order to explicate the larger modeling process.

ISOLATING STRATEGIES

The most obvious isolating strategies are "presencing barriers." Groups or individuals construct architectural and or social barriers around themselves to block the presence of others from their activities, or, at least, to keep them from seeing what they are doing. We have all closed a door or hiked into the woods or perhaps even climbed up to a treehouse, because we wanted to do something privately.

It may be noted that there is nothing intrinsically comforting about being looked at, no matter what activity one is engaged in. The contrary is frequently true. Argyle and Cook (1976) have convincingly demonstrated that gaze is a commonly encountered threat feature in infrahuman animals and, under certain specifiable circumstances, among human beings as well.

Many groups believe that exposing their model to outsiders would somehow weaken its content and thereby threaten the existence of the group itself. When groups build structural barriers, the structures become symbols of group membership to members and non-members alike. Groups may build these barriers as much for their own identity as for fencing others out. The modern country club provides us with an example of a structural barrier with such social implications.

Sub-groups wishing more than a modicum of independence from the larger society are also likely to hide some of their activities. Many societies, the Hausa and the Turks for example, have sub-groups which isolate activities according to sex. Wealthy Turks build special guest rooms in their homes which are for men only...where males can chat and share a cup of coffee or tea. The room is isolated from the rest of the house and male guests seldom witness the more mundane household activities (Stirling 1965:22). Among the Hausa, wedding ceremonies take place in both the bride's living compound and again in the compound of the groom. In each instance, the sexes celebrate the wedding separately (Smith 1957:32)

Similarly, the training of initiates is often in isolation, in order that the uninitiated do not learn model secrets.

Occasionally, sub-groups will be screened, rather than entirely hidden from view. Fence gaps or "holes" may permit outsiders to see a limited amount of sub-group activity. Sub-groups can use screens to control the image of themselves which they project before non-members. They can attract new members and elicit the curiosity of future initiates by allowing them to see the more attractive aspects of group activities. In some instances fence gaps are used in the validating process. Outsiders are allowed to view those aspects of group membership which do not conflict with the larger society's values.

Fence gaps can also be used strategically by sub-groups to discourage new members by permitting only acceptable activities to be viewed. (Many adolescent gangs and other terrorist groups use interaction screens in this manner).

Regardless of which group activities are witnessed through screens, fence gaps allow outsiders to speculate about the content of the group's value system. Speculating may lead to a good deal of awe among those who can't see everything. This awe also has positive and negative properties. If the group presents a positive image, those outside may look at insiders with envy and a hope that they too may one day be participants in the interaction. On the other hand, if negative activities are witnessed, those outside may fear the acts they see. Young boys who witness circumcisions which are performed as puberty rites may envy the physical symbol of group membership and look forward to the privileges associated with having the operation, but may simultaneously fear initiation as well.

All societies have marriage rules or at least some agreement as to what are preferred and non-preferred unions. Marriage rules may be described as universal presencing barriers by which groups deny certain selected individuals access to their model. In more cases than not, elderly modelers are involved in enforcing these marriage rules. They, in fact, often serve as intermediaries and as marriage brokers arranging the unions themselves.

The Truckese, who live on a small island in Micronesia, place a great deal of authority in the hands of the eldest men and woman of their lineage. When a couple wishes to marry, the oldest man and woman of the lineage must be consulted. They can rule out marriages between any members of the lineage who are younger than they are (Gladwin and Sarason 1953:124; Goodenough 1967:75; see also Herskovits 1937:126 [Haitians]).

Indeed, all cultures seen to recognize the likelihood of intimacy between marriage partners and the potential threat of model contamination if the wrong type of spouse is elected. Many cultures insist on publicly validating the bride's fitness as a marriage partner by having her demonstrate her virginity.

Among the Gilbertese the bridegroom's mother searches for blood on the couple's sleeping mat to prove her daughter-in-law's virginity. "She then descended alone to exhibit the mat to all eyes, whereupon taking up the cries of the old woman, the father and uncles of the bridegroom rubbed each a little of the virgin's blood upon his cheeks (Grimble 1921:31)." (I have been told that a similar custom occurs today in parts of the Mediterranean.)

CUSTODIAL BARRIERS

Other isolating strategies involve the custody of a model and its associate property. Isolating the content of a model by entrusting its care to the hands of a few respected individuals, may be called "sanctified keeping." This is an isolating strategy in which certain modelers are chosen to protect some symbol of group membership and/or certain reified model importances. Model symbols may include medicine bundles, community shrines, totem poles, and the like. A Torah is also an example. Sanctified keepers may also guard various technological and ritual skills which group members believe are essential for group survival. Sanctified keepers are chosen because their past performances are exemplary of model importances which group members wish to protect.

Among the Aranda, the same society on which Durkheim based *The Elementary Forms of the Religious Life*,

> The sacred objects of wood and stone (Churinga) stored in the totems secret storehouse are under the care of the headman and other old men of the totem. They alone can handle them. If women, uninitiated men, or strangers should stumble across the storehouse they would most likely be put to death. The old men would recognize the track of anyone venturing near who had no right to do so (Spencer and Gillen 1927:113; see also Cushing 1975:317, Stevenson 1970:304 (Zuni); Olson 1967:107 (Tlingit); for further examples of sanctified keeping).

Sanctified keeping may be employed to assure that decisions affecting a group are made by those within the social boundaries of membership, and then, only by those most capable of protecting group values. In the above example, Aranda men are not informed of *Churinga* secrets until old men deem them worthy (Spencer and Gillen 1927:113).

There seem to be two dimensions of sanctified keeping, maintenance on the one hand and control on the other. Maintenance of the model may be thought of as involving its perpetuation through time in an unaltered state. It may entail the embodiment of the model by its elderly keepers and sometimes, the care of a sacred physical object such as a medicine bundle which symbolizes the group. Control of the model implies that the model is not merely "passed along" but that it is, in addition, interpreted or changed in some other way by its keepers.

With respect to maintenance, sanctified keepers are chosen from modelers who embody the content of the model. For instance, among the Omaha Indians, the tribe divides the responsibility of "keeping" various tribal rituals. The division of responsibility is not arbitrary and represents the major geographic and kin groups within the tribe. In the "Southern" half of the tribal circle "Keepers" (generally elders) were in charge of rites dealing with the physical welfare of the people. The Keepers of the "Northern" half of the circle were custodians of rites pertaining to creation, stars, and status passages (Fletcher and La Flesche 1911:194-195).

Members of various groups may sometimes confuse the desire to protect the content of their model from outsiders with the desire to have decisions made from within their own ranks. Sanctified Keepers may believe that in order to protect a model, they must see to it that the model is not changed at all. These keepers may not realize that as a consequence of their having been entrusted with keeping the model, they must inevitably interpret it. In making decisions about it, they may in effect be modifying the model. They control the model since they alone make decisions about it, but they do not maintain it perfectly. In some instances, the desire of sanctified keepers to present a model as static may give rise to "spiritual constipation," limiting the judgments made by sanctified keepers to situations which are no longer relevant.

Sanctified keepers who maintain models are usually in charge of physically caring for some concrete symbol of the model. Among Plains Indian groups, elderly keepers carry around sacred bundles; among the Nubians, who live in Egypt, the ritual leader of women, *NAKIBA*, is custodian of the ancestral shrine; she performs minor religious acts; i.e., lighting candles, supervises cooking during certain celebrations, walks in processions, replaces tomb covers, etc. (Fernea 1966a:206). When the duties of sanctified keepers also include controlling model importances, they may use "magic" to dramatize these importances, perhaps by means of other sacred objects such as those used in divination. Such sacred objects may be used to awe other group members as well as to sanctify decisions made by sanctified model keepers. Recalling the Aranda sanctified Keepers of *Churinga*,

> "Old men visiting the stone can, by means of rubbing it and muttering a request to the contained...evil influence, to go out, cause the disease to be communicated to any individual or even group of men whom they desire to injure (Spencer and Gillen 1927:347)."

While sanctified keepers may maintain models simply by continuing to embody model importances and thus serving as examples for all group members, keepers must use additional strategies when they must control a model as well. They must, for instance, choose and train their own successors.

In some instances control is assured structurally by passing on the office of "keepership" hereditarily. Among the Omaha tribe discussed previously, "each gens had a family with the hereditary right to furnish the Keeper of the ritual of the gens. He was expected to instruct his son and so transmit to him the knowledge of the ritual and the right to perform it (Fletcher and La Flesche 1911:595)."

If a sanctified keeper becomes too old to physically perform all of his duties, he may continue to control his group's model by delegating authority to a close member of his family and still keep a few model secrets to himself. As the old man embodies all of the group's values behaviorally, he may maintain the model as well. The following example is from the Gilbertese:

> "Nam Binga is not the Elder of Kamokamo but since he is too old to walk constantly about the village, he has delegated the job of making announcements and issuing invitations in the name of the Elders of Makin to his own ...grandson (Lambert 1963:92)."

Sanctified keepers who are entrusted with controlling their group's models, in general, have a much tougher task than those who must maintain models. They are faced with potentially disruptive decisions, any of which may threaten their positions by making the "right decisions" as envious group members continually reevaluate the performances of their keepers. A decision resulting in the loss of control for other group members judged in retrospect to have been avoidable generally leads to a change in model keepership, a changing of the guard, so to speak.

The whole concept of "ownership" is a fencing strategy, and is often a special instance of sanctified keeping. When someone owns anything he or she controls it in the sense that he possesses the right to determine its use. Owners control access to their property and thereby literally fence in its use. Property can include money, land, animals, tolls, or even the right to perform various acts.

Among the Tellensi, "No one has an over-right to the farmland a man holds by right or inheritance or purchase. No one can dispossess him of it, prevent him from using it as and when he wills, or resume any that he leaves untilled (Fortes 1940:250)."

And, among the Tlingit Indians of the North West Coast, parents may allow their children to perform certain acts which they "own" (the Tlingit believe that the right to perform certain skills can be owned), but the children must return these rights to their parents if they get married (Olson, 1967:107).

Modelers who have custody over a society's importances protect their property by hiding its content behind a series of expected behavior patterns; only by following an intricate performance path which is revealed to them in carefully controlled stages.

This performance path resembles a situational control labyrinth in a number of ways. First, it stands as a process which begins with achieving entrance, which is the first step in understanding the ideology of a group. It continues with the gradual progression of the individual along certain predetermined and sometimes confusing pathways. The individual receives some guidance along the way; he is encouraged to copy the performances of others, for example. But, his efforts also depend to some extent on trial and error learning. Some particular turns in the labyrinth are more difficult and important than others; accomplishing these may be celebrated in "status passage ritual." And there are certain decision points and forks in the path which influence the amount of control eventually attained. Finally, the individual may achieve the center of the labyrinth, a position where mastery of the group's importances is presumed and where situational control is most assured.

As in real labyrinths, some individuals take longer to learn a path to the center than others. Some, in fact, get lost and never gain the center. Some may never even gain entrance. Unlike real labyrinths, however, the path may also be made easier for some, by positioned modelers who lead them on their way. Among the Natchez who lived in the lower Mississippi Valley, history was preserved through tradition. Teaching occurred in frequent conversations.

> The old men are the depositories of this, and as it has been very faithfully transmitted from generation to generation they call it "the ancient word." What contributes much to preserve it in all its purity is that they do not teach it to all the young people indifferently. This tradition is all theirs and the only authority on which they are able to base their reasonings...They therefore choose for this purpose those among the youths of whom they had the best opinion in order to teach them past things. Moreover, this choice is very easy for them, because the children are always under their eyes and the old men are in a good position to know them (Swanton).

BOUNDARY MAINTAINING CUSTOMS: IDENTITY DISPLAYS

There is an additional class of isolating strategies which have been referred to by Young and Bacdayan (1965:231) as "boundary maintaining customs." I think of these customs as "identity displays" which include a variety of stereotypic acts as well as physical signs of group membership such as circumcision, tattooing, or scarification. In order for identity displays to be effective as isolating strategies, they must be witnessed by non-group members who interpret what they see from a perspective somewhat different from that held by group members.

As in the case of constructing physical barriers between members and non-members of groups, identity displays become symbolic of group membership to insiders and outsiders alike.

The acts which compose identity displays are themselves the boundaries. Non-members either are not permitted to perform these acts, or, if they do perform them, their performances are judged to be inadequate by those group members who control the model.

Kroeber (1925:32) describes the following Yurok custom:

> A curious practice was followed in the Wohtek Deerskin dance following the Kepel fish dam... They danced downstream...Here the

old men made men tell what their fathers had paid for their mothers. Those of moderate ancestry were permitted to dance; the rich born and the illegitimate were both excluded.

Kroeber went on to explain that the performance of the dance presented a social hierarchy of villagers to all who witnessed it. Among the Yurok, one's social status was determined not only by what they possessed, but by what their fathers had given their mothers. The rich born obviously had high status. A bastard stood on the bottom of the social scale (Kroeber 1925:32). Performance in the dance was most important for those of moderate birth, whose status was most ambiguous.

Since identity displays are symbolic of group membership and group values it is important that decisions about them be made by experienced modelers within the group. When such decisions are made by such leaders, the group experiences the beneficial consequence of demonstrating that they control their own situation.

The Nicoberese believe that any experienced modeler has a right to contribute his opinions concerning the activities of group members. In some instances, all experienced men (all those inside the fence), act together, especially when it involves planning rites of intensification.

Two, three, or four years after the funeral...a council is held of all the elders of the village to consider the question of keeping the Ossuary Feast...If all are agreeable and able to contribute, they fix a day for the setting up of a post whereupon are to be placed... (Whitehead, G. 1924:197).

Identity displays are commonly expressed through language. The South African Thonga have passwords which they use to determine whether or not men have been circumcised.

Should I want to know if a man is initiated, I should say to him: "Mashindla bya ndjako, the best which must be opened from behind." If he answers at once: "Ngwenya, the crocodile," I know that he has been circumcised. But he must follow with the(se) words... There are also some obscene formulae which refer to certain diseases of women, of which not a word is told outside the Ngoma (Junod 1962:88).

In addition to telling an audience who is and who is not a member of a group, language can be used strategically by influential modelers to control the emerging composition of a group. In a variety of academic disciplines new jargon is being added all the time in the name of scientific development. In anthropology, for instance, terms describing the authority of male descendants within a household have changed over the past years, from "patriarchal" to "patripotestal," as "patrilocal" has changed to "virilocal." For all practical purposes the meaning of the terms within each pair is the same, but clearly the "wrong" choice labels one as anthropologist *manque*.

Food taboos serve a similar purpose. The notion that "taste cannot be disputed" is a limited one, for around the globe certain foods which are as nutritional and tasteful as any others are forbidden to group members. Adherence to these taboos serve as a further demonstration of group membership. Frequently, neighboring groups who do not observe the same taboos are the butts of each other's ridicule. A pattern of group naming which occurs with rather surprising frequency is one in which a given society calls itself by a name which means "human beings," and its neighbors by a name which means "cannibals," a reference to an extremely widespread and significant food taboo.

"Copying" is a necessary property of all group identity displays. This is most apparent with those boundary maintaining customs which show up as physical signs on the body or apparel of group members. It is probably reasonable to assume that a mass of people wearing very similar costumes have chosen this means of copying one another in order to display communalities that go far beyond the physical signs which are shared.

Sign copying generally occurs initially for an individual during formal status passages, which become rights of intensification for all of those present who display the identical physical sign. These ceremonies usually include some recitation of a group's value system or some other means of presenting verbally what the group has stood for in the past and some mention that the group should continue to stand for similar ideals in the future. Experienced modelers who embody group values are singled out somehow during these ceremonies, perhaps to give added emphasis to the timelessness of this group. In a sense, the old person gives the impression that the group has existed forever and the young person the impression that the group will last forever. As the person receives the physical sign which identifies him as a member of the group, he is simultaneously reminded of the fact that he must continue in other areas to copy the values of his group. The presence of elderly modelers is likely to impress upon him that copying may be a lifelong commitment.

Copying as a lifelong commitment is also impressed on others present during individual status passages, in so far as these passages are rights of intensification for the rest of the audience. Those who have been initiated but have not become senior group members are provided with an example whom they must strive to copy.

Among the Omaha, "In the Deer-Head gens on the 5th day after birth an old man of the same sub-gens as the infant ritually paints the infant and names the child (Dorsey 1884:246)." In this instance the act of painting the child is indeed a boundary that separates Omaha children from infants of other groups. And in addition, group membership is demonstrated, since only a person whom the child may copy in other behavioral areas (that is, a member of his same sub-gens) may perform the boundary maintaining display.

It should also be pointed out that this example reflects the fact that sub-groups within societies have rituals of their own replete with boundary maintaining customs. The dynamics involved in sub-group identity displays are identical with those that govern interaction between total societies. The Zuni, for instance, have a "meal with the Fathers" ceremony in which men who currently live with the families of their wives return to their families of orientation to share a meal.

"Early on the morning of the New Year, however, old men may be seen tottering from place to place, gathering up their married sons and conducting them to homes of their nativity (Cushing 1975:609)."

PACING STRATEGIES

Pacing strategies are fencing processes which are used by positioned group leaders to protect their model from misuse by others. Paving strategies protect the model by controlling takeovers and weeding out incompetent group members.

All organizations introduce the content of their value system to new members in stages. Even when it is in the best interest of the group for leadership to be transferred rapidly, a learning period follows the formal transfer of authority, during which the new leader is more or less on probation.

Society leaders hide - from even their most competent initiates - some information and artifacts which might allow them to assume control over their situations too quickly. The information needed to control the group situation is hidden inside a labyrinth of expected behavior patterns. It is accessible to inexperienced modelees only in stages as they learn to feel their way through the maze. "Stops" imposed in this behavioral labyrinth by those in control "pace" the flow of information to the less experienced.

Pacing produces a variety of consequences of which modelers are more or less aware. Pacing processes may be used strategically to regulate the influential hierarchy within a group. In academia, for instance, it is much more difficult to get tenure today than it was a few years ago. Faculty who are currently tenured are increasing the requirements for newcomers in order to protect their own positions as controllers. As a result of increased requirements, it now takes longer to become tenured.

Some pacing strategies appear to be present among all organizations who train new members, but a belief in "limited rewards" or "limited resources" seems to be a condition that accentuates these processes. This example, selected from a Nyakyusa (western Tanganyika) ethnography illustrates the condition:

> The introduction of courts and salaries has brought an entirely new element into the relationship between old and young chiefs. Only one of them can receive the salary and they commonly dispute about it. Quarrels are particularly frequent over the position of senior chief, for the presidency of a court carries with it a relatively large salary. Old chiefs cling to the position (which formerly was readily relinquished) after their sons have 'come out', and when they die their full- brothers still dispute the position... such a situation could not have arisen before 1926, for there was no comparable issue between them (Wilson 1951:284).

Creating an authority hierarchy, i.e., ranking the positions of individuals within a group, is the most common pacing strategy. A vivid example of this sort of pacing of course comes from the military. Ranking results in a situation in which all those who attain a rank higher than one's own are in a position to judge one's actions. Even within ranks, authority is organized in terms of time in grade. Judgment is thus a property of pacing processes. Ranking structures the process of pacing by specifying the occasions when judgments occur. Inside a control labyrinth, performances are reevaluated before each advancement to a higher rank.

We will see in the next chapter that modelers who make these judgments also engage in a wide variety of strategies to awe the less experienced so that they may continue to judge them authoritatively. Modelers foster fear, respect, and subsequent dependence in the less experienced, thus increasing the likelihood of the acceptance of the modelers' own judgments.

Ranking need not be formal; nor need it be consistent in all social settings. Indeed, in many societies, rank is assigned by participants situationally on the basis of experience. In Cuna society, for instance, an older man who knows the history of property is consulted in the case of boundary disputes (Stout 1947:3031).

Margaret Mead describes the situation in Samoa:

A man's attention is focused upon his behavior in relation to a situation, as host, as guest, as chief, as a member of the council, as a member of a chief's working group, as a fisherman beneath the leader, as a member of a war party in which his role is determined by his division membership in the village,...as the heir in his patrilineal line, as... the cross-cousin with a veto, in his mother's family, as the ranking member of one group, as the man of lowest rank in the next group he enters. Such a man does not develop a fixed response to others...(1937:296).

It might be added that ranking within groups is also a means of creating social borders. Ranking dramatized the differences between sub-groups in an organization, since members perform various identity displays which tell others the rank they occupy. Among the Todas, for instance, dairymen train apprentices. There are two grades of apprentices who dress differently and who are allowed different privileges (Rivers 1967:105).

Organizational hierarchies often use "mileposts" or ordered status passages to further control the progress of inexperienced members. Mileposts specify the order in which ranks may be achieved. Each initiate attempting to attain a particular model of situational control must follow a similar progressive path regardless of individual differences in ability. No milepost may be skipped.

If all initiates followed identical paths within the control labyrinth, and progressed at the same rate, they would simultaneously absorb a common set of values, a "collective conscience."

However, neither identical paths nor simultaneous advancement are necessary parts of pacing. Some persons are denied model secrets unless they are "born" into a particular path within the walls of the labyrinth, primogeniture for instance, or a specified caste. And some initiates who begin on the same path later take forks in the labyrinth leading to the control of different positions, rather than to the general goal of "social acceptance." In a sense, they become "specialists" instead of "generalists."

When an initiate enters an acceptable path, additional structural properties alter the context which surrounds the pacing process and consequently influence his progression. The following appear to be important factors which affect the context of pacing:

1. The number of persons being simultaneously paced. Each initiate may be treated individually or as a member of an echelon being paced together.

2. The province of modelers controlling the pacing. The control labyrinth may be divided into portions, each under the control of one modeler, or there may be an echelon of modelers with intermeshed responsibilities.

3. The number and significance of milestones.

a. The paths within the labyrinth may be continuous or may contain one or more milestones.

b. The modelers, the individuals in control of pacing, may change at each milestone, or alternatively one set of modelers may remain in control of the initiate throughout his career.

c. The mileposts may dramatize the acquisition of specific skills, maturity, or bodies of knowledge, or may simply mark the passage of time.

4. The position of the modelee witin the labyrinth. The modelee may be at the perimeter of the control labyrinth or approaching its center.

5. The extensiveness of the model itself. The path on which the modelee finds himself may lead to control over knowledge and skills which are specific or diffuse.

6. The ratio of modelers to modelees. The proportion of persons in control of the model may vary greatly with, in some cases, a great number of initiates on paths leading to a model controlled by a very few individuals or, on the other hand, there may be only as many initiates as there are modelers; in some cases, even fewer.

7. Differential reward associated with model control. Pacing processes vary with the nature of the rewards at the end of the path, some rewards of course being capable of exciting greater persistence in initiates than other rewards.

Pacing is always an attempt to regulate takeovers by assuring that incompetents do no gain control over model secrets, but the quality of particular pacing precesses within societies depends on the relationship between the above properties. For instance, an individual being trained by the current witchdoctor to become his society's one and only witchdoctor will face a different labyrinth than a series of boys being taught the responsibilities of warriors. In the first case the initiate is totally dependent on his teacher; in the latter trainees can additionally rely on one another.

Each of the above properties is related to whether modelees are being trained to take over models of individual control or whether they are being trained to control values associated with society in general. The relevant question is whether modelees are being trained to occupy specific positions or, instead to be acceptable members of the society at large. Things that all members of a group need to know are much more likely to be taught in a group than are skills associated with particular positions.

When there are only a few persons controlling a positional model, and there are rewards associated with this control, modelers have obvious reasons for regulating the progress of those in their control labyrinth. In order to assure that the trainees do not learn enough to take over too quickly, those in control feed information to them a little at a time.

All Truckese religious practitioners as well as craftsmen and magicians are owners of the knowledge necessary to exercise their specialties. In line with this is the expert's tendency to transmit his knowledge piecemeal until he is too old to exercise his skill...It is quite probable too that a pupil has definite obligations to his teacher in connection with the application of his knowledge...Obligations terminate only at a teacher's death (Goodenough 1967:55).

In this regard, modelers may decide to eliminate mileposts for their initiates, preferring instead to delay recognition of trainee achievements until they are ready to transfer control to them entirely. To assume a learning theory perspective for a moment, information fed piecemeal provides trainees with a fractional reinforcement schedule, which effectively increases the likelihood of their remaining in the control labyrinth.

The Trukese example is useful in that it emphasizes that the dimension of expected reciprocity, dealt with at such length by Mauss (1967), is inherent in all modeler/modelee relationships. During early progressions through control labyrinths, the balance of giving is in the hands of those who control information. As controllers are putting out more than they get back initially, those being trained become obligated to their teachers. Controllers may then use this feeling of obligation to continue to control the progress of their students and to encourage them to maintain models even after their teachers are deceased, as the following example from the Thonga (South Africa) illustrates:

A dying headman calls his kin together to utter his last wishes. He reminds them of his debts and of those debts owed to him. He also reveals the place where he has buried some treasure (Junod 1962:134).

Deathbed transfers allow those in control to continue a pacing process for an entire lifetime. "The knowledge of the medicine-men (nanga) is mostly hereditary. Before his death he transmitted his art to his son...(Junod 1962: 453-454).

The context of a pacing process is also influenced by the relative difference in experience between the person judging the performances and the performers themselves. The greater the difference in experience the more likely it is that the less experienced person will accept the judgement of his mentor. Chronological age, on the other hand, does not always make a difference. Controllers are more likely to be chronologically older than those whom they judge, when the information and subsequent control which they are transferring maintains a general societal or organizational model which is extremely stable. As discussed in earlier chapters, this is a condition in which those most experienced with a group's model are those who have lived with it for the longest period of time.

When ranking and mileposts are employed as pacing strategies, controllers of a given portion of the labyrinth are less likely to be elderly. When these conditions prevail, qualified judges need only to have completed the portion of the maze that those they judge are now in. The military again provide an example. Anyone of a higher rank is allowed to judge the performance of anyone who has not yet achieved that rank.

Age-grading is a structural condition imposed on groups of modelees to control takeovers in come parts of Africa. Age-grades are echelons of modelees who are paced so that they reach mileposts simultaneously. They are ordinarily paced by echelons of modelers as well. A classic example is provided by the Nyakyusa:

Until he marries each boy hoes his father's fields in his father's village and eats food cooked by his own mother at his father's house, but sleeps with his friends...A bachelor does not simply go home to eat by himself, but a group of bachelors...go round together eating at the house of one's mother in turn...The village begins with perhaps a dozen boys, and their younger brothers join them...but after some years...the younger ones begin to be refused admittance to the village: 'they are children.' The young ones then begin a village of their own...If (brothers)...belong to the same village that is because they are near each other in age, and were born in the same village, not because they are kinsmen (Wilson, M. 1963:20-21; see also Ottenberg 1965 for a description of the rather sharp division of political and legal authority in Afikpo [West Africa] age grades).

Before leaving the subject of pacing strategies, brief mention must be made of rituals which dramatized changes in individual statuses. Some social scientists have assumed incorrectly that status passages, particularly initiation ceremonies, simply mark the entrance of youth into adult society. A close analysis of the data reveal however that such events, particularly when they are ceremonialized, mark the movement from one stage of the model control to another. They tend to occur as individuals complete one portion of the control labyrinth and simultaneously enter another one. They celebrate movement through the labyrinth, rather than the accomplishment of unconnected elementary performances.

This is especially true of status passages which are celebrated for children. Let's consider the example discussed previously in which an infant was circumcised. It seems safe to assume that although the child had been admitted as a member of the clan, the kin present at the child's circumcision were aware that the infant had much to learn about his people's way of life. Again the involvement of older people in these ceremonies dramatized the lifelong commitment to group ideals for all present at the ceremonies.

Ceremonies for older group members awe those below who have yet to achieve that stage of development; there are rewards associated with the new statuses. These are awing as well.

WHEN THE CENTER IS A VACUUM

Given that in any society there may be a control labyrinth with certain known properties including hindrances between entrance and ultimate control, what then? Why should an individual choose to enter the labyrinth

211

and exert the effort necessary to attain control of the model? Why not ignore it?

One reason may be that full participation in the society is itself contingent on control of the model. The individual may have no choice if he is to be defined as a socialized adult - if, in other words, he is to achieve minimal situational control. Another reason, if entrance into the labyrinth is optional, is that certain material and social rewards accrue to the extent that one achieves control of the model by predetermined means. These rewards may be material, in the form of wealth or other valuable goods, or social, as when increased prestige results from the solution of the labyrinth.

However, whether entrance is required or optional is to some extent beside the point. The labyrinth by definition conceals something valuable and attainable at its center. That is, those who are aware of the existence of the labyrinth know that whatever it conceals - is something defined as socially valuable. This awareness provides sufficient reason for undergoing the hardships and frustrations associated with the mastery of the maze.

Empirically, what the center holds may not live up to the expectations of the modelees. Nothing could, if expectations are high enough. There may not be that much mystery in the world. As Goffman (1959:73f) has observed: "Often the real secret is that there is no mystery at all; the real problem is to keep the audience from finding this out."

More often the mundane nature of what has been concealed is not discovered by the modelee until he has, in fact, solved the labyrinth.

All the supplementary mystification which surrounds the masks and the performances not only contributes to masculine pride but heightens the atmosphere of secrecy and the sense of the uncanny as well. Sanctity and taboo further intensify these effects. None but the initiated may handle the masks or witness the transformations from ordinary person to masked man.

Yet virtually the only real secrets beneath all this elaborate cultural camouflage are the details of the internal structures of the masks and the procedures surrounding their construction (Valentine 1961:48).

By this time, of course, if pacing has been properly regulated, the modelee will have exerted sufficient effort and invested sufficient energy in the mastery of the model that he is unlikely to reveal the non-secret of the labyrinth to an uninitiated audience, and is more inclined to define the non-secret as justification enough for his expenditure of effort.

However, should his disappointment be inordinately high, and should he feel the rewards are insufficient, that he has been "faked out," certain options are open to him, and we will discuss these later.

PACING CONSEQUENCES

In the past several pages we have been discussing the strategies of pacing, particularly the technique of creating a control labyrinth around model importances and/or model property which symbolically represent these importances. We now turn to the consequences of pacing processes.

If one takes a functional systemic approach to pacing processes, pacing may be seen as a means of regulating the training of new group members. As a consequence of pacing, there are adequately trained replacements in line who will be called upon as soon as the system needs them. The pacing processes regulate the flow of information to those who will eventually replace those parts of the social system that are wearing out. Such an approach is useful in that it accounts for much of the variation in our data by providing us with a model for understanding how these relatively static cultures have maintained themselves so well over a considerable passage of time. Nevertheless, this approach does not account for significant variation in our data which cannot be explained in terms of system maintenance.

Pacing processes also retard the flow of information to initiates even when it is against "the best interest" of the larger society. Positioned group members are able by means of these processes to censor for a time, information which they might want to protect for themselves in order to maintain their own positions as aging influentials. In other words, it is possible to say that pacing processes are occasionally selfish.

Pacing processes do result in a context for controlling model takeovers. Whether or not these takeovers are supportive in terms of the general values in society will depend to a large extent on the properties of the particular pacing context.

CONTROLLING TAKEOVERS

In terms of the assumption presented in chapter I, that all groups wish their descendants at least as much control over their own situations as previous generations have had, it is easy to understand the relationship between pacing processes and the production of "properly trained" successors. All groups recognize that a certain amount of physical and social maturity is necessary before certain skills can be taught. Many ethnographies discuss the training of children in this regard. "When the child is old enough to walk" or "when he can talk" are traditional ways of expressing such maturity.

Pacing processes may result in successful successors if they also regulate the order in which certain information is passed on. In terms of our own educational experience, most of us realize that it is impossible to learn calculus without having learned the fundamental properties of numbers.

Through the property of judgment, pacing processes are able to weed out disloyal, disinterested or incompetent trainees from the roster of potential group leaders. The passage of time allows for periods of trial and error and most importantly a period of practice in which the inexperienced can copy the activities of older adults, and the experienced can judge the progress of their juniors. The Tanala who live in Madagascar have war games which are played by boys "under the direction, generalship and guidance of the old men who are very tough (Linton 1939:263)." The old men do something similar among the Mbuti Pygmies. There they pretend to be animals and the young boys learn to hunt by trying to capture the old men (Turnball 1965:114). The leadership qualities of the young trainees are also judged by peers and elders in order to select only the most competent to control the group in the future. Among the Nyakyusa:

> From the time boys begin to herd they recognize one of their number as a leader...He gains his leadership and his prestige by bodily strength...In many of the young groups there are already leaders appointed...If they have proved satisfactory their appointments are confirmed by the old village headmen; if not new ones are selected (Wilson 1963:22-23).

The long period of time that elapses as a result of pacing eliminates those trainees who are not sufficiently interested from positions of leadership. Many persons may wish to aid in maintaining a group's model by subscribing to its principles - group membership may indeed be very important to them - still, they may shy away from assuming the responsibility of making decisions about it. In fact, in the extreme, making decisions about model importances may be seen as a threat to the security generated as a consequence of group identity. In a sense, there is a limit to how much they feel they ought to know. For example, many Jews place a mezuzzah on their doorposts as a symbol of their group membership. Few of them however know the meaning of the Hebrew inscription which is written on a tiny piece of parchment and stored inside of the mezuzzahs. And only the most orthodox in terms of religious beliefs and practices and the leaders of the less orthodox are interested in controlling this information to the extent of "interpreting" its meaning.

Weeding out the overtly disloyal, those who not only don't want to become leaders but who openly flaunt their opposition to model importance, is even more critical. Many societies will banish the disloyal from the community, offering them the same status as those who were never admitted inside the fence in the first place.

This occurs, for instance, in Samoa where an elderly man accused of impregnating his granddaughter left his village in disgrace and lived elsewhere for two years, at the end of which time he was invited back (Maxwell 1978). In this case, the individual had violated those model importances associated with general social acceptance. In other cases, the community may be social rather than strictly geographic, and the model violated a highly specialized one, as when a lawyer is disbarred by his peers from further practice, or a soldier dismissed with a bad conduct discharge.

DEFINING STATUS RELATIONSHIPS: THE CONTEXT IN WHICH PACING PROCESSES OCCUR

Pacing processes provide a context in which status relationships are defined, and these may then persist without redefinition for a significant period of time. The processes, when they occur in the context of limited resources and many rewards for control, will result in a good bit of tension and competition between hierarchical levels. When a group begins together but is allowed to proceed through the control labyrinth at varying paces, depending on individual differences, competition is as likely to occur among members of the same cohort as it is between cohorts at different levels in the labyrinth. On the other hand, when a cohort of trainees is traveling through a maze together, pacing processes may result in a great feeling of solidarity (Young 1965).

In addition, stops in the labyrinth serve to keep seekers in awe of those who "have the goods" or more accurately, the information. As they proceed through the maze they are confronted with further stops which need to be overcome. Stops which "awe" are discussed in the next chapter.

REFERENCES

Ethnographic Sources

Cushing, F.H.: **Zuni Breadstuffs**, Reprint of Indian Notes and

Monographs, Vol. 8:1-673, 1920. AMS Press, 1975.

Dorsey, J.O.: **Omaha Sociology**, Annual Report of the Bureau of American Ethnology, Vol. 3:205-320., 1884.

Fernea, Robert A. (ed.): **Contemporary Egyptian Nubia**, Vol. II, New York: HRAFlex Book, 1966a.

Fletcher, A.C. and F. La Fleche: **The Omaha Tribe**, Annual Report of the Bureau of American Ethnology, Vol. 27:17-654, 1911.

Fortes, M.: "The Political System of the Tallensi," **African Political Systems**, M. Fortes and E. Evens-Pritchard (eds.), London: Oxford University Press, 1940.

Gladwin, T. and S. B. Sarason: **Truk: Man in Paradise**, Viking Fund Publications in Anthropology. Vol. 20:1-655, 1953.

Goodenough, W.H.: **Property, Kin, and Community on Truk**, Yale University Publications in Anthropology, Vol. 46:1-192, Hamden, Conn: Archon., 1967.

Grimble, A.: "From Birth to Death in the Gilbert Islands," **Journal of the Royal Anthropological Institute**, Vol. 51, pp. 25-54, 1921.

Herskovits, M.: **Life in a Haitian Valley**, New York: A.A. Knoff, 1937.

Junod, H.A.: **The Life of a South African Tribe**, New Hyde Park, New York: University Books, 1962.

Kroeber, A.L.: **Handbook of the Indians of California**, Bulletin of the Bureau of American Ethnology, Vol. 78:1-97, 1925.

Lambert, B.: **Rank and Ramage in the Northern Gilbert Islands**, PhD Dissertation, U.C. Berkeley, 1963.

Linton, R.: "The Tanala of Madagascar," **The Individual and his Society**, A. Kardiner (ed.), pp. 251-290. New York: Columbia University Press, 1939.

Nordenskiold, E.: "An Historical and Ethnological Survey of the Cuna Indians." (ed.), H. Wassen, **Comp. Ethnog. Studies**, 10:1- 686, Goteborg, 1938.

Olson, R.L.: **Social Structure an Social Life of the Tlingit In Alaska**, Anthropological Records, Vol. 26, Berkeley, CA., 1967.

Ottenberg, P.: "The Afikpo Ibo of Eastern Nigeria," **Peoples of Africa**, J.L. Gibbs Jr, (ed.), N.Y.: Holt, Rinehart and Winston, 1965.

Rivers, W.H.R.: **The Todas**, Atlantic Highlands, New Jersey: Humanities Press, 1967.

Smith, M.G.: "The Social Functions and Meanings of Hausa Praise-Singing," **Africa**, Vol. 27, pp. 26-43.

Spencer, B. and F.J. Gillen: **The Arvnla**, 2 Vols. London: MacMillan and Co., 1927.

Stevenson, M.C.: **The Zuni Indians**, Annual Report of the Bureau of American Ethnology, Vol. 23:1-634, 1970.

Stirling, Arthur Paul: **Turkish Village**, London: Weidenfeld and Nicolson, 1965.

Stout, D.B.: **San Blas Cuna Acculturation**, Viking Fund Publications in Anthropology, Vol. 9:1-124, 1947.

Turnbull, C.N.: **Wayward Servants**, New York, Garden City, New York, Published for the American Museum of Natural History (by) the Natural History Press, 1965.

Valentine, C.A.: **Masks and Men in a Melanesion Society**. Lawrence: University of Kansas Press, 1961.

Whitehead, G.: **In the Nicabor Islands**, London: Seeley, Service and Co., Ltd., 1924.

Wilson, G.: "The Nyakyusa of S. W. Tanganyik," **The Seven Tribes of British Central Africa**, Colson, E. and M. Gluckman (eds.), London: Oxford University Press, 1951.

Wilson, M.: **Good Company**, Boston: Beacon Press, 1963.

Other Sources

Argyle, M. and M. Cook: **Gaze and Mutual Gaze**, Cambridge: Cambridge University Press, 1978.

Goffman, E.: **The Presentation of Self in Everyday Life**, New York: Doubleday, Anchor, 1959.

Mauss, M.: **The Gift**, New York: W.W. Norton and Company, 1967.

Maxwell, R.J.: **Personal Communication**, 1978.

Mauss, M.: **The Gift**, New York: W.W. Norton and Company, 1967.

Maxwell, R.J.: **Personal Communication**, 1978.

Young, F.W.: **Intiation Ceremonies**, New York: Bobbs-Merrill Co., Inc., 1965.

CHAPTER 12

BREAKING OUT: The Emergence of Autonomous Selfhood in Women Through Psychotherapy and The Women's Movement

Irma G. Zuckerman

March, 1973

INTRODUCTION

Contemporary urban life has been characterized by profound unrest and intermittent break-out phenomena which express disillusion and despair both with the symbols and styles of our venerated value systems and the major institutions which embody and uphold them. The politics of confrontation has left in its wake a mood of impotent outrage, which, while alternately filling and clearing the sidewalks and TV screens of the nation, also infiltrates and penetrates the silent citadels of the public imagination.

Group after group has added its signature to the list of the disadvantaged, loudly proclaiming its stake in a more equitable distribution of modern-day spoils (the available goods, services and statuses which purportedly contain within them the promise of a better life). Even women have joined the ranks- solid citizens of primarily white middle class vintage, emerging entente width their own definitions of oppression into a viable and voluble self-interest group. The subject of the paper concerns these women, Empty, frustrated and bored on the one hand, and hopelessly locked in on the other by prevailing socialization and pacification patterns. The burgeoning women's movement of the late '60's was designed to politicized women's issues in rapid fashion, moving step-wise from education and group "consciousness-raising" at highly personalized levels to programmed action at more universal ones. Years later, despite advancing popularity, the Movement falls short of its political timetable and, to many observers, appears to serve a primarily psychological function. In an era when psychotherapies proliferate almost as rapidly as public demand, what functions could a woman's movement serve - especially for middle class women, who have, heretofore, constituted the largest consumer group for professional psychiatric services? The present study elucidates some of the processes that both the Movement and Psychotherapeutic systems and shows how they are interrelated. It explains the ways in which both are used by increasing numbers of women who seek to maximize autonomy under the complex and confusing conditions of a rapidly changing social life.

Psychotherapy and the Women's Movement are bother conceived of as liberating and identity-forming institutions. The study suggests their relationship is complementary rather than parallel or antagonistic. Experience in the Movement prepares a client-type who activates the liberating potential of therapeutic systems, gearing them less towards "fitting in" and more towards "breaking out" into varied and realistic alternatives.

It is important to point out the limitations of the study. It in *no way* purports and *holistic view* of the Movement or a description of the manifold processes subsumed therein. Women's Liberation is a powerful idea and an exceedingly complex and amorphous organization which contains within its scope wide-ranging types of women of varying degrees of commitment, engaged in diverse pursuits over differing time periods, which may only occasionally intersect along some major axis of change. In the study I have attempted to account theoretically for behaviors common only to a segment of women in the Movement; in the author's opinion, this segment is an especially significant one.

NATURE AND SCOPE OF THE STUDY

The study emerged from participant-observation in the Berkeley Women's Liberation scene over a two-year period ranging from early 1971 to the present. (By participant-observation I refer to: reading the feminist press, active membership in consciousness-raising groups and the frequenting of meetings, activities and places, bote public and formal and private and informal) In all this, one fact was immediately apparent: significant numbers of women were searching earnestly in ways that alternated between Movement and psychiatric thinking, despite the seeming contradictions between the two. It appeared possible that what the *Movement* supplied was *a missing link in the therapeutic process*, but one which most women found absent in the therapeutic experience itself.

The primary data for the study derives from 25 free-form interviews (averaging 3-3.5 hours in length) with educated, white middle class women ranging in age from 18 to 54. They were selected because of their involvement in both dimensions of liberation, the personal (psychiatric) and the social (the Women's Movement). Their initial experience in therapy (which was usually multiple and various in type) generally preceded their identification with the Movement by varying lengths of time (depending on age). With younger women, the therapy tended to be closer in time to entry into Women's Liberation, or even coincident with , or subsequent to, it.

Popular mythology and, occasionally, social scientific literature, abounds wit depictions of Movement women which vary from fearsome, man-hating monsters to pathetic failures, kooks, nuts or misfits. A more recent one, perhaps, is that of a sexually seductive Superwoman. In contrast, several assumptions underlay this study:

The problems of the so-called "clinical" population differ in degree rather than kind, from those of other women and are reflective of strains, conflicts and changing directions within the culture. The sensitivity and articulateness of these women make them superior "spokeswomen." What is occurring in their lives, presently, is a socially-precipitated crisis of value involving a reorientation of, and revolution for, the Self. Both psychotherapy and the Women's Movement, as popular modalities, provide contemporary symbols, structures and processes through which the desired and required changes can be achieved. Involvement in both represents the struggle to articulate and integrate what have heretofore for them been separate personal and social systems. by viewing these women as trail-blazers, we see their life course as etching out new pathways and multivariate solutions which may help clear the way for others: new ways out of old problems.

BREAKING OUT

"Breaking out", occurring over time, in which persons seek to optimize conditions (both inner and outer) for the emergence of a unique and increasingly autonomous self. The process in open-ended and has cut-off points along the way. It involves the balancing out of freedom and restriction, possibility and limitation through the gradual cultivation and exercise of critical judgement and individual choice.

Progression is episodic rather than continuous. The process is set in motion at critical life junctures where pain and suffering force a shift in perspective and a consequent reorganization of experience. At such times, a heightened awareness of limitation is succeeded by mobilized effort to remove it.

Essential to breaking out is its dualistic focus; there is a fundamental dialectic between (1) *Retrospective* modes of thought - i.e., moving backward in time to retrieve, review and reintegrate the past, and (2) *Prospective* modes, which reach forward in time to create the future. The backward-forward motion is reversible, but the two modes are interdependent and closely linked. Breaking out receives continued impetus from a

221

prospective focus. As new "freedoms from" emerge, they find their primary meaning only in relation to "freedoms for".

These modalities are inherent in everyday thinking processes, but have also been incorporated, systematized and maximized by major social institutions. Traditional psychotherapy, for example, may be thought of as help based primarily on retrospective modes, whereas Women's Liberation offers help which emphasizes prospective modes.

In out society, individuals in crisis often seek institutional sources of help. The women in this study were no exception. Perhaps because they led relatively isolated and protected lives, they were all the more impelled to seek conjoint or social means for working out their difficulties. Professional psychiatry has long been women's help-mate in this regard.

The social context of therapy today differs from what it was ten or twenty years ago. Psychotherapy in the '50's was mainly Freudian analysis and was limited to small numbers of select women who had both money and motivation. Therapy freed them retrospectively from disabling inner patterns and also channeled their energies into existing institutions; i.e., it monitored their passage through the educational system into professional or semi-professional careers. Women often emerged from such passage with personal freedoms which were unmatched by outer conditions. Their newfound chances for meaning and success in bother career and marriage were foreclosed by discriminatory social attitudes and limitations in the opportunity structure. Such women often settled in dingily at social and professional levels far below their capacities, or, if fortunate, gave up their own endeavors to experience vicarious satisfaction through the success of spouses. For others, new cries of liberation added fresh fuel to old fires.

By contrast today, Psychiatry serves a larger, less resourced and more skeptical body of women. In a growing climate of distrust, women question all institutional goals and outcomes, and seek, increasingly, non-traditional resources for furthering their growth and completing the unfinished tasks of therapy. By transcending institutional limitations, they attempt to discovert and defining goals and social conditions which more closely approximate the requirements of their newly emerging selves. In other words, the relative emphasis, the primary content and the embodying agency of prospection has undergone major shifts, with Women's Liberation replacing more conventional routes to freedom.

For purposes of this study, the breaking out process will be discussed in terms of three major stages:

(1) The Use of Retrospective Help - (Psychotherapy)

Initial freeing from family-type oppression through the learning of retrospective analysis.

(2) The Use of Prospective Help - (The Women's Movement)

The second freeing from larger units of oppression through the learning of prospective analysis.

(3) The Use of Retrospective/Prospective Help - (Psychotherapy) The synthesis of the two modes into a larger time perspective and the working out of realistic goals.

I - USE OF RETROSPECTIVE HELP

OPPRESSION IN THE FAMILY

The nuclear family has traditionally been the primary vehicle for transmitting the values of the culture. It may also be thought of as purveying its oppressiveness. The women in the study experienced their original oppression in the structural conditions of their homelife rather than the economic exploitation of the marketplace. These experiences were prototypical - i.e., they were duplicated later in other social contexts.

Families combined key characteristics in varying degrees: they were *growth-thwarting* and *restrictive* - whatever their linguistic style, parents were authoritarian and maintained a high measure of external control. They built in obsolescence and failure through *unrealistic* and *contradictory expectations* expectations. Merciless pressure to excel was seldom accompanied by friendly guidance or concern for the real problems or personal costs involved. Capable daughters were cherished less for competence than for dressing and behaving *very* prettily. Parents treated their children as *"non-persons."* Families operated as functional units with closed awareness regarding members as feeling persons. Personal closeness and expressiveness were minimal; there was little sense of being perceived and valued for oneself.

Early typifications of parents became translated into "generalized others" and stereotypes which subsequently ordered role-modeling and feelings about the self. Mothers were seen as either "hysterical, screaming bitches" or mute and helpless "martyrs", whose own ambitions and intellectual capabilities were sacrificed (with misgivings) for others. Even mothers who maintained successful careers were perceived as unhappy and emotionally unfulfilled.

Fathers, on the other hand, were oppressively idealized and often clung to as the major source of psychological security. Inexpressive calm was taken for strength and, by contrast with their own turbulent emotionality, a measure of good mental health. The women tried hopelessly to emulate this model, as well as their father's style of achieving worldly success.

Frequent relocation, cultural differences and/or the contingencies of death, illness and divorce, weakened the integration of these families into their local communities. The early lives of these women were characterized by aloneness and serious, introverted interests. Doing well in school was universal. It was the only route to social-type regards, but was also coveted as a private source of self-gratification. Nevertheless, these women were oppressed by an ambiguous sense of self, feelings of failure and low self-esteem, uncertain goals, and a dull sense of the future, The absence of compensatory sibling or peer-group relationships heightened their susceptibility to labels of "deviance" of "craziness".

BREAKING OUT INTO THE WORLD

Breaking out can often occur "naturally" when it coincides with normative developmental sequences or situational contingencies such as: moving away, finding new friends, going off to school, taking a job, becoming ill, getting married and/or pregnant, and entering politics. New social contexts afford structural opportunities for the learning of new behaviors and the testing out of established patterns. Uncomfortable feelings from the past and dysfunctional role-sets sometimes carry forward and intrude into the new situation. Or characteristics of the new environment may coincide with features of the old and serve to reinforce existing attitudes. for the women in question, this was a frequent occurrence.

Progression along the life course generally proceeded in two ways. These were (roughly) reflective of generational differences and a more generalized shift in styles and values. The first group was usually under 25. I will call them *dependents,* because their gratification was contingent upon others. The second group was generally over 25. I will call them *determined.* Their motivational impetus derived mainly from themselves.

After a brief sketch of both types of behavior and a short excursion into their development, I will show how, despite their divergence, both "careers" intersected at a later point in time.

The relatively comfortable circumstances under which both groups grew up spared them from harsh encounters with the economic world and its day-to-day struggles for existence. Their carefully circumscribed experience with larger social realities minimized the need to develop strong and independent coping skills.

The *dependent* group tests out its socialization to the feminine role by carrying it to its limits. The imperatives of a poor self concept and a new cultural license for relaxing impulse control impelled them to trade in long-range, conventionalized growth options for short range satisfactions in free-style loving. Aspirations were blurred and educational commitments interrupted. There were expressionistic break-outs into experimental forms: art, drama, drugs, deviant social groups, radical politics, communal living and mystical love affairs. The enormous urgency and high intensity of these experiences correlated with their brevity, velocity and consequent profusion. They burned themselves out. Occasionally roles were reversed and the man assumed the weak, dependent end of the parent-child spectrum. The results were no better.

Despite appearances, then, the over-investment (and consequent loss) of self in old-style loving resembled more, rather than less, the earlier, family-type model. The women felt constricted and restricted and angry at having given more than they received. Sexuality became differentiated increasingly from intimacy and enjoyment. The placing of all one's goodies in one psychosexual basket eventuated in male dominance, dependence or withdrawal. Women emerged feeling bruised, exploited and emotionally, socially and intellectually impoverished - more so because of accrued deficits in other spheres of interest. Radical politics, often the woman's first engagement with the larger social world, only reinforced these feelings; it offered another brand of doing for others what needed to be done for and, perhaps, by one's self.

By contrast, the break-out attempts of the *determined* were fewer, less drastic, more considered and sustained in effort, and more conventionally styled. Rather than burn out themselves, they held Self in abeyance while exhausting, instead the growth-possibilities inherent in major social institutions and the cultural mythologies which support them. Their academic course was longer and more continuous, eventuating for some in prospects for a PhD. Their self-concepts, compared to the *Dependent* group, were more delineated. They were, however, more self-critical than blaming of others and were more susceptible to guilt rather than rage; this operated to lock them in, rather than free them, from otherwise unbearable situations.

Their early break-outs were opportunistic, instrumental and socially programmed. They included service in the military, the church, industry and Social Welfare, and last but not least, marriage and motherhood. A few hardy souls appeared to by-pass the latter two by plunging headlong into careers the loneliness and personal emptiness of their lives forced an abrupt about-face as they approached biological deadlines at later stages of the life cycle. For most women, however, marriage and motherhood were unquestioned sequences at a time when "The Feminine Mystique" was still in vogue.

Marriage, as it turned out, became a slow agony of disillusion and disaster, an invisible withering of once tender hopes and feelings, and a hollow round of duties, roles and rituals from which the Self was gradually exiled. Physical comfort, respectability and economic security scarcely reduced the grim toll of dissatisfaction, rendered the more onerous by the need to maintain the social mask.

The devaluation, censure and inhibition of feeling displayed by husbands, reinforced earlier taboos against self-disclosure, and left the women feeling crippled and isolated, as though without a common language.

Breakthroughs into more intellectualized assertion were also disparaged; opinion, when female, was discounted as "irrational". Epithets like "castrating bitch" were powerful and frequent enough to stifle many a nascent intellect.

Small children were considered "woman's work". Cooperation was rarely available, even in emergencies. At everyone's beck and call, women were powerless to order their own priorities and schedules to meet the requirements of their own rhythms and fluctuations, daily, monthly or life-cycle. For sensitive women of creative temperament this was especially grueling. Even sexuality was a unilateral servicing operation - one of diminishing efficacy as the emotional gulf widened.

Efforts to widen one's social base by making new friends or taking on roles were also denigrated and obstructed. Work roles, when practicable, were escapist in nature and self-defeating, when perceived as further extensions of already overworked maternal functions in larger social contexts, or bureaucratic paper-pushing with a feminine flair.

In brief, the structural conditions of marriage approximated the primordial conditions of their home life, but with no graduation in sight. Marriage loomed like a jail-sell to which their jail-keeper husbands held the (monetary) keys. The prospect of release was prohibitive when it carried with it the additional penalty of stigma and the social opportunity of going nowhere (with small children in tow). These women lacked the conceptual tools to break through and reverse their own life sentences. Many struggled all the more valiantly to "fit in".

SEEKING HELP:

Breaking out in major ways is contingent upon three interrelated properties:

(1) The degree of oppression, restriction or control.

(2) The level of subjective awareness - i.e., tolerance for suffering, the meaning of the suffering, the ability to identify or define the problem, and knowledge that a way out exists.

(3) The quality and availability of resources - both internal (overall capacities, strengths and motivation) an external (immediacy of help, personal support and real opportunities).

Women usually waited until suffering reached critical proportions before seeking help (in itself a form of breaking out). Problems lay dormant for varying periods and generally erupted (in the guise of disabling symptoms) under the stress of new situational imperatives or conflicted interpersonal relationships.

or the *Dependent* group; it occurred in the middle to late teens, when there was full mobilization for the break with home. It occurred somewhat later in the *Determined* group, and was related to difficulties in marriage, work or school.

Therapy was frequently regarded as the last court of appeal when all else failed. Selection of therapist was a hit and miss affair, based less on personal matching of therapist, therapy and patient, than on criteria of availability, credentials and degrees, and professional reputation.

There were many tries with many therapists and therapies - somewhat random efforts to get at recurring difficulties. *Dependent*-type women such it out for shorter periods (generally 3-6 months or less; occasionally a year). They were more concerned with symptom remission and practicality, than with understanding. They found the conditions of psychotherapy almost as intolerable as their symptoms. The *Determined* group persisted longer (1-2 year periods and longer). They were more easily socialized to therapy as a way of life.

While a few women were thrust into psychoanalysis (because it was the thing to do), most experienced some version of psychoanalytic therapy, sometimes presented in a more eclectic framework.

CONTRIBUTIONS OF RETROSPECTIVE ANALYSIS

Classical forms of psychotherapy utilize retrospection (and introspection) to "work through" traumatic biographical events. They establish connections between troublesome symptoms in the present and their early origins in the past; they short circuit the system of archaic needs, behaviors and attitudes is undone, once seen in its appropriate social-historical context. The capacity to transcend oneself and critique oneself in action is a new freedom which increases and differentiates the range of *perceived* options, and places one squarely in charge of one's own (inner) life.

The interactional context of therapy also facilitates break-out from the past. It legitimizes self-expression and encourages the discharging of accumulated hurts and tensions. It is also restitutive offering partial recompense for earlier neglect by parents, by means of listening, acceptance and support.

Women benefitted differentially and to varying degrees by these aspects of the therapeutic situation. Some not at all. Minimally, it tided women over a crises, restored functioning and gave them someone to talk to. The conceptual and definitional aspects were critical for some women. Therapy helped develop symbolic tools for differentiating and dealing with ambiguous inner states. By far, the most important function of therapy and the one with greatest carry-forward, was the inculcation of questioning and the assessment of one's perspective as a conscious way of life. This laid the groundwork for future problem-solving.

The learning of retrospective analysis contributed to the breaking out process by first bringing about change in the *inner* conditions of life. It attended the birth of Selfhood by integrating a variety of past selves into an on-going sense of self, and by affirming that Self in action. It illuminated obscure chains to the past, creating an inner readiness for freedom. It then equipped the new-found Self with the tools and tasks of setting itself free.

TRANSITION TO PROSPECTION: RETROSPECTION TURNED UPON ITSELF

For the *Dependent* group, the severing of symbolic ties with family led to the cutting off of actual ties and to breaking loose into the navigable waters of an expansive social world. The *Determined* group, on the other hand, lacked alternatives, and reinvested the proceeds of therapy in the existing family structure. By bringing back into the situation a freer and better Self, they hoped to redesign a more congenial environment.

As the women proceed to test out the incipient promise of therapy and to implement newly learned behaviors, they became increasingly aware of nameless discomfort, disproportionate doubts and an agonized sense of betrayal - the very feelings that had put them in therapy; the old oppressiveness.

For many, these feelings had occurred during the therapy itself, but could not be expressed. They continued to smoulder beneath the surface, or break out into premature terminations.

As dissatisfaction continued and disparities widened between what was felt and what was ordained, the women became reflective and used retrospective analysis tuned on itself to clarify and codify their feelings about the psychotherapeutic process and the structural conditions under which it occurred.

This was a process which, in itself, took time; the amount varied according to the following contingencies:

(1) The *severity* of the crisis. The greater the incapacity, the greater the helplessness and the greater the need to believe in the power of the therapist and to postpone judgment. Results, moreover, were not always apparent. Germination and incubation of new ways proceeds below the surface and sometimes survives only through careful cultivation and the existence of favorable conditions.

(2) Empirical *testing* under real life conditions. When situations remain unchanged and constantly repeat themselves despite the application of new principles, the system becomes suspect.

(3) The *historical context* of therapy. Freudian therapy is the most restrictive form of all, and though still in vogue, it dominated the professional scene in the 50's and early 60's. The changing social climate of the 60's, with it's legitimation of questioning everything, was itself an

outgrowth, popularization and diffusion of retrospective principles among the masses. It strengthened the questioner's belief in his questioning (though it did not, at the same time, help him discriminate between his questions).

(4) *Comparison* with other therapies and therapists. Successive experiences in therapy enabled women to structure an otherwise ambiguous and highly charged field. Through comparisons and contrasts they developed finer discriminations about who met what need at what time and how.

These private ruminations about therapy had a common theme: the oppressiveness inherent in the treatment situation. It was still another case of coming full circle - of recognizing (a la retrospective mode) similarities between present and past oppression stemmed from two sources:

(1) The qualities of the therapist himself, which perpetuated the treatment of the women as non-persons.

(2) Structural limitations inherent in the method itself.

Emotional breakdown in women may be a particularly poignant thing, compounding and already horrendous sense of aloneness which stems from the shut-in quality of their lives. This aloneness, like solitary confinement, is peculiarly maddening in itself. It creates an overwhelming need for contact: the sense of another human presence, personal recognition and mutuality of response. Classic psychotherapeutic relationships overlook this need, or attempt to deal with it in purely rational always. Over and over in the interviews women voiced indignant protests about this grim, unyielding stance of impersonal objectivity (The resemblance to other male figures in their lives was far from coincidental). The cold, professional facade and the stony silence was felt to be dehumanizing, and, at times, humiliating and sadistic. It reinforced earlier feelings of rejection and perpetuated symbiotic relationships on the outside which needed to be, and could have been, broken if the therapeutic relationship had been more nurturing. Some women perceived that the clinical distance served the needs of the therapist and not the client. It provided him with "stilts" and a safe hiding place. Sometimes, if women persisted, they were lucky enough to come across warmer, more sympathetic types. This contrast was always a revelation and inspiration. Person qualities would then loom in importance as compared with training.

"I can make very strong statements about the differences...the woman was extremely helpful...and the man extremely unhelpful. He was not particularly sensitive anyway, and being a man was a hinderance...She treated me as a person...and was incredibly warm herself. She came out with, 'I feel...,' 'This is may opinion...,' so different from the Freudian impersonal, objective thing, which women find so intimidating and oppressive! It's awful!''

The authoritarian structure of psychotherapy and the inviolate nature of the psychiatric relationship protected the therapist from criticism and rendered his judgements infallible. The women were again kept in a childlike status and forced to swallow there misgivings or have them reinterpreted as "resistance". Though many felt they knew best about themselves, they went unheeded, and were sometimes discredited, discounted and disbelieved when reporting objective facts. The women's tentative constructs of reality were also easily bypassed and arbitrarily reformulated into terms they could seldom question, and perhaps never understand.

Retrospection had its built-in limitations and when therapy concentrated predominantly on the past, it distorted current reality and the significance of pressing, everyday problems and relationships. Therapists felt at home with the classical problems of sex and early infancy, steering comfortably away from issues concerning which neither temperament nor training had prepared them. In the meanwhile the severity of hr husband's emotional disturbance was overlooked by the experts and he committed suicide.

It appeared, then, that therapy was a unique, dyadic relationship which failed to deal with the external conditions of life needed to maintain the behaviors it generated. Women in unhappy marriages were encouraged to continue in them with the not so implicit assumption that any failure was *their* failure - not the failure of the partner, the structure of the institution, or the obvious mismatches involved.

Women who did manage to break out into the world found themselves unprepared to deal with the pressures, competition and inhospitable conditions they found. Few therapists understood the difficulty or helped them develop attitudes and behaviors necessary for success. Therapy, for the most part, harped on problems, weaknesses and blind spots. It often ignored strengths and untapped potential, which , if utilized, would have formed the foundation for healthy and independent functioning, and provided motivational impetus for breaking out of therapy. As it was, retrospective help lacked a prospective focus, and by perpetuating the notion of individual responsibility (primarily on the debit side) to absurd and unrealistic proportions, succeeded in perpetuating itself.

This retrospective assessment of retrospective therapy accomplished two things. It forced women to discriminate between good therapy and bad, and to develop personal guidelines for getting as much from the experience as possible. Success in therapy was seen to be contingent on a high degree of awareness about the processes taking lace, and a cultivation, rather than a surrender, of critical judgment. Stages, or ways of testing out the experience, seemed to suggest themselves:

(1) A vague uneasiness, confusion, dissatisfaction; a feeling that something's wrong.

(2) A trying on of therapist interpretations and a trying out of their attendant behaviors.

(3) Continued recognition when it doesn't fit, "click" and "runs counter to personal feeling".

(4) Comparison and contrast with new people and new experience.

(5) Discovering, or evolving, a formulation that "works".

Even with these guidelines, women became increasingly aware of the vast work left undone by therapy - which lay, seemingly, outside its province.

THE NEED FOR A PROSPECTIVE FOCUS:

As old-style loving failed for the *Dependents* and their new-found social orbits left them drained and empty, as the marriages of the

Determined group became worse, rather than better, the women suffered from pervasive feelings of inadequacy and inferiority and vacillated uneasily between highly discrepant measures of self-worth. They longed for a solid base for self-esteem, one which depended less on male regard and identification with male achievement than on a center of gravity within themselves and a confidence growing out of their own successes. They thought increasingly on instrumental roles which might accomplish this, roles which would bring about new and independent sources of gratification, visible and measurable achievements, and full adult status in what appeared to be a man-made world.

The need for new goals and roles became imperative. As the women tried themselves out in new situations and attended closely their own reactions, they recognized there was a *real price* to pay - the breaking out from structures and relationships which enslaved them to old ways, a *final* giving up of all symbiotic ties, in order to be a separate and autonomous self. This prospect filled them with terror. It meant aloneness again! Many are called, but few are chosen. It was a feat many dreamt of but few could accomplish - alone. They were ripe for a Movement, and for a different type of help. And when it happened, such help carried them swiftly and a long, long, way.

II - THE USE OF PROSPECTIVE HELP

JOINING THE MOVEMENT

Women emerged from their alternate courses in therapy in all stages of development, but with old anchorages at least partially loosened and built-in programming somewhat undone. The central questions seemed to be: "What do I want in my life?", and: How and where can I find new beginnings and new resources?

The advent of the Women's Liberation at such a juncture was truly Messianic. It promised both deliverance from suffering and the autonomy of *real* choices. No more hand-me down roles from parents and professionals, but instead, the possibility that hopes, so long obscure and so long held down, could find expression and realization in forms less alien to the emergent Self. Women's Liberation was traditional feminine docility and dependence. It placed the Self actively in charge of conditions favorable to its own survival - without the price of being alone.

As a social movement, Women's Liberation accomplished what individuals could not: it provided increased opportunity for freedom by creating a set of social structural conditions. This occurred along two dimensions:

(1) An Ideology:

The Movement developed *an ideology* based on the rhetoric of oppression. It offered a new socio-political perspective of women's situation, adding another dimension of awareness to those already in vogue. It defined women's liberation as a basic human right.

It offered an alternative construction of reality - an organizing framework for previously unexplained (or misunderstood) aspects of social experience.

It embodied a *Prospective* focus and the rhetoric of hope, aspiration and fulfillment.

(2) Social:

As an organized social base with widening membership, the movement also widened the security base and social circumference of individual members. It offered inspiration and protection while the following changes were in progress:

A. The shifting of "cutting points" (or tolerance range) for new or deviant-type behavior in the community through collective action and the sheer weight of numbers (This also reduced the need for psychiatric labels).

B. Providing both opportunity and resources for resocialization. Negative self-images were transformed by redefining the bases of self-worth and offering positive reinforcement from new significant others (women) in a context of consensus, group sharing, group validation and group support.

C. Providing a population reservoir for willing experiments in living with alternative lifestyles - people, places and activities for restructuring everyday living an relating.

The "careers" of both the *Dependent* and *Determined* groups intersected in the Movement. They both left (to varying degrees) the relative safety and familiarity of a closed system for an open universe filled with uncertainty, but rife with prospect. They could shift their gaze from looking backward to looking forward the equal adult status and the development of a full range of capacities. Characteristically, the "conversion" process was brief and explosive for the *Dependents* and long and considered for the others. Reading played a minimal part in such experiences; the new gospel was picked up by word of mouth. For the *Determined*, the quest was more multi-faceted.

The timing of "entry" to the Movement, like the timing of previous therapies, was generally related to crisis. For some, this coincided with initial experiences in therapy (to be discussed later); a few returned to therapy at this time, while for other, the Movement was a substitute. The crisis was one of break-up, or impending break-up, of a major relationship. The Movement provided emotional leverage for the break, reassurance during passage, an worm persons to fill the social vacuum.

For most women, small "consciousness-raising" groups, (the backbone of the Movement), which were small, informal, face-to-face weekly meetings in people's homes, became, in fact, a new kind of all-female family - an adult family of strangers. Entry into these groups was quick and easy. There were no prerequisites and no obligations.

The new family promised to reverse the original conditions of family oppression (mentioned earlier) by abolishing:

(1) Authoritarian control - and breaking out of normative rules. restrictions and hierarchical statuses.

(2) Anachronistic expectations - through autonomous goal-setting.

(3) Treatment as non-persons - through mutual acceptance as feeling persons.

A new expressive license in these groups lowered the barriers against self-disclosure. What had, for so long, been dept personal and private could now be made public through the media and the mechanism of such groups. Women, speaking together, spread the word, and further developed a language.

The Movement capitalized on the intense emotionality of the entry phase by capturing the expressive moment. Volcanic eruptions aided morale-building and public protest. The explosive energy of thousand private rages was welded into one, single bludgeoning instrument. Group sentiment, in groups of younger women, oscillated between the poetry of pathos and the rapture of revelation, the dirge of an outmoded way of life and the chanting of warrior songs; it was more subdued among the older women: a mood of conjoint commiseration.

Not all the women in the study joined consciousness-raising ("rap") groups. Some became involved in action-type organizations, such as N.O.W., or developed feminist projects in other social contexts.

LEARNING PROSPECTIVE ANALYSIS

Retrospective analysis offers a critique of self; prospective analysis critiques the social order. One expands the horizons of inner freedom; the other pushes out the frontiers of social freedom.

Prospective analysis is also historical: The roots of women's enslavement are to be found in the exigencies of a by-gone age which necessitated the ascension of male to positions of dominance. The perpetuation of this state of affairs in neither natural not inevitable, but falsely conceived. Women are not sick or inferior. They are powerless. Once they recognized this condition, they will rise to overthrow their oppressors.

The ramifications of this political theory are beyond the scope of this paper. They were also of lesser interest to the women involved, than their immediate, practical implications. The *Dependents*, however (partly because of recent radicalization), adopted the Marxian rhetoric and spoke in revolutionary terms. The *Determined*, characteristically, were more evolutionary-minded.

Like therapy, the Movement provided linguistic tools the name and describe what before was dimly felt, but not articulated. These words became new bases for action, which, in turn, were recognized and rewarded by the group. The words, in effect, had transformed power.

Prospective rhetoric added several new dimensions to the women's thinking. It was:

(1) De-neuroticizing

"Oppression" replaced "depression"; "victim" superseded "patient"; being "fucked up" was no longer a matter of "something's wrong with me", but, "I'm going somewhere positive"; "sickness" in the self was seen as the "sickness in the world". The target was no longer invisible, internal and located in the historic past, but was visible, external and locatable in the structural conditions of the here and now. The symbolic universe these women entered was one of wellness, growth, learning and change. The subsequent therapies these women selected reflected this (See later section), although the transformation inherent in such views was slow in coming, and considerable tension existed between the new ways of thinking and the old.

(2) De-conventionalizing

Prospective thinking abjured connection with the archaic past, with man-made theories, man-made institutions and masculine-type values of dominance and competitive individualistic success. It legitimized alternative ends and an ethic of cooperation and "sisterhood" as the means. It disavowed traditional roles.

(3) De-sexicizing

Integral to the analysis was the view of women as persons rather than sexual beings (or objects), and the salience of learned behavior over biological accident. Insistence on sexual role-playing was regarded as hedonistic male bias.

These shifting styles of thought had far-ranging consequences, moving from very personal levels outward to the social matrix. Those that will be discussed here can be seen as a series of stages: A New Prospective

Retrospect on Retrospective Help; A Re-orientation of the Self; and a Breaking Out into Alternative Structures.

A PROSPECTIVE RETROSPECT ON RETROSPECTIVE HELP

The feminist press waged a fiery and controversial attack on the psychiatric establishment. Professional roles were de-mystified; the infallibility of the experts challenged and their theory refuted as both preconceived and extinct. Women pointed out rampant sexism and highlighted built-in assumptions regarding the validity of conventional feminine roles.

Women's groups provided a gathering place for the wounded. "Radical Psych" groups in particular (these well be mentioned later on), attracted psychiatric casualties: failures, drop-outs, found little credence, choice or voice. Together, in such an ambience, women aired their hurts and grievances, compared and contrasted experiences, and, through retrospective sharing, differentiated criteria of helpfulness. The groups, then, began to function as a minor checking system on, and clearing-house for, local psychotherapy.

As women in this study reviewed their personal psychiatric histories they became indignant about previously unrecognized aspects. They realized before that their recurrent crises in relating had always been attenuated, but never really "dealt with", and the "intensity" of their conflicts was reduced, but never understood or resolved. They accounted for this now as: (1) Male chauvinism, which reinforced old patterns of behavior with men both inside and outside the therapeutic hour, and (2) Failure to take seriously the oppressive conditions in the external world and, consequently, to inculcate behaviors which were required to cope.

(1) Male Chauvinism:

Looking back, women recognized that they met therapist dominance, superiority and seductiveness with reciprocal roles abut which they were uneasy, but relatively unaware - i.e., falling in love, timid submission, dependency, and entreating for special favor. They rarely unlearned these within the context of the "therapeutic" relationship.

As members of a social elite, and men who themselves were pampered and looked after by women like those they treated, therapists thrived on traditional sex roles and, like many men, had little personal inclination to give them up. They perpetuated their own value system by "laying a male trip" on their patients - upholding sexuality, marriage and motherhood as the ultimate fulfillments to the possible exclusion of others. Blind to their own idealized images of women, therapists unconsciously projected them in a variety of subtle ways (smiles, interested glances, compliments, etc.), which were formative in their impact. Sometimes these ways were not so subtle.

Male (and male-type women) therapists, moreover, were felt to be incapable by many women of truly understanding their "struggle" as women. They felt that differences in biology, levels of sensitivity, life experience and integration into mainstream culture insulated therapists from the depths of female travail and frustration, especially when they themselves had difficulty explaining and expressing it. This problem was further compounded by traditional differences in modes of thinking and styles of expression; there was the same old dichotomy between cerebration and feeling, which caused so much trouble in the first place.

In couple therapy, women reported the male therapist to be male-identified - i.e., he related collegially and empathetically to the spouse, while castigating the woman (implicitly or explicitly) as emasculating, or as a childish trouble-maker.

Therapists themselves were seldom deeply at odds with the culture. They often deprived women of their chance to break out and grow, by too-quickly reducing the tension and anxiety which accompany real-life changes Instead of standing-by, sustaining and supporting women during a difficult period of turmoil and transition, it was easier, less troublesome and far commoner to subdue the patient with tranquilizers, divert her stirrings for the unexplored life into the usual sexual channels, or to impose upon her mute wonder and inarticulateness concerning her own felt needs and inclinations, some facile preference or interpretation of their own.

(2)Failure to Deal With the World:

Disposed by training to simplistic, undeterministic views of reality, therapists failed to appreciate the multitude of factors which impinged on their patients lives. Many could not understand the difficulties dealing with the outside world, or encourage, in relation to themselves, the kind of questioning, assertive and irreverent behavior that was needed in dealing with social institutions. The consciousness-raising groups sometimes made up for these deficits.

The Movement also supplied something for women who could not utilized therapy, despite their need for help (Either they could not tolerate the anxiety and ambiguity of the process and hoped for instant change, or damage in their early life was so severe they could open up deeply to no one, or they lacked goals and direction and a vocabulary with which to communicate their longings). For these women, Movement politics was congenial. There they could hide their despair behind a frenetic blaming of the system, and escape from troublesome symptoms by a never-ending involvement outside themselves. The Movement, like other organizations, programmed purpose into their lives. They also did well in encounter-type groups, where the fireworks of confrontation pre-empted personal preoccupations and jolted them into a ready-made identity.

A RE-ORIENTATION OF SELF

For most of the women, the next period was one of self-discovery and turning their sights froward to analyze their prospects. As they separated in varying degrees from old-style living and loving, they maximized their opportunity to heed, attend and give to themselves. Energy was withdrawn from others and invested in the Self. They geared into prospective thinking: wishing, imagining, projecting roles and anticipating their outcome, testing the self in action. This process was necessary in order to find personally compatible goals. It proceeded as follows:

(1) Differentiating what feels good and what doesn't feel good, likes and dislikes - i.e., establishing emotional tolerance ranges.

(2) Assessing competence - what one can and can not do - i.e., evaluating the true limits of one's capacities. This was often empirical, but sometimes not.

(3) Acquiring new images and role models. Talking with a wide variety of women - lawyers, grad students, teachers and artists, etc. - awakened new ambitions and showed it could be done.

(4) Taking risks - asserting feelings and opinions, arranging one's own clothes, schedules and activities to suit oneself, learning to tolerate criticism and toughen up to rejection.

(5) Seeking validation and nurturing from women instead of men.

(6) Increasing reliance on internal rewards - feeling good, satisfied, developing internal criteria of self-worth.

(7) Tolerating the tension and frustration involved in long-range goals, and the multiple stresses of new-found roles.

The women's choice of goals had much to do with age, life experience and stage of the life cycle. There tended to be a balancing out of experiences over time; whatever had been missing was sought for. Older women, who had been "big on career" and had tested themselves out in the world, longed more for the expressive side of life and sought the privacy and stability of a small, stable social unit, and the knowledge of biological maternity before it was too late. Having achieved a measure of independence earlier, they were eventually willing to surrender parts of it and to pay a higher price for love. These women were rare in the Movement, however. The major thrust was towards the development of instrumental roles.

Aspiration levels within both groups (*Dependent* and *Determined*) increased as they began to feel better and to take themselves seriously. The *Dependents* generally rejected marriage and motherhood, without having tried it. Contractual relations were seen as superfluous, and motherhood as dismal and draining (judging, perhaps, from their own mothers' experience). They were to much in need of nurture to think of caring for children, and they longed to use their bodies for pleasure rather than pain (childbirth). Their aspirations took the form of wanting to help other women who experienced the same difficulties as they did, they projected themselves into fields like social work, psychology, teaching and medicine, where they felt they could utilize their own learning experiences. Though instrumentally oriented, their motivation was not money, recognition or prestige, but the personal gratification which comes from touching someone else's life in a meaningful kind of way. They saw themselves developing skills within these fields. but using them "for the Revolution" and not within established agencies.

The *Determined* group had, for the most part, experienced marriage and motherhood and found them wanting. They felt the gratification ascribed to these roles was highly overrated - at least for themselves, and those they knew. This group was comprised of many gifted women, who, in their earlier school days, had glimpsed other forms of satisfaction - intellectual, artistic and even, for example, ice-skating. They turned towards these interests with renewed zeal, or, as suggested earlier, discovered other talents they had been previously unaware of. Many returned to academia for advanced degrees, motivated more by a need to fulfill themselves and do autonomous work, than to serve others. They were not averse to partaking of an equal share of the prevailing reward system, and began to organize or join interest groups on their own behalf. Like their *Dependent* sisters, they had not totally turned off to men, but no longer wished them to be the center of their universe. They were more pessimistic, or realistic, than the younger women, recognizing the disparity between their more differentiated need for love and the dearth of high-quality prospects.

Except for an occasional "drop-out", an amazing energy pervaded the lives of these women. Their orientation was not towards relaxation or pleasure, but towards work, or working things out, and this in the context of community. Even expressionistic ventures had an intensely serious, almost life and death quality about them.

BREAKING OUT INTO ALTERNATIVES

Self-discovery was not the isolating, introverted phenomenon it had been in the early lives of these women; not was it an uplifting, contemplative state. It was a conjoint search accompanied by a bursting forth of imaginative action programs and creative projects which carried these women into contact with real people in the real world. There was an enormous diversity of effort, some of which related to restructuring services, and some to restructuring everyday life.

(1) Restructuring Services:

This had a dual aspect: infiltrating the system and creating new structures.

Community-wide projects were numerous: R. ran for office and also developed affirmative action programs. L. Organized N.O.W. and a Bd. of education Task Force to investigate sexism in the public schools. X. started a class action suit on behalf of female investors. T. was involved in setting up a University Without Walls. J. engaged in speaking Tours and radio programming on the subject of changing sex roles. C. offered classes in Women" Literature to help raise consciousness in groups that might otherwise remain unreached. (Capital initials represent interviewees participating in this study).

New services developed by women for women. They were free and were organized on a non-hierarchical, non-professional basis. The guiding principle was: "Self-Help" - maximizing women" control over their own daily lives, and providing an alternative to exploitative public services. Breakaway and other groups offered wide-ranging classes from home repair and tire change to feminist research and child-care. The Women's Health Collective provided free and personalized medical care in an atmosphere of dedication. The Women's Refuge provided emergency services and "crashing" for transients. The Women's Center offered referral information on OK shrinks, medical men and other professionals in the community. The Women's Herstory Library housed a venerable collection of documents, present and past. Radical Psychiatry offered contract-type problem-solving for women in small groups which were safe and supportive in nature. New and imaginative groupings were developing all the time. Recently A. formed groups for women over 50. Announcements are printed in The Women's Newsletter.

(2) Restructuring Everyday Life:

Living Arrangements:

Dependents preferred group life in a variety of forms: form mixed or female collectives, to word or interest groups to moving in with a man.

The living quarters of *Dependents* were usually stark, ill-kept and barely utilitarian. By contrast, the *Determined* group retained its preference for single dwelling units and some modicum of beauty and order. Their environments reflected their own personalities, and showed a greater need to own their personal space.There was a preference for neighborhood, rather than close living arrangements.

These women also needed to protect their time, as well as their space. As they become increasingly tuned into themselves and deeply involved in the transformation of new "careers", they were able to drop the arbitrary scheduling of middle class life with its punctual, three meals a day, and surrender much of the ritualized activity that had been built into their previous lives. They lost interest in clothes, possessions, housekeeping and entertainment in order to allow more time for the thins that counted.

These women now showed an increased tolerance for aloneness and a grim determination to avoid domesticity. They insisted on an equal sharing of the tasks of daily maintenance, allowing their children to do much of the cooking, cleaning and looking after themselves. They hoped for an empathic division of labor instead of begrudging tokenism, but found few men who were interested in such arrangements. It was too soon to compromise.

Relating to Men:

While men were defined as enemy and the legitimate targets of pent up rage, few women wished to purchase their ticket to Self-hood at the price of no return. In calmer moments, they recognized men as merely less conscious, less conflicted victims of a system they had not themselves created; they saw "male chauvinism" as "insecurity" and a camouflage for weakness, rather than a show of strength. They hoped to find new ways of relating, though setting out to do so often seemed like an act of faith. There seemed to be a certain progression as they moved forward into the unknown:

A. Affirming Selfhood:

The revised self-image and the autonomous activity mediated by both therapy and the Movement resulted in higher self-esteem. As women began feeling better about themselves, they no longer needed men to fill a void, or lend meaning and importance to their lives. As alternate satisfactions grew, confidence grew and women became selective of quality in their relationships.

B. Risking Self-Disclosure:

It was necessary not only to be a Self, but to unmask, and become an authentic Self in relation to men. The expressiveness learned in the Women's Movement had to be carried forward into the outside world, and respect commanded for oneself as a feeling, thinking person. Anger, disagreement and opposition were easier to take out of hiding than more positive feelings. There was, for example, the need to stake out the territorial dimensions of Selfhood in any relationship, and the need to communicate tender longings for a shared intimacy. These became problematic.

C. Defining Femaleness:

In order to avoid being pulled back into old patterns and old ways of relating, most women needed to declare a moratorium in their relationships with men. This period served to heal old wounds, discharge bitterness, broaden one's social base and find out (at last) what it was one wanted from an intimate relationship, after all. (How could you ask, otherwise?) This defining proceeded in two ways:

(1) *Owning one's body* - This meant establishing a map of the physical and sensory self; exploring one's own body, developing an appreciation for it (independent of Hollywood/male standards), finding out what feels good and where, and how to be in control of one's own satisfactions. The Women's Movement legitimized the means to this end: self- stimulation and self-gratification.

(2) *Establishing a context for closeness* - Most women experienced sex

without love and tenderness and without release. There was a need to fuse physical and emotional closeness and to break down the kinds of personal barriers that characterized male dominated relationships. It was only in the safe, emotional context of being cared for that many women could initially let go. For this they turned increasingly to each other. The Movement legitimized love between women.

D. Apportioning Time and Energy:

Most women had not, as yet, achieved a satisfactory way of relating to men. They could only approximate their needs over time as they themselves were changing rapidly. These projections into the future were generally time-limited; they were a calculus based on balancing the nature of their particular need system at a given moment against the quality of the available supply system. Such projections, especially for the older women, were often dismal; male culture was felt to be lagging too far behind, and the women varied in their zeal as self-appointed catalysts. What emerged, then, was a projection of short-range relationships (if any), rather than one long one over all time. Short-term relationships could vary in accordance with the needs of a particular growth period. If, in addition, they were contract-free, there was easy exit. Who, after all, wanted to be locked in again?

Such relationships could not only be time limited and multiple, they could be concurrent and partial. Being an autonomous self meant that you could apportion time and energy according to your own needs - not always someone else's. Not all women felt this way. Some older women were less afraid of losing themselves in a relationship, and felt that real love involved commitment and a voluntary surrender. They could not, however, find partners who agreed with, or accepted them.

A very few women were fortunate in finding broad-minded, accepting men. Only one of these achieved what might be called a happy and fulfilling marriage. This was the result of: (1) Working out her own problems and independent career (with the help of 15 years of therapy), and (2) selecting a secure and stable man who could tolerate the unexpected, and (3) being innovative. X. has her own bank account, her own friends, interests and career. She sues her own name, to which she will soon add a PhD. The Movement provided leverage for these changes. Having delineated clear boundaries, X. is able to enjoy her marital relationship freely.

TRANSITION - RETROSPECTION UPON PROSPECTION

As women pressed on in the context of rapid change, and entered successive stages of the Movement, they experienced new tensions and conflicts, new doubts and uncertainties, which were vaguely reminiscent of the past. As they retrospected about the Movement, they recognized familiar "locked-in" feelings and a sense of the old oppressiveness. Retrospection brought them more clearly in focus.

THE PULL OF THE PAST

The momentum of outer life far exceeded the pace of inner development. The disparity grew between what was expected and professed, and what was personally experienced, As old needs, forsaken values and powerful internalizations exerted a backward pull, the distance between today and tomorrow doubled. There was the old disharmony between role and person, image and reality.

THE OPPRESSIVENESS OF SISTERHOOD

The Movement was not always ready to handle increased tension and anxiety. Women's groups, as such, were relatively unstable as new members came and went; they seldom lasted more than 3 months. Women entered at all phases of their growth, paced themselves differently, and cut out sooner or later, depending on their tolerance for change. Some were content with relatively minor modifications and left to return, perhaps at some later point. Others of more serious commitment, weathered out more drastic changes in a sea of constantly shifting faces.

While entry was quick and easy, the first flush of "I'm OK, you're OK" wore off under the clash of personalities, lifestyles, and divergent aims and approaches. As the Movement tried to consolidate under the banner of "Sisterhood", there was greater pull towards uniformity and less tolerance for difference. Individualistic orientations were frowned upon ("There are no personal solutions"). High degrees of anxiety were disruptive of group process and were either ignored or cooled out. Friends were not always available in time of need.

The non-hierarchical system, in closer observation, revealed powerful cliques and factions and a tyranny of types - i.e., vocal, verbal, domineering women who presided loudly over their quieter, less experienced sisters, converting Liberation into dogma.

Excessive talking and excessive "selfing" in groups carried its own dangers. When it was too rapid and too intense (as it often was), groups and people "burned out". There was a need for time, distance and intervening activity.

Similarly, the "gay" life did not always stand the test of time. The difficulties of working out a relationship transcended problems of sexuality.

It appeared, then, that *dominance*, *dissonance* and *personal distance* were problems of the new, ideal family as well as the old; that these were characteristics of all human systems, from the Self on outward, and were inherent in the structural conditions of all institutions and associations.

The feminist analysis itself needed de-mystifying, as women broke out conceptually and checked it increasingly against the facts of experience. "Maybe *all* people, not just women, want a different way." Like retrospective analysis, prospective analysis was also simplistic.

THE LIMITS OF PROSPECTION

Prospective thinking raised the sights of women; but as they moved out on all fronts to accomplish the goals they set for themselves, the conditions of everyday life proportionalized them and scaled down their dreams to size. The "careers" of their choice involved more difficulties than they realized. Hostility, ridicule, resistance of tokenism greeted their entry into high places. They lacked the wherewithal to cope strategically. The satisfactions from sudden intimacies, male or female, did not last and could not be counted upon. The longings for dependence, security and for being taken care of were still very strong; the responsibilities of freedom seemed onerous and confusing.

Between the grandeur of the ideal and the daily reality, the preoccupation with global issues and the growing personal preoccupations, lay a widening chasm which forced frenetic "Freedom Now!" attitudes into a larger time perspective. Utopian visions yielded to the humdrum pace of step-by-step solutions and the more modest accommodations that individual psyches and their immediate social contexts could allow.

The prospective gaze stumbled across reality and woke itself up. It engendered forward movement, but could not monitor the pace. It suggested a universe of possibility, when only facets could be realized.

Women who used retrospection to analyze prospective help from the Movement, found they were once more locked in to a closed system to which they had surrendered the keys of their critical judgment. As they reflected on learned distinctions which were once so vital and so compelling, and had recently delineated the contour of their lives, they recognized them as no longer so clear or so separate. The dualities of future/past, man/woman, inside/outside, dependence/independence, passive/active, dominance/submission, sick/well, giving and receiving had been dichotomized. They emerged now as ranges on a continuum along which each person travelled backward and forward in time at different historical junctures and at varying rates of speed. To break out of these categories was to break out once more from shelter and comfort, and the company of true believers. It was to experience once again the terror of aloneness and the frightening possibility of personal autonomy. Some women made the break - sooner or later; some women never did; still others sought another kind of help in order to define themselves, their limitations and their prospects more clearly and realistically.

III - THE USE OF PROSPECTIVE-RETROSPECTIVE HELP

The newly developed "consciousnesses" of the day held tremendous carry-forward power which, in the context of therapy, transformed the usage of retrospective help. The return to the experts was no longer son fearsome. Under revised conditions, retrospective analysis was easier, more positive and more productive. Women who returned to therapy after Movement experience, and women who engaged in both concurrently, found that:

(1) They were more *articulate*. They had a ready-made vocabulary for what once was too nebulous to talk about.

(2) They *elected* therapy and were not driven to it because of crisis.

(3) They had a stronger *awareness* of themselves and others which monitored therapist dominance and their own complicit behaviors.

(4) There focus was more *prospective*. They had a more *discrete* sense of their goals and purposes and the problems which intervened along the way.

(5) They were *reality-oriented*. They no longer sought naive escape from oppressive conditions, both inner and outer, but to work more diligently to overcome them. They projected what now were realistically attainable goals, of maximal rather than infinity range, within the limitations of the existing structure.

(6) They were *practically-oriented*, hoping to learn attitudes and behaviors which would be useful in realizing their prospects.

(7) They were highly *selective* in their choice of therapy, proceeding carefully and consciously on the basis of new criteria for judging compatibility and skill. They sought a personalized matching between the

mode of therapy, the type of therapist, the purpose of the therapy and the predilections of the patient. As therapists themselves reckoned with the new "consciousness" of the day, there was increasing likelihood of finding a good fit.

(8) They were more *questioning*. Their own intuitive and critical judgment replaced blind faith in authoritarian and authoritative verdicts.

The therapies women selected varied broadly in type, but the human qualities of the therapist were considered paramount. It was common for *Dependent* type women to choose "Feminist Counselors", women more nearly like themselves, with whom they could feel personally comfortable and sure of being understood. Such a relationship maximized the possibility of nurturance without the roller coaster heartaches contingent on working with a man. It also provided important and acceptable role models for women in search of feminine identity.

Determined type women considered other factors and were not averse to working with a man. Depth of method, degree of skill and the openness of the therapist to criticism were important qualifications.

The basic problems women brought back to therapy had a common core: how to relate instrumental roles and expressive ones, and how to integrate past orientations with future orientations. These problems had several interrelated dimensions:

(1) Relating to Men in New Ways:

As women took on new roles and responsibilities and learned to cope independently with the outer world, less energy was available for cultivating closeness in new and more satisfying ways. Part-time relationships and hit-and-run sexuality were promising in theory, but failed to satisfy deep-seated needs for continuity and care.

Many women longed to initiate relationships, but were held back from doing so by deeply ingrained conditioning and fear of rejection. Women who did take men in hand and tempted to bring them up to date often pushed too hard, too fast, too soon and then despaired of their newfound role as teachers.

As women experienced more aspects of their aggressiveness, competitiveness and dominance and came up against harsh obstacles in the outside work, they recognized potential commonalities which could unite them.

On the other hand, they despaired to recognized that many men were not ready for such a partnership, and felt helpless to create bridges in the meanwhile.

(2) The Fear of Success:

Women had difficulty fantasying themselves at the top and forcing their way against resistance and crushing pressures. They were fearful of losing male regard, and had few acceptable female models to emulate.

(3) Blocks in Creative Work:

Women were not used to considering themselves as creative. They felt internally blocked and fearful in relation to independent, creative thought, and hesitant in risking comfort and security to heed the uncertain voice of their imagination.

(4) Combining Love and Work:

Most women were conditioned to think in terms of a single or limited number of roles for themselves. Roles were often compartmentalized and women had difficulty moving comfortably from one to another.

As the dialectic of retrospection and prospection moves backward and forward through time, and women break out from all kinds of help, they will have learned a larger process which combines both modalities, and frees them to become their most cherished selves within the framework of the present.

IMPLICATIONS FOR FURTHER STUDY

The issues touched by this study of the breaking out process suggest many take-off points for further investigation.

(1) Other Comparison Groups:

The forms of breaking out in our culture are numerous and increasing. It would be interesting to compare and contrast the process described here with breaking out in, for example: Prisoners; Old People; Shut-ins; Astronauts; Artists; Religious Leaders; Scientists; Adolescents and Mental Patients.

(2) The Retrospective-Prospective Dialectic:

A further exploration of the use of time perspectives in the integration of self would be useful in relation to historical periods in which one form of another predominated. What about the implications of the "Here and Now"?

(3) Changing Conditions in Therapy:

(a) How does the changing client model affect the direction of psychiatric theory and practice? Who leads who,, and is there a change in emphasis?

(b) What effect will the new peer model and the declining emphasis on training have in the "products" of therapy?

(c) What implications does the "policing" of psychotherapy have for the freedom of thought of the therapist? Will he/she be ruled by individual whimsy and the politics of fashion, or does consumer protection itself have built-in safeguards?

(d) What are the limits of Self-Help modalities? What structural conditions exist within the cooperative framework?

(4) Whither Women?:

(a) What are the gains and losses women experience in their newfound freedoms? How alternative are the new forms of childcare, family life, and sexing and careering?

(b) What are the patterns of dominance in Women's Groups? Are these different from Men's?

(c) What are the problems women have with creativity and how could these be studied?

(d) How will the new instrumental roles hold up at later points in the life cycle? Will women live longer? Will they have missed biological maternity (if they have not experienced it)? Will there be a new breed of older women, who is less of a burden on the social system?

The present study is an opener to some of these questions and issues. As time moves on, it would be interesting to carry even this study forward under the rapidly changing conditions of the Movement today.

NOTES

CHAPTER 13

WOMEN ALONE IN URBAN PUBLIC PLACES:

Managing Approachability

Janet Tokerud

1975

The big city is a relatively hazardous environment these days. The incidence and visibility of muggings, rapes and other street crimes has increased significantly in recent years. Law enforcement efforts have proven woefully inadequate to the task of keeping street crime at a tolerable level. Personal safety in the public space of the city, once usually taken-for-granted, is now a difficult proposition. Cities are characterized by large, relatively transient and heterogeneous populations. These conditions create an environment filled for the most part with strangers. Living in the city means learning to get along in a "world of strangers" (Lofland, 1971). As strangers are not particularly noted for their reliability in coming to the assistance of fellow strangers in times of need, the urban environment poses the problem of self-protection to its inhabitants.

Much attention has been recently given to the problem of rape and to methods of prevention and ways women cope with rape. It is not my purpose here to add to the recent proliferation of literature on rape, but to address an equally important safety problem for women in the city: how to cope with the range of more commonly encountered assaults upon her person and sensibilities. These lesser sexual assaults may consist of verbal encounters, often lip-smacking suggestions of intimacy; visual encounters, the look up and down; personal space invasions; sometimes actual molesting; or prolonged engagements that continue after a woman has indicated she does not wish to be detained. Not so devastating when taken individually, these "little rapes,"[1] by their sheer frequency of occurrence, limit female mobility and inspire greater expenditures of energy in coping with them than does the more remote threat of rape. For the woman in the city, the acquisition of urban knowhow[2] consists to a great extent of learning how to manage her *appoachabiliity*.[3]

The type of approach varies to some extent according to the situation. Street hassles have a particular style, as do, for instance, hassles on the bus or in New York's subways. The characteristic urban public place is populated by strangers who have no other connection than that of being mutual occupants of a public setting. Approaches in such places, therefore, are between and among strangers. Unless the public place is under some sort of supervision, such as the supervision of a bartender of bus driver, a lone individual has few resources for protection other than herself.

My focus will be on the urban settings where women alone are particularly likely to be approached. My reference situations will be public transportation vehicles and terminals, coffee shops or eating places, and streets in densely populated areas such as downtown, ghetto and low-income neighborhoods. Because the main agenda of many bars is sociability, this setting will only be referred to when an extreme example is particularly helpful to the analysis. Occasional reference will be made to other situations where especially illustrative.

In my attempt to analytically describe the experience and tactical repertoire of the unescorted woman in public places, I have interviewed 19 women at length and talked with at least 50 other women, either singly or in small groups, on a more informal basis (in conversations without taking notes and without declaring our conversation an "interview"). I did not take a representative or statistically weighted sample in choosing interview subjects. My choice was based on three major considerations:

(1) Sampling women across a range of: age, marital status, employment status, and relative attractiveness.

(2) Doing a majority of interviews with women who have a reasonable modicum of first-hand experience alone in urban public places.

(3) Convenience and ease of obtaining the cooperation necessary to do a two-hour interview.

I obtained the interviews by mentioning my research topic to female acquaintances and interviewing either them or other women to whom they referred me, and by asking women interviewed for names of other women who might be willing to be interviewed.

Because my topic is on the heightened problem of approachability of women, I have chosen to emphasize the female half of the interaction and neglected to elaborate the approacher's definitions of the situation and interaction work except as it directly bears upon the female's interaction work. Over the time I was doing interviews of women, I spoke with a number of men about the male's side of the interaction and about their personal experience. After I completed my interviews with women, I interviewed five men at length. I have attempted to integrate the point of view of the male approacher into my theoretical framework (at least some key aspects of it that came through in my small interview sample) where it serves the overall analysis.

The product of my questions and these men's and women's answers forms the basis from which my concepts have been developed. My interview data is supplemented by information gained in a previous research effort wherein I did a content analysis of American etiquette texts from 1900 to 1972, focusing on the codes of etiquette regarding male-female interaction.[4] Etiquette writers have consistently devoted much attention to the protection of "ladies." Although in past times the situations in which women were present alone in public were fewer, careful and detailed instructions were given on how to preserve her integrity and reputation and minimize embarrassment. This extensive treatment of what I call a woman's problem of approachability suggests that it is a problem of underestimated importance. The problem remains. As the boundaries of action for women expand, responsibility has been shifting from protectors to self-protection.

SOCIOLOGICAL THEORETICAL BACKGROUND

My sociological analysis is part of the Symbolic Interactionist tradition. My basic units of analysis are individuals and social interactions. This is a microsociological study. My working assumption is that human activity is characterized by the symbolic interaction of actors with themselves and with Others. Human behavior is mediated by symbol construction and communication. How I define myself, my setting, myself to Others, Others' expectations of me, my expectations of Other, etc. at each point in an interaction, is central to what the interaction is and is becoming.

This paper focuses on a particular type of social interaction between specific classes of interactants and in a specific class of settings. I am interested in (a) face-to-face interaction, (b) between opposite sex strangers, in (c) urban public places. The interactionist perspective places social interaction on an equal plane with socialization and social organization. In a face-to-face meeting between strangers, persons with no mutually shared biographies (that they know of), who may have widely divergent social backgrounds, linguistic understandings and value assumptions, the emergent character of the interaction is heightened. In such an interaction there are few certainties. Both interactants must use all information available to them to "place" the Other in categories for action; yet, must do so tentatively and continuously throughout the interaction sequence.

For the lone female in the city, the management of approachability involves "instant" identity construction to define herself as only conditionally approachable in spite of cultural or micro-cultural stereotypes regarding the motives and sexual availability of women alone in particular settings. It also involves developing a psychological map of urban settings regarding setting occupants and agendas such that she may minimize the initiation of, control, terminate or entirely avoid approaches.

My survey of the sociological literature on rape, women and territory have yielded bits and pieces of the conceptualization that developed during my research. Lyn Lofland's dissertation, "A World of Strangers: Order and Action in Urban Public Space," provided a number of useful concepts and excerpts from her data that I used for secondary analysis. Another particularly relevant monograph is Sherri Cavan's *Liquor License* which focuses on behavior in public drinking establishments. Both of these authors acknowledge that women, specifically, have a problem with approach management in public settings. Lofland:

> ...if they make their relationship to the locale very clear, the encountered other is likely to grant appropriateness...despite the *not infrequent concerns of females* with keeping themselves aloof from surrounding males, this young woman was quite willing to engage the older man in conversation... (p. 280)

Cavan:

> I visited all establishments in the guise of a typical patron, attempting to be indistinguishable from other patrons present. The fact that the public drinking place is a setting open to all members of the community who have reached their majority made it unnecessary to justify my presence...But at the same time, being a female in what is customarily a male setting makes some difference. In the first place, there were bars from which I was categorically excluded, bars with a standing rule that they are open to males only. In the second place, some bars that are open to both males and females are typically patronized only by males, and in such establishments it would have been awkward, if suspicion-arousing, for me to enter alone. (pp. 16-17)

But neither of these authors, nor anyone else that I know of, have devoted adequate attention to this important problem that has become increasingly important with the increase in the extent of stranger-occupied public space.

None of them have elaborated the specific ways in which women cope with the problem of approachability, although for women the problem is particularly relevant.

This paper focuses on approach management in urban public places, concentrating on a category of persons for whom the problem of approachability is particularly acute. I will lay out some of the areas of action where an unescorted woman can take measures to protect herself from unwanted intrusions of privacy by contact from strangers. Individual sections of this paper address stages of approach management. In the first section of the text, I examine options to limit approachability that are available while one is still in "safe" territory: *pre-public planning*. Once preparations have or have not been taken and a woman crosses into public space, she begins the second phase of approach management: *minimizing approachability*. The second section deals with the tactics she can employ to defend herself against the level of generalized threat that she perceives. Last, I look at options she has open to her if approach is not prevented. This last section of the body of the paper covers basic tactics of repelling the approacher.

PRE-PUBLIC PLANNING

The first phase of managing approachability is pre-public planning. Preparation for traversing high-approach or high-risk settings can be strategic or incidental. A woman may choose her destination, the type of transportation to be used, the dress that will be appropriate, protective goods she wants to take with her, all with the thought of minimizing approachability - *or* she may make these decisions without giving the matter particular thought. She may have simply acquired habits of life which limit (or increase) approachability. In any case, while in "safe territory" prior to going "out," she has the opportunity to take precautions.

LIFE-STYLE CHOICES: AVOIDING

This paper is devoted to the *urban-dwelling* female. My focus is on women who fare forth in the city, at least some of the time, on their own. I am studying a phenomenon peculiar to a set of urban lifestyles. For some women the "hassles" I speak of have little meaning, because they have adopted life styles that effectively preclude the problem of approachability.

Marriage is a good start toward *avoiding* the problem, for example. A woman may marry a man who will support her and eliminate her need to *go out* and "make a living." He is home evenings and is a willing escort when she wants to go out at night and a willing errand-runner when something needs to be purchased, someone needs a ride, etc., at night. Even if she is not married, a woman may still make lifestyle decisions to avoid the problem. She may spend two-thirds of her paycheck on a "good" neighborhood and a car. She may live near or with her family - handy escorts. She may take a job and live only where she can park her car, so that she doesn't have to walk far to or from her car.

But, on the other hand, a woman may not "want to be rent-poor like my East Side friends."[5] She may go for a good job downtown that involves a daily walk. She may not be able to afford her own car, so may take the bus. She may not be willing or able to pay a high price for her peace of mind. She may enter the fray and manage her approachability as best she can. Or, of course, she may insist on her right to go where she pleases in "public" places and manage approachability as a matter of course. Whatever the reasons, a great number of women have, lately, been choosing urban lifestyles where the problem of approachability is *quite* relevant.[6]

ROUTE-ING

The social geography of the city is important to all city inhabitants. Lofland suggests, I think rightly, that in the modern city location is a more important identifier than appearance. Various settings in the city have their specific sets of people, acceptable behaviors and dress patterns. Dissociated from a particular setting and the normative overlay that accompanies it, a particular person's appearance or activity is very definitive. The same lone female behaving the same way will get "typed" an entirely different way in the Financial district as opposed to the Tenderloin district of San Francisco.

Choosing where, when and how one will traverse the urban terrain is critical. All other preparations depend on anticipation of the risk conditions one will be facing. Lack of forethought, a wrong turn or bus stop, or misinformation could make the smashing party dress into an invitation to trouble. The familiarity with one's own surroundings that is part of living in a more circumscribed environment is not so easily had in a big city. The first few months in a new city can be particularly stressful as a woman makes tentative forays through the city hoping that she will not blunder into situations for which she is not prepared. Sometimes an escort can be recruited to accompany her as she scouts out unfamiliar territory. However, while escorted it is often difficult to anticipate what the approachability configuration would be when unescorted.

Male informants unanimously emphasized the precedence of location in their assessment of a woman's approachability. Given that they find a woman desirable and have the impulse to approach, discouraging appearential or behavioral cues are often ignored if a woman is alone in high-approach settings. Negative signals, if noticed, can be summarily dismissed by the question "Why would she be here alone if she really wanted to be by herself?" Confronted by a lone female in certain situations, he may be moved by sex-role expectations, i.e. as one male informant put it, "All men don't want to be 'mach' but many men who don't, want to feel they have to be."

Once a woman gains familiarity with the parts of the city she usually traverses, intelligent route-ing depends upon her discretion. One of the older women I interviewed made this comment:

> I would suspect that I lead a fairly circumscribed life - as I said I've always ben timid, in some ways not. The old fashioned term is "decreet". "Discreet" means setting barriers.

Knowledge of setting agendas is necessary to intelligent route-ing, but knowledge is not always enough. The relative risk of path and means of transportation along that path is weighed against cost in time, money and convenience. Moving cars act as insulating shells that make an otherwise high-risk path a safe one. Likewise, unless one can afford to live in a good neighborhood (read "safe"), the trip to and from one's car (if one can afford a car) is a necessity that cannot be avoided. Subways may be the cheapest and quickest way to get around in New York City, but few single females dare take advantage of it.

Given the competing values of time and money, route-ing that virtually eliminates threats to the unescorted woman is more the exception than the rule.

ARRANGING APPEARANCE

A lone woman in urban public space is an approachability configuration that is determined by three major variables: her *appearance*, her *behavior* and the *setting*. Each of these variables exists as a meaningful dimension for both the woman alone and Others present in the setting who take note of her. Here we shall look at appearance as a factor in the approachability configuration.

Attractiveness, good looks, sex appeal - whatever one chooses to call it -

is perhaps the ingredient of appearance that determines approachability. Men say that some women are so good-looking that they can't help but stare, comment, whistle, or approach. They claim that given such a spontaneous attraction, all other factors about the situation are overridden.

That attractive women are more frequent objects of attention and approach is a taken-for-granted common sense understanding in our culture. The woman who goes out alone and does not wish to be conspicuous or be approached considers her own attractiveness as an important variable. She may make a calculated effort to "tone down" her natural appealing features (especially those she associates with sex appeal) if she feels it is necessary to reduce the attention she gets to a tolerable level. For example a large-breasted female may consciously choose to avoid "tight-fitting sweaters..." (Ann Landers column).

However, a woman's physical attractiveness is a particularly important personal feature in this society. Women interviewed feel that their attractiveness is a central part of a positive self-image. Without other particularly outstanding sources of self-esteem, a woman's attractiveness as reflected in mirrors and in the response of others is hard to part with. She likes to feel that she is attractive even if she "really doesn't care" what strangers on the street think of the way she looks. Besides, her attractiveness is often an important commodity. Great numbers of women are occupied in either the clerical or service professions, where it is often the case that a woman's physical attractiveness and even sexiness is practically a job requirement.

If attractiveness is the appearential main-spring of approachability, availability cues imbedded in appearance are primary overlay. If a lone female is seen as desirable, then whether or not she is available is of primary concern. Availability has as almost an insistent attention-getting force as does attractiveness.

If a potential approacher is interested in some degree of extended social interaction with a woman, it is of practical interest to know how available she is to such interaction. Is she desirous of approach? Has she dressed provocatively so that men will find her attractive and approach or so that they will see that she wants to be approached? There is a subtle but important distinction between dressing to communicate interest or disinterest in being approached, whistled at or "laid" and dressing to be attractive enough to be approached. As the "easy" woman is held in low esteem in our society, a woman who wishes approach may want to be attractive but not appear to be soliciting approach even though she wants it. Men interviewed respond both ways. Sometimes they respond to a woman because she appeals and don't dwell on her motives, other times (perhaps with those who are not so appealing?) they respond to "standard announcements that say she is open to approach." Signalling openness to approach opens one to a variety of impertinences as well. If she is seen as a loose woman or a whore, a woman is likely to meet with obscene gestures, remarks and stress. If a woman is open to approaches from strange men she is not a "lady", so the liberties of approach would not be an impropriety.

As men assess availability, they also assess potential threat; if she is not 100% likely to accept or tolerate an approach, some assessment is made of what a rejection might involve. If there is an audience to the approach encounter, the approacher is cognizant of how embarrassing it would be to be visibly turned down.[7] A "friendly" or lewd remark made to a woman on the street is great as long as the woman doesn't have a "snappy comeback" that makes the remarker appear foolish. It is probable that young women in their teens and early twenties are particularly subject to street-hassling because they are not expected to have the social skills to put-down such hasslers or *their* put-downs can be laughed off as childish.

ESCORTS AND PROTECTIVE GOODS

The use of "unescorted" to describe a woman alone suggests the central role escorting has had in the protection of women. The woman alone just doesn't look right; there's something missing - she doesn't have an escort! Not long ago one form of escort was an institution in this country - the chaperon. Although "escort" now usually refers to male escorts, the chaperon was typically an older (over 30) female. Parents are convenient escorts for children (also seen as needing protectors) and young girls. Husbands provide convenient escort service for married women. But single women beyond childhood may have considerable difficulty recruiting escorts for daily needs. Unlike the chaperon, the male escort is likely to prove a threat himself rather than a protector. Many more woman than those paying for an escort service have paid a price for the protection and "respectability" that a male escort provides. For want of "reliable" male escorts, female escorts are often used. The advantage of a female escort is that neither woman is indebted or put out, because both need escorts. The only problem in terms of approachability reduction is that two women together may still be seen as "open" to approach. Given the hassles and hazards of recruiting escorts, sometimes a woman says, "The Hell with it!" and just takes off on her own.

Dogs sometimes come in handy as escorts. A big, ferocious looking dog is likely to make the most desirous approacher think twice before he does anything that might offend its owner. One male informant who claimed that subtle signals to reduce approachability don't work, gave "large dog" as an example of a "strong signal" that does work. Dogs are most frequently escorts on walks. Although walking one's dog may provide many moments of peaceful solitude outside the confines of one's own home, dogs do not comfortably fit into many situations. It is rare that a woman can take a dog with her to work, for example.

Protective goods[8] in some ways function as surrogate escorts. Reading materials may be attended to as needed to control eye contact and signal alternative involvement. Purses may serve as useful props for the same purpose. A "wedding ring" may be worn as a symbolic escort.

Although my focus is more upon the social-psychological threats than the physical threats to unescorted women, another type of protective good deserves mention - weapons. Women rarely carry weapons visibly and therefore sacrifice any deterrent value such visibility might have. The occasional radical-feminist may wear a knife on her belt. Reports from those who have done so indicate, though, that harassment often increased considerably. A woman wearing a knife opens herself to approach or comment by her conspicuousness. Weapons are more typically carried in a purse or pocket. Most commonly used and recommended are: pocket knife, plastic lemon filled with ammonia, mace, hand gun, hat pin, or ice pick. Concealment of a gun is illegal, and mace is illegal in some states.

In summary, before she even enters the public space, a woman may take great measures to reduce the likelihood of unwanted approach or comment. Her whole lifestyle, particularly her choice of workplace and residence, may be bent to avoid unescorted time in public places. Her public appearance may be purposely subdued or desexualized. She may go to the expense of purchasing a car for transportation if she can afford one or may take circuitous routes to her destinations to avoid particularly "risky" situations. She may own a dog or gun or a library of paperbacks to arm herself for "trouble."

MINIMIZING APPROACHABILITY

Once preparations have or have not been taken and a woman steps out into the urban terrain on her own, she begins to actively *manage* her approachability. Women automatically adjust their demeanor and action to "fit" public places, just as most people automatically adjust their demeanor and action to what feels appropriate for any given setting. For the unescorted woman in the public space of the city, an important dimension of her adjustment involves *minimizing approachability*. Although many of the tactics for minimizing are taken for granted and not "calculated," they are nevertheless routinely employed.

The unescorted woman tailors her tactics to minimized approachability to the level of defensiveness she feels the situation requires. When she assesses the situation as a *high-approach* setting, she more actively employs tactics to reduce her approachability to a tolerable level. Her dress and hair style are now fixed conditions. If she is not familiar with the settings, she may temporarily bungle this part of approach management by relaxing and assuming that she is not in a high-approach situation when she actually is. However, after some observation and perhaps unpleasant surprises, she can immediately intensify her tactical efforts to prevent approach.

ROUTINE FEMALE MODESTY

Even in the low-approach setting, a number of basic behavioral precautions are routinely taken. In previous times and for those females who, sexual revolution or no, are still attempting to be "respectable," the "modesty" of "acting like a lady" is a behavioral absolute that is to be followed in the range of public places.

A greater degree of self-involvement or disinterest in one's social and physical environment is expected of women than of men. A woman is more properly the object of attention than the subject. Unless she is interested in *inviting* approach or increasing her approachability (and is willing to endure the stigma that may go along with doing so), a woman routinely avoids even momentary eye contact (particularly with males) and manages her body "modesty"; i.e., sitting with ankles crossed or keeping an upright posture in a chair. She is supposed to minimize her approachability to a greater degree than is expected of a male in similar circumstances. She properly presents a closed image, he properly, a more open image. Man the approacher, woman the approached. She need not look about and see the world and its inhabitants; they will come to her or, better yet, be presented to her by her guardians.

PROJECTING UNAPPROACHABILITY

In situations where being left alone is less easily maintained or where an unescorted woman is conspicuous by her mere presence, routine female modesty must be supplemented by other minimizing tactics. If her mere presence in a setting unescorted makes her a target for approach, routine female modesty is not enough by itself. She may have arranged her appearance to modify attractiveness, availability and threatfulness, but she is likely to act the part as well by manipulating the behavioral variable in the total approachability configuration.

Carriage and gait may not be just "modest" but downright purposeful and hurried. One etiquette writer suggests that a woman on the street should not turn her head from side to side as she walks but look where she is going. The implication was that she is not supposed to be enjoying herself by involvement in her public environment but is supposed to be practically oblivious to her surroundings; only there out of necessity as a means to get to her real destination. One female informant who claimed a genuine satisfaction from taking evening walks in solitude, said that whenever she passed anyone on the street at night she picked up her pace and accentuated her stride. She said:

A malingering walk would indicate that I'm not concentrating or that I'm available. The way you walk communicates.[9]

When asked about what makes a woman on the street approachable, men frequently note "tempo of her walk, casual relaxed body movements" as indicative of a "down to earth woman".." in touch with what is going on around her" who is more open to street involvements, and not so likely to respond with indignance to a stranger's overture. Also, this motion as opposed to "regimented, rigid walk, tight mouth, etc." is also just apparently more appealing and "sexy." They say that some women put out strong "vibes" that either indicate that they want to be approached or indicate that they want to be left alone. With this thought in mind, some women simply concentrate their minds upon sending out vibes that they are not "easy-pickin's" and believe that this will be apparent to the potential approacher. It is difficult to say what all the projection of "vibes" or the projection of unapproachability entails. Believers in "vibes" are usually believers in the popular folk wisdom that every woman who is raped was asking for it or wanted to be raped. Perhaps not surprisingly, women who frequently experience difficulty in being left alone when they want to be while unescorted in public places, take exception to the "vibes" theory.

.

They may admit that some women unquestionably "send out vibes" that invite approach, but express the firm belief that men rarely respond to subtle communications, especially subtle rejections. Most men and women did say that there are "nuts" and "some men who won't take 'no' for an answer," perhaps fairly prevalent in certain settings such as bus depots, who are not likely to respond to the most obvious signals.

The longer a woman is in a public place the more "suspect" she becomes. Loitering or engaging in activities that show no visible occupation, such as people-watching, resting, or thinking in public is less acceptable for a woman than for a man. Such a lack of visible occupation may make a lone woman conspicuous. She may be suspected of being a whore unless all other indications contradict that suspicion. Because of the unpleasant possibilities, women rarely engage in this type of behavior except when they are waiting for something or someone. Sitting on a bench at a bus stop nay be seen as legitimate until the bus is a half hour late.

To minimize the possibility of approach, unwelcome stares or public comment, women are *active* waiters. Frequent glances at a watch or clock, and frequent or concerted looking for the awaited vehicle or person, accompany a general display of impatient waiting. Active waiting serves notice that her lack of occupation is not willful and that her agenda is not open to unscheduled engagements because at any moment the object of her real business will appear.

Given a few props, the unescorted woman is much better equipped to demonstrate that she is occupied. A book can serve the dual functions of indicating her occupation and giving her an excuse to avoid eye contact. As mentioned earlier, many women regularly carry books with them when going about the city unescorted. Lyn Lofland describes in detail how a book can be used to minimized approachability in her description of the waiting style of "The Sweet Young Thing":

> She inevitably has a book or magazine in her possession and this is drawn from her coat or handbag the moment she has settled herself in a position. The book or magazine is never closely read; to become engrossed is to risk losing awareness and control of one's posture. In addition, it is essential to be on a constant lookout for any approaching danger. But while reading material receives little close attention, it is always conspicuously present, either lying on the lap or held out from the body with one hand, about midway between the lap and the face. Such a prop serves to demonstrate that she is tending to her own

affairs, not on the prowl for strange males and not the type of young lady who would invite attention by boldly staring about.[10]

Other possessions may serve to indicate one's busy-ness. A purse can always be sifted through and the items in it given careful attention. A checkbook could always be brought up to date. Unfortunately, this ruse is usually only effective for a short period, after which time it may indicate that one "has nothing better to do." Such busying activities are commonly associated with time-killing. Because of this they must be pursued animatedly and with a display of concentration to be convincing.

Smoking has little occupation-signalling value for a woman, but eating and drinking have some value as legitimate occupations. It is common, though, for a woman eating and/or drinking alone in public to bring her reading materials along, also. The combination is usually sufficient. The value of these activities in minimizing approachability seemed particularly evident at the Oakland Greyhound bus terminal. A majority of the unaccompanied men in the terminal were in the central lobby, typically occupied with looking around or actually strolling about. During a three-hour observation period, only four unescorted women sat in the main lobby. They were not looking around but were either tending to their belongings or were blankly staring in the direction of an unoccupied space. In an adjoining coffee shop, however, there were very few males and a great number of females, some accompanied and many unaccompanied. The women were usually eating or drinking *and* reading. None were idle.

LOCATING

The virtual segregation of males and females in the bus terminal exemplifies another minimizing tactic. When a woman chooses where to physically position herself in a setting, it may be done so that approachability is lessened. In the case of the Greyhound station, the waiting for a bus could just as easily take place in the coffee shop as in the regular lobby. Many public places are similarly segmented into sub-territories with differing "agendas" for interaction. Unescorted women typically locate themselves in the lowest approach sub-territory of a public setting, and they are expected to do so. If they don't, they are suspect. A woman is "inviting" approach if she locates elsewhere.

In the public drinking place, the segmenting is standard. There is typically a physical bar area, an area behind the bar, and usually an area with tables and chairs, each with its own agenda. Tables and chairs are for the self-contained groups or for individuals who wish to remain aloof from bar sociability. A woman sitting at the bar is considered out of place, fair game, or is just plain not allowed to sit at the bar at all. Sherri Cavan elaborates:

> Locating in the vicinity of the bar is generally preferred to locating away from it...Women are a notable exception...Thus to the extent that the physical bar is the center of social gravity of the public drinking place, women may frequently be found to be in the bar, but not of it. While they may be defined as open to overtures of sociability be their mere presence in the setting, their actual spatial location within the bar is often such that the probability of being contacted is lessened.[11]

In public places that are not really segmented, locating becomes a more improvised tactic. A woman might, for instance, sit at a table far away from others instead of at a table amidst many people. Her locating would be based on the "rules" of everyday sociability. In another instance, she might locate herself right next to a bus-stop sign at the curb, facing the street. In this way she makes it clear to all that she is a legitimate waiter.

Another dimension of optimal locating is the nearness of others who may act as witnesses or potential protectors. Although it may not happen so much as it does in the movies, there is some expectation in most public settings that if someone is obviously subjecting a "respectable-looking" woman to an unwelcome approach and she has no male escort to intercede, any other male present may intercede in her behalf.

Physical barriers may also be used in locating. A phone booth may be the perfect solution for the woman who has to wait for a bus at night or on any corner where street hassles are frequent. However, the see-through booth enclosure is no barrier to visual violation and actually may encourage it.

Tactics of minimizing approachability are employed against a generalized *threat*. There is no known quantity to deal with, only expectations based on information about oneself and the setting. One does not know for sure whether one's efforts are enough or too little, i.e. "You never know whether it's your not looking at them that helps or whether they have work to do or whether they want to talk with someone else, when they don't bother you." (woman interviewed). Also, to the extent one succeeds at this level in being unapproachable, one may be precluding opportunities for the occasional desired approach from the "right" person **and** just friendly conversation. The next section of the paper goes on to look at a more definite situation:

what happens when a woman is actually approached? How can she repel the unwelcome approach once she sees it?

REPELLING APPROACH

So far, my discussion of the unescorted woman in public places has dealt with pre-engagement contingencies of the approachability configuration. This section will be devoted to the kinds of interactions the unescorted woman takes part in when she is actual approached by a strange male. The first subsection deals with *deflecting* the initial overture. Subsequent subsections cover tactics and counter-tactics used as the engagement is prolonged or becomes a problem. If a single woman does not successfully deflect, she may *side-step*. If she does not successfully side-step, she may *relocate* or *leave the scene*. If that doesn't work, she may more aggressively *terminate* or ultimately, *defend* herself.

DEFLECTING

The woman alone in public who is seeking to minimize her approachability is on the alert for the slightest gesture of approach. If she truly does not want to be bothered at the moment, the unaccompanied female must reject an approach before she takes the time to inspect the desirability of the approacher. The initial overture of an approacher may often be deflected before an actual engagement has occurred. Initial gestures of approach frequently involve "getting someone's attention." Depending upon how obtrusive the opening signal is, one may be able to simply pretend that one does not notice, and, hopefully, reposition oneself in such a manner that the line of approach is blocked.

Approachers typically favor remaining at a distance and staring or walking by and staring until eye contact is made when making an overture. Once eye contact is made, he will get some idea of the woman's interest in further interaction. He does not expect a prolonged glance in return, but may hope for a smile. In public approaching, eye contact is analogous to getting one's foot in the door. The sophisticated female will keep alert enough so that as soon as eye contact is made, she instantly averts her eyes and turns in a direction that precludes further eye contact. If a woman is too relaxed she may accidently look directly into a pair of staring eyes and be caught or may be slow to avert. In these cases she may no longer pretend that an overture has not been made.

Deflecting is a general sort of tactic that can be applied to a variety of approach situations. On the street, as a male approaches in the opposite direction and begins to stare at a distance, an alert female immediately deflects his gaze by looking at the street or her purse. In particularly "bad" neighborhoods, a woman alone will routinely study sidewalk and scenery as she passes any male, expecting the worst. A problem may sometimes arise here. If a woman feels that she may still be encroached upon, she will want to "keep an eye on" the male so that she can protect herself. Looking far ahead as she walks and changing sides of the street to avoid the necessity of passing a strange male at close proximity is an extension of this type of deflecting that is used in settings of extreme risk, such as inner-city areas or most places after dark.

The lone female may also deflect aural overtures - be it a whistle, a "hey, baby" or an "excuse me" - so long as she can credibly pretend that she did not hear. She may even ignore a physical gesture, such as a light touch on the shoulder, so long as she is in a crowd and a touch might have been an accidental brush. The advantage of ignoring an opening gesture or remark is that it may have been made impulsely in a moment of daring or attraction. If success is not forthcoming, it is often the case that the impulse does not repeat itself. It may be unclear to the approacher whether or not his overture was noticed. He may try again, but he may in confusion turn his attention elsewhere. If so, he has escaped with no embarrassment, fuss or confrontation.

In close proximity she must quickly depart, with a studied casualness, of course, so that the approacher may not have the chance to intrude himself to the point where no pretense is possible.

When the pretense of unawareness is impossible, in many instances she may still successfully ignore the gesture and discourage further interaction. Both of these types of ignoring are highly recommended in etiquette texts. After all, a "lady" would not be approached by strange men on the street (or in a variety of other situations), so a lady is advised to insist on this definition of the situation:

> "She never should hear a rude remark, or see an impertinent glance, appearing to think it impossible that they could be intended for her."[12]

PURPOSES AND LINES OF APPROACH

Approaches vary considerably in method and in purpose. Some of the more typical purposes are: (1) to "pick up," (2) for sex, (3) to "get acquainted" with an attractive woman, (4) to flirt, or negatively, to sexually degrade, (5) just to look, (6) to make a conquest for an audience, (7) to ask assistance from a safe-looking stranger, i.e. ask for a match. The problem at first for the woman is that it is difficult to distinguish motive by the opening gesture of approach.

First-time encounters between strangers in public places have a developmental character. The longer the interaction, the greater the likelihood and opportunity to transform impersonal stranger-stranger sociability into persona male-female socializing. From the woman's point of view, disengagement at an early point in the interaction is preferable because the more personal things get, the more apt the disengagement is to be "messy."

SIDE-STEPPING

Ignorance works only up to a point. No one has much success ignoring a man who sits down at her table or walks up to her and says, "Well hello!" There is no denying at this point that she has been engaged and that some sort of disengagement is necessary. In a situation like this, a "lady" would probably look quizzically at the uninvited other and ask "Do I know you?" in a tone that indicates that there could be no other explanation for such an intrusion. This response and other one-liners make up the repertoire of side-stepping techniques. Request for a match, for example, would be met with either a shake of the head or a turn away. Employment of side-stepping tactics is complicated by a conflict in desires to be polite and desires not to encourage a prolonged engagement by one's friendliness. One female informant articulated this conflict very well in speaking of her experiences at age twelve:

"I always felt torn between warnings about being careful because your physical safety may be involved and norms of politeness. I was brought up to be a polite kid, as I think most of us are - not rude to strangers and so forth. Now it's something of a problem for a girl to decide who really needs directions or needs to know what time it is or is lost... and, who is really going to exploit those questions. And I remember really feeling uneasy trying to shuffle between those two values. I mean keep my wits about me and yet not hurt nice people."

A rather high-level discrimination must be made to distinguish between the approach for a legitimate and limited purpose and the approach for involvement. Etiquette writers rarely expect a young girl to be able to make these fine, yet important, distinctions.

"A young teen-age girl traveling alone on a train might reply

269

courteously to a man in the next seat who tried to open a conversation, 'I am sorry, but I am not allowed to talk to strangers.' She is too young to have discretion about such things, too inexperienced to distinguish between the forwardness of a man attracted to her youth and charm and the friendliness of another person who merely wants someone to talk to on a journey of several hours..."[13]

At some age, in the old days it was around 30, though, a woman is expected to have acquired the sophistication required to tell the good guys from the bad guys. Women typically create operational imagery of the good guys and the bad guys, which includes such elements as age, social class cues, race, neatness, or cleanliness of appearance, etc. This typing of approachers seems to have limited usefulness, though; women interviewed commented on numerous incidents where the good guys turned out to be the bad guys after all.

The conservative woman or the especially successful female adventurer rarely needs to resort to more drastic measures. She simply repels, repositions, or leaves the scene, with a mumbled excuse, at no more expense than perhaps slight embarrassment and/or a change in route. Side-stepping is successful and relatively easy disengagement at an early point in the interaction. However, ease of disengagement is determined partially by the tactics employed and partially by the degree of persistence of the approacher. In some situations, the other situational aspects of the approach configuration and character of the approacher are such that the approacher exhibits incredible persistence in the face of all sorts of polite rejecting behavior.[14] If an unescorted woman is faced with a very persistent approacher, or if she had not been alert, defensive or correct in assessing the legitimacy of the initial approach gesture(s), she may "have to" relocate or leave the scene.

RELOCATING OR LEAVING THE SCENE

Minimizing hassles at every opportunity, the unescorted woman's typical response to a unwanted engagement is to leave. She may excuse herself on some pretext and take the nearest available exit. In some cases she can simply relocate herself in the situation, perhaps changing seats or moving to the other end of the room:

If the stranger persists in his attentions, she should change her seat; if there are no seats and his overture is really offensive, as sometimes happens, say to the conductor as he comes through, "I wonder if you will arrange to change my seat!'' The conductor knows immediately what the trouble is and acts accordingly.[15]

She may have a sudden need to use the restroom, so that her relocation will not be an obvious rejection. If she thinks she can get away with it without embarrassment and her approacher has been particularly impertinent, she may venture to make a hostile remark as she departs.

Relocation will work only when the approacher is not persistent or where there is room enough to get out of the approacher's "range." If relocation is not desirable, the hassle may be curtailed by a complete exit. Maybe a taxi will have to be called in lieu of waiting for the bus. Other arrangements must be made. Some situations can be particularly stressful because it is impossible to leave on short notice. Airplanes, trains, and busses and subway trains passing through "bad" neighborhoods virtually preclude quick exits.

Another aspect of leaving the scene as a tactic to disengage is psychological. People (both men and women) tend to dislike being intimidated into retreat. My informants frequently chose to retreat, but certainly not without resentment. As one of them said, "No one likes to be a jellyfish." The choice to leave and admit to oneself that one's repertoire of tactics are not sufficient to "handle" the situation is most likely to be made when energy or self-confidence is low: one of my interviewees said her response depended on whether she felt "strong and competent or exhausted."

If the "easy way out" is not available or desirable, a hassled woman must stand her ground and *terminate*.

TERMINATING

Often the major reason for leaving the scene is to avoid making one. An important consideration in choosing disengagement tactics is how much embarrassment may result. An offense to the approacher may mean retaliation, which usually means a "scene," so frequently a woman being hassled will try to disengage with a smile. Excuses are thought up, indignation is kept under wraps, and patience is exercised. It is hoped that, given no encouragement, an approacher will either get the hint or get bored, and this is often the case.

Women don't always grin and bear it or retreat, though. Sometimes they actively repel intrusions. They say, "No!" She may "stare 'em down'' (the "cold stare"), as one of my informants frequently does, because she thinks "they aren't ready for it." Often a woman has one or two favorite put-downs, ranging from a curt "excuse me!" to a rather loud "fuck off." A notice at a woman's bookstore in Oakland requested suggestions for the ultimate put-down to use on impertinent approacher. Quite a few women wrote in their favorites.

Medea and Thompson recommend an aggressive rejection as both more effective and more enjoyable:

> "...At your next encounter, don't pretend his hand is only accidentally touching you. Don't make a sudden shift and retreat against the wall. Don't take his hand off your leg, only to have him touch you again. No. Stand up and yell, 'YOU GOD DAMN PERVERT, YOU'RE DISGUSTING!' Won't that be exhilarating?"

DEFENDING

In the last resort, a woman may be faced with an assault to her person, either for mugging, a fight or rape. If she is attacked, she is likely to be smaller than her assailant and less skilled in the combative arts. She may also have a "hang-up" about physical fighting because it is not supposed to be feminine. She likely has an image of herself as a relatively impotent fighter. She also is not used to being physically hurt, so may "fold up" at the first hint of actual violence. All these things combine to greatly disadvantage the typical unescorted woman.

Only if she has prepared for this moment does she stand a chance of escaping physical intimidation or even serious injury - psychological and physical. She may have a weapon that she knows how and is prepared to use. She may, like more and more women have been doing lately, have taken some instruction in self-defense. If so, she betters her chances. Even so, if the attacker has a gun, most authorities on rape advise her not to resist. Repelling approach is the last stage of approach management. At this stage one's final options appear. One has been hassled, detained or whatever and one must do something about it. This phase of management like the others can be handled effectively or ineffectively, partially by skill and partially by luck. It can be handled apologetically or aggressively.

CONCLUSION AND IMPLICATIONS

This paper focuses on approach management in urban public places concentrating on a category of persons for whom the problem of approachability is particularly acute. I have laid out some of the areas of action and interaction where an unescorted woman can take measures to protect herself from unwanted intrusions of privacy by contact from strangers. Individual sections of the paper address stages of approach management. The first section of the text examined options to limit approachability that are available while one is still in "safe" territory: pre-public planning. Once preparations have or have not been taken and a woman crosses into public space, she begins the second phase of approach management: minimizing approachability. The second section dealt with the tactics she can employ to defend herself against the level of generalized threat that she perceives. Next, we looked at what options she has open to her if approach is not prevented. This last section covered basic tactics of repelling the approacher.

Each woman who spends a fair amount of time unescorted in urban public places in some way combines the options open to her to establish a repertoire of tactics that can be employed to fit the range of situations she may encounter in the city. She may continually update this repertoire as she or her life circumstances change (such as a new job or residence in a new city or neighborhood) and as first- or secondhand experience teaches her something new. The revision in her tactical repertoire may simply consist of learning that the least provocative rejoinder to the "What's happenin', Baby?" from the man passing her on the street is a cheerful "Nothing much," rather than her previous silence and a frown. However, it may be drastic as in the case of cocktail waitress turned telephone operator. As a cocktail waitress (or many other "female occupations"), her option to dress down when taking the bus to and from work was severely curtailed. As a telephone operator, she now may wear conservative pants suits to work and expend much less energy on minimizing and repelling tactics.

The traditional pattern of intersexual behavior as regards the initiation of encounters between strangers or mere acquaintances has placed the male as the *ostensive* approacher and the female as the solicitor of approach. Signal reading by the male of subtle soliciting communications is crucial. Because the male is to be the initiator of interaction, female gestures of interest in engagement must be subtle so as not to *appear* to be themselves initiating the encounter. This expected subtlety results in the wide latitude in interpretation of female appearance and behavior as solicitation. The refrain of "she asked for it" after rape or a particularly abusive or embarrassing cross-sex interaction clearly evidences this latitude.

The traditional designation of males as approachers and females as approachable may be acceptable as a ritual in more protected situations such as perhaps exist in non-urbanized settings or a private party, but in the world of strangers *this pattern is no longer functional for women*. The risks, for the unescorted woman, involved in stranger contact of impertinences, hassling or rape are such that approachability must be controlled for self-protection and a modicum of privacy. Even the excessive amount of energy expended signalling disinterest, muting attractiveness, and avoiding particularly high-approach settings does not always ensure immunity from threat or intrusion.

The problem of approachability is not presently just a problem for unescorted women. Highly urbanized environments are characterized by the extensiveness of stranger-occupied public space. Approach management is necessarily practiced by all categories of persons, especially the lone individual. The options available to women for managing approachability are generally available to other persons as well, albeit, often taking different forms. Anyone could take the categories I have created or employed in this paper to analyze their own repertoire of tactics to manage approachability.

REFERENCES

1. Andrea Medea and Kathleen Thompson, Against Rape, (Farrar, Straus & Giroux: New York, 1974), pp. 49-54.

2. Lyn H. Lofland, "A World of Strangers: Order and Action in Urban Public Space," (Dissertation, Sociology Program, UCSF Medical Center, 1971).

3. For the purpose of this paper "approach" will be used loosely to refer to any type of verbal or visual overture and the line of interaction proceeding from it.

4. Janet Tokerud, "Etiquette and the Position of Women in American Society" (Unpublished paper, Sociology Program, UCSF Medical Center, 1973).

5. Judy Klemsrud, "Living With Fear in New York, New York Times Service, (San Francisco Chronicle, Jan. 24, 1973)

6. U.S. Census statistics show, as do a number of other demographic studies, that the number of single females, females living alone and female workers has been increasing significantly.

7. In this regard, it might be safer to approach the extremely attractive woman instead of the plain-looking one because it's not so embarrassing to be turned down by her.

8. Informant.

9. Lofland, pp. 241-242.

10. Cavan, p. 97.

11. Etiquette text: "She never should hear a rude remark, or see an impertinent glance, appearing to think it impossible that they could be intended for her."

12. Amy Vanderbilt, Amy Vanderbilt's Etiquette (Doubleday & Co., Inc.: New York, 1972 revised), p. 853.

13. A conventional wisdom regarding the seduction of females is that persistence pays off. Not "taking no for an answer" sometimes works. In Against Rape, the authors recount numerous episodes that started with "friendly" approaches but ended in rape because the female involved did not flatly refuse to continue the interaction until she no longer had that option.

14. Vanderbilt, pp. 853-854.

CHAPTER 14

LIFE AFTER PARENTING:

A Study of the Single Parent Empty Nest

Diane Lutovich

If you can see the time that your children are grown and out of the house, it is time to start thinking about how you want to live once your nest is empty. Any family finds it a shock to find themselves without children around, but for single parents the change is stunning - full of potential, either for sadness and loneliness or for the chance to formulate a brand new life.

Under the best of circumstances transitions are not easy. For single parents they can be even harder. In the first place, they might have no one intimately involved to turn to for mutual support or for making long-range plans. In the second place, they might have put an inordinate amount of their life on hold while raising children, working, keeping a home. Additionally, they have often forged a relationship with their children that is more intense, more intertwined, than parents and children in a nuclear family. Often, when saying goodbye to their children, they are saying goodbye to the last vestiges of family. Consequently, it is particularly important for the single parent to look ahead, to avoid being like the mother who while her daughter was packing, kept crying, "It happened so fast. I'm not ready. I didn't think it would end so soon."

PLANNING

Parents who don't start thinking ahead, and who realize they will be alone only upon seeing their youngest, or only; claim a diploma; or start packing their bags, are the ones who are lonely and distraught once their children are grown. It was a shame they didn't do some planning, because parents who did, are much more apt to be ready to embrace this next chance at forming a life.

Almost every parent I spoke to, no matter how well they had planned, experienced some loss and sadness when their children left. But those who had planned, or at least started to think about planning for the next stage, saw this sadness as temporary, and far from fatal.

PLANNING AS AN ADJUSTMENT PROCESS

Because of my own interest in the subject as a single parent for 17 years, about to pack my daughter off to college and feeling caught up in a whirlpool of conflicting feelings, I wanted to find out how other single parents dealt with this change in their lives. In talking with single parents, (mostly mothers but some fathers as well), it became clear that this emptying of the single-parent house involves a series of major adjustments.

Readiness: Among the more than fifty single parents with whom I talked, I found that those who were happiest had seen this final departure as a process, one with several stages, each stage requiring the parent to ask some hard questions and to, at least, start thinking about how to answer them. The earlier the parent started thinking about, and planning for the next stage, the easier the transition was. Most of the parents, in fact, who felt squared away with this next stage of their lives started making changes, or at least planning the changes they would make about the time their youngest or only child started high school. At the very latest, they started focusing on the future by the time the child was a junior in high school.

Whether the parent felt like Pat who said, "The timing is right. I can't wait to get on with my life," or Joan who said, "I feel cold and lonely - like I've lost my best friend." This transition, according to at least one parent, is "an important time in your life. I'd tell all single parents to get ready."

And how do parents get ready? It appears to start first with the realization that the time of being needed, of having children occupy so much time and thought, is but a finite period and will end. They realize that the children will make their own lives, leaving the parents to cope with theirs. Sarah, describing her own process, reported that, "You know, once he [her son] learned to drive, I saw less and less of him." She said that his growing independence reminded her daily of the time that he would be gone completely.

DETACHING

Ideally, the process of detaching works almost like a feedback system. The parent and the child, each thinking about his/her future, take tentative steps, one leading and one following. Those parents who felt their transition worked most smoothly, reported that their children took the first step out. Maybe the child started spending nights with a fiend, being involved with sports, getting a part-time job, or like Sarah's son, started spending more sports, getting a part-time job, or like Sarah's son, started spending more time in the car and away from home. The parent followed by adding one thing back to his/her life. One father started practicing his violin to prepare to audition for the community orchestra once his son was gone. Sarah, once she saw her son was moving on, started looking for summer teaching jobs in other parts of the world.

Another part of the teaching involves some emotional detaching. Often in itself, a difficult challenge for single parents who, for so many reasons, tend to be more involved with and dependent on their children. Thus the detachment can feel more like an "amputation," as one parent said. An extremely important factor in detaching and ultimately separating is whether the parents were able to hang on to some of their own dreams.

Something Apart: Those who were excited were people who, no matter how overwhelmed that they had been with their jobs as full-time single parent and, in most cases the bread winner, had managed to keep something outside their daily lives alive. They were able to nurture the seed of something that had been very important and/or would be important in the future. This dream not only got them through the rough spots, it provided the focus for the next stage. One parent said that when her children were at the worst of their adolescence and she was exhausted and feeling "it was never going to be easier," she would remember how much she had loved acting; how much she had enjoyed the few classes she had been able to sneak in. She said the day after her youngest child leaves home, she will be trying out for a part.

The enthusiastic parents then, even while preoccupied, had started detaching. They were able to keep a part of themselves free and it this part they could call upon. No matter how sad or frightened they might be, these parents had found or kept a focus "out there" - apart from their role as parent. These were the people who were ready to go after that which they had denied themselves during their years as a single parent. In some cases they looked at a rededication to work, return to school, or taking the risk of leaving a secure job to do something they always wanted to do. Some wanted new or different friends, some a lover, and others, just as eagerly wanted to have time to be by themselves, to find out what it was that really made them happy when they no longer had to answer to anyone else.

Being Alone: Several parents felt that one of the most important things they did to prepare was to practice being alone. One mother reported that when her daughter left for the summer before her senior year, she purposely did not make plans. She wanted to see how it would feel. And at first, she said it felt awful. She kept the television set on, not to watch but for the sound. By the second week, she was finding herself spending whole evenings satisfied. And by the time her daughter returned, she found she had to readjust to having her back. But she knew that when it was time for her daughter to leave the next time, she would hurt at first and then be just fine.

Many parents mentioned that they were not interested in finding a new mate. A number of parents, in this case all women, who had remained single to avoid the whole "mixing process", did not see finding a new mate as important. They had, as one mother explained, become "very capable of providing for myself. I don't think I could any longer give up my independence. I have waited a long time to be able to answer only to myself."

Stockpiling: Several parents reported they did a lot of "stockpiling" during the last year. They made special plans to do things with their child or invested the same things with special meaning. One father said that during his son's last year of high school, he and his son made a point of dinner and a movie every Sunday night. It was a special time and he saw it that way. She said that each time she made her son's lunch, she thought about "last times." She said that, while seeing the broader picture gave extra pleasure, it also reminded her that she would be ready to give it up.

Major Concerns: In addition to finding a way to detach, to practice being alone, to "stockpiling," parents who were ready, had started looking at some of the big questions. They started looking at the fears, concerns, choices and options they had.

Companionship: One of the major concerns had to do with companionship. Even while looking forward to the "return of peace and order," parents were aware that they would have to leave the house to spend time with another human being. For many of the parents who had gone right from their parents's home to their marriage and children, this represented an awesome departure. Other parents put money high on their list of concerns since any child support or AFDC would be ending. Lack of structure was a top concern of some - "What will keep me from flying of in to space?" one mother asked.

Others started looking for ways to compensate for what they knew they would miss most. Those who knew they did not want to be alone made other plans. Jack, who most feared the "silence," moved in with a widow and her two children the month before his youngest graduated from high school.

In fact, many parents, formed new adult relationships within a year of their children's leaving. For some it provided another chance to commit and continue. One mother announced that, three weeks before her daughter graduated from high school, she dreamt she [herself] had died and was being carried to her own funeral. But then she fell out of the coffin and started to laugh. The mother interpreted this as a clear sign she "was not dead yet" and in fact, met a man two weeks later - one she has great hopes of spending the rest of her life with.

Others, less thoughtfully, or so it seems, see remarriage as a way to avoid looking at their lives. Several parents who rushed into a new living relationship were very sorry within six months. And a high percentage of these relationships did not last very long.

Home Concerns: The other concerns most mentioned had to do with the family home (whether it was an apartment or grand suburban villa) and how best to "reward myself for a job well done." Betty, concerned about home and income, saw the "writing on the wall" when her youngest turned 15. She knew that she would be alone and would have no financial assistance. At that point, she sold the family home, bought a two bedroom condominium, quit her part-time job and threw herself into a new and demanding career. She said that her outside interest was good for her son, whom she had tended to "baby" since he was the last, and it gave her the income she would need. She said all of her children complained, but only a little.

Pat was a year away from the high school graduation of her youngest, but had the plans all worked out. She explained, "The last twenty years of my life have nothing to do with who I am or plan on becoming." She was set to lease her house out, rent a room in someone else's house and return to school full time. "I've done a good job," she said, "and now it's my turn."

And in many cases, the home presented a major obstacle for those eager to answer only to themselves. Those, who knew the home they had kept for their children was no longer right for them, had some important decisions to make. It was too isolated, to expensive, and too much of a burden. These parents had to walk a fine line between what their children expected and what they needed.

They tried wonderful things. One parent moved into a communal setting, another decided to housesit in a new community for at least a year. Others rented out a room, added a separate unit, or advertised for a roommate. Some joined the peace corps, and others moved back to be close to their own families. In many cases the children did object. But those parents who felt strongly about their own plans and future, were able to weather the disappointment of their children. They also found a way to make it right for everyone, at least in the long run.

Freedom: In their willingness to forge new ground, these parents made decisions that cut across many of their concerns. Because they had few role models, they had to be innovative if they were to use this new freedom as an opportunity to make a positive and happy life for themselves. And above all, they had to be willing to see themselves as worthy of the same nurturance and support they had provided for their children.

Those whose main concern was how they would handle the lack of structure or focus also planned accordingly. One woman who enjoyed cooking and providing for others and knew she would miss that, joined an organization which assigned her a home-bound person for whom she would cook and serve dinner to once a week. Many made commitments, volunteered and joined organizations like Big Brothers and Big Sisters.

Business: Laurie started her business when her daughter was a sophomore in high school. She knew that she could start building slowly and by the time her daughter graduated from high school, she was "totally invested in my business." " My daughter and I had forged a different kind of relationship and the only separation left was the physical one."

DEPARTURE

Even the way people handled their first night alone was telling. Several parents had planned both departure parties, so the change could be seen as a celebration, and a return party for themselves. Others sulked through this time. They could identify with the mother who, failing to put this change into a broader perspective, dwelled on the "emptiness, the loneliness," deciding *that* was what the rest of her life would be like. Or the mother who, on her first night alone, "woke up in the middle of the night, thought I was choking to death..... The doctor checked my lungs and heart and told me he thought I was having an anxiety attack... It was the strangest feeling. I never knew I would feel that way because I had always been so independent. But I always had the kids to distract me."

Parents who were ready to embrace this next stage of their lives were no less involved or committed. They had just made sure they never forgot there "would be life after children." They had started detaching, finding other ways to confirm themselves, having recovered or formulated dreams and were willing to innovate until they found what made them happy.

It's an old story. Parents who value themselves know what most wild creatures know. One need only watch the robin patiently sitting, feeding, teaching, and then, when the babies are ready to be on their own, they too, without a mate, take off, and fly high with the wind in their wings.

CHAPTER 15

DOING TIME:

Altered Perception of Time in Prison

Judith L. Lee

University of Tulsa 1975

Incarceration in a prison usually means a drastic alteration in a man's life circumstance. Man's place in society means a number of things. It has to do with the physical environment which in some manner he can call his own, and which by a variety of different ways, he comes to make personal in some way, if only by carving his initials into it. It means his social status, his relations to his family, his peers, his society. It means that particular niche that he fits into amidst the network of customs and values that form his world. This covers a lot of territory. To understand what happens to a person in prison is to understand the disintegrations of all these things.

When a man enters the society of the prison, the entire substance of this network of his life is in some way altered. His physical environment becomes circumscribed, to say the least. Personal space becomes a thing of the past. His relations with other people undergo a drastic change. What he has come to think of as his rights, however fundamental, are no longer rights but privileges. He loses his name. No longer can he present himself to the world as he wishes, with long hair or short, clean shaven or bearded, in overalls or a suit. He must cry and despair, ache, have nightmares, get an erection, pray, and relieve himself, before whom the institution decides he will do these things. What he knew in the other world of sex and masculinity, has no meaning in this one. The reasons he has always known for taking a bath or not, of doing a good job or not, of being friendly or not, no longer have any relevance in this new existence.

But, of all the changes which constitute his new situation, the most fundamental and personally jarring is that of Time. What once was the atmosphere in which his world floated (although he may rarely have averted to it), now becomes the very fabric of his existence. That thing, Time which was most basically his own, is no longer under his proprietor-ship. He no longer has a moment of which he can say, "This is absolutely my moment with which to do as I wish." He can no longer structure it; he can no longer have it serve to make him what he wants to be. It no longer heals him. It becomes his most basic problem.

"Doing time" is the major thing one does in prison.[1] The term, which at first appears to be a catch-all phrase for "serving a sentence," upon closer investigation turns out to be a profound expression of what the whole ordeal of prison is all about. All of us have been in situations where we have had to "do time", either on a job, or waiting for a friend, or savoring every minute of an all too short vacation. We are all aware of the bearing of our emotions on time's passage - fast or slow, heavy or light.

DATA

The data for this study were collected during a series of tape recorded interviews conducted at a work release center[2] in a fairly large southwestern city.

The participants, about 35 in all, volunteered to be interviewed. Each of the men were serving out their flat time. In the majority of cases, these men were repeaters. At least half of them had spent the majority of their adult life in prison. Each of the men had spent some time at the main maximum security institution, referred to as the "Walls," and most of them had spent the major portion of their sentences there. The offenses of the participants ranged from drug possession to multiple murder. While the assumption was that only the best behaved inmates ever got to a pre-release center, in reality, the only category of inmate that was not interviewed was someone with a severe psychological handicap. (See the appendix on Methodology for explanation of sample selection).

While the initial interviews were conducted formally at the Center, at least five of the inmates were interviewed on a continuing basis over a period of about nine months. This was possible because of the personal relationship that the interviewer was able to establish with a few of the inmates. Consequently in addition to interviewing these men, the writer was in a position to observe some of these inmates in a social setting removed from the Center, and to participate in peer group discussions. Any contacts made outside the Center were on an informal basis. The relationship of the interviewer to the institution was strictly academic. Cooperation was excellent.

The procedure of the interview was to ask a question such as "What was it like being at the Walls?" From there on, with the exception of one or two cases, no prodding was necessary except to probe certain key areas of interest. The interviews lasted from two to six hours apiece.

Most of the content of the interviews had to do with the time that the men had spent at the "Walls." There seemed to be a preoccupation with that phase of their incarceration and discussion flowed most freely in relating that experience.

EMERGENCE OF THE VARIABLE "DOING TIME"

Some key topics began to emerge from the preliminary interviews. Some of these included the political system among the inmates, hustles, personal relationships, sexual relationships, adjustment procedures, etc. One of the most significant phenomena to come out of the data was the inmates' concept of "*doing* time." Perhaps the first thing that strikes one about the phrase is the necessity to twist the language in order to get the concept across. In questioning the inmates about the terminology, it was ascertained that the use of the term connoted more than just a slang phrase. Rather, it captured one of the most problematic aspects of the inmates' lives.[3]

DOING TIME; WHAT IS IT?

THE PROBLEMATIC ASPECT OF TIME

This paper will analyze the process of "doing time." It makes the basic assertion that time becomes problematic under certain conditions. While these conditions are found in a variety of situations[4] ,they are epitomized in the prison setting. Under these conditions, the perception and experience of time undergoes a change. These are stages to the "doing time" process: first of all, there are periods at the beginning and the end of the prison term during which the "doing of time" is experienced in different ways. Secondly, there are conditions which aggravate "doing time," some of which are temporary and some of which "normalize" it to one degree or another. This altered experience of time has specific behavioral and attitudinal consequences which help to account for modes of accommodation of inmates, both psychological and social.

THE SUBJECTIVE EXPERIENCE OF "DOING TIME"

Heightened Awareness. The most obvious experiential aspect of the process of "doing time" is that the inmate becomes intensely aware of it for perhaps the first time in his life. Several of the inmates made the remark that up until the time they went to prison, they had tended to live a day at a time. This sudden confrontation with their sentence that they usually experienced upon entrance into the prison, gave them a perspective about time that had been missing until this point. They suddenly became aware of their age, of how much of their lives they considered wasted.

Preoccupation with Time. The inmates described a total preoccupation with the thought of time. This preoccupation takes several forms. First there is a sense in which one is aware of each moment, of having to live intensely aware of oneself with no possibility of distraction. Secondly, this awareness can take the form of the perception of time's dragging by slowly.

One week in that place can make a month go by. This is the sheer monotony of the experience. Thirdly, there is the preoccupation with one's sentence. At some point, each man had to come to grips with the length of time he knew he had to spend there. Each man seemed to be able to do his time by making up his mind to do "that much time."[5] A distinction must be made with the men who were doing life sentences. These men did not attempt to do a given amount of time. They took the attitude of not knowing how much time they had to do. To admit that one was going to spend the rest of his life there, would be to give up hope. So they set their sites on a parole date.

"Worrying". The actual "doing of time" was often described by the inmates as "worrying." The term seems to describe to process as well as suggest an explanation as to why the language must be twisted in order to describe what one "does" in prison. "Worrying" is a number of things: it is the tension brought about by the fretting over the time that the inmate has to do; it is the way in which time is done when one has not "adjusted" to the institution. Those who have not found a "system" by which to escape the tediousness of their time, or those for whom their "system" has ceased to be an effective escape for any reason, are said to do "hard time" and "worry" over their time. There are certain stages involved in "doing time" during which there is more intense "worrying." These will be discussed at length later.

Another aspect of "worrying" has to do with the way that prison ages a man. With two exceptions, the participants all looked at least five or six years older than their chronological age. All of them acted older than they looked. In being asked about this, they responded that their "time" had aged them, not in the sense of the years that age us all, so much as the "doing" of it, the "worrying" about it, the being constantly aware of it.

THE STAGES OF "DOING TIME"

The process of "doing time" has several discernable stages. The first is the adjustment period. Once the inmate gets through this initial difficult time, he has periods of "escape" during which he is able to avoid the thought of time. There can be more or less temporary breakdowns in the inmate's "escape system" by some crisis or by certain aggravating conditions within the prison. This is usually true of the days just previous to his release.

The Adjustment Period. A significant number of men could point to the occasion when they were first confronted with the problem of their time. For most of them, there was a juncture on the receiving cell[6] at which the burden of the years that they faced, simply overwhelmed them. The long sentence ahead of them became almost palpable. Following this confrontation came the realization that the inmate was either going to have to devise a way to "do this time," or else go insane. Several of the men described people who had "gone crazy" on the receiving cell because they let their time get to them. The men described their own recognition of the fact that they too could "go crazy."

Deciding to "do it" meant, first that they could do "this much" and no more.[7] Perhaps as a consequence of being able to do only so much, each man, once he could see daylight ahead of him, kept a calendar. Some could tell you how many hours they had left.

Secondly, "doing their time" meant that they had to find a "system." That's what they call "jelling." "But guys doing easy time, they jelling, they adjusted. They got a system." Nearly everyone agreed that the first year or so was the most difficult. There are so many things to get used to. Also, it took time to find the most effective way to blank the time out of one's mind.

The Period of Escape. There was a large number of men who, when they were first questioned, passed off the prison experience as trivial and not particularly difficult. This was a typical response. It could be partially a result of the attempt of the inmate to never let the institution know when they were bothering him. However, most of the men achieved a real conquest over their time temporarily, and learned to effectively escape the problems that it caused. In a later section, we shall consider some of the conditions that contributed toward an alleviation of the difficulty. Nonetheless, each inmate, before the end of the interview, also related experiences of doing really "hard time." While many of the men described to others who continually did "hard time," no one ever admitted to doing it all the time. There were some who seemed to find it harder to adjust than others.

"Hard time" seemed to be caused by certain aggravating conditions in the prison, which will be covered in detail later. It also recurred periodically when one's resistance had worn down.

Period Previous to Release. The period just previous to release can be both easier and harder at the same time for the same man. The knowledge that his days are numbered eases a great deal of the pressure. On the other hand, the anticipation of how he is going to cope, of whether his family will be there waiting for him, etc., makes the period a stressful one. The inmate who is about to be released is very conscious of tempo. Once again, he seems to live through each deliberate moment. With the end in sight, the slow passage of time is aggravating in a different way. Before it dragged because there was so much of it. He tried to escape the thought of it because there was so much ahead of him. Prior to release, however, it drags in a new way. There is so little left to do, but still each minute of time must be done. Often there is such anxiety that escaping the thought of it is impossible.

SUFFICIENT OBJECTIVE CONDITIONS WHICH GIVE RISE TO "DOING TIME"

There are certain conditions which, when found together, almost invariably result in time's becoming problematic. While these conditions are "writ large" in a prison, they are found in varying degrees, with varying manifestations in other settings. These conditions are: first, incarceration, by which is meant, (1) having a given duration of time in the situation, and (2) being physically confined. Second, there is the situation of having an abundance of time. Third, there is the lack of meaningful activity. And fourth, there is the lack of proprietorship over one's time, that is, the loss of personal autonomy. Each of these shall be considered in turn.

Incarceration. There are two elements of the prison situation which seem to contribute the most to the fact that time becomes problematic. The first is that of the sentence, or the given duration that the inmate knows he faces, as has been mentioned above. Suffice it to say here, that the fact that the inmate knows he faces a specified amount of time in this situation, plays a significant part in his attitude toward time, both in making it an encumbrance, and in how he will eventually face up to it. The sentence makes him feel trapped.

The second element is that of physical confinement. For the greater part of each day, the men are confined to a cell approximately 6' by 8'. In most cases, there are two men to a cell. Obviously, this limited space, shared by two people, greatly increases the mens' problem of having so much time and the probability of it getting on their nerves. Being confined to the prison grounds has like effects. In both cases, their options for distraction are greatly circumscribed.

The Abudance of Time. The abundance of time referred to here is the actual amount of time that the inmate finds that he has on his hands each day, and in total. This is distinct from the subjective awareness of the slowness with which life passes for him.

In addition to feeling trapped by a sentence he cannot control, the inmate is also faced with having this time on his hands. Not only does he have many months and years of time facing him, he also has approximately fifteen hours of each day to spend with one other man in 48 square feet of concrete cell. The inmates are usually locked at 4:00 or 5:00 p.m. each evening. From then until around 7:00 a.m. the next morning, their hours are their own to fill the best they can[8]. In the next two sections, we shall consider the problems of structuring which this entails.

Lack of Meaningful Activity. Finding something meaningful or even distracting to do in a small cell with another man is difficult enough. Added to this is the fact that even when the men are on their assignments or on the yard, there is little to do. The constant attempt to find a distraction becomes a vicious circle. Even the education courses, training courses, etc., are participated in not because they are worthwhile and fulfilling. Rather, they are a filler for the intrinsic uselessness of the time spent in prison.

Lack of proprietorship. So far, we have made mention of the problems of the actual abundance of time that the inmate has at his disposal, and of the perceptual correlate of that abundance, that it goes by slowly. Rather it is the fact that its abundance and its slowness are not at the disposal of the inmate that causes the real problem. He is not the proprietor of his life. As was mentioned above, the conditions of incarceration are a difficulty for him. But even more basically than that, he is not the proprietor of his time, because at the very most, the institution says to him, "Here, you can have your moment, but you can do with it only what I will allow you to do." The inmate has an abundance of time which is simultaneously given to him and taken away. It is because he loses the prerogative of structuring this life that time becomes an all consuming preoccupation.

The dilemma here is not that the inmate has no choices to make over how he will spend his hours. Rather, it is that the institution has full discretion over the degree to which he can structure it. The discretion that the institution uses is totally haphazard. Thus, the inmates are always laboring in a state of ambiguity. They become frustrated by the sameness of each day, the presence of "dead time." But over and over, it was mentioned that they had learned never to count on anything that was anticipated to provide a break in the routine.

There was no consensus on how much freedom a man had in making any choices about his immediate or remote future. Some men thought that anyone could get into an educational or training program simply by requesting it. Others thought that no matter how hard they tried, they had no say so about their future.

Not only were the men restricted in regard to their personal autonomy in planning their lives, but the policies of the institution seem to be inconsistent. Assignment to medium or minimum security institutions is made haphazardly or else with the aid of political maneuvering. Parole policies change with no warning.[9] Parole plans are made without the consultation of the prospective parolee[10]. In short, planning of any sort is discouraged by a variety of institutional necessities and institutional inconsistencies. The inmate's time is simultaneously given to him and taken away.

CONDITIONS WHICH AGGRAVATE THE CONDITONS OF "DOING TIME"

We have mentioned already those conditions which seem to necessarily result in causing time to become a problem. We shall now turn our attention to those conditions which aggravate the situation of the inmate and cause him to do "hard time."

Inability to Adjust. The first such condition is that of adjustment[11]. We have already mentioned the difficulty that the new inmate has. But even allowing for this, there seem to be some inmates that have more difficulty in finding a way with which to cope with incarceration than others[12]. They find it difficult to find a way to fill their time which does not seem absurd to them, or which absorbs their interest and attention. When asked about their observations of other inmates who seem to have this problem, there were no proposed solutions forthcoming.

Relationships Outside the Prison. An area that has great potential for making the time easy or hard is that of personal relationships. The degree to which this is a factor depends on the commitment that the inmate retains to those of the outside. For some of the men, a vital factor in their making it through the long months and years depends on the letters and visits of their wives or girlfriends, and other members of their families[13]. Mothers seemed to hold an especially important part. By the same token, the fact that they were separated from loved ones, unable to help them, and causing them concern, was one of the greatest causes of "worrying." A good indication of the importance of outside support is the impact of mail time. This is, perhaps, the most traumatic time of the day[14].

It is also very common for the inmate to break off all contact with family and friends when he goes to prison. The reason for this would seem to be that the disappointment of not receiving letters and visits is greater than not expecting them in the first place. Even among those who did not break off contact with their friends and families, many found their short and periodic visits more difficult to handle than no visits at all[15].

Despite the variety of degree of commitment that the men indicated, the one subject upon which there was unanimous agreement was that a man's relationship with his wife or girlfriend was the greatest single cause of worry. In the opinion of the respondents, the most crucial situation a man could face was the defection of his wife or "girl." It was probably also the most common. In every case where a man had kept contact with this person, he made it clear to the interviewer that it was not sexual fidelity that he expected, but that she not "get tight" with anyone else[16].

Relationships Within the Prison. An important factor in how a man's time is done is his ability to handle relationships within the prison. Does he choose his companions wisely, minding his own business, etc.?

A feeling of tension caused by the possibility of controversy with another inmate seems to be a universal experience among the participants. This tension seems to be tangible. It keeps the inmates constantly on the alert, limiting their ability to concentrate on anything else totally. It also seems to prevent them from being completely relaxed at any time. The degree of tension depends a good deal on the inmates' abilities to handle the pressures that surround them along with their "political contacts" within the prison power structure. Probably since the reputation of being "good people"[17] is top priority among survival skills, the respondents all presented themselves to the interviewer as people who minded their own business. This was in fact not the case[18].

The other important factor in this regard is a man's being able to find the person with whom he can "rap." However, having a true friendship was all but unheard of among the inmates[19]. There was nearly universal agreement that in order to do one's time, it was necessary to have somebody, at least for when the going got rough. There were some for whom companions were the most important means of psychological survival. There were others who tried to limit a really intimate relationship for times of crisis. But there were none who thought that another human being could be trusted totally.

Several of the inmates took great personal pride in the fact that they had helped someone over his worst time. There were several instances of men relating "sweating it out" over someone who had just received word about a girlfriend or wife who was breaking off a relationship, and whom they were trying to talk into not trying to escape, literally. In the section on "adjustment strategies" we shall consider the function of these relationships in more detail.

Lack of Privacy. The amount of privacy that a man desires and is able to have, has a bearing on how his time is spent and therefore, how "easy" it is. For many of the inmates, companionship is vital to their "system" of adjusting. But there are those who are more introverted and reflective, who must find a way of creating solitude in a cage. Time is easiest to handle when a person can handle it in his own way. In constant company of others, around whom the inmate may or may not feel comfortable, it is difficult to do the things that may alleviate the meaninglessness and frustration of his life.

This lack of privacy may result in a man's not adopting certain "systems" by which to while away his time. On the other hand, it becomes a necessity for him to create privacy which is strictly psychological, since physical privacy is no longer possible. What is more likely is that he will do things in the presence of his cellmate about which he nonetheless continues to feel uncomfortable. A man's bunk is sacred ground in which he may not be disturbed. It is the only refuge he has for writing poetry, for dreaming, for sexual release (either masturbation or homosexuality)[20].

Loss of Hope. The hope of parole was extremely important among those men doing life or very long sentences. Some of these men said that they succeeded in not thinking about their time until it became reasonable for them to hope for parole. Refusal for the first few times before the parole board was something that the men seemed to expect. However, this single political decision regarding no paroles for those accused of crimes of violence, was used again and again as an example of what can happen to

292

make a man lose hope. Hoping for a parole date was what made their time endurable. Without that hope, they had nothing to cling to. For some of these men, any hope of parole seemed extremely remote from the interviewer's point of view. Nevertheless, it was the only thing that kept them going.

CONDITIONS WHICH ALLEVIATE "DOING TIME"

There seem to be certain conditions of incarceration which significantly alleviate the experience of "doing time." Some of the conditions are only temporary. Others seem to "normalize" the situation on a more or less temporary basis.

Temporary Conditions. One of these instances occurs when the inmate's system is working and affords him some distraction from his condition. In this sense, all "systems" are designed with alleviation in mind.

A second circumstance occurs when the inmate has "schemed" to significantly "beat the Man." A good example of this is the inmate who hustles in a good supply of marijuana or some drug. (This is particularly satisfying when it is done without the assistance of the guards and administration, or better yet, when it is with their unknowing assistance). Any time an inmate can get the administration to do things his way without their being aware of it, his time has become a little easier. This becomes a way of life since most of the inmates consider themselves a good deal smarter than the guards. It would appear that this sort of "scheming" is done with a good deal of success.

The third situation of temporary alleviation occurs when a man becomes really involved and interested, either in his job or in his hustle, or in whatever means of escape he has concocted for himself. Thus in some instances, the inmate sees what he is involved in, not as escape, but as something which was really fulfilling to him. This is infrequent and lasts such a brief time as to be insignificant over the long run.

Normalizing Conditions. There are some instances in which the conditions of the prison approach a sort of subjective normality for the inmate. There are three situations in which this seems to be the case. The first is when a man is "institutionalized." According to the inmates, a man in prison becomes "institutionalized" when he is "happy" in the prison. Such a person is said to belong more inside the prison than on the outside. He is no longer able to cope with it. He comes back to the prison where he will be taken care of. "Institutionalization" is considered to be a permanent and irreversible state.

The second normalizing factor or condition is the instance in which the inmate finds that the prison is a refuge for him. Where the designation "institutionalization" is seen as a permanent state, the idea of prison being a refuge is not. It can be that the prison is a place to escape from things that trouble him on the outside. The prison provides a respite for him. There is also the possibility that the person can philosophically regard the prison as a temporary refuge.

The third condition is the situation in which a man is allowed some autonomy and/or recognition. Even being called by his name can relieve the tediousness of the prison existence for the inmate. There are other forms of autonomy foreign to the prison life style, most of which come about in classes and on some jobs, which are supervised by non-prison personnel, such as teachers, chaplains, etc.

EFFECTS OF THE "DOING TIME" EXPERIENCE: ATTITUDES AND BEHAVIOR

The "doing time" experience has very definite consequences in the formulation of an inmate's attitudes and values. Likewise, the ways by which the men deal with their time is very definitely an organizing factor in the day to day life of a prison. Let us briefly suggest how this is so, and then look closely at how "doing time" effects attitudes and behavior. "Doing time" has a great influence on the interpersonal relationships that a man engages in both during his incarceration as well as after his release. It affects his attitudes toward society. The recognition of the need to escape one's time results in the mens' preying on one another's vulnerability in this regard, and this way, is instrumental in setting the power structure among the inmates. Let us look at that these attitudinal and behavioral effects are so we can see this more clearly.

ATTITUDINAL CONSEQUENCES

Introspection. An important outcome of the inmate's experience of time is that, under the pressures of the situation, his mind becomes a kind of incubator. All of the men interviewed spent a lot of time in reflection[21]. To each respondent, this was a major element of the experience. This type of thinking, even when it hurts, is to be distinguished from a "system," which one uses deliberately to avoid "worrying."

A significant part of this reflection consists in analyzing all the reasons why the inmates had ended up in prison in the first place. They probe into their own personalities, their relationships with their families, and other situations that they had been in, trying to come up with the explanation of why they ended up the way they did. In most instances, they can resolve that they are no longer going to be the kind of person that they had been up to this point. These resolutions do not necessarily, or even mostly have to do with not returning to prison. Rather they center around how the inmate is going to handle his personal relationships, how he is going to live more according to his principles. An insight results in the inmate's seeing that his relationship to the law was tantamount to playing "cops and robbers," and that this was childish. He therefore would resolve to stop playing the game. Some of the inmates said that they thought it was harder to do time as they got older. Therefore, the time had come to stop flirting with the possibility of coming back to prison.[22]

This kind of reflection seemed to be the only thing that the inmates see as positive in their prison experience. They had come to know themselves better, something they would not have taken the time to do on the outside.

As important as the concept of "thinking" is the concept of "not thinking." The very purpose of having a "system" in fact, was to "not think." Just as there are men whose pattern it was to live in the past, there are those who do their best to avoid any thought of it. There was too much pain involved in not being a part of the things that they cherished. So too, there are those who find it too painful to look ahead. Even though hope was absolutely essential, most of the men had learned that it was far better to hope for nothing and be surprised than to hope for too much and be disappointed.

Consciousness of the Value of Time. The lack of proprietorship over his time, his life as it were, does two things to the inmates' concept of time. It serves to intensify his awareness of its value. Second, it makes him conscious that his time is being wasted[23].

As long as the inmate was on the street, free to distract himself, this awareness of time's value was missing. In the joint, every moment that hangs heavy on his hands is being taken from him. The inmate feels robbed of this part of his life. A natural consequence of this is that his resentment of the institution grows. While most of the inmates readily accepted the blame for their predicament, there was still some strong outrage at the prison for depriving them of their time, as well as other aspects of the prison experience[24].

BEHAVIORAL CONSEQUENCES ADJUSTMENT STRATEGIES-
ESCAPES AND SYSTEMS

Now that we have considered the changes in attitude and thinking that the inmate goes through in prison, we must turn our attention to those things he does which organize his days. It is important that the inmate find "things to do" which will occupy his time and keep him busy.

There are certain things which characterize the "escapes" and "systems" of the men which are fairly consistent. In the first place, it is unanimously agreed that every person must do his own time. This means that each one will have his own style of dealing with the monotony. There is very little that anyone can do, (or will dare do) to ease the "hard time" of another. There are instances, however, where one's running mate will make this effort. There are also instances where a man will attempt to console someone with whom he does not "run". Generally though, this situation is fraught with dangers. The consensus is that each man must do his own time.

Another characteristic is that the inmates feel constantly compelled to make their activities count for something so that the time is not totally wasted. Therefore, they try to find "escapes" that are physically or mentally advantageous.

Third, the "system" must be as absorbing as possible. It must leave little time for thought and be thoroughly distracting.

We shall now turn our attention to what some of these "systems" are.

Escapes and Systems. A system or escape is that pattern of activity in which an inmate engages for the express purpose of blanking out the consciousness of time. It is the observation of the inmates that a good many of the "things to do" participated in by the prison population, are a part of a person's system, his attempts to escape from and handle time, more effectively. This in no way detracts from the fact that a very important part of the motivation behind certain types of behavior arises from other sources. Unquestionably, many of these activities are based on considerations of economy, prison politics, mores, fear, sex, or just plain survival. Nonetheless, they are also "things to do." They take up time, they help it pass, they are an attempt to give meaning to the time spent in prison, and so they become part of a man's system.

Thinking. There are some types of thinking that are systems. A good example of this is a case of a man attempting to totally reconstruct the past in his memory. This man spent one year in solitary confinement. During this time he·was able to recollect in detail certain past experiences. He perfected this system to the point that he could reconstruct the thoughts that he had while sitting on the deck of his boat several years earlier. The past is for many the time when they were happy. They try to spend as much time there as possible, whether in their childhood or just reviewing some of the good times that they had on the street.

Another favorite topic of thought is the future. The inmate plans in detail what he's going to do when he is released. He plans how he is going to compensate for this "lost time," how he is going to be a better person, or for that matter, a better burglar.

The inmates also spend time thinking about the general condition of the world, or of the meaning of life. Some men go deeply into the questions of religion and philosophy. (This type of thinking is not limited to those who are more educated or seemingly more intelligent).

"Thinking" is a way of transporting oneself mentally out of the prison, "always wishing you were someplace else, basically daydreaming all the time."

Jobs. The fact that there is a need for men to create their own systems for helping time to pass arises partially from the fact that the institution provides very little to keep them busy. Therefore, one of the things to do is to drag out one's job as long as possible. While the men are on their jobs for eight hours, they are actually busy only a fraction of that period.

Hustles. Besides his job, almost all inmates have a "hustle," moonlighting, as it were. Hustles are primarily economic. There are some that are purely so, but most of them are "things to do" as well. At the upper end of the scale of hustles are gambling and money lending. At the lower end are those that are subservient, such as shining shoes. To one extent or another, each hustle becomes a man's thing to do as well as something which earns him money.

Drugs and Alcohol. Probably the most common of all the methods of escape are drugs and alcohol - drugs of course, being number one. Almost the first thing the inmates look for when they arrive at the prison is a drug contact. Alcoholic beverages too are very common. Many inmates stay high every day for months at a time.

Sleep. Very much related to the drug escape is that of sleep. To some extent, the purpose of finding drugs is to sleep. However, with or without drugs, sleep is a reputable system of its own. Those inmates who chose sleep as their system of escape said that they were gradually able to train themselves to sleep for eighteen to twenty hours a day, especially on the receiving cell or in isolation. But for those who do not go in for it in such a big way, sleep is still a very important means of escape. In the beginning, it literally provides the wings by which to leave the prison because all one's dreams are outside the walls. This means, however, comes to a very definitive halt, because there is a day on which one's dreams cease to be about the outside.

Homosexuality. Homosexuality is one of the biggest problems that incarceration offers to an inmate. No inmate that was interviewed admitted to participation in such activity. However, from their discussion of the subject, it is clearly their opinion that such activity is very much a way of "doing time," an alleviation of the loneliness, boredom and tension.

Music. For those who can afford to have stereos in their cells, listening to music becomes a great escape. Some of the men participated in music groups, spending a great deal of time practicing.

TV. Television is one of the most important diversions that there is. Men would go to great lengths to obtain a set. Consequently, TV repair was a much sought after skill.

Handiwork. For those who are inclined that way, art becomes the way out. Painting, drawing, leather work, are all favorites. Portrait artists are in great demand to do pen and ink portraits from photographs the inmates have.

Sports and Exercise. Sports and physical development are priorities among many of the inmates. Many of them felt it was a release of tension. For some of them, there was a marked preoccupation with their bodies. One man spoke of the different periods of his incarceration, measuring them in terms of baseball season, football season, etc. For many, every moment of free time was spent in the gymnasium.

Self Education. As was mentioned earlier, the inmates felt that they were being robbed of their time, and so felt a compulsion to make their time as productive as was within their power. One of the forms that this urge took was the discussion of how to do a better job of robbing a bank, of cheating at cards, of how to run a con game on the streets. And so, this type of education plays its part in "doing time."

There were, of course, other modes of education. Much time was spent in reading. Many of the men read as many as two or three books a day. To an extent, this meant paperback novels, but for many, the reading was much heavier than that. Although formal educational programs were almost nonexistent at this institution, several of the men used this opportunity to educate themselves. some did a good deal of writing, from poetry to philosophy and politics.

Rapping. Probably the most common system of "doing time" is rapping. It is perhaps more complex than it would appear. First of all, sheer survival depends on not rapping to the wrong person. Second, rapping is selective. Everything cannot be discussed with everyone. Obviously, rapping would be most fruitful if one could find the "significant other" with whom to rap. This is a big problem because true friendship is very difficult. Of course, everyone has those people to whom he feels he can talk. Nevertheless, it is an extremely rare person who feels that there is anyone to whom he can speak without reservation. Such friendship is too fraught with dangers. So, what must be one of the greatest needs for the men in order to do their time is, in many cases, impossible to fulfill.

In the end rapping itself turns against the inmate and turns his time to "hard time." Still, there are those who made rapping their major system, spending hours and hours at it. With rapping, as with thinking, there are things that you talk about and things that you don't. For some, the first thing they want to hear from someone new is what is going on on the outside. For others, this is a subject to be avoided. Some spend hours recalling earlier, more pleasant times. Others shun all reference to the things that they left. There are two reasons for this. One is that old memories are painful. The other perhaps more important reason, is that it is not safe for other inmates to "know your jacket," (past) lest they find some way to hold the information against you.

Then there is "joking your time off." People do not basically laugh very often in prison. There is nothing to laugh about. Laughing is a good way to do your time.

Summary. This paper has shown that the conditions of incarceration have a profound effect on the inmate's relation to time. As a consequence of this, he experiences time and its value in a new and often unique way. In order to cope with this onus, he adopts certain attitudinal stances. His value system is acutely modified. His relationship to loved ones, to the Establishment and to himself is altered, mostly for the worse.

Prisons have been called the microcosms of society. In many ways, a prison produces conditions in such an unadulterated state that are so intense, they are thought to be unique to prisons. They are not. In the next section, we shall consider some other situations which share the conditions which produce "doing time" and suggest ways in which they share the experience.

"DOING TIME" IN OTHER SETTINGS

The implication of this study of "doing time" are significant in other areas of society. The situation of the prison (that particular population and setting) explains one variation of "doing time." In order to develop this concept to a more sophisticated level it would be necessary to examine other contexts which the researcher sees as having similar conditions. There are at least two characteristics of discovery method of grounded theory that indicate the value of making such an investigation.

First, the concepts or core variables with which grounded theory deals are "trans-situational."[25] That is, they are applicable to contexts other than the substantive area which was the focus of the study. In this paper, the concepts as well as many of their properties are generic, and can be generalized to other settings.

Second, the concepts, drawn as they are from the reality of the respondents, usually strike a familiar chord in the experience of the reader even though he is a layperson in the substantive area or in the field of sociology. It is important therefore, to examine the concept of "doing time" in this light. It is believed that a scrutiny of the experience will produce an "aha" reaction in most who read it. Let us examine this idea. In what other contexts do people have a heightened awareness of time, become preoccupied with it, and become tense as a result of it?

The word "incarceration" could perhaps put one off, could limit the experience to the prison environment. But does it? In this society which is so highly mobile, does not the loss of freedom of movement suggest a type of incarceration? For the elderly person who is confined either by infirmity or because he can no longer drive, physical confinement can be a definite reality. Although the reasons for his confinement may alter drastically from that of a prison inmate, the reality of his experience is no less vivid. For him, time is something of which he is acutely aware and with which he is preoccupied. It is a source of tension to him.

The sentence which the elderly person serves is an indefinite one and one which is terminal. Chances are his circumstance will not alter sufficiently to remove his condition of incarceration.

The situation of military servicemen is even more similar to that of a prison inmate. His physical environment is definitely circumscribed by an authority, to a barracks, for example, or a ship or boot camp or whatever. His sentence is normally pretty well determined. And whatever it is, it is most likely too long. He probably has every day counted until his hitch is up.

Having an abundance of time is likewise common to the elderly and the serviceman as well as to many others. Anyone who has waited hours at an air terminal for a plane to be repaired knows the problem of having too much time on his hands.

The condition that complicates the amount of time, of course, is that of having nothing valuable or interesting to do. These conditions, taken together, serve to make the hours drag slowly. One has only to think of the common reference to the bored employee who is termed a clock watcher. Or again, one can call to mind the teacher who covered the face of the classroom clock with the sign, "Time will pass, will you?" and indeed, the time does pass, with agonizing slowness for the inactive elderly, the prison inmate, the person waiting in a hospital waiting room, the bored student, the lonely soldier.

The final condition that intensifies the experience of "doing time" is that of not having control over how one's time will be spent. The person stranded at the airport thinks, "If only I had brought my book." The elderly parson would perhaps rather be working, the student to be playing, the inmate and the soldier to be training for a job they want. None of these people has control over how they will spend their "sentence." Some, it must be recognized, have more control than others. But no one of them would be doing what he is doing were the decision his.

In each instance in which a person does time, he also finds a way to deal with it. Just as the prison inmate devises systems, so do the elderly, students, servicemen, bored employees and all those who wait for anything.

The systems, of course, differ with the circumstances. Servicemens' systems are fairly close to the prison inmate -- gambling, drugs, sleep, education, sex, etc.

Other groups too, participate in some of these same activities. Retired people often retire to games -- gold, poker, bridge, fishing and so forth. It is likewise reported that rates of alcoholism go up with retirement[26].

There are other preoccupations for the elderly -- their plants, their pets, their health. Things seem to need repair more often. Or at least there is some need to call the repairman more often. Could it be for company?

Bored students have innumerable ways of distracting themselves. They bring a toy to school, or a comic book or a transistor radio with an ear phone. Or perhaps they just annoy their fellow student. And on and on the list goes for bored housewives, hospital patients, asylum inmates, and so forth.

Whoever the people, wherever they are, if they live in the right circumstances in our society, they "do time". In a prison, as well as in other contexts where conditions are similar, time becomes problematic. Tempo is exaggerated. The person involved becomes preoccupied with time. He becomes anxious about it. The conditions are right when a person is confined to a limited space for a specific time. This time must be abundant and filled with little that is worthwhile and/or interesting. Finally, the person must have few options for how to fill the time.

Given these circumstances which must generally be present together, certain consequences follow. The time is seen as having greater potential in being spent another way. Certain strategies are employed to get through.

Time no longer passes. It must be *done*. Instead of being the atmosphere in which life is lived, it becomes tangible, something to be endured. Far from being that which heals, which allows growth, time becomes a problem, one which we must twist the language to express. That is "doing time."

METHODOLOGY

This paper was developed using the techniques of "grounded theory," as described by Barney Glaser and Anselm Strauss in their book, *The Discovery of Grounded Theory* (1967).

The purpose of grounded theory is to provide a framework by which theory can be scientifically and methodologically generated. Whereas much research is often more concerned with theory verification, grounded theory is concerned with insuring that the theory which is being verified has been methodologically and meticulously developed. Consequently, it cannot be subject to the criteria of verification research. Its purpose is different: its procedures are different; its sampling is different; its results are different.

As in all good sociological analysis, grounded theory emphasizes the development of inferences that are lucid, that explain the most variation in behavior, that are rich in conceptual detail, that have a great scope of applicability and that are useful in predicting human behavior. But over and above these criteria for good theory, this particular method puts great stress on the generation of inferences that are grounded in data. What then is the process of this development?

First of all, grounded theory proceeds from the assumption that "theory is process". It is an inductive method arriving at hypotheses. This process begins with the collection of raw data. This data is then qualitatively coded as a first step towards developing properties of the theory. From the preliminary coding, the major variables emerge, instigating further questions. Therefore, new data must be collected which is again coded.

Many substantive questions derived from previous data analysis are also addressed. If the answers are not found in the data, rather data collection is indicated. It is this consistent return to the data at each stage of development that validates the theory. The theory matures as elements of the data are integrated into the whole and the grounded network of relationships is established.

This "theory in process" procedure is called "theoretical sampling" by Glaser and Strauss:

"Theoretical sampling is the process of data collection for generating theory where the analyst jointly collects, codes and analyzes his data and decides what data to collect next and where to find them in order to develop by the emerging theory, whether substantive or formal. The initial decisions for theoretical collection of data are based only on a general sociological perspective and on a general subject or problem area (such as how confidence men handle prospective marks or how policemen act toward Negroes or what happens to students in medical school that turns them into doctors). The initial decisions are not based on a preconceived theoretical framework (1967:pg 45)."

A further word needs to be said about theoretical sampling as it differs from representative sampling. The purpose of theoretical sampling is to discover the categories of the phenomenon which is being studied and their interrelationships, so as to generate a theory. The scope of such sampling is determined by what is needed in order to enrich the theory, to discover more variation of data and different levels of relationships. This is opposed to representative sampling, the purpose of which is to gather accurate data on a representative sampling group of people. The group can then be taken to typify a larger group for the purpose of verifying the extent to which the properties of a theory pertain to a given population.

In grounded theory, a sample becomes "saturated" when no further categories or properties emerge from the data. When saturation occurs, there is no reason for further sampling, as the sampling task has been completed (i.e. the generation of theoretical categories). In representative sampling, on the other hand, the researcher continues to explore his sample no matter how many times his data is reiterated. The reason for this is that his purpose is to verify a theory using a representative group of people with the least amount of error possible.

REFERENCES

1. "Doing time " is used by many writers, and indeed by inmates, as a synonym for serving a sentence. In *The Felon* (1970), John Irwin classifies "doing time" as a "prison adaptive mode" which invovles: (1) avioding trouble, (2) finding activities to occupy time, (3) securing luxuries, (4) forming friendships, and (5) doing what is necessary to get out as soon as possible (pp. 66-67).

2. The work release center is a minimum security institution to which men are sent 60 to 90 days prior to their release. There they are given outside employment so that they will have some money when they are released. The men must return to the center at night. After they have been there a certain period of time, they are allowed first a twelve hour pass and then two twelve hour passes. This information was given by the inmates and verified by the staff.

3. Goffman notes that harshness alone does not account for the quality of life generated by an institution sch as a prison: "...rather, we must look to the social disconnections caused by entrance" (in Cressey: 1961, p. 66).

4. Other situations where the conditions for "doing time" are present will be discussed in the last section of this paper.

5. The state in which this research was conducted does not make use of the indeterminate sentence for adult offenders. John Irwin has some interesting things to say about the difficulties that the indeterminate sentence imposes on inmates in the California system (1970).

6. The receiving cell is located at the main institution. It is an isolation

area with the ostensive purpose of separating men in case they have communicable diseases. Oddly enough, they nonetheless, eat at the main dining area. Otherwise, they are completely isolated, although there may be two persons to a cell. They stay there until their FBI rap sheets arrive and they are classified.

7. No matter how much or how little a man had to do, it seemed intolerable to him. It seened that it would be impossible to do more. Some of the lifers recalled how they had tried to help men doing two years who were having a hard time.

8. There were also periods during the day when they were out in the yard. In this situation also, there was often little to do.

9. According to statute, a man could appear before the parole board at any time, at the discretion of the board members. After one third of the sentence had been served, their appearance before the board was mandatory. During one administration, however, certain classes of offenders were not allowed a parole.

10. A parole plan includes a job, a place to live, and a parole advisor. Often, these plans were arranged by families, friends, or agencies, with little or no communication with the prospective parolee.

11. Most of the imnates agreed that it was necessary to make some accommodation to prison life so as to keep some kind of peace with oneself. However, to give in any way to the institution, or to become satisfies with prison life, was considered anathema.

12. Since none of the respondents ever admitted to being one of those who were not able to adjust, one wonders whether or not it is a matter of pride to be able to handle prison life. There seem to be definite indications that one reason that no one admits that they do continual "hard time" is that such an admission would be giving in to the institution.

13. The location of the prison has important implications for the degree of contact that a man can keep with the outside. In this particular case, the prison is located at least one hundred miles from any metropolitan area of the state. For the families of many of the men, visiting there meant a long ride on a bus which arrived at night, requiring an overnight stay. Since many of the families were in the room at the same time, hearing was difficult and privacy impossible. Until recently, even letters were limited to one a day, and only from a very circumscribed correspondence list. All

these factors have a very dampining effect on any possible alleviation of lonely hours that contact with loved ones could afford.

14. Mail time is also traumatic in other institutional settings where residents are separated for long periods from loved ones. The author verified this specifically in regard to convents and military bootcamps. In all three settings, the whole day is climaxed by mail time. The day's success or failure depends on getting a letter or not.

15. Some of the inmates who did not have, or did not choose to have, visitors of their own, did visit with families of the friends. These visits did not take place at the maximim security institution, however. Visiting with other inmates' families alleviated the monotony of the daily routing. At the same time, it did not entail the emotional upheaval that visiting with one's own loved ones did.

16. It was not uncommon for inmates to mention that after having had one or two bad experiences with their wife or girlfriend, that they had learned not to develop deep and meaningful relationships. At least, the did not develop permanent ones. From now on, intimacy was expendable.

17. Being "good people" is defined exclusively as never snit anyone for any reason. This included hated police, as well as other inmates. Good people could be trusted never to incriminate anyone else, The consequences of this ethic could intail an added prison sentence or time in isolation.

18. The activities of some of the inmates indicated that they had to be snitches. Yet, under no circumstances would they admit that this was the obvious implication. These inmates upheld the "good people" ethic as vehemently as anyone during the interview.

19. It was nearly unanimously agreed that true friendship was inadvisable and unknown in prison. Many of the men were in prison in the first place because they had unwisely trusted a friend. But there were other reasons. If one was good friends with a person, then his enemies were yours also. By the same token, you were involving him in your affairs. Also being friends with one person limited one's possibilities with others. The pressures of prison life could force a person to snitch on you and involve you in something that could be very dangerous. Then too, being friends with someone meant that you had to go along with them in the things they wanted to do, limiting your alternatives. On the other hand there were certain "running mates" who trusted each other completely where matters of business were concerned. They would go to any lengths to help each

other out. Whether or not there was anything like affection is another question.

20. One could pay to be released from his cell or to have someone else released from their cell. Much homosexual activity was handled in this way.

21. The concept of "thinking" and "not thinking" that the writer has developed differs in importatn respects from Donal Clemmer's description of "reverie plus." In the first place, this type of "thinking" was not limited to those individuals with introspective personalities. Secondly, it seemed to be a direct function of the whole matter of "doing time," with its alsteration of the time experience, etc., and not just something one did as a leisure time activity, although there are certain aspects of "thinking" that match Clemmer's description (Clemmer: 1940).

22. There were a significant number of men who said that if the opportunity to do something illegal again presented itself and were attractive enough, they intended to get involved again. There were others who could spout the rhetoric about being reformed because they thought it appropriate. Still others really thought that they were ready for a straight life. Subsequent information indicated that they got in trouble again after they were released. They were probably sincere at the time.

23. In this connection Goffman makes the remark:

Among inmates in may total institutions, there is a strong feeling that time spent in the establishment is either wasted or destroyed or taken from one's life; it is time that must be "done" or "marked" or "put in" or "pulled"...This time is something its doers have bracketed off as such for constant conscious consideration not quite found on the outside (1961).

24. Sykes adds an interesting point in his *Society of Captives:*

Most prisoners are unable to fortify themselves in their low level of material existence by seeing it as a means to some high or worthy end. They are unable to attach any significant meaning to their need to make it more bearable, such as present pleasures foregone for pleasures in the future (Sykes: 1958; also see Goffman: 1961, p. 63).

25. In his unpublished doctoral dissertation, Stu Hadden refers to "basic social processes" as "trans-situational." The same holds for this core variable.

26. Reported in private conference in research done by the author for the University of Tulsa Preretirement Planning Program.

CHAPTER 16

NOTES ON THE EXPERT-LAYMAN RELATIONSHIP

Barney G. Glaser

1972

This study has provided us with a wealth of categories and basic processes pertinent to the expert-layman relationship. To be sure, the topic of this study gives only one set of values to these formulations, but it is easy enough to further extend, generalize and qualify them through comparative analysis with other kinds of relationships.[1] One need only, for example, think of the power of symmetry of other expert -layman relationships (such as the well-known ones of lawyer-client, student-teacher and doctor-patient) to discover a fuller range of bases for edge in power symmetry, or to discover conditions under which comparative bidding or generalling are appropriate.

This book has opened up the study of expert-layman phenomena far beyond the standard ones encountered in typical studies by going beyond the conceptions of control, autonomy and helping, to processes of bidding, gaining information, redesigning, inspecting, administering, evaluating, detailing work to temporal pacing, winning trust, obtaining and judging quality and closure, articulating, elsewhereism, generalling and so forth. But even with respect to the standard concerns of autonomy and control, our set of formulations on the patsy and the subcontractor gives us new ideas on what happens when the expert is not at such a great advantage in facing a vulnerable layman, as when doctors, lawyers and accountants face their typical, accepting clients. Also this book points up the often restrictive view of these studies from the standpoint of the limited number of variables -often preconceived as relevant - but from their limited densification and integration.[2]

Now let us go over some of these new processes and summarize their main hypotheses while generalizing and extending them somewhat through comparative analysis of other professional expert-layman relationships. And obviously, this chapter could serve as the beginning basis of another book on a formal theory of processes of the expert-layman relationship. Strauss and I accomplished this same transition in going from *Time for Dying* to our book *Status Passage*, where we comparatively analyzed the dying passage with many other status passages. And this author presented a formal theory of *Organizational Careers* by comparing several diverse studies on the subject. The method for this approach is delineated in Chapter 9 of *Status Passage*.[3]

This chapter, then, will be a small, fragmented formal theory of expert-layman relations. It will also illustrate what other hypotheses may be taken from this book and used or developed. Lastly, it will show methodologically how hypotheses developed about facets of the expert-layman relationship here can be broadened, extended and modified to the level of formal theory by comparative analysis with anecdotes and studies of other kinds.[4]

I shall organize this chapter under the three core categories pertaining to experts' relations with laymen: *choosing experts, power symmetry and elsewhereism*. The first category has to do with bidding experts, finding them, referrals, and judging whether or not to use experts. Power symmetry develops the traditional notions of autonomy and control on a processual basis which transcends current work. Elsewhereism focuses on the constant competition that laymen face with unseen others in claiming the time and work of an expert. Like the foregoing chapter, this chapter is written, by and large, from the perspective of the involved layman.

CHOOSING EXPERTS: BIDDING

Experts are chosen in several ways that indicate degrees of flexibility of choice.[5] At one end of the continuum is being *forced* through circumstances - like insurance, local monopolies, or public facilities - to accept the expert provided, and in particular, professional experts. In the middle of the continuum, there are experts *referred* both by other laymen -usually clients - and other experts, specialists to specialists. Referrals too can be forced, when only one expert is available for such referrals (e.g., a surgeon), but usually a few are referred from among a much larger aggregate.

Also in the middle of the continuum of the degree of flexibility is *comparative shopping*. When there are many experts to choose from, and many types and sub-types of them, the layman can, over a period of time and many trials, shop comparatively provided he ius not hooked by a particular one. Concerning health care, there are many specialist types within medicine for a disease condition, and many experts outside of medicine such as natural health food practitioners of various sorts[6] and practitioners of home remedies and myths.[7] As the layman compares results and prices and relationships, he can become quite flexible in choosing whom and how many experts to see.

As we have seen from this study, comparative bidding is a formalized, very flexible method of choosing an expert. It is basically a condensation and codification into a short period of what occurs with comparative shopping, but without the experience of work and the results which come with comparative shopping. As we have seen in Chapter III on detailing, this experience is supplanted by the experts development of trust in the layman that timing and results will occur as he has promised. The expert can go no further in the layman's particular case. The expert must rely on getting referrals from people with satisfied results and through showing his actual past work to the layman. Still, the layman must trust that he will also get the same quality and timing.

A crucial question regarding the use of bidding is, under what conditions experts will allow laymen to bid them? Not all experts appreciate the protection that bidding affords laymen from poor and/or high-priced experts, and the control afforded by the understanding and information gained--with its consequent allowing the layman some ability to inspect and judge quality, and administer cogently his particular work. This, of course, undermines the favorable dominance that professional experts have by virtue of their position and training: they see being a licensed doctor, lawyer or accountant should be protection enough for a client. "Why shouldn't people ask lawyers and doctors for bids?" They can save money and obtain quality without learning the hard way. But such experts do not like being invidiously compared, with a consequent undermining of the power of their positions. They expect to be accepted, *carte blanche*, with trust. They insist on faith. A layman with comparative notions must spend his money for visits while comparatively shopping, or surreptitiously comparatively bidding. Thus the experts do not know and do not give free bids as when there is a bidding system, however informal.

When they are aware of being compared, such experts, who as consultants have given what amounts to another bid, still will not take another's client. "Raiding" is unprofessional. Thus comparative bidding demands an ethical as well as a structural process base. It must be accepted as fair and just, not viewed as undercutting and raiding--as a form of unfair competition among experts. If a doctor does provide bids he is sure to lose his foothold in this referral network,[8] and thus be chastised by losing more clients than he has gained. This makes it hard for a layman who does shop comparatively to bid in order to switch experts who are aware of this. The layman is apparently the first visited expert's client, and a second expert would be fearful of taking over without the first's approval that the switch would be for the layman's good, and on some grounds that neither invidiously compare the two nor breach ethics. Of course, many questions remain for research on what further conditions - besides protection of the layman's interests and undermining of the expert's control - prevent bidding among many kinds of experts. For example, another condition is that bidding gives a degree of organization to an otherwise unorganized aggregate of clientele, which provides a source of lay pressure that professional experts would rather avoid.

Comparative bidding systematizes approaching and obtaining the maximum number of options for what goes on in all but some forced choosing of experts. The search is for protection against exploitation and incompetence, finding trust, understanding the best qualifications, and some control over quality, timing and costs (or some edge in the power of symmetry of the relationship).

Whereas professional experts expect imputed trust on the basis of having achieved a licensed position, bidding also provides trust through a build-up of understanding and details through comparisons as well as by licensing. One aspect of this build-up is that the expert can not sustain a *false front* to gain trust, as comparisons allow these laymen easily to see behind it. Being too sweet, double talkish, secretive or haughty is not effective. The next bidded expert probably will show that these styles are put on and are unnecessary to obtain quality. Bidding forces experts to play it straight. The expert wants a job, and then callbacks and referrals; he does not want to be dumped as a comparative phony.

The information gained by the layman during detailing is variously undermining of the trust expected by professional experts who insist on faith, and do not subject themselves to bidding. Information is a kind of evidence that demonstrates competence, and professional experts want this competence assumed without requiring demonstration of knowledge. Information-gaining also undermines the myth of secrecy of the professional's affairs and skills, thus eroding trust in the magic of the expert. Some professionalism is too complex to demonstrate satisfactorily so the professional can only variously impress the clients.

Further, the layman need not trust the expert as much since information gives him several offsetting powers. If the job is simple enough - as much law, accounting and medicine is - he can dispense with the professional and do-it-himself, an action offensive to experts (apart from such crucial exceptions as getting rid of unwanted patients as in some chronic illnesses.) Also, information gives the layman the ability to inspect work and temporally administer the expert to a "crowding" degree. Both are forms of control which experts - professional and unprofessional - rarely wish to yield. They think that the layman should follow their schedules and accept work as O.k., not cogently question or control on the basis of either. Even in bidding, experts give as little information as possible on how jobs will be done.

Whereas bidding provides a build-up of trust through comparing, detailing and playing it straight by the expert, in those expert-layman situations in which bidding is taboo and trust insisted upon *a priori*, any trust build-up is negligible until many days after the expert begins work - not, as in bidding, before work. At this point distrust may arise too late or trust be inconsequential; build-up provides only for follow-throughs, callbacks and referrals. For the expert, the positive consequence of the client's not putting trust in his professional skill to a test in choosing him before he has worked is that a doctor , say, can work on acutely ill patients without question, immediately, without being hindered by their subjective judgements. But when patients or clients have time, this delay in establishing evidenced trust until sometime after work begins can be costly to them. Bidding, then, is a sophisticated approach to resolving the dangers of haphazard, fortuitous choosing or long-term shopping. The lack of protection brought on by premature trust not only allows exploitation based on trust - the least danger - but allows being provided less-than-competent quality and skill, or provided with the wrong expertise, or delays in finding the correct specialists. Bidding limits these risks.

POWER SYMMETRY

Comparative bidding provides the initial basis for a near-equal balance in the power symmetry of the expert-layman relationship. Using comparative bidding, the layman develops good judgements on what to expect, to demand and pay for quality, timing and cost. This amounts to control over the expert. In contrast, the professional-client relationship is usually quite asymmetrical in favor of the professional, since it takes time to develop these judgments to a cogent degree. And there is seldom the time necessary until long into the course of a single, non-bidded, expert-lay relationship, even if such judgement eventually develops. Indeed, many patients are still ignorant of how to judge time, quality and cost after years with one doctor

-they lack a comparative perspective. In spite of having the time, they have no process, such as comparative bidding, by which they can systematically develop judgment.

The problem of power symmetry is complex. One cannot assume that an expert deserves a complete edge in power because of his position. (He may be an "inexpert expert" facing a knowledgeable layman, and his domination may not be just.) Conditions which are acute and serious, requiring instant expertise, demand an asymmetrical power relationship in favor of the expert: he is given *carte blanche* to act, as in emergencies. But when matters are not serious - though acute - or are long-range or chronic, then questions arise as to the justice in giving an expert such power asymmetry without proof of merit.[9]

But more to the point: to take over the job of expert or to control an expert, *a layman need not be an expert in general but only in his specific case.* This *is* enough expertise for him (but *not*, of course, enough for the expert). Indeed, on this detailed level, when the layman may know more than the expert, his judgments should, reasonably, prevail. This is starting to occur in cases of chronic diseases and in civil rights cases where intelligent or busy professionals allow or even advocate their clients' views.

It is from the asymmetrical professional-expert relationship that much of the "know-it-all/know-nothing" imagery emerges, with its consequent instant faith and yielding of dominance. *The mirror image of being a professional expert is being an obedient layman to other experts.* This is so inbred in professional experts that often they make the best patsys to experts in other fields! Thus a doctor turns himself over to a lawyer with complete, unquestioned trust on the basis of a mere referral. Knowing the patsy role through his own expertise, it is easy for him to do it when facing other experts. On the other hand, the bidded relationship teaches us how experts may become laymen to other experts so as to yield enough control while limiting domination although they are out of their own bailiwick. It gives to the relationship power symmetry while trimming or doing away with unquestioned trust and its contingent unprotectiveness and paranoia for the expert-turned-layman.

Imagery of what work is to be done by an expert is vital to its accomplishment. In an asymmetrical relationship based on instant trust, this imagery is not problematical during the beginning of the work. The layman makes no pretense at imagery and, with the barest details of his desire, leaves his fate in the expert's hands. But when power symmetry is a slightly shifting edge in balance, the respective image of a client and expert becomes problematic and possibly conflicting. This is why detailing is extensive in bidding - so that layman and expert both have a clear view of what is to come, and both agree. Obviously, professional experts prefer as little detailing as possible - even complete nondisclosure - so the layman's imagery will not conflict with and erode their power advantage. Such details as are disclosed are at a minimum, and legitimated by them alone.[10] This minimizes their loss of control in giving details, hence understanding, to the layman.

Imagery in the symmetrical expert-layman relationship, then, may easily lead to differential judgements *that matter* for the future course of the work - unlike the asymmetrical relationship. To keep the work going, as we have seen, the resolving of these differentials must be paced, and carefully, by each party. Many strategies (delineated throughout the book) resolve those differences. These are the strategies of reduction of anger or concern delays, discounting, listening and then doing what one considers best; also redesigning, intense detailing by the expert and by the layman, generalling strategies of pacing, generalling of orders, inspection and evaluations to the point where experts will not be stopped or quit (but do not proceed unfettered), playing patsy, information gaining, playing wise, pressuring, articulating, correctly paying, dismissing, controlling before being controlled, and negotiating, and so forth. These strategies do not come easy for many laymen who are accustomed to asymmetry in client-expert relationships.

But these same strategies, while resolving, *may also be used to generate* differential judgements and desires of imagery, which process can turn an asymmetrical relationship into a balancing symmetrical one if the layman has the temperament to try. For example, if a patient just gives orders out-of-hand to a doctor or lawyer, this would probably result in the expert's using the strategies of discounting and reducing with an allowable affect on asymmetry. But if the layman paces his orders to vulnerable junctures, such as at the end of detailing the case, or when a preliminary solution begins to be less than successful, or directs his orders at a para-expert in service of the expert; then he can start balancing the symmetry and developing control.

The layman cannot be shy nor waiver in telling a person who knows more than he what he ought to do. The layman must draw on his power to know his own specific case best - both technically and when applicable, with taste - and his power to reward, and his power to go elsewhere.

Part of pacing his orders is learning to leave an expert alone when he is working well and has sufficient imagery. To say something may stop the expert, and hinder the achievement of the layman's goal. The goal is *not* to dominate, but to achieve a goal with some controls in the layman's favor to secure what he wants. By definition, the expert is working for the layman's desires (though one can sometimes wonder about this in some asymmetrical relationships).

In our books on dying,[11] we have shown how the hospital staff manages patients for many purposes other than patients' welfare, e.g., nurses require an orderly ward too! The same process can apply in other client-expert relationships concerning administering and timing. When a layman wishes to right an asymmetrical relationship in order to gain some control, to be effective he must carefully gain enough information and pace his actions and words with the course of the expert's work. Inspections should be based on near-completions, or for corrections, or on the verge of errors - not before the expert has produced a viewable result, otherwise the layman's action will be premature and discounted. Administering should be attempted when temporal pacing is off, as for delays or for unhappy consequences for the layman elsewhere. Again the focus is on the goal - not on dominance - or the expert will not yield.

Well-paced interventions by laymen proportionalize the expert's imagery on the work, as the balance of power shifts toward symmetry. Give and take begins, pre-empting of control ceases; differential judgements emerge and are resolved. If enough laymen were to try to balance asymmetrical expert-lay relationships, they could change professional training and the professional practices. This is happening in some measure, as minorities, imbued with civil rights, demand better medical care. It happens as malpractice suits increase and as an individual rights are more guaranteed, as in the commitments of possibly insane people. Taking the asymmetry out of many expert-layman relationships is beginning to be frequent among the rebelling young in the realms of education, occupations, economics,health and politics. However, the balancing out of power asymmetrical relationships still does not provide the layman with the capability that we have seen in this study of being able legitimately to general many experts on an articulating basis. The structure of professional relationships is not often suited to the generalling of many lawyers or doctors. What generalling and articulating by a layman does accomplish is not manifest to those experts who are unaccustomed to fitting their own schedules to the bigger picture of a layman. The layman must do the best he can while keeping his own projects fairly out of issue. The layman in the professional relationship must depend on strategies, not on social structure, to gain and keep some control.

ELSEWHEREISM

This study offers a new variable of major importance in the course of expert-layman relationships and their outcomes: relative to one client, competitive demands from elsewhere upon the expert - or elsewhereism.[12] Stories are legion among laymen about delays from waiting for or missing their busy expert - and how fateful that is for them. I am reminded of a Los Angeles Times story about the woman who called her doctor, who was too busy elsewhere to see her. As her need was acute, a substitute doctor was sent by the answering service: he then hooked her on heroin and kept her hooked for many years! It is my contention that sociologists cannot talk of experts' servicing laymen without talking about how the service is articulated with demands from elsewhere, and how these affect quality and closure of servicing work. Busy doctors and lawyers often spread too thin are a problem to themselves and to clients regarding their timing and quality of service. Getting needed appointments by patients is a classic example of the problem. For example, one research study shows how people needing immediate psychiatric care are made to wait for two weeks by a busy clinic - over which time the problem disappears or changes drastically in the patient's view.[13]

Also, it is my contention that *how* a layman competes for an expert with laymen elsewhere - usually unknown, given the power of symmetry of the relationship - is important for understanding the course of an expert-layman relationship. For example, in our article on the social loss of dying patients,[14] we state that social loss may be a determinant of the amount and speed of medical and nursing attention. This proposition would have been more to the point had we followed through - on the hypothesis that people with low social value lack staff attention, with the idea that it is because they compete poorly with other people who are of a higher social value, of with experts' other affairs of more concern. This idea was surely documented in the data.

Elsewhereism primarily affects the pacing and articulation of the expert's work. As we have seen, this timing then can have quality and cost consequences. Either the expert has no time or he is delayed, cuts short his work, or finishes too fast because of demands from elsewhere - and the layman is in poor competition with these demands. If the demands are minimal or well articulated, however, the layman experiences no effect from elsewhereism. Inasmuch as most of these demands are not minimal and articulate, the layman is bound to feel elsewhereism, at least through short delays and often long ones. It is difficult for the expert not to pass on to a client the effects of elsewhereism: he can only cover so much with other experts or crews. Thus, when doctors have back-up colleagues, the colleagues too may be hard pressed by elsewhereism to back up the expert with his demanding client.

To the degree that elsewhereism is passed on, the layman must compete with other clients, with little or no knowledge of who are his competitors or what are the criteria of competition. He only finds out the barest information when the infrequent expert defends, explains or excuses his delay, and tells what has been going on elsewhere. The criteria of competition may vary from realistic to very difficult or impossible to meet. A mildly ill patient cannot win out against an emergency - he must wait. Patsys can outdo generals with prompt cash payments. The more an expert talks of his clientele, of course, the better astute laymen can learn how to compete for his time. An expert seldom talks this much, especially since it is information confidential to the professional relationship. Perhaps the best way to compete against high odds is the threat to go to another expert, to become an emergency, or to wait for a slack season. It is hard to get an accountant to do other work during "tax time," but afterwards he will. Many professional experts have slack periods.

The layman develops competitive power symmetry when, as a general, he must articulate several experts on the job - a structural property of the patsy-sub relationship - by delaying some experts and affecting others. But in professional expert-lay relationships and other kinds of servicing, where uneven balanced power obtains, the power gained from articulating is not as much since the layman does not general and articulate the work of several, say, lawyers on a legitimate structural basis.

A major property of elsewhereism, then, is the degree to which a layman is aware of with whom he is in competition. The practice of most professional experts is to say nothing respecting identity of their other clients, so clients must compete as best they can in the dark. As I have said, experts often only divulge properties of competing clients when excusing their tardiness. Most client-sets are an unknown aggregate to each other. But several structural conditions may obtain when knowledge of other clients becomes possible. Lay referral systems give this kind of knowledge on other clients as well as information on the expert, as do professional referrals although to a lesser degree. Information is given on the type and class of clients, not on particular ones, as in the lay system. Another condition is when many clients are grouped together in full view of each other such as in waiting rooms or in wards. The client can make judgements as to competitive ability in making appointments and warding off future delays. Unlike waiting rooms which just present an aggregate of types, hospital wards present a type of client, so competition criteria are clearer. If a client does not anticipate doing well, we can change wards; a medical or surgical emergency patient does not do well on a psychiatric ward. The less a layman knows how to compete, the more the expert can maintain his edge in power symmetry over him on when to see him and for how long.

When a layman is not getting the attention promised and needed, he can accurately assume he is not competing well with clients elsewhere. There are several conditions ascertainable by the layman that make for stiff competition which, with professional experts, usually is only of hourly or daily duration. The "best" experts in any field have several "prominent" clients, "good business" clients, or "deserving" clients who can easily crop up and take priority over an average client whatever his need and protest. Some clients make a practice of working for the position of a high priority client in order to obtain instant attention: they do not wish to worry about elsewhereism. For example, a corporation or businessman will flood a lawyer with business so he would not dare not to respond with instant attention to his slightest call. In consequence, a smaller client with a one-shot problem may find himself repeatedly bounced from the focus of attention. He, then, must pay for his place in the expert's clientele (and the larger system) with time and/or money. He must judge whether this "best man in town" expert is worth his time and money.

Another source of stiff competition knowable by the layman is the expert who is too busy by allowing himself to be spread too thin, whether or not he is among the best experts. He presents the layman with a constant rat-race of elsewhereism. No matter how well he articulates his practice, the large number of wanting clients are always interrupting and demanding. The phone is constantly ringing, the temporal demands are spotting and of short duration, but derailing for the layman who is seeking his expert's service. Even for crucial help, he can be made to wait a moment by the expert.

Other temporal conditions are the peak load hours and holidays which generate elsewhereism problems for any layman, and even for those experts who articulate client-sets well. Laymen generally avoid these times, unless they too become deserving clients - that is, feel that their sudden problem will compete well - or are forced to call an expert. Another temporal condition is the geographical swing of the expert and layman on the *fringes* - do not compete well with those near his geographical center. An expert can see more people in the center; temporally it is costly to go to the fringe to see one layman.

Another condition that generates baffling, stiff competition for the layman is the "squeezability" of elsewhereism. Whether it be a doctor, lawyer, accountant or sub, the question arises just how well, given the type of expertise and practice, the expert can squeeze in another client for a quick phone call or job while attending to a client's needs. High squeezability may allow an expert to take care of many other clients while the primary client does not know the difference: for example, in the well-articulated office, where the doctor goes from examination room to examination room while patients are being prepared. Low squeezability leads to constant interruptions and delays if the expert tries little jobs or calls in between and spreads himself too thin. The principal consequences of elsewhereism, as we have seen in Chapters IV and V, are delaying the layman and other experts. And, of course, delays also have their consequences.

In sum, besides what knowledge the layman may glean from the expert and the viewing of other clients which enables him to expect elsewhereism occurrences, he may also expect them on the basis of several conditions attending the practice of expertise. The expectation of elsewhereism is important because it causes delays in work or causes poor quality. These consequences in themselves have chain affects on future work, total projects, and other people (elsewhereism) whose fate is linked with the work. Delays of doctors are continually altering patients' schedules and subsequent experts do a good business in correcting previous experts' quality, some of which is caused by rushing.

As we have seen, in experts' work, delays may be caused by elsewhereism at any point: start, during and closure. The occurrence of elsewhereism is usually unpredicted exactly, but in general is expectable. The expert will warn if possible - the secretary calls - but in professional expertise he is often caught and cannot get away or even get to a phone. Thus the layman can expect surprises. Some professional experts are so used to such delays that their clients are never informed but simply left to understand on their own as the patients or surgeons or gynecologists. Experts, then, vary according to the mechanisms that they set up to inform laymen of elsewhereism demands which formally excuse delays. The mechanisms are associated with reduction and hooking strategies as discussed in Chapter V.

In response, the layman responds with some combination of understanding and anger. While anger gains some edge in power symmetry for the layman, in asymmetrical relations with professional expertise, anger usually does little good and the layman is left to understand or go elsewhere. If he cannot withdraw, he must rest and wait despite his anger. Withdrawal is harder when the expert and layman are well into the course of work. This is another reason why laymen lose their edge in power symmetry during the middle of work. It is at the beginning and at closure that they develop most of their power in symmetrical as well as asymmetrical relations.

We have seen that delays when expectable and of short duration generate a zone of tolerance and normality and do not occasion particular strategies beyond an attempt at understanding. But as the zone is breached, the layman will start ensuring an end of the delay by using strategies like reminding or verifying of time, or seeking a reaffirmed commitment. (For example, patients check with the secretary on whether they came at the right time.) If this does not eliminate delays, then "pushing" strategies come into play - the client applies direct demands and pressures through stressing imperative needs, making threats to withdraw, confronting over the breach, or making demands to know whey the delay? These strategies are familiar to any professional-client relationship. Lastly, anger may be used in full force irrespective of the consequences for the layman. The anger to be effective must be controlled and paced to gain an edge in power symmetry, otherwise it has no affect on the delay and may even occasion more; as when a patient is considered a "nut" and is custodialized by para-experts while waiting, or when a defendant is denied audience with counsel until he calms down.

The handling of delays become more complex when a layman must work with many experts (Chapter VI) which is not an usual condition in professional relationships of chronically ill patients. Here the problem is articulating a life-style elsewhere to jibe with the ever busy expert's schedule, which is seldom designed to consider the layman's elsewhereism. One can see that the problems of elsewhereism become quite complex when both layman and expert are articulating demands from elsewhere in order to work together. The typical first strategy is that of appointment-making, which the layman articulates to the expert's articulation because of initial asymmetry in power: the layman needs, the expert is busy.

I have barely touched the problems of temporal impact of elsewhereism brought out in this book and in considering comparatively the professional-client and other servicing relationships. I have merely opened the way to the problem but before closing this section I wish to touch briefly on the duality impact of elsewhereism. Experts set standard time periods for providing adequate quality, and these times are articulated with promised work for people elsewhere. The professional schedules of doctors and lawyers mirror this, and then the schedule cannot so mirror these professional charges for time and then the expert lets the job run. Lawyers' fee for service charges can become huge for open-ended care. Some clients elsewhere may demand excess time in order to get quality--emergency or surgery or lawsuits or accounting snags. To prevent disarticulation of the whole client--set, the expert may take time from jobs that can be "safely" rushed. The expert tries to keep up by dong less well on jobs with no exact quality requirements. Hence quality suffers and a layman is at least partly abandoned. Subs have more exact quality standards that are subject to the inspection of laymen and officials almost instantly. Professional quality is less clear and takes more time to emerge as being poor and perhaps worth correcting. Layman inspection of professional work is frowned upon, as we have seen. Even formal inspections by officials and other experts is discouraged, although some hospitals are developing genuine committees of peers to inspect certain treatments and procedures of surgical operations. Thus, criteria and inspection of quality vary widely in expert-layman relations; hence the effects on them of elsewhereism are varyingly difficult to ascertain. And the further consequence of gaining edge of power by laymen who have found poor quality is correspondingly harder in professional cases of low clarity.

Quality is intimately linked with closure: the two temporally intersect. To be finished on time is to have reached the desired degree of quality. Closure raises questions of guarantee of quality. Whereas subs must guarantee by statute, professionals have no such problem - save layman-instigated lawsuits. Once finished they are seldom held accountable for errors or corrections, sometimes they charge again if they do them. Thus, in professional relationships allowing closure is more hazardous for laymen. The increase in professional malpractice suits only indicates the problem, it does not resolve it. Professional responsibility and controls do not solve it either.[15] Formal inspections and legal guarantees are solutions, to be used or avoided depending on the expertise. They are used for non-professional servicing in areas. Professionals have avoided them, so elsewhereism can have more of a drawing away effect on quality. Perhaps the only control that laymen have is through withdrawal and lay-referral systems.[16] One source of continued asymmetrical power in professional-clients relationships is this lack of legitimized inspection of quality. That which occurs is *ad hoc*, specific, informal or consists of lawsuits which drag on and on.

In conclusion, this monograph indicates that in the explanation of behaviors occurring in expert-layman relationships - professional, non-professional, and many servicing relationships - three core explanatory variables are the processes of *choosing*, the balancing of *power symmetry* between expert-layman and the prevalence and force of *elsewhereism*. Using these complex variables, the sociologist can account for much if not most of the variation in expert-layman behaviors. This monograph also indicates that to use one without the other (such as the intense focus on autonomy reflected in the literature) is to miss the basic explanations of and belief in the complexity of what one is observing. The question is not just the autonomy of the professional, but this variable (which pertains to a dimension of power symmetry) in conjunction with choosing and elsewhereism - both of which affect the degree of autonomy as an expert's work progresses.

REFERENCES

1.See Barney G. Glaser, *Experts Versus Laymen: A Study of the Patsy and the Subcontractor,* (Sociology Press, 1972), and Barney G. Glaser and Anselm L. Strauss, *Status Passage*, (Chicago, Aldine Publishing, 1971, Chapter 9 and Barney G. Glaser, *Organizational Career: A Sourcebook for Theory*, (Chicago, Aldine Publishing Co., 1968) Introduction.

2.Barney G. Glaser, *Review:* of Eliot Freidson's *Profession of Medicine: A Study of Sociology of Applied Knowledge* (New York; Dodd Mead & Co., 1970), in *American Journal of Sociology*, (Sept. 1971) pp. 361-2.

3.*Ibid.* See also Anselm Strauss, *The Contexts of Social Mobility* (Chicago: Aldine Publishing Co. 1971)

4.On how fragmented theory can be broadened, see Anselm Strauss, "Discovery New Theory from Previous Theory" in Tomatsu Shibutani (ed.) *Human Nature and Collective Behavior*, (Englewood Cliffs, Prentice Hall, 1971).

5.On choosing professionals see Eliot Freidson, "The Impurity of Professional Authority" in Howard S. Becker et al, *Institutions and the*

Person: Papers Presented to Everett C. Hughes (Chicago, Aldine Publishing Co., 1968) pp. 27-31.

6.Richard R. Hanson, and Julius A. Roth, *In Quest of Optimal Health: The Natural Health Movement in the United States*, unpublished manuscript.

7.David - Hayes - Baptista, ''Judging the Medical Professions: Primary Concern by Chicano'', unpublished paper, University of California, San Francisco.

8.On referral networks in medicine see Eliot Freidson, ''The Profession of Medicine: A Sociological Analysis'' (New York, Dodd Mead, 1969) Part III.

9.The moral and consequential justification for such unfettered asymmetrical power in favor of the professional expert is dealt with at length in Freidson, *op. cit.*

10.See Barney G. Glaser and Anselm L. Strauss, *Awareness of Dying*, (Chicago, Aldine Publishing Co. 1965) PartII.

11.*Op Cit.* and *Time for Dying*, (Chicago, Aldine Publishing Co., 1967) and *Anguish: A Case History of a Dying Trajectory* (Mill Valley, The Sociology Press, 1970).

12.Elsewhereism effects the shape of the status-passage of an expert's client. See Barney G. Glaser and Anselm L. Strauss, *Status-Passage* (Chicago, Aldine Publishing Co. 1971) Chapter 3.

13.A study by Evelyn Peterson of making appointments for psychiatric help at a clinic by working class people presented in seminar at University of California Medical Center, San Francisco.

14.Barney G. Glaser and Anselm L. Strauss, ''The Social Loss of Dying Patients,'' *American Journal of Nursing*.

15.See Eliot Freidson, ''Processes of Control in a Company of Equals, *Social Problems.* XI (1963) pp. 119-131 and; Joanne Scherr, ''Reciprocal Dependence, Control and Peer Interaction; A Case Study of a Group Medical Practice,'' unpublished paper, University of California Medical Center.

16.On this see, Eliot Freidson, *Patients' View of Medical Practice* (New York: Russell Sage Foundation, 1961) Chapter 10.

CHAPTER 17

THE SENSUAL CONTEXT OF PHYSICAL TOUCHING

Carole Tyler

June 1973

People touching people is highly socialized process. Whether it is hugging a friend on a busy Street, offering a handshake to a new acquaintance or maneuvering a pathway through a crowded corridor, people are involved every day in face-to face interaction involving physical contact. That most of these interactions containing physical touching are managed with little effort in our daily lives gives support to a major assumption of this paper. That assumption is that the management of physical contact in our face to face interactions is largely influenced by a reservoir of assumptions or taken-for-granted social processes. It is generally only when we violate these assumptions that the power of a taken-for-granted process becomes obvious.

For example there would generally be a greater flexibility of the conditions concerning physical touch in a "mother-child" interaction than in many other interactions. However, even in this case, if there is not enough physical contact the mother is seen as "distant" or the child as "autistic": or if there is too much physical contact the mother is "smothering" and the child "overly dependent." Their interaction pattern is not socially acceptable and soon a wide variety of social structures and interaction tactics will be used to bring the interaction back into line.

It is the second assumption of this paper that there are a number of sets of conditions or contexts for physical contacting and each context has a different "recipe" or set of organized processes with which to manage the interaction. An interaction where the physical touching is labeled as "sexual" would be managed differently than one labeled "therapeutic". It is assumed that in everyday, face to face interaction that people use general clues to recognize what basic context is about to be used for physical touching and they then proceed to pick specific recipes for action based on the specific context. For example, a woman is in a doctor's office, recognizes a health or therapeutic context and responds in the interaction according to recipes associated with health.

From this last set of assumptions stems the specific purpose of this paper: to present the explanatory framework for the sensual context of physical touching.

The focus of the sensual context of touching evolved from a year's study on "experiential" or "sensory" massage. During 1972 and the beginning of 1973, this investigator gathered data through participant-observation, informal interviews and current literature. Most of the twelve informal interviews were with participants who claimed many years' experience with the world of "experiential" massage. In contrast, this investigator began gathering data as a participant-observer in experiential massage from the vantage point of a new recruit to the world of massage. Data was coded and analyzed using the strategies of grounded theory. The analysis of the data initially indicated the presence of four major contexts for physical touching. They were: (1) sensual, (2) sexual, (3) spiritual, and (4) therapeutic (or health). The continued analysis of the data from massage provided the best theoretical coverage to the "sensual" context.

So the task of this paper will be to present an explanatory framework for a specific context of physical contacting or touching, i.e., the sensual context. The rest of the paper will discuss, (1) the nature of the sensual context, (2) the generative conditions and structural processes, (3) the two key variables of the sensual context, and (4) the consequences of the sensual context.

THE SEXUAL CONTEXT OF PHYSICAL TOUCHING

The sensual context, as used in this paper, will refer to the complex integration of generative conditions, structural processes and face-to-face interactions which maximize the experience of pleasurable physical touching while "diffusing" the relationship interaction associated with the experience.

A number of unique aspects of this particular context can be drawn from noting its primary purpose, i.e. to *maximize the occurance and pleasurable experience* of physical touching in face-to face interaction between adults (who are frequently strangers). The use of "sensual touching" will mean the social interaction where two or more people engage in physical contact for the experience of tactile pleasure. It is composed of the experience of touching and being touched.

Any reference to "massage" will refer to "experiential massage" unless otherwise indicated. Experiential massage is a type of massage focussed on sensory awareness of the body. It is often associated with the organization of Esalen and with the concepts of "self-awareness" and "personal growth''.

GENERATIVE CONDITIONS

There are numerous factors which provide fertile ground for the occurrence of the sensual context of touching. Among the most obvious of the recent trends in Western America are the emphasis on technological priorities, the mind-body dichotomy, the "future" and "achievement" orientation of the people, and the increasing geographic and social mobility of our time.

The conceptual framework for sensual touching in many respects seems to be a response to a society which has blindly stressed things, intellectual abilities, future rewards, work and change-change-change!

Many of these generative conditions will be discussed in the body of the paper in relation to a specific variable or specific influential factor. Suffice here to present the list of major influences on the sensual context.

CONTRIBUTING STRUCTURAL PROCESSES

Esalen: Esalen was a social organization which provided important contributions to the maintenance of the sensual context of touching. The first contribution was that of "codification". Esalen was frequently referred to as an original source for many of the ideas and practices incorporated in the sensual context. Esalen was an organization that had been a "pioneer" in the area of exploring and developing many types of "awareness". The awareness pertained to both mind and body, with the emphasis on the immediate involvement or experience of the senses of the mind and body. Esalen is credited with identifying many of the factors which maximize the "Experience", e.g. focusing on "here and now", focusing on the immediate feelings, and increasing the personal exploration of the immediate unknowns for the purpose of "personal growth" or "self-fulfillment". One of the many subdivisions that developed from the activities of Esalen was a focus on sensory awareness of the body, and specifically sensual massage. It is this particular "off shoot" that the sensual context of this paper relates to.

A second contribution of the organization of Esalen was its ability to *legitimize* those activities which derived from the organization or those people who could claim some type of attachment to it. Especially since physically touching for pleasure is, in general, a restricted social activity and since "massage", specifically, carries a heavy moral stigma, the efforts at expanding the "people base" of sensual touching requires legitimizing the sensual context to society. Esalen seems to be one of the more acceptable legitimizing sources.

The third contribution offered by the Esalen organization was the recruitment, training and developing of "expertise" for the practitioner of sensory touching. As the idea of sensory massage began to widen its "people base", the organizers of "massage workshops" would frequently refer to their "training at Esalen" or an "Esalen type massage" or a history of having studied with a "master" at Esalen. Besides continuing to be a way to establish an individual's "expertise", the organization of Esalen was also used as a means of differentiating one practitioner from another, e.g., "that masseuse gives more of a sensory awareness than that one."

Workshops: The more immediate structural process which facilitated the sensual context of touching was the "massage workshop". This structure was especially important for the people newly recruited to sensory touching. The "workshop" associated itself with the concept of "learning", "personal growth", education and followed the legitimating processes used by Esalen. The second factor which the "workshop" offered is that it maximized the possibility of participants being able to change and explore new ways of managing "people touching for pleasure". A "workshop" infers taking time away from the usual everyday life to focus on one specific problem and "work" at alternative ways of dealing with it. It also usually means leaving the usual environment and traveling to a new environment, hence heightening the possibility that new alternatives might develop.

In summary, both Esalen and massage workshops are social structures which provide important conditions for the sensual context.

CORE VARIABLES

This section of the paper will present the two key variables which are integral to the sensual context; the major factors influencing each variable including the tactics used to maximize the conditions of the sensual context, and the variety of consequences stemming from the sensual context.

The two key variables integral to the sensual context are the sensual experience and the diffuse relationship. These are separate factors within the sensual context and will be considered in terms of their unique contributions. However, what makes them essential to the context is not only their unique qualities, but the processes and interaction which emerge between the variables.

An indication of their interdependence can be given by noting that for both variables, the first two influential factors are the same, i.e., differentiation of out-there and right-here and differentiation of sensual and sexual. Therefore, it's essential for each variable to handle the major factors, but the consequences of one variable will have consequences for the other and eventually for the entire sensual context. It is this complex, fluid interaction involving these two variables which accounts for the wide variations in the sensual context.

The Sensual Experience

The essence of the sensual context of touching is to heighten the ability to include physical touch in an interaction and to heighten the sensory pleasure of physical touch. There are four major factors which contribute to maximizing the experience of sensual touching. they will be discussed in the following order: 1) differentiation of "out there" and "right here", 2) differentiation of sensuality and sexuality, 3) presence of ability and skills, and 4) body exposure.

Differentiation of "out there" and "right here": It is important that the focus of space and time be limited to the "here and now". The sensory context of touching expects the experience to relate to the immediate responses of the body senses. Therefore, it is important to funnel attention to what is happening to oneself "right now" and "right here". While this focusing on immediate body experiences facilitates the awareness of sensuality, the inattention to the "out there" is equally as necessary to the sensory context. The "out there" concept includes past or future experiences, habits, worries, activities, etc. which would hinder the ability to become fully aware of the immediate sensual experience. There are a variety of structural processes and interaction tactics which assist the participant in using the "right here/out there" differentiation. Current literature has informed the public of the American dilemma of a person using energy either to rectify his past or bring success to his future. In other words, a man immersed in his past and future and no connection with the present. One of the features that "personal growth" organizations like Esalen contributes to the sensual context is their influence of informing the public about the "here and now" orientation.

Other tactics used by participants more directly in the context itself include minimizing the discussions about "out there". A few examples are, not talking about where you came from, what you do for a living, what your plans are for the future, or what your family is like. (As will be discussed later, this lack of clues as to the social or personal identity of individuals is also useful in "diffusing" the relationship.) When verbal discussions occur, they generally focus on the immediate environment or activity occurring. The major tactic which minimizes the instrusion of the "out there" world is that the majority of the interaction time in the sensual context is non-verbal.

This process of differentiating the worlds of "right here" and "out there" assist the participant in two ways. The first is by maximizing the conditions under which sensory awareness will be heightened. The second is by creating a special "right here" (ie at this workshop, in this home, at this time, with these people) where the "outside" assumptions concerning interactions with physical touch might be suspended. What might carry a variety of restriction or stigmas "out there" can be temporarily and safely experimented with "right here". Although this differentiation becomes extremely critical to a new recruit, some variations continue to be used by long term "massage buffs" depending on how well they integrate sensual touching into their overall personal and social identities.

Differentiation of sensual and sexual: One of the key factors in maximizing the sensual experience is formulating the differences between a sensual context and a sexual context. The sensual context attempts to heighten the ability to be sensually aware of the whole body. In contrast, the sexual context is focussed on only experiencing the erotic areas of the body and is specifically oriented toward achieving sexual orgasm. This differentiation is important for at least two reasons. First, it guides activities of the sensual context in exploring the sensual capacities of the whole body, which in turn expands the parts of the body and the variety of experiences which can be included in the context. Second, it becomes an alternative context for "people touching people" which doesn't assume the social limitations of the "sexual" context.

Physical touching that's pleasurable is so quickly aligned with sexuality in our everyday life, that even when there are social structures (e.g. massage workshops) designed to use a sensual context, additional tactics are needed to emphasize the differentiation. The new recruit soon understands that participants do not have sexual orgasms while with the group at a "massage workshop". The physical space used for sensual touching is often a large room or area where everyone is exposed to everyone else. This arrangement would be in contrast to the private space associated with a sexual context. Another tactic used is humor. Many jokes are told about the stereotypes of the sexual context (e.g. prostitutes, homosexuals, swingers). These jokes offer some valuable clues for the initial separation of the sensual and sexual contexts.

Presence of ability and skills: To the surprise of most participants, this factor cannot be assumed and passed over. There is a level of ability which is necessary in order to maximize the experience of the sensual context.

A unique feature of this context for physical touching is that it requires the interaction of at least two persons, with a division into active and passive roles. There are skills associated with both the active and the passive role, plus additional skills needed for facilitating "team work" of all involved. The techniques needed while "getting" touched (passive role) revolve around increasing the ability of identify and respond to the sensuality of the body. Many adults talked of having "lost touch with their body," others talked about never having been aware of immediate feeling states in the body, "When the teacher first said to feel the sensation travel down my leg to my foot, I thought she was crazy." Many tactics are used to facilitate awareness of bodily states. Mental images are often used, "Imagine you are floating on a cloud ... what does it feel like?" Other tactics include how and when to breathe in order to heighten the sensual experience.

The person "giving" the touching (active role) has a different set of skills. This participant uses skills to experience personal pleasure in the activity while also using a variety of techniques to give pleasure to the partner. The "giver" in the sensual context is often surprised that a slight variation in pressure, speed or motion can produce vastly different sensual responses - both for the giver and the getter. It is while learning the craft of experiential massage that many neophytes get a variety of "lessons" on *how to* massage the feet, of *how to* oil the body. etc.

It becomes evident that abilities and skills are necessary in maximizing the sensual experience.

Body exposure: In the efforts to maximize the sensual experience of physical touching, the sensing context confronts many of the implicit social rules pertaining to people exposing their bodies. Potentially the best means to heighten the awareness of the body sensations is to have the whole body available without clothes interfering. Hence is raised one of the biggest problems of the participant who is considering entering the sensual context -- being *nude among strangers*. It would be hard to even list the variety of personal and social problems that emerge when dealing with the bodily exposure factor. Use of the sensual context is found on a continuum from maximum exposure to minimum exposure. (However, the optimal situation would have maximum exposure.) An example using the "minimal exposure" is given by one of the informants who was asked to enter a high school and focus on sensory awareness. The masseuse satisfied all the social rules by focusing for two hours on massaging the feet.

DIFFUSE RELATIONSHIPS

While the participant is actively involved in maximizing the experience of tactile pleasure, he is also faced with the equally important task of managing the human relationships required of the sensual context. The context requires two or more people engaged in physical touching. It also requires that the primary focus be on the sensual experience, not on the individual people involved in the experience. The management of these two key variables strains many of the taken-for-granted ways of handling interactions on physical touching. Hence, a variety of conditions, factors and interaction tactics emerge which account for the "diffuse relationship".

The diffuse relationship is a process of interacting in the sensual context where the sensual experience is maximized while the "personal" identities of the participants are minimized. The relationships are primarily used to enhance the goal of the sensual context, therefore, many conditions and interaction tactics emerge to facilitate a participant's focus on the process and not on the individuals who assist the process. *Who* makes it happen is not the issue; that it *happens well* is the goal.

The generative conditions are especially influential to the diffuse relationship. A society on the move and of constant change has direct implications for people's everyday management of physical touching. On the one hand, it has been responsible for minimizing the satisfaction from touching which used to be associated with intimate long term relationships (family and friends.) On the other hand, a mobile society has maximized the conditions of necessitating short-term friendships. It is not uncommon for people to believe "here today, gone tomorrow" about personal relationships. Many friendships are formed with an assumption of an existence "now" and no plans for a future. In this specific study, most of the participants were in a single marital state. This means that a high percentage were divorced, separated, temporarily without a partner or "paired" but with a contract where additional partners were mutually agreeable. The single state may be one of the consequences of a mobile society and one of the important sources of motivation for entering the sensual context.

This leads to the discussion of the other major factors which maximize the "diffuse" relationship. These factors include: differentiating "out there" and "right here", differentiating sensuality and sexuality, and using the "bonding" and "reciprocity" properties of relating in the sensual context.

Differentiating "out there" and "right here": The conceptualization and management of time and space is as important for the diffuse relationship as it was for the sensual experience variable. An important means of keeping the relationship secondary to the experience is by minimizing the associations with people's identity "out there". It limits the possibility of choosing a partner based on his "out there" social standing, activities, etc. It also limits the expectations of a relationship continuing in the "out there" world once the sensual context is discontinued. The past and future associations with a relationship are minimized and the relationship is primarily conceptualized and managed in terms of the "task" of sensually experiencing. The pressures to relate to others in terms of the here/now/task orientation has the consequence of changing many of the criteria "normally" used in partner selection. The shift represents a change from "what you hope to gain 'out there' by the relationship", to "what can the partner immediately supply". Examples of the new criteria are: is the person good at massage? or, can the partner provide the type of sensual experience wanted? or, who's available to practice particular techniques?

Dirrerentiating sensuality and sexuality: The differentiation of sensual from sexual when using the sensual context has important implications for maintaining the diffuse quality of the relationship. In the sensory context maximum exposure is wanted to sensual conditions. An important tactic for accomplishing this is to promote continual changing of the partners who touch. This minimizes sexuality while maximizing sensuality. Although any given set of partners may interact for several hours, there is the assumption that maximum sensual exposure comes from expertise and variety of partners and exchanging the active/passive role of touching. One of the major obstacles to maintaining this focus on the sensual experience is a structural or congenitive shift to a sexual experience where the "person" involved becomes important. When the interaction shifts to a sexual context, the "recipes" or assumed guidelines also shift and interaction problems occur.

There are numerous structural and interactional tactics which encourage the differentiation of sensual and sexual. On a *social organization level*, the experiential massage group does not publicly want to be identified with the "massage parlors" of prostitutes. The sensory massage groups are directed toward improving their social image by becoming "professionals". In terms of this paper, they are attempting to lose the restriction and negative social connotation of a sexual context by moving into and maximizing the sensual context. On a *face-to-face interaction* level, the sensual context *maximizes* the occurrence of touching in many ways. The sexual context carries numerous social limitations on who may touch, whom, when and where. For one example, the sex-identity of the partner is secondary to the experience in the sensual context, but if two men were touching each other in a sexual context they would be responded to as "homosexuals" and obstacles would occur in their interaction.

In summary, the sensual context keeps the relationships diffuse by minimizing the importance and the public occurrence of sexual interaction. The differentiation is especially important at the social organization level and during the indoctrination of new recruits.

Using the "bonding" and "reciprocity" properties: another factor in maximizing the diffuse relationship is adopting a moderately positive affective "bonding". The concept of "caring" is frequently identified as an important element of the sensual relationship. This can serve two purposes: first, it can differentiate the "caring" of the sensual context from the "loving" of the sexual context. Second, if offers a positive, but not highly charged, emotion to accompany the diffuse relationship. The emotion of caring is more easily transferred from partner to partner or can even be more easily spread to a generalized effect about "all the people" involved - a " community" feeling.

Reciprocity: The activity of physical touching in the sensual context emphasizes both getting and giving, or active and passive roles. Therefore, the process of reciprocity maximizes the potential of sensually experiencing by maximizing the usual variation allowed in the basic properties of giving and getting in a touching interaction. The sensual context "loosens" the usual restrictions and patterns on the who, what, where and when associated with physical touching.

In conjunction with the diffuse relationship, the "who" of reciprocity is not as important as the ability to connect with the type of experience wanted. An experience can be reciprocated often by a variety of people or partnerships. Coinciding with the nature of the key variable the "sensual experience", the "what" of the experience is of primary importance. The ability to fulfill a growing variety of sensual experiences demands the reciprocity meet the types of experiences needed. The "where" of the sensual context is again fluid. Although a person may spend an hour giving a backrub, he may negotiate to continue to "give" to the next partner, but focus on the head. Or another alternative is to negotiate with a partner and reciprocate the active-passive roles for a length of time. The "when" of reciprocity is the most elastic of all. The time of sensual context can vary at massage workshop from one hour to many days. Whether you equalize getting and giving with a particular person is not as relevant in reciprocity as that the people of the entire group are able to contract for satisfying experiences. So, the person whose back you rub one day, you may not necessarily touch again.

In summary, the management of reciprocity represents one of the best examples of the complex interplay of the key variables. The sensual context provides a reciprocity process which maximizes the sensual experience while also maximizing the diffuse relationships.

CONSEQUENCES

A variety of positive and negative consequences stem from the use of the sensory context of physical touching. The positive outcomes fall into two groupings. One group is comprised of participants who find the sensory context satisfying and continue to return to the original social structure in order to use the context. An example is periodically signing up for another massage workshop. The second group is comprised of participants who find the sensory context satisfying and begin to spread the sensory context into other parts of their lives or people in their lives. The "spreading" usually takes place into one of the following areas: the sexual, the friendships or the work-career. In these three areas the sensory context did not tend to replace any major practices but was used to supplement or synergize the existing processes.

The negative outcomes seemed to fall into one group that had problems handling the sensory experience variable, a second group that had problems with the diffuse relationship variable, or a third group where the juggling or integration of both variables was unsatisfactory.

Some problems associated with the first group include: participants not managing the body exposure; not finding pleasure in sensual touching; or not developing skills to handle the sensual experience.

some problems associated with the second group include: participants not managing sexuality between partners (fears of homosexuality and jealousy within triad are common obstacles) or not differentiating a "right here" relationship from an "out there."

The third group would speak of a more generalized dislike for the entire experience. For this group there would be problems associated with the inability to suspend or transform an original moral stigma attached to the sensual context. In this case, both the experience and the relationships within the context were unmanageable.

SUMMARY

This paper has presented an explanatory framework for the sensual context for interactions of physical touching. The writer has identified major generative conditions, structural processes and key variables of the sensual context. The constant interaction of the major variables was illustrated, as was a variety of interaction tactics used to maximize the sensual context. A number of consequences were pointed out with a major implication being the continued spread of the sensual context into essential areas of the everyday world of face-to-face interaction.

CHAPTER 18a

Reprinted from *The Journal of Criminal Law, Criminology and Police Science*,Vol. 63, No. 2, 1972

DEPRIVATION OF PRIVACY AS A "FUNCTIONAL PREREQUISITE":

The Case of The Prison

Barry Schwartz

Besides the loss of freedom, besides the forced labor, there is another torture in prison life, almost more terrible than any other - that is compulsory life in common.

I could never have imagined, for instance, how terrible and agonizing it would be never once for a single minute to be alone for ten years of my imprisonment. At work to be always with a guard, at home with two hundred fellow prisoners; not once, not once alone!

Fyodor Dostoevsky

The House of the Dead

Entitlement to privacy and its protection varies in scope and certitude from one social organization to another. A basic assumption in this analysis is that the prison is a place which allows very little of both. The sociological question then becomes "What accounts for attenuation of the right to privacy in prison and in what ways does deprivation enter into its organization and into the lives of its inmates?"

In addressing these questions our focus will be on the maximum security institutions[1] that have come to symbolize the "pains of imprisonment."[2] Although such places do not reflect the variation in organization of contemporary prisons, they do highlight the regimenting and custodial forms that are found to some degree in all of them. In these classic institutions we also find the most radical denial of privacy. In addition, the maximum security prison merits our attention because, to a greater extent than any other kind of institution, it sets in relief a distinctly modern form: the rational administration of human lives, to which the deprivation of autonomous withdrawal is functionally related.

REGIMENTATION: MASS PROCESSING AND MASS STORAGE

Bureaucratic administration and privacy. The bureaucracy is notable for its purely technical superiority over other forms of organization with respect to speed, precision, and continuity in the administration of things and records. This instrument for the "discharge of business according to calculable rules and without regard for persons"[3] has become a paradigm for ordering the lives of men in prisons. A way of regimenting work flow is there harnessed to the problem of regimenting people. This is possible because of rational administration is a technique whose applicability is altogether independent of contents. It represents, so to speak, "pure means." Thus, just as things can be moved en masse through the different phases of a productive process, so men in batches can be moved according to an unambiguous time schedule through the sequence of points in a daily activity cycle. Similarly, while materials may be placed together in a stored inventory and their records safely packed into a systematic file, men can be stored together in such a way that the whereabouts of anyone is secure and continually known.

The interactional consequence of this arrangement in prisons is that inmates are almost continually in one another's presence or in sight of authorities. But co-presence is precisely that consequence which complicates employment of the bureaucratic mode. That model causes trouble because, unlike the physical material of the factory or administrative bureaucracy, the objects of penal bureaucracy have selves which are oppressed by continual social contact and monitoring. This sense is related to the universal but distinctly non-rational assumption that "an ideal sphere lies around every human being ...[which] cannot be penetrated, unless the personality value of the individual is thereby destroyed."[4] If we endorse another assumption, advanced first by Durkheim[5] and later by Shils,[6] that the personal sphere is a sacred one, then its violation may be said to entail profanation--or, as it is put nowadays, a "mortification" of self.[7] At question is how and why this comes about in the context of the prison.

The strictly legalistic account focuses on rights. It holds that by making a public nuisance of himself, the prisoner merits the investment of a special despised status that entails forfeiture of the right to a protective sphere of privacy. But this formulation does not take us far enough, for it raises rather than solves the problem of whether violation of privacy is purposively instrumental in stripping a convicted man of his dignity or whether his loss of dignity is occasioned, as a mere by-product, by a denial of privacy that is organizationally rather than penally grounded. In Tappan's words, "The deprivation of 'civil rights' may be conceived to be either an auxiliary punishment in itself or the incidental consequence of conviction and sentence, not intended to be specifically punitive but merely protective of public interests and of official convenience."[8] There is reason for us to emphasize the second of these conceptions. While loss of civil entitlements may legitimate invasion of an inmate's privacy, it does not account for the condition of this violation--which undermines the dignity of jailed *suspects* as well as *convicted* men and denies personal reserve in other non-penal but totally institutionalized settings. Suspension of the right to privacy thus derives from the social organization of prisons and not from the legal status of persons found in them.

Of course, the privacy of an imprisoned man may be violated in a manner that takes retributive account of his status. This is seen in many ways. For example, there is the rude, harshly indifferent demeanor of guards; the deliberate exposure of inmates for the sake of punishment or mere harassment; the ridiculing of inmates in connection with exposure of their past, their person, or even their correspondence;[9] there is humiliation of having to denude oneself before contemptuous overseers (who are today more often than not members of rival groups in a larger society). But however unbearable, and whatever part they play in the seething discontent of many of our prisoners, these degradational modes are not the source of deprivatization; they merely exploit that source. They represent, in other words, the consequences and not the sociological condition of inmate exposure, which is notable not in its retributive aspect abut for its consistency with the affectively neutral imperative of efficiency "without regard for persons."

Typical forms of bureaucratic disregard may be identified and analyzed in terms of what they do to those who are subjected to them.

FORCED EXPOSURE

The innumerable kinds of profanation effected by mass administration of persons causes us to look for a paradigm, an exemplary form of institutionalized exposure. Perhaps the most humiliating is that having to do with a man's most unique possession, his body. The prison's mass denudation rituals exemplify (though by no means exhaust) the ways this valued possession can be transformed into an altogether neutral object. A concrete instance is found in the efficient manner one penitentiary currently welcomes its guests:

> "Everybody strip bare-ass!" yelled the sergeant. We all stripped standing up and stuffed our belongings in the bags, which the old convict dragged off down the corridor.
>
> After we had been standing bare-assed on the concrete for about half an hour the sergeant strutted down the corridor and unlocked the door. It was a large square-shaped room with shower heads jutting out from the walls at four-foot intervals....
>
> "In and out," the fat sergeant shouted. "Two minutes!"
>
> There were about twenty shower heads. A man got under each one, and the rest stood milling about in the center of the room.
>
> "*Everyone* in," the sergeant screamed. "Two men to a shower...three men to a shower. *Everyone* in."
>
> The rest of the men jammed into the space under the shower heads until all stood elbow to ass waiting for the water to come on.[10]

The two sources of degradation herein depicted correspond to the fact that social distance is instrumental to as well as affirmative of personal honor. One not only withholds himself from others by reason of his inherent dignity; he also maintains that dignity precisely because of his right to conceal actions and imperfections that would otherwise discredit the self that he publicly presents. This is not a matter of hypocrisy; it is a matter of face.[11] Because it reveals a person's imperfections and makes them the focal point of attention, forced exposure contradicts the socially valued attributes the person claims for himself; it constitutes a painful loss of face--whose linkage to mass processing techniques is confirmed in another "reception" setting:

> The grimy gang of new arrivals rushes toward the showers--a gallop of bare feet smacking on the tiles of the wide corridor. The first ones in run into the last of the group coming out, cleansed and ridiculous. Their physiques are grotesque: Men dredged up and thrown together by the accident of their misfortune are usually misshapen and ugly in the nude, deformed by their misery. They gesticulate, shiver, struggle with heaps of clothes.[12]

Humiliation is intensified when the inmate must expose himself before an audience rather than co-participants preoccupied with their own shame.

Sinclair provides an example:

> They searched Jurgis, leaving him only his money, which consisted of fifteen cents. Then they led him to a room and told him to strip for a bath; after which he had to walk down a long gallery, past the grated cell doors of the inmates of the jail. This was a great event to the latter--the daily review of the new arrivals, all stark naked, and many and diverting were the comments.[13]

An even more extreme form of abasement imposed by impersonal, rational processing is exposure of the body in undignified postures, such as those required to perform common bodily functions. Such needs are accommodated in many prison settings by open rows of toilets. But sometimes accommodation takes on in addition a very regimented form. A radical instance is found in the Chinese political prison:

> An aspect of their isolation regimen which is especially onerous is the arrangement for the elimination of urine and feces. The 'slop jar' that is usually present in Russian cells is often absent in China. It is a Chinese custom to allow defecation and urination only at one or two specified times each day--usually in the morning after breakfast. The prisoner is hustled from his cell by a guard, double-timed down a long corridor, and given approximately two minutes to squat over an open Chinese latrine and attend to all his wants. The haste and the public scrutiny are especially difficult for women to tolerate. If the prisoners cannot complete their action in about two minutes, they are abruptly dragged away and back to their cells.[14]

The body's exposure moreover renders it susceptible to physical as well as visual exploitation. As one ex-convict puts it:

> The young prisoner, who in lieu of a shortage of passive homosexuals might face advances himself, is well advised to acquire a good degree of modesty about his body. He should dress and undress quickly, and not hang around the shower room, but shower with dispatch, preferably when the shower room is least crowded. If he does not mind his ass, somebody else will.[15]

Such considerations as these demonstrate the way deprivation is grounded in the regimental process (timed activity in blocks); in so doing they confirm the interactional grounding of the self. The dignity that an individual claims for himself may serve as the very condition of interaction in civil life, with its characteristic mutual protection of face and correspondingly sharp differentiation of public and private life. But this mode of interaction is inconsistent with rational men-management in prison. There a man's monopoly on his self and the denial of its use or inspection by others is an entitlement that has no place. Consequently, interaction can there exude but one nuance, namely, indiscretion, tactlessness and the vulgarity that is natural to those who have ceased to be mindful of their own and others' sphere of personal reserve.[16]

FORCED SPECTATORSHIP

A prisoner is mortified and vulgarized not only by having to continually expose himself as he is moved and stored in the company of others; he is also defiled by being subject to *their* exposure. This distinction requires an amendment to the notion of "information control" which, as used by Goffman,[17] refers to the manner in which individuals, by the selective granting and withholding of facts about themselves, supervise the impressions they make upon others. This usage is too restricted, for the individual must also shield himself against noxious information elicited by others. The prisoner is therefore profaned because he cannot keep himself uninstructed; he is contaminated by the receipt as well as the transmission of demeaning information. In Van den Haag's words, his privacy is invaded because he is *compelled* to sense or participate in the activities of others.[18] A sample of this kind of exposure is found in one of our larger prisons' "night storage" sections.

> Even in your cell you had to live without privacy....The constant hubbub made letter-writing difficult: prisoners in the tier shouting, laughing, screaming from cell-to-cell--like the monkey house in the zoo--and that in competition with the blare coming over the PA system, which was used more often for piping in commercial radio programs than for announcements.

> [T]he weirdest sounds in the world come out of the prison at night...the snores, the nightmares, the groaning and the sighs, the talkers in their sleep who could be arguing their case in court, fighting with their wives, selling door to door. So turning off the PA system and snapping off the lights at taps is an empty gesture; the hubbub continues pretty much as before.[19]

Exposure to others may take interactional as well as auditory forms. This occurs when individuals are stored in one another's physical presence in common dormitories or cells. This most common form of community, the very act of living together, becomes unnatural when the supportive, oppositional form of periodic separateness is denied.[20] Serge's lamentations on this subject are exemplary:

Three men are brought together in a cell by chance. Whatever their differences, they must tolerate each other; relentless intimacy twenty-four hours a day. Rare is the day when at least one of them is not depressed. Irritable or gloomy, at odds with himself, he exudes a sort of invisible poison. You pity him. You suffer with him. You hate him. You catch his disease....The presence of a slob fills the cell with snoring, spitting, belching -nauseating smells and filthy gestures.

Each does his business in front of the other two. But perhaps the worst intimacy is not that of bodies. It is not being able to be able to be alone with yourself. Not being able to remove your face from the prying glance of others. Betraying, with every tic, at every moment, the secret of an obtusely disturbed inner life.[21]

The oppression of forced relationships was perhaps most pronounced among southern work forces, where prisoners were not merely locked into one another's presence but bound physically (during sleep, at least) to one another by chains, whose jingling racket made the slightest movement, the most otherwise inconspicuous muscular twitch, a public gesture.

Besides purely interactional stress, deprivatization may entail moral defilement. We refer here to contamination through contact with a profane being, a kind of exposure that brings the individual into a forced social relationship with despised persons who are normally kept away by conventional distancing practices. However, selective association in accordance with honorific (as opposed to instrumental) criteria is inconsistent with strictly rational men-management. The complaint of an anti-Semite illustrates the unhappy unions so efficiently created:

Another warden came up with a pair of handcuffs and coupled me to the little Jew, who moaned softly to himself in Yiddish....

Suddenly, the awful thought occurred to me that I might have to share a cell with the little Jew and I was seized with panic. The thought obsessed me to the exclusion of all else.[23]

Violation of collective privacy. Moral defilement may occur in reference to groups as well as individuals. For example, the imposed intimacies and associations of the prison, along with its regimented "life style," extends beyond its walls to desecrate what are often prisoners' most sacred possessions: those who live and wait for them on the outside. Visits from these people are a technical bother, imposed by some irrational, irresistible humanistic impulse. To satisfy administrative efficiency, visits are often molded to the bureaucratic imperative by being scheduled and conducted in blocks. In few other contexts do suffocating closeness and utter isolation so perfectly coincide. The following (nineteenth century French) arrangement is neither historically nor culturally unique:

> To have an interview with his kinsfolk the prisoner is introduced, together with four other prisoners, into a small dark coop....His kinfolk are introduced into another coop opposite, also covered with iron bars, and separated from the former by a passage three feet wide....Each coop receives at once five prisoners; while in the opposite coop some fifteen men, women, and children--the kinsfolk of the five prisoners--are squeezed. The interviews hardly last for more than fifteen or twenty minutes; all speak at once, hasten to speak, and amidst the clamor of voices, each of which is raised louder and louder, one soon must cry with all his strength to be heard. After a few minutes of such exercise, my wife and myself were voiceless, and were compelled simply to look at each other without speaking....She used to leave the reception hall saying that such a visit was a real torture.[24]

In this way, a group's boundaries may be violated, the principle of its exclusive intimacy mocked, its very existence rendered insignificant and ridiculous. Members thereby become common to one another. The specific and incomparable features of a social relationship are destroyed by violation of its collective privacy. In the words of a recent military prisoner:

> Whether at the farm camp or in the penitentiary, the visiting room is crowded with adults and children. Husband and wife grow apart because they are undergoing profound changes--especially if they are young--and they never have the time nor the right atmosphere to communicate what is happening inside one another....The only consolation that current visiting practices in Federal prisons bring is the opportunity for the inmate and his family to renew their faith in the existence of one another. Otherwise, visiting, as surely as imprisonment itself, functions to destroy family ties.[25]

ELEMENTARY FORMS OF INTRUSION

Up to now, we have dwelled upon "coincidental" aspects of exposure, which are so designated because they embody *in their pure form* not surveillant intent on the part of care-takers but occur merely as a by-product of regimented, mass activities.; Being a "residual" part of those activities, coincidental exposures are in no way instrumental to the goals of the organization itself. This form is to be distinguished from "programmed invasions of privacy" (otherwise known as "surveillance"), which are carefully planned and executed by institutional officials. Though often confounded empirically, these two forms are analytically distinct, with their difference based on contrasting contributions to the organization as a whole. Whereas the function of coincidental exposures is manifestly neutral with respect to organizational goals, the programmed kind are not only instrumental but absolutely essential to their achievement. The latter are thus explicitly purposive rather than residual in nature.

While coincidental exposure involves "horizontal visibility," whereby peers are reciprocally open to one another's observation, programmed invasions of privacy introduce a "vertical" dimension characterized by unilateral observation by superordinates. Programmed invasions of privacy moreover do not replace but are normally superimposed upon coincidental forms.[26]

CUSTODY VS. PRIVACY

The condition of programmed intrusion to be found in the orientation of its subjects. When there is official confidence in their commitment to the goals and orderly operation of the system, inmates may be left to themselves. However, when obedience and loyalty cannot be taken for granted overseers are compelled to exercise continual rather than periodic surveillance.[27] The latter case finds it s most pronounced exemplar in the prison, for here presence as well as compliance is problematic. Radical attenuation of privacy in prison may thus be subsumed under the general rule that where membership and participation in an organization is involuntary, social order must be coercively maintained; individual conformity can then be ensured only by means of surveillance.[28]

Dominant features of prison surveillance programs may be described.

First there is the problem of "boundary maintenance" or defense against intrusion of foreign matter that could prove subversive to prison security. Means of dealing with this problem find their functional equivalent in the customs inspection that safeguard collective integrity at the expense of the individual's. An instance from an early twentieth century French prison is exemplary:

> Two or three hulking guards strut out in front of a line of naked men. "Open your mouth! Bend over!...More...lower, dammit, you jerk, lower!...legs apart... come on...Next man forward!' A fat thumb prods the inside of a suspicious jaw. A guard with a crumpled *kepi* inspects the rear end of a tough-looking mug who has been put over the bar; the bar is designed to make you bend over in such a manner that any object hidden in the anus is supposed to be revealed....[29]

The custody orientation negates privacy in innumerable other ways. These include such purposive intrusions as periodic headcounts, nightly checks, inspections or shakedowns of prisoners' living areas and belongings. Whatever tends to disturb visibility is forbidden. Behavior within the cell itself may be strictly regulated; variation in cell conduct would only create "static," which makes information gathering more difficult. The home is therefore designed to be a public rather than a private place. For example, in one classic setting

> A camp bed...is folded in the morning at a signal. Even in case of illness, it is absolutely forbidden to lie down during the day without the doctor's permission....Inside the Judas, the spy-hole, an eye whose metallic blinking is heard every hour when the guards make their rounds....Whistling, humming, talking to yourself out loud, making any noise, is forbidden.[30]

Furthermore, prisoners must continually hold themselves open for monitoring--sometimes even when asleep. Thus, a rule in one state penitentiary reads: "When the lights go out at the designated hour go to bed at once and remain quiet.... Sleep with the head uncovered to enable the officer to see you."[31] Similarly, in contemporary federal and military prisons inmates must participate in the violation of their own privacy by assigning power of attorney to the warden and his representatives, giving them the right to censor their mail. (Refusal to sign means forfeiture of the right to receive and send letters.)[32]

Incidentally, just as lack of privacy during visits banalizes a prisoner's relationship with this family, mail censorship (justified as security against escape and dissemination of information about other prisoners), by prohibiting communication about anything but the most innocuous details of prison life, reduces a social bond and its members to the level inanity. Some nineteenth century French prisons showed themselves to be less hypocritical about the whole matter by allowing inmates to communicate with the outside only by signing their names to a printed form![33]

But other sources of subversion must be anticipated. In context of the climate of distrust that prevails in most security-oriented prisons, inmates may not be expected to even go to the toilet without causing trouble. For this reason toilets in cells (many with attached sinks for washing) are typically in full view of guards. The following instance contradicts those who would interpret this arrangement as a mere architectural convenience:

> As soon as the room was in darkness, I threw back the covers and tiptoed over to the toilet in the corner. I had painfully waited until I could have the dark concealment from a piercing eye at the spy hole in the door. That little aperture was the very last invasion of my privacy and rights, and filled me with resentment. Suddenly a light flashed on and remained until I had finished my business and returned to my bed.[34]

In some situations the prisoner is even denied the freedom to dispose of his bodily wastes in private. Thus, within some isolation units, toilets are flushed by a device along the wall outside. After seeing to his needs an inmate must signal the overseer, who inspects the contents of the commode through an opening before flushing. (In this way, the occupant is prevented from stuffing the bowl with sheets and clothing.) One prison went even further:

> Across from the offices there are windows opening on the latrines, allowing the guards, without moving, to keep an eye on the squatting men. The latrines open onto narrow paved courtyards. The clean-up squad comes in there every day to empty the tanks in the hope of recovering forbidden objects. The perfection of jail! The administration even looks into your excrement.[35]

In maximum security institutions custodial concerns reach a very high pitch during the time an inmate is visited by civilians. In going to meet a visitor the prisoner may first have to be stripped naked and searched; this procedure is generally repeated when the visit is over in order to ensure against exchange of contraband. Apprehension over security also gives rise to physical or normative barriers which prevent family members from touching or even approaching one another.[36] Moreover, it is well known that in many instances their conversations are taped.[37] This practice is said to be particularly common when a jailed inmate awaiting hearing or trial is visited by his attorney.[38]

By finding nothing connected with his life that cannot be exposed and rendered general, the inmate may attribute no specific significance to his own being. The escape orientation can therefore express itself not only by the act of going over or under a wall but also by self-dispatch to another world through suicide. This contingency, which would imply an intolerable degree of inmate autonomy,[39] is one to which guards are especially sensitive:

> When they come by your cell around 5:00 A.M. you were supposed to move to let them know you were alive. And if by chance you were in a deep sleep - too sound to hear them on the early morning round - they'd reach in through the bars and grab a leg to see if you were still warm.[40]

This kind of surveillance is especially intense on death row: "The guard watched me while I ate," writes a condemned man. "When I wrote letters the guard would pass me a pen [and] watch me use it."[41] Here also continual illumination denies even the cover of darkness, a condition that periodically provides some measure of privacy in more conventional confinement. "Spotlights hung outside, aimed into each cell," writes another condemned man. "They were turned on every evening at sundown and remained lit until sunrise."[42]

INFORMATION NETWORKS

Up to now we have dealt with surveillance only in terms of assessment of current activities of inmates. To maintain order, however, governors of penal institutions must not only know what a prisoner is doing; they must also know what he is going to do. For this, data to be projected into his future are required from the inmate's past. Also, such non-observable current behaviors (like intentions and plans secretly communicated to another) as evade the primary monitoring system must be uncovered by a secondary system, which takes the form of a comprehensive and well organized information network. Thus, just as we have described organizational arrangements that minimize audience segregation, so we must point to structural features of the prison which overcome the privacy ensured by dispersion and segregation of information.

Knowledge about prisoners flows along three kinds of channels. First, there are official operational contacts, exemplified by one staff member requesting and obtaining information about an inmate from another. In civil society many of these contacts would be considered as unheard-of violations of the principle of privileged communication. For example, a caseworker might need to consult the physician in deciding on an inmate's job assignment--or the psychiatrist, in assessing whether or not a certain prisoner is likely to be a "trouble maker." As one inmate put it, "Privileged communication with a psychiatrist (or for that matter with any physician) is non-existent.... To confide in the prison psychiatrist is, essentially, to confide in the chief warden."[43] Secondly, prison administrators obtain information about inmates through an intelligence network manned by "stoolies" or "rats." Perhaps Leopold's is the most cogent testimony of its effectiveness:

> The deputy explained to me...'If you figure to do something and tell your best friend in here, that makes three of us that know it! For the moment his arithmetic stumped me a trifle, but I was to learn that it represented the sober truth.[44]

Thirdly, there are centralized contacts which are part of the standard administrative procedure. These include "exposure ceremonies." At one penitentiary, for instance, "as each shift comes to work, the day's new men are brought to the guard's room, their record and charge read to guards [in their presence], and then they are returned to their cells."[45] Also included are staff meetings where all overseers come together to pool information on an inmate. Or overseers might periodically receive questionnaires by which inmate performance in diverse respects is assessed and recorded.

All information thus obtained flows toward and is collated within a single repository, the case folder. Into this data bank are also filed biographical data, medical and psychological reports, photographs, written communications between inmates and staff, descriptions of many verbal transactions, frequency and nature of rule infractions, names of visitors and frequency of their visits, addressees of correspondence, confiscated letters, prison savings records, and all other observations of inmates' lives that are capable of transcription.

This flow of information from multiple sources toward a unique center is symbolic of the classic conception of mass surveillance, the panopticon, where from a central vantage point the activities of all prisoners may be surveyed at will. This kind of architectural support has been relaxed in the construction of contemporary prisons, thanks to the availability of sophisticated electronic means. The eyes and ears of the overseer may now be replaced by the more efficient television camera and microphone.[46]

Nevertheless, the panopticon principle continues to govern the flow of information, which remains centripetal in nature.

A NOTE ON DEPRIVATIZATION AND THE INMATE SUBCULTURE

It may be argued that while deprivatization is initially oppressive, inmates eventually accommodate themselves and learn to live with it. Ward and Kassebaum, however, provide data which show the opposite to be the case: as time passes, lack of privacy is increasingly designated as the most difficult aspect of adjustment to prison life.[47] This observation coincides with Glaser's, which shows most inmates to be oriented toward voluntary isolation rather than integration.

The continuing desire for privacy in the face of forced interaction may constitute one of the most important facets of the prison experience. This is a dilemma to which Bettelheim points in another totally institutionalized setting, the kibbutz. He suggests that persons who find themselves continually in the presence of others must repress the hostile feelings that inevitably emerge in normal interaction with them; otherwise, relationships would be in constant turmoil.[49] Moreover, repression may often involve a "reaction formation" through which a person exhibits compulsive, exaggerated solidarity with those whose presence he secretly wishes to avoid. Through this mechanism the very negation of privacy becomes its substitute.

In a social organization like the kibbutz, characterized by relative equality of statuses, compulsive solidarity might encompass superordinates as well as peers; however, where statuses are rigidly differentiated and their encumbents hostile to one another, feelings of unity are likely to have members of one's status group as their referent. This consideration, in conjunction with our earlier observation, helps explain the manifestly bizarre coexistence of two contradictory tenets within the "inmate code," namely, the well-know commands "Do your own time," and "Be loyal to your class, the cons."[50] The assumption that solidarity stands as a psychological alternative to its sociological antithesis , voluntary reserve, helps to make this contradiction intelligible.

It remains to say that inmate solidarity is more "mechanical" than "organic" in nature, tending to be based upon likenesses rather than interdependence of heterogeneous parts.[51] Such a characteristic is conditioned by lack of privacy, according to the principle that differentiation, or the development of ego boundaries and maturation of idiosyncratic and/or ego creative inclinations, presupposes a substantial measure of voluntary withdrawal.[52] This idea we suppose, informs the conception of the prison as a "homogenizing" (as opposed to "differentiating") setting which tends to level initial individual differences.[53]

We have here, in any case, the condition of a vicious cycle. On the one hand, lack of privacy lends itself to the development of a homogeneous or compact oppositional subculture; on the other, solitary opposition toward administration and staff makes for increased surveillance and lessened privacy. The very ordeal of deprivatization thus leads to a process which entails privacy-suppressing rather than privacy-amplifying reactions.

CONCLUSION

We have tried to show that the right to privacy is attenuated in prison by two structural obstacles, the technique of regimentation and the imperative of custody, which correspond to organizational means and ends respectively. We have also tried to demonstrate how these barriers to privacy enter into and de-humanize the lives of inmates. At question is whether the prisoner deserves something better, on the grounds of either his humanity or his citizenship. Neither the first (moral) nor the second (legal) ground can be herein informed. Rather, what is sociologically at stake in expansion of the right to privacy is its basis in and consequences for social organization.

That a protective private sphere should surround the individual is not an idea that prevails for its own sake. Social organizations can after all allow for only as much privacy as is compatible with their objectives and means. While the efficient operation of some groups require that members be insulated from observation, others, like maximum security persons, cannot achieve their goals unless members are arranged in such a way as to be continually visible. Moreover, groups cannot leave it up to members to comply in making themselves available for monitoring; whatever its extent, lack of privacy must be built into the structure of the organization itself. This is to say that the right to privacy is never granted, appropriated or extended unless the organizational conditions for such grants, appropriations or extensions exist. Privacy can endure, then, only within a context of organizational (rather than normative) supports. Rights cannot be imposed upon a system built around the presupposition of the absence. Privacy is therefore non-negotiable, given a particular form of social organization. This means that the degree of privacy is a *property* of that organization.

So phrased, however, this (functionalist) perspective deceptively resonates fatalism. It connotes the same pathos that during the 1950's and early 1960's permeated so much of the sociological literature on the prison.[55] But fatalism masks the fact that social structure is itself negotiable (despite its often not being subject to negotiation itself). Accordingly, by focusing on the solid, utilitarian basis of inmate visibility and exposure, functional theory helps pinpoint foci of and directions for change. In so doing, of course, that theory demands that we assess the price to be paid in expanding prisoners' right to privacy, which must entail contraction of collective rights to security and organizational efficiency.

But to be sensitized to the costs of change is not to be counseled against it. Thus, if highly efficient regimentation through mass processing and storage is inimical to the value of privacy, a measure of cost-efficiency may be candidly renounced in its favor. "Perhaps an ideal solution," writes Glaser, "involves single-room housing for inmates, away from dayroom area with a means by which inmates can [open and] lock their rooms, even though the custodians also have master keys...."[56] Though more expensive than dormitory or cell-block living, this arrangement is employed in several institutions housing penitentiary-type inmates. It is one method of balancing the costs and benefits of privacy. Similarly, if the custody orientation encroaches too far upon the right to privacy, surveillant modes associated with it may be reconsidered, with costs related to violation of house rules and escapes accepted. Some institutions have taken steps in this direction by relaxing visiting codes (even unto conjugal visiting) and doing away with all forms of mail censorship. The minimum security concept also embodies this alternative. Finally, if collection and distribution of (mostly degrading and sometimes false) information about inmates unduly violates their privacy, its flow may be curtailed, with a minimum amount of data given to staff by privileged custodians and sanctions applied for both negligence and overinquisitiveness. Once again, such self-restriction may entail a price in terms of the prison's capacity to fulfill its obligations.

Just as we attend to the costs of organizational change we must also stop to assess its benefits. While lessened surveillance places a great burden on trust, it may also build trust and obviate the tension and hostility that its absence entails. And while respect for an inmate's rights concerning his own body and his own past may impede custody and security, it may also promote the dignity that would make them less necessary. Finally, and perhaps most importantly, the provision of more private living space, while involving greater expense, may reduce contact with and exposure to other inmates and so help shift the differential association and influence ratio in favor of the staff.[57]

In brief, a corollary to the idea that oppositional inmate solidarity is in part a functional alternative to privacy is that privacy may serve as an alternative to solidarity. This is to say that when its benefits and costs are compared, expansion of the right to privacy may be in the interests of the prison as well as its prisoners. But this is an empirical question which we can do no more than raise.

REFERENCES

1. This focus is mainly through the eyes of inmates themselves--or, more precisely, a non-random sample of that class of inmates which has recorded its experiences in writing. Autobiographical data naturally involve pitfalls, particularly in respect of systematization and representativeness of observation. But they do inform certified knowledge by portraying the color and nuances of prison life, features that are ignored or muted by more systematic data collection methods. Indeed, the unique value of autobiographical data rests on its very bias. For it may be assumed that the sensibilities tapped through autobiography are more acute and articulate than the impressions of the more representative but less perceptive persons on whom so much of the sociological literature depends.

2. G. SYKES, SOCIETY OF CAPTIVES 63-83 (1966).

3. Weber, Bureaucracy, in FROM MAX WEBER 25 (H. Gerth & C. Mills ed. 1958).

4. Simmel, Types of Social Relationships by Degrees of Reciprocal Knowledge of Their Participants, in THE SOCIOLOGY OF GEORG SIMMEL 321 (K. Wolff ed. 1950).

5. Durkheim stated, "The human personality is a sacred thing; one does not violate it nor infringe its bounds...." E. DURKHEIM, SOCIOLOGY AND PHILOSOPHY 37 (1953).

6. The modern version of the Durkheimian theme is advanced in Shils, Privacy: Its Constitution and Vicissitudes, 1970 CENTER FOR SOCIAL ORGANIZATION STUDIES 98. In this view, the sacredness of charisma of its "center" diffuses throughout the social order unto its very "periphery," so that each group member partakes of a measure of charisma and is entitled to deferential avoidance according to his proximity to central persons, roles and institutions. There is moreover a minimum of appreciation of privacy to

which all persons are entitled:

Intrusions on privacy are baneful because they interfere with an individual in his disposition of what belongs to him. The 'social space' around an individual, the recollection of his past, his conversation, his body and its image, all belong to him. He does not acquire them through purchase or inheritance. He possesses them and is entitled to possess them by virtue of the charisma which is inherent in his existence as an individual soul--as we say nowadays, in his individuality--and which is inherent in his membership in the civil community. They belong to him by virtue of his humanity and civility.

Id. at 98. A similar point is noted in Benn, Privacy, Freedom, and Respect for Persons, in PRIVACY 1-26 (J. Pennock & J. Chapman ed. 1971).See also E. GOFFMAN, INTERACTION RITUAL 62-70 (1967).

7.E. GOFFMAN, ASYLUMS 14-35 (1961).

8.Tappan, The Legal Rights of Prisoners, 293 ANNALS OF THE AMERICAN ACADEMY OF POL. AND SOC. SCIENCE 109 (1954). For a more recent statement see Vogelman, Prisoner Restrictions, Prisoner Rights, 59 J. CRIM. L.C. & P.S. 386-96 (1968).

9."In weekly shakedowns of the cells," complains an inmate of a well-known penitentiary, "they read the mail and then they make derogatory remarks later about people mentioned in the letters." Chicago Tribune, Nov. 16, 1971, 1A, at 4.

10.J. GRISWOLD, AN EYE FOR AN EYE 11-12 (1970).

11.E. GOFFMAN, supra note 6, at 5-45.

12.V. SERGE, MEN IN PRISONS 16 (1969).

13.U. SINCLAIR, THE JUNGLE 158 (1905).

14.Hinkle & Wolff, Communist Interrogation and Indoctrination of Enemies of the State, 76 A.M.A. ARCHIVES OF NEUROLOGY AND PSYCHIATRY 153 (1956).

15.H. LEVY 7 D. MILLER, GOING TO JAIL 148 (1971). Another form of physical exploitation is the forced medical examination, administered in blocks. E. WALLACH, LIGHT AT MIDNIGHT 244-45 (1976), provides an example from a Russian labor camp:

'Ready everyone? Let's go spread our legs.' Hilde was waiting for us.

'I'm not going,' I said in disgust....

'Come on Erica,' Irma said, 'There is no way out of this.'

In the hall of the dispensary, waiting in line, I felt like throwing up. The door to the examination room was open. Nadja, the sanitation officer, sat at a table, checking off the names. The Hippopotamus, the shapeless, sullen female doctor, stood in the middle of the room like a prize fighter, her sleeves rolled up to the elbow, her right hand in a glove. Five girls crowded in line before the jack, one was on it, on her back, her legs up. Without a word, Hippo went up, pushed her right arm into the girl, pressed on the stomach with her left, called something to Nadja, and pulled out. "Next!' she barked as she held her right hand for one second under the dribble of a cold water nail. The whole procedure had taken no more than one minute.

16.Schwartz, The Social Psychology of Privacy, 73 AM. J. OF SOC. 749 (1968).

17.E. GOFFMAN, STIGMA 41-104 (1963).

18.Van Den Haag, On Privacy. in PRIVACY 152 (J. Pennock & J. Chapman ed. 1971).

19.I ZIMMERMAN, PUNISHMENT WITHOUT CRIME 152-53 (1964).

20.For a more complete discussion of the tension management functions of privacy, see Schwartz, supra note 16, at 741-52.

21.V. SERGE, supra note 12, at 53-54.

22.This arrangement is hilariously depicted in L. ELDER, CERE-MONIES IN DARK OLD MEN 123 (1965).

23.A.H. SMITH, EIGHTEEN MONTHS 14, 17 (1954).

24.P. KROPOTKIN, IN RUSSIAN AND FRENCH PRISONS 270-71 (1971).

25.H. LEVY & D. MILLER, supra note 15, at 48-49.

26.But this superimposition, presupposing the principle of rational methods of people-processing, and storage, is historically unique. For example, the Pennsylvania System which prevailed in the early nineteenth century as the first model of penitentiary organization, was based upon the non-compromised principle of absolute (auditory and visual as well as physical) segregation of prisoners. Here visibility was vertically structured so that inmate privacy was subject to violation by superordinates only. Even Auburn's "silent system"--the first regression from the Pennsylvania ideal--allowed inmates to come into one another's presence only during working hours; at all other times prisoners dwelled in their private cells. Though they have persisted in certain parts of the world, these pre-modern forms are from a contemporary standpoint distinctly irrational in organization, for, besides driving prisoners made, they sacrifice a substantial measure of cost-efficiency, attainable through mass processing and mass storage. For an authoritative summary regarding these early penitentiary systems see H. BARNES 7 N. TEETERS, NEW HORIZONS IN CRIMINOLOGY 335-47 (1959).

27.This is not to say that surveillance is uniquely determined by inmate attitudes and orientations. In L. LAWES, TWENTY THOUSAND YEARS IN SING SING (1932), for example, the author describes the 1843 counter reformation at Sing Sing. The newly elected state administration, which had looked askance at the 'laxity' caused by earlier reforms, tightened things up by fresh appointments. "The method of constant supervision in those days," writes Lawes, "is impressive." "Not for a moment was the prisoner permitted to stray from the vigilant eye of the guard or keeper. Every gesture was regulated. Every movement keenly watched. The 'cat' hovered over the prison with hungry eyes, ready to descend at the least provocation. Prisoners were checked and rechecked, watched, warned, and punished for the slightest violation of the rules." Id. at 76-77.

28.A. ETZIONI, A COMPARATIVE ANALYSIS OF COMPLEX ORGANIZATION 14 (1961). See also Kelman, Processes of Opinion Change, 25 PUBLIC OPINION QUARTERLY 57-78 (1971).

29.V. SERGE, supra note 12, at 15-16 (Not even incumbents of sacred statuses are exempt from this desecrating procedure. See, e.g., P. BERRIGAN, PRISON JOURNALS OF A PRIEST REVOLUTIONARY 36 (1967).

30.V. SERGE, supra note 12, at 31, 52.

31.Wolfgang, Rules for Inmates, in THE SOCIOLOGY OF PUNISHMENT AND CORRECTION 89 (M. Wolfgang ed. 1962). Further discussion of privacy in connection with sleeping arrangements is found in Schwartz, Notes on the Sociology of Sleep, Soc. Q. 485-99 (1970).

32.See H. LEVY & D. MILLER, supra note 15, at 4.

33.See P. KROPOTKIN, supra note 24, at 319.

34.H. BATTLE, EVERY WALL SHALL FALL 61-62 (1969).

35.V. SERGE, supra note 12, at 121.

36.An excellent example of the latter is found in A. SOLZHENITSYN, THE FIRST CIRCLE 190-93 (1968).

37.A. WESTIN, PRIVACY AND FREEDOM 130 (1970).

38.Id. at 130, 190, 204, 352.

39.see, e.g., J. STEINER, TREBLINKA 81-83 (1968).

40.See I. ZIMMERMAN, supra note 19, 161.

41.Id. at 96.

42.J. RESKO, REPRIEVE 20 (1956). The condemned are even denied the dignity of dying in private, for tradition requires that their agony be witnessed. The final horrifying contortions become a public spectacle. See I. ZIMMERMAN, supra note 19, at 121-22:

He was sitting in the chair; they were adjusting the electrode to his right leg....They dropped the mask over his face--is it to spare the witnesses? Or is it to give you an illusion of privacy in your dying? Elliott made it strong. O'Loughlin's body strained forward against the straps, then slumped. The mouth sagged open; the mask doesn't hide your mouth.

43.H. LEVY & D. MILLER, supra note 15, at 103-04, 105.

44.N. LEOPOLD, LIFE PLUS NINETY NINE YEARS 91 (1957).

45.R. NEESE, PRISON EXPOSURES 46 (1959).

46.The capacity of impersonal surveillance is rather formidable, as is seen in a recent advertisement in one of the leading correctional journals:

Now you can tighten security, even if you are short of trained correctional officers. The patented Tri-Pan Closed-circuit TV system uses remote control to move the camera along a lateral track, besides panning and tilting to provide a clear view of cell interiors and corridors.

(Advertisement, 31 AM. J. CORR. 27 (Nov.-Dec. 1969). We can only point to the question of how electronic surveillance, by replacing pivotal figures in the prison, might affect its organization.

47.D. WARD & G. KASSEBAUM, WOMEN'S PRISON 16 (1965).

48.D. GLASER, THE EFFECTIVENESS OF A PRISON AND PAROLE SYSTEM 98 (1964).

49.B. BETTELHEIM, THE CHILDREN OF THE DREAM 130-31 (1970).

50.Sykes & Messinger, The Inmate Social System in THEORETICAL STUDIES IN SOCIAL ORGANIZATION OF THE PRISON 8 (R. Cloward ed. 1960).

51.This is not to deny the very pronounced differentiation of roles within inmate subcultures. We mean to say that these roles tend to be united mainly by principles (the "inmate code") which are shared by their incumbents--as opposed to mutual dependence in respect of services, which is definitive of organic solidarity.

52.See Simmel, Privacy is not an Isolated Freedom, in PRIVACY 77 (J. Pennock & J. Chapman ed. 1971) where the author states: "Openness is almost inevitably linked to homogeneity....To maintain a difference, a degree of isolation against the outside is necessary, thus reinforcing what boundaries exist against external influence."

53.See Wheeler, The Structure of Formally Organized Socialization Settings, in SOCIALIZATION AFTER CHILDHOOD 78 (O. Brim & S. Wheeler ed. 1966). The notion of prison as a "homogenizing setting" is qualified, but not contradicted, in Schwartz, Pre-Institutional vs. Situational Influence in a Correctional Community, 62 J. CRIM. L.C. & P.S. 532-42 (1971).

54.This notion is succinctly expressed in Coser, Insulation from Observability and Types of Social Conformity, 26 AM. SOC. REV. 29 (1961), where the author states, [I]nsulation from observability and access to it are...important structural elements in a...[social organization]." See also R. MERTON, SOCIAL THEORY AND SOCIAL STRUCTURE 343 (1964).

One shortcoming of this approach (and a limitation of the present paper) is that it tends to deflect attention away from the numerous strategies inmates use to privatize their existence. These include illegal accumulation of private property, distinctive ways of wearing uniform apparel, staking claim to personal territory in diverse parts of the institution, etc. See especially E. GOFFMAN, supra note 7, 173-320.

tion]". See also R. MERTON, SOCIAL THEORY AND SOCIAL STRUCTURE 343 (1964).

One shortcoming of this approach (and a limitation of the present paper) is that it tends to deflect attention away from the numerous strategies inmates use to privatize their existence. These include illegal accumulation of private property, distinctive ways of wearing uniform apparel, staking claim to personal territory in diverse parts of the institution, etc. See especially E. GOFFMAN, supra note 7, 173-320.

55. This tendency has been exemplified by Gresham Sykes in many of his influential writings and, in particular, in G. SYKES SOCIETY OF CAPTIVES 130-34 (1966).

56. D. GLASER, supra note 48, at 155.

57. Id. at 150-51.

CHAPTER 18b

Reprinted from *American Journal of Sociology*, Vol.73, No. 6, May 1968

THE SOCIAL PSYCHOLOGY OF PRIVACY

Barry Schwartz

ABSTRACT

Patterns of interaction in any social system are accompanied by counter-patterns of withdrawal, one highly institutionalized (but unexplored) mode of which is privacy. There exists a threshold beyond which social contact becomes irritating for all parties; therefore, some provision for removing oneself from interaction and observation must be built into every establishment. Such provisions subserve the action patterns for which they provide intermission. Privacy, which is bought and sold in social establishments, reflects and affirms status divisions, and permits "local-ized" deviation which is invisible to the group as a whole. Privacy thereby insulates against dysfunctional knowledge. Rules governing entrance into and exit from privacy are most clearly articulated on the level of the establishment and are reflected in its physical structure and in proprieties concerning the uses of space, doors, windows, drawers, etc. The report ends with a discussion of identity and its relation to the freedoms of engagement and disengagement.

Patterns of coming and staying together imply counterpatterns[1] of withdrawal and disaffiliation which, as modalities of action, are worthy of analysis in their own right. Simmel makes the identical point in his essay, "Brucke and Tur": "Usually we only perceive as bound that which we have first isolated in some way. If things are to be joined they must first be separated. Practically as well as logically it would be nonsense to speak of binding that which is not separate in its own sense....Directly as well as symbolically, bodily as well as spiritually, we are continually separating our bonds and binding our separations."[2] Simmel, however, ignores the question of how separation subserves integration - of how men are bound by taking leave of one another as well as by their coming together. One sociologically relevant approach to this problem is through the analysis of privacy, which is a highly institutionalized mode of withdrawal.

THE GROUP-PRESERVING FUNCTIONS OF PRIVACY

Withdrawal into privacy is often a means of making life with an unbearable (or sporadically unbearable) person possible. If the distraction and relief of privacy were not available in such a case, the relationship would have to be terminated if conflict were to be avoided. Excessive contact is the condition under which Freud's principle of ambivalence most clearly exercises itself, when intimacy is most likely to produce open hostility as well as affection.[3] Issue must therefore be taken with Homans' proposition, "Persons who interact frequently with one another tend to like one another" (providing the relationship is not obligatory).[4] The statement holds generally, but misses the essential point that there is a threshold beyond which interaction is unendurable for both parties. It is because people frequently take leave of one another that the interaction-liking proposition maintains itself.

Guarantees of privacy, that is, rules as to who may and who may not observe or reveal information about whom, must be established in any stable social system. If these assurances do not prevail - if there is normlessness with respect to privacy -every withdrawal from visibility may be accompanied by a measure of espionage, for without rules to the contrary persons are naturally given to intrude upon invisibility. "Secrecy sets barriers between men," writes Simmel, "but at the same time offers the seductive temptations to break through the barriers."[5] Such an inclination is embodied in the spy, the Peeping Tom, the eavesdropper, and the like, who have become its symbols.

"Surveillance is the term which is generally applied to institutionalized intrusions into privacy. And social systems are characterizable in terms of the tension that exists between surveillant and anti-surveillant modes. Much of our literature on the anti-utopia, for example, George Orwell's *1984,* which depicts the dis-eases of excessive surveillance, is directed against the former mode. But dangers of internal disorder reside in unconditional guarantees of invisibility against which many administrative arms of justice have aligned themselves. On the other hand, surveillance may itself create the disorder which it seeks to prevent. Where there are few structural provisions for privacy, social withdrawal is equivalent to "hiding." For Simmel, "This is the crudest and, externally, most radical manner of concealment."[6] Where privacy is prohibited, man can only imagine separateness as an act of stealth.[7]

Since some provisions for taking leave of one another and for removing oneself from social observation are built into every establishment, an individual withdrawal into privacy and the allowance of such a withdrawal by other parties reflects and maintains the code that both sides adhere to. Leave taking, then, contains as many ritualistic demands as the act of coming together. Durkheim, like Homans, is not altogether correct in his insistence that the periodic gatherings of the group are its main sources of unity.[8] After a certain point the presence of others becomes irritating and leave taking, which is a mutual agreement to part company, is no less a binding agent than the ritual of meeting. In both cases individual needs (for gregariousness and isolation) are expressed and fulfilled in collectively indorsed manners. The dissociation ritual presupposes (and sustains) the social relation. Rules governing privacy, then, if accepted by all parties, constitute a common bond providing for periodic suspensions of interaction.

If privacy presupposes the existence of established social relations its employment may be considered as an index of solidarity. Weak social relationships, or relationships in the formative stage, cannot endure the strain of dissociation. By contrast, members of a stable social structure feel that it is not endangered by the maintenance of interpersonal boundaries. This point is of course well reflected in the Frostian dictum, "Good fences make good neighbors."

PRIVACY HELPS MAINTAIN STATUS DIVISIONS

It is also well known that privacy both reflects and helps to maintain the status divisions of a group. In the armed forces, for example, the non-commissioned officer may reside in the same building as the dormitoried enlisted man but he will maintain a separate room. The officer of higher rank will live apart from the non-commissioned, but on the same base, often in an apartment building; but officers of highest status are more likely to have private quarters away from the military establishment.

In organizational life the privacy of the upper rank is insured structurally; it is necessary to proceed through the lieutenant stratum if the top level is to be reached. In contrast, the lower rank, enjoying less control over those who may have access to it, find their privacy more easily invaded. Even in domestic life persons of the lower stratum lack "the butler" by means of whom the rich exercise tight control over their accessibility to others.

Privacy is an object of exchange. It is bought and sold in hospitals, transportation facilities, hotels, theaters, and, most conspicuously, in public restrooms where a dime will purchase a toilet, and a quarter, a toilet, sink and mirror. In some public lavatories a free toilet is provided--without a door.

Privacy has always been a luxury. Essayist Phyllis McGinley writes: "The poor might have to huddle together in cities for need's sake, and the frontiersman cling to his neighbor for the sake of protection. But in each civilization, as it advanced, those who could afford it chose the luxury of a withdrawing place. Egyptians planned vine-hung gardens, the Greeks had their porticos and seaside villas, the Romans put enclosures around their patios.... Privacy was considered as worth striving for as hallmarked silver or linen sheets for one's bed."[9] In this same respect Goffman comments upon the lack of front and back region differentiation in contemporary lower-class residences.[10]

The ability to invade privacy is also reflective of status. The physician's high social rank, for instance, derives perhaps not only from his technical skill but also from his authority to ignore barriers of privacy. However, this prerogative is not limited to those of high status. We must not forget the "non-person" who lacks the ability to challenge the selfhood of his superiors. Goffman cites Mrs. Frances Trollope: "I had indeed frequent opportunities of observing this habitual indifference to the presence of their slaves. They talk to them, of their condition, of the faculties, of their conduct exactly as if they were incapable of hearing. ...A young lady displaying modesty before white gentlemen was found lacing her stays with the most perfect composure before a Negro footman."[11] In general society the assumption of the social invisibility of another is looked upon as indecency, that is, as a failure to erect a barrier of privacy between self and other under prescribed conditions.

The general rule that is deducible from all of this is that outside of the kinship group an extreme rank is conferred upon those for whom privacy shields are voluntarily removed. The prestige afforded the physician is exaggerated in order to protect the self from the shame which ordinarily accompanies a revelation of the body to a stranger, particularly if he is of the opposite sex. Likewise, the de-statusing of the servant is necessary if he is to be utilized for purposes of bathing, dressing, etc.

Persons of either high or low rank who have access to the private concerns of their clients are subject to definite obligations regarding both the manner in which secret knowledge is to be obtained and, most importantly, the way in which it is treated once it has been obtained. Explicit or implicit guarantees of confidentiality neutralize the transfer of power which would otherwise accompany the bestowal of private information. Both the possession of an extreme rank and the assurance of confidentiality thus legitimize the "need to know" and the intrusions which it makes possible.

Up to this point we have tried to indicate privacy's stabilizing effect upon two dimensions of social order. Withdrawal subserves horizontal order by providing a release from social relations when they have become sufficiently intense as to be irritating. Privacy is also a scarce social commodity; as such, its possession reflects and clarifies status divisions, thus dramatizing (and thereby stabilizing) the vertical order. But we must recognize that privacy also opens up opportunities for such forms of deviance as might undermine its stabilizing effects. However, privacy admits of *invisible* transgression and therefore serves to maintain intact those rules which would be subverted by the public disobedience that might occur in its absence.

Moore and Tumin, in their discussion of the function of ignorance, stated: "All social groups...require some quotient of ignorance to preserve esprit de corps."[12] And Goffman has made it clear that every establishment provides "involvement shields" for its members wherein "role releases" may take place, particularly deviant ones.[13] As Merton puts it:

Resistance to full visibility of one's behavior appears, rather, to result from structural properties of group life. Some measure of leeway in conforming to role expectations is presupposed in all groups. To have to meet the strict requirements if a role at all times, without some degree of deviation, is to experience insufficient allowances for individual differences in capacity and training and for situational exigencies which make strict conformity extremely difficult. This is one of the sources of what has been elsewhere noted in this book as socially patterned, or even institutionalized, evasions of institutional rules.[14]

Thus, each group has its own "band of institutionalized evasion" which expands and contracts as conditions change. Rose L. Coser, in this connection, has considered observability in terms of the social status of the observer. She indicates that persons of high rank tend to voluntarily deprive themselves of visibility by signaling their intrusion with a prior announcement.[15] The deviation band, then, is normally condoned by both the upper and lower strata.

Moore and Tumin stress the importance of preventing deviation from being known to the group as a whole.[16] No doubt, a publication of all of the sins, crimes, and errors that take place in a social unit would jeopardize it's stability. The preoccupation of the press with sensational deviations from norms might be considered from this point of view. Similarly, the more one person involves himself with another on an emotional basis the more both will need private facilities to conceal nasty habits and self-defaming information from each other. If the child, for instance, became suddenly aware of all the non-public performances of his father, and if the latter were aware of all the perversions that are privately enacted by his offspring, a father-son relationship characterized by mutual admiration would be impossible. This same point is illustrated in well-adjusted marriages which depend not only upon mutually acceptable role- playing but also upon the ability of both parties to conceal "indecent" performances. This presupposes a modicum of physical distance between husband and wife. Simmel, in addition, adds that a complete abandon of one's self-information to another "paralyzes the vitality of relations and lets their continuation really appear pointless."[17]

Privacy enables secret consumption. We observe, for example, the adolescent practices of smoking or drinking in their locked rooms. Similarly, "Women may leave *Saturday Evening Post* on their living room table but keep a copy of *True Romance* ('something the cleaning woman must have left around') concealed in their bedroom."[18] However, some modes of secret consumption have come into the public light. The erotic "girlie magazines," for example, no longer need be employed privately by the middle-class male since the advent of the *Playboy* magazine. As some activities emerge from secrecy others go underground. Thus, the person who nowadays finds pleasure in the Bible will most likely partake of it in private rather than in a public place or conveyance. These new proprieties are perhaps specific instances of a general rule set down by Simmel, that "what is originally open becomes secret, and what was originally concealed throws off its mystery. Thus we might arrive at the paradoxical idea, that, under otherwise like circumstances, human associations require a definite ratio of secrecy which merely changes its objects; letting go of one it seizes another, and in the course of this exchange it keeps its quantum unvaried."[19]

Incidentally, just as the person must employ proper language for the public situations in which he finds himself, he is required to maintain an appropriate body language as well. Differing postures must be assumed in his public encounters. But public postures do not exhaust the many positions of which the human body is capable. Anyone who has maintained a single position over a long period of time knows that the body demands consistent postural variation if it is to remain comfortable and capable of good role performance. Privacy enables the person to enact a variety of non-public postures and thus prepares him physically for public life.

It should be stressed that the absence of visibility does not guarantee privacy. The hypertrophied super-ego certainly makes impossible the use of solitude for deviant objectives. The person who is constantly in view of an internalized father, mother, or God leads a different kind of private life than those possessed by a less demanding conscience. This reveals an interesting paradox. Privacy surely provides for some measure of autonomy, of freedom from public expectation; but as Durkheim so persistently reminded us, the consequences of leaving the general normative order are moral instability and social rootlessness. (It is for this reason that secret societies compensate for the moral anarchy inherent in pure autonomy by means of ritual.)[20] Is it then possible that, through privacy, the ego escapes the dominion of the public order only to subordinate itself to a new authority: the super-ego? In some measure this is certainly the case, but one may also venture to suggest that the super-ego, like the social structure whose demands it incorporates, has its own "band of institutionalized evasion." The super-ego cannot be totally unyielding, for if every deviation of the ego called into play its punitive reaction the consequences for the self would be most severe.

PRIVACY AND ESTABLISHMENTS

It was earlier noted that rules or guarantees of privacy subserve horizontal and vertical order. Such rules are embodied in the physical structure of social establishments. Lindesmith and Strauss, for instance, have noted that proprieties concerning interpersonal contact and withdrawal are institutionalized in the architecture of buildings by means of a series of concentric circles. Specific regulations permit or forbid entry into the various parts of this structure, with a particular view to protecting the sacred "inner circle."[21] A more specific instance of the physical institutionalization of norms is found in the case of the bathroom, whose variation in size and design is limited by the requirement that body cleansing and elimination be performed privately.[22] This norm is reinforced by the architectural arrangements in which it is incorporated. The fact the bathroom is only built for one literally guarantees that the performances which it accommodates will be solos. However, this normative-physical restriction admits of more complicated, secondary proprieties. Bossard and Boll write:

> The fact that the middle-class family rises almost together, and has few bathrooms, has resulted in a problem for it, which has been resolved by a very narrowly prescribed ritual for many of them—a

bathroom ritual. They have developed sets of rules and regulations which define who goes first (according to who must leave the house first), how long one may stay in, what are the penalties for overtime, and under what conditions there may be a certain overlapping of personnel.[23]

The very physical arrangement of social establishments thus opens and shuts off certain possibilities for interaction and withdrawal, and creates a background of sometimes complex ritual in support of a foreground of necessary proprieties. Needless to say, the form taken by such ritual is always subject to modification by architectural means.

Charles Madge also urges the architect to take explicit account in his designs of the ambivalences of social life. Men, for example, are given to both withdrawal and self-display. This duality, notes Madge, requires an "intermediate area" in housing projects such as a backyard or garden which separates the home or inner circle from the "common green."[24] But it is one thing to so divide our physical living space as to insure ourselves of interactional options; it is another to regulate the interactional patterns that the division of space imposes upon us. The latter task is most efficiently met by the door.

Doors.--McGinley has referred to the door as a human event of significance equal to the discovery of fire.[25] The door must surely have had its origin among those whose sense of selfhood had already developed to the extent that they could feel the oppression of others and experience the need for protection against their presence. Continued use of the door very probably heightened that feeling of separateness to which it owed its creation. Doors, therefore, not only stimulate one's sense of self-integrity, they are required precisely because one has such a sense.

The very act of placing a barrier between oneself and others is self-defining, for withdrawal entails a separation from a role and, tacitly, from an identity imposed upon oneself by others via that role. Therefore, to waive the protection of the door is to forsake that sense of individuality which it guarantees. As Simmel points out, some measure of de-selfing is characteristic of everything social.[26]

I would like now to discuss various kinds of doors, including horizontal sliding doors (drawers) and transparent doors (windows). I shall also treat walls as relatively impermeable interpersonal barriers, in contrast to doors, which are selectively permeable.

Doors provide boundaries between ourselves (i.e., our property, behavior and appearance) and others. Violation of such boundaries imply a violation of selfhood. Trespassing or housebreaking, for example, is unbearable for some not only because of the property damage that might result but also because they represent proof that the self has lost control of its audience; it can no longer regulate who may and who may not have access to the property and information that index its depths.[27] The victim of a Peeping Tom is thus outraged not only at having been observed naked but also for having lost control of the number and type of people who may possess information about her body. To prove this we note that no nakedness need be observed to make Peeping Tomism intolerable.

"Alone, the visual feeling of the window," writes Simmel, "goes almost exclusively from inward to outward: it is there for looking out, not for seeing in."[28] This interdiction insures that the inhabitants of an establishment may have the outside world at their visual disposal, and at the same time it provides for control over their accessibility to this world. But, whereas the shade or curtain may be employed to regulate accessibility between the private and public spheres of action, situational proprieties are depended upon for protection in public. One such norm is that of "civil inattention" which has been elaborated by Goffman.[29]

Unlike the window, "the door with an in and out announces an entire distinction of intention."[30] There must be very clear rules as to who may open what doors at what times and under what conditions. The front and back doors are normally the only doors that any member of a family may enter at any time and under any circumstances. A parent may enter a child's room at any time and may inspect and replenish drawers, but visiting friends may not. But the parent must learn that some private doors (drawers) may not be opened (although they may be to friends); if they are, new receptacles for ego-indexes will be found, for example, the area between mattress and spring. The child, however, must never inspect the contents of the drawers of his parents nor enter their room at night. Thus the right of intrusion is seen to be an essential element of authority, whose legitimacy is affected by the degree to which it is exercised. Correspondingly, authority is dependent upon immunity against intrusion. Cooley notes that "authority, especially if it covers intrinsic personal weakness, has always a tendency to surround itself with forms and artificial mystery, whose object is to prevent familiar contact and so give the imagination a chance to idealize...self concealment serves, among other purposes, that of preserving a sort of ascendency over the unsophisticated."[31] In this same connection, Riesman writes:

> As compared with the one room house of the peasant or the "long house" of many primitive tribes, he (the inner directed child) grows up within walls that are physical symbols of the privacy of parental dominance. Walls separate parents from children, offices from home, and make it hard, if not impossible, for the child to criticize the parents' injunctions by an "undress" view of the parents or of other parents. What the parents say becomes more real in many cases than what they do....[32]

Moreover, it is possible to map personal relations in terms of mutual expectations regarding intrusion. The invasion of various degrees of privacy may be a duty, a privilege, or a transgression, depending upon the nature of the interpersonal bond. And, clearly, expectations regarding such impositions may not be mutually agreed to.

Parental obligations concerning the care of a child override the child's rights to seclusion and place him in a position of social nakedness wherein he has no control over his appearance to others. However, to be subject to limitless intrusion is to exist in a state of dishonor, as implied in the rule against "coming too close." This point is made in Simmel's discussion of "discretion" as a quality which the person-in-private has a right to demand of another who is in a position to invade his seclusion.[33] Compromises between child and parent are therefore necessary and generally employed by the manipulation of the door. For example, the bedroom door may be kept half open while the child sleeps, its position symbolic of the parents' respect for the youngster's selfhood. Furthermore, a general temporal pattern might emerge if a large number of cases were examined. During infancy the door to self is generally fully open;[34] it closes perhaps halfway as a recognition of self development during childhood, it shuts but is left ajar at pre-puberty, and closes entirely--and perhaps even locks--at the pubertal and adolescent stages when meditation, grooming, and body examination become imperative. Parents at this time are often fully denied the spectatorship to which they may feel entitled and are kept at a distance by means of the privacy that a locked door insures.

There are also certain situations wherein husband and wife must remain separate from one another. A spouse, for example, must generally knock before entering a bathroom if the other is occupying it. This is a token of deference not to nudity but to the right of the other party to determine the way he or she wishes to present the self to the other. This rule insures that the self and its appearance will remain a controllable factor, independent of the whims of others, and it contributes to self-consciousness as well. This is seen most clearly in total institutions like the armed forces where open rows of toilets are used first with some measure of mortification and later with a complete absence of consciousness of self. In such doorless worlds we find a blurring of the distinction between "front and back regions," between those quarters where the self is put on and taken off and those in which it is presented.[35] In conventional society those who confuse these two areas are charged with vulgarity.

In contrast to the door, the wall symbolizes "separation" rather than "separateness" and denies the possibility of the encounter and withdrawal of social exchange. It strips away that element of freedom which is so clearly embodied in the door. "It is essential," notes Simmel, "that a person be able to set boundaries for himself, but freely, so that he can raise the boundaries again and remove himself from them."[36] In privacy, continues Simmel, "A piece of space is bound with himself and he is separated from the entire world."[37] But in enforced isolation man is bound *to* space. While the door separates outside from inside, the wall annihilates the outside. The door closes out; the wall encloses. Yet doors are converted into walls routinely, as is seen in the popular practice of "sending a child to his room" for misdeeds and the like. In this sense, many homes contain private dungeons or, rather, provisions for transforming the child's room into a cell - which forces upon us the distinction between formal and informal imprisonment.

Privacy is not dependent upon the availability of lockable doors. Goffman, for example, discusses "free places" in the institution where inmates may, free of surveillance, "be one's own man...in marked contrast to the sense of uneasiness prevailing on some wards."[38] In addition there is "personal territory" established by each inmate: for one a particular corner; for another a place near a window, etc. "In some wards, a few patients would carry their blankets around with them during the day and, in an act thought to be highly regressive, each would curl up on the floor with his blanket completely covering him; within the covered space each had some margin of control."[39] Thus do men withdraw from others to be at one with themselves and to create a world over which they reign with more complete authority, recalling Simmel's observation that "the person who erects a refuge demonstrates, like the first pathfinder, the typically human hegemony over nature, as he cuts a particle of space from continuity and eternity."[40]

In summary, islands of privacy exist in all establishments and throughout even the most intimate household. These islands are protected by an intricate set of rules. When these rules are violated secret places are sought after, discovered, and employed as facilities for secret action. These places and their permeability constitute one type of map, as it were, of interpersonal relationships and reveal the nature of the selves participating in them.

Privacy, property and self. - Implied in any reference to a private place is its contents, personal property. One perhaps more often than not withdraws into privacy in order to observe and manipulate his property in some way, property which includes, of course, body and non-body objects.

There are two types of objects: those which may be observed by the public (and which may be termed personal objects) and those which are not available to public view (private property). Private property, as we are using the term, may be further delineated in terms of those intimate others who may have access to it in terms of visibility or use. Some private objectifications of self may be observed by family members, but some may be observed by *no one except the self.* There is no doubt that these latter objects have a very special meaning for identity; some of these are sacred and must not be contaminated by exposing them to observation by others; some are profane, and exposure will produce shame, but both are special and represent an essential aspect of self and, from the possessor's point of view, must not be tampered with.

It is because persons invest so much of their selves in private and personal things that total institutions require separation of self and material objects. When individualism must be minimized private ownership is always a vice worthy of constant surveillance. In such situations the acquisition and storage of personal things persist in the form of the "stash," which might be anything from a long sock to the cuff of one's pants.[41]

It follows that those who have direct or indirect access to the belongings of others or to articles which have been employed by them in private ways enjoy a certain amount of power which, if judiciously employed, may serve their interests well. Hughes observes:

> It is by the garbage that the janitor judges, and, as it were, gets power over the tenants who high-hat him. Janitors know about hidden love affairs by bits of torn-up letter paper; of impending financial disaster or of financial four-flushing by the presence of many unopened letters in

the waste. Or they may stall off demands for immediate service by an unreasonable woman of whom they know from the garbage, that she, as the janitors put it, 'has the rag on.'' The garbage gives the janitor the makings of a kind of magical power over that pretentious villain, the tenant. I say a kind of magical power, for there appears to be no thought of betraying any individual and thus turning his knowledge into overt power.[42]

But, certainly, power need not be exercised to be effective. The mere knowledge that another "knows" invokes in the treatment of that other certain amount of humility and deference.

DEPRIVATIZATON

We have attempted to show that the possibility of withdrawal into well-equipped worlds which are inaccessible to others is that which makes intense group affiliations bearable. But we have also seen that men are not always successful in protecting their invisibility. Accidental leakages of information as well as the diverse modes of espionage threaten the information control that privacy is intended to maintain. But information control also consists of purposeful information leakage and even of the renunciation of secrecy. Just as men demand respite from public encounter they need periodically to escape themselves, for a privacy which lacks frequent remissions is maddening. The over-privatized man is he who is relieved of public demand only to become a burden to himself: He becomes his own audience to performances which are bound for tedium. Self-entertainment is thus a most exhausting business, requiring the simultaneous performance of two roles: actor and spectator. Both tire quickly of one another. When privacy thereby exhausts itself new and public audiences (and audienceships) are sought.

Moreover, we are led to relinquish our private information and activities by the expediencies and reciprocities routinely called for in daily life. We all know, for example, that in order to employ others as resources it is necessary to reveal to them something of ourselves, at least that part of ourselves which for some reason needs reinforcement. When this occurs (providing support is forthcoming), two things happen. First, we achieve some degree of gratification; second, and most important, our alter (or resource) reveals to us information which was heretofore withheld, for self-revelation is imbued with reciprocal power: It calls out in others something similar to that which we give of ourselves. There is both mutual revelation and mutual gratification. It is easy to see that when stress or need is prolonged this process may become institutionalized: Intimacy is then no longer an alternative; it is enforced, and private activity becomes clandestine and punishable. The deprivation process approaches completion when we are not only penalized for our withdrawals but feel guilty about them. A housewife who had probably undergone the deprivatization process confided to Whyte: "I've promised myself to make it up to them. I was feeling bad that day and just plain didn't make the effort to ask them in for coffee. I don't blame them, really, for reacting the way they did. I'll make it up to them somehow."[43]

But loss of privacy among conventional folk is free of many of the pains of social nakedness which are suffered by inmates and by others undergoing total surveillance. The civilian voluntarily subjects himself to publicity and is relatively free of the contamination of unwanted contacts. His unmaskings are selective and subject to careful forethought. The intruder is chosen rather than suffered; indeed, his resourcefulness depends upon his ability to "know" his client-neighbor. Therefore, in civil life, we find valid rationalization for our self-revelations. The demand that we "be sociable" is too compelling and too rewarding to be ignored by any of us.

But a substantial self-sacrifice is made by those who actually believe themselves to be what they present to public view. An awareness of the masquerades and deceptions that are part of good role performance is necessary to recall ourselves to our *own* selfhood and to our opposition to that of others. We must indeed deceive others to be true to ourselves. In this particular sense privacy prevents the ego from identifying itself too closely with or losing itself in (public) roles. Daily life is therefore sparked by a constant tension between sincerity and guile, between self-release and self-containment, between the impulse to embrace that which is public and the drive to escape the discomfort of group demands. Accordingly, our identities are maintained by our ability to hold back as well as to affiliate. Thus Goffman writes:

> When we closely observe what goes on in a social role, a spate of sociable interaction, a social establishment - or in any other unit of social organization - embracement of the unit is not all that we see. We always find the individual employing methods to keep some distance, some elbow room, between himself and that with which others assume he should be identified.

Our sense of being a person can come from being drawn into a wider social unit; our sense of selfhood can arise through the little ways in which we resist the pull. Our status is backed by the solid buildings of the world, while our sense of personal identity often resides in the cracks.[44]

For Goffman, privacy is one of "the little ways in which we resist the pull" of group commitments and reinforce our selfhood.

FOOTNOTES

1.The initiation of a social contact generally entails a withdrawal from a preceding one. Therefore, men may withdraw into new social circles as well as into seclusion. In this particular sense it would be most exact to employ the term "contact-withdrawal," as opposed to a single term for engagement and another for disengagement. However, this distinction does not apply to movements into privacy.

2.Georg Simmel, "Brucke und Tur," in *Brucke and Tur* (Stuttgart: K.F. Koehler, 1957), p. 1.

3.Sigmund Freud, *Group Psychology and the Analysis of the Ego* (New York: Bantam Books, Inc., 1960) pp. 41-42.

4.George C. Homans, *The Human Group* (New York: Harcourt, Brace & Co., 1950), p. 111.

5.Georg Simmel, "The Secret and the Secret Society," in Kurt Wolff (ed.), *The Sociology of Georg Simmel* (New York: Free Press, 1964), p. 334.

6.*Ibid.*, p. 364.

7.*Ibid.*

8.Emile Durkheim, *The Elementary Forms of the Religious Life* (Glencoe, Ill.: Free Press, 1947), pp. 214-19.

9.Phyliss McGinley, "A Lost Privilege," in *Province of the Heart* (New York: Viking Press, 1959), p. 56.

10.Erving Goffman, *The Presentation of Self in Everyday Life*(Edinburgh: University of Edinburgh, 1958), p. 123.

11.*Ibid.*, p. 95.

12.Wilbur E. Moore and Melvin M. Tumin, "Some Social Functions of Ignorance," *American Sociological Review,* XIV (December, 1949), 792. See also Barney Glaser and Anselm Strauss, "Awareness Contexts and Social Interaction," *American Sociological Review,* XXIX (October, 1964), 669-79, in which social interaction is discussed in terms of "what each interactant in a situation knows about the identity of the other and his own identity in the eyes of the other" (p. 670). A change in "awareness context" accompanies acquisitions of knowledge, provisions of false knowledge, concealment of information, etc.

13.The "involvement shield" and Everett C. Hughes' concept of "role release" are elaborated in Erving Goffman's *Behavior in Public Places* (New York: Free Press,1963), pp. 38-39.

14.Robert K. Merton, *Social Theory and Social Structure* (New York: Free Press, 1964), p. 343.

15.Rose L. Coser, "Insulation from Observability and Types of Social Conformity," *American Sociological Review,* XXVI (February, 1961), 28-39.

16.Moore and Tumin, *op. cit.* (see n. 12 above), 793.

17.Simmel, "The Secret and the Secret Society," *op. cit* (see n. 5 above), p. 329.

18.Goffman, *The Presentation of Self in Everyday Life, op. cit.* (see n. 10 above), p. 26. Needless to say, many instances of the employment of privacy for "secret production" could be given.

19.Simmel, "The Secret and the Secret Society," *op. cit.* (see n. 5 above), pp. 335-36.

20.*Ibid.,* pp. 360-61.

21.Alfred R. Lindesmith and Anselm L. Strauss, *Social Psychology* (New York: Henry Hold & Co., 1956), p. 435. However, in an interesting statement, McGinley announces the death of the very idea of the "inner circle": "It isn't considered sporting to object to being a goldfish. On the same public plan we build our dwelling places. Where, in many a modern house, can one hide? (And every being, cat, dog, parakeet, or man, wants a hermitage now and then.) We discard partitions and put up dividers. Utility rooms take the place of parlors. Picture windows look not onto seas or mountains or even shrubberies but into the picture windows of the neighbors. Hedges come down, gardens go unwalled; and we have nearly forgotten that the inventor of that door which first shut against intrusion was as much mankind's benefactor as he who discovered fire. I suspect that, in a majority of the bungalows sprouting across the country like toadstools after a rain, the only apartment left for a citadel is the bathroom" (*op. cit.* [see n.

9 above], pp. 55-56).

In contrast, Edward T. Hall observes: "Public and private buildings in Germany often have double doors for soundproofing, as do many hotel rooms. In addition, the door is taken very seriously by Germans. Those Germans who came to America feel that our doors are flimsy and light. The meanings of the open door and the closed door are quite different in the two countries. In offices, Americans keep doors open; Germans keep doors closed. In Germany, the closed door does not mean that the man behind it wants to be alone or undisturbed, or that he is doing something he doesn't want someone else to see. It's simply that Germans think that open doors are sloppy and disorderly. To close the door preserves the integrity of the room and provides a protective boundary between people. Otherwise, they get too involved with each other. One of my German subjects commented. "If our family hadn't had doors, we would have had to change our way of life. Without doors we would have had man, many more fights.... When you can't talk, you retreat behind a door. ...If there hadn't been doors, I would always have been within reach of my mother" (*The Hidden Dimension* [Garden City: Doubleday & Co., 1966], p. 127. For a discussion of the norms regulating privacy among the English, French, Arab, and Japanese, see pp. 129-53).

22.Alexander Kira, *The Bathroom* (New York: Bantam Books, Inc., 1967), pp. 178-84. The requirement of complete privacy for personal hygiene is only a recent phenomenon (see pp. 1-8).

23.J.H.S. Bossard and E.S. Boll, *Ritual in Family Living* (Philadelphia: University of Pennsylvania Press, 1950), pp. 113-14 (cited by Kira, *op. cit.* [see n. 22 above], pp. 177-78).

24.Charles Madge, "Private and Public Places," *Human Relations,* III (1950), 187-99. F.S. Chapin (in "Some Housing Factors Related to Mental Hygiene," *Journal of Social Issues,* VII [1951], 165) emphasizes that the need for relief from irritating public contact must be consciously and carefully met by the architect. On the other hand, Kira writes: "There are problems which cannot be resolved by architects and industrial designers alone, however; they also pose a challenge to the social scientists and to the medical and public health professions. This is an area in which the stakes are enormous and in which little or no direct work has been done." (*Op. cit.* [see n. 22 above], p. 192.)

25.See n. 21 above.

26.Simmel, "The Secret and the Secret Society," *op. cit.* (see n. 5 above), p. 373.

27.The law recognizes the psychological effect of such criminal acts and provides additional penal sanction for them. Wolfgang and Sellin report that "the chain store is more outraged by theft from a warehouse, where the offender has no business, than from the store where his presence is legal during store hours." Moreover, "the victim of a house burglary is usually very disturbed by the fact that the offender had the effrontery to enter the house illegally....For these and similar reasons, breaking and entering as well as burglary carry more severe sanctions in the law" (Marvin E. Wolfgang and Thorsten Sellin, *The Measurement of Delinquency* [New York: John Wiley & Sons, 1964], pp. 219-20.

28.Simmel, "Brucke und Tur," *op. cit.* (see n. 2 above), p. 5.

29.Goffman, *Behavior in Public Places, op. cit.* (see no. 13 above), pp. 83-88.

30.Simmel, "Brucke und Tur," *op. cit.* (see n. 2 above), p. 4.

31.Charles Horton Cooley, *Human Nature and the Social Order* (New York: Schocken Books, Inc., 1964), p. 351.

32.David Riesman, *The Lonely Crowd* (Garden City: Doubleday & Co., 1953), p. 61. Another characterologist, William H. Whyte, suggests that "doors inside houses...marked the birth of the middle class" (*The Organization Man* [Garden City, N.Y.: Doubleday & Co., 1956], p. 389).

33.Simmel, "The Secret and the Secret Society," *op. cit.* (see n. 5 above), pp. 320-24. Similarly, Erving Goffman writes, "There is an inescapable opposition between showing a desire to include an individual and showing respect for his privacy. As an implication of this dilemma, we must see that social intercourse involves a constant dialectic between presentational rituals and avoidance rituals. A peculiar tension must be maintained, for these opposing requirements of conduct must somehow be held apart from one another and yet realized together in the same interaction; the gestures which carry an actor to a recipient must also signify that things will not be carried out too far" ("The Nature of Deference and Demeanor," *American Anthropologist,* LVIII [June, 1956], 488).

34.The absence of ability among infants and children to regulate the appearance and disappearance of their audience does not mean that privacy or separateness is not an important feature of their development; the privacy need is simply expressed differently. The infant, for example, can sometimes remove himself from the field of stimulation by going to sleep or wriggling away from the adult who holds him. This is probably why pathology resulting from overcontact is less likely than that due to undercontact, for the former is far more easily regulated by the infant than the latter. At a later stage of development, the infant learns that he can hold back and let go in reference not only to sphincters but to facial expressions and general dispositions as well. He comes to view himself as a causal agent as he inherits the power of voluntary reserve. When the child is locomoting he first confronts privacy imposed against him by others and begins to define himself in terms of where he may and may not go. On the other hand, his ambulatory ability gives him enormous control over his audience, a power in which he delights by "hiding." Espionage is practiced as well and suspected in others-whereby the condition of shame begins to acquire meaning for the child. These incomplete comments suffice to illustrate the point that the privacy impulse is not at all inactive in infancy and childhood. They further suggest that each stage of development has its own mode of privacy, which may be defined in terms of the ego's relationship to those from whom privacy is sought and the manner in which withdrawal is accomplished.

35.Goffman, *The Presentation of Self in Everyday Life, op. cit.* (see n. 10 above), pp. 66-86.

36.Simmel, "Brucke und Tur," *op. cit.* (see n. 2 above), p. 4.

37.*Ibid.,* p. 3.

38.Erving Goffman, "The Underlife of a Public Institution," in *Asylums* (Garden City, N.Y.: Doubleday & Co., 1961), p. 231.

39.*Ibid.,* p. 246. For more on norms regulating territorial conduct in face-to-face encounters, see Nancy Felipe and Robert Sommer, "Invasions of Personal Space," *Social Problems,* XIV (May, 1966) 206-14; and Robert Sommer, "Sociofugal Space," *American Journal of Sociology,* LXXII (May, 1967), 654-60.

40.Simmel, "Brucke und Tur," *op. cit.* (see n. 2 above), p. 3.

41.Goffman, *Asylums, op. cit.* (see no. 38 above), pp. 248-54.

42.Everett C. Hughes, *Men and Their Work* (Glencoe, Ill.: Free Press, 1958), p. 51.

43. Whyte, *op. cit.* (see no. 32 above), p. 390.

44. Goffman, *Asylums, op. sit.* (see no. 38 above). pp. 319-20.

CHAPTER 19

THE STAGES OF FRIENDSHIP FORMATION

D. Kelley Weisberg

May 1973

Friendship is a highly processual social relationship. As a process, it had a beginning, development and oftentimes a termination. This paper will touch on the developmental stag of friendship formation under the generative condition when former friendships have been temporarily suspended because of cross-cultural relocating and the individual must thus make new friends in a new setting.

Twentieth century man is man in motion. He is frequently relocating himself from one geographic area to another. Always a major consequence of relocating is the disruption of a familiar social matrix. This social matrix consists of three elements: intimate interpersonal relationships with family members, intimate interpersonal relationships with friends, and casual interpersonal relationships with acquaintances.

After relocating, some connection with the disrupted former social matrix is often retained with friends and family members by means of phone calls and letters. However, when two conditions are operative - the greater the distance of relocating, and the greater the temporal duration of relocating - the loss of intimate relationships with friends and family members is more devastating to the individual.

Of the two elements of the former social matrix, friends and family members, obviously the individual cannot replace family members. However, he can make new friends in the new setting and thereby re-people *this* element of his social matrix.

Three steps can be delineated in the process of making friends. Two steps occur in the beginning phase: meeting, where one encounters potential friends, and making contact, where one first initiates and interaction, and the step in the developmental stage of maintaining contact.

MEETING

Meeting people must occur in order for an individual to make friends. By "meeting," the author means encountering a pool of potential friends. The term is not taken to signify here the initial contact. That will be considered in the second stage of friendship formation, making contact.

Meeting potential friends is contingent upon a number of variables. One variable is the predisposition to make friends. Other variables include: the availability of certain resources (e.g., time and energy), and a physical setting conducive to meeting people.

PREDISPOSITION

For an individual to make and meet friends, he must desire friends. He must be open to the idea of, that is, predisposed to meeting people.

Individuals have different capacities for having friends and for having specific types of friends. For some individuals, the number of friends or the number of certain types of friends they may desire in their social matrix may be finite. Having several close friends, for example, or having one lover or one marital partner, may be sufficient for an individual. He may, hence, be sated or "saturated" and not desire other friends or specific types of friends. Indeed, some people can "saturate" on the level of no friends - being satisfied with only their own company (e.g., the recluse, the loner).

The predisposition to meeting people, then, may be affected by the condition which this author terms "friendship saturation."[1] When this condition is operative, the necessary predisposition for meeting people (or for meeting specific types of people - such as potential lovers or marital partners) will not be present. Under this condition, then, this first necessary step in the process of friendship formation will not occur.

The cross-culturally relocating student, however, is the opposite of the "friendship saturated" individual. This individual has previously often had a full social matrix, but upon relocating is experiencing a social matrix completely devoid of friends. Under the condition of relocating, the loneliness and aloneness generated by the disruption of ties with former social matrix often operate to promote in the individual a heightened willingness and openness to meeting people. The cross-culturally relocating student, hence, often deeply feels a predisposition to meeting people and to making friends in the new culture. (The importance of liveliness in promoting this predisposition to meeting people had been recognized by other authors as well).[2]

In addition to the predisposition to meeting people, another variable, available resources, affects meeting. The individual must be willing to expend the resources necessary for meeting people. Among these resources are time and energy. The individual must have available to him a ready supply of time and energy.

TIME

Meeting people takes time. The individual has at his disposal a finite source of time. One-third of his twenty-four hour day is expended in sleeping time. Obviously, this constitutes a time in which meeting cannot occur. Meeting, however, can occur during most other times, e.g., work time, school time, eating time, free time.[3]

The individual can, and often does, structure time to optimized the possibility of meeting people. By managing his time, he can place himself in situations where he will be most likely to meet potential friends. That is, he may choose to spend work time, school time, eating time or free time in situations involving natural opportunities for interaction with others.

Putting oneself in such situations requires that one plan time. Often extended periods of time are necessary for doing so.

Time may have to be planned for deciding where to go to meet people, in grooming for the meeting, in gaining access to the meeting site and in waiting in the site.

Meeting potential friends can, of course, occur without planning and after a slight expenditure of time. In many instances the individual does not have to consciously structure time for meetings to occur. Indeed, such accidental unstructured and unplanned meetings occur frequently and are a common experience of anyone who has made friends.

However, for some people and especially for the cross-culturally relocating student, this step in the process may demand excessive expenditures of time. Much time may be spent abortively while the individual tries to meet people but does not succeed. Certain conditions (such as language difficulty, passivity, shyness, a difference in social customs) may result in such abortively-spent meeting time for the cross-culturally relocating individual and will be discussed later.

Often individuals may be "time saturated" and not have at their disposal available time to meet people. Time saturation most frequently results from the demands of employment and/or parental responsibilities.[4] Time saturation, like the condition of friendship saturation, may function to minimize the likelihood of meeting potential friends.

The cross-culturally relocating student, however, is not usually time saturated and does have at his disposal available time to meet people. Not being a parent (as most foreign students are single) and not being employed because of visa restrictions, he spends he daily time studying and going to class. Free time is frequently interspersed in these activities. Hence, the cross-culturally relocating student often has and abundant source of available time to meet people.

ENERGY

Energy is still another resource necessary for meeting people. Just as the individual has a finite source of time, the individual also has a finite source of energy at his disposal. The condition of "energy saturation" too will affect meeting people.

High demands of energy output may be felt by individuals experiencing ill health. Energy demands on emphysema victims, for example, mitigate against meeting because respiratory disability restricts mobility.[5] In some instances, individuals in poor health may actually have an abundant source of time at their disposal, but may not have sufficient energy available for meeting new people. Such is often the case with multiple sclerosis victims.[6]

The condition of energy saturation which often befalls the cross-culturally relocating student at the beginning period of relocating ("culture fatigue") has been well documented.[7] In this initial period, the demands of adjusting are so high that the individual often does not have a supply of available energy for meeting. Only after this period of energy saturation passes does the individual have more energy at his disposal.

However, energy expenditure remains problematic for the cross-culturally relocating student as considerable energy is necessary for him to meet people because of the generative conditions of his situation. Not only is he unfamiliar with his setting, but he is also unfamiliar with the language of his host. Therefore, in addition to the energy normally expended in the actual presentation of self in interaction,[8] he must also expend considerable energy in communication during meetings. Energy is required for finding the right words to express his thoughts, in translating his thoughts into words, and in understanding what is being said to him.

Oftentimes, the amount of energy that is required to meet people is unavailable or deemed to be too great to pay for meeting. Under this condition, meeting will not occur because many individuals may in fact structure time to conserve energy by avoiding meeting people through such tactics as going to bed, reading or simply staying home. Thus it can be seen that just as friendship saturation and time saturation minimized meeting possibilities, so functions the condition of energy saturation.

Other resources often necessary for meeting include: a mobility source, money and a place to invite people. Automobiles or other sources of transportation may be necessary in order to gain access to pools of potential friends. Walking, of course, is the most common mobility source. Yet, for some individuals, especially the aged and the ill, even this resource may be unavailable and may therefore limit opportunities for meeting people.[9]

Similarly, not having available cash may minimize meeting possibilities, if cash is required to gain access to certain meeting sites. In addition, not having a place to invite people may affect meeting in some instances.[10] These resources have been specified here, although not particularly problematic for the cross-culturally relocating student, because they may affect meeting for some individuals.

SETTING

In addition to a necessary predisposition and a supply of available time and energy, meeting may also be affected by a physical setting that is conducive to meeting possibilities. Individuals may in fact consciously select settings bearing in mind the need to meet people. The cross-culturally relocating student may choose to live in a dormitory in order to meet people rather than choosing a private apartment. Settings such as college dormitories constitute what Hall terms "sociopetal"[11] settings: settings tending to bring people together.

Indeed, certain areas within a setting may be more sociopetal than others because of their physical layout. Meetings in a college dormitory, for example, will be more likely to occur in common lounges, common bathrooms, television rooms or dining halls. Similarly, meetings within a large university will be more likely to occur in small seminar-type classes than in large lecture halls. Individuals desiring to meet people can therefore structure and manage their time so as to expend it in these sociopetal areas within certain settings.

Some settings provide opportunities for meeting specific types of people. Individuals can also structure and spend their time in settings which will maximize the possibility of meeting those people possessing specific characteristics they may desire in friends. For example, in the case of the cross-culturally relocating student who desires to meet other relocating individuals, he can and often does, select settings which highlight his nationality - e.g., native organizations and associations. In these settings, the individual will increase his chances of finding people who talk who talk his language, eat the same type of food and share the common culture.

Such settings, formed by people who enjoy certain activities or interests and who seek out other people who enjoy the same thing, are termed by this author "clientele-specific" settings. Gay bars and gay baths are examples of such "clientele-specific" settings serving homosexuals wanting to meet members with their own sexual preference who are interested in sexual encounters.[12] Certain bars function similarly for swingers who are interested in meeting other couples to "swing with."[13] Religious settings similarly provide opportunities for people to meet others of their religious preference. Disability-highlighting settings (such as centers for the deaf, the blind) function similarly to aid handicapped people to meet others like themselves.

The list of "clientele-specific" settings, of course, is endless. The main characteristic of all these settings is, like the native organizations of the cross-culturally relocating student, the settings attract individuals who figuratively talk the same language and share the common culture. Hence, the individual need only discover such settings in order to maximize possibilities of meeting those people he desires to befriend.

The existence of certain social psychological and structural conditions, then, operates to affect the possibility of meeting people. The social psychological condition consists of a predisposition to meet - a predisposition often heightened in cases of intense loneliness of aloneness. The structural conditions include an availability of such resources as time and energy and a physical setting which is conducive to meeting people either because of its sociopetal nature or because of its function to promote meetings for a specific clientele.

MAKING CONTACT

After a meeting has occurred, the next step in friendship formation is making contact. In this step, the individual interacts in an initial encounter with the other whom he desires to befriend.

Making contact in order to be successful has to be a dyadic interaction, a "two-way street," so to speak. That is, both parties have to be willing to interact. If one party is not willing, the interaction will not proceed beyond a "one-liner." Once again, we see that a predisposition is a necessary condition for friendship formation.

Time and energy are also essential resources in this stage of the friendship formation process. An available source of time is necessary for the initial contact, e.g. the taking of time to interact with the other. It can be seen that making contact is difficult in such settings as busy city streets or supermarkets precisely because individuals in these settings do not generally have at their disposal the time necessary for interaction.

Energy, too, is necessary for making contact. One often overlooks the amount of energy involved in sheer vocalization. However, for such energy-saturated individuals as emphysema victims, limited energy supplies (because of extreme oxygen shortage) may interfere with vocalization and make this stage of the friendship process problematic. Cross-culturally relocating individuals similarly experience high energy demands for vocalization - not because of any oxygen shortage, but rather because of the high energy output necessary for conversing in a foreign language. (Although vocalization does not constitute the only energy drain for cross-culturally relocating individuals, it is a major contributing factor to their culture fatigue).

FORMS OF MAKING CONTACT

Generally making contact, this initial interaction, is accomplished by means of verbal communication. In order to make contact, the individual needs something to talk about. Oftentimes an "opener" or opening gambit provides this essential element.

Salutations and greetings all serve as such verbal opening gambits.[14]Opening gambits may include other forms, such as: self-introductions, comments or questions about the other, comments or questions about neutral subjects, or comments about an activity that both parties are engaged in.

Self-introductions serve as frequently used opening gambits. A self-introduction may encompass telling the other one's name such a "Hi, my name is Jack." Or, it may also include furnishing additional information about oneself - "Hi, I'm a psychology student here."

Self-introductions may be quite direct, as in the above examples. Or, oftentimes, they may be much more subtle. In some instances the individual may in a covert way present information about himself to the other - information which is intended to make the other aware of his desirable attributes. A humorous example is given in *The Sensuous Man*[15] when after twice stepping purposely on a woman's foot in a crowded conveyance, the man apologizes, saying : "I'm not usually so clumsy. I'm a bit wobbly today because I just got off the yacht.''

Another form of opening gambit is the other-directed comment or question. Questions addressed to the other may include such examples as ''Hi, are you new here?'' or ''What's your name?'' Often the other-directed statement may include a compliment. ''My, that's a nice dress you're wearing'' or ''You have such beautiful eyes,'' are examples of compliments proffered by men intending to make contact with women.

Opening gambits may include comments or questions about neutral subjects. The time and the weather furnish subjects for often used opening gambits.

Opening gambits can also arise from an activity that both parties are currently engaged in. The most common opening gambit at a dance, for example, is ''Would you like to dance?'' or at a bar, ''Would you like a drink?'' These opening gambits, like the openers discussed above, function to promote further interaction between the two parties.

Making contact is often problematic for the cross-culturally relocating student. Because he is unfamiliar with the language of his host country, he is hence unfamiliar with the culture's opening gambits. Assuming that the necessary predisposition for making contact is present and the necessary time and energy are available, making contact requires a facility with the opening gambits - a facility which often the cross-culturally relocating individual does not possess.

The relocating individual may not be familiar with the phrases used in opening gambits or with the whole gamut of gambits. Only knowing, ''hi, how are you?'' for example, may mean that the individual is lost if a different opener is ''thrown'' at him (such as ''what's happening, man?''). In addition, the individual may not know whether an answer is required to the opener, whether to simply repeat the opener (''how are you?'' - ''how are you?'') or whether to respond to the opener with a new question entirely (''how are you?'' - ''how are things with you?''). Oftentimes, he may be puzzled as to whether the opener is meant to be taken literally. Does ''how are you?'' require a detailed elaboration of one's physical are mental state, for example? This difficulty can be further seen by one student's response to the question ''how do you do?'' with ''how do I so what?''

For many cross-culturally relocating individuals, other elements of the opener sequence may prove problematic. The duration of the opener may puzzle the foreign individual. American opening gambits are often quite brief, last only several seconds. After exchanging salutations, Americans often separate and go their own ways. For some cross-culturally relocating individuals, this brief opener seems unnatural and is often interpreted that the other party does not desire interaction.

Some cross-culturally relocating individuals may be troubled by the absence of physical contact in American openers. Many cross-culturally relocating individuals originate from cultures whose opening sequence includes touch.[16] Openers in may countries when strangers first make contact, for example, may include a handshake, a touch upon the arm or a playful punch. The absence of physical contact in openers may signify for the foreign individual a lack of warmth or interest on the part of the other.

In addition the physical distance utilized during American opening gambits may be problematic for cross-culturally relocating individuals. Individuals from Latin American countries, for instance, are more comfortable with less physical distance between the interacting parties than Americans are accustomed to. For individuals from these cultures, the greater physical interaction distance may also signify a lack of warmth or interest on the part of the other.

Another element of the opening sequence may prove problematic for the cross-culturally relocating individual. Not being familiar with the new culture, the individual may share only a limited part of what Schutz terms the culture's "socially distributed knowledge."[17] They may, hence, not be conversant on many topics which arise in the initial contact. As one relocating student explained:

"I didn't know any topics to talk to Americans about when I came. I didn't know anything about Vietnam - about ecology or courses being offered - or football or basketball - or current events. I didn't know anything about these things in the beginning. We don't have football or basketball in my country...It's hard to talk to Americans if you have nothing to talk about."

COMMON DENOMINATORS

For the cross-culturally relocating student, a "common denominator" often facilitates making contact. This common denominator may serve both as an opener and as a carry-through for a conversation. The most common denominators include: common background, common language or common status.

A common background or common language eliminates both the problem of the foreign culture's opening gambits and of the culture's unfamiliar socially distributed corpus of knowledge. Sharing a common background or language results in both parties being able to converse in a familiar language (with familiar openers) and on familiar topics (which often concern their country).

Similarly, a common status (such as that of student) may also facilitate making contact. The common status provides a conversation topic on a familiar subject, such as the common discipline or common student problems. Like a common background, a common status partially resolves the problem of coping with the culture's unfamiliar socially distributed corpus of knowledge, as the foreign individual is on somewhat familiar ground (although the individual still has to function in interaction in an unfamiliar language).

Making contact, however, remains problematic for the cross-culturally relocating student due to several conditions. One such condition is the unfamiliar language. Difficulty with the language of the host country causes interaction strain as conversations do not proceed smoothly. The foreign individual often has to request that the other slow his conversation pace, that the other repeat statements frequently, or explain statements frequently.

Conversation with more than one other may produce even more strain in interaction for the relocating individual. In this situation, conversation may proceed even more rapidly than in a dyad. The rapidity of the triad interaction may provide less opportunity for the individual to interrupt to request clarification, repetition or explanation.

Another condition which affects making contact for the cross-culturally relocating student is passivity or shyness. Making contact necessitates a certain amount of aggression, of putting oneself forward. Because of the language difficulty, many cross-culturally relocating students are reluctant to "put themselves forward." By so doing, their foreignness and their foreign accent and difficulty with the language becomes even more apparent and may cause them considerable embarrassment.

When originating from cultures with different social customs, some cross-culturally relocating students manifest higher degrees of passivity in making contact. The social customs or etiquette of some cultures (primarily Oriental) dictate that the individual refrain from making contact on his own initiative.[18] Instead, making contact is socially sanctioned only when facilitated by a third party. When passivity in making contact is present because of a difference in social customs, then, making contact is less likely to occur.

It can thus be seen that making contact, this second step in the process of friendship formation, is highly problematic for the cross-culturally relocating student because of the generative conditions of his situation. Such factors as language difficulty, a lack of familiarity with opening gambits and with the culture's socially distributed corpus of knowledge, passivity or shyness and a difference in social customs operate to make this step difficult for individuals originating from other cultures.

MAINTAINING CONTACT

If a relationship, in which the parties have just met and made contact, is to become a friendship, there must be a maintenance of contact. This stage of friendship formation, maintaining contact, involves the largest expenditure of resources. These resources include the aforementioned time, energy, mobility, money, and in addition, social psychological resources such as caring sharing, trust, concern and affection.

Maintaining contact with friends can be accomplished by means of face-to-face interaction and by distant interaction (phone calls, letters). This author would not go as far as saying that "frequent interaction seems to be a necessary condition for a strong and viable relationship," as some authors have argued.[19] The present author would rather assert that oftentimes friendships may be sustained without either of the above forms of maintenance. Friendships, in fact, may often be suspended or "put in storage" to be brought out and renewed at a later date with little effect on the relationship. For the purposes of this paper, however, the author shall limit discussion of maintaining contact in friendship to face-to-face interaction.

Maintaining contact requires a large expenditure of time. Time is expended primarily in exchanging information - such as biographical sketches, present, past and future problems and personal feelings and sentiments. Much time is thus expended doing things together. Activities involving both individuals also require large expenditures of time. The phenomenon termed a "strain toward totality"[20] signifies not only the inclusion of larger and larger segments of self in the friendship relationship, but also the inclusion of ever-increasing proportions of one's time.

In the maintenance of a friendship, other resources such as energy, mobility and money are also expended. Just as maintenance is time-taking, so is it energy-taking. Although some amount of energy is required for conversation, the highest demands of energy are required for participation in activities. Under the previously discussed condition of energy saturation, maintenance often proceeds only on the level of conversation. Energy saturation, then (similar to time saturation, of course) will not only affect meeting and making contact, but will also affect maintaining contact.

Mobility is also required for maintaining contact. The individual must have a mobility source for maintenance in order to gain access to the other, or to gain access to activity sites. Decreased mobility functions similar to energy saturation and time saturation to affect maintenance of contact.

Money may be another resource necessary for maintenance of friendship. Although money is not required for maintenance on the level of conversation, money may be necessary for gaining access to the other or to activity sites.

Maintenance also requires an expenditure of social psychological resources. These resources may include: caring, sharing, trust, concern and affection. The expenditure of these resources often results in an ever-growing closeness, or intimacy, between the two parties. It could be said that these resources provide the social psychological glue that cements individuals in the friendship.

Individuals are constantly investing resources in the friendship relationship. They only invest their time, energy, mobility and money in the relationship, but also invest large portions of their social psychological resources. The investment of such resources may be likened to an individual's investment in a bank. Just as individuals build up a principal, so do individuals build up closeness in a friendship. Because of the "deposit" of these valuable resources, relationships are not easily disposed of, as can be seen in the case of marital relationships.

Extending the banking analogy, because of the high degree of investment in the relationship, individuals expect returns, e.g. reciprocity. These returns may include: dependability, caring, support (financial and/or emotional), trust, companionship, and often sexual exclusivity. This expectation of returns may be termed the "norm of reciprocity."[20]

When returns are not forthcoming or are deemed insufficient, the maintenance of the friendship may be affected. Maintenance can also be affected, of course, by other conditions. These conditions may include death or relocating. Unlike death, which terminates a friendship, relocating only necessitates the suspension of the relationship.

Thus in summary, for the relocating individual, meeting friends, making contact and maintaining contact are stages of a process which begins upon arrival in the new culture. Upon departure from the culture, maintaining contact often continues with the new-found friends through letters. Upon arrival in the home culture, the process comes full circle.

The social matrix formed in the new country has now been disrupted and friendships at home which had formerly been suspended will be reactivated and maintained through face-to-face interaction. And often, in the home country the friendship process begins once again after relocating - meeting new friends, making contact and maintaining contact.

CONCLUSION

The process developed in this paper has significance, of course, for the cross-culturally relocating student. Although specifically valuable for this population, the foregoing study also has import for many other individuals for whom friendship formation becomes problematic because of the disruption of their normal social matrices. Such individuals to whom this study might be especially relevant include: the recently-widowed, newly relocated businessmen and their families, relocated college students, the military and their families, prisoners, people seeking distant medical treatment and institutionalized mental patients. In addition, this information would also unquestionably be valuable to those individuals who are involved with the proceeding populations in providing them with assistance and counseling.

From a survey of the foreign student literature and the literature concerning friendship, it was apparent to this author that scant attention has been paid to the interactional difficulties experienced therein specifically by cross-culturally relocating students. A recognition of these interactional difficulties would not only be an important contribution to the literature, but it might also aid in making the friendship formation process less problematic for these individuals by highlighting their dilemma for foreign student advisors who assist these individuals.

Further studies would certainly be valuable to verify, modify or elaborate the concepts developed here and to explore their significance in relationship to other populations. Hopefully, such research would generate additional useful interactional conceptual models.

APPENDIX

METHODOLOGY

Data for this study consisted of informal interviews with foreign students and foreign student advisers and field observations. Interviews were conducted over a fourteen month period during 1971-72 in two settings: the University of California, San Francisco Medical Center, and the International ("I") House of the University of California at Berkeley.

The sample contained 20 foreign students enrolled on the San Francisco and Berkeley campuses. The students, 10 males and 10 females, were between the ages of twenty and thirty-five. The median age was 25. The majority of foreign students interviewed were living in university residence halls.

Nationals from the following countries were included in the sample population: China (Hong Kong and Taiwan), Cuba, Finland, France, India (3), Italy, Korea, Nigeria, Pakistan (2), Peru, Sweden (2), Thailand (2), Turkey and Vietnam. Students represented a variety of academic disciplines: anthropology, biochemistry, business administration, chemistry, chemical engineering, civil engineering, finance, mathematics, mechanical engineering, medical technology, nursing, operations research, pharmacy, and pharmaceutical chemistry. One-half of the students were studying on the graduate level; one-half on the undergraduate level. The duration of the students' study sojourn in the United States ranged from one to five years.

Respondents, with two exceptions, were unmarried. Most (18 students) had traveled alone to the United States and settled alone without other family members.

All students has prior training in English before coming to the United States. The average period of prior study was six years. However, language ability in terms of speaking and understanding (according to estimations of the researcher), varied from poor to excellent.

Field work consisted of several stages. First, interview data with foreign students were collected. The interviews were predominantly informally structured. Formal structure comprised only the first few moments of each interview, e.g. obtaining preliminary background data (age, sex, country, academic discipline, residential location and prior English training). Informal structure then prevailed.

In the initial period of interviewing, students were asked to discuss all

393

problematic areas of adjustment. Responses ranged from eating, sleeping, financial and interpersonal problems to problems of climate, language and etiquette. Later, the interpersonal area emerged as the most frequently mentioned and the most problematic area of adjustment (as specified by the majority of respondents). Interviews then focused exclusively on this aspect.

Participant observations of foreign students' activities proceeded concurrently with the interviewing stage. observations focused on foreign students' activities and interactions within the two residential settings of Millberry Union (University of California, San Francisco) and International House (Berkeley). In the final stages of research, the data were coded and analyzed, based on the constant comparative methods of grounded theory.[22]

REFERENCES

Bartell, Gilbert. 1971 Group Sex. New York: Signet Books.

Berne, Eric. 1972 What Do You Do After You Say Hello? New York: Bantam Books.

Bott, Elizabeth. 1952 Family and Social Network. London: Tavistock Publications.

Davis, Marcia. 1970 Transition to a Devalued Status: The Case of Multiple Sclerosis, doctoral dissertation, University of California, San Francisco, School of Nursing.

De Grazia, Sebastian. 1964 Of Time, Work and Leisure. New York: Doubleday Anchor Books.

Fagerhaugh, Shizuko Y. 1973 "Getting Around with Emphysema," American Journal of Nursing, 73:94-99.

Gilmour, George R. 1962 "Freshman Dating Patterns," unpublished paper, University of San Francisco.

Glaser, Barney and Anselm Strauss. 1967 The Discovery of Grounded Theory: Strategies for Qualitative Research. Chicago: Aldine Publishing Co.

Goffman, Erving. 1959 The Presentation of Self in Everyday Life. New York: Doubleday Anchor Books.

Gouldner, Alvin W. 1960 "The Norm of Reciprocity: A Preliminary Statement," American Sociological Review, 25:161-178.

Guthrie, George M. and Margaret S. McKendry. 1963 "Interest Patterns of Peace Corps Volunteers in a Teaching Project," Journal of Educational Psychology, 54:261-267.

Hall, Edward. 1969 The Hidden Dimension. New York: Doubleday Anchor Books.

Harvey, Will. 1972 How to Find and Fascinate a Mistress (and Survive in Spite of it All). New York: Pocket Books.

Hess, Beth . 1972 "Friendship," in Martha White Riley, Marilyn Johnson and Anne Forer (ed.) Aging and Society. New York: Russell Sage Fdn.

Howard, Alan. 1973 "Symposia in the Flesh -- an Inside Look at Gay Baths and Other Places to Meet Your Friends," Popular Psychology, 6:25-31.

Lawton, M. Powell and Bonnie Simon. 1968 "The Ecology of Social Relationships in Housing for the Elderly," The Gerontologist, 8:108-115.

Lopata, Helena Znaniecki. 1969 "Loneliness, Forms and Components," Social Problems (Fall), 248-262.

M . 1971 The Sensuous Man: The First How-To Book for the Man Who Wants to Be a Great Lover. New York: Dell Books.

McCall, George J. 1970 Social Relationships. Chicago: Aldine Publishing Co.

McCall, George J. and J.L. Simmons. 1966 Identities and Interactions: An Examination of Human Associations in Everyday Life. New York: Free Press.

Nelson, Joel I. 1966 "Clique Contacts and Family Orientations," American Sociological Review, 31:663-72.

Ortega y Gasset, Jose. 1957 Man and People. New York: W.W. Norton and Co.

Schutz, Alfred. 1962 "Common Sense and Scientific Interpretation of Human Action," in Collective Papers, Volume I, The Problem of Social Reality.

Szanton, David L. 1966 "Cultural Confrontation in the Philippines," in Robert B. Textor (ed.) Cultural Frontiers in the Peace Corps. Cambridge, Mass.: MIT Press.

Udry, Richard and Mary Hall. 1965 "Marital role Segregation and Social Networks in Middle-Class, Middle-Aged Couples," Journal of Marriage and the Family, 23:392-95.

Weisberg, Deborah Kelly. 1971 "A Cross-Cultural Study of Social Interaction," unpublished honors thesis, Brandeis University.

1. The condition of friendship saturation as it affects the predisposition to meeting people for the aged is discussed by Hess (1972). Hess hypothesizes that for the aged the number an type and intensity of friendships desired by individuals at this particular period in the life cycle are lessened. Hess and Lopata (1969) also discuss the condition of friendship saturation as it affects widows.

2. Nowhere is the importance of loneliness for promoting a predisposition to meeting people as highlighted as in the "how-to" books for men to meet women. See Harvey (1972) and M (1971).

3. For an excellent discussion of man's management specifically of work time and leisure time, the reader is referred to the work by De Grazed (1964). This author, however, would question De Grazia's classification of friendship solely as a leisure time activity. De Grazia seems to ignore here both the existence and importance of friendships in other "times."

4. Hess (1972:361) states that the demands of time upon the individual are dependent in part upon a person's age, e.g., higher demands are felt by the young and middle-aged, and especially by those who are parents. In her assertion that the highest demands of time are felt by those with familial responsibilities, she is supported by Bott (1952:60-9, 180), Nelson (1966) and Udry and Hall (1965).

5. See Fagerhaugh (1973) for a discussion of the energy demands on emphysema victims.

6. The etiology of the decreased sociability of multiple sclerosis victims is much more complex than the energy saturation discussed above, For further elaboration see Davis (1970).

7. "Culture fatigue" refers to the phenomenon experienced immediately after entry into a new culture. Szanton (1966:49) defines the term as "...the physical and emotional exhaustion that almost invariably results from the infinite series of minute adjustments..." See also Guthrie and McKendry (1963).

8. This paper will not discuss the interactional elements of the presentation of self, referring the reader instead to Goffman's work (1959) on this subject, especially the chapter on "Performances." It will merely be stated in passing that Goffman notes the expenditure of energy necessary for meeting people (for "projecting one's social front") and that the expenditure is greater with individuals with whom we are unfamiliar.

9. Lawton and Simon (1968) have termed the decreasing mobility of the aged "the environmental docility hypothesis," finding that aged persons deprived of mobility tend to be limited in their opportunities of meeting people.

10. The necessity of such resources as car, cash and apartment for meeting has been noted for college freshmen by Gilmour (1962).

11. For a detailed discussion of sociopetal settings see Hall (1969).

12. For a discussion of who homosexuals meet in gay baths, the reader is referred to Howard (1973).

13. M (1971:56) emphasizes this technique of identifying oneself immediately by occupation;, interests of income level, so as to manifest one's qualifications as an "eligible" male.

14. For further elaboration in the decisive importance of the salutation the reader is referred to Ortega y Gasset's chapter (1957) on "Reflections on the Salutation." Berne's book (1972) is also useful for its pertinent discussion of the salutation (both "hello" and the handshake) in the psychiatric context of physician-patient relationships.

15. M (1971:56) emphasizes this technique of identifying oneself immediately by occupation, interests or income level, so as to manifest one's qualifications as an "eligible" male.

16. For a cross-cultural comparative study of physical contact and interaction distance in salutations, the reader is referred to this author's "A Cross-Cultural Study of Social Interaction," (1971).

17. For a discussion of the term see Schutz (1962).

18. Lopata (1969) also notes that passivity may affect friendship formation for widows upon the death of their spouses especially if their husbands formerly took the initiative in arranging contact with others.

19. See Mc Call and Simmons (1966:189).

20. The term "a strain toward totality" was first used by Simmel in his discussions of friendship and the dyad. McCall (1966,1970) further elaborates on the phenomenon in relationships. A citation from the latter work illustrates the phenomenon:

"If interacting with alter is enjoyable, why not interact with him more? If yachting with alter is fun, why not ask him down to the club? In this way, the strain to spend more time with alter gives rise to a strain to include more activities..." (1970:187)

21. For a discussion of the normative standards of reciprocity involved in relationships see Gouldner (1960).

22. See Glaser and Strauss (1967).

CHAPTER 20

Reprinted from *American Journal of Nursing*, Vol. 64, No. 6, June 1964

THE SOCIAL LOSS OF DYING PATIENTS

Barney G. Glaser

Anselm L. Strauss

Inevitably, a social value is placed on a patient, and that value has much to do with the impact on the nurse of his dying and, frequently, on the care he receives. So the authors have discovered in a study they, with a nurse faculty member, Jeanne Quint, are making of hospital personnel, nursing care, and dying patients at the University of California Medical Center. A clear recognition by the nurse, of the evaluating she does, can help buffer the impact and make it easier for her to determine nursing needs objectively.

When a patient dies, a nurse feels a loss. In fact, she may experience three kinds of loss. One may be personal loss. Some nurses become involved with patients for such very personal reasons as friendship, similar age, or transference. A second kind is work loss - fighting to save a patient, then losing them. The third kind is the subject here - social loss.

In our society we value people, more or less, on the basis of various social characteristics: for example, age, skin color, ethnicity, education, occupation, family status, social class, beauty, "personality," talent, and accomplishments. Each dying patient embodies more or less of these social characteristics, each to a different degree. The total of the valued social characteristics which the dying patient embodies indicates the social loss to family, occupation, and society on his death.

Nurses tend to react to this degree of social loss with relatively consistent sadness, distress, and efforts at care. Their reactions are most noticeable on wards that have large ratios of high social loss patients (for instance, pediatrics) or low social loss patients (for instance, geriatric wards in state hospitals). However, one can see it virtually any place in which patients die.

A clear recognition of her social loss appraisal may well help a nurse to avoid inequitable attention to different types of dying patients.

CALCULATING SOCIAL LOSS

Perhaps the single most important characteristic on which social loss is based is age. Americans put a high value on having a full life. Dying children are being cheated of life itself, a life full of potential contributions to family, an occupation, and society. They are a loss to the coming generation. By contrast, aged people have had their share of life; they have made their contributions to family, occupation, and society. Their loss, while felt, will be less than if they were younger. Patients in the middle years are in the midst of a full life, contributing to families, occupations, and society. Their loss is often felt as the greatest, for they are depended on the most. It is tragic to see dying a young woman who is married to a devoted husband, charming, educated, and who has three young children. A nurse told us, "I feel most involved with mothers." Or, "I was very involved with a young man who died with rapidly advancing carcinoma. He had a wife, our age, who was a nurse and who had a baby just before he died. He was to be an x-ray technician."

Thus, age is a gauge for a patient's actual and potential social worth. As a gauge, it becomes a baseline for judging in combination other factors. For example, education is more important for calculating the social loss of a middle-year adult than a child or an aged person, since in the middle years education is most put to use.

Age is an apparent characteristic, as are such others as beauty and charm, social class, or skin color. But the nurse must learn about certain other characteristics a patient has - talent, accomplishments, family status, occupation, and education. The longer a nurse works around a dying patient, the more likely she is to learn of his occupation, accomplishments, talents, fame, and family status. Further, she is more likely to learn the degree to which his loss will matter to occupation and family. Family members of dying patients visit frequently, and over time the degree which the patient will be missed after death becomes clear.

This learning usually becomes a collective operation among nurses, as they frequently share their variously discovered facts about the patient. A product of this sharing of information can be consensus among ward nurses about the social loss of the patient. However, consensus does not have to occur, since nurses with the same information can vary in their appraisals of social loss. Lack of consensus is most probable when some of the social loss characteristics of the patient are at odds - as in the case of an elderly man with a very important job, but with no family to care for.

PATIENT'S SOCIAL LOSS STORY

As nurses learn more about the social characteristics of a patient, and learn more about the degree of social loss involved in both apparent and learned characteristics, they continually balance out these factors. Thus, over time, a story is in continual development about the patient as factors are added, adjusted, and subtracted; we term this the patient's social loss story.

This story, then, is a product of the nurse-patient relationship carried over time, which in many cases can be months or even years. Obviously, on some wards which keep patients only a short time - such as premature infant nursery, intensive care unit, emergency - there is only a short social loss story. On these wards nurses may act and feel mainly on the basis of apparent characteristics. They have little time to learn about their patients' other social characteristics.

As the social loss story develops, it becomes an entity apart from the patient, though its calculus may better mirror the patient's potential social loss. The story is told to other nurses almost as if no patient were really involved. It is very sad to hear a story of a young boy run over by a streetcar, or a woman with three children who is dying. It is sad whether or not the patient is himself currently cheerful. Nurses thus react to the dying patient;s social loss story as well as to the patient himself. A prime source of this separation is the generic basis of the social loss story: valued social characteristics, which are themselves something apart from any one person.

The social loss story gains an historical aspect as nurses learn more of the past meaning of the patient's present characteristics. They learn where a patient is from, what he has been doing and, therefore, what loss his death will be fore family, occupation, and society. For example, it is a great loss when a medical student dies of cancer, and this loss is increased when nurses learn the young man had decided to be a doctor in his early teens like his famous father. Similarly, it appears a loss when a dentist is dying, but this loss is somewhat reduced when it is learned that he has spent the last few years of his life hustling marijuana on skid row. The loss of a premature infant may not seem so great when it is discovered that the mother had already lost three premies and did not fully expect this one to live either.

The historical and present aspects of social loss stories derive their meaning from the anticipated future. Thus the story spells out the loss for family members, to occupation, to society--all of which remain to go on without the dying person. In some cases, so the story may say, a family will fall apart without the father's paycheck, or a business will collapse, or a nation will feel the loss of a VIP. In other cases, such as the adolescent who, in a wild car drive, kills himself and four others, or the Mexican farm worker with cancer, little social loss may be anticipated by nurses. (In the adolescent's case, some nurses may feel a social gain!) For projections into the future, a nurses' imagination easily fills in details.

Social loss stories terminate or stop developing in various ways. For low social loss patients, they may scarcely begin before nurses lose interest. Typically the story stops at a patient's death, because the body is disposed of and the family disappears. With this egress of people all further news of the patient ends, and very few nurses check on what happened afterwards. They become caught up in the care of new patients. The story may also stop when a patient becomes comatose and family visits taper off. In this instance, social death has set in for patient, family, and nurses, and may last for days, weeks, or months before physical death finally occurs. The story may also stop in cases of lingering illness when family members have accepted the coming loss and grieved as much as humanly possible.

Sometimes the story goes on after death. This occurs in the case of a surprise death which does not allow enough time beforehand for story development. After the death the staff members sit around and hash out, with what little information they have among them, the social loss of the patient. Story development after death can also occur when family members return or send letters to the nurses, telling what has happened since the patient's death. Some striking stories are never forgotten among nurses; the relating of the story brings out again, and perhaps develops further, the social loss involved. One such striking case is that of a nurse, with one child, who let herself die from a nonsterile abortion in order to protect, it was assumed, her lover and the abortionist.

IMPACT OF SOCIAL LOSS

The principal impact of social loss on nurses is on their feelings. Low social loss patients may hardly bother them; high social loss patient can be very upsetting. The secondary impact of social loss is on patient care. Low social loss patients tend to receive minimal routine care. In some few cases, low social loss patients may receive less then routine care. For example, at peak hours on emergency wards, when the staff must engage in split-second priority decisions concerning attention and treatment, low social loss patients can easily be forgotten for several minutes.

High social loss patients often receive more than routine care. Extra "good will" efforts are made to talk with them, to keep up their spirits, to make them comfortable, and to watch for sudden changes in their condition. However, if the high loss of such a patient is too upsetting for the nurses, he may find himself, like the low social loss patient, receiving only routine care.

Many conditions serve to balance off the effects of social loss on nurses. An important one is the use of standard "loss rationales" to reduce being upset in the face of low or high social loss. People dying from a Friday night knife fight, or the adolescent on the verge of death who has killed others in a wild care drive, have their low social loss reinforced by an "it's their own fault" rationale. That rationale helps to stifle excessive efforts or minimize feeling upset by the tragedy. Being upset at the death of high social loss patients, such as the young mother or father, is typically reduced by rationales to the effect that "It was a blessing he passed on, he was in such pain." Old age rationales are "He had a full life," "He had nothing more to life for." The typical rationale for the loss of premature babies is "He probably had brain damage and couldn't have a (socially) useful life." Or for dying children, "You wouldn't ask him to suffer any longer, would you?" "Don't you think he is happier?" Thus these loss rationales--based on social worthlessness, having a full life, enduring pain, and defects pointing to no potential for a normal life--provide "good reasons" for discounting the impact of high social loss patients or accepting lack of concern with low social loss patients.

Some dying and deaths are not readily handled by loss rationales. It is hard to give good reasons for the accident or the surgery that considerably reduced a patient's life. What emerges are reasons that may increase the distress of social loss. One nurse said in the case of surgery, "I think I feel worse if I know that the patient might have done all right without surgery. They may have lived. Especially a young person. If I cannot explain it to myself, then I feel worse about it. If I can't make an explanation for someone dying, it seems irrational." In such cases, the death is senseless, and the impact consequently greater.

The greater the number of social loss factors the patient embodies, the greater will be the impact of his death on his nurses. For example, the death of a young man is probably less likely to be upsetting than that of a young man with a wife, children, and a highly respected profession. A low social loss factor can cancel the effects of high social loss factors, such as our skid-row dentist or the case of brain damage which renders impossible future contributions to society.

Various properties of the wards also affect the impact of social loss on nurses. On wards where many patients die, nurses can get accustomed to seeing repeatedly the same degree of social loss. This reduces its impact. In contrast, the surprise death of a mother on a ward which seldom has dying or death can have a very strong social loss impact on nurses. Closely associated with frequency of death on a ward is the type of ward patient. For instance, the same frequency of death on a geriatric ward is easier to take than on a pediatric ward. Some wards are filled with lower class patients, other with middle class or upper class. Still others cater to no particular type of patient.

Another property that changes the effects of social loss is the patient's length of stay on the ward. On wards which generally keep patients for a very short time, the impact of social loss is mainly based on apparent characteristics. On wards with slow turnover, the impact is based also on learned characteristics and on the resulting story development, as the balance of loss factors changes. It is difficult to generalize which conditions lead to greater impact. Some nurses who find it difficult to face death and dying on cancer wards, where patients linger for months, many take it much more easily on ICU, where patients either die or leave within a few days. Closely linked with length of stay is the pace of nurses' work. The quick turnover wards tend to keep the nurses very active with intensive care, which is a buffer to the impact of social loss. On the slow turnover wards, the nurses may dwell on the social loss of their patients.

IMPORTING VALUES

Is nurses' response to social loss professional? We do not believe this response is a result of professional training, skills, or attitudes. Indeed, becoming upset in the face of high social loss may hinder the professional requirement of composure in the face of dying and death. Variations in patient care based on social loss also hinder the professional ideal of treating all patients in accordance with their medical needs. The morale of a dying patient needs to be maintained irrespective of, say, his social class or "personality."

Thus we believe that nurses are responding as human beings born into our particular society--a response not necessarily in conflict with professional responses, but not falling within the group of professionally prescribed responses. Nurses import into the hospital the values of our society and act accordingly.

Can or should importing social values into the hospital be professionalized? This is difficult to say. It goes on; it cannot be stopped. But what surely can be done is to become deliberately aware of the importation so that responses to social loss will not hinder professional requirements of composure and care. If understanding the impact of social loss will help a nurse maintain her composure in the face of dying, she will not be forced to avoid patients whose tragic plight is just too much to take. She can also offset some of the untoward effects of social loss evaluation by realizing that socially important dying patients are not the only ones who sorely need extra efforts of good will in their care.

Quanititative Research Grounded Theories

CHAPTER 21

AN INTRODUCTION TO THE SOCIOLOGY OF TAXATION

Fred W. Taylor

May 1972

The following paper was written in 1972, before the inflation of the 1980's made all the numbers look very small, and long before the tax reform of 1986 eliminated or curtailed some of the provisions of the federal income tax which I discuss. Nevertheless, the basic logic of the argument remains valid: the tax system generates economic inequalities and potential class conflict.

Tax inequalities are now more complex and subtle than in 1972. As tax reform has reduced the emphasis on tax sheltered investments, it has increased emphasis on structuring compensation to defer taxation. But the tax provisions of President Clinton's first budget just passed in August of 1993 tend to reintroduce important sources of inequalities which I discussed in 1972, i.e., real estate deductions and a differential capital gains rate.

A sociology of the state budget would clearly involve three fundamental processes, taxation, expenditure, and the complex political and administrative processes according to which decisions about taxation and expenditure are made. Although all three are highly interrelated, I want to focus on one, taxation, for purposes of discussion in this essay. I want to outline some of the basic dimensions of a sociology of taxation which, I argue, is necessary in order to understand some aspects of recent American politics.

Basically I wish to show that the tax system in the United States is a complex system of socially structured inequalities according to which different groups, depending more on their position in the American political economy than on their level of real income, are liable to different forms and different levels of taxation. As the proportion of the total economic flow of American society that is redistributed through the tax system and the state budget has increased four or five fold in this century, the economic consequences of the socially structured inequalities in the tax system have been multiplied. As a result, the modern American state is emerging in the latter half of the 20th century as a critical arena of economic stratification. And this tax stratification has contributed to some important aspects of post-war American politics.

TAX GENERATED ECONOMIC CLASSES

The historical process in which the American state in the 20th century has come to create economic classes through the process of taxation and expenditure, has been one in which as existing tax structures have been transformed in order to meet increased demands for revenue, the consequences of the systematic economic inequalities inherent in these tax structures have been multiplied. This historical process has been driven by the absolute growth in the proportion of national income redistributed by the state through the process of taxation and expenditure. Underlying this general increase in the level of taxation, are three major changes in the structure of taxation: the creation of the graduated income tax during World War I; the vast extension of the income tax during World War II; and the increase in state and local taxes since 1950.

TABLE 1

UNITED STATES TOTAL GOVERNMENT REVENUE AND EXPENDITURE, AND TOTAL

REVENUE AS A PERCENT OF NATIONAL INCOME

Year	National Income[1] (billions)	Total Federal, State and Local Revenue[2] (billions)	Total Federal, State and Local Revenue[3] (billions)	Revenue National Income (%)
1913	34.8	3.0		8.6
1922	63.1	9.3		14.7
1927	81.7	12.2		14.9
1929	87.6			
1930	75.7			
1931	59.7			
1932	42.5	10.3	12.4	24.2
1933	40.2			
1934	49.0	11.3	12.8	22.8

1936	64.9	13.6	16.8	21.0
1938	67.6	17.5	17.7	25.9
1940	81.6	17.8	20.4	21.8
1942	137.7	28.35	45.6	20.6
1944	182.6	64.8	109.9	35.5
1946	180.9	61.5	79.7	34.0
1948	223.5	67.0	55.1	30.0
1950	241.9	66.7	70.3	27.6
1952	292.2	100.2	99.8	34.3
1954	301.8	108.3	111.3	35.9
1955	331.0	106.4	110.7	32.2
1957	364.0	129.2		35.5
1960	414.5	152.1		36.8
1963	481.9	180.3		37.4
1964	518.1	192.4		37.2
1965	562.4	202.6		36.1
1966	616.7	225.6		36.6

[1] Source: *Historical Statistics of the United States, Colonial Times to 1957,* series F-7, p.139; and *Statistical Abstract of the United States,* no. 462, p. 317.

[2] *Historical Statistics,* Series Y-384, p. 722; and *Statistical Abstract,* 1969, no. 579, p.407

[3] *Historical Statistics,* Series Y-412, p. 723.

As Table 1 shows, total federal, state and local government revenue as a percentage of national income has increased during every war and generally remained at the level achieved in wartime, during subsequent periods of peace. Beginning at less than 9% of national income before World War I, total federal, state and local revenue increased during the war and remained at about 15% of national income throughout the 1920's. During the Depression, total government revenue increased to between 20 and 25% of national income, although early in this period, absolute government revenue actually declined, and the increased percentage is altogether due to the drastic decline in national income in the 1930's.

In the late 30's and early 40's, war preparation kept proportional government revenue at these higher levels in spite of large increases in national income. With our entrance into World War II, and especially following the vast extension of the federal income tax in 1943, total government revenues increased again, reaching 35.5% of national income in 1944.

After the war, total government revenue dropped briefly to just below 30% of national income, but during the Korean war it rose again to World War II levels where it remained throughout the Cold War. Finally in the late 1950's, with increased social expenditures by all levels of government added to already high military expenditures, total government revenues increased further and hovered throughout the 1960's at about 37% of national income.

The present steeply graduated structure of the federal income tax was instituted to meet the cost of World War I. Originally the idea of a federal income tax was a radical, populist idea for transferring the burden of taxation from property tax paying farmers to the commercial and industrial rich, but the effective implementation of the income tax has always come during war.

The first income tax was imposed in the first revenue act of the Civil War. Its scales varied during the period it was in force, but it effectively taxed about 1% of the population from 1863 until it was allowed to expire in 1871. Following the elections of 1892, a second income tax law was proposed which would have imposed a flat 2% tax on income above a personal exemption of $4000. It was adopted by the Democratic "billion dollar Congress" in 1894, but in 1985 the Supreme Court held the income tax to be an unconstitutional "assault upon capital."

Following the adoption of the 16th amendment in 1913, the present income tax was instituted, but it was an exceedingly modest tax by modern standards. It imposed a 1% tax on net income exceeding an exemption of $3000 for an individual and $4000 for a husband and wife, plus a surtax beginning at an additional 1% on net incomes from $20,000 to $50,000 and increasing gradually to 6% on net incomes over $500,000. Only with the entrance of the United States into World War I was the federal income tax restructured into its modern steeply graduated form. Exemptions were reduced to $1000 individual and $2000 joint in 1917, and rates were temporarily increased, reaching a high of 6% on the first $4000 above the $2000 joint exemption, and extending theoretically to 77% on net income above $1,000,000.

Nevertheless, in spite of this transformation of the federal income tax during World War I into the outlines of the present system as it affects high income taxpayers, the federal income tax was still limited to the relatively rich. For even in 1920, the year in which more taxable returns were filed than in any year before 1940, only 5.5 million individuals or married couples out of a population of 106.5 individuals filed income tax returns. Between 1925 and 1936, the number of taxable returns filed did not exceed 2.9 million, and the number reached a pre-World War II high in 1939 of only 3.9 million out of a population by then of 131 million.

During World War II, however, the federal income tax was extended from a graduated tax on the relatively rich to a largely ungraduated mass tax. As Table 2 shows, while personal exemptions were reduced four times from $1000, individual, $2000, joint in 1939, finally to $500, individual and $1000, joint in 1944 and 1945, the basic tax rate was progressively increased from 4% of the first $4000 of taxable income in 1939, finally to 23% of the first $2000 of taxable income in 1944 and 1945.

The consequence of this vast extension of the federal income tax was that in the four years from 1939 to 1943, the number of taxable individual and joint income tax returns filed increased tenfold, from 3.9 million in 1939 to over 40 million in 1943, and the total federal personal income tax paid increased from less

TABLE 2

Income year	Personal Exemptions		# of taxable returns filed (millions)	Tax rates for Married Couples	
	Single	Married		Lowest Bracket	Highest Bracket
				Rate Amnt. of Income	Rate Amnt of Income
	No dependents				
'24			4.5		
'27			2.4		
'29			2.4		

			'30 2.0				
			'31 1.5				
			'32 1.9				
			'33 1.7				
1936-39	$1000	$2500	'36 2.86	4%	$4000	79%	$5,000,000
			'37 3.33				
			'38 3.00				
			'39 3.90				
1940	800	2000	'40 7.44	4.4	4000	81.1	5,000,000
1941	750	1500	'41 17.50	10.0	2000	81.0	5,000,000
1942-43	500	1200	'42 27.64	19.0	2000	88.0	200,000
			'43 40.22				
1944-45	500	1000	'44 42.35	23.0	2000	94.0	200,000
			'45 42.65				
1946-47	500	1000	'46 37.92	19.0	2000	86.45	200,000
			'47 41.58				
1948-49	600	1200	'48 36.41	16.6	2000	82.13	200,000
			'49 35.63				
1950	600	1200	'50 38.19	17.4	2000	84.36	200,000
1951	600	1200	'51 42.65	20.4	2000	91.0	200,000
1952-53	600	1200	'52 43.88	22.2	2000	92.0	200,000
			'53 45.22				
1954-63	600	1200	'60 48.06	20.0	2000	91.0	200,000
1964	600	1200		16.0	1000		
1965-70	600	1200	'65 53.70	14.0	1000	70	200,000

than $891 million in 1939 to $14.45 billion in 1943. But as the income tax was extended for the first time to millions of low income taxpayers, it became for the majority of taxpayers an ungraduated tax, since during the war over 60% of all taxpayers paid at the basic flat rate of 19 or 23%.

The basic formal structure of the federal personal income tax remained about the same from World War II until recently when rates have been slightly lowered and exemptions increased. Tax rates were reduced briefly in the late 1940's, but they were returned to war-time levels in 1951 and 1952, where they remained until 1964. In 1964 and 1965 rates were reduced somewhat for all income classes, and in 1971 a low income allowance further reduced rates on the lowest incomes.

Similarly in 1948 the personal exemption was increased slightly to $600 per person, where it remained until 1970, when it was increased to $625, and scheduled to increase yearly to $750 by 1973. But the formal stability of exemptions and tax rates from World War II to 1964, and even the seeming reduction of rates since then, obscure a critical change in the social significance of the federal income tax which has taken place in the post-war years.

Although the basic personal exemption remained fixed at $600 per person from 1948 to 1970, consistent, and since 1965, pronounced inflation during this period effectively extended income tax liability to all but the most destitute (and a few of the richest) individuals in American society. And although the formal rate schedule remained roughly constant from the war to 1964, and then was even reduced, inflation of incomes and prices has effectively raised the tax rates and increased the tax burden on most taxpayers. For with inflating incomes and prices, an individuals' rising dollar income reaches into higher and higher tax brackets even though his real income may remain constant, either relative to other people's incomes, or even absolutely, with respect to purchasing power and a standard of living. (For an example of what this means for a family of $3000 income, see Appendix I).

Only during World War II, when the federal income tax was greatly extended as we have discussed, did total federal taxes for the first time exceed total state and local taxes. The ratio of total federal taxes to total state and local taxes increased from about .625 in 1940 to about 1.44 in 1944, and up to 2.2 in 1950. But since 1950, state and local expenditures have increased much more rapidly than federal expenditures. Thus while total federal taxes increased by 129% from 1950 to 1966, state and local taxes increased by 176%. By 1966 the ratio of total federal taxes to total state and local taxes was back down to 1.83, and clearly this trend has continued in the last five years.

The significance of this change for the structure of taxation can only be appreciated by realizing that individual and corporate income taxes contribute only about 14% of total state and local taxes, while property and sales taxes contribute about 77% of total state and local taxes. And clearly this relative distribution is continuing, for between 1960-69, while six states adopted state income taxes, 10 states adopted state sales taxes.

In the late 1960's and early 1970's, state and local taxes have been increasing at about 14% annually. In 1970, total property tax amounted to $34 billion. On a nationwide average, property tax has increased from $48 per capita in 1950, to $91 per capita in 1960, to $126 per capita in 1966, to $140 per capita in 1968, to $160 per capita in 1970. In 1972, in several large cities and their suburbs, property tax will reach $300 per capita.

TAX GENERATED SOCIAL INEQUALITIES

In the period since World War II, the American state is creating tax classes through the system of taxation and expenditure. As taxes have been extended to larger numbers of taxpayers through the extension of the federal income tax, and through new and increased state and local taxes, and as the general level of all taxes has risen, the economic inequalities between social groups, that are inherent in the structure of each tax are multiplied. The result is that the tax structure as it has developed since World War II is a system of socially structured inequalities based on socially varying effective liability to taxation.

There are two general types of tax inequalities. The first type is the inequality between people of different incomes, in general between the relatively rich and the relatively poor. I call this type economic inequalities, because it is the type of tax inequality that economists have studied. Although this is the initially obvious type of inequality to look for in an economic system, I will try to explain why it is sociologically less significant than the second type.

The second type is the inequality between people of generally the same level of income. It has its origins in some of the more profound economic inequalities, but carries over into more sociologically significant inequalities among the relatively affluent. I call this type of inequality sociological inequalities, not because sociologists have studied it, but because sociologists ought to.

413

During the post-war years, liberal sociologists and economists made several assumptions about the growth of the middle class, the distribution of income, and the tax system in American society. In general they assumed that the middle class was growing because incomes were becoming more equally distributed within the populations. And they assumed that one factor in the equalization of incomes was the tax system which was dominated by the progressive federal income tax.

But in the 1960's, as substantial data became available about long-term trends in the distribution of wealth and income in the post-war period, it became clear that neither wealth nor income were becoming more equally distributed. This recognition contributed to two related developments. In general, sociologists, economists and other intellectuals were led to take a new look at the phenomenon of poverty, and at the poor, because if incomes were not becoming more equally distributed, then the gap between rich and poor was increasing. And specifically with respect to the tax system, considerable doubt was cast on the role of the tax system in contributing to the equalization of incomes, if in fact that equalization of incomes was not taking place.

Among the problems of the poor which economists began to take an interest in during the 1960's, was the problem of just what was the tax burden of the poor, and what was the relative tax burden of the poor compared to that of the more affluent. In other words, certain economists were led actually to investigate to what degree, if any, the tax system is really progressive.

Like the federal equivalents, state individual income tax is slightly progressive. But since state and local taxes consist overwhelmingly of property and sales taxes, both of which are steeply regressive, the overall burden of state and local taxes is clearly regressive over all income groups. In sum, as the following table shows, total federal, state and local taxes impose the heaviest average burden on the recipients of the lowest incomes, and on those in the "over $15,000" class.

TABLE 3

TAXES AS PERCENT OF INCOME, 1965

Income Classes	Federal	State and Local	Total
Under $2000	19	25	44
$2,000- 4000	16	11	27

4,000- 6000	17	10	27
6,000- 8000	17	9	26
8,000-10,000	18	9	27
10,000-15,000	19	9	27
15,000 and over	32	7	38
Total	22	9	31

Two comments should be made about the figures above for the tax burden of the very poor. First, the income figures exclude transfer payments from the government, which in the lowest income group exceed the amount paid in taxes, and thus significantly modify the total exchange between poor persons and the state. However, all poor persons do not receive transfer payments, and, as a UCLA economist has pointed out recently, not all the poor pay taxes; thus, the critical figure for assessing the tax burden on the poor would really be the tax burden on the poor who pay taxes.[1] Second, as we noted above, since state and local taxes are increasing much more rapidly than federal taxes, and since state and local taxes are highly regressive, the tax burden in 1972 is undoubtedly even more regressive than the figures above indicate for 1965.

Those who focus on economic inequalities correctly point to the inequity of our present tax system which taxes the very poor so severely. And the standard criticisms of the tax system are based on analysis of this type. Thus, for example, with respect to the income tax, it is often pointed out that the basic features of the tax rules give an advantage to the affluent, and the advantage is directly proportional to the level of taxable income.

The split income provision, according to which a couple's total income is split exactly in half between husband and wife so that in effect each will be in the lowest possible tax bracket, is advantageous only to those whose incomes fall above the basic tax rate, and it is more advantageous the higher the tax rate bracket. As Ferdinand Lundberg has calculated, under the current tax rules, while to have a wife saves a man with a taxable income of $8000 only $250; it saves a man with a taxable income of $20,000, $1690; a man with a taxable income of $50,000, $5,530; and a man with a taxable income of $100,000, $10,310.[2]

Similarly, deductions for homeowner's mortgage interest and taxes are advantageous only to those who own their own homes, and are advantageous in proportion to income, since a man in the 20% bracket saves 20% of his interest and taxes, while a man in the 50% bracket saves 50%.

The same principle applies to nearly every form of tax deduction. *Deductions apply only to those who itemize them, and their value is directly proportional to a taxpayer's taxable income.* Thus while the provisions of the income tax effectively mitigate its impact on the affluent for whom it is the major tax, no similar provisions mitigate the impact of state and local sales and property taxes on the poor for whom these taxes are the major source of being taxes. But while the economists' analyses of the structure of taxation in the United States allow us to judge the relative equity of the tax structure vis a vis the poor, the struggling, and the modestly affluent, their conclusions have only negative significance for the sociology of taxation. We are able to say only that taxation is not consistently progressive, and that low and moderate income groups who oppose the present structure of taxation are not necessarily irrational.

There is little sociological significance in economists' analyses for two reasons. First, because economists wish to make the most systematic possible use of their data, they are constrained to limit their independent variable to dollar income alone. Although they wish to analyze the absolute and relative tax burden of the rich and the poor, they are constrained to identify the relevant groups for comparison as "income classes." All American society is divided into those families and individuals with incomes "under $2,000," "$2,000-4,000," and so on up to "over $15,000." Thus in spite of the thoughtful consideration given to the optimal definition and measures of economic categories such as "income," and "tax burden," their conclusions are largely irrelevant to the sociology of taxation. For the concept of "income class" according to which they identify social groups, obscures every social variable except money income, and as a result, corresponds to no real social divisions in American society. Further, the *gross* statistical methods on which economists depend require that they lump together as one group, "over $15,000," several of the critical contending groups that I believe are created by the process of taxation. And finally, *at every income level, the basic statistical techniques of determining* <u>*average*</u> *tax rates, completely obscures the equally interesting fact of unequal taxation of individuals with approximately equal incomes.*

"BEING TAXED" - "PAYING TAXES"

The second reason that economists' analyses of relative tax burdens are not relevant to a sociology of taxation is that the relative tax burdens of the rich and poor is not really a salient issue in the formation of self-conscious, hence potentially political, groups. Taxation is not a significant issue to the poor not only because most complex issues are not significant to the poor, but also because the process of "being taxed" is very different for the poor, and much less politically arousing, than is the process of "paying taxes" for the more affluent.

By this I mean that the taxes which most effect the poor and the struggling, such as sales tax, property tax shifted to them in the form of added rent, utility tax, social security, and even federal income tax which is entirely withheld from wages, are more or less concealed taxes added onto normal expenditures at the point of payment, or subtracted from earnings before earnings are disbursed. These taxes are collected bit by bit, day by day. But even more important, with the exception of the federal income tax withheld, and here too, for the very poor who may not even file a tax return, these taxes are continuously collected, but remain *forever untotalled*. And for those low income individuals who do file federal income tax returns, complete withholding, the short form and the standard deductions make the tax paying process simple and *socially unobtrusive*.

In contrast, the taxes which most affect the modestly affluent and wealthier, have precisely the opposite character. Property tax levied on the property owner, even if impounded with mortgage payments, and federal and state income taxes, even when withheld, are annually totalled up and brought to the center of the taxpayer's consciousness. And for these taxpayers, the need to use the longer income tax form, and to itemize deductions, and the attendant tension involved in whittling away as much as possible from taxable income, make the filing of federal and state income tax complicated and *socially intrusive*.

In addition, many of the more affluent taxpayers are in part or altogether outside of the withholding system. These individuals must pay property taxes semi-annually, and federal and state income taxes by quarterly estimates, all of the funds for which must be withdrawn from income already received and in the possession of the taxpayer. And for individuals who run their own or other's corporations, federal corporation tax is paid in two lump sum payments in the year after the end of the tax year. For these reasons, the *social process of "paying taxes" for the relatively affluent is very different from the social process of "being taxed" for the relatively poor*.

TAXATION AS A SOCIAL ISSUE

But it is not only the different social processes of being taxed and paying taxes that set the moderately affluent apart from the poor with respect to their relation to the tax system. Among the relatively affluent there is a further distinction. For those whose income comes only in the form of a regular weekly or monthly salary or wage, although the process of paying taxes may be socially intrusive, very little control is possible over the general level of taxes they pay. But for those whose occupation consists of making choices, either in business activities or investments, the tax system, with its "tax consequences," is a critical variable in their daily economic lives.

In fact it is possible to conceptualize the *tax system as a vast and pervasive motivational system*, allocating rewards and penalties for different kinds of economic activities, in the context of which most significant economic choices are weighed. Thus on the basis of the differing social relations the poor and the more affluent have to the tax system, I would argue that even though the poor may pay a higher portion of their income in taxes, it is only among the modestly affluent and wealthier that taxation becomes a significant social issue and a potential basis for political group formation.

SOCIOLOGICAL INEQUALITIES - TAX STRATIFICA-TION

In contrast to economic inequalities between rich and poor, there are also inequalities between taxpayers with approximately the same income. It is these inequalities which I call sociological inequalities. Since these inequalities occur most significantly among those groups for whom taxation is a socially and politically significant issue, I believe these inequalities are fundamental to a sociology of taxation. It should be clear, however, from the summary above, that sociological inequalities cannot easily be studied through economic analyses. Further, although I would like to study at first hand the actual process either of "being taxed" or of "paying taxes," among different groups and different types of business, neither I nor any other sociologist to my knowledge has yet done this.

Consequently we are obliged to fall back on the method of analyzing the logical possibilities of particular taxes, in order to identify the principal sources of variation in the incidence of the tax. In the following discussion I want to make this preliminary analysis of two particular taxes, the federal income tax, and the local property tax, and in each case to identify the source of sociological inequalities from which tax stratification arises.

The federal income tax, and to a lesser degree state income taxes modelled on its provisions, impose varying tax burdens on groups occupying different structural positions in the American social economy. The basis for this variation is that the *income tax does not tax wealth, but rather income, and it taxes income derived from wealth or property differently than it taxes income derived from work.* The basic process by which income from wealth or property is taxed less severely than income from work, is the process according to which current income is deferred in the form of appreciation which can subsequently be retrieved at an opportune time in the form of capital gains which are taxed at one-half the rate of ordinary income.

Property consists basically of real estate and capital goods on one hand and corporate stock on the other, and for each the process of deferring current income and converting it to capital gains takes a slightly different form. For real estate and capital goods the process is accomplished first by allowing deductions against current income for all expenses of holding the property such as interest and fees on loans, property taxes, insurance, repairs, management, etc., and second, by allowing the deduction of depreciation, not of land, but of buildings and capital assets, as an expense, even when the property in question is actually appreciating in value. Additionally, deferred income built up in the form of equity can be transferred from one piece of real estate to another by trading rather than selling, thereby postponing indefinitely any tax on the deferred income. But, although the income is deferred, it need not be unavailable, because one can borrow against the deferred income without paying taxes on the income realized. And the interest paid on the borrowed funds is fully tax deductible against any income the borrowed funds may generate.

For property in the form of corporate stock, current income is deferred for future realization as capital gains because most corporations pay out in dividends only about one-half of current earnings. The retained earnings remain in the corporation, build its assets, provide it with funds for further investment, and therefore raise the value of the corporation's stock. In addition, the owner of corporate stock also ultimately has current income deferred to the usually significant extent that the corporation, as an owner of real estate and capital goods, defers current income through the process outlined in the paragraph above. And just as the holder of real estate equities may use his income, even though it is "deferred," the owner of appreciated corporate stock may borrow against the stock without realizing any taxable income, and the interest is tax deductible against any income the borrowed funds may generate.

However, not only can income from property be deferred in the form of appreciation and then realized as capital gains, but also, under varying post-war tax rules, those with sufficient wealth in the form of depreciable assets, such as buildings and equipment, are able to convert on paper large portions of current income beyond their direct income, from the property being depreciated, to capital gains which will be taxed only at some future date. And they can do this without actually changing their flow of disposable income.

The basic mechanisms for this conversion are the investment credit and depreciation. Investment credit, which is put into effect from time to time "to stimulate investment," allows the purchaser of a capital asset to deduct a portion of the capital expenditure directly from his tax in the year of the investment. Excess credits may be carried forward (or back) to other years. Depreciation allows owners of capital assets to deduct a certain fraction of the value of the asset from current taxable income each year over a specified "life" of the asset.*

The critical point is that the investment credit and rapid depreciation allow owners of capital assets , in proportion to the value of the eligible assets they own, to write off against current income much more than simply the income produced by the assets themselves.** To be sure, whatever is written off in credits or depreciation reduces the owner's "cost basis" in the asset, so that when the asset is sold, tax must be paid on the difference between the resulting "cost basis" and the selling price. But that tax, when it is paid, will be largely at capital gains rates.

Thus, current income is converted to capital gains and the tax is postponed several years. In a situation in which the individual's or corporation's holdings of depreciable assets is growing, the process of deferring current income from taxation can be effectively limitless. But in any case, in the financial world in which wealthy individual investors and corporations operate, in which cash flow is critical, to postpone taxes for several years, and thus to have the use of the cash flow for several years, is equivalent to having the money, for in several years the money deferred from taxes reproduces itself.

THE WEALTHY'S FORMULATION OF TAX ADVANTAGE

Clearly, the basic features of the federal income tax were not created by chance. That the federal government should primarily tax income rather than wealth, and that within the structure of the income tax such substantial advantages should be given to those who possess property, are so clearly in the interests of the very wealthy in American society that it would be naive to assume that the very wealthy or their representatives have not played a critical role in the initial construction and subsequent modification of the federal tax system. Thus my research hypothesis with respect to the historical development of the income tax is that representatives of the very rich in American society played a critical role in the formulation of the federal tax laws, and have since played a critical role in modifications of the tax law through their piece meal struggles to protect the wealth of the very wealthy and to deflect the state's search for additional revenue onto other sectors of society which are less well represented in the political system.

One persuasive item of indirect evidence for this hypothesis is the remarkable degree to which the same families which were the wealthiest families in the United States in the early years of this century, before the income tax, remain the very wealthiest families in the United States today. In fact the remarkable stability of the American elite from the end of the 19th century to today suggests the degree to which representatives of this elite have succeeded in controlling the consequences of the tax system for their own ends.

TAX STRATIFICATION: THE FINANCIAL ELITE

But even though the purpose of certain basic provisions of the federal income tax laws may be to protect the wealth of the very wealthy, and even though these provisions may in fact accomplish that purpose well, protecting the wealth of the very wealthy does not in fact exhaust their consequences. For, no matter with what self-interest particular tax measures have been promoted, once they have been enacted as law or administrative regulation, most are at least theoretically available to all.

As a result, the provisions written into the tax laws to aid the very wealthy, not only do that, but also give rise to an entire set of secondary consequences which are of great interest for a sociology of taxation. For example, if the mechanism of deferring income in property discussed above, allows the very wealthy to significantly limit their liability to taxation, that same mechanism allows some of the simply affluent, who could never have legislated their own tax loophole, to limit their liability to taxation, too.

But since the access to provisions of the tax laws by which one's liability to taxation is limited depends on having certain sources of income and a certain arrangement of assets, these provisions, although theoretically available to all, are in practice differently accessible to different groups in American society. *And it is on the basis of this differential access to the means in the tax laws of limiting tax liability, that the process of stratification through the tax system is going on.* I refer to the differential incidence of the federal income tax as a process of stratification because on the basis of the tax system, otherwise similar individuals with similar amounts of real income are subjected to quite different rates of effective taxation on the basis of the nature and source of their income and their "tax intelligence." Although presently the degree of tax class consciousness varies, it seems appropriate to conceive of differentially taxed groups as tax classes, because the process of tax stratification has significant objective economic consequences.

It is not necessarily that the amount of differential in any one year be large, even though it can easily amount to 10 to 25% of an individual's total yearly income. Since the process of income taxation is an absolutely continuous process, to which the total income flow of a moderately affluent individual is subjected, the consequences of the process of differential taxation are continuously compounded. Especially among moderately affluent groups in which families have enough income to avoid consumer debt, and possibly to accumulate a little wealth, differential taxation over a period of years can make the difference between some wealth and none at all. And under certain conditions, the accumulation of wealth facilitates the further limitation of tax liability. Thus stratification on the basis of access to the means of limiting tax liability is a continuous process with permanent, cumulative, and compounding economic consequences.

The basic process of paying income tax involves paying a percentage, based on a graduated table of rates, of the difference between an individual's gross income, adjusted for some of the expenses, if any, involved in making that income, and the deductions allowed against that income. For those few or no deductions, a standard deduction of a percentage of adjusted gross income is allowed. In the post war years, up through 1970, that percentage was 10% of adjusted gross income up to a maximum for a married couple, of $1000. (By 1972, it will have been increased to 15% up to a maximum of $2000). Thus without access to any other means of limiting tax liability, a married couple has been protected from the full impact of the theoretical tax rates only to the very modest extent of 10% of their income, and only up to the cut-off point of an adjusted gross income of $10,000. And since, between 1954 and 1963, the federal income tax rate on taxable income between $8,000 and $10,000 was 26% for a married couple and 34% for a single individual, (since 1965 the rates are 22% and 25% respectively), the economic consequences of access to means of limiting tax liability are substantial.

And these consequences have come to affect increasing numbers of people. For if in 1950, much less than 10% of all families had adjusted gross incomes of more than $10,000, by 1970, possibly as many as 25% of all families had adjusted gross incomes above $10,000. Thus, during the post war years, as the tax structure has remained roughly fixed, with rates reduced only a little, but as typical incomes have risen into higher and higher tax brackets, *increasing numbers of moderately affluent taxpayers are becoming subject to the process of tax stratification on the basis of their differential access to the means of limiting tax liability.*

For all taxpayers, but especially for the approximately 25% of families with gross incomes exceeding $10,000, effective liability to taxation depends on the relation of the taxpayer to a complex set of structural conditions. On the one hand, one can specify certain conditions under which individuals are able to use the provisions of the tax laws favoring property. The general condition is having a primary or secondary occupation that involves investing capital for profits rather than working for a wage or salary. But that clearly depends on having a certain level of freely disposable income, having leverage or credit, having financial sophistication adequate to calculate the tax advantages, having access to tax favored investments, and having interest and skill sufficient to manage the investments satisfactorily. And these conditions are interrelated. Under certain conditions of knowledge and access, the amount of disposable income and credit necessary to "work" the tax system varies. I believe, however, that it really requires first hand, comparative observation to generalize about which groups among the less than very rich, have the greatest access to tax advantages, and under exactly what conditions they have that access.

On the other hand, it is possible to point to two general groups who without special knowledge and planning do not in the normal course of their economic lives have much access to tax advantages. To be sure, these are large groups, into one of which the majority of middle and upper class taxpayers fall. It is for these groups, almost exclusively, for whom the theoretical progressive tax rates actually apply.

The first are independent business and professional men, who while they may own the property on which their business is located, derive most of their income from their own efforts, and thus realize a high income relative to their capital investment. Such individuals, until they reach the scale at which, if they are permitted, they can incorporate, have very little opportunity to defer income from taxation. Instead of retaining earnings to be realized later as capital gains, independent business and professional men must receive all their net business income as personal income in the year in which they earn it. Thus for them, a high income year is invariably an even higher tax year. The second are the rapidly growing numbers of bureaucratic employees, from skilled labor to administration, who are steadily employed, and who earn all their income in the form of wages or salary from which federal income tax is fully withheld.

There are three cross-cutting conditions that under certain circumstances limit the effective tax liability of certain individuals within each group. The first is simply that to the extent that individuals in either of these circumstances have sufficiently high incomes and sufficiently large amounts of disposable funds to make tax favored investments, and to the extent that they have the knowledge or advice to do so, they can limit their liability to taxation to a certain degree. It is this condition under which independent businessmen, doctors, lawyers, and corporation executives, but also less highly paid employees such as government functionaries and college professors, acquire real estate, which provides deferred income in the form of appreciation and a current tax write-off in the form of depreciation.

Since these individuals are principally occupied in other professions or employments, their tax oriented investments must have a certain character. And in fact in the post-war years an entire "industry" and category of occupations has grown up consisting of individuals who arrange and manage such "tax-planning" investments. The proliferation in the 1960's of real estate syndicates, and most recently of "real estate trusts" which operate like mutual funds for investing in real estate, indicate the degree to which as incomes rise through the tax structure, increasing numbers of relatively unsophisticated individuals are being compelled to invest in real estate, as the most easily accessible means of limiting their tax liability.

The second cross-cutting condition is that among independent business and professional men, tax liability can be limited by failing to report certain amounts of income. According to Melvin J. Ulmer, an IRS survey in the summer of 1970 discovered that

> Of 300 doctors whose returns were examined, it was found that about half had failed to report a "substantial amount of their income," especially Medicare and Medicaid payments. In some instances the "omission exceeded $100,000."[3]

The magnitude of the difference in effective taxation between independent business and professional men and those who receive income in the form of wages and salary which is fully subject to withholding, is suggested by the results of an earlier study which showed that income from sources other than salaries and wages is underreported for tax purposes by one-third.[4]

This conclusion is based on a comparison of the income individuals report on confidential surveys by the Census Bureau and the Commerce Department with the income they report for taxes, but the figure of one-third does not represent entirely concealed income because it includes legal as well as illegal exclusions. To a certain extent the tendency of independent business and professional men to avoid taxation by underreporting income is not altogether a property of the tax system; it is rather an indication of the degree to which economic activity even in the United States is not fully rationalized and subjected to complete accounting. And on the other end of the income spectrum there is a corresponding degree of income from part-time labor that is unreported and untaxed. But it is the theoretically high progressive rates of taxation to which these relatively high income individuals with few other means of limiting their tax liability are uniquely subjected, that motivates these individuals, who have the opportunity, to conceal significant amounts of income.

The third cross cutting condition with respect to which certain individuals in the group that receives relatively high incomes exclusively in the form of wages or salary limit their liability to taxation, is the opportunity to make use of the provision according to which corporations can deduct from their corporate taxable income any "ordinary and necessary business expense."*

Whatever income an employee receives in the form wages or salary, is taxable to the employee, but most income an employee receives in the form of business expense, is not taxable to the employee. Of course, at the highest levels of corporate employment, non-salary compensation may well constitute the major part of an employee's actual long-term income, for this is effectively what stock options and pension plans are. In addition, corporate owned airplanes, boats, vacation homes, and corporate subsidized club memberships, contribute to non-salary compensation. But at less exalted levels of corporate employment, certain employees are able to combine much of their traveling, eating in restaurants, entertainment and party-giving with some form of business activity. And the process of compensation in the form of subsidized business expenses extends well down into the corporate ranks of executives and salesmen. While the amounts involve are often relatively small compared to the amounts for top executives, an additional $2,000 to $5,000 of tax-free subsidized living and entertainment expenses for a man earning $12,000 to $30,000 a significantly sets him apart in effective taxation from a skilled worker or technician earning straight salary, or a bureaucrat or administrator employed by a non-profit or public agency at the same level of pay.**

LOCAL TAXATION

In addition to the federal income tax, the local property tax also has stratifying consequences. For the purposes of this discussion, I disregard renters, who although they may be heavily burdened by property tax shifted to them, seldom really make the connection between the rent they pay and the property tax. Ironically, although the property tax is one of the few taxes on wealth, it bears overwhelmingly on those whose only wealth is their homes. And since it taxes a form of illiquid wealth, it bears no necessary relation to ability to pay.

In order to understand the property tax, we must come to some conclusion about evaluating its burden. While it would seem obvious to relate the amount of property tax to the value of a home, this is not necessarily correct, because the critical value of the home over which the taxpayer has control is the value at the time of purchase. Subsequent increases in value require no increase in the installment payment, and bring no income until the property is sold, and yet they result in higher property taxes. For this reason, C. Lowell Harris, a Columbia University expert on the property tax, argues that a homebuyer capitalizes in the purchase price of the home the present level of property taxation at the time of purchase, and that therefore the appropriate measure of the relative burden of property tax on a taxpayer is the amount of increased taxation to which the homeowner is subjected after the purchase of his home. If we accept that reasoning, certain consequences follow.

First, because in the post-war years, property values have risen and property taxes have risen even more, the burden of the property tax is more severe on those whose incomes are not rising. For although the property tax may be apportioned roughly on the basis of ability to pay at the point of initial purchase, it only remains equitably apportioned for those individuals whose incomes continue to rise as rapidly as their home appreciates.

Second, the burden of the property tax is more severe on those who have owned their present home for longer periods of time. This group includes those whose incomes are not rising, such as the elderly and the less affluent who are steadily employed in one location. For among homeowners, the more affluent tend to be more mobile, thus higher income individuals who do move frequently are able to capitalize anew the present level of property taxation with each move.

Finally the burden of the property tax is more severe on those who do not itemize their deductions for federal and state income tax, because property tax paid is deductible for those who do itemize their deductions. Not only do higher income individuals more frequently itemize their deductions, also within the groups of those who do itemize, the higher the taxable income of the property taxpayer, the lower the proportion of effective tax to theoretical tax, because an individual in the 20% federal income tax bracket pays in effect 80% of his nominal property tax, while the individual in the 42% bracket pays in effect only 58% of his nominal property tax.

Clearly these conditions of property tax stratification are not independent. The categories of older people, people who have resided in the same house for longer times, people with lower incomes, people who do not itemize deductions on federal tax returns, and people whose incomes are not rising as rapidly as property values, are to a high degree, mutually inclusive categories.

But one critical question from the point of view of this essay is in what ways and to what degree do the stratifying processes of the federal income tax and local property tax overlap. The groups which benefit most from the federal income tax, such as the very wealthy, and the simply affluent who invest in real estate and capital assets in order to use the tax advantages of the very wealthy, are clearly also the ones who are least burdened by the local property tax. Independent business and professional men, and bureaucratic employees who receive all their income in the form of salary or wages, the groups on whom the federal income tax is most burdensome, are, to the extent that they have high incomes relatively less burdened by the property tax. The more recently and more modestly affluent, such as skilled laborers and various middle-level white collar employees, whose total family incomes are approaching or have recently exceeded the $10,000 cut-off point for the standard deduction, but whose incomes are not increasing as rapidly as their homes are appreciating and the property tax increasing, are broadly speaking the type of individuals who increasingly are becoming relatively burdened with respect to both the federal income tax and local property tax. Finally the elderly, and other whose incomes are not increasing at all, and may actually be decreasing, are relatively more burdened by the property tax than the federal income tax.

TAX POLITICS

The foregoing analysis of the potential stratifying consequences of the federal income tax and the local property tax suggests several types of persons which would be most likely to oppose the present structure of one or both taxes, and to be in conflict with other groups over taxation. And while it is beyond the scope of this essay to present an extended explanation of several political movements in terms of tax stratification, I would like to point out the degree to which the preliminary analysis I have presented is consistent with what we know about several post-war political movements.

Since World War II, there have been three periods of intense tax politics, the early 1950's, the early 1960's, and the late 1960's and early 1970's. In the early 1950's and early 1960's, tax politics were focused primarily on the federal income tax, and were bound up with right wing movements. By the 1970's tax politics involve a complex set of issues related to all levels of taxation, but especially property tax.

Right wing movements in the post-war years have been at least symbolically concerned primarily with "Communism," but what has confounded students of these movements is that right wing anti-communists seem to be overwhelmingly concerned with internal communism, within the United States. But what is meant by "internal communism?" As more lucid right wing commentators point out, when they speak of communism they mean to pierce the liberal rhetoric surrounding what they regard as genuinely socialist institutions, of which the principal examples are the welfare state and the income tax which makes it possible. Consequently one of the few substantial political initiatives that bound right wing groups together in some semblance of a program in the 1950's and even into the early 1960's was the campaign for the adoption of the "Liberty Amendment," which would repeal the 16th amendment authorizing the federal income tax.

Although it is perhaps incorrect to characterize McCarthyism as a movement, we can regard McCarthy as an organizing symbol around which a great deal of political resentment was expressed. Simply to indicate the way in which McCarthyism is related to tax politics, let me cite one major observation by three students of McCarthyism. Martin Trow, in this study of McCarthyism in Bennington, Vermont, found that, in Bennington anyway, independent businessmen, of all occupational categories, were most likely to support McCarthy. But also, Trow found that among small businessmen and others, what he identified as "nineteenth century liberals," those who were opposed both to large corporations and to labor unions were most likely to support McCarthy. He argued that McCarthy appealed to individuals who opposed the concentration of power in the liberal welfare state, as represented both by large corporations and labor unions. This argument has often been cited in support of the thesis that support for McCarthy and other right wing movements in times of prosperity reflects the economically "irrational" status conflicts of older declining status groups with newer aggrandizing groups, rather than real economic conflicts. By my analysis of the stratifying consequences of the federal income tax, independent businessmen, for whom the theoretical progressive tax rates tend actually to apply, were by the early 1950's in tax class conflict with large corporations and the (Eastern) corporate elite over the funding of the welfare state. And they were in a similar tax class conflict with organized labor over what the content of the welfare state would be. Only the real economic conflict over federal income taxation makes sense of Republican businessmen's political hostility directed against both large corporations and the welfare state.

S.M. Lipset, in his essay in the 1962 edition of *The Radical Right*, argues on the basis of a large compilation of survey data on McCarthyism that while in general, favorable response to McCarthy is associated with membership in the Republican party, and with lower-socio-economic status, nevertheless, especially among Republicans within any given occupational or educational group, higher socio-economic status ("a measure of the style of life of the respondent, largely reflecting income") is associated with favorable response to McCarthy. If we translate that finding into the terms of our analysis of tax stratification, it means that especially among Republicans, among individuals with the same level of education or the same job, a higher income and a resulting higher tax bracket, are associated with favorable response to McCarthy.

Finally Michael Rogin, in his recent analysis of McCarthyism, lays great stress on the real significance of the Korean war and the objective concern about Communism in foreign relations as an important determinant of general support for McCarthy. But Rogin makes the very important distinction between political leaders who supported McCarthy and non-political respondents to surveys who simply indicated a degree of favorable or unfavorable response. With respect to leaders who actively supported McCarthy, Rogin argues that they are distinguished by being very active local Republican leaders. My research hypothesis is that these local Republican leaders were drawn from two groups which were relatively oppressed by post-war taxes. One group would be only moderately prosperous business and professional men and their wives. The other group would be more wealthy local elites. But to the extend that the local Republican leaders who supported McCarthy represented substantial wealth, it was new wealth. As Rogin points out, of the 17 wealthy leaders of the Committee of 10 Million, only 2 had inherited their wealth. But the point is not that these local leaders suffered from status insecurities; rather, either moderately affluent, or trying to accumulate wealth under the wartime and post-war income tax, these local Republican leaders were in tax class conflict with the inherited (pre-income tax) family and corporate wealth of the Eastern Republican elite. And they had every reason to oppose this Republican elite, because it was not only acquiescing in but also actively promoting the post-war system of taxation and expenditure of the American state.

The John Birch Society, and the right-wing "anti-communism" it stood for in the early 1960's, represented a similar anti-welfare state, anti-large corporation position that is consistent with the tax politics of independent businessmen and professionals. And in fact, as S.M. Lipset points out in his essay written in 1962, the Birch Society "upholds an economic program promoting the interests and values of the small stratum of moderately well-to-do businessmen and professionals." In an analysis taken from the California Poll in 1962, Lipset found that

> Basically the Birch Society appeals most to well-to-do Republicans, and somewhat more to the Catholics among them than to the Protestants. These findings suggest that the Society's appeal is most effective among those to whom economic conservatism and fear of Communism are crucial issues.[5]

Lipset points out that in general in the United States, tolerance for civil liberties is associated with greater education. Thus it is understandable that among Democrats opposition to the Birch Society increased with increasing education. What is interesting from our points of view, however, is that among Republicans, favorable response to the Birch Society increased with increasing socio-economic status and education. Lipset also points out that among those who feared communism, those whose greatest fear of communism was directed to internal communism were the strongest supporters of the Birch Society. I have tried to suggest that such a fear is closely related to perceptions of the welfare state and the income tax which supports it. And it is interesting to note that in a footnote, in which Lipset means to suggest simply the relatively high, if newly acquired status level of Birch Society supporters, Lipset quotes a study of Congressional mail which compared the letters received by Senator Fulbright in response to his attacks on McCarthy, to the letters received by Senator Kuchel in response to is attacks on the Birth Society. The study concludes:

> Birch mail is much more moderate in tone than McCarthy mail, even though it may be as extremist in objective. It is better written and better reasoned.... The great bulk of the mail came from people who acknowledged membership in the Birth Society or from sympathizers.... Many of the writers seem genuinely concerned over the rise of Communism.... But many of them seem *more aroused mover social-welfare legislation, income taxes, and foreign aid* than they are over Communism. (my emphasis)[6]

In 1962, Lipset was still trying to find status discrepancies to explain the phenomenon of support for the Birch Society. Now while clearly there are other social determinants such as social class, educational background, and occupational community, involved in the process according to which a relatively well-to-do business or professional man, or his wife, pressed to actually pay the theoretically high progressive tax rates, while large corporations and the corporate elite manage to limit their liability, becomes either an advocate of income tax reform, or of income tax repeal. But to deny the significant role of actual tax stratification in this process implies a serious ignorance of the sociology of taxation.

But what is even more interesting about these two instances of extreme radical right activity, is the timing of the most severe activity. For, the extremes of radical right activity correspond to the two times during the post-war period during which the income tax was most burdensome to moderately affluent taxpayers. The timing of McCarthyism and the changes in the income tax are probably both due to another event of the time, the Korean war. Nevertheless it is worth pointing out that as shown previously in Chart 2, income tax rates were raised three years in a row, in 1951, 1952, and in 1953, finally reaching virtually to the level of 1944-45. (They were slightly lowered for 1954, to the level at which they remained until 1964). It seems to me that McCarthyism arose at the critical juncture in the history of the American state, where it became clear that even though the Korean War was over, the American state and the levels of taxation that made it possible were going to remain in the form created during World War II.

The Korean War is the first war in this century after which taxes were not reduced substantially. After World War I, taxes were reduced sharply, and after World War II, taxes were reduced substantially for a few years. Following the Korean War, taxes remained at war-time levels. For older businessmen and professionals, whose incomes rose fastest following World War II, it must have been shocking to confront a national tax system that required them to pay in federal income taxes an amount easily equal to their total income in a year before World War II. For in fact, in the early 1950's, an older couple with no remaining dependents might easily have paid a tax of $3000 on an income of $15,000.

RIGHT WING AND TAX DISCRIMINATION

Similarly, the early 1960's, the years in which the John Birch Society and other right wing organizations most recently flourished, or at least attracted the greatest attention, was the period during which the federal income tax imposed the greatest burdens on moderately affluent taxpayers. For the rate structure put into effect in 1954, which was only slightly below 1944-45 levels, had by the early 1960's become truly oppressive to moderate income families with no special means of limiting tax liability. As both prosperity and inflation pushed the incomes of businessmen (and also the wages of skilled labor and the salaries of bureaucratic employees) higher and higher, these types of individuals became liable to taxation at rates that were intended for the considerably more well-to-do at the time the rates were set in the early 1950's.

For example, taking an income of twice the median family income as a hypothetical typical income of a moderately affluent family, between 1950 and 1963, this family's income would have increased from $6,638 to about $12,800 ($13,138 in 1965). And if we assume a family of four, which claims the standard deduction, we get the following effective income tax rates for a moderately affluent family: In 1950, when twice the median income was $6,638, a family of four earning this amount paid $622, or 9.4% of their total income, and paid at the rate of 17.4% on the next few hundred additional dollars of income. In 1954, when twice the median income was $7,000, a family of four earning this amount paid $780, or 11.3% of their total income, and paid at the rate of 20% on their next few hundred dollars of income. But by 1963, when twice the median income was $12,800, a family of four paid $2,044, or 16% of their total income, and paid at the rate of 26% of their next few hundred dollars of income. Thus between 1954 and 1963, when the formal rates remained constant, the effective tax rate (the percentage of total income paid in federal income tax) on a family of four earning twice the median income, increased by 42%!

While 16% of total income is not in itself an intolerable burden of taxation, it must be borne in mind that the federal income tax is only one among several taxes, including local sales and property taxes which were increasing during this period. But for both 1964 and 1965, federal income tax rates were reduced, so that by 1965, a family of four earning twice the median income for that year, an income of $13,138, paid $1571 in federal income tax, a figure representing 12% of their total income. As one would expect, in the middle of the 1960's radical right politics on a national level, and moderately affluent opposition to the federal income tax dropped off, or at least faded from public attention.

DIFFUSE TAX OPPRESSION

Recently opposition to taxation has become more general and diffuse in American society. One reason is that by 1970, perhaps as many as 25% of American families had income in excess of $10,000, the level at which the standard deduction cuts off. And as more and more bureaucratic employees, whose only significant means of limiting their liability to taxation is either the standard deduction or the deduction of their home mortgage interest and property tax, increasingly receive incomes in higher and higher tax brackets, the bulk of those non-poor who are relatively oppressed by taxes has shifted from independent business and professional men to the larger numbers of wage and salary employees.

Several consequences can be traced back to this shift in the character of the groups relatively oppressed by taxation. First, there has been a tremendous proliferation of tax preparing services. These services attempt to use the provisions of the tax laws to limit the taxation of individuals whose income and assets do not really fit the categories of the tax laws. Thus their basic recourse is to fabricate itemized deductions. Recently in California, when several hundred tax preparers were investigated, about one-half were found to be preparing fraudulent returns.

The phenomenon of tax preparing services seems to indicate two things: First the degree to which relatively unsophisticated individuals in American society have been propelled into progressive tax brackets from which they can be protected only by illegitimate deductions; and second, the degree to which these individuals are sufficiently conscious of the process of paying taxes that they will spend considerable money trying to save a little more.

Recent changes in the tax laws clearly have been designed to deal with the problem of the sizeable numbers of taxpayers who have been converted by inflation from the category of being taxed, to the category of paying taxes. Personal exemptions were raised in 1970, 1971, and 1972. And the standard deduction was increased from its previous level of 10% up to $1,000, to 13% up to $1,500 in 1971, and finally to 15% up to $2,000 in 1972. This change, which extends the standard deduction up to 15% of an income of $13,333.00, besides giving a small tax break to moderately affluent taxpayers who do not own their own homes (in the range of $8,000 to $13,300), performs the critical function of cutting probably in half the number of families whose gross income is beyond the limits of the standard deduction.

TAX STRATIFICATION: GROUPS

The process of stratification on the basis of the federal income tax thus reached a temporary peak in the early 1950's, in the early 1960's, and at the end of the 1960's. Recently steps have been taken to alleviate, somewhat, if not the worst of the inequalities, at least those aspects of the tax system that create the greatest consciousness of oppressiveness. Nevertheless, tax stratification is an ongoing process, but one for which the level of consciousness varies according to certain conditions. One of the reasons for this is that the stratified groups are often quite remote, and only in an indirect economic relation which is mediated by the state. Thus much of tax politics up to this time has taken the form of opposition to taxation *per se*, and only secondarily opposition to other groups less burdened by taxation.

As the present character of the modern state comes more and more to be seen as permanent and unalterable, it seems clear that the conflict over taxation will come to be seen as it really is, that is, a conflict between different groups over their relative contributions to the state budget. Heretofore, however, it has often been easier to see the relation between taxpayers and certain tax receivers, such as public employees, or welfare recipients, then it is to see the relation between one group of taxpayers and another. None of these reservations exist on the level of local taxes, however, where the privileged and disprivileged usually coexist within the same community. This is clearly one reason why presently the strongest opposition to taxation, although it often is an opposition to both income and property taxes, seems to exist on the local level.

As we have noted, the property tax imposes relatively greater burdens on those whose home is their only investment, whose incomes are not rising as rapidly as property values and the property tax, who live in one place for a long time, and who do not have a high income. What is particularly striking is that it would seem that the federal income tax and the local property tax are tending to impose the greatest burdens on the same groups of people. For as the bulk of urban home owners, through inflation, come to have incomes which fall into progressive tax brackets from which they have no means of limiting their liability except home ownership, then the two groups tend to become the same.

Unfortunately, little empirical research has been done on the opposition to the property tax. Impressionistic evidence from the current Democratic primary election campaigns suggests that Democratic candidates believe the same middle income groups feel themselves pressed both by income and property tax. And although the press interprets the tax positions of the various Democratic candidates as conservative concessions to George Wallace's following, the press has simply failed to appreciate the degree to which tax stratification is creating an oppressed class as surely as mortgage lending created a debtor class among farmers in the late 19th century.

Further impressionistic evidence from local politics in San Francisco suggests that the groups who are most strongly opposed to local property taxes are also the groups who are most strongly opposed to school bussing. It is interesting to note that this is at least plausible on the grounds that nationwide (in 1960), while about 64% of white families own their own home, only about 38% of black families own their own home. Thus the property tax is predominantly a white issue. And further it seems that it is lower income home owners who are both relatively oppressed by property tax and most threatened by blacks in their neighborhood schools.

These statements, however, are simply hypotheses for research. The relation between the politics of federal taxes and the politics of local taxes, and the relation between opponents of property tax and school financing and opponents of school bussing are questions, on a local level, that a political sociology of the modern state, informed by a sociology of taxation, might deal with.

TAX BASIS OF STRATIFICATION

In this essay, I have argued that one important element of a sociology of the modern state is a sociology of taxation. And I have tried to outline some preliminary aspects of a sociology of taxation, arguing along the way that the process of taxation in the United States can be understood as a relatively autonomous process of economic stratification. As a concluding remark, I would like to indicate the relation I see between the analysis I have presented here and the historical development of social fact and sociological theory. In his discussion of economic stratification, Max Weber outlines an historical theory of the changing bases of economic stratification from ancient times to the present. Although he qualifies his historical generalization with the observation that at any given time, there are always present processes of economic stratification in several economic markets, he nevertheless argues that the dominant source of economic stratification has evolved in the Western world from the credit market, to the commodity market, and finally to the labor market.

The great shift, which has been going on continuously in the past, and up to our times, may be summarized, although at the cost of some precision: the struggle in which class situations are effective has progressively shifted from consumption credit toward, first, competitive struggles in the commodity market and, then, toward price wars on the labor market. The 'class struggles' of antiquity...were initially carried on by indebted peasants, and perhaps also by artisans threatened by debt bondage and struggling against urban creditors. For debt bondage is the normal result of the differentiation of wealth in commercial cities, especially in seaport cities....Debt relationships as such produced class action up to the time of Cataline. Along with this, and with an increase in provision of grain for the city by transporting it from the outside, the struggle over the means of sustenance emerged. It centered in the first place around the provision of bread and the determination of the price of bread. It lasted throughout antiquity and the entire Middle Ages. The propertyless as such flocked together against those who actually and supposedly were interested in the dearth of bread. This fight spread until it involved all those commodities essential to the way of life and to handicraft production. There were only incipient discussions of wage disputes in antiquity and in the Middle Ages. But they have been slowly increasing up into modern times. In the earlier periods they were completely secondary to slave rebellions as well as to fights in the commodity market.

The propertyless of antiquity and of the Middle ages protested against monopolies, pre-emption, forestalling, and the withholding of goods from the market in order to raise prices. Today the central issue is the determination of the price of labor.[7]

From the point of view of the beginning of the 20th century, Weber argues that there have been three broad historical stages in the history of economic stratification. From the point of view of late in the 20th century, however, I would argue that we are entering onto a fourth stage, the stage in which in addition to stratification in the credit, commodity and labor markets, stratification on the basis of taxation in the modern state is becoming an increasingly critical source of economic class formation. While historically the sources of economic stratification, and hence of economically based political conflict, have been in civil society, presently, the state itself is emerging as a critical source of economic stratification and political group formation. As Tocqueville put it, when he confronted an earlier transformation of the relations between society and politics, "A new science of politics is needed for a new world."

APPENDIX I

As an example of the changing social significance of the federal income tax, on Table 1 I have calculated the tax on an annual income of $3000, along with the changing position of an annual income of $3000 in the national distribution of incomes in several years since 1939. In 1939, when only about 16% of all families and unattached individuals had before-tax incomes of $3000 or more, an individual with an income of $3000 paid $68 in federal income tax, and a family of four with an income of $3000 paid no tax. In 1944, when more than 48% of all families and unattached individuals had before-tax incomes of $3000 or more, at the peak of the war-time tax rates, an individual with an income of $3000 paid $585 in federal income tax, and a family of four with an income of $3000 paid $275 tax. In 1950, when more than 60% of all families and unattached individuals had incomes of $3000 or more, before tax rates were raised to finance the Korean war, an individual with an income of $3000 still paid $428 in federal income tax, and a family of four with an income of $3000 paid $104 tax. But by the period from 1954 to 1963, at the end of which nearly 80% of all families and unattached individuals had before-tax incomes of $3000 or more, nevertheless, an individual with an income of $3000 paid $488 in federal income tax, and a family of four with an income of $3000 paid $120. Or in short, during the post-war period from 1950 to 1963, when the median income for families (these figures exclude unrelated individuals) rose from $3319 to about $6400 ($6569 in 1965), and thus when a family income of $3000 fell (by these figures) from more than 90% to less than 47% of the median family income in the United States, the federal income tax for an individual with an income of $3000 actually rose from $428 to $488, and for a family of four with an income of $3000, actually rose from $104 to $120. In 1964 taxes were reduced for all taxpayers, although the subsequent surcharge restored approximately one half of the former reduction. And accelerated inflation continued to raise equivalent real income into higher and higher dollar brackets. Still, in 1969, an individual with an income of $3000 paid $322 in federal income tax, and a family of four paid $4. Only in 1970 did a family of four with an income of $3000 cease to be subject to federal income tax, which in 1970 for a family of four, began at $3600.

TABLE 4

FEDERAL INCOME TAX ON AN INCOME OF $3,000

Year	Tax Individual	Family of 4	% of all families and unattached individuals with yearly income less than $3,000.
1939	$ 68.00	$ 0.00	84%
1944	585.00	275.00	52
1950	428.00	104.00	40
1954-	488.00	120.00	
1963	488.00	120.00	20%*
1969	322.00	4.00	

* These percentages become less accurate as they decrease because federal income tax data understates the number of low income individuals and families.

REFERENCES

1.Yung-Ping Chen, The Direct Tax Burden on the Poor and Elderly, Department of Economics, UCLA, 1970.

2.Ferdinand Lundberg, The Rich and the Super-Rich, 1968., pp. 412-413.

3.Melvin J. Ulmer, The New Republic, Nov. 7, 1970.

4.Glenn D. Morrow, National Tax Journal, Sept., 1963, cited by Ulmer.

5.S.M. Lipset, "Three Decades of the Radical Right," in Daniel Bell, The Radical Right, 1964, p. 431.

6.Ibid, p. 438.

7.Max Weber, "Class, Status, Party," in Gerth and Mills, From Max Weber, 1958, p. 185-186.

Page 15

* Depreciation and investment credit are the area in which tax concessions to industrial and manufacturing corporations are most directly and quietly made. The 7% investment credit was in effect during most of the 1960's, and reinstituted by the Nixon administration in 1971. The Nixon administration also enacted a new "Asset Depreciation System" (ADR) under which capital assets other than real estate may be depreciated more quickly than previously, resulting in larger write-offs of current income. The changing rules of depreciable lives and accelerated depreciation methods would be critical historical variables in a sociology of taxation.

** Recently under the Nixon administration's ADR system, the IRS has explicitly abandoned its previous requirement that assets cannot be depreciated faster than they are actually replaced.

Page 20

* Since corporations pay income tax at a flat rate presently of 48% on taxable net income above $25,000, all corporate expenses, either in the form of wages and salaries, or in the form of business expenses, have a real cost to a corporation that has more than a minimum of taxable income, of only 52% of the nominal expenditure.

Page 21

** The tax on the next $2,000 of income for a married man with a taxable income of $12,000 is $500, and the tax on the next $5,000 of income for a married man with a taxable income of $30,000 is $2140).

CHAPTER 22

Reprinted from *Science*, March 6, 1964 Vol. 143, No. 3610, pp. 1012-1014.

COMPARATIVE FAILURE IN SCIENCE

Barney G. Glaser

A recent study shows that this is not incompatible with stable careers for basic research scientists.

A perennial problem for some scientists is their feeling of comparative failure as scientists. This problem becomes clearer if we consider two major sources of this feeling that are inherent in the very nature of scientific work. (i) In science, strong emphasis is placed on the achievement of recognition[1]; (ii) the typical basic scientist works in a community filled with "great men" who have made important and decisive discoveries in their respective fields; they are the acknowledged guiding lights. These esteemed scientists, who have attained honors beyond the reach of most of their colleagues, tend to become models for those who have been trained by them or who have worked under them. As Eiduson has put it in her recent psychological study of basic research scientists[2]: "Scientists are idols-oriented."

To take these honored men as models is important for training as well as for a life in research. During training, one learns to think creatively. Emulation of these models results in the internalization of values, beliefs, and norms of the highest standard. This emulation of the great continues and guides the scientist in his research work, however individual in style his work may be.

But it is precisely here that a feeling of comparative failure may arise. In emulating a great man the scientist tends to compare himself with the model. He estimates how closely he has equaled his model in ability to adhere to high standards of research, to think of relevant designs, to devise new methods, to write clearly, to analyze data. In addition, because of the strong emphasis on attaining recognition for research contributions, the scientist perhaps will compare his own degree of success with his model's to gauge how he himself is doing. In using the great man's achievements and the recognition accorded him as criteria, the scientist may be motivated to strive continually and unremittingly toward greater heights[3]. On the other hand, he may see himself, over time, as a comparative failure for not having attained a comparable amount of recognition[4].

Eiduson brings out the dynamics of this problem for scientists (see endnote 2, p. 189): "The model, then, is the ego ideal figure, who represents the ultimate position and in fact, defines what a scientist should do, how he should think, how he should act. *By comparison, everything else is inevitably of lesser worth* [italics mine]. We have seen the way the scientists in this group rebuke themselves as they become old, distracted, sit on committees or government advisory boards, or become administrators - and thus move away from the ideal. From this picture it is obvious that the scientist is hard on himself. He has a built-in, clearly marked scalar system, along which attitudes and kinds of performances are measured. When he moves away and deviates from the pattern, he becomes a maverick, or a person who has tossed aside the flaming torch."

AVERAGE SUCCESS

With this problem in mind, I recently made a study of the organizational careers of basic research scientists, one purpose of which was to ascertain the consequences, for the scientist's career, of receiving or not receiving an average amount of recognition[5]. At the time of the study, these scientists were employed in a government medical research organization devoted to basic research. This was a high-prestige organization from the standpoint of scientists and was run much as though it were a series of university departments. The study is relevant to this discussion in showing something of the career history of basic research scientists, who are today in increasing proportions leaving the university setting to become affiliated with high-prestige organizations devoted to basic research. In these contexts organizational scientific careers are still primarily dependent on professional (not organizational) recognition[6].

By "average amount of professional recognition" I mean supervisor's favorable evaluation of the quality of the scientist's current research, and proper credit, through publication and through acknowledgment in the publications of others, for his contribution to the cumulative knowledge in his field. This definition gives the three major sources of recognition within reach of the typical scientist: references from superordinate colleagues, publication, and publication acknowledgments in the work of others. This "average" degree of professional recognition is attained by most of the country's scientists at any one time and by practically all scientists at one time or another. This degree of recognition is in marked contrast to the highly regarded, and restricted, high-prestige honors (in the form of awards, prizes, grants, lectureships, professorships, and so on) that are part of the professional recognition accorded those scientists who make great and decisive discoveries - the "great men."

Three general aspects of scientists' careers were studied: performance; security in, and advancement of, position; compatibility with others, and satisfaction with one's location in science. With respect to performance, and average degree of recognition was found basic to high performance. That is, recognition resulted in the scientist's devoting more of his own time to research; this, in turn, resulted in high-quality scientific performance, as judged by the researcher's closest professional colleagues.

Since, of course, such performance on the part of many individuals is the basis of organizational prestige, it was not surprising to find the organization providing, in return, a stable scientific career for a scientist who received average professional recognition. The scientists accorded this degree of recognition, in contrast to those accorded less, felt more satisfaction in their jobs and salaries. They tended to be more optimistic about their chances of promotion, and their rate of promotion was higher. With respect to the conditions for research - a most important consideration for basic-research scientists - they fare considerably better than scientists not accorded average recognition. They had more freedom to work on their own ideas, had more chance for originality, had more chance to use their current abilities and knowledge as well as to gain new abilities and knowledge, and had generally better research facilities and supplies. In sum, the "average" recognition accorded them was sufficient to give them security and advancement in their scientific careers.

Lastly, with average recognition, the high-quality performance and steady advancement could be achieved in a setting that provided personal satisfaction. The scientists accorded average recognition, again in comparison to those accorded less, were more content with their research and non-research colleagues. More of them felt intense interest in working with close professional associates. They were more satisfied with their assistants and with the other scientists, the organization leaders, their own supervisors and the directors of their particular institutes. They felt strengthened through belonging to work groups, such as sections and laboratories. They depended more on personal contacts for scientific information, both inside and outside the organization. They participated more in seminars, meetings, and the activities of professional clubs and other small groups.

Closely linked with this compatibility with their associates was a satisfaction with their location in the community of organizations of science.

The scientists accorded average recognition, in comparison to those accorded less, felt strongly attached to their respective institutes and organizations. Indeed, they were more satisfied with the organization's reputation in the scientific world, and more of them felt that a sense of belonging to an organization which had prestige in both the scientific and the general community was of utmost importance. In comparing their own organization (from the standpoint of what job factors they deemed most important) with the "best" of universities, hospitals, industrial research organizations, and government research organizations, one of them consistently reported that their organization was generally better. In sum, the context of their careers in science was highly favorable.

Together these findings suggest that an average amount of recognition has a generally stabilizing effect for the careers of the scientists within the high-prestige organization of the study. (Even for individuals who received little or no recognition, the pressure on careers was not so great as to cause an exodus from the organization or from science itself. The great majority of these men thought the lack of recognition was only temporary and planned to continue in the organization, trying to advance knowledge.)

These findings suggest that career stability based on average professional recognition is probably found in other organizations similar in nature to the basic-research organization of this study, and that in organizations of lesser standing even less recognition may assure career stability.

In the light of these findings it appears that the feeling of comparative failure that may result when the average scientist judges his lesser success by the considerable success of his "great man" model tends to occur in many instances within the context of a stable, promising career. Further, most scientists can gain, if they do not have it currently, the degree of recognition necessary for a stable career. Comparative failure, then, is an evaluation resulting from a social comparison. It is not to be taken as absolute failure (loss of position as a scientist). A comparative failure can still be successful; an absolute failure is thorough.

THE SCIENTIFIC CAREER:

A CARNIVOROUS GOD?

Comparisons with great men are, however, taken not as comparative but as absolute failure by Kubie in his famous article "Some unresolved problems of the scientific career"[7]. Kubie warns future scientists of the perils ahead when devoting themselves to that "carnivorous god, the scientific career." His criteria in warning of potential failure, are absolute (not comparative) judgments, based on the careers of the more notable great men of science. For example, he talks of the "ultimate gamble which the scientist takes when he stakes his all on professional achievement and *recognition* [italics mine], sacrificing to his scientific career, recreation, family, and sometimes even instinctual needs, as well as the practical security of money." Implying again that the scientist whose success falls short of the great man's is an absolute failure, he characterized the young scientist as having "a self-deceiving fantasy: that a life of science well may be tough for everyone else, but that it will not be for him," and as having "ambitious dreams; unspoken hopes of making great scientific discoveries; dreams of solving the great riddles of the universe."

Kubie states that the young scientist "dreams unattainable dreams." More directly relating his judgments to great men, he cautions against choosing science as a career, because of the "many failures it took to make one Pasteur." He states that most young scientists, in using great men as models, unwittingly set themselves up to become failures: "...most young men view their prospect solely by identifying with their most successful chiefs, never stopping to consider how many must fail for each one who reaches this goal." Without making the distinction between absolute and comparative failure, this last statement clearly implies the former.

Admittedly, from this standpoint many must fail and few will attain the stature of their models, but they should be informed that most can gain the fundamental degree of recognition indicated in my study as necessary for a promising career in science. Surely the career to which they commit themselves need not be, as Kubie says, "devoid of security of any kind, whether financial or scientific."

Furthermore, these young men should be encouraged to enter science and take great men as their models, for most will be the artisans who do the commendable, but not earth-shaking, research which accumulates to form the foundation for the future decisive advances. Kubie himself has recently, although somewhat ambivalently, recognized this, in comparing the typical scientist with the internationally famous scientist [8]: "These little known and unrewarded men are the expendables of science. They are no less essential than are the few who reach their goals. Therefore, until many years have passed it would be hard to weigh which of these two men had had the more profound impact on scientific knowledge."

Perhaps my discussion draws the kind of "implication" from "statistics" that Kubie is looking for in future research when he says in his article on the scientific career: "It is the...duty of scientists and educators to gather such vital statistics on the life struggles of a few generations of scientists and would-be scientists and to make sure that every graduate student of the sciences will be exposed repeatedly to the implications such data may have for its own future." Career decisions are perhaps among the most important determinants of a man's fate, and anything which contributes to an understanding of the career in science may help people make these decisions more wisely.

REFERENCES

1. Merton accounts for this in the following manner: "...Originality can be said to be a major institutional goal of modern science, at times, the paramount one, and recognition for originality a derived but often as heavily emphasized goal" [R.K. Merton, Am. Sociol. Rev. 22, 640 (1957)].

2. B. T. Eiduson, Scientists: Their Psychological World, p. 167 (Basic Books, New York, 1962).

3. See O. Klapp, Heroes, Villains and Fools (Prentice-Hall, Englewood, N.J., 1962), pp. 18-24 for some functions of role models. I have reference to the function of "providing the individual with self-images and corresponding motivation."

4. In their comprehensive statement on careers, Becker and Strauss note the relative nature of failure: "Of course, failure is a matter of perspective. Many positions represent failure to some but not to others." [H. S. Becker and A. Strauss, Am. J. Sociol. 15, 257 (1956)]. The relative nature of failure can be seen in marked contrast to its absolute nature when a person simply has failed to keep a position. On absolute failure, see E. Goffman, Psychiatry 62, 451 (1952).

5. B. G. Glaser, Organizational Scientists: Their Professional Careers (Bobbs-Merrill, Indianapolis, 1964).

6. C.V. Kidd. Personnel Admin. 15, No. 1, 16 (1952); W. Kornhauser, Scientists in Industry (Univ. of California Press, Berkeley, 1962). pp. 131-133.

7. L. S. Kubie, Am. Scientist 41, 569 (1953); ibid. 42, 104 (1954) [reprinted in M. R. Stein, A. J. Vidich, D. M. White, Identity and Anxiety (Free Press, New York, 1960) and in B. Barber and W. Hirsch, The Sociology of Science (Free Press, New York, 1962)]. The remarks by Kubie

are based on 30 years' observation. He sees these observations as "random," but their consistently negative character suggests that, by and large, they are observations of his analysands and are random only in that context. My references are to but one short section of an excellent article.

8. ------, <u>Daedalus</u> 91, 304 (1962).

CHAPTER 23

Reprinted from *Administrative Science Quarterly*, Vol. 8, No. 3, December 1963

ATTRACTION, AUTONOMY, AND RECIPROCITY IN THE SCIENTIST-SUPERVISOR RELATIONSHIP

Barney G. Glaser

This paper explores the basis of work integration between the scientist and his supervisor in an organization devoted to basic research. The analysis uses a three-dimensional model of role integration: (1) mutual attractiveness, why they get together; (2) reciprocity; and (3) autonomy, how they stabilize working together. The recognized competence in research of both parties is shown to be a source of mutual attraction, reciprocity in work and maintenance of autonomy.

Shepard has noted that the "objective evidence" on the scientist-supervisor relationship is "meager." He suggests three sources of resistance by research laboratories to its study: (1) "The traditions of science organization prescribe formal, impersonal relations but give little direct guidance for close collaborative relations." (2) "A relatively low value is placed on collaboration in much of scientific education: the student is taught to do independent work." (3) "Personal and group relations are regarded as peripheral considerations in research, so that it is something of an imposition, if not an indignity, to have to be concerned with them." In sum, "there is no room for the concept of supervision in the traditions of science organization. So little importance is attributed to personal and social matters as factors in scientific work that they are relegated to the category of ethics"[1] To be sure, this notation was made in 1956; however, while there has been some subsequent research there is still meager objective detailed evidence on this strategic relationship, as a brief study of the comprehensive footnotes of two recent books on scientists will establish.[2]

In contrast, the supervisor's relationship to his subordinates has been the object of much study in other types of organizations. In a recent consolidation of findings on the role of the supervisor in formal organizations, supervision of scientists is not mentioned indicating again the meager evidence to date.[3] One reason this relationship has been of much interest for research in other organizations is that the supervisor is potentially a "controllable variable." He can be taught appropriate styles of supervision. This may be another latent reason for resistance to its close study in research organizations, since it conflicts with the value of autonomy in the institution of science.

Beyond adding to the evidence on the scientist-supervisor relationship, my intent in this paper is to present a generalized model of the work integration between the scientist and his supervisor. It is my hope that this model will help guide further research and thought on the scientist-supervisor relationship as well as help consolidate what diverse evidence already exists.

Just as supervisors of scientists, because of their powers of evaluation, facilities procurement, protection, support, and sponsorship, are very important to their supervisors' research as well as their successes, scientists are important to their supervisors' research and careers.[4] At the core of this interdependence is the work that scientists and supervisors do, both for themselves and for one another. In attempting to formulate a basis of work integration between the scientist and his supervisor, this analysis employs a three-dimensional model: (1) mutual attractiveness, (2) reciprocity in work, and (3) maintenance of autonomy. According to this model, mutual attractiveness accounts for the initial establishment of a work relationship; reciprocity and autonomy explain how that relationship is stabilized to persist for a sufficient time. I shall attempt to show that socially recognized competence in research, particularly for the subordinate, is a source of attractiveness, adequate reciprocity, and the maintenance of autonomy.

The data for the analysis consist of answers to survey questionnaires in 1952 by the total resident research staff (332) of a large government medical research organization devoted almost exclusively to basic research.[5] Secondary analysis of data collected some years ago for other purposes is uniquely well suited for exploratory work of a theoretical intent. The resulting general properties can be applied to many current locations, while the specific descriptions of a particular place which yielded the properties may have changed. Thus, whether or not the specific descriptions to follow will have current relevance for the present members of the organization under consideration is questionable. However, the general formulation to be developed will undoubtedly have much current relevance to the members of many research organizations throughout the community of science.

To develop, not test, a model, it is sufficient to explore plausible relations between variables, and not necessary to build a strong case on hard fact. Accordingly, I shall use somewhat crude indices and consider many consistent and highly suggestive differences that led to an integrated picture of the work relationship of the scientist and his supervisor. Since I am only suggesting, not testing, my language will be spared the qualification rhetoric required in more rigorous demonstrations, and my inferences will be designed to present a generalized formulation of a dynamic process rather than describe a real situation in static detail. In my opinion, this generalized formulation has a high probability of applicability to current places of basic research.

In this analysis I deal primarily with paired responses for each of the 332 scientist-supervisor relationships: a scientist's response about himself or his supervisor is combined with a supervisor's response about himself or his subordinate scientist. Findings yielded by this type of "relational" data[6] are particularly compelling, serving as a check on the accuracy of each party's view. It also rounds out the full meaning of the relationship, in contrast to studies whose total source of information on a social relationship is the perspective of only one participant.[7] Thus these relational data allow one to operationalize better a core unit of sociological theory - the social relationship.

Two variable tables are not included simply because there are too many of them; however, I do present (after the statement to which they refer) differences in the text indicating both the direction and the magnitude of the relation between two variables. And insofar as direction and magnitude are sufficient for replication by other social scientists, knowledge of the proportions upon which differences are based is not essential. The base numbers for each relationship never vary: high recognition (144) and low recognition (188). All statements about scientists with recognition are comparative; that is, they are based on a comparison with scientists who have low recognition. Thus I take grammatical liberty of saying "scientists with recognition" for "scientists who have achieved high recognition." I also use "scientist" interchangeably with "subordinate."

MUTUAL ATTRACTION

Two essential aspects of role integration are (1) the attractiveness of each party for the other, and (2) whether or not attractiveness becomes a basis for association.[8] Socially recognized competence in research is a basis for mutual attraction between scientist and supervisor under the following structural conditions. In the institution of science, recognition for research validated that one can live up to the exacting requirements of being a scientist by indicating past achievement, present competence, and potential future contributions.[9] The organization under consideration gives priority to this institutional emphasis; a memo to all personnel makes it clear that a successful organizational career is contingent on achieving professional recognition.[10]Thus this section demonstrates that the possession of this institutionally and organizationally valued quality accounts for the mutual attraction of both scientists and their supervisors for their current work.

MEASURE OF RECOGNITION

For the typical scientist, two major forms of professional recognition are supervisor evaluations and publications. Although the questionnaire did not include information on actual supervisor evaluation or on actual publications, it did include two items that measure felt recognition from supervisors and in publications.

They are:

A. How do you feel about how your chief makes evaluations about the quality of work you are doing? - (1) accurate, (2) partly accurate, (3) no attempt, and (4) no answer.

B. In scientific or other professional papers about work to which you have made some contribution, is proper credit given to your own contribution by means of authorship or acknowledgement? - (1) always, (2) usually, (3) seldom, and (4) no opinion.

Over half the investigators feel they receive adequate recognition from the supervisor (53 per cent say "accurate") and in publications, whether by authorship or acknowledgment, (72 per cent say "always"). To form an index of felt professional recognition, I have dichotomized each item between the highest category and all others. This dichotomization occurs as close to the median as possible and at a statistical breaking point. In many cross-classifications of each item with other variables, the direction of association consistently changed between the highest category and the remaining categories. When these two variables are combined into an index of felt recognition, 44 per cent of the investigators are high on both items, 37 per cent of the investigators are high on one item, and 19 per cent are low on both items.

For further analysis I dichotomize the index into high and low, distinguishing those who are high on both items from all others. There are three justifications for this: (1) in many cross-classification checks the middle group proved to be more like those low on both items than those high on both items. Therefore, the index is reducible on statistical evidence;[11] (2) only a dichotomized variable is necessary to establish general relations between variables; (3) the dichotomization is at the median, saving cases for necessary cross tabulation.

I have shown in other publications that this index of felt recognition approximates actual recognition to a degree sufficient for an exploratory analysis.[12] This is also substantiated by many relations between variables in this report. For example, a supervisor who chooses a scientist on the basis of recognition must be responding to the actual recognition that generated the scientist's felt recognition. Publication credits and current research are both visible and a standard basis in science for judgments of competence. On the other hand, one's feelings about his recognition, even if expressed to his supervisor, are surely not a basis for this kind of judgment.

THE SUPERVISOR'S VIEWPOINT

Supervisors were asked to list in order of importance up to fifteen people within the organization with whom some contact is of greatest significance to them in their work. Within the first seven choices more of those subordinates with recognition are chosen by their supervisor (21 per cent);[13] this difference persists to the fifteenth choice.

Insofar as "some contact" means association, this finding also indicates that the supervisor follows through in associating with the subordinate who has the attractive quality of recognition. That this association takes place is substantiated by other data. According to supervisors who were asked to report on how frequently they contact each subordinate and under what conditions most of these contacts occur, more of those scientists with recognition have daily contact with their supervisors (22 per cent) and who enjoy this contact very much (13 per cent).

THE SCIENTIST'S VIEWPOINT

For the competent scientist this work relationship with the supervisor is mutual. More scientists with high recognition choose supervisors, who have chosen them, as significant to them in their own work (21 per cent). Furthermore, the scientists with high recognition tend to choose those supervisors whom they judge to be professionally well-qualified to make sound suggestions, comments, and judgments about their research. That this attractive quality of their supervisor is a criterion for their choice is indicated by the virtual disappearance of the relation between scientists' recognition and choice (12 per cent) when appraisals of qualification are removed (2 per cent and 0 per cent); the "choice" relation thus depends upon this intervening factor (Table 1).[14]

Given this finding, we can readily understand that more of the scientists with recognition find contacts with their supervisor very enjoyable (32 per cent) and that more are satisfied with the number of these contacts (25 per cent).

In short, the mutual attraction and association that results in an integrated work relationship between supervisor and subordinate is based on each party's research competence. Moreover, both parties find this relationship enjoyable and engage in it, often daily, on a person-to-person basis. In general, research

Table 1. The competent scientist chooses the competent supervisor.

	Scientist's recognition		
	High	Low	Difference
	%	%	%
The scientist chooses his supervisor as one of five most significant people for his work...	90 (144)	78 (188)	+12
Scientists who choose supervisor among first five people and who judge supervisor as: Fully qualified	93 (130)	91 (96)	+2
Less qualified	64 (14)	64 (92)	---

organizations tend to select supervisors on the basis of scientific competence only when the institutional organizational goals coincide.[15] As we noted above, the organization in this study meets this condition, thus accounting for the existence of many competent supervisors with whom competent subordinates can establish integrated work relationships.

RECIPROCITY IN WORK

Once the work relationship of scientist and supervisor is established, the question arises as to how it is stabilized. One source of stability is reciprocity in work of mutual helpfulness;[16] another is the maintenance of individual autonomy in the context of mutual dependence. I will discuss reciprocity in this section and autonomy in the next.

Research competence attracts scientists and supervisors to one another because of the potential to engage in a work relationship of mutual benefit. This focus on competence means that the chances are maximized that each will help the other, and that neither will nor can exploit the other and that the end result of their individual and/or joint work will be interdependence of successes. If one party goes without the help of the other or tries to exploit the other, then reciprocity in work does not obtain, and the mutual attraction based on research competence will lead to an unstable work relationship. (I say unstable because one party, especially since he is competent, would have no reason to prolong the integrated work relationship if he is exploited or derives no help from it.) It is the purpose of this section to show that reciprocity does exist between scientists with recognition and their supervisors.

THE SUPERVISOR'S VIEWPOINT

Supervisors indicate in several ways that integration with scientists with recognition is useful in their own work. They report that the activities of more of those subordinates with recognition are usually very helpful to them (18 per cent), and more of these subordinates' activities or decisions have a direct or indirect effect on their work (18 per cent). Consistent with these data is the slight tendency of supervisors to view these competent scientists as familiar with the everyday aspects and problems of their job (11 per cent). This familiarity, probably gained in daily, personal contact, would increase the subordinates' ability to be helpful. Supervisors also view these subordinates with confidence, that is, as people whose sincerity, motives, and intentions are to be trusted.

THE SCIENTIST'S VIEWPOINT

In comparing the reports of scientist and supervisor on whether or not the other is helpful, more scientists with recognition are involved in a mutually helpful work relationship with their supervisor (26 per cent: Table 2). Other data reported

Table 2. The mutual helpfulness in work relationship.

Helpfulness*	Scientist's recognition		
	High	Low	Difference
	%	%	%
Mutual	65	39	+26
Scientist only helps	2	9	-7
Supervisor only helps	30	33	-3
None	3	19	-16
	(144)	(188)	

*Scientist and supervisor report on each other

by subordinates further indicate the helpfulness of the supervisor. More scientists with recognition say that their supervisor's activities and decisions have a direct or indirect effect on their work (18 per cent); more find their supervisor very stimulating for their work (45 per cent); more think their supervisor is thoroughly familiar with the everyday aspects of their job (40 per cent). These data reinforce the above finding that competent scientists try to choose professionally well-qualified supervisors to be involved in their research. More scientists with recognition also report that they have confidence in the sincerity, intentions, and motives of their supervisor (35 per cent), and that they can rely on their supervisor to back them up effectively in getting approval from higher-ups for expenditures and projects (28 per cent). This latter finding also indicates that the supervisor actively becomes the subordinate's organizational work sponsor rather than merely fulfilling the formal requirement of making references.

Only 20 out of the 332 scientists are possibly exploited by their supervisors (scientist only helps: Table 2); and this potential is not related to recognition. The chances are small that unfair gain from a subordinate's talents exists, and, if it is not based on the socially recognized competence of scientists. Insofar as competence is a visible and attractive quality, and since the competent scientist is likely to be in demand by other supervisors, it is a likely source of control over exploitation. The scientist with recognition, should his present relationship not be going well, could readily establish another of greater reciprocity.

Thus, mutual attraction based on competence results in a stable research work relationship between scientist and his supervisor because of mutual helpfulness and the absence of exploitation. This reciprocity in work results in and is supported by each party's familiarity with the other's work and by mutual trust.

AUTONOMY

Stability in this integrated work relationship depends also on the autonomy that both the supervisor and the subordinate are able to maintain while allowing themselves and their work to become interdependent. The importance of autonomy for insulating the research scientist from the undue influence of others (both within and outside science), thereby insuring the highest levels of motivation, performance, and creativity, is attested to by the emphasis it receives in the literature on the institution of science and by the extensive research on this problem.[17] It is thus important to investigate the conditions under which a competent scientist can participate in an integrated work relationship with his supervisor (and vice versa) without a crippling sacrifice of autonomy.

Supervisor's Viewpoint. It seems likely that, concomitant with the subordinate's access to and impact on his supervisor's work, some controls limiting the supervisor's vulnerability should exist. According to the supervisors, such controls over subordinates do exist. They report that more of their subordinates with recognition can be influenced by them with respect to work-related activities (18 per cent); and these are precisely those scientists who, because of their integrated work relationship, most affect their supervisors. This specific influence, while deriving, in part, from the many general controls supervisors have over the subordinates' fate in career and work, may also derive from the charisma of the supervisor.[18] This controlled helpfulness of the integrated subordinate thus explains the supervisor's granting trust and familiarity with their work.

These various findings on attraction, reciprocity, and autonomy indicate that supervisors see integration with subordinates having recognition as useful for their work, and feel good about the ensuing relationship. Insofar as these consequences are anticipated by supervisors, they may also motivate their choice of these competent subordinates for a work relationship.[19] This, then, means that these anticipated consequences are additional reasons why recognition is an attractive quality of scientists.

SCIENTIST'S VIEWPOINT

We already have some answers to the question of how the subordinate maintains his autonomy. Insofar as his recognition will also make him attractive to other, especially higher-ranking, scientists, he has a measure of control over his supervisor; should the present relationship be too constraining, he can readily enter into another. Another potential course of subordinate control is the impact he has on the supervisor's research; in order to maintain his autonomy, the scientist has the possibility of either increasing, withdrawing, or otherwise changing that impact.

However, the scientist's autonomy is specifically vulnerable (more so than that of the supervisor) when the supervisor helps him. How can he accept this help without its curbing his own bent of mind? On the other hand, why should the supervisor continue to help him if he is not accepting the help? To answer these questions, I have endeavored to trace out a few of the factors enabling the competent subordinate to utilize the supervisor's help without either constraining his autonomy or rendering the help ineffectual.

First, scientists with recognition do not tend to render their supervisor's help ineffectual in order to maintain autonomy. More of those subordinates with recognition get effective help (37 per cent: Table 3), which, I suggest, is an important benefit of their integrated work relationship. Since the supervisors' helpfulness is interrelated with their effect on their subordinates' work (Coefficient of Association = .45), this means both that their helpfulness tends to have much effect and that having much effect is very helpful.

Table 3. The effect of the supervisor's help.

Scientist says supervisor is:		Scientist's recognition		
Helpful	Effective	High	Low	Difference
		%	%	%
+	+	66	29	+37
+	+	16	11	+5
-	-	13	32	-19
-	-	5	28	-23
		(144)	(188)	

Second, one way that subordinates with recognition tend to maintain their autonomy while allowing their supervisor to affect their work is to influence him with respect to precisely those activities that will affect their own research. This is illustrated by the tendency of the relationship between scientist's recognition and supervisor's effect (18 per cent) to diminish when influence over supervisor is removed (10 per cent and 13 per cent); indicating that the "effect" relationship depends upon this intervening factor (Table 4).20

Table 4. The scientist's influence over his supervisor's effectiveness

	Scientist's recognition		
	High	Low	Difference
	%	%	%
The scientist says the activities of his supervisor affect his work...	79	61	+18
	(144)	(188)	
Scientists whose supervisors' activity affects their work and whose influence over these activities is:			
a great deal or quite a bit	86	76	+10
	(66)	(38)	
moderate, little or none	70	57	+13
	(78)	(150)	

This influence over the supervisor, a product of the scientist's integrated work relationship with him, becomes a mechanism for controlling any undue effect that the supervisor's help may have on the scientist's research.21 If the integrated work relationship did not yield this control, it would not be as stable, since fewer subordinates with recognition would allow their supervisor to affect their research when they lack sufficient measure of counteracting control. And, to carry this to its logical conclusion, if the supervisor had no effect on the subordinate's work, there could be no help and hence no mutual helpfulness; this means that mutual attractiveness would have led to nought, and the relationship might dissolve.

The existence of this influence over the supervisor is corroborated by other data. More of those scientists with recognition report that the actual relationship they have with their supervisor with regard to work problems or assignments (26 per cent) and to substantial new expenditures for equipment or assistance (26 per cent) is either one of the supervisor's consulting with the subordinate before he makes his own decision or one of joint decision. Consultation and joint decision, products of an integrated work relationship, are thus two ways in which scientists can exert influence over the supervisor's effect on their research.[22] Moreover, more of those subordinates with recognition state that the relationship they have with regard to work problems or assignments (21 per cent) and new expenditures (21 per cent) is the one they prefer, indicating that the actual relationship is, in part, a result of influence over their supervisor.

In summary, the following process may be inferred from the scientist's viewpoint. The subordinate with recognition tends to establish an integrated work relationship with his supervisor, resulting in the supervisor's being very helpful and having a substantial effect on his research. This effect does not threaten the subordinate's autonomy. He can considerably influence, particularly through joint decision and consultation, the very activities of the supervisor that will affect his research, especially those activities regarding work assignments or problems and new expenditures. Joint decision and consultation, as mechanisms of control, also derive from his integrated work relationship.

SUBORDINATES WITH LOW RECOGNITION

By no means does this integrated work relationship take place in a vacuum. It is potentially highly visible to the other subordinates of the same supervisor. No matter how many subordinates a supervisor may have (two to fourteen), he still has an equal or nearly equal number of scientists with high and with low recognition. Most scientists with recognition (130 of 144), while tending to enjoy an integrated work relationship with their supervisor, do not have an exclusive relationship with him.

Tables 2 and 3 suggest what happens to subordinates with low recognition while the supervisor more fully devotes himself to working with the scientist with high recognition. First, 32 per cent of the scientists, irrespective of recognition, report that their supervisor is very helpful, while, according to their supervisor, they do not give help in return (Table 2). This suggests that such formal elements of supervision as guidance and support of research occur independently of degree of recognition and work integration.

Second, more of the subordinates with low recognition give no help to and receive no help from their supervisors (16 per cent: Table 2). This indicates that the lack of work integration of those subordinates with low recognition with their supervisors can have an element of mutual work rejection within the formal framework of guidance and support. Also indicated by this finding is an independence of the scientist from his supervisor (such as it may be) based on mutual rejection.

Of note in Table 3 is that subordinates with low recognition are affected by their supervisor's activities and decisions while receiving little or no help (19 per cent) or are neither affected nor helped (23 per cent). Whereas the former pattern implies and element of dominance in their supervisor's guidance and support, the latter implies an element of rejection by their supervisor, an well as the possibility of forced independence. In short, those scientists who lack sufficient socially recognized competence tend to be faced with an unintegrated work relationship with their supervisor that can be characterized as one of guidance and support, imbued with elements of rejection, dominance, and forced independence.

However, subordinates with low recognition - whether rejected by, dominated by, or independent of their supervisor - are always present and possibly competing with prestigious subordinates for the time and help of the same supervisor. As these subordinates gain sufficient recognition or find other bases to attract their supervisor into a work relationship they will fare better in the competition. In this sense, the integrated work relationship with a supervisor must be continuously maintained by the subordinate with recognition in a context of proximate competitors making legitimate demands on the same supervisor and potentially becoming just as attractive to him for a mutually advantageous work relationship. On their side, all but the most attractive supervisors of scientists are continually competing for the most competent available junior colleagues.

DISCUSSION

In this exploratory research I have developed a three-dimensional model of stable work integration between the scientist and his supervisor, both of whom are engaged in basic research. This model accounts for why they get together - (1) mutual attractiveness - and why they stay together - (2) reciprocity in work, and (3) maintenance of autonomy.[23] In this case, the principal source of all three dimensions is acknowledged competence in research: it makes a scientist or supervisor attractive, forecasts his ability to be helpful to the other, and gives him a level of control over his own research and career.

This model of integrated work relationship is a generalized formulation. For the parties involved it is a relationship in process. Both supervisors and subordinates will be continually engaged in its inception, establishment, maintenance, and termination. The relationship may be inked in time with a specific piece or series of research. Any one party may be involved in more than one integrated work relationship, and each relationship may take place at different stages of development. This probability applies to supervisors who are also subordinates and who have many subordinates, as well as to subordinates who have more than one superior.

The integrated work relationship is most likely a property of supervision in other organizations devoted to basic research. I suggest this because it is compatible with the "colleague authority" system of science that "emphasizes a relationship of association, alliance and working together, and, at the same time, accepts whatever inequality in status may be present";[24] and, too, because organizations whose research goal is the same as that of the institution of science tend to select supervisors of their scientific competence.[25] Supervisors competent in research appear necessary for this relationship.

Since "the dominant pattern in industry is not to select research administrators on the basis of scientific competence,"[26] the applied research and development organization may not support such a relationship between supervisors and subordinates. In industry, management seeks research supervisors who are primarily oriented toward the organization rather than toward the profession, whose competence is primarily administrative, not scientific, and who exercise tight control over work. This type of supervisor engages most comfortably in "executive authority" - direct, arbitrary, and paternalistic - in which he does not need to consider the view of subordinates or to defer to the competencies of people in lower-ranking positions.[27] Since scientists generally resent and resist this type of supervision, the possibility of developing the kind of integrated work relationship described in this paper would, therefore, be blocked. However it remains for future research to establish to what degree and on what bases an integrated work relationship obtains between scientists and supervisors in applied research organizations.

I have analyzed the source, nature and existence of the integrated work relationship in this paper. It remains for further research to show its consequences for each party and for the research organization. For example, in the beginning of the paper I suggested that a scientist and his supervisor are, in part, dependent on each other's successes with respect to advancing their own careers and research conditions. The integrated work relationship described here will most likely feed back to more interdependence of research and career successes for the subordinate with recognition and his competent supervisor. This will probably enhance their chances for receiving further recognition of achievements; and hence for becoming more "attractive" to each other (although they may part after one or a few mutual successes) and to other scientists and significant laymen.

This cumulative process of individual successes then increases the scientific creativity and output of the research organization, hence its prestige in science. Another important question is whether or not this output is greater than the output of research organizations depending upon an integrated work relationship of a kind that is more compatible with "executive authority."

Other possible consequences of this relationship for the subordinate are to develop further his abilities as a researcher, to give him a reliable sponsor for his future career and research endeavors, and if the supervisor is a "great man," to allow him better to internalize the values and standards of his field from an "ideal" role model. With respect to the supervisor, those successes of his subordinates, in which he shares, help him remain in the organization in the later stages of a career, with full research support, with continued promotion potential, and, moreover, if he has enough such subordinates, in command of a prestigious tiny empire.

REFERENCES

1. Herbert A. Shepard, Superiors and Subordinates in Research, The Journal of Business, 29 (1956), 266-67.

2. William Kornhauser, Scientists in Industry (Berkeley, CA., 1962), pp. 56-73; and Simon Marcson, The Scientist in American Industry (New York, 1960), chs. 7, 8, and 9.

3. Peter M. Blau and W. Richard Scott, <u>Formal Organizations: A Comparative Approach</u> (San Francisco, CA, 1962), ch. 6, "The Role of the Supervisors."

4. Most discussions on the scientist-supervisor relationship focus on the problems and plight of the scientist, not the supervisor. For the few discussions of the research supervisor's dependence on subordinated, see on the tender motivation of subordinates as a control over supervisors, Glen D. Mellinger, <u>Interpersonal Factors in Research: Part II</u> (Ann Arbor, MI, 1957), pp. 48-49.

On hedging, a mechanism by which the supervisor handles this dependence on subordinate's successes see Marcson, op. cit., pp.113-115. Hedging allows the subordinate to work on a pet idea part time. If the idea works out the supervisor receives credit for encouraging it; if it does not, the supervisor is not discredited since he has not risked much on it. On conditions preventing supervisors from engaging in "correct leadership styles," see Barney G. Glaser, <u>Organizational Scientists: Their Professional Careers</u> (Indianapolis, Bobbs-Merrill, 1964), ch. 9.

5. I am indebted to Donald C. Pelz of the Survey Research Center, University of Michigan, for providing these data.

6. "Relational properties of members are computed from information about the substantive relationships between the member described and other members," Paul F. Lazarsfeld and Herbert Menzel, "On the Relation between Individual and Collective Properties," in Amitai Etzioni, ed., <u>Complex Organizations</u> (New York, 1961), p.431; see also James Coleman, "Relational Analysis," in Etzioni, op. cit., pp. 449-451.

7. Blau and Scott, op. cit., pp. 145-48.

8. Peter M. Blau, A Theory of Social Integration, <u>American Journal of Sociology</u>, 65 (1960), 546.

9. Robert K, Merton, Priorities in Scientific Discovery, <u>American Sociological Review</u>, 22 (1957), 640.

10. Charles V. Kidd, Resolving Promotion Problems in a Federal Research Institution, <u>Personnel Administration</u>, 15 (1952), 16.

11. On reduction see Allen Barton, "The Concept of Property Space in Social Research," Paul F. Lazarsfeld and Morris Rosenberg, eds., <u>Language of Social Research</u> (Glencoe, Ill., 1955).

12. Glaser, op. cit., Variations in the Importance of Recognition in Scientists' Careers. Social Problems, 10 (1963), 268-276; The Impact of Differential Promotion Systems on Careers, IEEE Transactions in Engineering Management, 10 (1963), 21-24; The Local-Cosmopolitan Scientists, American Journal of Sociology (to appear).

13. As a reminder to the reader of the meaning of this form of evidence notation (21 per cent) this difference indicates that more of the scientists with high recognition, as compared to the scientists with low recognition, are chosen by supervisors. Further, the relationship between choice and recognition is positive in direction and of a 21 per cent magnitude.

14. To be sure, this finding also suggests that the competent supervisor helped the scientist achieve his recognition in the first place as well as being chosen for his competence, if we consider the judgement of qualification as an antecedent, not intervening, factor. However, the essential idea still remains that the supervisor was chosen for his competence by a competent subordinate, who proved his merit by achieving recognition. For the original formulation of elaboration analysis of which this is the MI type, see Paul F. Lazarsfeld, "The interpretation of Statistical Relations as a Research Operation," in Lazarsfeld and Rosenberg, op. cit., pp. 115-124.

15. Kornhauser, op. cit., pp. 56-58.

16. Shepard has shown that a university research group's "stability depends upon another condition...the possibility of reciprocation." In his case it was the exchange of technical information between engineers and their technicians. Herbert A. Shepard, The Value System of a University Research Group, American Sociological Review, 19 (1954), 456-462. See, on the "ethic of mutual aid" between scientists, F. William Howton, Work Assignment and Interpersonal Relations in a Research Organization, Administrative Science Quarterly, 7 (1963), 508-510. Howton discusses the general professional right of one scientist to ask another for information and counsel. In our case reciprocity in work emerges also from the interaction between scientist and his supervisor on the job. Whether it is also based on a general ethic is a moot point.

17. On the value of independence or autonomy in the institution of science see Robert K. Merton, Social Theory and Social Structure (Glencoe, Ill., 1957), p. 453; Bernard Barber, Science and the Social Order (Glencoe, Ill., 1952), p. 89; Charles V. Kidd, Basic Research-Description versus Definition, Science, 13 (1959), 369. With respect to the problem of

autonomy applied specifically to the scientist-supervisor relationship, both Shepard, Superiors and Subordinates..., and Marcson, Organization and Authority in Industrial Research, <u>Social Forces</u>, 40 (1961), 80 et passim, devote themselves to bringing out the differences between the traditional supervisory relationship in organization and that type required for maintaining the scientist's autonomy. For research on the autonomy problem in this relationship, Robert C. Davis, "Factors Related to Scientific Performance," <u>Interpersonal Factors in Research: Part I</u> (Ann Arbor, Mich., 1957), pp. 14-26; Donald C. Pelz, Some Social Factors Related to Performance in a Research Organization. <u>Administrative Science Quarterly</u>, 1 (1956), 310-317; Kornhauser, op. cit., pp. 62-73; and Marcson, <u>The Scientist in American Industry.</u>

18. The persona charisma of the supervisor of a scientist is an aspect of this relationship that bears research. Since the world of science is studded with charismatic models, it is important to know to what degree the typical supervisor is charismatic. Modifying somewhat Weber's classic definition to apply to lesser leaders, Etzioni defines charisma as "the ability of an actor to exercise diffuse and intense influence over the normative orientations of other actors," Amitai Etzioni, <u>A Comparative Analysis of Complex Organizations</u> (New York, 1961), p. 203. Research in this area may be usefully stimulated by Etzioni's chapters 9 and 10. For a discussion of "evokers of excellence" in science, a type of charisma, see Robert K. Merton, "'Recognition' and 'Excellence": Instructive Ambiguities" in <u>Recognition of Excellence</u> (New York, 1960), pp. 314-320. For other points on charismatic role models in science, see Bernice T. Eiduson, <u>Scientists: Their Psychological World</u> (New York, 1962), ch. 5; and Lawrence Kubie, Some Unsolved Problems of the Scientific Career, <u>American Scientist</u>, 41 (1953), and 42 (1954); and Glaser, <u>Organizational Scientists: their Professional Careers</u>, ch. 12.

19. On anticipated consequences and motives, see C. Wright Mills, Situated Actions and Vocabularies of Motive, <u>American Sociological Review</u>, 5 (1940), 905-906.

20.Thisin MI type elaboration, see endnote 10.

21. This type of influence has been shown to be associated with high-quality performance by Davis, op. cit., and Shepard, Superiors and Subordinates..., p. 266. It has also been shown to be a crucial factor in communication accuracy between the scientist and his immediate supervisor, Mellinger, op. cit.

22. See Marcson, The Scientist in American Industry, pp. 78-84, for a full discussion of the importance to the scientist of participation with his supervisor in decisions affecting his research.

23. This paper was begun in January, 1958. Hence, this research was conducted independently, but simultaneously with Alvin W. Gouldner's important theoretical work on functional autonomy, functional reciprocity, and exploitation, in which he called for empirical research on these ideas. It is important to compare the system model of interdependence I have developed through research with that developed by Gouldner through theoretical inquiry. To account for its persistence he uses two dimensions of an interdependent system: "functional autonomy," enabling a party "to resist total inclusion into the system" and "functional reciprocity," "a system of independent parts engaged in mutual interchanges." To these dimensions I add another for the study of interdependence: mutual attractiveness, accounting for initiation and establishment of interdependence. See Gouldner, The Norm of Reciprocity: A Preliminary Statement, American Sociological Review, 25 (1960), 161-178; and "Reciprocity and Autonomy in Functional Theory," in Llewellyn Gross, ed., Symposium on Sociological Theory (New York, 1959), pp. 241-270.

24. Marcson, Organization and Authority in Industrial Research, p. 75. For the original formulations of colleague authority see Talcott Parsons and A. M. Henderson, eds., Max Weber: The Theory of Social and Economic Organization (New York, 1947), pp. 58-60, n. 4, and p. 402

25. Kornhauser, op. cit., p. 58.

26. Ibid. On the debate "whether or not the administrator has to be a scientist," see Norman Kaplan, The Role of the Research Administrator, Administrative Science Quarterly,4 (1959), 24-25; and Research Administration and the Administrator: U.S.S.R. and U.S., Administrative Science Quarterly, 6 (1961), 56-59.

27. Marcson, Organization and Authority in Industrial Research.

CHAPTER 24

Reprinted from *The American Journal of Sociology*, Vol. LXIX, No. 3, November 1963.

THE LOCAL-COSMOPOLITAN SCIENTIST

Barney G. Glaser

In contrast to previous discussions in the literature treating cosmopolitan and local as two distinct groups of scientists, this paper demonstrates the notion of cosmopolitan and local as a dual orientation of highly motivated scientists. This dual orientation is derived from institutional motivation, which is a determinant of both high quality basic research and accomplishment of non-research organizational activities. The dual orientation arises in a context of similarity of the institutional goal of science with the goal of the organization; the distinction between groups of locals and cosmopolitans derives from a conflict between the two goals.

Several studies in the sociology of occupations and of organizations have concluded that some professionals in organizations tend to assume a "cosmopolitan" orientation that manifests itself in the approval of colleagues throughout their professional world, in focusing on a professional career, and in a concomitant lack of loyalty to and effort for the organization. Other professionals tend to assume a "local" orientation that manifests itself in their lesser commitment to the profession, in more concern with the goals and approval of the organization, and in focusing on an organizational career.[1] With the growing movement of scientists into research organizations, there has been some interest by sociologists of science in studying the many problems and strains generated by the often conflicting professional and organizational demands and practices that, in turn, generate the adoptive cosmopolitan and local types of orientations.[2] A partial list of these problems might include varying incentive systems, differential emphasis in publication of research results, types of authority and supervision related to the professional need of autonomy, divergent and conflicting influences on work situations, assignments and research problem choices, budgets of time and money, kinds of compatible work groups, focus of performance, multiple career lines and commitments.

The major goals of many research organizations, particularly industrial research organizations,[3] are, of course, not consistent with the major institutional goal of science: advancing knowledge by basic research. They often emphasize goals of application, product development, and expert service. The scientist seeking a professional career (one based on pursuing the institutional goal) in an organization of this type becomes a "cosmopolitan," by and large directing his efforts to professional goals, rewards, and careers. Insofar as the cosmopolitan is always looking within the community of research organizations for better professional positions and conditions[4] and has little "local" loyalty to inhibit his mobility, the result is a high organizational turnover. A professional career may be impeded by a too-long stay in the industrial context. Indeed, insofar as the industrial organization needs basic research, it becomes detrimental for it to try to induce the cosmopolitan to focus his efforts on the major organizational goals - product development, application, and service - since that refocusing may reduce the quality of his basic research contributions.[5]

Whereas studies of industrial research organizations have usually found scientists who have either a primarily local or cosmopolitan orientation, I shall try to demonstrate a local-cosmopolitan orientation among highly motivated scientists in an organization devoted to the institutional goal of science. The congruence of goals reduces in considerable measure, if not completely, the strains between organizational and professional requirements that tend to generate distinct local and cosmopolitan types. My principal criterion for ascertaining the general orientation of these investigators will be the directions of their work effort. First, I investigate the general performance-reward process of science; then I investigate the efforts of those who do well in their scientific performance to meet organizational demands. From these findings on their professional and organizational contributions, I infer that the orientation of these scientists is both local and cosmopolitan. I conclude with a discussion of the implications of this formulation for the developing theory about local and cosmopolitan orientations of professionals in organizations.

The data for the analysis consist of answers given to survey questionnaires in 1952 by the total resident research staff (332) of a large government medical research organization devoted to basic research.[6] In addition, some letters and documents give further information on the organization. My demonstration will be an effort to explore for plausible relations between variables, not to develop a strong case built on hard fact. While secondary analysis is well suited for exploratory work, to achieve the latter with old data is probably impossible. Accordingly, I shall use somewhat crude indexes and consider small differences that are consistent, highly suggestive, and that lead to an integrated picture of the local-cosmopolitan process. Since I am only suggesting, not testing, my language will not be riddled by the qualification rhetoric required in more rigorous demonstrations; my inferences will be designed to guide future research on local-cosmopolitan theory along (I believe) useful lines; and my primary effort will be to generalize as opposed to describing a real situation in detail.

THE PERFORMANCE-REWARD PROCESS

Motivation. In the institution of science perhaps the most important goal for the typical scientist is to advance the knowledge in his field by some form of basic research. A scientist, especially in training but throughout his career, is constantly reminded by colleagues that it is his job to advance knowledge by some increment, large or small. He internalizes the goal, and becomes, using Parson's term, "institutionally motivated" to achieve it.[7] Therefore, before we know anything about the distinctive personality of this or that scientist, we can hypothesize that to some degree he will be motivated to advance knowledge by virtue of his professional training and that his research performance will tend to vary directly with the degree of his institutional motivation.

Insofar as the research scientist is motivated to advance knowledge, both his research work on problems, hypotheses, and methods as well as his results are centrally involved because he has the potential for advancing knowledge at either stage.[8] Irrespective of failures in results, he may have been quite original in his research work, and vice versa, he may have run rather a routine project into a contributing result.

As a measure of motivation to advance knowledge, I have selected the following two items that tap the (a) work and (b) result stages of the advancing knowledge process.[9]

"How much do you want? How important is (it) to you?"

(a) Freedom to carry out my own ideas; chance for originality and initiative.

(b) Contributing to basic scientific knowledge

Degree of importance: (1) utmost, (2) considerable, (3) some or little, (4) no opinion.

Over half the investigators felt both freedom and contributing were of the utmost importance. Each item was dichotomized between "utmost" and the remaining categories since this was where the direction of association consistently changed in cross-classification with criterion variables. The two items were fairly strongly related (coefficient of association = .70). Investigators were considered to have high motivation if they felt both freedom in work and contributing results were of the utmost importance. Fifty-six per cent (186) of them were in the category. Among those of lower motivation, 27 percent (89) were high on one item and 17 percent were low on both items.

For further analysis I dichotomized the index into high and low, distinguishing those who were high on both items from all others. Three justifications for this are: (1) In many cross-classification checks, the middle group proved to be more like those low on both items than those high on both items. Therefore, the index is reducible on statistical evidence.[10] (2) We only need a dichotomized variable to establish general relations between variables. (3) The dichotomization is at the median, saving cases for necessary cross-tabulation.

Performance. The performance score (developed three months after the survey data were collected) consisted of the assessments by colleagues in the work situation of each investigator's current research.[11] Each assessment was based on five criteria: (1) originality and creativeness, (2) wisdom and judgment, (3) rigor of thought and precision of methods, (4) persistence, industriousness, and efficiency, and (5) contribution to the work of others. Three criteria (2, 3,and 4) focus directly on the research work, and two (1 and 5) focus mainly on research results. Thus, this index is based on the same aspects of advancing knowledge as the motivation index. Bearing out my hypothesis on the positive relation between motivation and performance, 19 percent more of the highly motivated scientists (compared to those with less motivation) have been judged by their colleagues to have high quality performance.

Recognition. Concomitant with the development of institutional motivation is the expectation of reward for achievement of the institutional goal.[12] The strong institutional emphasis of science on this achievement-reward pattern is noted by Merton: "originality can be said to be a major institutional goal of modern science, at times the paramount one, and recognition for originality a derived, but often as heavily emphasized, goal."[13]

The institutional emphasis on professional recognition holds for the research organization under study.[14] A memo to all personnel described the promotion process as follows:[15] The immediate supervisor recommends the investigator to the institute director for promotion. If the latter agrees, he recommends the investigator's case to the promotion board. The board then thoroughly examines the investigator. A sample of his publications is read; prior and current supervisors are asked about him; and his qualifications are judged in terms of the following criteria: (1) quality of work he has engaged in, (2) capacity to develop, (3) capability in relation to other investigators, (4) reputation in his field, (5) personal characteristics and ability to get along with others, and (6) ability in the non-scientific work associated with his present and prospective position. If he passes this examination, he is recommended for promotion to the director of the organization, who follows the advice of the board in most cases.

The first four criteria clearly relate to the investigator's professional recognition by focusing on his past, present, and potential ability to advance knowledge. I have shown elsewhere that professional recognition is also positively linked with getting along with others and with accomplishing non-scientific work.[16] Given the emphasis on professional recognition for advancement, it seems reasonable to assume that this reward (recognition) for achievement will maintain motivation for further achievement.

The promotion process clearly indicates the importance of two types of professional recognition: (1) the immediate supervisor's evaluation and (2) publications. Therefore if each type of recognition is measured and combined in an index, we can approximate completeness in measuring both the fundamental range of professional recognition required by the organization, and an important patterned form of professional recognition for research work and results. Thus all three indexes are based on the two broad stages of advancing knowledge.

The questionnaire did not include information on actual supervisor's evaluation nor did it include information on actual publications (extent or quality). It did include two items that measure felt recognition from supervisors and in publications. They are:

A. "How do you feel about the way your chief makes evaluations about the quality of work you are doing?" (1) accurate, (2) partly accurate, (3) no attempt, (4) no answer.

B. "In scientific or other professional papers about work to which you have made some contribution, is proper credit given to your own contribution by means of authorship or acknowledgment?" (1) always, (2) usually, (3) seldom, (4) no opinion.

Over half the investigators feel they receive adequate recognition from the supervisor (53 percent say "accurate") and in publications, whether by authorship or acknowledgment (72 percent say "always"). To construct an index of felt professional recognition I have dichotomized each item between the highest category and all others. This dichotomization occurs as close to the median as possible, and at a statistical breaking point. In many cross-classifications of each item with other variables, the direction of association consistently changed between the highest category and the remaining categories. In combining these two variables into an index of felt recognition, 44 percent of the investigators are high on both items; 37 percent of the investigators are high on one items; and 19 percent are low on both items. I have dichotomized the index between high and all others (low) for the identical statistical and substantive reasons earlier applied to the motivation index.

As suggested, professional recognition tends to maintain institutional motivation in this organizational context. Nineteen percent more of those scientists who feel they have achieved high recognition (compared to those with low recognition) are highly motivated to advance knowledge.[17]

Process. The next step is to show in one table the following process: recognition for advancing knowledge (which indicates pat performance) tends to maintain motivation (a time sequence based on common observation), which in turn tends to result in high quality research performance (measured three months later). This will give us the basic links of the circular, general performance-reward process in science: research performance leads to professional recognition, which maintains motivation to advance knowledge, which in turn leads to more performance.

In Table 1 the magnitude of association between recognition and performance is diminished when the intervening effect of motivation is removed. Therefore, high motivation tends to be a link between attaining recognition and accomplishing high quality research performance, thus tentatively demonstration the performance process.[18] As a social pattern, this circular process will continue if the performance measured here results anew in recognition.

At this point I wish to suggest that, besides research performance, it is also possible to predict behavior associated

TABLE 1

Recognition, Motivation, and Performance

	Recognition (percent)		
	Average	Less	Difference
High performance	56	44	+12
	(144)	(188)	
Proportion with high performance			
and: High motivation	60	53	+7
	(96)	(90)	
Low motivation	46	37	+9
	(48)	(98)	

with research on the basis of intensity of institutional motivation. This is borne out by one indicator of research behavior: the amount of time in a typical work week the scientist puts into "performing my own professional work (or work under the guidance of my chief) such as research, professional practice, professional writing, etc." Fifteen percent more of the highly motivated investigators who work 21 hours a week on their own research have a high quality performance score.

In combining motivation, personal research time, and performance, Table 2 demonstrates that the highly motivated investigators will tend to put more time into their own research work, and that this time, in turn, will tend to result in higher quality performance.[19] The magnitude of association between motivation and performance is diminished when the intervening effect of personal research time is removed.[20] This finding adds a subsidiary link to the performance-reward process.

TABLE 2

Motivation, Research Time, and Performance

	Motivation (percent)		
	High	Low	Difference
High performance	57	38	+19

	(186)	(146)	
Proportion with high performance who put:			
Twenty-one or more hours per week into own research.	60	43	+17
	(142)	(89)	
Less than twenty-one hours per week into own research.	48	35	+13
	(44)	(57)	

SCIENTISTS AS ORGANIZATIONAL MEN

As a link in the performance process, time in own research has direct relevance to the research organization. Insofar as this process supposedly results in the continual fulfillment of the institutional goal of advancing knowledge, one might be tempted to say that this is favorable for the organization since this is why the research organization has been created. *But is this process favorable?* Scientists in any organization have other activities and duties, besides their own personal research, that must be accomplished as part of their organizational commitment. The typical investigator cannot be his own scientist all week long, as is indicated by the fact that the median number of hours put into "own professional work" in a typical week is 29.8.

The question, therefore, arises as to whether investigators with high motivation sacrifice their other organizational commitments for their personal research because of strong desires to advance knowledge.[21] If they do, and since this factor is a link in the performance process, then perhaps the above findings have unfavorable consequences for the organization. This process may require too much time for personal research, which may be disruptive for the organization as regards the scientists' fulfilling their other organizational commitments.

Table 3 provides one answer to this question. The extra time that the highly motivated scientists put into their own research is carried forward, as their weekly time schedule accumulates, with no sacrifice to other professional and organizational activities or commitments. The longer hours put into their own research (15 percent difference) are maintained by highly motivated investigators as time is consecutively added on (1) for other professional productive work (14 percent difference), such as performing services for others and working with close colleagues; (2) for non-productive professional work (21 percent difference), such as attendance at meetings and seminars, reading and dealing with people other than close research associates; and (3) for a total work week (17 percent difference), which includes all other organizational activities beyond their professional ones.

TABLE 3

MOTIVATION AND WORK ACTIVITIES

Consecutive addition of hours per week spent on various work activities	Motivation (percent)		
	High	Low	Difference
*Own research: twenty-one or more hours............	76	61	+15
*Plus other professional productive work: thirty-six or more hours........	63	49	+14
*Plus non-productive professional work: forty-one or more hours............	69	48	+21
*Plus other organizational activities for total work week: fifty-one or more hours...................	65	48	+17

In fact, in response to the question, ''How much time per week are you now spending on activities which could be shifted to other people or eliminated without impairing your present scientific or other professional work?'', more highly motivated investigators suggested that less time be shifted to other people. Thus, in line with not sacrificing organizational work for their own research, the highly motivated investigators are less ready than those with low motivation to shift any additional work load of organizational life upon other men. Indeed, it would have been understandable if they had been more ready to shift activities not directly pertinent to their professional pursuits to their personnel, since they are motivated to advance knowledge, and any activity that intruded into this effort might appear burdensome. It would seem, then, that high institutional motivation tends to make these scientists both hard-working investigators and hard-working organizational men.

THE DISTINCTION BETWEEN COSMOPOLITAN AND LOCAL

This finding suggest that those scientists who are highly motivated to advance knowledge will be assets to the organization in two ways: (1) achieving the organizational goal, which is the same as the institutional goal of science, and (2) meeting non-scientific organizational requirements that take time from research. Thus, the organization will tend both to persist and to maintain its prestige (through accumulated individual successes) within the community of scientific organizations. The latter aim is very important for attracting and recruiting more capable, highly motivated scientists. Persistence and maintenance of prestige through achievements of the institutionally designated goal need not always be related. There are numerous examples in the literature that show that attempts to meet requirements for persistence can subvert organizational goals.[22]

This finding - that both research and non-research activities seem important and compatible to highly motivated scientists - indicates, by the criterion of direction of work efforts, that these scientists are both cosmopolitan and local oriented. They are oriented to achievement of the institutional goal and honorary rewards, and hence toward professional colleagues everywhere and toward success as members of their profession. They are also oriented to their responsibilities within the organization that provides them with the facilities for advancing scientific knowledge and thus gaining recognition, and with a prestigeful base for that cluster of organizational rewards called a promising career.

Further data support the presence of the dual orientation among highly motivated scientists. As hard-working cosmopolitans oriented to all professional colleagues they are more interested in contacts outside the organization as source of information, in a move (if necessary) to a university environment (however, motivation does not account for more plans to move), and in belonging to an organization with prestige in the scientific world. Also, they feel a greater sense of belonging to and involvement with professionals within the organization. With respect to the professional or institutional goal, any suggestion of a change from basic research as the only organizational goal to its coexistence with applied research will be cause for concern.

As hard-working locals, the more highly motivated investigators desire an important job in the organization and association with persons who have high status and important responsibilities. In addition, more of them have a strong sense of belonging to the organization and are interested in higher level jobs that are most compatible with the institutional goal. That is, they tend to be interested in the supervision of subordinate scientists rather than in supervision of the organization.

In sum, this congruence of organizational and institutional goals generates a local-cosmopolitan scientist when the scientist is highly motivated to advance basic knowledge. Devotion to both profession and organization is, in this case, not incompatible, as it tends to be for scientists in industry.

LOCAL-COSMOPOLITAN THEORY

This dual orientation of highly motivated scientists is especially important since, with few exceptions, the research literature characterizes scientists as either cosmopolitan or local. They are presented as two distinct types of scientists whose orientations and activities are, if not directly opposed to each other, not related. Shepard, in discussion dilemmas in industrial research, has said, "The research staff itself is likely to be divided into what Robert Merton calls the 'cosmopolitans' and 'locals'."[23] In his book on industrial scientists, Marcson reports that "It is possible to distinguish between two types of laboratory staff people - professionally oriented and organizationally oriented."[24] Peter reports of a seminar on problems of administering research organizations, "In the first two of the seminars, some time was spent discussing another bimodal distribution of scientists, those described as 'cosmopolitan' and those called 'locals'."[25]

I suggest that cosmopolitan and local can also be seen as two dimensions of orientation of the same scientist, each activated at the appropriate time and place as determined by the organizational structure within which he works. The question now arises as to whether or not there is a conflict between my findings of a cosmopolitan-local orientation and the body of literature that treats the two orientations as distinct. Is one view more correct than the other? If we ask the question,"Under what conditions has each distinction emerged?" then we find that each of the views is accurate and applicable to the particular organizational situation under analysis.

The distinction between cosmopolitan and local scientists emerged during the study of research organizations in which the institutional goal of advancing knowledge is more or less in conflict with a major organizational goal of applying knowledge, For example, in reviewing industrial research organization studies, Shepard states that the scientist's "motto" is "How much do we know about this?" whereas the businessman's motto is "What is the value of this to the company?"[26] This conflict results in a "problem person" in the cosmopolitan and in a "good employee" in the local.

Scientists take sides in the conflict according to their goal priority; hence the social scientist studying the organization uses this criterion to divide scientists into two groups. The cosmopolitan group creates little problem in primarily pursuing the company goal and career. In sum, this distinction is a device for understanding organizational problems such as communication of results, turnover, multiple career lines, differential incentive systems, needs for loyalty versus expertise, and so forth.[27]

Cosmopolitan and local as dual orientations of the same scientist emerged on our analysis of a research organization that emphasized the institutional goal. As there was little or no conflict between goals, there was no necessity to take a priority stand, or of being split into groups. Because of this congruence of goals, a local orientation helps to maintain the opportunity to pursue research and to have a career at a highly prestige locale, both thoroughly consistent with the cosmopolitan orientation.[28] In using the notion of dual orientation, we end up talking of organizational benefits, not problems.

Further, I have found this dual orientation among highly motivated scientists, whereas Shepard, as well as the other authors cited, talks of all scientists. Thus, the two conditions that generate the emergence of either groups of cosmopolitan and local scientists, or scientists with a cosmopolitan-local orientation, are (1) compatibility of the organizational with institutional goal, and (2) highly motivated scientists versus all scientists.

One of the exceptions to viewing local and cosmopolitan scientists as different groups in the literature on scientists is the "mixed type" offered by Kornhauser.[29] The "mixed type" is oriented to both company and profession and is interested in "facilitating the utilization of technical results." This applied orientation existed under the conditions of a conflict between the institutional goal and the company goal and is an accommodation seemingly in favor of the company. Thus, to date we have two general types of local-cosmopolitan scientists arising under different sets of specific conditions: (1) the basic research local-cosmopolitan and (2) the applied research local-cosmopolitan.

Table 4 locates the various general orientations of scientists to organizations and\or professions likely to be generated by the two cited conditions: (1) congruence of institutional and organizational goals and (2) degree of institutional (or professional) motivation.

TABLE 4

SCIENTISTS' ORIENTATION

Institutional and Organiztional Goals	Professional Motivation		
	High	Medium	Low
Same.	Basic research. Local-cosmopolitan.		Local.
Different	Cosmopolitan.	Applied research. Local-cosmopolitan.	Local.

Last, the concern among the scientists in this study over the potential organizational emphasis upon the applied research goal suggest a few hypotheses about possible changes. If the organization starts to emphasize applied research, those highly motivated to do basic research may give up the basic research cosmopolitan-local orientation and become a definite group of cosmopolitans. The professional motivation of some may drop a little and then they are likely to become applied research local-cosmopolitans. The potential conflict between institutional organizational goals may generate these changes, which then could result not only in the loss of benefits to the organization cited in this paper but also in the accumulation of problems cited by those writers who have developed the distinction between cosmopolitan and local as two types of scientists.30

REFERENCES

1.The terms "cosmopolitan" and "local" were first used by Merton to describe different types of community leaders (Robert K. Merton, Social Theory and Social Structure [Glencoe, Ill.: Free Press, 1957], pp. 187-420). For a formulation of cosmopolitan and local as organizational types see Alvin W. Gouldner, "Cosmopolitans and Locals: Toward an Analysis of Latent Social Roles", Administrative Science Quarterly, II (1957-58), 281-306, 444-80; see also Alvin W. Gouldner, "Organizational Analysis", in Robert Merton, Leonard Broom, and Leonard Cottrell (eds), Sociology Today (New York: Basic Books, 1959), pp. 64-74; Leonard Reissman, "A Study of Role Conceptions in Bureaucracy," Social Forces, XXVII (1949), p. 308; Theodore Caplow and Reece J. McGee, The Academic Marketplace (New York: Basic Books, 1958), p. 85 and passim; Harold Wiensky, Intellectuals in Labor Unions (Glencoe, Ill.: Free Press, 1956), pp. 129-53; Warren G. Bennis et.al., "Reference Groups and Loyalties in the Out-Patient Department," Administrative Science Quarterly, II (1958), pp. 481-500.

2. William Kornhauser, Scientists in Industry (Berkeley: University of California Press, 1962), esp. chap. v; Simon Marcson, The Scientist in American Industry (New York: Harper & Bros., 1960); Donald C. Pelz, "Some Social Factors Related to Performance in a Research Organization," in Bernard Barber and Walter Hirsch (eds), The Sociology of Science (New York: Free Press of Glencoe, 1962), p. 357; Herbert A. Shepard, "Nine Dilemmas in Industrial Research," Administrative Science Quarterly, I (1956), 346; Hollis W. Peter, "Human Factors in Research Administration," in Rensis Likert and Samuel P. Hayes, Jr. (eds.), Some Applications of Behavioral Research (Paris: UNESCO, 1957), p. 142; Clovis Shepard, "Orientations of Scientists and Engineers," Pacific Sociological Review, Fall, 1961, p. 82. Robert Avery, "Enculturation in Industrial Research," IRE Transactions in Engineering Management, March, 1960, pp. 20-24; Fred Reif, "The Competitive World of the Pure Scientist," Science, CXXXIV (1961), 1959.

3. Kornhauser, op. cit., p. 133; Leo Meltzer, "Scientific Productivity in

·

Organizational Settings," Journal of Social Issues, No. 2 (1956), p. 38; Marcson, op. cit., pp. 81-82, 104; Shepard, op. cit., p. 347.

4. Kornhauser, op. cit., p. 130.

5. Ibid.; see also Shepard, op. cit., and Pelz, op.cit., p. 358.

6. I am indebted to Donald C. Pelz of the Survey Research Center, University of Michigan, for providing me with these data.

7. Institutional motivation has been dealt with extensively in: Talcot Parsons, Essays in Sociological Theory (Glencoe, Ill.: Free Press, 1954), chaps. ii, iii, Merton, op. cit., pp. 214, 531, 555, 558-59; Robert K. Merton, "Priorities in Scientific Discovery," American Sociological Review, December, 1957, pp.640-41. It should be noted that advancing knowledge as I deal with it here is institutional, a part of a normative pattern, not a mode of orientation that is simply natural to man. Thus, I make the distinction between institutional motivation (motivation based on internalized norms and goals) and typical human motives (assertive, friendly, ambitious, egotistic, etc.) as elements of concrete motivation.

8. Advancing knowledge is a process that, for any one scientist, is composed of many events. This process has at least two broad stages: research work and research results. Bernard Barber, in talking of "inventions and discoveries," says "they have two aspects, that of process and that of products, and these aspects must be distinguished" (Science and the Social Order [Glencoe, Ill.: Free Press, 1958], p. 193).

9. I follow the procedure for index construction outlined and discussed by Paul F. Lazarsfeld, in Merton, Broom, and Cottrell (eds), op. cit., chap ii, pp. 47-67; in "Evidence and Inference in Social Research," Daedalus, LXXXXVII, No. 4 (1958), 100-109; and with Wagner Thielens, The Academic Mind (Glencoe, Ill.: Free Press, 1958), pp. 402-7.

10. On reduction of property space see Alan Barton, "The Concept of Property Space in Social Research," in Paul F. Lazarsfeld and Morris Rosenberg (eds), The Language of Social Research (Glencoe, Ill,: Free Press, 1955).

11. This performance score cannot be construed as a measure of recognition, since, to be sure, the scientists were not made aware by the research team of their colleagues' evaluations. The essence of recogniton is that it is a known reward for one's work. For a complete discussion of the construction of this index of research performance see Donald C. Pelz et al.,

Human Relations in a Research Organization (Vol. II; Ann Arbor: Institute for Social Research, University of Michigan, 1953), Appendix S; and Interpersonal Factors in Research (Ann Arbor: Institute for Social Research, University of Michigan, 1954), Part I, chap.i, Appendix A.

12. See Parsons, op. cit., pp.53-54, 143-44, 230-31, 239, for the formulation that institutional norms reciprocally define relations between two classes of people or two positions.

13. Merton, "Priorities...," op. cit., p. 645.

14. This is not the only government medical research organization that bases promotions on professional recognition. There would seem to be many others. Miltzer reports for his national sample of 3,000 physiologists that publication productivity for those in government was the same as those in the university and that publication was as strong a factor in promotions in both contexts (Meltzer, op. cit.).

15. Charles V. Kidd, "Resolving Promotion Problems in a Federal Research Institution," Personnel Administration, XV, No. 1 (1952), 16.

16. See my Organizational Scientists: Their Professional Careers (Indianapolis: Bobbs-Merrill, forthcoming), chaps. vi and vii, and see below for the relation of performance process to accomplishing non-scientific work.

17. For other evidence that recognition supports motivation see Donald C. Pelz, "Motivation of the Engineering and Research Specialists" (General Management Series, No. 186 [New York: American Management Association], p. 30). He reports that for a national sample of 3,000 physiologists, the number of publications and acknowledgements is positively related to intensity of motivation.

18. Various sources exist for a full discussion of Lazarsfeld's elaboration analysis of which this is the MI type. For the primary source see Paul F. Lazarsfeld, "Interpretation of Statistical Relations as a Research Operation," in Lazarsfeld and Patricia L. Kendall, "Problems of Survey Analysis," Continuities in Social Research, eds. Lazarsfeld and R. K. Merton (Glencoe, Ill: Free Press, 1950), chap. vii. One could say that the table also shows that motivation leads to recognition, which in turn leads to performance (14 percent and 16 percent are less than 19 percent). But this is the same process I have described in the text. For motivation to result in recognition implies that there was some performance intervening; for

recognition to lead to performance implies that there was some motivation intervening.

19. I have based this finding on the one-time sequence. It is also possible that some investigators may have developed a high degree of motivation because of putting in more than 21 hours per week. Hard work could generate interest. Therefore, we may have another time sequence in the performance process of longer hours in research leading to high motivation which results in high performance. However, this is not so. In comparing proportions downward in Table 2 among those with high motivation, 12 percent more who work 21 or more hours a week on their own research have a high performance score. The original relation between time in own research and performance is 11 percent. Therefore, high motivation, instead of being an intervening variable between time and performance, is a condition that creates a slightly stronger relation between the two. This is, of course, the time sequence I have originally assumed, which shows it is the sequence that prevails in the population under study.

20. I use the " 21 or more hours a week" break in the distribution, since it is at this point that the consistent direction of association between time and motivation changes. The distribution ranges from 7 percent who work less than 15 hours a week on their own research to 7 percent who work over 46 hours a week.

21. That this is an important consideration for the organization is indicated by one of the six criteria used in evaluating the scientists for potential promotions: "Writing or editorial ability, effectiveness on boards and committees, ability to organize his and others' work, administrative judgment and other traits relevant to his performance on his current job and the job for which he is being considered" (Kidd, op. cit.). This criterion indicates that the scientist's worth to the organization is based also on the non-scientific work he has been asked to do.

22. The foremost example is Philip Selznick's TVA and the Grass Roots (Berkeley: University of California Press, 1953).

23. "Nine Dilemmas...," op. cit.

24. Ibid., p.18.

25. Ibid.

26. Ibid. A conflict in goals is also the criterion for separating local and cosmopolitan scientists used by Marcson, op. cit., and Peters, op, cit.

27. That the distinction between types of scientists has much potential use in the analysis of problems surrounding the research organization's need for both loyalty and expertise is forcefully brought out in Gouldner, "Cosmopolitans and Locals," op. cit., pp. 465-67.

28. Blau and Scott, op. cit., pp. 70-71, in comparing county agency caseworkers and Bennis' data on professional nurses, note that opportunities for a professional career in an organization coupled with restricted opportunities in competing organizations generate local orientations among professionals. Whether they still remain cosmopolitan or not was not discussed. Their analysis is, therefore, consistent with mine on the local dimension.

29. Kornhauser, op. cit., p. 122. Another exception is Avery's (op. cit.), "The career question confronting the technical man is not, typically, whether to commit himself wholly to localism or cosmopolitanism. Rather he is likely to be constrained to try to extract advantages form both sources." Gouldner (op. cit.) and Blau and Scott (op. cit.) also have mixed types in their tables but do not discuss them in text. They focus on the distinct groups. Caplow and McGee also note a mixed orientation among professors in high-prestige university departments (op. cit.), p.85 (see also Warren G. Bennis, op. cit., pp. 481-5000.

30. For an analysis of the generation of cosmopolitan and local factions because of a change in goals see Paula Brown and Cloves Shepard, "Factionalism and Organizational Change in a Research Laboratory," Social Problems, April, 1956, pp. 235-43.

CHAPTER 25a

Reprinted from *The Academic Mind: Social Scientists in a Time of Crisis*; The Free Press of Glencoe, IL, 1958, Chapter 3.

A MEASURE OF APPREHENSION

P.F. Lazarsfeld

W. Theilens, Jr

In the spring of 1954 Robert M. Hutchins, in a popular magazine, expressed the opinion that the spirit of the teaching profession was being crushed. A few months later the Fund for the Republic commissioned the present study. Russell Kirk and other conservatives voiced skepticism: How could one expect that a study financed by the Fund would do anything but confirm its president's conviction? In the liberal camp Sidney Hook felt that Hutchins' statement was exaggerated. Characteristically, no one raised the question of what the statement meant and by what devices it could be proved or disproved. To this topic, the present chapter is devoted.

Brief thought needs to be given first to the implications of such an undertaking. An extreme position would be that Hutchins' statement is self-evident, and that its meaning and intent would only be perverted by an empirical investigation. No one can deny that many professors were investigated. Quite a number were dismissed, several probably without justification. It is only common sense that if some members of a social group are singled out for attack, the whole group may became frightened. Besides, this argument might continue, statistical data would only veil the moral implications of the situation. There are fifteen million Negroes in this country; if fifteen were lynched, would it not be absurd to say that this is only .0001 per cent?

The moral issue and the descriptive effort should not be confused. Our task is to analyze, as accurately as possible, the feelings of social scientists during the difficult years and to spell out some of the implications of their attitudes and experiences. A call, if necessary, for remedial action must be left to other agencies. Just as chemists hope that their discoveries will not help people to poison each other, so the social scientist expects that his findings and his language will not be misused.

THE BASIC MATERIAL

CHAPTER I and Appendix 3 have acquainted the reader with the general ideas used to formulate classifications of our 2,451 teachers. Similar procedures were used to establish a measure of what we shall call apprehension. The first step was to conduct a series of detailed interviews with a number of college professors, who were prevailed upon to describe in detail any situation encountered in their capacity as teachers which had somehow made them feel uneasy. We asked them to remember as much as they could of both important and trivial experiences which create problems in a teacher's professional career, experiences they had already encountered or which might arise in the future.

From these preliminary interviews we selected a list of about twenty relatively specific experiences. Questions were then worded so that the respondent simply had to say whether or not these things had happened to him. It was necessary to present a large number of situations related to academic life which might cause a teacher concern or induce him to act contrary to his convictions; depending on personality and background factors, one man's apprehension might express itself in regard to his publications, while for another relations with students or with neighbors might be more indicative.

The strategy behind this procedure deserves a moment of reflection. Long before surveys like this one existed, philosophers wondered how to make distinctions between people and put them into different classes for analytical purposes. William James, for instance, in *The Meaning of Truth*, says:

Suppose, e.g., that we say a man is "prudent."

Concretely, that means that he takes out insurance, hedges in betting, looks before he leaps....As a constant habit in him, a permanent tone of character, it is convenient to call him prudent in abstraction from any one of his acts.

In the fifty years since this was written, the basic idea expressed has become the pivot of much empirical research. But it has been amended in three respects. For one, we would not expect a prudent man always to hedge in betting or always to take out insurance; we talk today about the probability that he will do so. Secondly, we no longer assume that we can arbitrarily divide people into those who are prudent and those who are not. We accept the idea that all such traits or attitudes form a continuum which may be divided into segments only for practical convenience. Finally, we know that the number of indicators to be used for such a classification may be very large, and various subsets of indicators may be chosen according to the purpose of the study at hand. Among college students, for instance, we would find little betting and rare occasions for taking out insurance. Thus we might use as indicators of prudence whether a student always makes a note when he lends a book, whether he always locks his dormitory room, and so on.

In the spirit of this tradition twenty-one items were included in the questionnaire to gauge a professor's apprehension. But further screening was necessary to select the items most suitable for the classificatory task on hand. It developed that a few units did not signify what we had expected. In one such case, we had inquired as to whether in hiring a teaching assistant the respondent would wonder about the candidate's political background; 40 per cent answered in the affirmative. But the comments and explanations added by teachers revealed an ambiguity. For many, such concern was indeed a matter of self-protection and a sign of apprehension. But for others it was a policy based on long-established convictions. Other items turned out to be too limited in applicability. Almost half of the respondents, for example, had no opportunity to act as sponsors for student organizations, and so a question regarding caution in accepting such sponsorship was discarded.

As a result of this sifting, eleven items remained suitable for an index of apprehension. These were then subjected to a further analysis. On the basis of their wording, they were divided into two groups, one pertaining to feelings of worry about security, the other pertaining to precautionary behavior. The singling out of these two dimensions of apprehension will be described first. Finally, we made use of statistical tests to pick the small group of items which were most appropriate for classifying all the respondents.

WORRYING

Of the eleven items remaining after the preliminary screening, six contained a phrase such as "have you worried," or "do you ever find yourself wondering," or "have you ever thought about the possibility," in connection with such matters as gossip, delayed promotion, or other difficulties resulting from an expression of political opinion. The term "political" was always explicitly used to shift the focus away from issues of professional competence, scientific controversy, or moral problems which might otherwise have overly guided respondents' answers. In Table 3-1, the wording of the questions is reproduced, together with the distribution in percentages of the 2,451 answers to each.

The variation in the number of affirmative answers to these questions is considerable and not without interest. The first three items, reported by about the same proportion of teachers, all have

TABLE 3-1

DISTRIBUTION OF ANSWERS TO A SERIES OF ITEMS INDICATING "WORRY"

1. Have you worried about the possibility that some student might inadvertently pass on a warped version of what you have said and lead to false ideas about your political views?

Yes 40%
No 58
Don't know 2
Never encount'd -
Total 100%

2. If you were considering a move to another college, have you wondered if that college would ask anyone at your present college about your political background and the political biases you might have in your teaching?

Yes 37%
No 57
Don't know 4
Never encount'd 2
Total 100%

3. Do you ever find yourself wondering if because of your politics or something political you said or did that you might be a subject of gossip in the community?

Yes 37%
No 61
Don't know 1
Never encount'd 1
Total 100

4. Have you ever wondered that some political opinion you've expressed might affect your job security or promotion at this college?

Yes 27%
No 72
Don't know -
Never encount'd 1
Total 100%

5. Have you ever wondered if there was something political you said or did that would cause you to become unpopular with any group of alumni?

Yes 16%
No 82
Don't know 1
Never encount'd 1
Total 100%

6. Have you ever thought about the possibility that the Administration of the college has a political file or dossier on every faculty member, including yourself?

Yes 17%
No 82
Don't know 1
Never encount'd -
Total 100%

one element in common: once one has expressed an opinion, events are set in motion over which one may not have control. The difference between the figures for the second and fourth items probably reflects an element of reality in the academic tradition: a teacher's opinions are undoubtedly more likely to keep him from getting a job than to cost him one he already has.

The last two situations in this list are much less frequently reported. The alumni are considered a more remote hazard, perhaps because they are less likely to learn what the professor says than the people resident in the community, and because in some schools the influence of the alumni is slight to begin with. The term dossier in the last item may well have a cloak and dagger implication to which only the especially distrustful are responsive. While the answers to each question are certainly affected by many elements in the wording, it is still worth noticing that the most frequently experienced item refers to damage caused "inadvertently"; the Machiavellian designs implied in the final item are much less often visualized by teachers.

An important way of understanding the meaning of such a list is to study the relation of answers to the various items to each other. The same amount of worry can be expressed by quite different indicators according to the specific circumstances in which a respondent teaches. Still, there are certain interrelations which prevail more generally. Gossip is most frequently paired with the other situations; it is, so to say, the most characteristic of all the worrisome eventualities in the list. The three items which specifically refer to jobs (items 2, 4, and 6) form an interrelated group; an affirmative answer to one is especially likely to go together with the two others. The suspicion of a political dossier kept by the administration is particularly unlikely to be linked with the fear of inadvertent misrepresentation by students. This suggests perhaps that there are really two types of respondents revealed by these questions: those who felt that the difficult years were the result of unfortunate circumstances in which some people were almost unintentionally victimized, and those who saw the world more as a place in which bad people are deliberately out to hurt the good ones.

The reader should not be misled by our choice of the term "worry" to describe these questions. It is undoubtedly true that in answering them affirmatively a teacher expressed concern for his job security and uncertainty about his freedom of opinion. However, it need not only mean concern with his own position. It may also express a general sensitivity to academic freedom or political constraint. A man who thinks the college administration has a political dossier on the faculty might have nothing to fear himself and yet worry considerably that such practices prevail. Affirmative answers could therefore indicate worry about oneself combined with concern about the civil liberties situation in the college at large (This idea will be further developed in the next chapter).

On the other hand these affirmative answers might not only express worry about professional matters; they could well be the result of broader personal anxieties, the responses of people who also worry every day about whether they have left a lighted cigarette in their office or whether their children will fall off a swing.[1]

CAUTION

The remaining five questions had a different character. In these, teachers were not asked whether they had worried, or what they had felt, but whether they had actually done something to forestall some of the consequences which caused them concern. Had they toned down their writings in order to avoid controversy? Were they more circumspect in their discussions with other people? Just as the items of Table 3-1 are indicators of worry, those in Table 3-2 could be called indicators of caution.

In comparing Tables 3-1 and 3-2, one notices that the proportion of affirmative answers for the caution questions is likely to be smaller than for the worry items. This may be partly because it requires more honesty to concede that one is actually "pulling in his horns" than to reveal a general mood of concern. But it also makes good sense to find that a general feeling of concern was more pervasive than were concrete precautionary moves.

Questions 8 and 9 in Table 3-2 have one element in common: they give the respondent an opportunity to justify his careful behavior with the idea that free expression of opinion might embarrass others. Item 7, as we shall soon see, also has an alleviating element: it can mean that one has the courage of one's opinions but wants to be sure that they are clearly understood by others. This probably explains why the first three precautionary situations in Table 3-2 are more frequently asserted than the last two. As noted above, it is not surprising that conceding real

TABLE 3-2

DISTRIBUTION OF ANSWERS TO A SERIES OF ITEMS INDICATING "CAUTION"

7. Do you occasionally go out of your way to make statements or tell anecdotes in order to bring home the point directly or indirectly that you have no extreme leftist or rightist leanings?	Yes 27% No 71 Don't know 2 Total 100%
8. Have you occasionally refrained from expressing an opinion or participating in some activity in order not to embarrass the trustees or the college administration?	Yes 22% No 75 Don't know 2 Never encount'd 1 Total 100%
9. Do you find yourself being more careful now and then not to bring up certain political topics with your colleagues in order not to embarrass them?	Yes 18% No 81 Don't know 1 Total 100%
10.Do you find in your recommendations of reference materials to students	Yes 12% No 85

that you are more careful today not to recommend something that might be later criticized for being too controversial?	Don't know 2 Never encount'd 1 Total 100%
11.Have you toned down anything you have written lately because you were worried that it might cause too much controversy?	Yes 9% No 85 Don't know 4 Never encount'd 2 Total 100%

changes in one's professional activities is acknowledged by only a small number of respondents.2 It is quite possible that our figures underrate the frequency with which this actually happens. It is therefore important to remember that we don't mean to use any of these figures by themselves for describing the social reality. They are part of a larger set of indicators which, when taken together, will permit us to distinguish various levels of apprehension. We will provide a possible corrective in Chapter VIII on the specific subject matter of the last two items. Respondents were asked whether their colleagues had changed their publication and teaching practices in the course of the difficult years. The number of affirmative answers, when talking about others, was about 8 per cent higher than when respondents referred to themselves, even though one out of five respondents had formed no judgment. Many of the reports professors face about their own reactions will be matched in Chapter VIII against the observations they made on their colleagues.

The caution items of Table 3-2 are related to each other. As could be expected, teachers who affirmed one of the two final professional items were also likely to affirm the other. Not so strongly, but still quite noticeably, the second and third situations which refer to avoiding embarrassment were likely to be reported by the same respondents. Additional suggestive insight is gained by tabulating the worry against the caution items. The highest worry-caution interrelation occurs between the fear of misrepresentation by students, and the tendency to make sure that one is not considered an extremist. Some respondents, it appears, are especially concerned over having their views quite clearly understood by others. The wish not to embarrass the administration is paired, relatively

491

strongly, with concern for one's job; tact appears to have a certain practical utility.

Looking at the whole picture revealed by the eleven questions, we face a dilemma of interpretation. Should we say that "only" one out of ten professors have been affected in their writings, or should we be appalled by the fact that thousands of college teachers have taken such precautionary steps? A similar moral issue, if one less central to academic institutions, is raised by the first item in Table 3-2. Is it a token of awakened patriotism or a sign of weakened moral fibre when more than a quarter of an academic community feels obliged to go out of its way to express its loyalty? We leave these decisions to the reader.

THE INTERRELATION BETWEEEN WORRY AND CAUTION - APPREHENSION

INDEX

We can divide respondents into those who give a "yes" answer to one worry item, at most, and those who concede two or more. The same can be done with caution items. These two divisions together classify our respondents into the four groups shown in Table 3-3. In the upper left corner are those who report neither worry nor caution (1,184 cases or 48 per cent); 719 people (29 per cent) express considerable worry but report at most one precautionary move. Seventeen per cent (423 cases) are both worried and cautions. Only 125 respondents affirm a sizeable number of caution items but hardly any worry.

We can look at Table 3-3 in the following way. If teachers are not strongly worried (first column), they would seldom have reason to be cautious; actually the 125 cases who feel differently are surprising and will be discussed later. If teachers are worried, they may or may not make concrete precautionary moves (second column). Worry and caution can be considered different levels of an underlying attitude which we call apprehension.

A relatively low degree of apprehension is expressed mainly in feelings of worry and uneasy anticipation; as apprehension increases, it affects one's external behavior and leads to actual changes in one's work and social conduct. It is this formulation which will now be converted into our definitive instrument, the apprehension score. Henceforth we will be interested in the distinction between worry and caution only for certain special purposes; in general, we consider them the inner and outer manifestations of an underlying attitude of apprehension.

TABLE 3-3

OUR RESPONDENTS CROSS-CLASSIFICATION ACCORDING TO THE NUMBER OF CAUTION AND WORRY ITEMS THEY ANSWER AFFIRMATIVELY

Number of caution items	# of worry items		
	0,1	2-6	Total
0,1	1,184	719	1,903
2-5	125	423	548
Total	1,309	1,142	2,451

From our eleven items six were selected to form the final apprehension index. They include the first four of Table 3-1 (worry about misinterpretation by students, about one's future employment chance, about community gossip, and about security in one's present job) and the last two of Table 3-2 (being more careful about reference material, and toning down one's writing). The choice of these six items was first based on general considerations of content and then verified by a statistical procedure. The two caution items selected were those closest to a teacher's professional activities. We eliminated the last two worry items for substantive reasons. The one which referred to alumni was, as mentioned before, too dependent upon actual variations in the role which such groups can play in a college. And specific tabulations convinced us that the item referring to a possible administration dossier had an overdramatic implication which prevented a number of respondents from giving an affirmative answer.

There remained the final task of showing that the six items selected for our index really were indicators of an underlying sentiment of occupational apprehension, a latent dimension along which respondents could properly be classified. We can give here only the general idea of such a statistical test and its main outcome.

Suppose we were able to look into people's feelings and see directly the degree of apprehension they experience. Then we would expect the following relationship between this basic measure and the different items which we use as indicators: the more apprehensive a group of respondents, the more likely are they to answer an item affirmatively. Bur each of the indicators will have a somewhat different relationship to the underlying sentiment. Some will readily come to the fore as apprehension increases, others will be asserted only at a very high level of apprehension. Obviously we don't have such a direct measure. Nevertheless it is possible to derive mathematically the curves which relate general apprehension to the propensity of reporting each of the specific symptoms. In figure 3-4, the horizontal direction represents the basic underlying dimension. Along the vertical direction we have plotted for each question the probability that teachers give an affirmative answer. These curves are sometimes called tracelines because they permit us to trace how characteristic an indicator is at various levels of basic apprehension.

Take, for instance, the first three questions reported in Table 3-1. They are answered in about the same frequency. Forty per cent are worried about student misrepresentation, 37 per cent about their future job, and an equal 37 per cent the community. Now, let us look at their tracelines in Figure 3-4.

The gossip item (3) is represented by a practically straight line. This must be understood as follows: people with little apprehension are very unlikely to be concerned about the repercussions of their political opinions in the community, but the likelihood increases in direct proportion to the degree of underlying apprehension. The concern about one's future job (2) presents a different picture. Its probability at the outset rises somewhat more sharply; at the lower degrees of apprehension people are a bit more likely to worry that an expression of opinion could jeopardize their chances to move elsewhere. But, on the other hand, at a high degree of apprehension this worry is less prevalent than the concern with gossip. After all, gossip is an ever-present danger while comparatively few people think far into the future or seriously consider that they will ever have to move to another college.

The item regarding student misrepresentation (1) is again quite different. First, we notice that at the onset its traceline is higher. This shows that even people who are not apprehensive at all reckon with student misrepresentation as part of the inevitable hazards of their occupation. And for quite a while, ass apprehension rises, the probability of this concern doesn't increase very much. But then, at the higher levels of apprehension, it shoots up, and in the end becomes dominant.

For comparative purposes, we have added the traceline of the caution item which deals with the toning down of one's writing (11). The probability that a teacher will assert such a move appears only very late on the right side of our graph, but them it rises steeply. This confirms our general interpretation that such changes in professional practices are indicators of rather extreme apprehension, but even there they are not very likely to occur.[3] Such an analysis of tracelines is the statistical method by which the meaning of an underlying concept is clarified. The kind of apprehension which our index measures is such that fear of community repercussions to one's opinions is what one might call the most typical expression; its probability increases proportionately to the increase of the underlying feeling itself. Concern about one's future job appears earlier than fear of local gossip. The harm students can do is taken more in stride, and worry about it characterized only a rather advanced state of apprehension. Typically, the most acute form of apprehension is reflected in actual changes in professional activities.

The procedure we have just sketched could, if we wished, now also permit us to classify each respondent in a statistically precise way. But that would mean pushing the method to an extreme not warranted by the practical purpose of our study. Rather, we shall proceed as before, and classify our respondents simply by counting the number of items they answer in the affirmative. This leads to the distribution of scores presented in Table 3-5.

TABLE 3-5

DISTRIBUTION OF SCORES ON THE APPREHENSION INDEX

Apprehension score	Number of respondents	Percentage of respondents
0	742	30%
1	600	24
2	454	19
3	336	14
4	193	8
5	99	4
6	27	1

Total   2,451   100%

We can compare the distribution of these scores with the types developed from Table 3-3. We may call unapprehensive all those with a score of 0 or 1. The rest (46 per cent) can be called apprehensive, with a very apprehensive group comprising those who have a score of 4 or higher. The picture presented in Table 3-6 ensues.

TABLE 3-6

TWO WAYS OF ESTABLISHING LEVELS OF APPREHEN-SION

Type		Apprehension score	
Neither worried nor cautious	51%	Low (0,1)	54%
Worried but not cautious	31	Medium (2,3)	33
Worried and cautious	18	High (4-6)	13
	100%		100%

*Excluding respondents reporting caution but little worry (125)

The two classifications match fairly well, and the apprehension score turns out to be somewhat more conservative; it describes 46 per cent of all the social scientists as apprehensive. This classification is, of course, meant mainly for comparative purposes. We shall devote several chapters to reporting what types of social scientist are relatively more apprehensive and what situations make for a higher or lower frequency of apprehension in terms of this score. This is all an index should legitimately be used for. Indeed, this self-restraint is not confined to the kind of social research work of which this report belongs. The physicist can measure temperature by Fahrenheit, Celsius, etc. He can tell whether it is hotter in the suburbs or downtown. But he should not be asked how many hot days there were in New York City this year, because he does not know whether "hot" means above 90 degrees or above 95 degrees. Of course, there develops in each city a social tradition of what is considered "hot." In London newspapers the weather makes headlines if the thermometer rises above 85 degrees. In this sense it would be a legitimate problem of empirical inquiry to ask what score people would consider the onset of dangerous or unusual apprehension. Repeated studies permitting comparisons over various historical periods would give a clue, but we have no such material. It is our impression, from reading numerous questionnaires in full detail, that two or more out of six items answered affirmatively do indeed indicate apprehension in the colloquial sense of the term. Whether or not this is correct must be left to future inquiries. One merit of our effort may be that it provides the first bench mark for a continued effort.

We turn to a more necessary task. The fact that people answer questions does not tell what the answers mean. The tracelines described earlier give some of the answers. Additional insights can be obtained in a variety of ways.

ADDITIONAL INFORMATION

Many of our respondents added comments of their own on the six questions after they had chosen between the alternatives presented to them. Quite often these remarks shed light on the interpretation given to questions by respondents. It is possible to show, by briefly summarizing this material, that any differences in understanding could not have markedly affected our statistical results.

A group of 400 questionnaires was selected at random and scrutinized for the observations added by respondents in the course of answering checklist questions. Altogether 315 comments were recorded by interviewers on the six items included in our index. About two-thirds of these reinforced or explained the interpretation of apprehension we gave to the checkmarks. For instance, one respondent, worried that expressing his political opinions might affect his job security, specified the area about which he was concerned:

You have to be careful in domestic and state politics. I avoid them. It is embarrassing.

Another professor, who said that he was now more careful regarding controversial reference material, explained his motivation:

This is because students are more apprehensive that readings will reflect on them.

Conversely, unapprehensive respondents often explained their "no" answers. In regard to misrepresentation by students, for instance, many respondents refused to be worried because they felt that such incidents were part of their job.

Any teacher who would worry about that should stop teaching -

because I think that in teaching often people listen with half an ear and them go out and make statements about what you said. Also you should be strong enough in your own ideas to refute them if necessary.

Others were not worried because they had confidence in the administration.

It has happened to me but I have never worried about it. I am confident that the whole climate of administration is such as to discount warped student versions.

Conservative respondents often remarked that they didn't need to be cautious because their thinking was in tune with the opinion prevailing in the community.

About 10 per cent of the comments, however, indicate that the checkmarks which form the basis of the statistical treatment did not always catch the real meaning of the respondents' answers. In qualifying a "yes" answer, respondents sometimes said they were worried about the consequences of an expression of opinion, but then added that their worry shouldn't be taken too seriously.

I haven't lost any sleep over it. I'm young and mobile and not worried about security.

It's been just incidental thought on my part, as to what effect my words might have. But it has not been a sense of fear.

In most of these cases the qualifications centered around the interpretation of items used in the question. These people wanted to say that they had considered he possibly dangerous implications of free expression of opinion but were not really worried about them.

The qualifications of "no" answers are somewhat more complex. Some of the respondents said that they had not refrained from frank expression in their writing although they could think of rather characteristic exceptions.

Wait a minute. I haven't toned sown, but I have refrained from writing letters to editors, etc., that I would have written on segregation - some letters I have felt the urge to write.

Others said that they had already made protective moves. They said "no" to an apprehension item, but added remarks like these:

But I might point out to students that what they are going to read might be criticized by some people.

In a state college I have to be careful about socialized medicine. If I do refer to it, I refer to a conservative reference.

It should be remembered that in all these cases the response was statistically classified as not showing apprehension.

We found that when the 400 respondents were taken together, the qualifications tended to cancel each other. An affirmative answer which was qualified to a "no" occurred as often as a qualification in the other direction. This means that if we were to shift all the "misplaced" apprehension checkmarks and reclassify every teacher accordingly, the relationships to other factors, reported later in this volume, would remain much as they appear at present except that they might show slightly greater strength.[4]

We also have some statistical information which provides additional support for the apprehension index. The score should be higher among teachers who have a realistic reason for concern. This could occur either because they have actually been attacked, or because some previous association is open to misinterpretation. A commonsense classification of vulnerability in such terms should correlate well with the apprehension score. We know whether or not a professor had been involved in an incident; furthermore, our interviewer inquired as to whether the respondent had ever been a "member of a political group which advocated a program or a cause which has been unpopular or controversial."[5] The frequency apprehension among the four resulting groups of teachers is shown in Figure 3-7.[6]

FIGURE 3-7

VULNERABILITY AS RELATED TO APPREHENSION

Involved in personal incident	Member of a controversial organization	% apprehensive	Average apprehension score
Yes	Yes	75% (138)	2.85
Yes	No	71% (128)	2.67
No	Yes	56% (605)	1.90

No	No	36% (1562)	1.30

If teachers were actually attacked, they were quite likely to be apprehensive; for these respondents the further effects of past membership were slight. Without a concrete incident, though, the potential dangers of a controversial membership made quite a difference. We report two kinds of measures in Figure 3-7 to show these results. In the bars the percentages of respondents with a score of 2 or more are recorded. The column at the right shows the mean score, the average number of items affirmatively answered by each group. Both measures verify our expectation and imply that the apprehension index is a reasonable and sensitive instrument.7

We can therefore accept a surprising finding with the confidence that it has substantive importance and is not due to the use of a faulty instrument. For if we compare the extent of apprehension in various groups of schools, we find small variations only, as can be seen from Figure 3-8.

FIGURE 3-8

APPREHENSIVE RESPONDENTS IN NINE TYPES OF COLLEGES

Type of College	% apprehensive	Average apprehension score
Private - Large	51% (497)	1.72
- Small	46% (326)	1.59
Public - Very Large	48% (431)	1.69
- Large	50% (390)	1.92
- Small	37% (113)	1.36
Teachers colleges -	45% (195)	1.46
Protestant -	44% (291)	1.56
Catholic - Large	38% (93)	1.45
- Small	14% (115)	0.66

The small Catholic schools, it is true, have few apprehensive teachers.8 Otherwise very little difference appears. The apprehension rate is the same in the smaller private schools as it is in Protestant and teachers colleges. Size, also, matters little. This is unexpected, because in Chapter I we saw how different these groups of schools are in many respects, and in Chapter II that some had come under considerably more attack than others. If these same school groups are so similar in their apprehension rates, a congeries of factors ought to exist which results in such a relatively even distribution. For one, perhaps apprehension itself is a complex experience which might have different meaning in the context of various school types. Again, we must investigate what makes an individual professor apprehensive; maybe personal differences are large, but are balanced by differences between schools which need to be studied. The next four chapters will explore all of these questions.

REFERENCES

1. At an early stage of this study we contemplated the insertion of a number of questions which would directly gauge this generalized anxiety for each respondent. In pre-tests, however, it was found that social scientists, well-acquainted with personality tests, resented answering such questions. In a mailed questionnaire subsequently sent to some of the teachers we had interviewed, Professor Riesman inserted an item of this type, and again met with the same difficulty.

2. The item on toning down one's writing has a somewhat different meaning for productive professors than for those who do very little writing. Information on this point is given in Appendix 8C.

3. The worry item on security in the present job (4) has a traceline lying between the gossip item and the one on student misrepresentation. Item 10 on reference material has a traceline very similar to item 11. In order not to crowd the graph, these two tracelines have been omitted. For an elementary introduction to this technique see: P. F. Lazarsfeld, ed., **Mathematical Thinking in the Social Sciences** (Glencoe, Ill.: The Free Press, 1954), Chapter 7. The reader should not be misled into the idea that we have an independent measure of apprehension against which the frequencies of the various items are plotted. The opposite is true. The statistician studies the interrelations of the items with each other. From those he derives the tracelines, and they in turn establish what the apprehension index actually means. The mathematical outcome never fits the empirical data completely. The degree of "misfit" can be seen from the fact that two of the tracelines

show at the left side of Figure 3-4 slight negative probabilities, which of course should nor occur; not would the student item go above the probability 1.0 if the whole set of data fit the model more closely. Still, the general trend of the tracelines remains valid.

4. Characteristically, the qualitative remarks do indicate that the expression of worry is slightly exaggerated while the reports of cautious behavior underrate the actual occurrences.

A rather interesting sidelight can be added. As will be seen later, the colleges were divided into those where the administration protects the faculty against attacks from the outside and those where it doesn't. Respondents from unprotected colleges make about twice as many qualifications to their answers as those who teach at a more secure place. The tendency to feel ambivalent in talking with an outsider seems then in itself to be an indicator of a difficult situation.

5. Thirty-one per cent acknowledged controversial affiliations. Of these, one-fifth were involved in an episode of the kind described in the previous chapter. Among those who had not belonged to such an organization, only one out of twelve had been in trouble.

6. Eighteen cases for which no information on past affiliation was available are excluded.

7. The mean score is more sensitive than the proportion with a high score; the latter, however, is much easier to compute and to understand intuitively. It will be used in this report except in a few cases where the mean score will help us to make direct distinctions. Also, since there are relatively few teachers reporting personal incidents and since past memberships make for little difference in their amount of apprehension, the 138 and 128 respondents will be combined henceforth as a single, most vulnerable group.

8. They include a number of girls' colleges staffed by nuns.

CHAPTER 25b

Reprinted from *The Academic Mind: Social Scientist in a Time of Crisis*: The Free Press of Glencoe, IL, 1958, Chapter 4.

THE NATURE OF APPREHENSION

P.F. Lazarsfeld

W. Theilens, Jr.

We have considered a teacher apprehensive if he was concerned with the consequences his political opinions might have for his professional reputation and his job security - a somewhat vague description. Apprehension conceived in such terms can find expression in a variety of ways. It can mobilize a person to face danger, or it can make him unfit for action. It can be the result of private experiences, or an attitude developed among groups of people about a common situation in which they find themselves. It can be the expression of a discerning mind, or it may result from an uneasy inability to understand what is going on in the world. What kind of apprehension emerges in this study?

APPREHENSION AND ACTIVISM

A number of items in our questionnaire dealt with varying aspects of teachers' willingness to take an active stand on issues of academic freedom. We may make use of their statistical relation to apprehension to shed considerable light on its nature, and on the position of social scientists during the difficult years.

Two of these questions, given in Table 4-1, presented teachers with hypothetical situations. Those who favored the speech or the debate were then asked what they would do if the president of the college were to ban the event. In the case of the controversial speaker, 40 per cent of the whole sample said they would protest vigorously to the president; regarding the debate on China, 55 per cent stated they would.[1]

TABLE 4-1

TWO QUESTIONS TO GAUGE RESISTANCE

"Suppose you were faculty advisor to a student organization here on this campus that proposed inviting Owen Lattimore, Far Eastern expert (now under indictment in Washington), to speak at a public meeting here. Do you think Lattimore ought to be allowed to speak here or not?"

Not allowed = 14%, Don't know or = 6%, Allowed = 80%

no answer, Total= 100%

"There has been a good deal of discussion recently about whether or not the proposed admission of Red China to the U.N. is a proper subject for intercollegiate debate. How do you feel about it - do you approve or disapprove of intercollegiate debates on the admission of Red China to the U.N.?"

Disapprove = 3%, Don't know or = 2%, Approve = 95%

no answer, Total = 100%

While we cannot know whether the intention to protest would be carried out in a real situation, the mere claim indicates at least a teacher's impulse to act in defense of his convictions. Figure 4-2 shows that the intention to stand up for freedom of expression is more frequent the more apprehensive a person is.

Thus the apprehension of these social scientists did not prevent them from taking strong positions on civil liberties, even to a strange interviewer of whose discretion they could not be completely assured. However, this seems the case only up to a point. Once the degree of apprehension as measured by our index reaches a score of 3, the proportion of activistic responses flattens out and at the highest level; in each instance, a slight reverse tendency sets in.

TABLE 4-2

APPREHENSIVE PROFESSORS ARE MORE LIKELY TO PROTEST AGAINST ADMINISTRATIVE INTERFERENCE WITH STUDENT ACTIVITIES

Proportion who would vigorously protest ban on the controversial speaker

(Low Range)

0 29% (742)

1 38% (600)

2 45% (454)

3 50% (336)

4 50% (193)

5 & 6* 47% (126)

(High Range)

Proportion who would vigorously protest China debate ban

0 45%

1 54%

2 60%

3 65%

4 66%

5 & 6* 59%

* Because they are so small separately, the two groups with the highest apprehension scores have been combined in this Figure and in those which follow.

Some might, of course, speculate as to whether the two protest questions did not merely elicit fantasies of courage, but another set of questions dealt with what the teachers actually did, rather than what they might do. Our respondents were asked what magazines concerned with public affairs they read. Let us select three magazines which are widely considered somewhat left-of-center and which, therefore, might at the time have been subject to censure by prevailing community opinion.2 We see in Figure 4-3 that the

FIGURE 4-3

APPREHENSIVE PROFESSORS ARE MORE LIKELY TO READ LIBERAL MAGAZINES

Apprehension Score

Proportion who read *The Nation*

0 11%

1 15%

2 16%

3 22%

4 23%

5 & 6 21%

Proportion who read *The New Republic*

0 12%

1 17%

2 20%

3 24%

4 30%

5 & 6 26%

Proportion who read *The Reporter*

0 20%

1 28%

2 37%

3 40%

4 47%

5 & 6 42%

liberal magazines were more often read by apprehensive respondents; and again for all three we find at the highest level of apprehension a slight decline much like that in Figure 4-2.

At another point in the interview we asked the following question:

Leaving aside Communist Publications, which publications that teachers like yourself might receive do you feel are likely to be attacked as being subversive? Any others?

If a respondent indicated a periodical which he himself read as possibly dangerous, we took this as a token of defiance, for he was telling us that he continued to do something which might lay him open to attack. The upper part of Figure 4-4 shows that such behavior occurred much more frequently among apprehensive than among nonapprehensive: there is a slight decline.

FIGURE 4-4

PROPORTIONS OF PROFESSORS WHO READ A MAGAZINE OR BELONG TO AN ORGANIZATION WHICH THEY CONSIDER DANGEROUS

(Apprehension Score)

Proportion who read at least one magazine which they feel is likely to be attacked as being subversive

0 13%

1 19%

2 26%

3 34%

4 44%

5 & 6 38%

Proportion who are members of at least one political organization considered likely to be attacked

0 6%

1 11%

2 17%

3 19%

4 18%

5 & 6 20%

When similar questions on organizations were asked, no single group stood out enough to permit statistical counts. When we combined all those considered likely to be attacked, 13 per cent of the social scientists reported memberships. Once more, in spite of the danger involved, such membership was increasingly more frequent among those with higher levels of apprehension. The lower part of Figure 4-4 provides the evidence. (Here, incidentally, the decline sets in only at score 6, which is not separately shown.)

We thus arrive at a rather far-reaching conclusion. There is indeed widespread apprehension among these social science teachers, but in general it is hardly of a paralyzing nature; the heads of these men and women are "bloody but unbowed." Only for the respondents with the highest apprehension scores (about 5 per cent of the entire sample) is this perhaps no longer quite so true. While they too are considerably more activistic than the average, they show slightly fewer signs of resistance than the next most apprehensive group. It could be that on this high level of apprehension some paralysis has begun to set in.

The statistical relation between apprehension and activism, as found in Figures 4-2 and 4-4, is undoubtedly the result of a complicated mechanism. We are dealing with a middle level of apprehension, so to speak. This is far from the atmosphere of security in which one would expect a profession to do its best work; but at the same time in the spring of 1955 it had not reached a level of demoralization which would rule out resistance to restraints on academic freedom. What might have happened if the situation had become worse is, of course, impossible to say. Actually, at the time of our field work, the difficulties had passed their peak in some respects. The elections of 1954 and the censure of Senator McCarthy had brought a change in the tone in which legislative investigations were conducted. With the end of the Korean War, the feeling of the country at large calling for intense vigilance had somewhat slackened. Perhaps as a refection of this calmer atmosphere, the sense of apprehension of the professoriate at the time of our study might be said to have reached a kind of uneasy equilibrium, with the pressures arising during the difficult years and the responding forces of moral resistance almost balancing each other. Some further observations about this can be made.

CAUTIOUS ACTIVISM

The attentive reader may have been struck by an apparent contradiction in our analysis. We have just seen that the more apprehensive professors are willing to engage in activities which in some circumstances involve an element of risk. But it will be remembered from the previous chapter that an important element in our index of apprehension was caution: a tendency to be wary in one's professional activities and personal conduct.

We are thus faced with strange finding that a considerable number of our respondents are actually cautious activists. While professing defiance in some matters, they concede withdrawal in others. How can we explain the fact that many professors who refrain from discussing politics, express fewer controversial opinions in public, and are more circumspect in their writings, at the same time read magazines or belong to organizations which they know are controversial, and are confident that they would vigorously oppose a president who interfered in campus intellectual activities?[3]

To clarify this phenomenon of cautious activism we will first draw on the qualitative remarks volunteered by many professors when they themselves felt their pattern of replies might sound paradoxical. For some teachers the apparent contradiction is quickly revealed as no more than a separation between the attitudes and behavior appropriate to the campus and those befitting the larger community. These teachers felt that, while they are free to do and say what they please in the academic arena, considerable caution and restraint are necessary in off-campus activities if repercussions are to be avoided. A professor of political science at a West Coast state university was quite explicit:

> There is no pressure put on me within the university about what I do in the classroom. There has been pressure outside the university on the administration by groups to get me fired because of public statements I have made. These activities and statements are off campus.

Sometimes such a position was accompanies by a feeling of considerable bitterness. One cautious activist told how he had been criticized for his membership in a controversial organization:

> Not from the university. There my political activities are welcomed. It's the community - the ignorant and suspicious people who don't know the facts.

Corresponding to this difference in kinds of pressures, some professors were willing to take a stand on the campus as long as the matter could be kept within its confines. A political scientist at a state university, when asked whether he would protest a president's ban of a student discussion, answered:

> I would not protest publicly, but would within the university. I would not issue a press release, but use the channels through which we go in the university.

At a college in the Mountain States a respondent said he had toned down some of his writing, and went on to explain:

> I had to be careful because it would get beyond the university and people who read it would judge me entirely on what I wrote.

Here the idea seems to be that the mores of academia require that a man's total intellectual personality be taken into account, while in the outside world remarks might be torn out of context and misinterpreted.

We shall see later that, generally the professoriate feel safer on the campus than outside its walls. No wonder then that they would answer a series of questions in a cautious or a courageous vein according to whether they interpret them in an intramural or extramural context. This distinction has serious implications. How can a teacher ever be sure which of his opinions will be confined to the campus? We should expect considerable uncertainty, a tendency to surround what one says or does with all sorts of precautions. And this is indeed a second element of which some respondents were well aware. Many of them do want to stand up for their convictions, but they become strategists who hold their ammunition for situations where the aim seems attainable, and make concessions on the issues which, in the present temper of the time, they consider undebatable. A professor of government at a New England university expressed this position quite clearly in reporting an episode where he agreed with a restrictive move of the president:

> There may be circumstances under which the president might feel this action a better way to protect academic interests in freedom. There are times when we do need to make concessions to achieve some important matter.

This attitude of "saving one's ammunition" was especially likely to emerge when these cautious activists wanted to be sure that they were not misrepresented as Communists. A professor of political science in another New England college made the following statement:

> When I was a member of the Progressive Party many critics equated support of the Progressive Party with sympathy toward Communism. It therefore became necessary for me and other academicians supporting the Progressive Party to explain repeatedly that our support had nothing to do with sympathy toward Communism.

At a state university on the West Coast a professor of economics was deeply disturbed that a display of loyalty became necessary in order to clarify his true position:

> I nearly got fired because of the loyalty oath. I resented very deeply the fact that it had to be signed and before the Korean War refused to sign and helped lead the opposition. Then South Korea was invaded and I was afraid the issues would get mixed up with patriotism and

Communism, so I signed.

One should not overlook the difficulties implied in this position. Men and women who oppose Communism may find it quite degrading if they feel forced to reiterate their private convictions in order to satisfy suspicious critics. While they agree with the condemnation of Communism, they fear they may be setting a dangerous precedent on the broader issue of the free expression of opinions. If forswearing heresy becomes general practice, they may some day find themselves in a precarious position if they should deviate from the prevailing mood of the time. As a result, professors often feel embarrassment and even guilt. They are not extremists, but they dislike having to prove it. This came out particularly clearly when we asked respondents whether they occasionally went out of their way to demonstrated that they had no extremist leanings. A history instructor in a small Eastern liberal arts college said:

> When I lecture on Marxism I probably am led to spend greater time giving my disagreements with it than previously.

And then he added:

> I'm embarrassed to say so.

It is surprising how similarly these experiences were worded by men who taught under quite different circumstances. An anthropologist at a New England college (neither of the two previously mentioned) described the matter as follows:

> If you say something critical of the American government, for instance, you feel obliged to say something equally critical of Russia. You go out of your way in this respect to make you position clear. That's one of the bad effects of this whole current climate.

This sense of feeling obliged to show that one is on the right side is rather subtle, and probably not many of our respondents were aware of it or able to articulate it for the interviewer. It is therefore possible that our indicators of apprehension may underrate its statistical frequency. The teacher just quoted would be entirely justified in saying that he did not refrain from expressing his opinions; yet in some way his teaching had been distorted. One professor stated in so many words how difficult it is to describe such an ambivalent position. Discussing the general effects of the difficult years, he illustrated from his own case:

> These trends have the effect of making people more concerned to

conform to acceptable views. I find myself tending to be more cautious in presenting new ideas. My conscious attitude is "Go to Hell!"; but subconsciously I am influenced.

The complicated mixture of caution and activism appeared particularly in the answers to the following item:

Have you recently wanted to express publicly a political point of view on something, and despite your worry that you might be criticized for saying what you did, you said it just the same?

A third of the respondents reported such an experience, and surprisingly, there was a very sharp increase of this claim as we compare respondents with increasing caution scores.[4] The figures are given in Figure 4-5.

FIGURE 4-5

THE MORE CAUTIOUS PROFESSORS MORE OFTEN REPORT DEFIANT EXPRESSIONS OF OPINION

(Number of Cautious Responses*)

0 (1174) 23%

1 (729) 37%

2 (311) 45%

3 (168) 52%

4,5 (69) 62%

The question conjured up what undoubtedly was a big problem for many respondents during the difficult years: whether it is nobler in the mind to exercise judicious restraint or to take arms against a sea of troubles. One might expect that the particularly cautious teachers would not be the ones to express controversial opinions. However, Figure 4-5 shows that the contrary is true. The question inquires into two things: worry, and action in spite of it. The more cautious professor was, we know, more worried. Yet more often he spoke out - a Hamlet on the campus, with all his hesitations. But why did the resolution tend to be on the side of courage?

PUBLIC AND PRIVATE COURAGE

Let us visualize a college in which an academic freedom case has arisen. A series of incidents has made a teacher controversial and the administration is inclined to dismiss him. They would like to get faculty approval for this, however, and so they call a meeting to put their case for the dismissal. This presents no problem for many of the teacher's conservative colleagues: they approve the contemplated action. Other faculty members, who feel strongly about academic freedom, welcome an opportunity to take a stand and even prepare a joint statement. The middle-of-the-road professor, however, may find himself under cross-pressures. On the one hand he does not want to put himself in jeopardy; signing the statement opposing the administration may some day bring him under attack. He is also threatened if he does not sign. The prevailing mood of the college fraternity is not conservative, as we shall see in the next chapter. If he refuses to sign, he will probably be considered "yellow" by the colleagues he meets every day. While outside forces such as legislative committees may have harsh and definite means to do him damage, he cannot underestimate the subtle deprivations to which his immediate professional environment could subject him. Most members of the faculty involved in this imaginary situation would have to make up their minds one way or another. But some might be "lucky": on the day of the decisive meeting they may be sick or away from the campus on unavoidable business. Then they cannot be blamed by their colleagues for not having signed the petition in favor of the accused colleague; nor will they later have to suffer for having signed it.[5]

This leads to a useful, though crude, distinction between private and public courage, where the frame of reference is the professional community. The professor decides that if a situation develops where he must take a visible stand he may have to chance it and join his peers. But when he thinks he can escape unnoticed, he prefers to be more cautious. If we look more closely at the items which were indicators of caution and those which were indicators of activism, the former appear to refer more to private and the latter more to public situations. Activism was indicated by willingness to protest if the president interfered with the academic freedom of students, and by remaining with an organization or continuing to read a magazine which could become embarrassing. These items have a strong element of visibility. Friends would notice if one were not to sign a protest or if one were suddenly to drop one's membership or, to a lesser degree, cancel a subscription. In addition, these are reactions to situations requiring a decision one way or another. A colleague is likely to request that one join a protest; an officer of an organization is sure to urge continuation of membership.

The items indicating caution are quite different. Being careful not to bring up certain political topics with one's colleagues is not visible because it means simply not doing something when there is no specific occasion for doing it; the same is true for the tendency to make occasional remarks showing directly or indirectly that one has no extremist leanings. Toning down one's writings or being more circumspect with one's reading lists can easily go unnoticed by colleagues, especially if the change is slow and not attached to specific challenge situations. Thus caution can be exercised without being noticed. Perhaps instead of public and private courage we might speak of its expected and spontaneous versions. Whatever the terms, our material points to an important distinction.

We mentioned earlier that speaking one's mind seemed safer on the campus than on the outside. Now this can be added: not speaking one's mind on the campus, not sharing the general mood of resistance, would also be inadvisable. Left to their own devices many teachers might have considered caution the better part of wisdom. But when the need arose to stand up and be counted, it was safer to do so. In a way, this is an unusual situation. For the most part we think of people's private thoughts as being more "dangerous" than those they express in public. In matters of academic freedom, however, the teacher seems inclined to be courageous in public and cautious in private. This is so because he really deals with two publics. What at times appears dangerous to the larger community is proper in the eyes of one's peers, and they are the ones who matter more.

Thus the community of teachers seems to have made its individual members better men than they would have been if left to their own devices. In intellectual matters we are inclined to think that a man thinks best if he works alone; the derision attached to "committee work" is well known. In matters of morale, the situation is different, at least as long as no panic situation is involved.[6] This last qualification deserves stress. Our study characterized a specific state of affairs where the dangers threatening from the larger community are not as great as the consequences which would ensue from disapproval on the part of one's professional group. There is no doubt that a changed historical situation would make a considerable difference. If matters grew worse, then private caution and diminution of campus courage would undoubtedly begin to go hand in hand. Still, for those concerned with the integrity of the professoriate, ours is an important result. A professional group such as a college faculty is characterized by frequent and continuous face-to-face contact. If, in such a group, there is a tradition of freedom, this climate of opinion can hold in line many who would otherwise break down under attacks from the broader community. From a policy point of view, then, any strengthening of such local traditions of academic freedom may have disproportionate influence on individual attitudes.

Let us see how far this analysis has progressed. We are attempting a composite picture of the state of mind which is indicated by a sizeable apprehension score. We found a strong element of defiance intertwined with fear for one's job or for one's reputation. However, this defiance was tempered by a variety of precautionary moves. To continue a previous figure of speech: middle level courage and middle level fear are in a somewhat unstable equilibrium. Apprehension seems, indeed, to be a good term to describe this sentiment.

But our picture of it would be incomplete without still another dimension: a general sensitivity to problems of freedom of expression and individual liberty, regardless of whether one is himself a potential victim. We shall call it alertness to academic freedom.

APPREHENSION AND ALERTNESS TO ACADEMIC FREEDOM

We know from Figure 3-7 of the preceding chapter that increased vulnerability means increased apprehension. The respondents can also be described according to their general concern with matters of civil liberties. Two items were included in our questionnaire for this purpose.

(1) How closely do you follow civil liberties problems and issues in the news?

(2) Do you find yourself discussing civil liberties issues and problems with your friends, colleagues, or family members?

The checklist answers and the distribution of replies are shown in Table 4-6.

TABLE 4-6

DISTRIBUTION OF ANSWERS TO TWO QUESTIONS REGARDING GENERAL INTEREST IN CIVIL LIBERTIES

Follows civil liberties news:	Discusses civil liberties issues:
More than most other news 34%	Fairly often 42%
As much as any other news 55%	Just occasionally 44%
Not as much as other news 11%	Hardly ever 14%
Total 100%	Total 100%

On the basis of these two questions we can form a crude index by dividing people according to whether they gave two, one, or no affirmative answers. (Affirmative here means "more than most other news" for the first item in Table 4-6 and "fairly often" for the second.) It is not surprising, of course, that personal vulnerability is related to concern with civil liberties. A person who had been involved in an incident, or thinks he might be one day because he has belonged to a controversial group in the past, is likely to follow pertinent news more carefully and to discuss such matters more often. This can be seen in Figure 4-7.

Beyond this we want to show that, regardless of a teacher's own vulnerability, he will be more concerned with civil liberties if he is more apprehensive. This would indicate that apprehension does not just imply fear for one's own position, but also signifies alertness to the general state of academic freedom and the threats to which it is exposed. Confirmation for this general statement is provided in Figure 4-8. As in Figure 4-7, the whole sample is classified according to vulnerability and concern with civil liberties. Only now each point shows the percentage of respondents who have an apprehension score of 2 or more.[7]

This Figure confirms what we already know: the more vulnerable a teacher the more likely he is to be apprehensive. The new information appears in each of the three lines for teachers having a particular degree of vulnerability. If only fear for personal security contributed to apprehension, within each vulnerability level the proportions of apprehensive teachers should remain constant. A glance at the three lines shows, however, that apprehension is noticeably affected by the respondent's intellectual concern with civil liberties. We conclude, then, that this alertness is one more element involved in the general complex of apprehension.

ADDITIONAL OBSERVATIONS

We have singled out the elements which, in combination, make up the mental set of apprehension: fear (or anxiety, if one prefers the term) not strong enough to paralyze resistance and defiance; activism ambivalent enough not to be tantamount to undaunted courage; alertness to the general problems of academic and civil liberties which goes well beyond mere concern with one's own security.

One might ask how these several elements affect each other. Do professors want to do something about a state of affairs and then become fearful about the possible consequences of their act? Or when they are worried about their own security do they turn to collective action as a result? Does alertness to danger lead to worry about their own situations, or does this work the other way around? Undoubtedly all of these interconnections exist. Moreover, different people go through different processes and there can be mutual interaction between these various elements within the same person over a period of time. Were we to observe individuals for long periods, we would undoubtedly find each of the elements we distinguish sometimes playing the role of cause and sometimes of effect; whenever studies with repeated observations have been carried out, such a network of mutual effects has appeared. But our study was restricted to a cross-section at one point in time, which permitted us occasional glimpses into the past of our respondents. While we can analyze the nature of apprehension and its various components as it existed in the spring of 1955, we can only surmise the dynamics of its development.

Two additional observations deserve mention. One relates to the 125 respondents who were singled out in Table 3-3: the teachers who expressed very little worry but who reported that they had nonetheless become much more cautious in their professional activities and in their contacts with colleagues and the community at large. To begin with, prudence is probably a natural state of mind for these respondents. As they watched the scene during the difficult years, they did not feel in any way threatened themselves. When they favored caution it was because they had become more firmly convinced of certain beliefs: a faculty should not embarrass its administration, nor subject its students to controversial reading materials. If a professor had a sizeable score, this did not necessarily mean that the difficult years had made him fearful for his job or more sensitive to civil liberties; it might only mean that the pertinent items in our questionnaire gave him an opportunity to reaffirm his basic attitude of caution.[8] (A keen observer of the contemporary college scene who heard about our study expected that this kind of anxiety would be quite widespread among the professoriate: according to his expectations, they would not have become professors if they had not been scared to begin with. Although we did not explore this matter directly, our general findings fail to support this interpretation.)

Our second observation pertains to a surprising negative result in our data. We had expected many professors to view the incidents of the difficult years as an indignity to their profession. To study this possibility we provided a question which would single out teachers who felt a threat to the status of the professor on the American scene. In the beginning of the

517

interview, as described earlier, respondents were asked if the greater public concern with the political opinions of college teachers they had noticed had proved harmful. Anticipating that the answers volunteered to this question might be phrased only in the most general terms, we provided a checklist on which the professors were asked to choose one of four designated consequences of the difficult years. Two of these - ''impairing the intellectual role of the college'' and ''discouraging constructive public discussion'' - offered a choice between repercussions felt by the college itself or by the democratic process in general. Almost three-fourths of the respondents chose one of these two alternatives. A third category was political in nature (''It prepares the ground for totalitarianism''); this was checked by 7 per cent. But what about the view in which we were most interested: ''It degrades the academic profession''? Only sixty individuals selected this alternative! Although the first two broadly stated choices may have detracted from the two more specific ones, if the connection between the incidents of the difficult years and the status of the academic man had been an urgent concern for respondents, certainly more than sixty of them would have chosen the degradation of the academic profession as the most harmful effect of public concern with the politics of professors. We cannot tell whether more indignation of this kind might have been elicited if a more detailed and clinical probing had been attempted. But we have scrutinized the approximately 3,000 free answers which referred to ''harmful effects.'' Even including all comments which by any stretch of the imagination would be relevant, at most 100 contained references to indignities of some sort affecting the professorial role.

Indignation, then, is apparently not an important element in the complex of apprehension we have analyzed in this chapter. Perhaps one reason lies in the occupational inferiority feelings which we described in Chapter I. If so many teachers feel that laymen have little respect for professors, then it is understandable that degradation of the academic profession would not be seen as a major consequence of attacks and investigations. Recently Professor Arthur Schlesinger, Jr., stated as a matter of fact what for us was a hypothesis. In a review of a number of books on academic freedom, he said: ''What is really at issue has not been so much 'academic freedom' itself as it is the self-respect and reputation of the academic profession.''[9] Our data seem to indicate that Dr. Schlesinger and the authors of the present volume are too small a sample to permit general conclusion based on their own feelings.

REFERENCES

1. The alternatives offered were: "protest vigorously," "just say you disagree and leave it at that," or "accept his order and not say anything." The last alternative was chosen by 5 per cent on both questions. Just prior to our study President Eisenhower had made the statement that debate on Red China should not be prohibited even in military colleges. Doubtless as a result of this, only 3 per cent of our professors were in favor of such a prohibition, while 14 per cent would keep students from inviting a controversial speaker. Thus a comparison of the two questions contributes to our general knowledge of opinion formation. Seventy years ago a famous British political scientist, Dicey, argued that once a law has been adopted its underlying principle "acquires prestige from its mere recognition by Parliament." The power to confer legitimacy to ideas can rest with many forms of authority. In this case an utterance of the President seems to have done it.

2. There are, of course, other liberal magazines, but they are not read by a sufficiently large number of persons to yield meaningful results.

3. The actual findings are beyond doubt. We can parallel Figures 4-2 to 4-4 in this chapter by using only the caution items (see Table 3-2) to classify our respondents. The frequency of the activism items either increases with the caution of the respondents or remains substantially the same. The figures have been relegated to Appendix 8D.

4. The word "recently" in this question is important. We were only interested in such activities which occurred at a time when the respondent presumably was already apprehensive. We had intended to ask a similar question regarding recent joining of organizations. By a typographical mishap, however, the word "recently" was omitted, making the question (No. 6/5) useless.

5. It is fortunate that priority disputes between playwrights and university professors are rare. Several months after this paragraph was written, the following lines from a famous musical comedy came to our attention:

The lord above made man to help his neighbor,

No matter where, on land or sea or foam,

But with a little bit of luck,

When he cones around you won't be home.

We consider the similarity of idea and wording a valuable confirmation.

6. Similar observations have been made by students of the Army in several countries. See S. A. Stouffer, et al., The American Soldier, Vol. II. (Princeton: University Press, 1949), especially Chapters iii and iv, and the paper by Shils and Janowitz, Public Opinion Quarterly, XII, No. 2, 1948. In the preceding discussion we have used this notion of "support by the primary group" in a rather conjectural way. More specific evidence will be found in the sixth and the tenth chapters.

7. The proportions for each point in Figure 4-8 are computed against the "base figures" given in Figure 4-7. There, for instance, the reader can easily see that 52 per cent (815 professors) of the 1,562 having low vulnerability also have a low concern with civil liberties. Now from Figure 4-8 we learn that 29 per cent (237 cases) of the 815 have, nevertheless, an apprehension score of 2 or more. This would be the residual group (about 10 per cent of the whole sample) whose apprehension is probably accounted for by personality characteristics only.

8. A different pattern seems to prevail in a few of these cases: some teachers previously had deviant leanings, then became converted to the conservative point of view, and no longer worry because they feel that their newly-acquired caution has made them secure.

9. In The Journal of Higher Education, June, 1956, pp. 341-42.

CONCLUDING REMARKS

Most of the above articles were the written products which came from seminars, in the 70's, on the theoretical analysis of data. They are not "just say so" papers. Rather, they are what results from the work of beginning grounded theorists who are willing to wrestle with what emerges from the data. They are bonfide, good examples of the beginnings of doing grounded theory, which is the position which so many readers of this volume are in. As beginnings, these theories are no less "good", they just lack the polish of mature, older authors. The have the essential, emergent theoretical ideas (concepts).

The authors focus on a core variable which processes a problem. They allow the emergent. They figure out how to integrate their categories and properties into a theory. Though some papers are underanalysed, they still have tapped relevance with variables that fit and work. They write substantive theory that deals with the emergent main concern of the subjects. And as said above, although the articles are dated, the core variables or basic social processes are not. They are timeless and relevant with appropriate modification for current times and places.

The obvious exceptions to the above is (1) the Lazarsfeld chapters on apprehension which example the beginning of core variable, inductive theory methodology. Lazarfled was my teacher and mentor for inductive research and analysis. He taught me, and so many others, methodology (the theory of method) and how to generate and to write methdology.

(2) The works of Barry Schwartz, which are totally outside the grounded theory teaching network, show that others who are sensitive to what is emergent in the data almost automatically do grounded theory, albeit without the methodological refinements.

Much of my book, *Theoretical Sensitivity*, came from the seminars in which the above papers were generated. It was my policy always to have a student doing methodological notes on exactly what we were doing, using grounded theory methodology, as we analyzed each student's data. The notes ended up as most of *Theoretical Sensitivity*.

In conclusion, the reader should skip and dip in this reader as he or she looks for models for constructing one's own grounded theory.

Barney G. Glaser, PhD